Investment Management Certificate

CW01643317

STUDY TEXT

Unit 2 – Investment Practice

Syllabus version 10

In this December 2012 edition

- A **user-friendly format** for easy navigation
- **Exam tips** to put you on the right track
- A **Test your knowledge** quiz at the end of each chapter
- A full **index**

BPP LEARNING MEDIA

Published December 2012

ISBN 978 1 4453 9592 0

e ISBN 978 1 4453 9097 0

British Library Cataloguing-in-Publication Data
A catalogue record for this book
is available from the British Library

Published by

BPP Learning Media Ltd
BPP House, Aldine Place
142-144 Uxbridge Road
London W12 8AA

www.bpp.com/learningmedia

Printed in United Kingdom by Ricoh

Ricoh House, Ullswater Cresent
Coulsdon CR5 2HR

Your learning materials, published by BPP Learning Media Ltd, are printed on paper sourced from sustainable, managed forests.

A note about copyright

Dear Customer

What does the little © mean and why does it matter?

Your market-leading BPP books, course materials and e-learning materials do not write and update themselves. People write them: on their own behalf or as employees of an organisation that invests in this activity. Copyright law protects their livelihoods. It does so by creating rights over the use of the content.

Breach of copyright is a form of theft – as well being a criminal offence in some jurisdictions, it is potentially a serious beach of professional ethics.

With current technology, things might seem a bit hazy but, basically, without the express permission of BPP Learning Media:

- Photocopying our materials is a breach of copyright
- Scanning, ripcasting or conversion of our digital materials into different file formats, uploading them to facebook or emailing them to your friends is a breach of copyright

You can, of course, sell your books, in the form in which you have bought them – once you have finished with them. (Is this fair to your fellow students? We update for a reason.)

And what about outside the UK? BPP Learning Media strives to make our materials available at prices students can afford by local printing arrangements, pricing policies and partnerships which are clearly listed on our website. A tiny minority ignore this and indulge in criminal activity by illegally photocopying our material or supporting organisations that do. If they act illegally and unethically in one area, can you really trust them?

Contents

The IMC Unit 2 Investment Practice Syllabus

The Study Text reference in the right-hand column below indicates the chapter and section in which each learning outcome is covered. For example learning outcome 18.2.5 is covered in Chapter 9 section 2.4.

Syllabus Item		BPP Ref Chapter–Section
18: ASSET CLASSES Demonstrate an ability to evaluate the characteristics, inherent risks, behaviour and correlation of asset classes		
18.1 Equity Capital Characteristics		
18.1.1	Identify the characteristics, and the risks to the investor, of the various classes of equity capital.	9 – 1
18.1.2	Explain the reasons for issuance of preference shares and the implications to the investor.	9 – 1.2
18.1.3	Explain the characteristics of Global and American Depository Receipts.	9 – 1.3
18.2 Equity Issuance		
18.2.1	Distinguish between primary and secondary share issuance.	9 – 2
18.2.2	Explain the key features of the following equity issuance methods: - Placing. - Intermediaries offer. - Offer for sale. - Offer for sale by subscription.	9 – 2.2
18.2.3	Define and explain the purpose of a rights issue, a scrip issue and a stock split.	9 – 2.4
18.2.4	Calculate the theoretical ex-rights price and the value of the right (nil-paid) given the cum-rights price, the issuance ratio and the subscription price.	9 – 2.4
18.2.5	Calculate the theoretical ex-scrip price given the scrip ratio and the cum-scrip price.	9 – 2.4
18.2.6	Evaluate the options open to an investor in response to a rights offer and explain the effect on the investor's wealth.	9 – 2.4
18.2.7	Explain the motivations behind a company buying back its own shares.	9 – 2.4
18.3: Equity Valuation		
18.3.1	Calculate a holding period return for an ordinary share, comprising capital gain and dividend income.	9 – 3.8
18.3.2	Explain the components, assumptions and limitations of the dividend discount model (Gordon's growth model).	9 – 3.3
18.3.3	Calculate the present value of a share using the dividend discount model.	9 – 3.3
18.3.4	Calculate an estimated growth rate for dividends using historic data or using return on equity and a retained earnings ratio.	9 – 3.3
18.3.5	Explain the reasons for a company's chosen dividend policy.	9 – 3.3
18.3.6	Explain the practical constraints on companies paying dividends.	9 – 3.3

Syllabus Item		BPP Ref Chapter–Section
18.3.7	Explain the importance of the dividend yield and dividend cover in stock analysis.	9 – 3.3
18.3.8	Calculate dividend yield and dividend cover.	9 – 3.4
18.3.9	Distinguish between and evaluate the merits of relative valuation models and absolute valuation models and between historic and prospective measures of value.	9 – 3 16 – 5.3
18.3.10	Calculate a basic earnings per share.	16 – 5.1
18.3.11	Explain what is meant by diluted earnings per share.	16 – 5.2
18.3.12	Explain the rationale for the use of the following ratios in equity valuation: - Price-earnings. - Price to book. - Price to sales. - Price to cash flow. - Enterprise value (EV) to earnings before interest tax, depreciation and amortisation (EBITDA).	9 – 3.6 16 –5.3
18.3.13	Calculate price-earnings (both historic and prospective), price to book, price to sales, price to cash flow ratios for a company.	16 – 5.3
18.3.14	Apply the company ratios in part 18.3.12 above to the valuation of another given company.	9 – 3.6
18.3.15	Explain the possible shortfalls of using each of these price multiples in corporate valuation.	9 – 3.6
18.3.16	Explain the basics of Free cash-flow based valuation methods (FCFF, FCFE) and Residual Income Valuation methods.	9 – 3.7
18.3.17	Define (financial) gearing and evaluate the effect on required equity returns and thus dividend valuations.	9 – 3.3 16 – 4
18.3.18	Explain the measures of economic value added (EVA) and market value added (MVA).	9 – 5.12
18.4: Equity transaction costs		
18.4.1	Explain and identify transaction costs associated with dealing in UK equities.	9 – 2.5
18.4.2	Calculate the total transaction costs for an equity transaction, given the appropriate data.	9 – 2.5
18.4.3	Evaluate the impact of alternative trading platforms, facilitated by MiFID, on transaction costs associated with equity dealing.	9 – 2.5
18.5: Fixed Interest Securities – characteristics		
18.5.1	Explain the structure and characteristics of the various types of fixed income instruments issued in the UK including government bonds, index linked bonds, corporate bonds and Eurobonds.	8 – 1
18.5.2	Understand the rationale for and risks to the issuer and holder of a convertible, callable or putable bond.	8 – 1.6

Syllabus Item		BPP Ref Chapter–Section
18.5.3	Explain clean (quoted) and dirty pricing.	8 – 2.3
18.5.4	Understand the valuation methodology for fixed income securities.	8 – 2.2
18.5.5	Calculate the price of a fixed income security given its maturity, coupon and yield.	8 – 2.2
18.6 Fixed Interest Securities – risk and return		
18.6.1	Identify the components of return of fixed income securities.	8 – 3
18.6.2	Explain the main risks faced by bond holders and how these risks can be addressed.	8 – 5.1
18.6.3	Explain the two components of interest rate risk (price and reinvestment risk).	8 – 5.2
18.6.4	Explain the nature of the relationship between yield and price.	8 – 3.6
18.6.5	Analyse the factors that affect the sensitivity of a bond's price to a change in required yield.	8 – 5.2
18.6.6	Define and calculate the (Macaulay) duration of a bond.	8 – 5.2
18.6.7	Define and calculate the modified duration of a bond.	8 – 5.2
18.6.8	Calculate, given the duration of a bond, the change in price given a change in required yield.	8 – 5.2
18.6.9	Explain the convexity error that arises from using duration to estimate a change in bond price using duration.	8 – 5.2
18.6.10	Define credit risk as it affects bonds.	8 – 5.3
18.6.11	Explain the role of the major credit rating agencies.	8 – 5.3
18.6.12	Interpret the key classes of rating on the scales published by the major rating agencies.	8 – 5.3
18.6.13	Explain the concept of debt seniority.	8 – 1.6
18.6.14	Identify key features and financial ratios considered by credit rating agencies in conducting a corporate rating.	8 – 5.3
18.7: Fixed Interest Securities – yields and the yield curve		
18.7.1	Define and calculate: - Flat yield. - Gross redemption yield (GRY). - Net redemption yield (NRY). - Grossed-up NRY.	8 – 3
18.7.2	Explain when each of the above measures may be appropriate to use.	8 – 3
18.7.3	Define the yield curve.	8 – 4.2
18.7.4	Explain the theories that contribute to explaining the shape of the yield curve.	8 – 4.3
18.7.5	Define forward and spot interest rates.	8 – 4.4
18.7.6	Explain the relationship between forward rates, spot rates and the GRY.	8 – 4.5

Syllabus Item		BPP Ref Chapter–Section
18.8: Fixed Interest Securities – transaction costs		
18.8.1	Explain and identify transaction costs associated with dealing in UK fixed interest securities.	8 – 1.4
18.8.2	Calculate the total transaction costs for a fixed interest security transaction, given the appropriate data.	8 – 1.4
18.8.3	Contrast trading methods for fixed interest securities with equities and examine the impact on trading costs.	8 – 1.4
18.9: Property		
18.9.1	Distinguish between the commercial and residential property markets.	10 – 1.2
18.9.2	Understand the rationale for investing in property.	10 – 1.2
18.9.3	Identify the main investors in the commercial property market and the characteristics of the principal commercial property sectors.	10 – 1.3
18.9.4	Explain how the direct commercial property market works with regard to: ownership and lease structures; buying and selling; costs, the valuation of property and investment performance measurement.	10 – 1.2, 1.5, 2
18.9.5	Identify the risks associated with property investment, both direct and indirect.	10 – 1.4
18.9.6	Explain the routes to indirect property investment.	10 – 1.6
18.9.7	Identify the transaction costs associated with property investment.	10 – 1.5
18.10: Cash and Cash Equivalents		
18.10.1	Explain the main characteristics and risks associated with cash deposits and money market instruments (Treasury Bills, CDs, CP, FRNs).	7 – 1, 3
18.10.2	Calculate the discount and quoted yield on a UK Treasury Bill.	7 – 3.2
18.11: Alternative Investments		
18.11.1	Explain the characteristics of the main commodity derivatives, including, energy, softs/biofuels, metals, emissions, weather.	12 – 10
18.11.2	Identify the main commodity derivative indices, including GSCI, DJAIG and RICI.	18 – 5.4
18.11.3	Explain how commodity exposure can be viewed as a hedge against inflation and 'event' risk.	11 – 1 18 – 5.3
18.11.4	Understand the role of the Investment Property Databank indices in the market.	12 – 11
18.11.5	Explain the advantages and risks of investing in 'alternative' investments, including gold and antiques.	11 – 2
18.12: Correlation between asset classes		
18.12.1	Identify the correlation between the various asset classes (equity, fixed interest, property, cash and alternative investments) and explain its relevance to asset allocation.	17 – 4.3
18.12.2	Explain the limitations of correlation analysis in extreme market conditions.	17 – 4.3

Syllabus Item		BPP Ref Chapter–Section
18.13: Pricing, liquidity and fair value		
18.13.1	Explain the relationship between pricing, liquidity and fair value for the asset classes of equity, fixed interest, property, cash and alternative investments.	17 – 4.3
19: INVESTMENT PRODUCTS Demonstrate an ability to analyse the characteristics, inherent risks, behaviours and relevant tax considerations of investment products		
19.1.1	Compare and contrast investing through direct investments in securities and assets compared with investing through indirect investments.	13 – 1.2
19.1.2	Distinguish between open and closed ended funds.	13 – 1.4
19.1.3	Distinguish the features, risks and benefits of unit trusts, investment trusts and open-ended investment companies.	13 – 2, 3, 4, 8
19.1.4	Explain the additional benefits and risks of investing in split capital investment trusts.	13 – 4
19.1.5	Explain the key features and objectives of Exchange Traded Funds (ETFs) and Exchange Traded Commodities (ETCs).	13 – 6.2, 8
19.1.6	Explain the key features and objectives of Venture Capital Trusts and Enterprise Investment Schemes.	13 – 7
19.1.7	Explain the features and objectives of - Private client funds. - Hedge funds and funds of hedge funds. - Structured products. - Wraps and other platforms.	13 – 5, 6.3, 6.4, 9
19.1.8	Identify the characteristics and advantages of Individual Savings Accounts (ISAs), Child Trust Funds (CTFs), National Savings and Investments, Life assurance based investments and Defined Contribution pension arrangements.	13 – 7, 10, 11
20: DERIVATIVES AND OTHER INSTRUMENTS Demonstrate an ability to analyse the characteristics, inherent risks of Derivatives and Other Instruments		
20.1: Derivatives		
20.1.1	Distinguish between forwards, futures and options.	12 – 2.1
20.1.2	Explain the nature, trading and settlement of exchange traded derivatives.	12 – 2.1, 2.6
20.1.3	Understand the motive for using a futures contract rather than a trade in the underlying asset.	12 – 2.2
20.1.4	Explain the nature of, and reasoning behind, a contango and backwardation market.	12 – 2.5
20.1.5	Define the 'basis' of a futures contract.	12 – 2.5

Syllabus Item		BPP Ref Chapter–Section
20.1.6	Know the contract specifications of the following NYSE Liffe contracts: - Short term interest rate (STIR) futures. - Long Gilt futures. - FTSE 100 futures.	12 – 2.3
20.1.7	Explain the possible uses of the above contracts in an investment management context.	12 – 2.3
20.1.8	Understand the concept of index arbitrage.	12 – 2.6
20.1.9	Distinguish between American style and European style options.	12 – 3.8
20.1.10	Explain time value and intrinsic value relating to an option premium.	12 – 3.8
20.1.11	Identify when an option is in-the-money, out-of-the-money, or at-the money.	12 – 3.8
20.1.12	Calculate the time value of an option, given the premium, strike price and current market price.	12 – 3.8
20.1.13	Explain the factors that determine the premium of an option.	12 – 3.8
20.1.14	Calculate the maximum profit, maximum loss and the motivation behind the following option strategies: - Long and short call. - Long and short put. - Long and short straddle. - Long and short strangle. - Long and short butterfly. - Covered call and protective put.	12 – 4
20.1.15	Explain the use of futures and options in hedging an equity portfolio.	12 – 2.2
20.1.16	Calculate the number of FTSE 100 futures or options contracts required to hedge a portfolio with a specified beta value.	12 – 2.3
20.2: Selling short, Stock Lending and Contracts for Differences (Swaps)		
20.2.1	Explain the mechanics and uses of short selling.	12 – 8
20.2.2	Explain the role of stock lending in the markets, and the benefits to the participants.	12 – 8
20.2.3	Explain the nature of contracts for differences.	12 – 5
20.2.4	Explain the nature of, and motivations behind: - Interest rate swaps. - Currency swaps. - Equity swaps. - Inflation swaps.	12 – 9
20.3: Convertibles and Warrants		
20.3.1	Explain the nature of convertible bonds and convertible preference shares.	12 – 7
20.3.2	Calculate a conversion price, value and premium.	12 – 7
20.3.3	Explain the component parts of the valuation of a convertible bond (namely straight bond value, call option value, dilution effect and conversion ratio).	12 – 7

Syllabus Item		BPP Ref Chapter–Section
20.3.4	Define a warrant.	12 – 6.1
20.3.5	Distinguish between a warrant and a call option.	12 – 6.1
20.3.6	Explain the key features of covered warrants.	12 – 6.2
20.4: Credit derivatives		
20.4.1	Explain the purpose mechanics and implications of a credit default swap (CDS).	12 – 9.5
20.4.2	Explain the risks to the financial system resulting from the proliferation of credit derivatives.	12 – 9.5
21: Investment Theories and Models Demonstrate an understanding of the merits and limitations of the main investment theories		
22.1: Risk and Return and the Importance of Diversification		
21.1.1	Explain the 'normal' trade-off between risk and return and the concept of 'dominance' between investment strategies.	5 – 2.4
21.1.2	Explain the implications of assuming returns are normally distributed.	5 – 2.2
21.1.3	Explain the importance of risk-measurement in the analysis of investments, and why ex-ante and ex-post measures of risk may be very different.	5 – 1
21.1.4	Identify the commonly used measures of risk in investment analysis and fund management.	5 – 2.2
21.1.5	Explain the shortfalls of standard deviation as a measure of investment risk.	5 – 2.6
21.1.6	Explain the meaning of drawdown as a measure of risk.	5 – 2.6
21.1.7	Understand the impact on changing levels of price volatility over time and how this affects predictions such as tracking error and downside risk.	5 – 2.6
21.1.8	Understand the importance of correlation in constructing efficient portfolios and the difficulties, limitations and meaning of correlation coefficients.	5 – 2.3
21.1.9	Calculate correlation coefficients from standard deviation/covariance of two investments.	5 – 2.3
21.1.10	Explain diversification and its role in constructing efficient portfolios and its limitations during extreme market conditions.	5 – 2.3
21.1.11	Explain the meaning of Value at Risk (VaR) and its advantages and disadvantages for risk management.	5 – 2.5
21.1.12	Analyse and explain other types of investment risk including inflation, currency, interest rate, fraud and counterparty risk.	5 – 2
21.2: Models of Return and Risk		
21.2.1	Explain the concept of investments being exposed to a number of common factors which partially explain their return and risk profile ('arbitrage pricing theory').	5 – 6

Syllabus Item		BPP Ref Chapter–Section
21.2.2	Identify the assumptions behind the single-factor Capital Asset Pricing Model (CAPM) and identify other factors in common use.	5 – 5.1
21.2.3	Explain the limitations of the CAPM model.	5 – 5.1
21.2.4	Define the segmentation of risk into systematic (factor) risk and unsystematic ("investment specific") risk.	5 – 2.3
21.2.5	Calculate the total risk given some systematic and unsystematic components.	5 – 2.3
21.2.6	Calculate the expected return on a security by applying the CAPM through interpreting the beta of a security.	5 – 3.1
21.2.7	Explain how the beta may be derived from a scatter chart of historic returns.	5 – 4.3
21.2.8	Calculate the beta of an investment given the systematic risk of the investment and the risk of the market.	5 – 4.3
21.2.9	Calculate the beta of an investment given the variance of the market return, and the covariance of the investment return with the market return.	5 – 4.3
21.2.10	Calculate the beta of a portfolio given the component betas and the investment weightings.	5 – 4.4
21.2.11	Explain how different asset class returns may be related, for example Merton models relating fixed income risk to equity.	8 – 5.3
21.3: The Efficient Markets Hypothesis (EMH) and Behavioural Finance		
21.3.1	Explain the key concepts of the EMH.	6 – 7.2
21.3.2	Explain the limitations of the EMH.	6 – 7.2
21.3.3	Explain the basic concepts of the behavioural finance school of thought including heuristics and framing.	6 – 7.3
21.3.4	Evaluate the evidence on market anomalies in relation to both EMH and behavioural finance interpretations.	6 – 7.3
21.3.5	Examine the concept of 'financial amnesia' and the role of behavioural factors in its promotion.	6 – 7.4
21.3.6	Explain the notion of 'bubbles' in financial markets.	6 – 7.4
22: Investment Management Principles Demonstrate an understanding of the principles of investment management		
22.1: Investment Management Principles – fixed income		
22.1.1	Explain the following bond portfolio management techniques: - Cash matching /dedication. - Immunisation. - Contingent immunisation. - Anomaly switches. - Policy switches. - Credit risk management. - Riding the yield curve.	17 – 6.4, 6.5

Syllabus Item		BPP Ref Chapter–Section
22.1.2	Calculate the theoretical gain from riding the yield curve.	17 – 6.4
22.1.3	Calculate duration for a bond portfolio.	17 – 6.5
22.1.4	Explain the benefits and risks of using barbell and bond portfolio strategies.	17 – 6.5
22.2: Fund management styles		
22.2.1	Distinguish between a 'top-down' and 'bottom-up' approach to fund management.	17 – 3.4
22.2.2	Distinguish between active and passive fund management and explain the costs/benefits to the investor.	17 – 3.3
22.2.3	Distinguish between strategic and tactical asset allocation.	17 – 4
22.2.4	Explain the major investment styles prevalent in the fund management industry (including socially responsible investing – SRI / environmental social governance investing ESGI).	17 – 3.5, 3.6
22.3: Liability driven investment (LDI)		
22.3.1	Explain the benefits and risks of an LDI strategy.	17 – 1.5
22.3.2	Explain the process of a liability driven investment strategy.	17 – 1.5
22.3.3	Evaluate some of the techniques used in LDI.	17 – 1.5
22.3.4	Explain the use of basic measures of risk used in LDI.	17 – 1.5
23: INVESTMENT PERFORMANCE MEASUREMENT Demonstrate an understanding of the principles of investment performance measurement		
23.1: Total return and its Components		
23.1.1	Explain the importance of returns analysis in the portfolio management process.	19 – 1
23.1.2	Identify the components of total return for a bond or equity portfolio.	19 – 2
23.1.3	Calculate the income, capital and total return over a single period for an equity or bond portfolio.	19 – 2
23.1.4	Calculate the reinvestment return on income over a specified investment horizon.	19 – 2
23.1.5	Explain how returns are decomposed for different asset classes such as equities (sector/stock/interaction effect) and fixed income (shift/twist/spread return).	19 – 3.2
23.2: Money weighted and time weighted returns		
23.2.1	Identify the data requirements to calculate a - Money weighted return; and - Time weighted return.	19 – 2.3, 2.4
23.2.2	Calculate respectively, from such data, the - Money weighted return; or - Time weighted return.	19 – 2.3, 2.4
23.2.3	Interpret time-weighted and money-weighted returns.	19 – 2.3, 2.4

Syllabus Item		BPP Ref Chapter–Section
23.3: Choosing a benchmark, comparisons with investment objectives, base portfolio, indices		
23.3.1	Explain the purpose of benchmarking.	19 – 3.2
23.3.2	Identify the characteristics of an appropriate benchmark.	19 – 3.2
23.3.3	Identify the key types of benchmark used in the investment management industry.	19 – 3.2
23.3.4	Explain how to construct a benchmark portfolio comprising global equities.	19 – 3.2
23.4: Performance measurement including risk adjusted returns		
23.4.1	Explain the importance of risk analysis in performance evaluation.	19 – 3.3
23.4.2	Explain and interpret the following risk adjusted measures of return: - The Sharpe measure. - The Treynor measure. - The information ratio. - Jensen's alpha.	19 – 3.4
23.4.3	Calculate the Sharpe, Treynor, information ratio and Jensen measure.	19 – 3.4
23.4.4	Explain how total return can be decomposed into the following: - Risk-free return. - Return due to choice of benchmark. - Return due to market timing. - Return to diversifiable risk. - Pure selectivity.	19 – 4.2
23.4.5	Explain tracking error and its limitations.	5 – 2.6
24: THE MACRO-ECONOMIC ENVIRONMENT Demonstrate an understanding of the macro-economic environment and its impact on investment.		
24.1 The macro-economic environment		
24.1.1	Identify the main long term UK and global socio-economic trends.	6 – 8.1
24.1.2	Identify key economic indicators and explain their trends.	6 – 8.1, 8.2
24.1.3	Understand the relationship between and importance of the main World economies.	6 – 8.3
24.1.4	Explain economic and financial cycles including their predictability and regional differences.	6 – 8.3
24.1.5	Identify international differences in consumption, credit and savings	6 – 8.2
24.2 Determination of National Income, the circular flow of income, consumption, the multiplier, the paradox of thrift, foreign trade and income determination		
24.2.1	Distinguish between GDP and GNP.	6 – 9.2
24.2.2	Explain the difference between real and nominal GDP.	6 – 9.2

Syllabus Item		BPP Ref Chapter–Section
24.2.3	Explain the components of the circular flow of income.	6 – 9.1
24.2.4	Distinguish between injections into, and withdrawals from ('leakages') the circular flow.	6 – 9.1
24.2.5	Distinguish between national income and GNP.	6 – 9.2
24.2.6	Distinguish between classical economics and the Keynesian and Monetarist schools of thought.	6 – 9.3, 9.4
24.2.7	Explain the major components of the Keynesian model.	6 – 9.4
24.2.8	Explain Keynesian equilibrium.	6 – 9.4
24.2.9	Calculate the Keynesian multiplier given the marginal propensity to consume (mpc) or propensities to withdraw (tax, import and save).	6 – 9.4
24.2.10	Explain the paradox of thrift.	6 – 9.1
24.3: Inflation, Unemployment, Fiscal and Monetary Policy and the role of Central Banks		
24.3.1	Describe fiscal policy and its influence on aggregate demand.	6 – 10.4
24.3.2	Explain the role of debt in the business cycle.	6 – 10.4
24.3.3	Explain the problems associated with fiscal policy.	6 – 10.4
24.3.4	Define money supply (from 'narrow' through to 'wide').	6 – 10.5
24.3.5	Describe the fractional reserve banking system.	6 – 10.5
24.3.6	Define the money multiplier and identify its determinants.	6 – 10.5
24.3.7	Calculate the potential money multiplier given a cash reserve ratio.	6 – 10.5
24.3.8	Explain the transmission mechanism whereby monetary policy influences economic aggregates.	6 – 10.5
24.3.9	Define inflation and explain how it is measured in the UK.	6 – 12.1
24.3.10	Define unemployment and explain how it is measured in the UK.	6 – 12.5
24.3.11	Explain the relationship between inflation and unemployment.	6 – 12.5
24.3.12	Explain how inflation targeting operates in the UK.	6 – 11
24.3.13	Distinguish between the different approaches to the control of inflation taken by the major central banks.	6 – 11.5
24.3.14	Explain the other tools (including Quantitative Easing (QE)) used by central banks to manage the economy and in particular inflation.	6 – 10.5
24.3.15	Explain the impact of bank capital and liquidity requirements and the move towards macroprudential regulation on the macro-economy.	6 – 10.5
24.3.16	Explain the role of securitisation on credit growth and the wider macro-economy.	6 – 10.5
24.4: The foreign exchange market, government policy and exchange rates, fixed floating and managed exchange rates, and the balance of payments		
24.4.1	Explain how changes in supply and demand for a currency will affect its value on the foreign exchange markets.	6 – 13.1
24.4.2	Identify the key components of the balance of payments.	6 – 13.5

Syllabus Item		BPP Ref Chapter–Section
24.4.3	Explain the relationship between the supply and demand for a currency and the underlying transactions represented in the balance of payments.	6 – 13.1
24.4.4	Distinguish between a fixed, floating and a managed exchange rate ('dirty-floating' regime).	6 – 13.1
24.4.5	Explain the economic benefits and costs of a fixed exchange rate mechanism.	6 – 13.1
24.4.6	Explain an optimal currency area (OCA) and identify the advantages and disadvantages of implementing a single currency in an OCA.	6 – 13.5
24.4.7	Explain the implications of persistent global imbalances of trade and capital.	6 – 13.8
24.4.8	Explain the notion of purchasing power parity as a forecasting tool for exchange rates.	14 – 3.2
24.4.9	Explain the effectiveness of monetary and fiscal policy in fixed and floating exchange rate regimes.	6 – 13.1
24.4.10	Understand the nature and basic operations of the foreign exchange market.	14 – 1
24.4.11	Explain the nature of exchange rate risk and how it can be managed.	14 – 1.6
24.4.12	Explain spot and forward exchange rates.	14 – 2
24.4.13	Calculate forward rates using interest rate parity (IRP).	14 – 2
24.4.14	Explain the concept of purchasing power parity (PPP).	14 – 3.2
24.4.15	Distinguish between IRP and PPP.	14 – 3.3
24.4.16	Explain the International Fisher effect.	14 – 3.3
25: MICRO-ECONOMICS Demonstrate an understanding of micro-economics		
25.1: Demand and supply		
25.1.1	Explain the laws of supply and demand.	6 – 2.1
25.1.2	Distinguish between movements along demand and supply schedules and shifts thereof.	6 – 2.1
25.1.3	Identify the factors that cause a demand or supply schedule to shift.	6 – 2.1
25.1.4	Describe, calculate and interpret own price elasticity of demand and its impact on total revenues.	6 – 3.2
25.1.5	Identify the factors that determine own price elasticity of demand.	6 – 3.2
25.1.6	Explain, calculate and interpret the concept of cross elasticity of demand (as applied to substitute and complementary goods).	6 – 3.4
25.1.7	Explain, calculate and interpret elasticity of supply and its dependence on the flexibility of factors of production.	6 – 5.1
25.2: The costs of production; marginal costs, average costs and total costs		
25.2.1	Distinguish between explicit (accounting) costs and opportunity (economic) costs.	6 – 4.1

Syllabus Item		BPP Ref Chapter–Section
25.2.2	Explain the concept of normal, supernormal and sub-normal levels of profit.	6 – 4.1, 5
25.2.3	Define fixed costs, variable costs, marginal costs, total costs and average costs.	6 – 4.1
25.2.4	Explain the shapes of the short-run marginal cost, average variable cost, average fixed cost, and average total cost curves.	6 – 4.2
25.2.5	Explain the law of diminishing marginal returns and its impact on the shape of short-run cost curves.	6 – 4.2
25.2.6	Explain the relationship between total revenue, average revenue and marginal revenues for a normal demand schedule.	6 – 3.2
25.2.7	Explain the relationship between marginal cost and marginal revenue and how this determines the profit maximising level of output for a firm.	6 – 5.1
25.3: Short and long run costs, economies and diseconomies of scale		
25.3.1	Define short-run and long-run in the context of cost behaviour.	6 – 4
25.3.2	Explain the notions of economies of scale, a minimum efficient scale and diseconomies of scale and their impact on the shape of the long-run average cost curve.	6 – 4.3
25.3.3	Explain the relationship between long run marginal costs and long run average costs and explain how this determines the level of output for productive efficiency to arise.	6 – 5
25.4: Perfect competition and monopoly		
25.4.1	Identify the conditions that characterise a perfectly competitive ('price-taker') market.	6 – 5.1
25.4.2	Explain the conditions of long-run equilibrium for a price-taker.	6 – 5.1
25.4.3	Explain the market mechanics through which only normal levels of profit can be earned by price takers in the long-run.	6 – 5.1
25.4.4	Explain the relationship between short run supply and marginal cost for a price-taker.	6 – 5.1
25.4.5	Describe the shape of the long run supply curve for a perfectly competitive industry.	6 – 5.1
25.4.6	Explain the decision by a price taker facing economic losses to either continue to operate or shut down.	6 – 5.1
25.4.7	Identify the conditions that characterise a pure monopoly.	6 – 5.2
25.4.8	Explain the conditions of long run equilibrium for a monopoly.	6 – 5.2
25.4.9	Distinguish between the equilibrium price, output levels, and productive efficiency of a monopoly compared to a perfectly competitive firm.	6 – 5.2
25.4.10	Explain price discrimination and the conditions under which it will prevail.	6 – 5.2
25.5: Commonly used methods of assessing industries/companies		
25.5.1	Understand how business cycles may affect relative industry performance.	6 – 6.1
25.5.2	Explain Porter's five competitive forces that drive industry competition.	6 – 6.3

Syllabus Item		BPP Ref Chapter–Section
25.5.3	Explain the product life cycle and the characteristics of each phase (introduction, growth, maturity and decline).	6 – 6.2
25.5.4	Explain the concept of strengths, weaknesses, opportunities and threats (SWOT) analysis and its role in corporate evaluation.	6 – 6.4
25.5.5	Explain the 4Ps marketing mix (product, price, promotion and place) in the context of analysing competitive advantage and threats.	6 – 6.5
26: Statistics and Financial Mathematics Demonstrate an ability to apply statistical and financial mathematics techniques		
26.1: Sources of Data		
26.1.1	Distinguish between primary and secondary sources of data.	2 – 2.1
26.1.2	Identify examples of primary and secondary data.	2 – 2.1
26.1.3	Distinguish between a population and a sample.	2 – 2.2
26.1.4	Explain the key sampling methods.	2 – 2.3
26.1.5	Distinguish between continuous and discrete data.	2 – 3
26.1.6	Define categorical data and explain how it can be converted to ordinal data.	2 – 3
26.1.7	Interpret a frequency and relative frequency distribution.	2 – 4.2
26.1.8	Explain the use of the following in the presentation of data: - Lorenz curve. - Pie chart. - Bar chart. - Histogram. - Scatter plots. - Graphs.	2 – 4.3
26.2: Summary Data		
26.2.1	Define, explain and calculate the following measures of central tendency for both raw data and interval data: - Arithmetic mean. - Geometric mean. - Median. - Mode.	3 – 2.1
26.2.2	Distinguish between symmetric and skewed data.	3 – 2.7
26.2.3	Explain the relationship between the mean, median and mode for symmetric and skewed data.	3 – 2.7
26.2.4	Define, explain and calculate the following measures of dispersion for both raw data and interval data: - Standard deviation (population and sample). - Variance. - Range. - Quartiles and percentiles. - Inter-quartile range.	3 – 3

Syllabus Item		BPP Ref Chapter–Section
26.2.5	Explain the notion of probability distributions and identify the properties of the normal distribution.	5 – 2.2
26.2.6	Explain the notion of statistical significance in the context of investment decisions.	5 – 2.2
26.3: Correlation and bivariate linear regression		
26.3.1	Explain the least-squares regression technique in deriving a line of best fit.	3 – 4.4
26.3.2	Distinguish between the dependent and independent variable.	3 – 4.4
26.3.3	Interpret the intercept and gradient components of a regression line.	3 – 4.4
26.3.4	Calculate a forecast value for the dependent variable given the regression line equation.	3 – 4.4
26.3.5	Explain and interpret the correlation coefficient in the context of linear regression.	3 – 4.5
26.3.6	Explain the shortfalls in the application of linear regression to forecasting including correlation does not imply causation and the pitfalls of data-mining.	3 – 4.3
26.3.7	Explain the concept of autocorrelation and appreciate the impact of extreme events on correlation	5 – 2.2
26.4: Index numbers		
26.4.1	Explain the purpose of an index value.	18 – 1
26.4.2	Calculate an index level for the current year, given the base year data and the current year data.	18 – 1
26.4.3	Explain the role of financial market indices in fund management.	18 – 4.1
26.4.4	Explain and calculate a price relative for a share.	18 – 2.1
26.4.5	Calculate and interpret a simple arithmetic index.	18 – 3.2
26.4.6	Calculate an index level having re-based the index series.	18 – 1.3
26.4.7	Calculate and interpret a geometric index.	18 – 3.2
26.4.8	Calculate and interpret a market value weighted index.	18 – 3.4
26.4.9	Understand the composition and construction of key global bond and equity market indices.	18 – 4.3, 5
26.4.10	Explain the relevance of free-floating indices.	18 – 4.2
26.5: Simple and compound interest		
26.5.1	Distinguish simple interest from compound interest.	4 – 2
26.5.2	Calculate simple and compound interest over multiple periods.	4 – 2
26.5.3	Distinguish a nominal (simple) annual interest rate from an effective (compound) annual rate.	4 – 2.3
26.5.4	Calculate the annual compound rate given the nominal rate and the frequency of compounding.	4 – 2.3
26.5.5	Calculate the annual nominal rate of interest given the annual compound rate and the frequency of compounding.	4 – 2.3

Syllabus Item		BPP Ref Chapter–Section
26.5.6	Explain the concept of continuous compounding.	4 – 2.3
26.5.7	Calculate the effective continuously compounded rate given the nominal rate.	4 – 2.3
26.6: The time value of money – present and future value calculations, annuities, perpetuities, and mortgages		
26.6.1	Calculate and interpret future values for: - Single sums. - Annuities.	4 – 3.2
26.6.2	Calculate and interpret present values for: - Single sums. - Annuities. - Perpetuities.	4 – 4.2
26.6.3	Calculate equal instalments on a repayment mortgage given the present value of the borrowings, the fixed mortgage rate and the term of the borrowing.	4 – 4.6
26.7: The internal rate of return and net present value		
26.7.1	Calculate and interpret the net present value of a series of investment cash flows.	4 – 4.2
26.7.2	Calculate and interpret an internal rate of return.	4 – 5.2
26.7.3	Explain how NPVs and IRRs can be used in investment decision making.	4 – 7.1
26.7.4	Explain the limitations of each technique.	4 – 7.1
26.7.5	Explain why decisions using each technique may conflict.	4 – 7.1
26.7.6	Explain the scenarios in which multiple IRRs may occur.	4 – 7.1
27: ACCOUNTING Demonstrate an understanding of accounting principles		
27.1: Fundamental Precepts		
27.1.1	Explain the legal requirement to prepare financial statements.	15 – 3.1
27.1.2	Explain the concept of a company being a separate legal entity, and the purpose of the preparation of the accounts.	15 – 1.1
27.1.3	Define 'small companies' for the purpose of financial statement preparation and explain the relevance of this definition.	15 – 9
27.1.4	Explain when accounts may be required to be prepared under IFRSs rather than UK GAAP.	15 – 2.5
27.1.5	Explain the role of the auditor.	15 – 3.2
27.1.6	Identify, in outline, the reasons for auditors issuing a qualified report.	15 – 3.2
27.2: The Balance Sheet		
27.2.1	Explain the purpose of a balance sheet.	15 – 5
27.2.2	Identify and explain the key balance sheet categories and content.	15 – 5.2
27.2.3	Distinguish between capital and revenue expenditure.	15 – 7.5

Syllabus Item		BPP Ref Chapter–Section
27.2.4	Explain the valuation of non-current assets.	15 – 6
27.2.5	Calculate depreciation under the straight-line and reducing balance methods.	15 – 6.2
27.2.6	Calculate the profit or loss on disposal of a non-current asset.	15 – 6.2
27.2.7	Explain the principles behind the valuation of inventories.	15 – 6.3
27.2.8	Explain the effects of first-in-first-out and last-in-first-out valuations on inventory values and profits.	15 – 6.3
27.2.9	Identify the types of current and non-current liabilities that typically appear in financial statements.	15 – 5.2
27.2.10	Explain the concept of a provision.	15 – 5.4
27.2.11	Explain the treatment of contingent liabilities within financial statements.	15 – 5.4
27.2.12	Explain the treatment of pension costs in financial statements.	15 – 5.4
27.2.13	Explain what is meant by a post-balance sheet event.	15 – 6.5
27.2.14	Distinguish among authorised, issued, paid up and called up share capital.	15 – 5.4
27.2.15	Explain the effect of the following on a balance sheet: - Rights issue. - Bonus/scrip issue. - Stock split. - Share repurchases.	15 – 5.4
27.2.16	Identify and explain the main types of reserve found in the balance sheet.	15 – 5.4
27.3: The accounting treatment of financial instruments		
27.3.1	Identify the various classifications of financial instrument and outline the accounting treatment of each.	15 – 6.6
27.4: The Income Statement and Statement of Changes in Equity		
27.4.1	Identify and explain the classification of expenses based on nature or function.	15 – 7.3
27.4.2	Explain the principle of revenue recognition.	15 – 7.3
27.4.3	Identify the following different levels of profit and understand which classes of expenses are considered in arriving at each level: - Gross profit; - Trading (or operating) profit; and - Net profit.	15 – 7.3
27.4.4	Explain the objective of a statement of changes in equity.	15 – 7.4
27.4.5	Identify the information to be reported in a statement of change in equity.	15 – 7.4
27.5: The Cash Flow Statement		
27.5.1	Explain the purpose of a cash flow statement.	15 – 8
27.5.2	Identify the classification of cash flow activities.	15 – 8
27.5.3	Calculate net cash flow from operations given operating profit (or vice versa) and the relevant balance sheet movements.	15 – 8

Syllabus Item		BPP Ref Chapter–Section
27.6: Group Accounts		
27.6.1	Define and distinguish between corporate investments, associated companies and subsidiaries.	15 – 10.2
27.6.2	Explain the purpose of group accounts.	15 – 10.2
27.6.3	Define a minority interest and explain how it is represented in the financial statements.	15 – 7.3
27.6.4	Explain how goodwill arises in acquisition accounting.	15 – 5.4
27.6.5	Explain the treatment of goodwill and intangible assets in the group accounts, including amortisation, useful lives and the requirement for impairment reviews.	15 – 5.4
27.7 Major Accounting Ratios		
27.7.1	Distinguish between profitability, liquidity, and gearing ratios.	16 – 1
27.7.2	Define and calculate return on capital employed.	16 – 2.1
27.7.3	Define and calculate return on equity.	16 – 2.4
27.7.4	Explain how return on capital employed can be broken down into profit margin and asset turnover.	16 – 2.1
27.7.5	Define, calculate and interpret - Operational gearing. - Financial gearing. - The current ratio. - The quick ratio (acid test).	16 – 2.5, 3.1, 3.2, 4
27.7.6	Explain the effect of the following on the major accounting ratios: - Rights issue. - Bonus/scrip issue. - Stock split. - Share repurchases.	15

1 Introduction to Investment Management

INTRODUCTION

Investment management involves identifying client objectives and constructing portfolios to meet these objectives. The manager must operate within the confines of the risk tolerance of the client.

We will consider the role of the investment manager as well of that of the trustee, the person with responsibility for looking after the assets.

Investment management may be conducted at an institutional level for companies or at an individual level. Furthermore there are different approaches and philosophies behind managing money, ranging from hands-on active approaches, to more passive approaches.

Often collective products such as unit trusts and exchange traded funds are used to enable investors to achieve a broad array of securities for a small initial outlay. We will look at both the advantages and disadvantages of these products.

CHAPTER CONTENTS

Chapter Learning Objectives

There are no syllabus learning objectives associated with this chapter, it is purely to establish a framework for what follows.

1 Investment Management – An Overview

1.1 Definition

Investment management is the management of an investment portfolio on behalf of a private client or an institution, the receipt and distribution of dividends and all other administrative work in connection with the portfolio.

1.2 Purpose and considerations of investment management

Investment management involves the investment of a client's assets in order to meet a number of key objectives. The objectives will vary from investor to investor and, consequently, the process of investment management must start with a detailed consideration of the fund's objectives in order to determine the appropriate investment policies.

Broadly speaking, the **objectives of funds** fall into one of two categories.

- **To maximise returns**, i.e. positive net worth individuals looking for a portfolio to match their risk/return preferences.
- **To match liabilities**, e.g. pension funds, where the aim is to match assets and liabilities or minimise any mismatch.
- To satisfy the fund's objectives, the investment manager needs to know certain factors about the client, such as
  - Time horizons
  - Liabilities to be met
  - Liquidity needs
  - Risk aversion/tolerance
  - Tax status
  - Other preferences and legal constraints, e.g. ethical or religious considerations

This is required for at least three reasons.

- It is a prerequisite to the initial portfolio structure.
- It influences the types of portfolio adjustment that can be made.
- It, consequently, influences portfolio performance.

1.3 The regulatory framework for the investment manager

The regulation of the UK financial services industry continues to evolve. Prior to the advent of the 1986 Financial Services Act, the industry was completely self-regulating.

The Financial Services Act was not a detailed legal code as one might anticipate, but rather a statutory framework which made provision for the recognition of detailed rules produced by the investment industry itself – the self-regulatory aspect of the regulatory structure.

A key element of the system was the Financial Services Act 1986, which contained the basic premise that those conducting investment business in the UK obtain authorisation. On 30 November 2001, the **Financial Services and Markets Act 2000 (FSMA)** came into force. Whilst practitioner and consumers are actively consulted it is the FSA, a public authority, that co-ordinates the regulation of the industry.

The provision of investment management services constitutes a **regulated activity** as defined by FSMA. Thus, any firm providing these services requires **authorisation**.

On 1 November 2007 further changes to the regulatory environment occurred with the introduction of MiFID, a European directive aimed at opening up the European market.

1.4 The role of the investment manager

While an individual investor may choose to manage his own money, the majority of investors in the UK are turning towards institutional investment management to safeguard their assets. One of the reasons for this is that commissions have come down for institutional investors, while commissions for private customers remain high. Unless customers are undertaking large transactions, they may be limiting their access to the marketplace.

Equally, it is important for an investor to buy a range of assets. This restricts the level of risk he may face but, with only a limited amount of capital, it may be impossible at today's commission rates for an investor to spread his money over a portfolio wide enough to minimise risk. Consequently, it makes sense for small investors to pool their money into large funds that can be invested on their behalf by professional fund managers.

To safeguard the assets of the individual investors, funds are frequently managed under trust. This means that **all of the fund's assets** are registered in the name of the trustees, rather than the managers, with the managers only having authority to undertake particular transactions, e.g. buying or selling securities, on behalf of the trustees.

1.5 The role of the trustee

1.5.1 Introduction

Sometimes a fund is managed under trust and the role of the trustee is to protect and control the trust property. It is the responsibility of the trustee to invest the trust property, though this role is frequently delegated to a fund manager.

If the fund is managed under trust and there are no specific instructions for its investment in the trust deed, the trustee must invest the funds in accordance with the Trustee Act 2000. Where there are specific investment criteria laid out in the trust deed, the trustee must ensure that these are not breached by the fund manager.

In performing this role, a trustee must, under the terms of the Trustee Act 2000, act with a duty of care, ensuring the suitability of an investment to the trust.

1.6 Overview of the investment management process

The process of investment management involves the investment of a third party's assets in order to meet a number of key objectives. The objectives will vary for each investor and, consequently, the process of investment management must start with a detailed consideration of the fund's objectives and constraints.

1.6.1 The approach to investment management

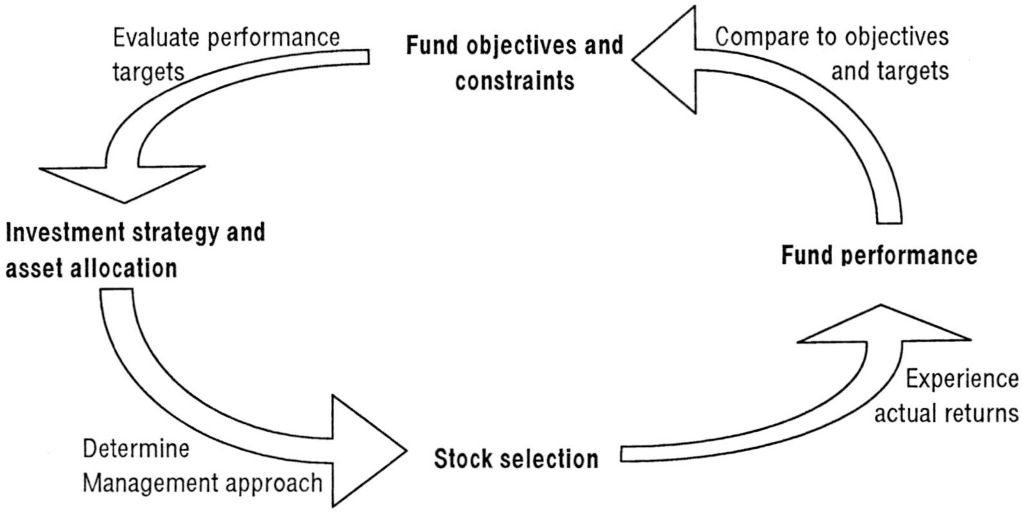

The fund management process is not a linear one which is completed once the final stage has been undertaken, rather it is a process of continuous review ad refinement in the light of changing client needs and market circumstances.

The initial stage, however, is the consideration of the client's, hence the fund's, objectives and constraints. These objectives and constraints, once defined and evaluated, direct the fund manager towards certain asset classes and away from others, leading to the development of an investment strategy and an initial strategic asset allocation.

Having determined a strategy, the manager now needs to consider his management approach which directly leads to his stock selection.

Having now established a portfolio, the manager will experience the returns over time and must assess whether they are sufficient to satisfy the client's needs which then needs to be fed back in to the performance targets for the following period, possibly leading to revisions of the investment strategy, asset allocation, stock selection etc. In addition, any changes in client's objectives that may arise will need to be factored into this process.

That is, investment management must be viewed as a continuous iterative process of refinement.

1.7 Diversification

As mentioned above, one of the key benefits of employing a fund manager is that the investor's funds are being pooled with those of other investors. This pooling allows the investor's money to be spread over a range of assets.

In any investment there are two sorts of risk – the general **market risk** of investing in shares or bonds and the **specific risk** of any individual investment. For example, if an investor were to put all their money into the shares of a company, there would firstly be the risk that the market in all shares would fall, causing the value of the investment to fall, and secondly the risk that the specific company itself may suffer from a specific incident causing the share price to fall.

If an investor is able to buy more investments, he will be taking on board specific risks of different companies. Eventually, there will be a situation where, because of specific risks, some of the investments will fall but others will rise. Overall, through this process of **diversification**, investors are able to rid themselves of the specific risk of a stock. It is, however, **impossible to remove the market risk**.

2 Risk/Reward Profile

Fundamental to an understanding of investment management is an appreciation of the relationship between risk and reward, that is

Formula to learn

High Risk = High Return

Investments offer a range of risk and return which can be summarised as follows.

Investments and Risk

Low Risk	**National Savings Certificates** **Bank and Building Society A/Cs** (Including money market deposits) **Gilts Held to Redemption** **Gilts Sold Before Redemption** (Here, there is the risk of a fall in the value of the stock)
	Local Authority Issues
	Corporate Bonds (Dependent on the credit rating)
Medium Risk	**Life Assurance Policies**
	Unit Trusts, OEICS and Investment Trusts (Obviously certain schemes carry greater risk than others)
	Shares and Property (Ranging from 'blue chips' to penny shares in small dynamic companies)
High Risk	**Warrants, Futures and Options** (However, there is only a limited risk in purchasing an option or a warrant since here only the premium can be lost)

Before offering any investment advice, it is vital to ensure that the risk and returns match the customer's criteria.

3 Institutional Investment Management

3.1 Introduction

In the period since 1945, the power of the institutional investor has grown dramatically in line with the decline in individual investors.

Share ownership 1963

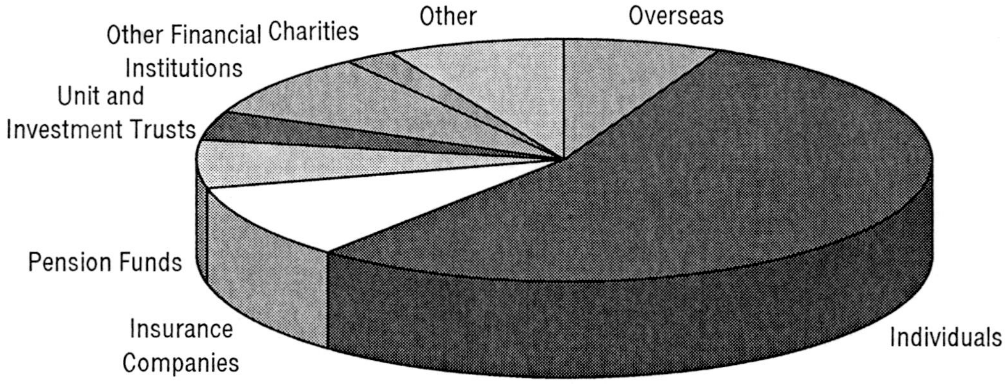

Share ownership 2010

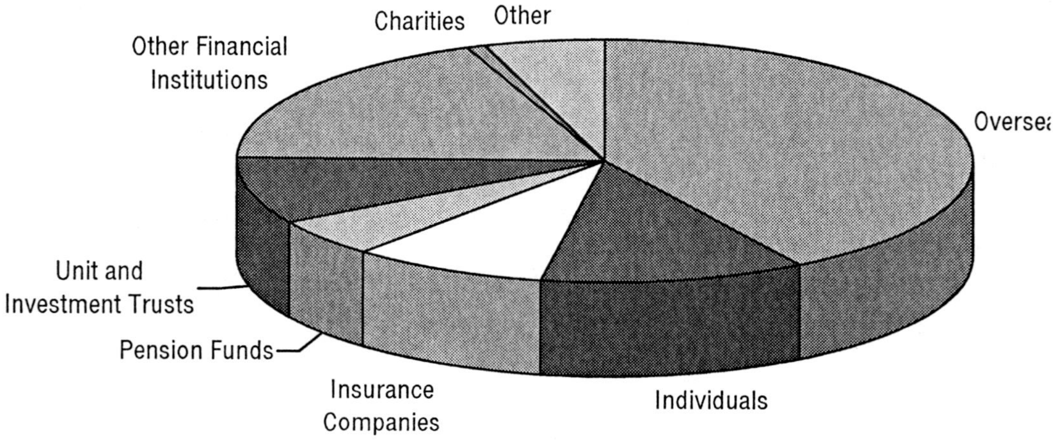

3.2 Types of fund

A variety of funds exist. Each has its own particular risk/reward profile stemming from

- Its initial objectives, return maximising/liability matching.
- The value and time horizons of the liabilities it has to meet (if any).
- The assets it can invest in.
- The liquidity they require within the fund.
- The risk they can tolerate in the fund.
- Its tax status.
- Legislation governing its powers.

3.2.1 Pension funds

A pension fund represents a pool of money to be invested now to achieve either a specific return as a **proportion of salary** (final salary or **defined benefit schemes**) over a number of years, or a general increase in value (**money purchase or defined contribution schemes**).

Generally speaking, pension funds have fairly **long-term** horizons and, as such, are prepared to take on board a higher degree of risk since any shortfall in the fund can be made up in future investment performance.

Pension funds also have to keep control over the real rate of return that they earn since their liabilities, the pension payments, will be expanding in line with inflation.

Defined pension schemes are not allowed to make profits or losses so must aim to ensure that their assets cover their liabilities both now and on a projected basis (in the future). Assuming for a fund that assets cover liabilities at present, the primary driver of their required return, the required **Actuarial Rate of Return**, is how rapidly the fund liabilities are growing. This will be driven by such factors as

- Current employee length of service and ages – influencing likely ultimate length of service
- Potential wage inflation rates
- Current pensioner ages and pension rights
- Mortality rates

As a consequence, pension funds tend to invest in slightly more speculative assets, such as **equities** and **property**, with only a small proportion of the fund in fixed interest instruments. They will tend to be substantial holders of index-linked stocks, partly because these guarantee real returns over a period of time, but also because the bonds themselves tend to have fairly high durations and are, therefore, sensitive to movement in real interest rates.

Note that as the age profile of contributions changes, the asset mix is likely to change. With **young** contributors the fund is likely to focus heavily on **equities**. This results in a greater **mismatching** between the assets and the liabilities. However, as the contributors get **older** the focus is likely to switch to **bonds** since they will provide greater price stability in the short term. This also provides more direct matching of the assets against the liabilities.

UK pension funds tend to have a much greater proportion of equities in their portfolios than Continental European pension funds.

3.2.2 Life assurance companies

In common with pension funds, life assurance companies tend to have reasonably **long-term** liabilities and are, once again, able to take on board a higher degree of risk. Again, this tends to involve a high proportion of their assets being invested into equities and property with only a small proportion being invested into the fixed interest markets.

As a **long-term** fund, life assurance companies are able to take reasonably higher degrees of risk and may be tempted towards bonds of higher duration.

3.2.3 General insurance companies

General insurance companies have a much **shorter liability profile** than life funds. In essence, insurance is like taking a bet. The insured person pays the company the premium. The insurance company makes money if they are able to take in this premium and earn investment income on it, which exceeds the amounts of any claims arising on the policy. Since claims are likely to arise in the immediate future, for example in the next five years, they are unable to take substantial risks, forcing them to invest a greater proportion of their fund into 'risk-free' government securities. Whilst the returns may not be as high, the fund simply cannot take any risk.

Both life assurance funds and general insurance funds are closely monitored to ensure that the solvency of the company is in no way called into question. Overall, this tends to make both of them more risk-averse than pension funds, but there is a marked difference between life assurance companies and general insurance companies in the risk/reward profile they adopt.

3.2.4 Collective investment schemes

Collective investment schemes are operations where a large number of small investors pool their money together to achieve a large fund that is placed under professional investment management. These funds can be in the form of unit trusts, OEICs or investment trusts. In essence, there is not a great deal of difference between the three types of trust, barring a degree of regulatory difference.

The overall objectives of each fund are determined in advance in the trust deed. This states the objective in terms of risk/reward profile and may indicate the appropriate markets in which to invest. For example, it may be felt worthwhile for an investment manager to establish a unit trust investing in highly speculative fixed interest instruments, such as bonds with very high durations in order to maximise returns for its investors.

On the other hand, other groups of investors may wish to have their money placed into reasonably secure short-term liquid issues generating a reasonable income flow. Each scheme will have its own particular emphasis and a selection of stocks, and a strategy will be determined by this emphasis.

3.2.5 Discretionary customers

Discretionary customers are, generally speaking, high net worth individuals who place their funds under management with a broker. As with collective investment schemes, the objectives of these individuals vary. Some customers may be looking for rapid capital appreciation with minimal income flows, whilst others may be looking for a secure portfolio with a guaranteed flow of income. Either way, a discretionary portfolio will be put together for the private client.

Once again, it is the duty of the investment manager to ensure that he understands the objectives of the individual customer and that the objectives are consistent with the customer's circumstances. With regard to discretionary agreements for individual customers, there are a number of important rulebook procedures under the FSA's rules which need to be adhered to.

4 Individual Investment Management

4.1 Fundamental criteria for providing investment advice

One of the Principles for Businesses, *Customers: Relationships of Trust*, issued by the FSA requires that the firm obtain information about its customer. This ties in with the specific rule on suitability that requires the firm to give suitable advice based on the information it knows or might reasonably infer about a customer.

This information will normally be obtained through the use of a customer questionnaire. If the customer does not respond to the questionnaire it will not prevent the firm from acting on his or her behalf. However, it will limit the protection that the customer receives.

4.1.1 Key information

1. **The customer's income**
2. **Present net assets**

   Is the customer a homeowner?

   What other investments does the customer have?

3. **Tax position**

   Is the customer a higher rate taxpayer? If so, only certain instruments will have the appropriate features. One of the most effective investments for a higher rate taxpayer is **short-dated low-coupon gilts**. The advantages of these stocks are that as low-coupon stocks they trade below par, and will be redeemed at par within the next seven years generating a tax-free gain.

4. **Their investment objectives**

   Some investors may be prepared to take on substantial levels of risk. Others may require that their capital remains safe whilst producing a steady flow of income. An investment that lends itself to the latter objective is a floating rate note. Since it carries a regular coupon, which varies with the market return, it tends to retain its par value.

   Other investors will not be concerned with the income flows from an investment but wish their portfolio to be biased towards capital growth.

5 The Investment Management Process

5.1 Introduction

There are three activities involved in the investment management process, specifically

- Asset allocation.
- Market timing.
- Stock selection.

Each of these activities is outlined briefly below.

5.2 Asset allocation

Asset allocation is the allocation of the funds available between the various instruments or financial markets.

All fund managers require a knowledge of asset allocation according to more fundamental principles. This is perhaps the most subjective area of fund management, and one where there will never be a single correct answer. Given the same fund and client, it is unlikely that any two fund managers would produce exactly the same asset allocation and make exactly the same investment decisions. However, it would be reasonable to assume that any allocations would have a broadly similar effect. The justification for this last statement is that the fund manager has a legal and professional duty to base the asset allocation on the client's wishes with particular regard to the criteria discussed above when identifying the client's objectives, specifically the following.

- Matching liabilities.
- Meeting any ethical considerations.
- Remaining within risk tolerances.
- Maximising fund performance.

There are three basic rules the fund manager should bear in mind when trying to satisfy the client's investment objectives.

- The fund manager should take every step to diversify risk, a process requiring an understanding of the different risk factors affecting all the investments in which he may be investing as well as the impact of foreign exchange.
- The fund manager should be aware that the best way to match the client's liabilities if they are fixed in money terms is by investing in bonds, since this will generate cash flows from interest and redemption proceeds which will allow the liabilities to be met as they arise.
- Asset allocation is effectively a compromise between matching investments to client liabilities and investing assets in more attractive markets in order to maximise fund performance.

5.3 Market timing

Market timing involves adjusting the sensitivity of the portfolio to anticipated changes. A fund manager engages in market timing when he does not agree with the consensus about the market, i.e. he is more bullish or more bearish than the market, and rebalances his portfolio to take advantage of this view.

5.4 Stock selection

Stock selection is the selection of the specific stocks within each asset class. The precise approach adopted depends on the investment management style adopted, i.e. active or passive.

6 Investment Management Style

There are two overall styles that the investment manager can adopt. On the one hand, an active investment manager is one who intervenes with the portfolio on a regular basis, attempting to use individual expertise in order to enhance the overall return of the fund. Passive investment management, on the other hand, establishes a strategy which, once established, should guarantee the appropriate level of return for the fund. These are, perhaps, two extreme versions of investment management. There are alternatives that represent hybrids between the two extremes.

CHAPTER ROUNDUP

Purpose of investment management

- Investment management is the management of an investment portfolio on behalf of a private client or an institution.
- The objective of the fund/investors will either be to match future liabilities or to maximise returns within given risk parameters.
- Whilst the investment manager will take primary responsibility for managing the money, the role of protecting the assets is often passed over to a trustee.

Types of funds

- There are two main types of pension scheme: defined benefits schemes which pay a proportion of final salary at retirement; and defined contribution schemes which pay a pension based on the amount of contributions and investment performance up to retirement.
- Life assurance and general insurance companies also invest the premiums they receive to generate returns.
- Collective investment schemes include unit trusts, investment trusts and open-ended investment companies (OEICs). All offer investors benefits of diversification, professional fund management and the opportunity to invest in worldwide assets.
- The investment management process involves asset allocation, market timing and stock selection.
- Investment managers may follow an active process of trying to outperform the market, or a passive approach of merely aiming to track the market.

Pre-requisites for an investment management

To carry out his responsibilities correctly the investment manager must understand and be able to determine

- Investment returns and risks.
- Investment values.
- Details about the characteristics, returns, risks and valuation of the various assets available.
- How a funds performance should be assessed.

and it is these areas that are covered in subsequent chapters.

2 Data and Data Presentation

INTRODUCTION

Data can be displayed in a variety of different ways. Where there is lots of data, rather than showing a raw mass of numbers, it may be clearer to use tables, charts and graphs to convey the information.

We will look at both sample and population data and explore various presentation methods including bar charts and Lorenz curves.

CHAPTER CONTENTS

Chapter Learning Objectives

26 Statistics and financial mathematics

Demonstrate an ability to apply statistical and financial mathematics techniques

26.1 Sources of data

26.1.1 **Distinguish** between primary and secondary sources of data.

26.1.2 **Identify** examples of primary and secondary data.

26.1.3 **Distinguish** between a population and a sample.

26.1.4 **Explain** the key sampling methods.

26.1.5 **Distinguish** between continuous and discrete data.

26.1.6 **Define** categorical data and explain how it can be converted to ordinal data.

26.1.7 **Interpret** a frequency and relative frequency distribution.

26.1.8 **Explain** the use of the following in the presentation of data.

- Lorenz curve.
- Pie chart.
- Bar chart.
- Histogram.
- Scatter plots.
- Graphs.

1 Introduction

Analysing investment opportunities involves the collection, assimilation and presentation of a large amount of information regarding the security under consideration. This is true regardless of whether the investment manager is using fundamental analysis, technical analysis or quantitative analysis, though differing types and levels of information would be required for each.

For example, a technical analyst studying equities would require detailed information regarding the past price movements of a share and would wish to be able to appreciate the information as easily as possible. Clearly, he could obtain a list of the values the share has taken each day for, say, the past five years. However, this is unlikely to be the most convenient form. Some kind of chart, plotting share prices against time, would obviously be much more suitable from the point of view of showing trends, and hence much more useful.

A fundamental analyst would probably wish to appreciate the changes in the fundamental factors that influence the performance of the company and hence the value of its shares. He would, perhaps, wish to study any changes that have taken place in the context of a wide range of economic variables such as inflation rates, interest rates, exchange rates, etc. Again, it is important to be able to appreciate the information contained within such data, and hence again a chart plotting these factors and how they have moved over time may be the most appropriate form.

Our considerations are

- How do we collect data, i.e. what sources are available?
- What different types of data could we collect and what unique factors may each type have?
- How can this data be presented in the most convenient and useful form?

2 Definitions

2.1 Sources of data

Learning objectives

26.1.1 Distinguish between primary and secondary sources of data.

26.1.2 Identify examples of primary and secondary data.

2.1.1 Primary data

The collection or generation of new data in relation to a specific project or task is referred to as collection of **primary data**. Primary data may be obtained through the use of such techniques as

- Scientific investigation/research.
- Observation.
- Discussion.
- Questionnaires/market research.

Clearly, since it is produced as a result of research into a specific project or task, it is relatively time consuming and hence expensive to obtain.

2.1.2 Secondary data

There are many companies and government agencies whose role is to collect and distribute/sell information. Such existing data is referred to as **secondary data**. For those who originally collected the data, it was primary data. However, its use by others would not require any new original investigations, hence they would regard it as secondary data.

In the financial markets, in particular, there are an extensive number of secondary data sources available, both in written publications and on computer databases. These will probably provide the initial source of any analyst's data due to their immediate availability and relatively low cost. However, this may need to be followed up by some original research of the form described above.

Published sources of secondary data

The following are frequently used sources of published secondary data.

- Government publications such as
  - The *Annual Abstract of Statistics* and the *Monthly Digest of Statistics* which provide general statistical information regarding the economy covering such factors as population, employment, production, transport, energy, etc.
  - Monthly *Economic Trends* and monthly *Financial Statistics* which provide more detailed economic data such as money supply information, interest rates, balance of payments figures, etc.
  - *Regional Trends* and *Social Trends*, both annual publications, which provide more specialist regional and social data regarding population trends, employment, etc.
  - The *Employment Gazette*, providing detailed labour market data such as employment, unemployment, earnings, etc.

- *Bank of England Quarterly Bulletin*, showing a variety of different economic indicators such as interest rates, inflation rates, etc.
- *Federal Reserve Bulletin*, produced monthly by the US Federal Reserve, showing similar information in relation to the US.
- International Monetary Fund's *International Financial Statistics*.
- The Bank for International Settlement publishes data regarding international banking cash flows.
- The World Bank and OECD (Organisation for Economic Co-operation and Development) provide a range of international economic data.

Computerised sources of secondary data

The following are examples of frequently used computerised sources of secondary data.

- **Datastream (part of Thomson Reuters)** and **Bloomberg**, which all provide historical data regarding securities' prices and a range of other economic variables.
- **Extel (part of Thomson Reuters)**, which provides summarised data and statistics, such as P/E ratios obtained from company accounts.

2.2 Sampling and populations

Learning objective	26.1.3 **Distinguish** between a population and a sample.

2.2.1 Introduction

When we are gathering information it is important to appreciate the distinction between a sample and the full population. Have we asked only a few people their opinion or have we asked everyone? The terms are fairly easy to understand when we are talking about, say, an election where the whole population can vote. The terms are, however, used more broadly in relation to data gathering.

2.2.2 Population

The **population represents all the members of a specifically defined group**. When undertaking some investigation it is important to clearly define the population you are considering. It may, for example, be

- Everyone of voting age in the UK.
- Everyone of voting age living in London – clearly this is a subset of the above population, however, if we are only interested in people living in London, e.g. local elections, then they would represent our **full** population and the views of someone who did not live in London would be irrelevant.
- Everyone living in a particular street if we were interested in views regarding parking restrictions in that street.
- All UK companies.
- All UK listed companies – clearly a subset of the above.
- All FTSE 100 companies – again, a subset of the above.

The important point is that we must be able to clearly define the group of items that we are interested in. Any item that falls within that definition will be a member of the population.

2.2.3 Sample

We may wish to consider every item in the population, e.g. the population of voters at a general election. However, due to the costs involved in investigating the full population, it is more common to investigate a **sample**.

A sample represents a subset of the full population that has been selected for investigation. For example, in establishing the Consumer Price Index (CPI), the prices of a sample of items are investigated rather than all goods available. The CPI is, however, taken to be representative of all goods, i.e. we investigate a sample to provide information regarding the full population.

2.3 Sample selection

Learning objective	**26.1.4 Explain** the key sampling methods.

2.3.1 Introduction

If we are going to select a sample which we hope will enable us to draw some conclusions about the full population, then it must be representative of the full population. We will, therefore, need to take great care in the selection of our sample and in determining the size of our sample. Sample selection may be either

- Random; or
- Non-random.

2.3.2 Random sampling

A **random sample** is one where **every item in the population has an equal chance of being selected**. If such a sample is large enough, it should be representative of the population. Indeed, the margin for error can be statistically evaluated when such a technique is used correctly.

The difficulty lies in achieving a purely random sample. For example, if we wished to establish voting intentions we would need to select people from everywhere in the UK. Simply conducting a survey in the centre of a few large cities would probably exclude the possibility of obtaining the views of a substantial part of the population. As a result, though we may randomly test the city dwellers by this method, it is not a pure random sample.

2.3.3 Non-random sampling

The example above clearly illustrates the difficulty, in certain circumstances, of obtaining a good random sample. We may, therefore, need to select a sample on another basis that will, to a degree, involve an element of judgement. This, by definition, will mean that we are excluding some of the population.

Quota sampling

A popular non-random sampling technique is a quota sampling, where a sample is selected which it is believed will be representative of the full population. Help with this may be obtained from sources such as census information that will enable us to get a picture of the proportion of the population displaying a range of characteristics. A sample can then be selected which displays these characteristics and, hence, should be reasonably representative. This is the typical approach utilised in market research.

Panelling

Panelling is where a hopefully representative sample is selected to provide continuous information over a period of time. Television viewing figures are obtained in this way. A panel of individuals report on their viewing habits – the television companies do not know what everyone is watching all the time!

Postal or telephone surveys

We may try to achieve a random sample by undertaking a postal or telephone survey enabling us to obtain very large coverage of the population. This will not be a random sample, however, since not everyone has a telephone (hence they cannot be selected) and not everyone would choose to respond to a postal survey. Indeed, there is a reasonable chance of obtaining an atypical response since the 'average' person may not reply and only those with strong or extreme views do.

2.3.4 Sample size

The larger the sample, the more likely it will be to represent the full population. Indeed, if we continue to extend a sample we will ultimately test the full population.

Conversely, the smaller the sample, the less representative it is likely to be. Clearly, asking just one person their opinion at general election time will provide very little useful information from the point of view of assessing the likely voting patterns and election result.

3 Types of Data

Learning objective

26.1.5 Distinguish between continuous and discrete data.
26.1.6 Define categorical data and explain how it can be converted to ordinal data.

The data that we utilise may be obtained from various sources and may represent either a sample or the full population. It may also take a variety of forms.

Continuous data

Continuous data is data that can take any value whatsoever. Real life statistics such as height, weight, temperature, etc. fall within this category.

Discrete data

Discrete data is data that can only take certain specific values, such as whole numbers. In the financial markets, data is most frequently of this form as money changes hands in whole units.

Categorical or nominal data

Categorical or nominal data is data that has been classified into a **number of distinct categories**. The collection of this type of data is seen on census forms and market research questionnaires, where a box is ticked in response to questions such as 'Which of the following newspapers do you read?' (followed by a list of popular dailies), 'Do you drive a car?', 'Did you vote at the last election?', etc.

To process such data on a computer, we may assign a number to each of the bands. However, this number does not convey any other information and cannot be used to calculate such statistics as the standard deviation (covered later). Such data can only be used as a simple statistic, such as – 30% of people drive cars.

Ordinal data

Ordinal data is data that has been classified into a **number of distinct ranked categories**. The star system for hotel ratings is an example of such a system, or the classification of degrees into firsts, seconds and thirds.

When assigning numbers to this type of data for processing, care should again be taken in trying to draw statistical conclusions. Once more, the calculation of, say, a standard deviation (covered later) would be inappropriate and only such measures which are based on the position within the order, such as the median (also covered later), should be considered.

4 Data Presentation

4.1 Introduction

Having gathered our data, we now need to find a way of presenting it in a useful form for analysis.

Example

We have gathered the following data regarding the weekly sales volumes of packets of cornflakes from 200 shops.

26 59 51 41 27 33 39 28 47 30 41 51 44 41 30 48 31 35 27 22
42 39 48 32 42 45 38 56 22 55 52 25 41 34 36 52 40 42 37 34
33 36 38 28 34 32 42 43 36 31 29 38 34 39 28 43 47 39 41 30
58 32 42 35 40 50 26 22 31 47 36 32 38 20 21 44 50 33 37 42
46 45 31 38 39 52 25 39 34 41 37 37 35 44 32 51 39 36 24 38
51 41 27 35 31 48 30 41 44 22 59 26 47 28 39 33 27 41 51 30
25 52 37 42 40 52 36 34 41 34 39 42 22 56 38 45 42 32 48 55
38 29 41 39 47 43 28 39 34 30 36 33 36 43 42 32 34 28 38 31
32 36 37 33 50 44 21 20 38 42 32 58 31 22 26 50 40 35 42 47
37 37 24 36 39 51 32 44 35 38 45 46 34 39 25 52 39 38 31 41

Clearly, this just looks like a list of random numbers, so how can it be presented in a useful form?

4.2 Tables

Learning objective | **26.1.7 Interpret** a frequency and relative frequency distribution.

4.2.1 Introduction

The tabulation of data provides a means of summarising the raw data in a more convenient and usable form, whilst retaining the detailed content, i.e. values involved.

4.2.2 Frequency distribution

A **frequency distribution** groups the data into **bands of specific values** and displays the **frequency of occurrence** of each band.

Tabulating into a frequency distribution represents a very powerful way of presenting and summarising data, though care needs to be taken in the selection of the size of the bands, as illustrated by the following tabulations of the above data.

Solution

Version 1 – Band size of 1

One potential frequency distribution for the above data would be to group it by each possible value giving (where f represents the frequency of observation, i.e. the number of shops selling each observed number of packets).

Sales	f	Sales	f	Sales	f	Sales	f
20	2	30	6	40	4	50	4
21	4	31	10	41	12	51	6
22	4	32	8	42	12	52	6
23	0	33	8	43	4	53	0
24	2	34	8	44	6	54	0
25	4	35	6	45	4	55	2
26	4	36	10	46	2	56	2
27	4	37	8	47	6	57	0
28	6	38	12	48	4	58	2
29	2	39	14	49	0	59	2

This format, however, does not appear to provide a substantial improvement over the raw data.

Version 2 – Band size of 4

An alternative, and perhaps more useful, presentation would be to group this data into equal groups, as follows.

Sales Range	f	Units Sold
20-23	10	212
24-27	14	360
28-31	24	716
32-35	30	1,002
36-39	44	1,658
40-43	32	1,328
44-47	18	818
48-51	14	698
52-55	8	422
56-59	6	346
	200	7,560

This format is clearly more manageable and usable. We can now easily see a trend in the figures that was far from apparent in the raw data or the original frequency distribution.

Version 3 – Band size of 10

Summarising into wider equal groups produces the following.

Sales Range	f	Units Sold
20-29	32	798
30-39	90	3,150
40-49	54	2,338
50-59	24	1,274
	200	7,560

Clearly, in this last case, a lot of trend information is lost, and if we enlarged the bands further the situation would become worse.

4.2.3 Relative frequency distribution

A relative frequency distribution displays the same data as a **percentage of the sample or population size**, rather than as actual observed frequencies.

A relative frequency distribution would, possibly, be more appropriate where a **more direct comparison between bandings** is desired or where the sample size has been exceptionally large and the scale of the numbers may obscure their understanding.

Solution

The second alternative above (version 2) could be represented as a relative frequency distribution as follows.

Sales Range	f	Units Sold
	%	%
20-23	5	2.81
24-27	7	4.76
28-31	12	9.47
32-35	15	13.25
36-39	22	21.93
40-43	16	17.57
44-47	9	10.82
48-51	7	9.23
52-55	4	5.58
56-59	3	4.58
	100%	100.00%

We can now easily see that 15% of stores achieve sales of between 32 and 35 packets a week, which represents 13.25% of the total sales volume.

Cumulative frequency distribution

An extension of the above ideas would be to prepare a **cumulative frequency distribution**. This could be used in addition to either the frequency distribution or the relative frequency distribution and would show the number/percentage of a sample or population with a value less than or equal to a given figure.

Solution

Illustrating this idea in connection to the relative distribution we established above gives

Sales Range	f		Units Sold	
	%	Cum %	%	Cum %
20-23	5	5	2.81	2.81
24-27	7	12	4.76	7.57
28-31	12	24	9.47	17.04
32-35	15	39	13.25	30.29
36-39	22	61	21.93	52.22
40-43	16	77	17.57	69.79
44-47	9	86	10.82	80.61
48-51	7	93	9.23	89.84
52-55	4	97	5.58	95.42
56-59	3	100	4.58	100.00
	100%		100.00%	

We can now easily see 39% of stores achieve sales of 35 units or less and contributed just 30.29% of the total sales volume.

4.2.4 Data interval/band width

As we said at the outset, frequency distributions (basic, relative or cumulative) provide a very powerful way of presenting data. However, the selection of the data interval or band width is essential to the meaningfulness and usefulness of the data presented, and needs to be done with great care on the basis of the individual data being considered. There are no rules regarding this aspect of data presentation.

This is, perhaps, an even more acute problem when we are considering continuous data where we must be very careful to ensure that all items are included within a band, but only within one band. For continuous data, bands will need to be described as, for example

- Greater than or equal to 20 but less than 24.
- Greater than or equal to 24 but less than 28.
- Greater than or equal to 28 but less than 32, etc.

4.3 Graphs and charts

Learning objective

26.1.8 Explain the use of the following in the presentation of data: Lorenz curve; pie chart; bar chart; histogram; scatter plots and graphs.

4.3.1 Introduction

Tables provide a useful way of presenting information and retaining the detailed values, though sometimes the detail in the numbers may obscure the understanding slightly. It is possible that the same level of information can be conveyed more easily and intuitively by the use of graphs or charts.

There are a variety of different methods of producing charts which are each suited to different applications. We consider below some of the more fundamental types.

4.3.2 Lorenz curve

A **Lorenz Curve** is a visual representation of the **two cumulative frequency distributions** against each other. It shows the proportion of items on the x-axis that contribute a proportion of values on the y-axis and is often used to represent income distribution where we may find the following.

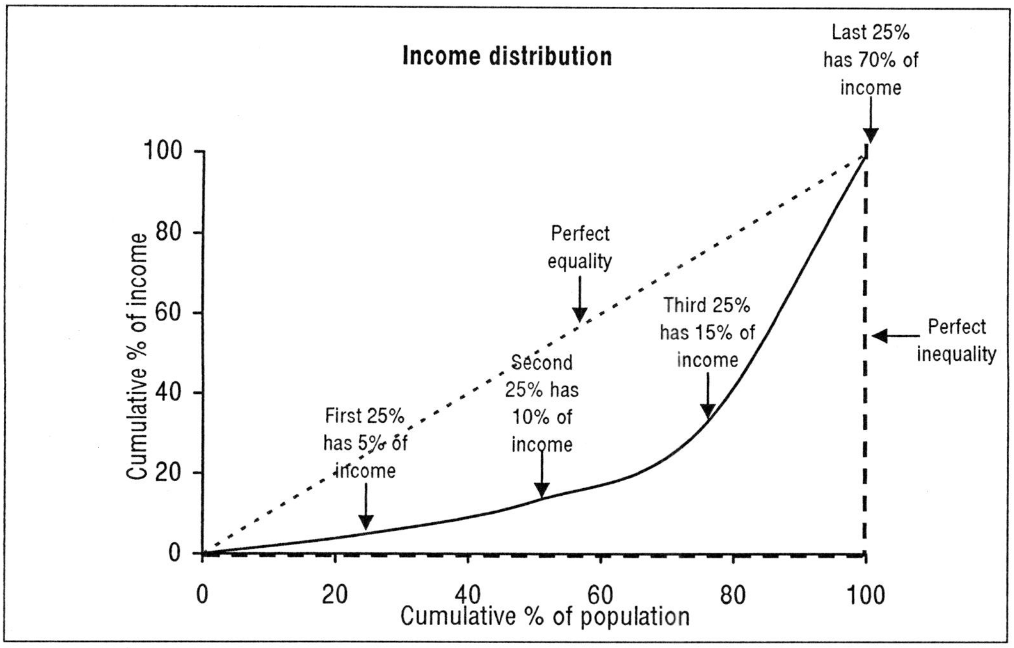

If, say, income was evenly distributed across the entire population then the Lorenz curve would be the straight line shown above, the line of perfect equality. In an equal distribution 25% of the population would have 25% of the income, 50% of the population would have 50% of income, 75% of the population would have 75% of income etc – percentage of population and percentage of income being balanced.

If, on the other hand, all income was earned by just one individual then the curve would be the line of perfect inequality shown above.

Perfect equality and perfect inequality are two extremes and in any other situation we would have a Lorenz curve between these two extremes, ie below the line of perfect equality but above the line of perfect inequality with

- A more even distribution giving a straighter the line (a line close to the even distribution)
- A more unequal distribution giving a more extreme curve (a line closer to perfect inequality)

So for any distribution where we are looking at positive cumulative percentages it must be that the Lorenz curve

- Cannot rise above the line of perfect equality
- Cannot fall below the line of perfect inequality
- Demonstrates a convex shape with an increasing slope

Any curve that does not have these attributes is not a valid Lorenz curve.

4.3.3 Pie charts

A pie chart provides an alternative way of representing **relative frequencies** by dividing a circle (the pie) into sections (slices) whose area is proportional to the relative frequency. It is of most use when communicating **categorical data**.

Since a circle spans 360° and we wish this to represent the full sample/population, i.e. 100%, then we will use 3.6° to represent each 1%, e.g. 22% = $22 \times 3.6° = 79.2°$ on the chart.

A pie chart for the above relative frequency distribution would appear as follows.

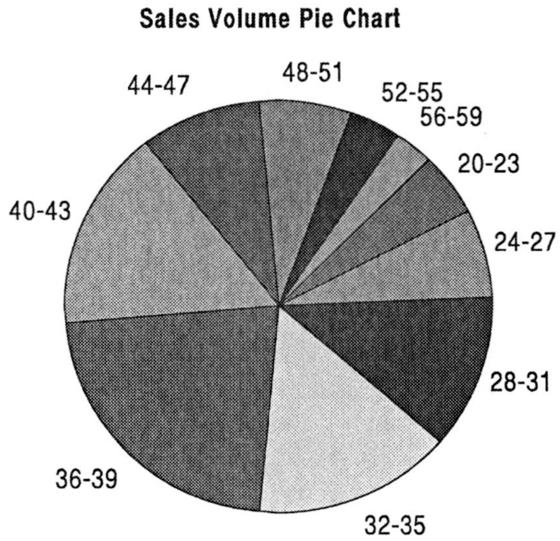

4.3.4 Bar chart

A **bar chart** represents, through the **height of a bar**, the number or percentage of items displaying a particular characteristic.

Example

Suppose our sales volume data can be sub-analysed into the following cross tabulation showing the number of stores and their volumes by region.

Volume	North	South	East	West	Total
20-29	8	8	9	7	32
30-39	22	23	25	20	90
40-49	11	15	15	13	54
50-59	4	5	9	6	24
	45	51	58	46	200

We could construct the following bar chart to illustrate the number of stores by region.

4.3.5 Component bar chart

If we wished to use this graph to convey further information, we could construct a **component bar chart**, breaking down the number of stores by region and by sales volume as follows.

Stores by Region and Sales Volume

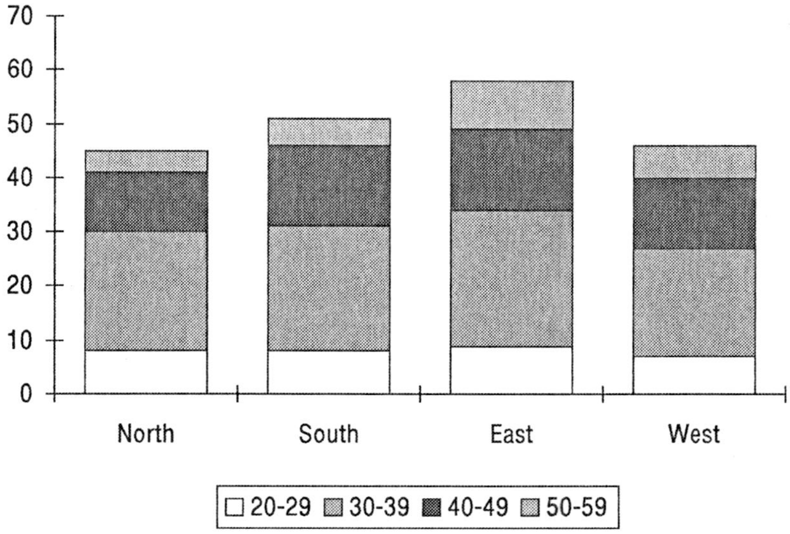

4.3.6 Histograms

A histogram displays the **number or percentage of items falling within a given band through the area of a bar**.

Generally, a histogram is used to describe circumstances where one bar is used to represent a range of values for **continuous data**. Where discrete data is grouped (as in the above example, where we group into bands four-wide), it may be represented as a histogram as if it were continuous, as follows.

Sales Volume Histogram

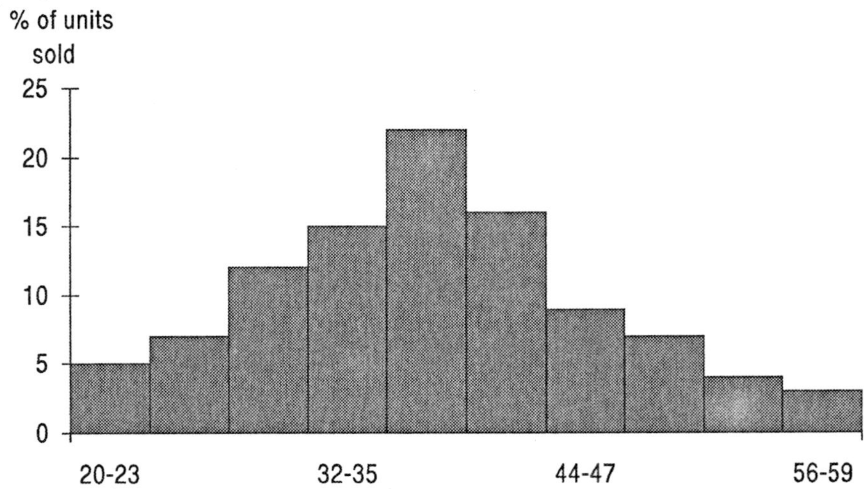

One problem that may arise in relation to a histogram is where the extreme bands are simply described as greater than something or less than something. For example, if the extreme bands in the diagram above were simply described as ≤ 23 and ≥ 56, i.e. they are not bounded. How do we decide what width to make the band?

There are no strict rules regarding this and it will require a degree of judgement on behalf of the researcher. If a definite upper and lower limit are known, then these will provide obvious bounds. If they are not, a bound will need to be assumed, since the histogram cannot be drawn unless all areas are bounded.

One consequence of this, however, is how tall we make the band. In completing the histogram, one thing that we will need to bear in mind is that **if any bands are wider than any others, their heights will have to be scaled down proportionally to ensure that the area of that band still reflects the number of items.** This problem is most likely to arise in the context of the extreme bands, however it may also be applicable to other bands of differing widths.

For example, if three bands each contain 24 items but the bands are one, two and three units wide respectively, then their heights will be 24, 12 and 8 respectively, so that they each have an area of 24.

4.3.7 Graphs and scattergraphs

Introduction – basic graphs

One of the most effective ways to demonstrate the relationship between two items is to plot them on a graph, where the values of one of the factors is plotted along the horizontal axis (the x-axis) and the corresponding values of the other factor are plotted along the vertical axis (the y-axis). We may then be able to use this graph to try to make some predictions.

Independent v dependent

By convention, the variable thought to be responsible for causing the change (the **independent variable**) is plotted along the x-axis, and the variable whose value is driven by this x value and whose change we are seeking to predict (the **dependent variable**) is plotted up the y-axis.

A frequent requirement is to plot how something has changed with **time**. In this situation the item alters **with time**, i.e. the item is the dependent variable, time is the independent one. Time cannot be altered, i.e. time could never be the dependent variable. Hence we plot time along the x-axis and the item along the y-axis.

Example

The sales achieved by a company over the past ten years have been as follows.

Year	£000
1999	1,000
2000	1,210
2001	1,450
2002	1,730
2003	2,080
2004	2,490
2005	2,990
2006	3,590
2007	4,300
2008	5,160

Plot this data on a graph.

Solution

Clearly the sales vary with time, i.e. sales is the dependent variable, time is the independent one (we could not make time go faster by selling more units!). Hence, we plot time along the x-axis and sales along the y-axis, giving the following **scattergraph**.

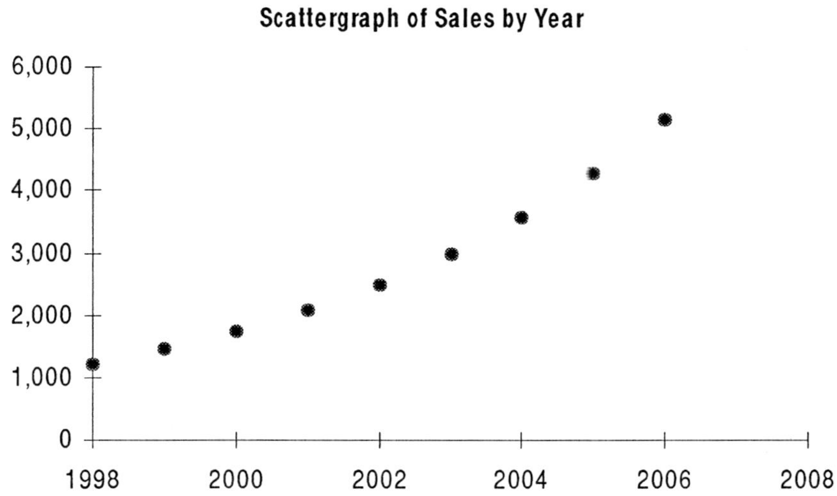

Alternatively, this data may be represented by a graph in which those points are joined by a smooth line, as follows.

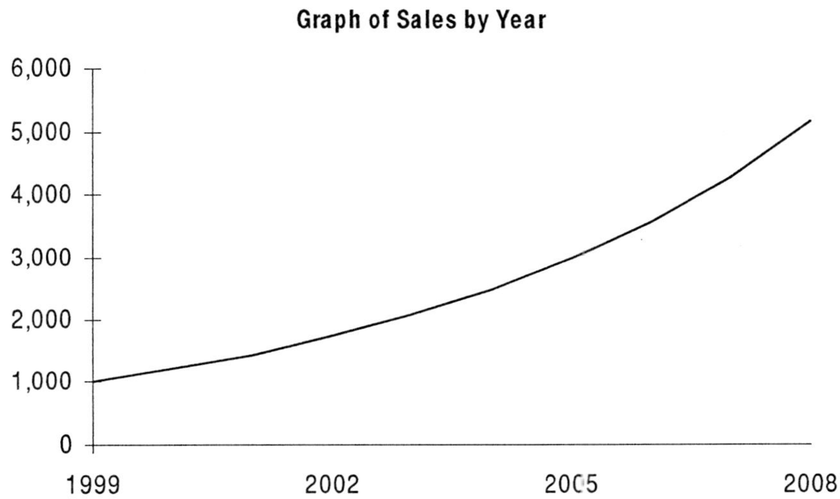

This graph shows a trend of rising sales values, which is clearly very positive for the company.

Unfortunately, curves do not lend themselves well to extrapolation, or predicting forward, hence this may not be the preferred presentation and we may find the semi-logarithmic graph described below more useful.

Axis values

When drawing a graph, the selection of the y-axis values is of fundamental importance. Clearly, we should select y-axis values that are representative of the data being graphed. It would be fairly unrealistic in our example above to show the y-axis going up to, say, £600m, as the data would hardly appear at all.

Axis scale – rates of change and semi-logarithmic graphs

Of equal importance to the usefulness of a graph is the selection of the scale. The illustration above shows a trend of accelerating growth in sales. When we are in the position that we wish to establish the rate of change, it may be more appropriate to utilise a semi-logarithmic scale, effectively plotting the log of the value instead of the value itself on the y-axis.

On such a graph, if something is growing at a constant rate it will appear as a straight line which will be much more useful for prediction purposes. In addition, any move away from steady growth would be highlighted by this graph. If the item's growth rate increased then the graph would become steeper. Conversely, if the growth rate slowed, the graph would become flatter.

If we plot the above figures on a semi-logarithmic graph we obtain the following.

Semi-Logarithmic Graph of Sales by Year

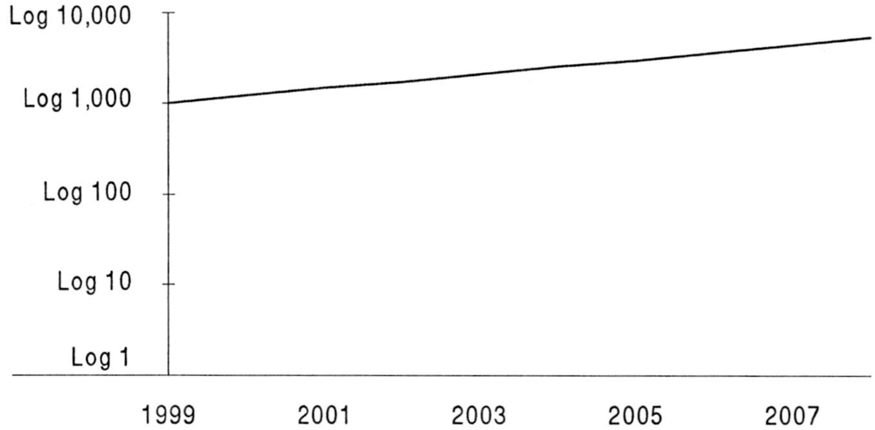

What we can see on this graph is that a ten-fold increase in value is represented by the same vertical distance, hence its appropriateness for illustrating constant growth which compounds in this way.

Chapter Roundup

Data source

- Data can be distilled into primary data, which relates to the collection of new data, and secondary data, which arises when existing data is distilled and packaged together into publications.
- Secondary sources include government statistics, Bank of England reports, IMF statistics.
- Computerised secondary sources include Datastream, Bloomberg, Extel.

Populations and samples

- A population represents all the members of a specifically defined group.
- A sample represents a subset of the full population.
- Samples can either be
  - random, where every item has an equal chance of being selected.
  - non-random such as
    - quota sampling.
    - panelling.
    - postal and telephone surveys.

Types of data

- Continuous data is data that can take any value whatsoever. Discrete data is data that can only take on specific values, such as money, which changes value in whole units.
- Categorical data is data that has been classified into a number of distinct categories (ie categorised). Ordinal data is data that has been classified into a number of distinct ranked categories (ie categorised and ordered).

Tables

- Frequency distributions group the data into bands of specific values and display the frequency of occurrence of each band. Relative frequency distributions show proportions or percentages rather than frequencies.
- Cumulative frequency distributions can be used to show the number of items with a value less than or equal to a given figure. Cumulative relative frequency distributions show the proportion or percentage with a value less than or equal to a given figure.

Graphs and charts

- Lorenz curves are a visual comparative representation of the two cumulative frequency distributions.
- Pie charts represent an alternative way of representing relative frequencies.
- A bar chat displays the number or percentage of items falling within a given band through the height or length of the bar.
- A histogram displays the number or percentage of items falling within a given band through the area of a bar.
- Scatter graphs can be plotted to establish if a relationship exists between an independent variable (x-axis) and a dependent variable (y-axis).

TEST YOUR KNOWLEDGE

Check your knowledge of the chapter here, without referring back to the text.

1. Would data obtained through scientific research be classified as primary or secondary data?
2. Is panelling a form of random sampling?
3. Is temperature an example of continuous or discrete data?
4. What is ordinal data?
5. How does a relative frequency distribution differ from an ordinary frequency distribution?
6. What is a Lorenz curve?
7. Is the dependent variable on a scattergram shown on the 'y' or the 'x' axis?

Test Your Knowledge: Answers

1. Primary data.

   (See Section 2.1)

2. Panelling is a non-random sampling method.

   (See Section 2.3.3)

3. Continuous data (since it can take on any value, e.g. 24.269876 degrees centigrade).

   (See Section 3)

4. Ordinal data is data that has been classified into a number of distinct ranked categories.

   (See Section 3)

5. A relative frequency distribution converts the data into a percentage rather than an actual observed value.

   (See Section 4.2.3)

6. A visual representation of the two cumulative frequency distributions against each other.

   (See Section 4.3.2)

7. 'y'-axis.

   (See Section 4.3.7)

3 Statistical Analysis

INTRODUCTION

Statistical analysis encompasses the areas of location and dispersion measures, and regression and correlation analysis.

Location measures are used to condense down data into a central measure, an average figure. Dispersion measures tell us about the spread of data, ie its variability or volatility. Investment risk is often measured by the volatility, therefore the greater the volatility, the greater the spread of possible values and the larger the perceived risk of the investment. We would expect the spread of returns from a share to be greater than the spread of returns from a bond and this spread of data around a central point is frequently measured by the standard deviation.

Regression is a technique for identifying whether a relationship exists between two variables. Correlation tells us about the strength and the direction of the relationship.

CHAPTER CONTENTS

Chapter Learning Objectives

26 Statistics and Financial Mathematics

Demonstrate an ability to apply statistical and financial mathematics techniques

26.2 Summary data

26.2.1 **Define**, **explain** and **calculate** the following measures of central tendency for both raw data and interval data.

- Arithmetic mean.
- Geometric mean.
- Median.
- Mode.

26.2.2 **Distinguish** between symmetric and skewed data.

26.2.3 **Explain** the relationship between the mean, median and mode for symmetric and skewed data.

26.2.4 **Define**, **explain** and **calculate** the following measures of dispersion for both raw data and interval data.

- Standard deviation (population and sample).
- Variance.
- Range.
- Quartiles and percentiles.
- Interquartile range.

26.3 Correlation and bivariate linear regression

26.3.1 **Explain** the least-squares regression technique in deriving a line of best fit.

26.3.2 **Distinguish** between the dependent and independent variable.

26.3.3 **Interpret** the intercept and gradient components of a regression line.

26.3.4 **Calculate** a forecast value for the dependent variable given the regression line equation.

26.3.5 **Explain** and interpret the correlation coefficient in the context of linear regression.

23.3.6 **Explain** the shortfalls in the application of linear regression to forecasting, including 'correlation does not imply causation' and the pitfalls of data mining.

1 Introduction

1.1 Aim of location and dispersion measures

In a certain world, we would always know what is going to happen, e.g. what dividend return a share is going to offer, or how the stock market in general is going to perform. As a result, we would be able to make perfect investment decisions.

In a more realistic world, we do not know such factors for certain. We may be able to make an estimate based on technical analysis of previous performance or fundamental analysis of relevant factors. However, we would have to accept that this forecast is likely to be incorrect and that the true position may vary away from this estimate.

In performing our technical analysis, we would review past returns and how these have varied, hoping that these may give us some guide to the future, though bearing in mind the dangers of making this link. It is in this context that **location and dispersion measures may be of use to the investment manager**.

The purpose of location and dispersion measures is to indicate the

- Central/long run average value/return achieved – **location**.
- The variability or spread of values around this point – **dispersion**.

In the context of, say, shares these measures will provide us with an indication of

- The expected future **returns** from the share (all other things being equal).
- The **risk** we are facing (the potential variability of the returns about this expected return value) in holding the shares.

1.2 Considerations

There are a number of different measures outlined individually below, of which each has its own advantages and disadvantages.

The main consideration when undertaking any calculations is the way in which the data is presented. There are three possibilities with which we may be faced.

- Raw data.
- Tabulated data.
- Grouped data.

We will provide examples of each of these and show how the location and dispersion measures may be calculated for each.

1.2.1 Raw data

Raw data is where the data is presented as a simple list of figures or values that may or may not be ordered.

Example

The example we will use is the following ordered series of raw data.

1, 2, 3, 3, 4, 5, 5, 5, 6, 7, 8, 9, 20.

1.2.2 Tabulated data

Tabulating data is a useful method for summarising large volumes of **discrete data**, i.e. data that can only take certain values, such as whole numbers.

Example

The example we will use to illustrate this form of data presentation is

Value x	Frequency f
1	20
2	40
3	60
4	50
5	10
	180

1.2.3 Grouped data

Grouping data is a convenient way to summarise **continuous data**, i.e. data that can take any value within a range.

Example

The example we will use to illustrate this form of data presentation is

Range	Frequency f
0 to $4.\dot{9}$	30
5 to $9.\dot{9}$	50
10 to $14.\dot{9}$	40
15 to $19.\dot{9}$	10
	130

NB: $4.\dot{9}$ represents 4.9999.... (four point nine recurring), and hence the first range represents any number in the range greater than or equal to zero to less than five. Questions may use 4.9 to end such a range. They are not intending to exclude any items between 4.9 and 5.0, rather they are using 4.9 to indicate any number less than 5.

BPP LEARNING MEDIA

2 Location/Central Measures

2.1 Introduction

Learning objective

26.2.1 Define, explain and **calculate** the following measures of central tendency for both raw data and interval data: arithmetic mean; geometric mean; median and mode.

There are four location measures that we need to be familiar with.

- Arithmetic mean
- Median
- Mode
- Geometric mean

2.2 Arithmetic mean

2.2.1 Calculation

The arithmetic mean is the simple average that we are probably all used to. It is calculated by adding up (arithmetically) the observed values and dividing by the number of observed values. Again, the only difficulties arise in the way in which the data is presented.

2.2.2 Raw data

The calculation of the arithmetic mean can be mathematically expressed as

Formula to learn

$$\bar{x} = \frac{\sum x_i}{n}$$

where

$\bar{x}$ = the arithmetic mean

x_i = the observed values

$\sum$ represents the summation (i.e. the total) of those observed values

n = number of observed values

This could alternatively be shown as (and will certainly be calculated as)

Formula to learn

$$\bar{x} = \frac{x_1 + x_2 + x_3 + \cdots + x_n}{n}$$

Although the initial formula is the one we will be stating.

Solution

$$\bar{x} = \frac{\sum x_i}{n} = \frac{1+2+3+3+4+5+5+5+6+7+8+9+20}{13} = \frac{78}{13} = 6$$

2.2.3 Tabulated data

With tabulated data we will have many items with the same value (in the same band). If an item appears, say, 20 times, then rather than adding it in 20 times to the numerator of the fraction, we simply add 20 times the value as one figure.

The calculation of the arithmetic mean for tabulated data can thus be achieved using

Formula to learn

$$\bar{x} = \frac{\sum f_i x_i}{n}$$

where

$\bar{x}$ = the arithmetic mean

x_i = the observed values

f_i = the frequency with which those values have been observed

$\sum$ represents the summation (i.e. the adding together) of those following values

n = number of observed values

Solution

Value x	Frequency f	Frequency fx
1	20	20
2	40	80
3	60	180
4	50	200
5	10	50
	n = 180	$\sum f_i x_i$ = 530

Hence

$$\bar{x} = \frac{\sum f_i x_i}{n} = \frac{530}{180} = 2.94$$

2.2.4 Grouped data

The calculation for grouped data requires us to make the assumption that values are evenly spread within each range so we can, therefore, **evaluate each range based on its midpoint**. Having done this, the calculation is identical to the calculation for tabulated data.

The calculation of the mean for grouped data is

Formula to learn

$$\bar{x} = \frac{\sum f_i m_i}{n}$$

where

$\bar{x}$ = the arithmetic mean

m_i = the midpoint of the range

f_i = the frequency with which values in the ranges have been observed

$\sum$ represents the summation (i.e. the adding together) of those following values

n = number of observed values

Solution

Range	Midpoint m	Frequency f	Frequency fm
0 to 4.$\dot{9}$	2.5	30	75
5 to 9.$\dot{9}$	7.5	50	375
10 to 14.$\dot{9}$	12.5	40	500
15 to 19.$\dot{9}$	17.5	10	175
		n = 130	$\sum f_i m_i$ = 1,125

Hence

$$\bar{x} = \frac{\sum f_i m_i}{n} = \frac{1,125}{130} = 8.65$$

2.2.5 Comments

We should note in relation to the arithmetic mean that the calculated **mean is not necessarily one of the possible values**. This can easily be seen from the raw data example and the tabulated data example.

In addition, since all observed values are considered, this measure can **be severely distorted by extreme values**.

Example

Suppose in our raw data example the last observed item had been 100 rather than 20. The mean would then be

$$\bar{x} = \frac{\sum x_i}{n} = \frac{1+2+3+3+4+5+5+5+6+7+8+9+100}{13} = \frac{158}{13} = 12.15$$

when clearly the majority of observed values are less than nine.

2.2.6 Summary of arithmetic mean

Raw data

Formula to learn

$$\bar{x} = \frac{\sum x_i}{n} = \frac{x_1 + x_2 + x_3 + \cdots + x_n}{n}$$

Tabulated data

Formula to learn

$$\bar{x} = \frac{\sum f_i x_i}{n}$$

Grouped data

Formula to learn

$$\bar{x} = \frac{\sum f_i m_i}{n}$$

2.3 Median

2.3.1 Calculation

The **median** is the value of the **mid-item in an ordered arrangement of the observed data**. The **mid**-item number to consider will be given by

Formula to learn

$$n_m = \frac{n+1}{2}$$

That is, if we had five observed values, the median would be the value of item number

$$n_m = \frac{5+1}{2} = \frac{6}{2} = 3^{rd} \text{ item}$$

in an ordered arrangement (i.e. the third item in an ordered arrangement).

Clearly, if there are an even number of items this calculation will not produce a whole number. In this case, the median will be a simple average of the mid-two values either side of this point. For example, if we had six items, then this formula would produce

$$n_m = \frac{n+1}{2} = \frac{6+1}{2} = \frac{7}{2} = 3.5^{th} \text{ item}$$

Hence, we would take a simple average of the value of the third and fourth items.

2.3.2 Raw data

For raw data, we need to find out the value of the mid-item in the ordered arrangement.

Solution

Our raw data example had 13 values, hence the median would be item number

$$n_m = \frac{13+1}{2} = \frac{14}{2} = 7^{th} \text{ (i.e. the seventh item in the ordered arrangement)}$$

If we look to the ordered list of values {1, 2, 3, 3, 4, 5, **5**, 5, 6, 7, 8, 9, 20}, the seventh item is the second 5, hence

Median = 5

2.3.3 Tabulated data

For tabulated data, we would again need to find the value of the mid-item which would turn out to be the value associated with one of the rows.

Solution

The item to consider is given by

$$n_m = \frac{n+1}{2} = \frac{180+1}{2} = \frac{181}{2} = 90.5^{th} \text{ item}$$

Value X	Frequency f	Cumulative f
1	20	20
2	40	60
3	60	120
4	50	170
5	10	180
	n = 180	

There are 20 items of value 1 and 40 items of value 2, hence, we have seen 60 items before we see an item valued at 3. There are 60 items valued at 3, taking us up to a cumulative total of 120 items. Hence, the 90.5th item is one of these, i.e. the median item has a value of 3.

2.3.4 Grouped data

Again, for grouped data, we would need to find the value of the mid-item.

Solution

The median for this example is item number

$$n_m = \frac{n+1}{2} = \frac{130+1}{2} = \frac{131}{2} = 65.5^{th} \text{ item}$$

Range	Frequency f	Cumulative f
0 to $4.\dot{9}$	30	30
5 to $9.\dot{9}$	50	80
10 to $14.\dot{9}$	40	120
15 to $19.\dot{9}$	10	130
	130	

If we look at the cumulative frequency above, we see that we have seen 30 items in total by the end of the 0 to $4.\dot{9}$ band and 80 in total by the end of the 5 to $9.\dot{9}$ band. The 65.5th item therefore falls within the range 5 to $9.\dot{9}$ (5 to 10), indeed it should be the 35.5th (65.5 – 30.0) item in that band. On the **assumption that the items are evenly spread throughout this range**, the median will be given $\frac{35.5}{50}$ into this 5 to 10 band, i.e.

$$\text{Median} = 5 + \left[\frac{35.5}{50} \times (10-5)\right] = 8.55$$

The general expression for this is

Median = Start value of band + Fraction of distance through band × Width of band

or

Formula to learn

$$\text{Median} = \text{Start value of band} + \frac{\text{Median item} - \text{Cumulative number to start of band}}{\text{Number of items in band}} \times \text{Width of band}$$

And applying it to the above where the median was the 65.5th item gives

$$\text{Median} = 5 + \frac{65.5 - 30}{50} \times (10 - 5) = 8.55$$

as before.

2.3.5 Comments

The median will **either be one of the actual observed values** (if there is an odd number of items), **or a simple average of the mid two items** (if there is an even number).

Unlike the arithmetic mean, the median will **not be affected by the size of extreme values**, since it only ever considers the most central values in the ordered list, but will be affected by the addition of extreme items since the total number of observed values will change.

2.4 Mode

2.4.1 Calculation

The mode is the most frequently occurring item in the observed data on the basis that the more central items should occur most frequently in a **Normal distribution**.

2.4.2 Raw data

Solution

Based on our example above, the mode is 5 since this occurs three times in the range

1, 2, 3, 3, 4, **5**, **5**, **5**, 6, 7, 8, 9, 20.

2.4.3 Tabulated data

When we consider the tabulated data

Value	Frequency f
1	20
2	40
3	60
4	50
5	10
	180

we can see that the most frequently occurring value is, again, three, as there are 60 occurrences of the value 3. Therefore, the mode is 3.

2.4.4 Grouped data

For the following grouped data, the mode falls within the range 5 to $9.\dot{9}$ as there are 50 items in this range.

Range	Frequency f
0 to $4.\dot{9}$	30
5 to $9.\dot{9}$	50
10 to $14.\dot{9}$	40
15 to $19.\dot{9}$	10
	130

This is the limit of the accuracy we can achieve, i.e. the Modal **Range** = 5 to $9.\dot{9}$.

We **cannot establish a single value within this range** since we assume that the items are **evenly distributed throughout the range**, hence all are equally likely – they occur as frequently as each other.

2.4.5 Comments

By definition, the mode **must be one of the actually occurring items** (unlike both the median and mean).

The unfortunate problem with this measure is that **there may be several modes** if a number of items occur with equal frequency. For example, if there were a third 3 instead of a 4 in the raw data example then there would be three 3s and three 5s, and hence there would be two modes, 3 and 5. Indeed, if we had the following data: 1, 6, 7, 8, 36, each would be a mode since each only appears once. As a result, the mode may be of limited value as a central measure since, in extreme cases as above, it gives little or **no indication of central tendency**.

Since it is the most frequently occurring item, by definition it is **unaffected by extreme values**.

2.5 Geometric mean

2.5.1 Calculation

The geometric mean is calculated by taking the nth root of the product of the n observed values. Again, the only difficulties arise in the way in which we are presented with the data.

2.5.2 Raw data

Formula to learn

$$\bar{x} = \sqrt[n]{x_1 \times x_2 \times x_3 \times \cdots \times x_n}$$

where

$\bar{x}$ = the geometric mean

x_i = the observed values (i going from 1 to n)

n = number of observed values

Solution

$$\bar{x} = \sqrt[n]{x_1 \times x_2 \times x_3 \times \cdots \times x_n}$$

$$= \sqrt[13]{1 \times 2 \times 3 \times 3 \times 4 \times 5 \times 5 \times 5 \times 6 \times 7 \times 8 \times 9 \times 20}$$

$$= \sqrt[13]{544{,}320{,}000} = 4.70$$

$$= \sqrt[13]{2.5^3 \times 7.5^5 \times 12.5^4 \times 17.5^1}$$

$$= \sqrt[13]{158{,}417{,}967{,}359} = 7.27$$

2.5.3 Tabulated and grouped data

The geometric mean can also be calculated for tabulated data and for grouped data but due to the complexity of the calculation it is not included in the syllabus for this examination.

2.5.4 Comments

Usefulness

The geometric mean may be most appropriate as a central measure when we are considering growth or inflation which compounds each year, i.e. builds on top of the previous years, rather than simply adding to it.

Example

A share price rises and falls by the following amounts each month over a six-month period.

+5%, +4%, +2%, –3%, –1%, +3%

What is the average growth per month over that period?

Solution

To appreciate the solution, we need to consider the value at the end of six months of each £1.00 invested at the start of the period.

After the first month, this £1.00 will have grown by 5% to £1.05, i.e.

New value = £1.00 × 1.05 = £1.05

where 1.05 is 1 + the growth rate of 5%, expressed as a decimal, i.e. 1 + 0.05.

This £1.05 will then grow in the next month by 4% to £1.092, i.e.

New value = £1.00 × 1.05 × 1.04 = £1.092

By the end of the six months, the value will have grown to

New value = £1.00 × 1.05 × 1.04 × 1.02 × 0.97 × 0.99 × 1.03 = £1.1017

NB: The general term we are using to compound up the values each period (known as the Compound factor (CF)) is given by

Formula to learn

Compound factor (CF) = (1 + r)

where r = the growth rate expressed as a decimal, i.e. +5% = +0.05 giving

CF = (1 + 0.05) = 1.05

and –3% = –0.03 giving

CF = (1 – 0.03) = 0.97

If we now wished to work out the average growth rate, then it would be

$$(1+\bar{x}) = \sqrt[6]{1.1017} = 1.0163$$

$\bar{x} = 0.0163$ or 1.63%

Tutor tip

People often have difficulty entering this into the calculator, the key strokes for this example are

[ⁿ√x] 6 (▶) 1.1017 = where (▶) is the right Replay button

i.e. an average growth rate of 1.63% per month.

The full relationship here may be expressed as follows

Formula to learn

$$(1+\bar{x}) = \sqrt[n]{(1+x_1)\times(1+x_2)\times\ldots\times(1+x_n)}$$

Relationship to arithmetic mean

The geometric mean **will understate average growth/returns, etc. compared to the arithmetic mean**, as a comparison of the results of the above examples demonstrates. This fact can be most easily appreciated by considering the impact of an extreme item with an observed value of zero. The arithmetic mean, which works by adding the values together, will have a value so long as there are other non-zero values observed. Since the geometric mean works by multiplying together all the relevant items, if any one of them is zero then the product, and hence the geometric mean, will be zero.

2.6 Weighted average

One final variation on the average is the weighted average that is useful for determining the return on a portfolio of securities.

Example

A portfolio holds two securities with the following returns

Security	Return
A	10%
B	14%

If we invest 25% in A and 75% in B what will be the return on the portfolio

Solution

The mean of the returns of the two securities can be easily seen as 12 % [(10 + 14)/2]. If our portfolio held A and B in equal proportions then this would be the portfolio return but if the portfolio weightings are not 50:50 then its return will be biased towards that of the higher weighted holding.

If we held 100% in A the portfolio return would be 10%.

If we held 100% in B the portfolio return would be 14%

If we held 50% in A and 50% in B then we would get the mid point return of 12%

With the selected weighting the portfolio return can be calculated as the weighted average of the two returns as follows

Security	Return	Proportion	Weighted
	r	p	pr
A	10%	0.25	2.5
B	14%	0.75	10.5
			13.0

2.7 Relationship between mean, median and mode

Learning objectives

26.2.2 **Distinguish** between symmetric and skewed data.

26.2.3 **Explain** the relationship between the mean, median and mode for symmetric and skewed data.

2.7.1 Perfectly symmetrical population

In a **perfectly symmetrical population**, (e.g. 1, 2, 2, 3, 3, 3, 4, 4, 5) with the mean being the most commonly occurring item, the mean, median and mode would have the same value, because

- The average (arithmetic mean) would be the midpoint (the median).
- The mean would be the most frequently occurring item (the mode).

We could represent such a distribution as

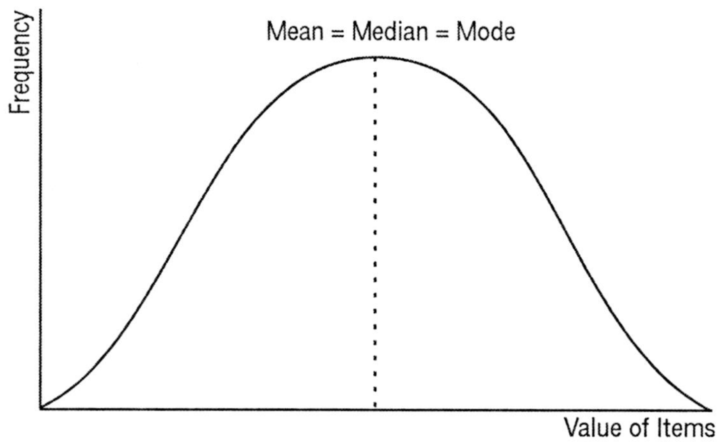

If, however, we added just one extremely high value in this otherwise symmetrical distribution, then

- The mode would be unaltered – the most commonly occurring item is unaltered.
- The median would now be slightly higher since there is now one more item.
- The mean could be significantly higher depending on how extreme the additional item is.

2.7.2 Positively skewed distribution

If we extend this idea to consider a number of asymmetrical items, producing a **positively skewed** distribution, i.e. one where the **more extreme items lie above the mode**, we would find the relationship between the three measures to be

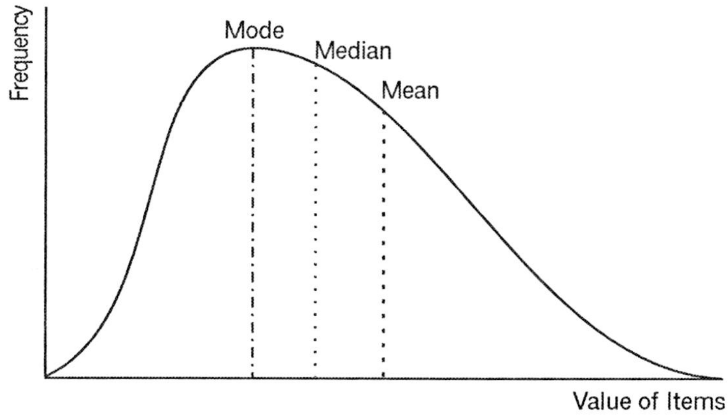

i.e. **mode < median < mean**

2.7.3 Negatively skewed distribution

Similarly, for a **negatively skewed** distribution (one where the **more extreme items fall below the mode**) we would find

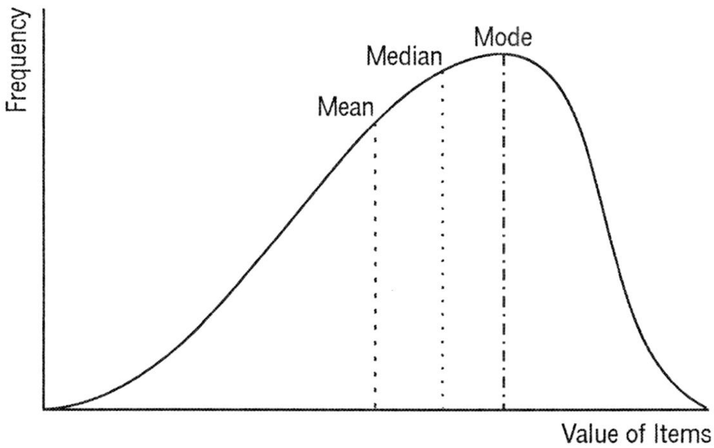

i.e. **mean < median < mode**

3 Dispersion Measures

Learning objective	**26.2.4 Define**, **explain** and **calculate** the following measures of dispersion for both raw data and interval data: standard deviation (population and sample); variance; range; quartiles and percentiles and interquartile range.

3.1 Introduction

Dispersion measures aim to tell us how broadly **spread** a range of values are around the observed central point. For, say, the returns offered by a share, the location may provide the expected return and the dispersion may provide a measure of risk.

Different measures are appropriate depending on how the central point has been calculated. The measures that we need to be aware of are as follows.

Location Measure	Related Dispersion Measures
Arithmetic Mean	Standard Deviation Variance
Median	Range Deciles Interquartile Range Percentiles
Mode	N/A
Geometric Mean	N/A

3.2 Standard deviation and variance

3.2.1 Calculation

The standard deviation, as we noted above, is a dispersion measure that is related to the arithmetic mean. The idea behind the calculation is to establish how far each observed value falls from the mean, the standard deviation being a function of this divergence, and the variance being the square of the standard deviation.

The greater the divergence of the observed values from the mean, the greater the standard deviation (or risk).

3.2.2 Population

When we are considering the total population of values with no omissions, the approach, as for location measures, varies slightly depending on how the data is presented, though in outline the calculation of the standard deviation is

- Calculate the arithmetic mean $\bar{x}$.
- Calculate the difference between each observed value and the arithmetic mean $(x - \bar{x})$, the sum of which must be zero since some items lie above the mean and have positive values and some below the mean and have negative values.
- Square the differences to remove the negative signs from those lying below the mean, i.e. we are now considering just the absolute value (or square of the value) of the differences, ignoring whether they lie above or below the mean.
- Sum these squared differences.
- Calculate the average of these squared differences by dividing by the number of observed values.
- Take the square root of this average to cancel the effects of our earlier squaring up.

Since we square the differences up, then later take the square root, the units of the standard deviation will be the same as those for the mean, i.e. if the mean is the average number of miles travelled in several journeys, the standard deviation will also be in miles.

3.2.3 Raw data

Stating the above as a mathematical expression for the calculation of the standard deviation for raw data gives

Formula to learn

$$\text{Standard deviation} = \sigma = \sqrt{\frac{\sum(x-\bar{x})^2}{n}}$$

and the calculation of the variance is

Formula to learn

$$\text{Variance} = \sigma^2 = \frac{\sum(x-\bar{x})^2}{n}$$

i.e. the variance is simply the square of the standard deviation.

Solution

We calculated earlier that the mean of this population was $\bar{x}$ = 6. To calculate the standard deviation it would be most convenient to tabulate the data as follows.

x	$(x-\bar{x})$	$(x-\bar{x})^2$
1	–5	25
2	–4	16
3	–3	9
3	–3	9
4	–2	4
5	–1	1
5	–1	1
5	–1	1
6	0	0
7	1	1
8	2	4
9	3	9
20	14	196
	0	276
		$\sum(x-\bar{x})^2$

Giving

$$\text{Standard deviation} = \sigma = \sqrt{\frac{\sum(x-\bar{x})^2}{n}} = \sqrt{\frac{276}{13}} = \sqrt{21.23} = 4.61$$

and

$$\text{Variance} = \sigma^2 = 4.61^2 = 21.23$$

Tutor tip

The above calculation illustrates the idea, exam calculations are most likely to be limited to four or five numbers.

3.2.4 Tabulated data

The calculation for tabulated data must take account of the frequency of each observed value within each band, and hence the frequency of each observed difference, by multiplying the square of the difference for the band by the number of items in that band. Thus the standard deviation can be calculated as follows.

Formula to learn

$$\text{Standard deviation} = \sigma = \sqrt{\frac{\sum f(x-\bar{x})^2}{n}}$$

The calculation of the variance is

Formula to learn

$$\text{Variance} = \sigma^2 = \frac{\sum f(x-\bar{x})^2}{n}$$

This can easily be illustrated by correctly banding our raw data from above as follows.

x	f	$(x-\bar{x})$	$f(x-\bar{x})^2$
1	1	–5	25
2	1	–4	16
3	2	–3	18
4	1	–2	4
5	3	–1	3
6	1	0	0
7	1	1	1
8	1	2	4
9	1	3	9
20	1	14	196
	13		276
	n		$\sum f(x-\bar{x})^2$

The sum of the squared differences again giving 276.

Solution

In the previous part to this example we calculated the arithmetic mean as 2.94, which we show again below. Our full calculation of both the mean and the standard deviation could be laid out as follows.

x	f	fx	$(x-\bar{x})$	$f(x-\bar{x})^2$
1	20	20	–1.94	75.272
2	40	80	–0.94	35.344
3	60	180	0.06	0.216
4	50	200	1.06	56.180
5	10	50	2.06	42.436
	180	530	–	209.448
	n	$\sum f_i x_i$	–	$\sum f(x-\bar{x})^2$

Hence

$$\bar{x} = \frac{\sum f_i x_i}{n} = \frac{530}{180} = 2.94$$

$$\text{Standard deviation} = \sigma = \sqrt{\frac{\sum f(x-\bar{x})^2}{n}} = \sqrt{\frac{209.448}{180}} = \sqrt{1.1636} = 1.079$$

and

Variance = $\sigma^2 = 1.079^2 = 1.1636$

3.2.5 Grouped data

The calculations for tabulated and grouped data are almost identical, except we use the **group midpoint** as the observed value as we saw for location measures above.

Solution

Our full calculation of both the mean and the standard deviation for the grouped data example could be laid out as follows.

Range	m	f	fm	$(m-\bar{m})$	$f(m-\bar{m})^2$
0 to $4.\dot{9}$	2.5	30	75	–6.15	1,134.675
5 to $9.\dot{9}$	7.5	50	375	–1.15	66.125
10 to $14.\dot{9}$	12.5	40	500	3.85	592.900
15 to $19.\dot{9}$	17.5	10	175	8.85	783.225
		130	1,125	–	2,576.925
		n	$\sum f_i m_i$	–	$\sum f(m-\bar{m})^2$

Hence

$$\bar{x} = \frac{\sum f_i m_i}{n} = \frac{1,125}{130} = 8.65$$

$$\text{Standard deviation} = \sigma = \sqrt{\frac{\sum f(m-\bar{m})^2}{n}} = \sqrt{\frac{2,576.925}{130}} = \sqrt{19.8225} = 4.45$$

and

Variance = $\sigma^2 = 4.45^2 = 19.8225$

3.2.6 Population summary

Raw data

Formula to learn

$$\text{Standard deviation} = \sigma = \sqrt{\frac{\sum(x-\bar{x})^2}{n}}$$

Tabulated data

Formula to learn

$$\text{Standard deviation} = \sigma = \sqrt{\frac{\sum f(x-\bar{x})^2}{n}}$$

Grouped data

Formula to learn

$$\text{Standard deviation} = \sigma = \sqrt{\frac{\sum f\left(m-\overline{m}\right)^2}{n}}$$

3.2.7 Sample

When calculating the standard deviation based **only on a sample of the values**, the calculation described above is unlikely to give a realistic measure since it may **not consider a representative sample of variations**. To give an extreme example, if a sample of one item is selected from a population it will not be possible to calculate a standard deviation, since this item, being the only one observed, will be the mean and hence there will be no divergence of observed items from this mean.

Clearly, therefore, we cannot calculate the standard deviation when we only consider one value. Similarly, the standard deviation for small samples are likely to underestimate the true standard deviation, since the values chosen may not be representative (it is unlikely that we will select the extremes in a small sample).

As a result, it is usual to use **Bessels approximation** in the calculation of the standard deviation, that is divide down by **n – 1**, rather than n. This ensures

- No standard deviation can be calculated when the sample size is one since that would involve dividing by zero.
- Calculated standard deviations are slightly enlarged, since division by n – 1 produces a larger value than division by n, e.g. 16 ÷ 4 = 4, 16 ÷ 5 = 3.2.
- As the size of the sample increases towards the size of the full population, deducting one from the denominator will have an increasingly insignificant effect until the standard deviation is (approximately) identical to that calculated using the above equations for the full population.

The calculations therefore become

Raw data

Formula to learn

$$\text{Standard deviation} = \sigma_{n-1} = \sqrt{\frac{\sum (x-\overline{x})^2}{n-1}}$$

Tabulated data

Formula to learn

$$\text{Standard deviation} = \sigma_{n-1} = \sqrt{\frac{\sum f(x-\overline{x})^2}{n-1}}$$

Grouped data

Formula to learn

$$\text{Standard deviation} = \sigma_{n-1} = \sqrt{\frac{\sum f\left(m-\overline{m}\right)^2}{n-1}}$$

Tutor tip

In a gapfill question, if you are unsure whether a question involves a population or a sample, calculate as a sample and make a note in the exam feedback function. In a multiple choice question, if both population and sample answers are offered as options then again calculate as a sample and make a note in the exam feedback function.

3.3 Range and interquartile range

3.3.1 Introduction

As we noted above, the range and interquartile range are measures of dispersion most frequently associated with the median.

3.3.2 Range

The range is the distance between the highest and lowest observed values.

It may be expressed as

Formula to learn

Range = Highest observed value – Lowest observed value

As such, it is **completely dependent on** (and sensitive to) **the two most extreme values**, and takes **no account of the frequency of occurrence of** any items or the values of any of the other items. As a result, it may be of little use in determining most likely variations. Consider each of our three initial examples in turn.

Raw data

Our series of raw data was 1, 2, 3, 3, 4, 5, 5, 5, 6, 7, 8, 9, 20.

Solution

The range will be

Range = 20 – 1 = 19

Tabulated data

Our tabulated data had five values from one to five.

Solution

The range will therefore be

Range = 5 – 1 = 4

NB: This is unaffected by the frequency of occurrence of the two extreme values, it is simply the difference between them.

Grouped data

To calculate the range for the grouped data, we again need to make the assumption that values within the range are evenly spread throughout that range, hence the lowest value in any range will be the value marking the bottom of that range and the highest value will be the value marking the top of the range.

Our grouped example had four groupings, the extreme ends being 0 and 20 (19.9).

Solution

As such the range is

Range = 20 – 0 = 20

3.3.3 Interquartile range

The interquartile range tries to give a measure of spread that is **more representative** of the observed values. It is calculated by placing the values in ascending order, dividing them into four quarters, or **quartiles**, each containing the same number of items, and measuring the **difference between the top of the first quartile and the top of the third quartile**. Hence, it measures the range over the central-most 50% of the population and should, therefore, be a more representative measure since **extremes are excluded**, i.e. it is **insensitive to extremes**.

The **median** itself, being the mid-item in an ordered list, marks the **top of the second quartile**. Note, however, that for the purposes of this exam we will only need to be able to calculate this measure for raw data.

Example

To calculate which items we need to consider, we use item numbers.

$n_1 = \frac{1}{4}(n + 1)$ to give the item marking the top of the first quartile.

$n_2 = \frac{2}{4}(n + 1)$ to give the item marking the top of the second quartile, i.e. the median item.

$n_3 = \frac{3}{4}(n + 1)$ to give the item marking the top of the third quartile.

The median and interquartile range are given by

Median = x_2

Interquartile Range = $x_3 - x_1$ (referred to as 'the middle 50%')

where

x_1 = the value associated with item n_1

x_2 = the value associated with item n_2

x_3 = the value associated with item n_3

3.3.4 Raw data

Solution

There are thirteen items, therefore

$$n_1 = \frac{1}{4}(13+1) = \frac{14}{4} = 3.5^{th} \text{ item}$$

We therefore need to take the average of the third and fourth items, which are both three, hence $x_1 = 3$.

$$n_2 = \frac{2}{4}(13+1) = \frac{28}{4} = 7^{th} \text{ item}$$

The median is therefore the seventh item, hence $x_2 = 5$.

$$n_3 = \frac{3}{4}(13+1) = \frac{42}{4} = 10.5^{th} \text{ item}$$

We therefore need to take the average of the 10th and 11th items, which are 7 and 8, hence $x_3 = 7.5$.

Thus

Median = $x_2 = 5$

Interquartile Range = $(x_3 - x_1) = 7.5 - 3 = 4.5$

3.3.5 Percentiles

Percentiles are calculated in a similar way to quartiles, indeed a quartile is just a specific instance of a percentile. Quartiles calculate the spread from the $\frac{1}{4}$ point (or **25th percentile**) to the $\frac{3}{4}$ point (or **75th percentile**). In a similar way, we could calculate the spread over any selected range where the percentile indicates how far through the population we are looking.

4 Regression and Correlation

4.1 Introduction

4.1.1 Relationships

In many business situations, we are trying to establish whether a relationship exists between two factors and what exactly that relationship is. For example, if we consider the profits that a company may generate, a company's profit is clearly a function of its sales revenues and its costs. The higher the sales, the higher the profits; the higher the costs, the lower the profits.

Many other relationships also exist in business, investment and economics. For example, in investments it is generally believed that a higher risk will result in a higher return from a security. In economics, it is generally believed that wage rates and inflation go hand-in-hand, with high pay increases corresponding to high levels of inflation.

Where such relationships exist, it would be very useful to be able to quantify them. If we were able to do this, we would be placed in a much better position to make business/investment/economic forecasts and decisions.

4.1.2 Regression and correlation analysis

Regression and correlation analysis provides the means of achieving this aim. If, for example, we plotted the profits achieved each month against the sales that have been generated we may find the following.

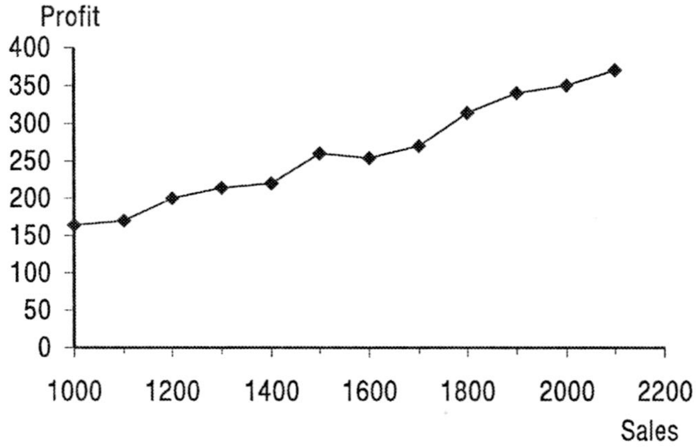

The data on which this is based are

	Jan £'000	Feb £'000	Mar £'000	Apr £'000	May £'000	Jun £'000	Jul £'000	Aug £'000	Sep £'000	Oct £'000	Nov £'000	Dec £'000
Sales	1,000	1,300	1,700	2,000	2,100	1,800	1,900	1,600	1,500	1,400	1,200	1,100
Profit	165	215	270	350	370	315	340	255	260	220	200	170

There clearly appears to be some kind of relationship here along the lines that we would expect, i.e. higher sales result in higher profits. What we want to be able to do is establish the relationship between profits and sales such that if we could project a sales figure we could establish the associated profit.

One way we could try to achieve this would be to take a ruler, place it over this graph and try to visibly draw the line that achieves the best fit to the points noted. In the example above this may well produce a reasonable result since all the plotted points appear to fall in a fairly straight line. This technique would certainly give a rough and ready indicator but could not be considered precise.

Regression and correlation calculations add a degree of precision to this idea. In outline, these two calculations establish the following.

- **Regression** – the equation of the line of best fit mathematically, giving a much more accurate result than the visibly drawn line.
- **Correlation** – an indication of the accuracy or strength of the relationship, i.e. whether this line is a good or poor explanation of the relationship between the two variables.

4.2 Uses of regression analysis

The uses of regression and correlation analysis are to aid the estimation/forecasting of data and provide an indication of the validity of the forecasting.

We have already given an indication of how this relationship could be used if it could be ascertained through regression analysis. How valid or useful the result is, however, may well depend on exactly how we intend to use it, i.e. do we wish to use it for

- **Interpolation**, where we try to estimate the profits that will arise from sales **within** the already observed range?
- **Extrapolation**, where we try to predict the profits that will arise **beyond** (either above or below) the observed range of sales?

4.2.1 Interpolation

Using the result of our regression analysis for the purposes of interpolation, e.g. estimating profit levels arising from sales within the noted range, should provide reasonable results since there will be some fairly close data to support the conclusions we arrive at.

4.2.2 Extrapolation

Using the results of regression analysis to extrapolate beyond the end of the noted data ranges, i.e. to estimate profits arising from sales levels above £2.2m or below £1.0m, could be dangerous since we do not have the data to support the results we will be estimating. It is quite possible that a relationship that appears linear over a short range of values turns out to be non-linear when we move beyond those values, making any extrapolated results worthless or even dangerous.

We can, however, use the data to establish an expected value or forecast, and use the variability of the data to try to establish confidence limits within which we can be sure, with a given degree of confidence, that the observed value will lie.

4.3 Major limitations

Learning objective

26.3.6 Explain the shortfalls in the application of linear regression to forecasting including 'correlation does not imply causation' and the pitfalls of data mining.

We have commented above on one major limitation, which is the danger involved in extrapolating results. Regression and correlation analysis does, however, have some other limitations that we discuss below.

4.3.1 Linear relationships

Regression and correlation analysis can be used with reference to linear relationships only. The calculations are designed to produce the equation of the straight line that best fits the noted points and an indication of the accuracy of that fit.

The reason that we assume a straight line relationship is convenience and the fact that many relationships will be approximately linear. However, although many of the relationships we may wish to establish may be linear, there will be some that are not.

4.3.2 Spurious relationships

In our analysis, we are trying to establish the relationship between two variables. Typically, we will hypothesize **causality**, i.e. that one factor is causing the other to change. It is quite possible, however, that two variables appear to be related but are, in truth, completely unrelated. Consider for example the following graph.

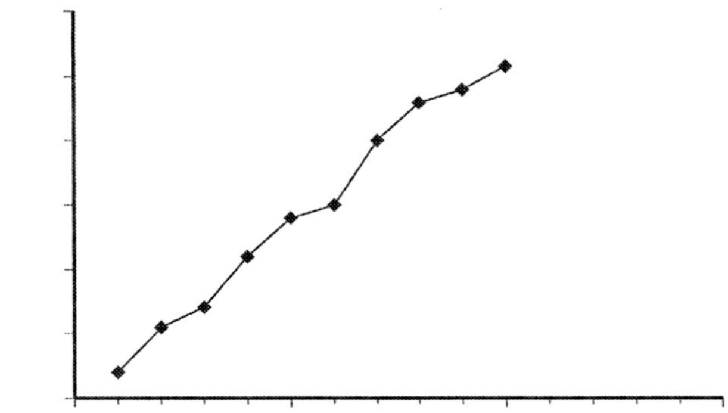

Do ice cream production levels really determine the number of wasp stings that are suffered in the summer? It seems unlikely that it does intuitively, and if it did, ice cream production would certainly have been banned.

What we are observing here is a spurious relationship. A more likely reason is that both the frequency of wasp stings and the level of ice cream production are related to a common factor, say the number of sunny days. The greater the number of sunny days, the greater time people will spend outdoors, the more ice cream they will eat and the more wasp stings they will suffer.

We must be very careful in our regression analysis in determining that a relationship actually exists between the two sets of variables. Regression analysis in itself does not prove causality.

Whilst reasonably easy to appreciate in this example, spurious relationships are harder to determine in economic analysis. Economics is not a precise science and exactly what economic variables are relevant in any circumstances is not always perfectly clear. As a result, economists frequently undertake the process of sorting through large amounts of data looking to pick out information that may be relevant – a process otherwise known as **data mining** which can easily lead to such spurious relationships.

4.4 Regression analysis

Learning objective 26.3.3 **Interpret** the intercept and gradient components of a regression line.

4.4.1 Linear relationships

If we plot a straight line on a graph where y is the vertical axis and x is the horizontal axis, then the equation of a straight line would take the form

Formula to learn

$$y = a + bx$$

where

a = the intercept, i.e. the height at which the line cuts the y-axis
b = slope, i.e. the change in the value of y per unit change in the value of x

Graphically, this would appear as follows.

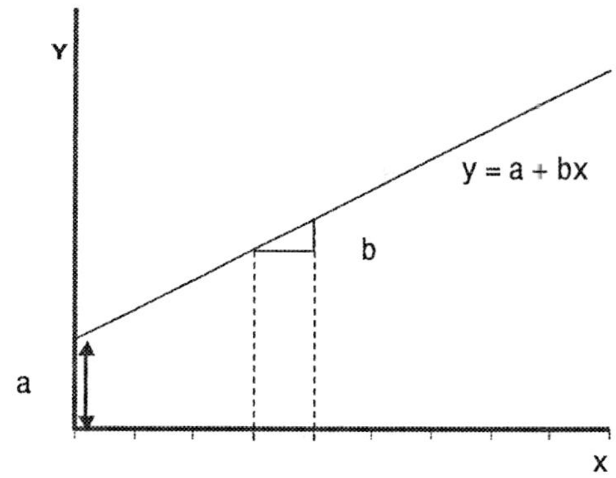

Note that the specific notation used may vary. For example, instead of saying y = a + bx, we could say y = α + βx or y = c + mx. Typically, when we are dealing with a population, we use the form y = α + βx and when we are dealing with a sample taken from a population, we use the form y = a + bx. Whatever notation is used, a and b (or their equivalents) are referred to as the parameters.

4.4.2 The variables and the relationship

Learning objective

26.3.2 Distinguish between the dependent and independent variable.

Tutor tip

Note that the syllabus does not require you to be able to calculate regression coefficients.

If we plot our variables on such a graph, regression analysis gives us the value of the factors a and b which determine the relationship. To do this, however, we must firstly determine which variable should be plotted along the x-axis and which along the y-axis, which depends on the form of the relationship.

If a relationship exists between two variables, then the value of one will drive/determine the value of the other, i.e. we have cause and effect. This is referred to as **bivariate** or **simple linear regression**.

Independent variable – x-axis

The variable whose value does the driving, the cause, is known as the **independent variable** (x). This variable should always be plotted along the x-axis.

The independent variable is the predictor variable. If we can identify a value for the independent variable, we can then use this to predict a value for the dependent variable.

Dependent variable – y-axis

The **dependent variable** (y) is a variable whose value is driven by the independent variable (x), i.e. the effect.

It is the value of the dependent variable (y) that we will be wishing to predict by interpolation or extrapolation from given expectations regarding the independent variable (x).

4.4.3 Regression coefficients

The output from regression analysis is the two coefficients a and b which determine the relationship between the two variables.

The meaning of b

The gradient of the line is represented by b. For example, if b = 2, it indicates that if the value of x increases by 10, the value of y increases by 20. If b is positive, it indicates an upward sloping line, i.e. the value of y is directly proportional to the value of x. If b is negative, it indicates a downward sloping line, i.e. the value of y is inversely proportional to the value of x. For example, if b = –2, then an increase in the value of x by 10 would cause a decrease in the value of y by 20.

The meaning of a

This gives the value of y when x is zero. For example, if we were to look at consumption (y) compared to income (x), individuals will consume a certain amount regardless of their level of income – their non-discretionary expenditure.

Using the coefficients

Learning objective | **26.3.4 Calculate** a forecast value for the dependent variable given the regression line equation.

The regression line can be used to estimate a value for y given a value for x. For example, assume that we have the following regression line

$$y = 30 + 0.8x$$

where

y = weekly expenditure
x = weekly income

If weekly income is £500, what is the weekly expenditure?

$$y = 30 + (0.8 \times £500)$$
$$y = £430$$

The error term

A regression equation is often expressed in the following form.

$$y = a + bx + e$$

The e is an error or disturbance term. If the regression line represents the best linear unbiased estimate of the relationship between x and y, the error term will have a random variable with a mean of zero. It reflects the fact that we cannot guarantee that the value of y will actually be as predicted by the regression equation. On a random basis, the actual value will lie both above and below the predicted value.

Calculating a and b

Learning objective | **26.3.1 Explain** the least-squares regression technique in deriving a line of best fit.

The method of estimating the parameters a and b is referred to as the **least squares method**. The idea is that in calculating the regression line, we want it to be the line of best fit. This implies that all the actual values on the graph are reasonably close to the line. It is usually not possible to make all the values very close at the same time, since we are constructing a straight line and consequently some values will have to be further from the line than others.

Therefore, what we do is minimise the **sum** of the vertical distances of each value from the straight line being drawn. In performing the calculation of the sum of the vertical distances, the distances are squared. This ensures we only consider the absolute value of any distance (squared) since the square of any number is always positive. It also ensures that large distances from the line are avoided, since the squaring process exaggerates the larger distances. This is referred to as minimising the **sum of the squared errors**.

The formulae for calculating the coefficients a and b are as follows.

$$b = \frac{\sum xy - n\overline{x}\overline{y}}{\sum x^2 - n\overline{x}^2} = \frac{\text{covariance (x,y)}}{\text{variance (x)}}$$

$$a = \overline{y} - b\overline{x}$$

Giving the equation of the relationship as

y = a + bx

The justification for the formula for calculating a and b and an illustration of the least squares method are in an appendix at the back of this chapter. Note, however, that this is provided for information only and is **not** required knowledge for the exam.

4.5 Correlation

The purpose of the correlation measure is to measure the strength of the relationship between two variables. In the context of regression analysis with only one independent variable, the correlation coefficient will give an indication of how accurately the regression line matches the observed values.

4.5.1 Correlation coefficient

Learning objective | 26.3.5 **Explain** and **interpret** the correlation coefficient in the context of linear regression.

The correlation coefficient is a relative measure indicating how two variables move with respect to each other. It is also referred to as Pearson's correlation coefficient. When a correlation coefficient is calculated by reference to a sample of data, it is referred to by the symbol r. When it is calculated by reference to the whole population, it is referred to as ρ (pronounced **rho**).

The correlation coefficient measures the direction and degree of linear association between the two variables.

A correlation coefficient will have any value between +1 and –1 and the meaning of the correlation coefficient can best be understood by considering the extremes.

Perfect positive correlation (correlation coefficient = +1)

If two variables are perfectly positively correlated then they move up and down together and in proportion.

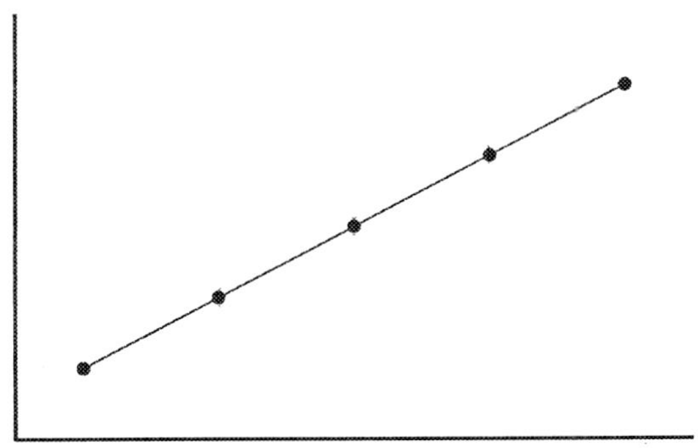

Here, it can be seen that the line is upward sloping and all the actual values of y are exactly the same as the predicted value given the regression line.

Non-perfect positive correlation (0< correlation coefficient < 1)

If two variables are positively correlated, but not perfectly positively correlated, we will have something like this.

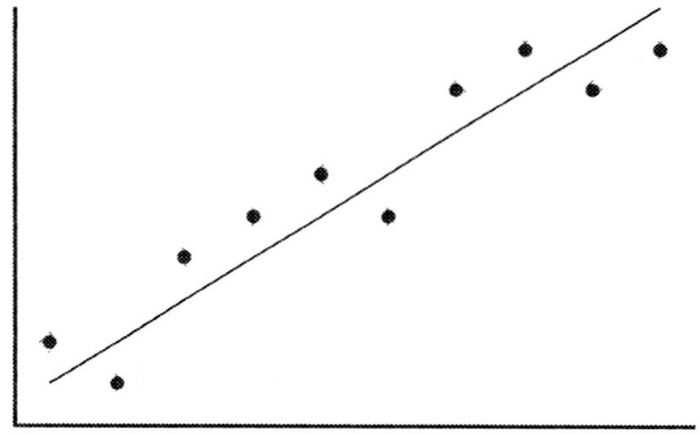

Here, it can be seen that there is a positive relationship between the two variables – as the value of x increases, so does the value of y. However, the relationship is not exact and so this is not perfect correlation. The correlation coefficient here may be +0.8, for example.

Perfect negative correlation (correlation coefficient = –1)

If two variables are perfectly negatively correlated then they move up and down in exact opposition and in proportion.

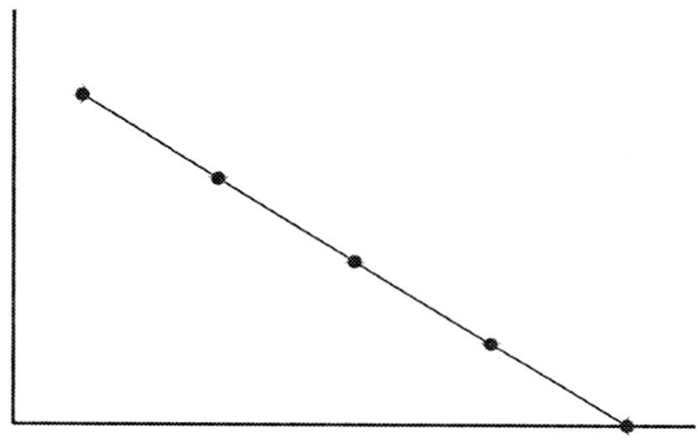

Once again, all the actual values of y are as predicted by the regression line, meaning that the relationship is perfect. However, the slope is downward, indicating a negative relationship.

Uncorrelated (correlation coefficient = 0)

If two variables are uncorrelated then they move independently of each other, i.e. if one goes up, the other may go up or down or not move at all.

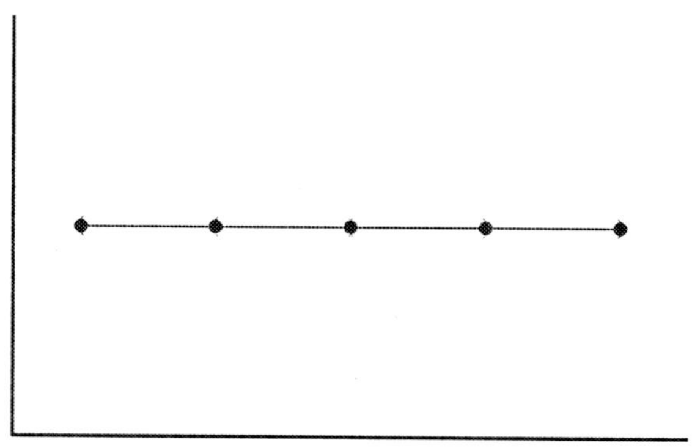

In this case, it can be seen that the value of y is independent from the value of x – it does not change regardless of the value of x. An alternative presentation of zero correlation would be to have points randomly scattered across the whole of the diagram.

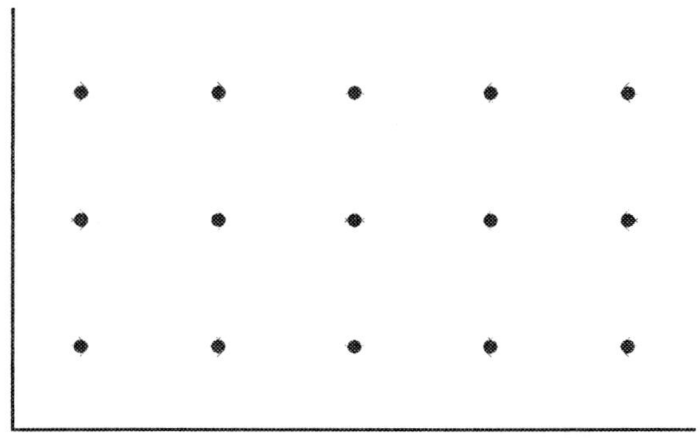

In between perfect correlation and no correlation, there are relationships between variables of varying strength. Generally, a correlation coefficient of 0.5 would be viewed as moderate correlation. Values of less than this would be viewed as weak correlation while values above this would be viewed as strong correlation.

4.5.2 Conclusion

There are two relevant factors in a correlation coefficient, the sign (+ or –) and the value. Their effects are

- Positive correlation implies that variables move up and down together, negative correlation means that they move in opposition.
- The value of the figure, ignoring the sign, gives an indication of the strength of the relationship, the closer to a value of 1 the stronger the relationship.

Note the link between the correlation coefficient and the b coefficient in the regression equation. If the correlation coefficient is positive/negative, b will also be positive/negative, respectively. If there is no correlation (correlation coefficient = zero), b will be zero. In this latter case, there is no point in drawing the regression line.

The b coefficient gives more information than the correlation coefficient since it not only shows the direction of the relationship, it also shows by how much the dependent variable will change. However, use of the b coefficient involves the limiting assumption that the dependent variable is a function of the independent variable. It is not necessary to designate a dependent and independent variable when calculating the correlation coefficient.

Also note that a high correlation coefficient does not **prove** causality, as noted above with reference to spurious correlation.

4.5.3 Calculating the correlation coefficient

Tutor tip

> Note that the syllabus does not require you to be able to calculate the covariance, though you may be given it in order to calculate the correlation coefficient using the following formula.

Quick approach

The formula for calculating the correlation coefficient of x and y is as follows.

$$cor_{x,y} = \frac{\sum xy - n\overline{xy}}{\sigma_x \sigma_y} = \frac{\text{Covariance}(x,y)}{\sigma_x \sigma_y}$$

The **covariance** is a number related to the correlation coefficient. It is calculated as follows, given a sample of data.

$$\text{cov}_{x,y} = \frac{\sum(x-\bar{x})(y-\bar{y})}{n-1}$$

You may be given a covariance and the standard deviations (or variances – watch out!) of the two variables, then be asked to calculate the correlation coefficient.

4.5.4 Coefficient of Determination – r^2

The coefficient of determination shows what proportion of the total variation in the value of y can be explained through the regression line by changes in the value of x.

If the correlation coefficient is 0.9 then

$r = 0.9$

$r^2 = 0.81$

Hence

0.81 or 81% of the variations in the value of the dependent variable can be explained by changes in the independent variable and 0.19 or 19% of the variations in the dependent variable are not accounted for.

Chapter Roundup

Statistical measures

- Data may be presented as raw data, tabulated data or grouped data.
- The mean, median and mode are all examples of location measures which can be used to tell us about past performance and average returns achieved. They may be used in an attempt to assess future returns.
- Standard deviation and variance are both dispersion measures associated with the arithmetic mean which tell us about the spread of values around that point and can be used in determining the risks of an investment.

Mean, standard deviation and variance

- Arithmetic mean is
  - Not necessarily an observed value
  - Greatly affected by extremes
- Calculations

	Raw Data	Tabulated Data	Grouped Data
$\bar{x}$ =	$\frac{\sum x_i}{n}$	$\frac{\sum f_i x_i}{n}$	$\frac{\sum f_i m_i}{n}$
Population Standard Deviation (σ) =	$\sqrt{\frac{\sum(x-\bar{x})^2}{n}}$	$\sqrt{\frac{\sum f(x-\bar{x})^2}{n}}$	$\sqrt{\frac{\sum f(m-\bar{m})^2}{n}}$
Sample Standard Deviation (σ_{n-1}) =	$\sqrt{\frac{\sum(x-\bar{x})^2}{n-1}}$	$\sqrt{\frac{\sum f(x-\bar{x})^2}{n-1}}$	$\sqrt{\frac{\sum f(m-\bar{m})^2}{n-1}}$

It is perhaps easiest to remember the tabulated data version for the full population only. These are the most general ones since

- For raw data, $f_i = 1$ for each item.
- For grouped data, remember to use the midpoints.
- For sample **standard deviation**, divide by $n - 1$ rather than n.

Geometric mean

- $\bar{x} = \sqrt[n]{x_1 \times x_2 \times x_3 \times \cdots \times x_n}$
- Useful for compounding relationships
- Understates the mean compared to the arithmetic mean
- or when using compound growth rates or returns

$$(1+\bar{x}) = \sqrt[n]{(1+x_1) \times (1+x_2) \times \ldots \times (1+x_n)}$$

Median, range, interquartile range

- Items to consider for median and interquartile range (and associated values) are

$$n_1 = \frac{1}{4}(n+1) \quad \text{value} = x_1$$

$$n_2 = \frac{2}{4}(n+1) \quad \text{value} = x_2$$

$$n_3 = \frac{3}{4}(n+1) \quad \text{value} = x_3$$

- Calculations

Measure	Comment
Median = x_2	Unaffected by extremes
Range = Highest – Lowest	Considers only extremes
Interquartile Range = $x_3 - x_1$	Unaffected by extremes
Percentile = Percentage point through population	Unaffected by extremes

- For grouped data

$$\text{Median} = \text{Start value of band} + \frac{\text{Median item} - \text{Cumulative number to start of band}}{\text{Number of items in band}} \times \text{Width of band}$$

- The range and interquartile range provide information on the spread of data, the range is completely a function of extremes the inter quartile range is unaffected by extremes.

Mode

- Mode = most frequency occuring item
- Must be an observed value
- Unaffected by extremes

Relationship between measures

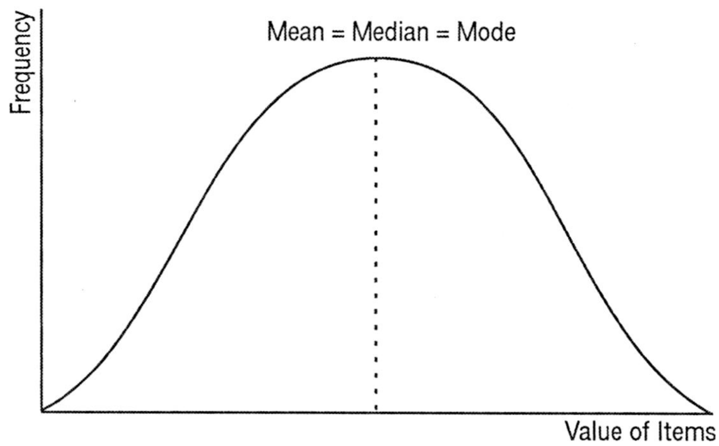

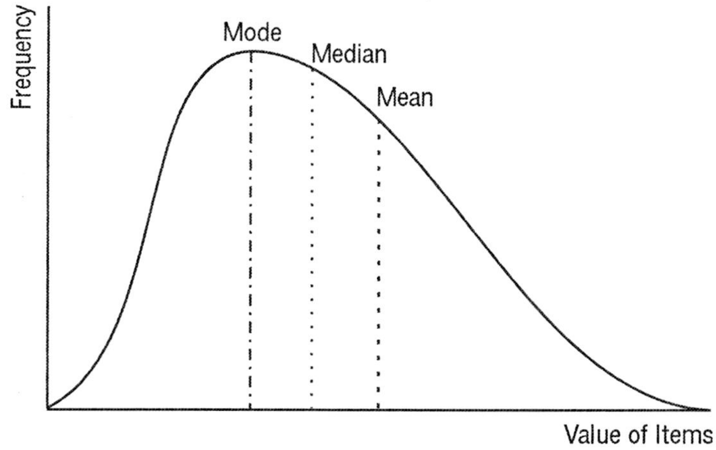

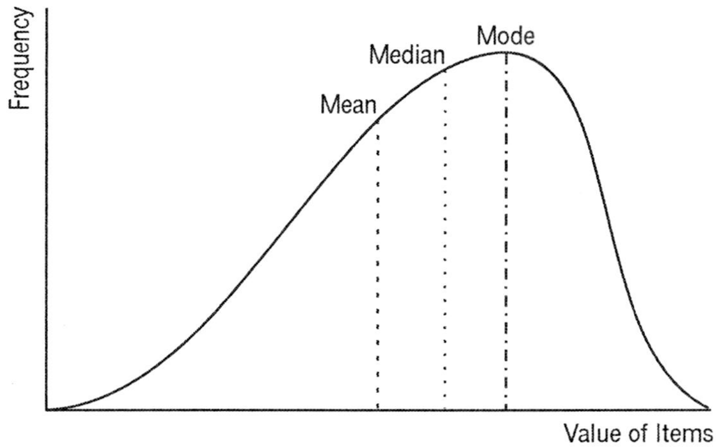

Regression and correlation

- Regression is used to establish if a relationship exists between two factors. A regression calculation provides a line of best fit.
- Correlation indicates the strength of the relationship between the two variables.
- Regression: y = a + bx

$$b = \frac{\text{Covariance (x, y)}}{\text{Variance (x)}} = \frac{\sum xy - n\overline{xy}}{\sum x^2 - n\overline{x}^2}$$

$$a = \overline{y} - b\overline{x}$$

- Correlation coefficient (r): $Cor_{xy} = \frac{\text{Covariance (x, y)}}{\sigma_x \sigma_y} = \frac{\sum xy - n\overline{xy}}{\sigma_x \sigma_y}$
- r^2 = Proportion of the change in the value of the dependent variable that is explained by changes in the independent variable.
- Interpolation is where we use the regression line to estimate future results from data within an already observed range. Extrapolation is where we try to estimate results from beyond our existing range of experiences and data.

TEST YOUR KNOWLEDGE

Check your knowledge of the Chapter here, without referring back to the text.

1. The arithmetic mean will always be one of the observed values. *True or false?*

2. Calculate the arithmetic mean and the geometric mean from the following series of data:

   5%, 6%, –2%, 10%

3. Which of the following is not a measure of location

   A Mode
   B Range
   C Median
   D Mean

4. A positively skewed distribution occurs when

   A More extreme items lie below the mode
   B More extreme items lie above the mode
   C Less extreme items lie above the mode
   D There are no extreme items

5. What does the range calculate?

6. What is regression looking at two variables also known as?

7. What is the method for estimating the parameters 'a' and 'b' in a regression calculation known as?

8. A correlation coefficient of +0.5 is referred to as

   A Perfect positive correlation
   B Perfect negative correlation
   C Positive correlation
   D Negative correlation

9. A security has annual rates of return over the last seven years of –9%, 12%, –19%, 22%, 28%, –5% and 2%. What is the geometric mean return?

10. Over the last seven years, the returns on a particular fund have been as follows

    2%, 7%, 6%, 13%, 11%, –5%, –3%

    What is the average return as measured by the arithmetic mean?

11. Securities A and B have expected returns of 12% and 16%, respectively. If 25% of a portfolio is invested in security A with the rest invested in B, what is the expected portfolio return?

12. The probability distribution of annual returns from investing in company A is given below.

Return %	Probability
10	0.1
20	0.7
30	0.2

What is the mean and standard deviation of the annual rate of return on this investment?

13. A portfolio manager believes that the outlook for the UK equity market for the next year will depend crucially on exchange rate and interest rate developments. In particular, he identifies three possible states of the world with their associated probabilities of occurrence and equity market returns.

State of the World	Probability	Rate of Return (%)
No change	0.2	8
£ joins Euro	0.4	26
Euro collapses	0.4	15

Calculate the expected return and standard deviation of the return on the UK equity market for the next year.

14. A monetarist economist believes he knows the relationship between monetary growth and subsequent inflation. In addition, he has views on the likelihood of different monetary regimes in the next year. The table below summarises his views.

Monetary Growth	Probability	Rate of Inflation (%)
Non-existent	0.2	1
Moderate	0.4	5
Fast	0.4	12

Calculate the expected inflation rate and the standard deviation of the inflation rate given his views.

15. The probability distribution of annual returns from investing in a company is given below.

Return %	Probability
10	0.4
15	0.4
5	0.2

What is the standard deviation of the annual rates of return on this investment?

TEST YOUR KNOWLEDGE: ANSWERS

1. False, the arithmetic mean is not necessarily one of the observed values.

   (See Section 2.2.5)

2. Arithmetic mean = $\frac{5+6-2+10}{4} = 4.75\%$

   Geometric mean = $\sqrt[4]{(1.05 \times 1.06 \times 0.98 \times 1.10)} - 1 = 4.66\%$

   (See Sections 2.2 and 2.5)

3. Range is a measure of dispersion

   (See Section 2)

4. B

   (See Section 2.6.2)

5. The highest observed value less the lowest observed value.

   (See Section 3.3)

6. Simple linear regression/bivariate linear regression.

   (See Section 4.2)

7. The least squares method.

   (See Section 4.4.2)

8. C

   (See Section 4.5.11)

9. Geometric mean = $\sqrt[7]{0.91 \times 1.12 \times 0.81 \times 1.22 \times 1.28 \times 0.95 \times 1.02} - 1$

   $= 1.032 - 1 = 0.032$ or 3.2%

   (See Section 2.5)

10. Arithmetic mean = $\overline{x} = \frac{2+7+6+13+11-5-3}{7}$

    $= 4.4\%$

    (See Section 2.2)

11. $r = 0.25 \times 12\% + 0.75 \times 16\% = 15\%$

    (See Section 2.6)

12.

p	r	pr	$r-\bar{r}$	$(r-\bar{r})^2$	$p(r-\bar{r})^2$
0.1	10	1	–11	121	12.1
0.7	20	14	–1	1	0.7
0.2	30	6	9	81	16.2
	$\bar{r}$ =	21			29.0

Expected return = $\bar{r}$ = 21%

Standard deviation of return, $\sigma = \sqrt{29}$ = 5.39%

(See Section 3.2)

13.

State of world	p	r	pr	$(r-\bar{r})^2$	$p_i(r-\bar{r})^2$
No change	0.2	8	1.6	100	20.0
£ joins €	0.4	26	10.4	64	25.6
€ collapses	0.4	15	6.0	9	3.6
		$\bar{r}$ =	18.0	σ^2 =	49.2

Expected return = $\bar{r}$ = 18%

Standard deviation of return, $\sigma = \sqrt{49.2}$ = 7%

(See Section 2.2 and 3.2)

14.

p	i	pi	$(i-\bar{i})$	$(i-\bar{i})^2$	$p_i(r-\bar{r})^2$
0.2	1	0.2	–6	36	7.2
0.4	5	2.0	–2	4	1.6
0.4	12	4.8	5	25	10.0
	$\bar{i}$ =	7.0		σ_2 =	18.8

σ = 4.34

(See Section 3.2)

15.

p	r	pr	$r-\bar{r}$	$(r-\bar{r})^2$	$p(r-\bar{r})^2$
0.4	10	4	–1	1	0.4
0.4	15	6	4	16	6.4
0.2	5	1	–6	36	7.2
	$\bar{r}$ =	11		σ^2 =	14.0
				σ =	3.74%

(See Section 3.2)

APPENDIX

Note: this is provided for information only and is **not** required for exam.

Calculating the regression coefficients

The formulae for calculating the coefficients a and b are as follows.

$$b = \frac{\text{Covariance }(x, y)}{\text{Variance }(x)} = \frac{\sum xy - n\overline{xy}}{\sum x^2 - n\overline{x}^2}$$

$$a = \overline{y} - b\overline{x}$$

Giving the equation of the relationship as

$$y = a + bx$$

Though it is not obvious what these equations are doing, they are calculating the line which results in the minimum sum of squared deviation of the observed points from that line, i.e. calculating the line for which the points show a minimum divergence. This could be illustrated graphically as follows.

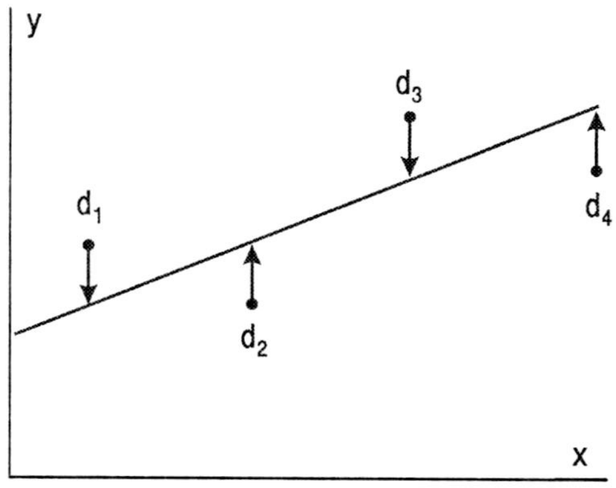

In other words, what these formulae provide are the values of a and b for which

$$\sum_{1}^{n} d_i^{\,2} = d_1^{\,2} + d_2^{\,2} + d_3^{\,2} + \cdots + d_n^{\,2}$$

is minimised and hence the line provides the closest possible fit to all the points.

Example

We will use, for this example, the data regarding the relationship between sales and profits noted in our introduction above. Note that you should not be expected to do these calculations and therefore, at most, need only briefly review this example.

Solution

Dependent and Independent Variables

In this scenario, the profit is clearly dependent upon the sales generated. The company, through the activities of its sales force, can directly influence the level of sales but they cannot directly influence the level of profits – the profit is a consequence of the sales. We will therefore take sales as the independent variable and profits as the dependent variable.

Dependent and Independent Variables

Alternative 1

Using

$$b = \frac{\text{Covariance}(x, y)}{\text{Variance}(x)}$$

NB: We do not need the sixth column of this table here; we refer to it when calculating the correlation coefficient later.

x (Sales)	y (Profit)	$(x-\bar{x})$	$(y-\bar{y})$	$(x-\bar{x})^2$	$(y-\bar{y})^2$	$(x-\bar{x})(y-\bar{y})$
1,000	160	(600)	(100.4167)	360,000	10,083.5069	60,250.0000
1,300	215	(300)	(45.4167)	90,000	2,062.6736	13,625.0000
1,700	270	100	9.5833	10,000	91.8403	958.3333
2,000	350	400	89.5833	160,000	8,025.1736	35,833.3333
2,100	370	500	109.5833	250,000	12,008.5069	54,791.6667
1,800	315	200	54.5833	40,000	2,979.3403	10,916.6667
1,900	340	300	79.5833	90,000	6,333.5069	23,875.0000
1,600	255	0	(5.4167)	0	29.3403	0.0000
1,500	260	(100)	(0.4167)	10,000	0.1736	41.6667
1,400	220	(200)	(40.4167)	40,000	1,633.5069	8,083.3333
1,200	200	(400)	(60.4167)	160,000	3,650.1736	24,166.6667
1,700	170	100	(90.4167)	10,000	8,175.1736	(9,041.6667)
19,200	3,125			1,220,000	55,072.9167	223,500.0000

$$\bar{x} = \frac{19,200}{12} = 1600$$

$$\bar{y} = \frac{3,125}{12} = 260.416667$$

$$\text{Variance}(x) = \frac{1,220,000}{12} = 101,667$$

$$\text{Variance}(y) = \frac{55,072.9167}{12} = 4,589.4097$$ Note, this is not needed here but is referred to later

$$\text{Covariance}(x,y) = \frac{223,500}{12} = 18,625$$

$$b = \frac{\text{Covariance}(x, y)}{\text{Variance}(x)} = \frac{18,625}{101,667} = 0.18320$$

$$a = \bar{y} - b\bar{x}$$

$$= \frac{3,125}{12} - 0.18320 \times \frac{19,200}{12}$$

$$= 260.417 - 293.115$$

$$= -32.70$$

Giving the equation of the relationship as

$$y = -32.70 + 0.18320x$$

Alternative 2

Using

$$b = \frac{\sum xy - n\overline{xy}}{\sum x^2 - n\overline{x}^2}$$

NB: We only need the first four columns of this table here; we refer to the fifth column when calculating the correlation coefficient later.

x (Sales)	x^2	y (Profit)	xy	y2
1,000	1,000,000	160	160,000	25,600
1,300	1,690,000	215	279,500	46,225
1,700	2,890,000	270	459,000	72,900
2,000	4,000,000	350	700,000	122,500
2,100	4,410,000	370	777,000	136,900
1,800	3,240,000	315	567,000	99,225
1,900	3,610,000	340	646,000	115,600
1,600	2,560,000	255	408,000	65,025
1,500	2,250,000	260	390,000	67,600
1,400	1,960,000	220	308,000	48,400
1,200	1,440,000	200	240,000	40,000
1,700	2,890,000	170	289,000	28,900
19,200	31,940,000	3,125	5,223,500	868,875

$$\overline{x} = \frac{19{,}200}{12} = 1600$$

$$\overline{y} = \frac{3{,}125}{12} = 260.416667$$

$$b = \frac{\sum xy - n\overline{xy}}{\sum x^2 - n\overline{x}^2}$$

$$= \frac{5{,}223{,}500 - 12 \times 1{,}600 \times 260.416667}{31{,}940{,}000 - 12 \times 1{,}600^2}$$

$$= \frac{223{,}500}{1{,}220{,}000} = 0.18320$$

$$a = \overline{y} - b\overline{x}$$

$$= \frac{3{,}125}{12} - 0.18320 \times \frac{19{,}200}{12}$$

$$= 260.417 - 293.115$$

$$= -32.70$$

Giving the same equation we established earlier using Alternative 1 of

$$y = -32.70 + 0.18320x$$

Interpretation of results

From this we can say

Profit = –32.70 + 0.18320 × Sales

In this context, we can interpret this result as

- The company has fixed costs of £32,700 – the level of loss when the sales are zero.
- The company generates a profit margin of 18.320% (0.18320) as every extra £1 of sales generates an extra £0.18320 of profits.

Calculating the correlation coefficient

The formula for the correlation coefficient can be shown to be

$$\text{Cor}_{xy} = \frac{\text{Covariance}(x, y)}{\sigma_x \sigma_y} = \frac{\sum xy - n\overline{xy}}{\sigma_x \sigma_y}$$

Though both alternative formulations look a little complicated, the various terms that need to be inserted can be established using the tabular calculation we used for establishing the regression coefficients and adding one more column.

Example

Calculate the correlation coefficient for the regression line established in our earlier example involving the determination of a profit figure from a sales figure.

Solution

Alternative 1

Using

$$\text{Cor}_{xy} = \frac{\text{Covariance}(x, y)}{\sigma_x \sigma_y}$$

We calculated the covariance and the variances under Alternative 1 earlier as

$$\text{Variance (x)} = \frac{1{,}220{,}000}{12} = 101{,}667$$

$$\text{Variance (y)} = \frac{55{,}072.9167}{12} = 4{,}589.4097$$ Note, this is not needed here but is referred to below

$$\text{Covariance (x,y)} = \frac{223{,}500}{12} = 18{,}625$$

Hence

$$\sigma_x = \sqrt{\text{Variance (x)}} = \sqrt{101{,}667} = 318.8521$$

$$\sigma_y = \sqrt{\text{Variance (y)}} = \sqrt{4{,}589.4097} = 67.7452$$

$$\text{Cor}_{xy} = \frac{18{,}625}{318.8521 \times 67.7452} = 0.86224$$

Alternative 2

Using

$$Cor_{xy} = \frac{\sum xy - n\overline{xy}}{\sigma_x \sigma_y}$$

Based on the data calculated in the Alternative 2 table earlier

$$Cor_{xy} = \frac{5{,}223{,}500 - 12 \times 1{,}600 \times 260.416667}{\sqrt{\left[31{,}940{,}000 - (1{,}600)^2\right]\left[868{,}875 - (260.416667)^2\right]}}$$

$$= \frac{223{,}500}{\sqrt{[1{,}220{,}000][55{,}072.916667]}}$$

$$= \frac{223{,}500}{259{,}208.333} = 0.86224$$

This answer is probably along the lines that we would have expected. It is positive, which indicates that profits increase as sales increase, and it is relatively close to one, indicating a reasonably strong relationship between the two.

4 Discounted Cash Flows

INTRODUCTION

Returns on investments will be improved by reinvesting income earned. The process of reinvesting income and so generating interest on interest is known as compounding.

We can forecast the amount by which an investment will grow if we know the compound rate and the time period of the investment. This final value is called the terminal value.

Likewise if we know we will receive a payment in x number of years, we can work backwards to compute the value today. This is calculated using present value calculations.

Discounted cash flow is the technique used to compute present values. The concept is fundamental to many of the techniques used when undertaking financial valuation and will be utilised in later chapters.

CHAPTER CONTENTS

Chapter Learning Objectives

26 Statistics and financial mathematics

Demonstrate an ability to apply statistical and financial mathematics techniques

26.5 Simple and compound interest

26.5.1 **Distinguish** simple interest from compound interest.

26.5.2 **Calculate** simple and compound interest over multiple periods.

26.5.3 **Distinguish** a nominal (simple) annual interest rate from an effective (compound) annual rate.

26.5.4 **Calculate** the annual compound rate given the nominal rate and the frequency of compounding.

26.5.5 **Calculate** the annual nominal rate of interest given the annual compound rate and the frequency of compounding.

26.5.6 **Explain** the concept of continuous compounding.

26.5.7 **Calculate** the effective continuously compounded rate given the nominal rate.

26.6 The time value of money – present and future value calculations, annuities, perpetuities and mortgages

26.6.1 **Calculate** and interpret future values for

- Single sums.
- Annuities.

26.6.2 **Calculate** and interpret present values for

- Single sums.
- Annuities.
- Perpetuities.

26.6.3 **Calculate** equal instalments on a repayment mortgage given the present value of the borrowings, the fixed mortgage rate and the term of the borrowing.

26.7 The internal rate of return and net present value

26.7.1 **Calculate** and interpret the net present value of a series of investment cash flows.

26.7.2 **Calculate** and interpret an internal rate of return.

26.7.3 **Explain** how NPVs and IRRs can be used in investment decision making.

26.7.4 **Explain** the limitations of each technique.

26.7.5 **Explain** why decisions using each technique may conflict.

26.7.6 **Explain** the scenarios in which multiple IRRs may occur.

1 INTRODUCTION

Central to all our theories regarding the valuation of securities is DCF (Discounted Cash Flows) and the time value of money. It is therefore essential that we thoroughly understand this topic and the relevance of the measures that we derive.

The various valuation ideas are based on the dividend valuation model which states that

"The market value of a security is the present value of the future expected receipts, discounted at the investors' required rate of return."

We will see this idea time and time again, hence the importance placed on the basics.

2 THE TIME VALUE OF MONEY AND INTEREST RATES

Learning objectives	26.5.1 **Distinguish** simple interest from compound interest. 26.5.2 **Calculate** simple and compound interest over multiple periods

2.1 Introduction

A starting point is the realisation and appreciation of the time value of money, which we will all be aware of as a result of the payment (or possibly the receipt) of bank interest.

Bank interest can take one of two forms

- Simple interest; or
- Compound interest.

Each of which are illustrated below with the aid of the following example.

2.2 Simple interest

If a bank account were to offer a **simple interest** rate, then the interest received each year would be based on the **original capital invested only**. Hence, in relation to the above example, we would have the following solution.

Example

£100 is deposited in an account paying interest at 10% per annum (simple interest). How much interest will be earned during, and what will be the value of the deposit at the end of

- The first year?
- The nth year (say 5th)?

Solution

First Year

The interest earned in this year would be based on the capital originally invested (£100) and the simple rate of interest (10%). The interest could be calculated using the formula

Formula to learn

$$i_1 = D_0 \times r$$

where

i_1 = interest earned by the end of the first year (time = 1)

r = interest rate stated as a decimal, here 10% or 0.10

D_0 = original capital invested at the start of the first year (time = 0)

Giving

$$i_1 = £100 \times 0.10 = £10$$

At that date, the deposit will be worth £110.

n^{th} Year

With simple interest, the interest generated each subsequent year will be exactly the same, since it is only based on the original capital invested. Hence, we can apply the same formula to calculate this year's interest as

$$i_n = D_0 \times r$$

giving for the fifth year

$$i_5 = £100 \times 0.10 = £10$$

We can see that the value of our deposit is growing by £10 each year.

In conclusion, with simple interest, we earn the same amount of interest each year. At the end of n years, the total interest we will have earned will be

$$n \times \text{Annual interest}$$

or

$$i_{tot} = n \times (D_0 \times r)$$

which, when added to our starting capital of D_0, gives the value of our deposit as

$$D_n = D_0 + n \times (D_0 \times r)$$

Applying this to the above example gives

$$D_5 = D_0 + n \times (D_0 \times r) = £100 + 5 \times (£100 \times 0.10) = £150$$

which is perhaps the result we expected. Five years' interest at 10% per annum should add a total of 50% to the value of the deposit with flat interest.

2.3 Compound interest

Learning objectives

26.5.3 Distinguish a nominal (simple) annual interest rate from an effective (compound) annual rate.

26.5.4 Calculate the annual compound rate given the nominal rate and the frequency of compounding.

26.5.5 Calculate the annual nominal rate of interest given the annual compound rate and the frequency of compounding.

2.3.1 Annual compounding

Interest rates are described as **compound interest** if, in each year, interest is earned on the **total value of the deposit at the start of the year**, i.e. original capital plus any interest previously earned. With compound interest, we receive interest on our previous interest.

Example

£100 is deposited in an account paying interest at 10% per annum (compound interest). How much interest will be earned during, and what will be the value of the deposit at the end of

The first year?

The nth year (say 5th)?

Solution

First Year

The interest earned in this year would be based on the value of the deposit at the start of the year, i.e. the capital originally invested (£100) and the compound rate of interest (10%). The interest could again be calculated using the formula

$$i_1 = D_0 \times r$$

where

i_1 = interest earned by the end of the first year (time = 1)

r = interest rate stated as a decimal, here 10% or 0.10

D_0 = original capital invested at the outset (time = 0)

Giving

$$i_1 = £100 \times 0.10 = £10$$

At that date, the deposit will be worth £110, which we could have calculated directly using the formula

$$D_1 = D_0(1 + r) = £100 \times (1 + 0.10) = £100 \times 1.10 = £110$$

where D_1 = the value of the deposit at Time 1. We can see that, so far, this is identical to the simple interest example above. However, this is only true for the first year.

n^{th} Year

With compound interest, the interest generated each subsequent year will be based on the value of the deposit at the start of each year. We could state this in a formula as

$$i_n = D_{n-1} \times r$$

In order to calculate the interest for the fifth year, we would need to know the value of the deposit at the start of the fifth year/end of the fourth year. From our Year 1 illustration above, we noted that the value of the deposit at the end of the first year/start of the second was given by

$$D_1 = D_0(1 + r)$$

This amount would then grow by the end of the second year/start of the third year to

$$D_2 = D_1(1 + r) = D_0(1 + r)^2$$

In a similar way, we could calculate the value of the deposit at the end of each subsequent year as

$D_3 = D_2(1 + r) = D_0(1 + r)^3$ – end of third/start of fourth

$D_4 = D_3(1 + r) = D_0(1 + r)^4$ – end of fourth/start of fifth

$D_5 = D_4(1 + r) = D_0(1 + r)^5$ – end of fifth/start of sixth

which could be described generally as

$D_n = D_0(1 + r)^n$ – end of nth/start of $(n + 1)^{th}$

Hence, at the end of the fourth year/start of the fifth the value of the deposit would be

$$D_4 = D_0(1 + r)^n = £100\ (1 + 0.10)^4 = £100 \times 1.1^4 = £146.41$$

and, hence, the interest generated in the fifth year would be

$$i_5 = D_4 \times r = £146.41 \times 0.10 = £14.641$$

taking the value of the total deposit up to £161.051 (£146.41 + £14.641) by the end of the fifth year, which we can confirm with the formula

This is a larger sum than under simple interest, since we are getting interest on our previously earned interest.

$$D_5 = D_0(1 + r)^5 = £100\ (1 + 0.10)^5 = £100 \times 1.1^5 = £161.051$$

2.3.2 Non-annual compounding

Generally, bank and building society accounts quote an annual interest rate that is liable to be compounded, though the compounding may be more regular than once per annum. There is no standard in relation to the frequency of compounding. Bank accounts regularly compound monthly, while instant access building society accounts are frequently compounded quarterly, though many are six-monthly or annually.

Generally, two rates are quoted.

- A flat rate.
- An Annual Percentage Rate (APR).

What are these quotes and what difference does this make to our deposit?

Flat Rate

Example

£100 is deposited in an account quoting an annual flat rate of 10% compounding quarterly. Calculate the interest earned and value of the deposit by the end of the first year.

Solution

A flat rate of r per annum which compounds n times a year would generate interest of $\frac{r}{n}$ each period, i.e. with a flat rate of 10% compounding quarterly (four times per annum), the interest generated each period would be $\frac{10\%}{4} = 2.5\%$.

We can now suppose that we are generating an interest rate of 2.5% per period, hence at the end of four periods (one year), the value of our deposit will have grown to

$$£100\ (1 + 0.025)^4 = £100 \times 1.025^4 = £110.38$$

which is slightly more than when interest is compounded annually.

Example

£100 is deposited in an account quoting an annual flat rate of 10%, compounding monthly. What is the value of the deposit at the end of one year?

Solution

The rate per month would be $\frac{10\%}{12}$ = 0.83333%.

Hence, at the end of 12 months (one year), the value of our deposit will have grown to

$$£100\ (1 + 0.0083333)^{12} = £100 \times 1.0083333^{12} = £110.47$$

which is slightly more than when interest is compounded both annually and quarterly.

What we can conclude is

- The more frequent the compounding, the better.
- The higher the interest rate, the greater the benefit of frequent compounding.

Annual percentage rate

We can see from the above that if the interest compounds monthly we have generated interest of £10.47 over the first year based on our initial £100 deposit – an effective rate of 10.47%. This effective rate is the APR. It tells you exactly how much you will earn over a year (or pay if you are borrowing) based on the flat rate and the frequency of compounding.

Pulling the ideas together, n periods at a rate of $\frac{r}{n}$ each period must equate to one full year at the APR, ie

$$(1 + \text{APR}) = \left(1 + \frac{r}{n}\right)^n$$

2.3.3 Continuous compounding

Learning objectives

26.5.6 **Explain** the concept of continuous compounding.

26.5.7 **Calculate** the effective continuously compounded rate given the nominal rate.

Introduction

Interest rates tend to be quoted in annual terms, i.e. the interest rate is per annum regardless of the frequency of the payments. If we are quoted such a rate of interest, then the actual annual return we receive will depend on how frequently it is compounded.

Example

We are quoted a rate of 32% p.a., this may be 16% each half year or 8% per quarter or 2.667% per month or 0.0877% per day. If we compound these up to get the actual annual rate that we will earn we get

Compound Period	Calculation	Actual Rate (%)
Annual	$1.32^1 - 1$	32.00
Half yearly	$1.16^2 - 1$	34.56
Quarterly	$1.08^4 - 1$	36.05
Monthly	$1.02667^{12} - 1$	37.14
Daily	$1.000877^{365} - 1$	37.69

As we can see, the actual rate is increasing, but tending towards a limit. This limit is given by

Formula to learn

$R = e^{rt} - 1$

where

e = exponential constant (2.7182818)
r = quoted annual rate as a decimal
t = time period being considered as a proportion of a year

Thus, over one year, converting the 32% rate to a continuously compounding rate gives a return of

$$R = e^{rt} - 1$$
$$= 2.7182818^{0.32 \times 1} - 1$$
$$= 1.3771 - 1$$
$$= 0.3771 \text{ or } 37.71\%$$

a slightly higher rate than the daily one, as it compounds continuously.

Tutor tip

The calculator key strokes for this calculation are

[e□] 0.32 [×] 1 [▶] 1 [=]

where ▶ is the right Replay button and [e□] is accessed by pressing [Shift] then [ln]

3 Terminal/Future Values

3.1 Introduction

A **terminal value** or **future value** is the value of a deposit at the end of a period of time having received interest over that period, i.e. D_n is the terminal value in the above examples.

A **present value** is the equivalent value of the same deposit before the effects of interest, i.e. D_0 is the present value in the above examples.

Calculating terminal or present values for investment opportunities provides a means of appraising them. Indeed, as we noted at the outset, the calculation of a present value provides a method for evaluating a security, i.e. determines its market value.

All calculations with regard to these ideas utilise the concept of **compound interest**.

3.2 Terminal/future values

3.2.1 Introduction

Learning objective

26.6.1 Calculate and interpret future values for: single sums and annuities.

Terminal/future value calculations consider

- Each cash flow generated by an investment.
- The timing of the cash flow.

They calculate how much cash could be generated to the end of the investment period if the earlier returns were banked each year to generate additional compound interest.

If the returns plus the interest that they can accumulate exceeds the total that could be generated had we simply banked the cash at the outset rather than buying the investment, then we accept the investment.

The decision criteria could be stated as
"An investment should be accepted if it produces a surplus in cash terms after accounting for interest."

Example

Two alternative investments to banking £100 are investments A and B, both of which will terminate in three years. Investment A will return £41.00 per annum for the next three years, giving a total return of £123 and a total profit of £23. Investment B will return £134.00 at the end of the third year, a profit of £34.

Which investment opportunity is superior and which, if either, should be accepted if the interest rate is 10%?

Solution

Since we can receive 10% per annum on any cash generated, then the effects of selecting A or B would be as follows.

Investment A

Time	Balance b/f £	Interest for Year £	Receipt at Year End £	Balance c/f £
1	–	–	41.00	41.00
2	41.00	4.10	41.00	86.10
3	86.10	8.61	41.00	135.71

Undertaking investment A will result in cash in the bank of £135.71 at the end of the three years – this is its terminal value.

Investment B

Investment B will result in a receipt of £134.00 at the same time, hence this is its terminal value.

Bank Account

Time	Balance b/f £	Interest for Year £	Receipt at Year End £	Balance c/f £
1	100.00	10.00	–	110.00
2	110.00	11.00	–	121.00
3	121.00	12.10	–	133.10

Banking the £100 today will result in cash in the bank of £133.10 at the end of the three years.

Conclusion

Both investments produce a better end position than the simple investment in the bank. Investment A will result in £2.61 more cash (£135.71 – £133.10) and Investment B £0.90 more (£134.00 – £133.10). Comparing the two, Investment A now appears preferable to Investment B.

It would certainly seem that it is in the investor's interest to pay more attention to the cash flows expected from an investment and to the timing of these cash flows than to consider solely the level of profit.

Alternative solution

An alternative way of dealing with the example would be by compounding the interest on each flow individually, using our earlier compound interest ideas.

Investment A

Time	Cash Flow £	Compound Factor	Terminal Value £
1	41.00	1.10^2	49.61
2	41.00	1.10^1	45.10
3	41.00	1	41.00
Terminal value at t_3			£135.71

Investment B

Time	Cash Flow £	Compound Factor	Terminal Value £
1	0.00	1.10^2	0.00
2	0.00	1.10^1	0.00
3	134.00	1	134.00
Terminal value at t_3			£134.00

Here, we have compounded each flow by adding on interest at 10% per annum for the number of years remaining until the end of the investment lives. To achieve this, we have in each case multiplied the cash flow by the compound factor, which in general terms may be written as

Formula to learn

Compound factor with n years to run $= (1+r)^n$

where r is the rate of interest expressed as a decimal (here r = 0.10) and n is the number of years' compounding required.

Clearly, the calculations have produced the same result, but the method used here is somewhat neater. We have compounded the flows to produce what is termed the terminal value of each flow.

Again, this can be compared to the £133.10 terminal value from the bank account to show that the investments are both worthwhile.

3.2.2 Net Terminal Value

The net surplus or deficit from the investment (£2.61 for Investment A, £0.90 for Investment B as calculated above) is known as the Net Terminal Value (NTV), and since it is positive, indicating a surplus, the investments are worthwhile and should be accepted. Had it been negative, indicating a deficit, we would have rejected the investments.

Rather than calculating separately the terminal values of the investment and the bank account, we can combine them in one net terminal value calculation, as follows.

Investment A

Time	Cash Flow £	Compound Factor	Terminal Value £
0	(100.00)	1.10^3	(133.10)
1	41.00	1.10^2	49.61
2	41.00	1.10^1	45.10
3	41.00	1	41.00
Net terminal value at t_3			£2.61

Here, we are considering the £100 invested initially as a cash outflow on which we will lose interest. In turn, we get the investment inflows that generate interest, but it is the net difference we are interested in.

Investment B

Time	Cash Flow £	Compound Factor	Terminal Value £
0	(100.00)	1.10^3	(133.10)
1	0.00	1.10^2	0.00
2	0.00	1.10^1	0.00
3	134.00	1	134.00
Net terminal value at t_3			£0.90

3.2.3 Depreciation

Applying depreciation

So far, we have considered only the idea of appreciation, i.e. values growing with time. Exactly the same relationship can be used to deal with depreciation on a reducing balance basis by making r negative rather than positive.

Example

An asset with a cost of £50,000 is to be depreciated at a rate of 30% per annum on the reducing balance basis. What will be its net book value at the end of the

First year?
Third year?

Solution

First Year

Using the relationship

$$D_n = D_0(1 + r)^n$$

gives

$$D_1 = £50,000 \times [1 + (-0.30)] = £50,000 \times 0.70 = £35,000$$

Third Year

Using the same relationship gives

$$D_3 = £50,000 \times [1 + (-0.30)]^3 = £50,000 \times 0.70^3 = £17,150$$

Calculating the depreciation rate

The above approach is fine providing we are given the depreciation rate and asked to determine the net book value. What if we are told that we need to depreciate an asset to a certain net book value by the end of its useful life and are required to calculate the depreciation rate?

Example

A machine costs £50,000 and is to be depreciated to £20,480 over four years under the reducing balance method. What is the rate of depreciation?

Solution

Using the same relationship, we have

$$D_n = D_0(1 + r)^n$$

This time, we know D_0, D_n and n, and we are trying to solve for r. Rearranging this equation gives

$$\frac{D_n}{D_0} = (1+r)^n$$

Hence

$$1+r = \sqrt[n]{\frac{D_n}{D_0}}$$

giving

$$r = \sqrt[n]{\frac{D_n}{D_0}} - 1$$

and applying this, we get

$$r = \sqrt[4]{\frac{£20,480}{£50,000}} - 1 = 0.8 - 1 = -0.2$$

The negative sign denotes depreciation rather than appreciation, i.e. depreciation a rate of 20%.

3.2.4 Continuous Compound Factor

If, but only if, we are told that the rates we are applying are continuous then we need to apply the continuous compounding ideas discussed above. In this situation the compound factor that results from these ideas that can be used for terminal value calculation is

$$1 + R = e^{rt}$$

Example

What is the terminal value of £100 after eight months when the continuously compounded rate is 5%

Solution

$$TV = 100 \times e^{0.05 \times 8/12} = £103.39$$

Tutor tip

The key strokes here are

100 [×] [e□] 0.05 [×] 8 [÷] 12 [=]

3.3 Conclusion

Net terminal values will be useful for evaluating individual investments or investments with the same end date. If, however, we are trying to evaluate investments with different end dates, then we cannot compare the terminal value of one directly to the terminal value of the other.

For example, how could we compare the terminal value of Investment A of £135.71 at the end of three years, to the terminal value of a third investment of £150 at the end of six years?

In order to do this comparison, we must compound the interest out to a common end date. Here, six years would be sensible. However, this method will get very cumbersome, especially if we have some investments that will continue forever and never terminate, such as an investment in irredeemable gilts.

4 Present Values and Net Present Values

4.1 Introduction

One way of accounting for the interest is by compounding the flows and calculating the terminal values, as we have just seen. However, as we stated earlier, if we are to compare investments, we will have to calculate to a common date, say, the end of the longest investment time. An alternative approach is to use present values where we take the common date as the present.

4.2 Present values

4.2.1 Introduction

Learning objective — **26.6.2 Calculate** and interpret present values for: single sums; annuities and perpetuities.

Present value calculations consider for any investment

- Each relevant cash flow; and
- The timing of the cash flow

and calculate how much cash we would need to have invested now to generate these same amounts of cash at these same future dates.

If we can get the same amounts of cash at the same future dates by investing less upfront now, then we should accept the investment.

Example

Two alternative investments to banking £100 are Investments A and B, both of which will terminate in three years.

Investment A will return £41.00 per annum for the next three years; Investment B will return £134.00 at the end of the third year.

Which investment opportunity is superior and which, if either, should be accepted if the interest rate is 10%?

Solution

Investment A

Investment A generates the following cash flows.

Time	Cash Flow £
1	41.00
2	41.00
3	41.00

Looking at each of these in turn, how much cash would we need to invest now at our 10% rate of return to have £41.00 in each year?

Year 1

If we invest x now, then in one year it will grow to $x \times 1.10 = 1.10x$. Since we know that this is £41.00, then we can calculate x as

$$1.10x = £41.00$$

or

$$x = \frac{1}{1.10} \times £41.00$$

$$x = £37.27$$

Year 2

Similarly, x invested now will grow to $x \times 1.10^2 = 1.21x$ after two years, hence

$$1.21x = £41.00$$

or

$$x = \frac{1}{1.21} \times £41.00$$

$$x = £33.89$$

Year 3

And x invested now will grow to $x \times 1.10^3 = 1.331x$ after three years, hence

$$1.331x = £41.00$$

or

$$x = \frac{1}{1.331} \times £41.00$$

$$x = £30.80$$

Conclusion

Putting these all together, we have

Time	Cash Flow £	Discount Factor	Present Value £
1	41.00	$\frac{1}{1.10^1}$	37.27
2	41.00	$\frac{1}{1.10^2}$	33.89
3	41.00	$\frac{1}{1.10^3}$	30.80
Present value at t_0			£101.96

In total, the present value of these receipts is £101.96. This means that, given the 10% rate of return, we would be indifferent between £41.00 each year for three years and £101.96 now.

Rather than compounding up the cash values for interest generated to the end of the investment, we are **discounting down**, i.e. reducing future cash values to their equivalent value today.

This discounting is effectively the reverse of our compounding process and in a similar way, we could apply a general formula for any year.

Formula to learn

$$\text{Discount factor at time}_n = \frac{1}{(1+r)^n}$$

where r is the **discount rate**, i.e. rate of interest expressed as a decimal (here r = 0.10) and n is the number of years' discounting required.

Solution

Investment B

Calculating the present value for Investment B gives

Time	Cash Flow £	Discount Factor	Present Value £
3	134.00	$\frac{1}{1.10^3}$	100.68
Present value at t_0			£100.68

This means that we would be indifferent, given the 10% rate of return, between £134.00 in three years and £100.68 now.

4.2.2 Bank

What is the present value of our option to bank the cash for a comparison? Under this option, we left the cash in the bank until Year 3 when it had grown to £133.10. This is then the cash flow to discount giving

Time	Cash Flow £	Discount Factor	Present Value £
3	133.10	$\frac{1}{1.10^3}$	100.00
Present value at t_0			£100.00

This one really proves the idea, as it shows that we would be indifferent between £133.10 in three years and £100.00 now, which stands to reason as to get £133.10 in three years, we will need to invest £100.00 in the bank now.

4.2.3 Net present value

Learning objective — 26.7.1 **Calculate** and interpret the net present value of a series of investment cash flows.

The present value of Investment A is £1.96 higher than could be expected from the bank. Investment B has a present value which is £0.68 higher than that from the bank. These represent the **net present values** of these investments.

In a similar way to net terminal values, we could calculate a net present value in one go, rather than calculating separately the present value of the investment and the banking option, as follows.

Solution

Investment A

Time	Cash Flow £	Discount Factor	Present Value £
0	(100.00)	1	(100.00)
1	41.00	$\frac{1}{1.10^1}$	37.27
2	41.00	$\frac{1}{1.10^2}$	33.89
3	41.00	$\frac{1}{1.10^3}$	30.80
Net present value at t_0			£1.96

You will note in this that the cash flow at Time 0 (now) is not discounted. £100 now is worth £100 now. Discounting takes account of the time value of money.

Investment B

Similarly, for Investment B, we get

Time	Cash Flow £	Discount Factor	Present Value £
0	(100.00)	1	(100.00)
3	134.00	$\frac{1}{1.10^3}$	100.68
Present value at t_0			£0.68

Conclusion

For an accept or reject decision, the criterion is as before – a positive net present value (NPV) indicates a cash surplus after accounting for interest and therefore we should accept. A negative NPV indicates a cash deficit and we should therefore reject.

If we were to choose between various investments, we would now simply select the investment with the highest NPV.

4.3 Discount factors

4.3.1 Single cash flow discount factor

We established above that the general term for a discount factor to be applied to cash flows at Time_n is

Formula to learn

$$\text{Discount factor at Time n} = \frac{1}{(1+r)^n}$$

The above formula is suitable if we are only dealing with a few cash flows, or have a spreadsheet model to cope with a large number, but what if this is not the case? There are some other situations for which we can establish discount factor formulae to make manual calculations more straightforward, specifically in the situation of

- Level annuities; and
- Level perpetuities.

4.3.2 Annuity discount factor

An annuity describes the situation where we have equal annual cash flows for a set period, such as in investment A above. Here, we have £41.00 received at the end of each of the next three years and, so far, we have appraised each flow separately.

However, since for all the receipts we are multiplying the relevant discount factor by £41.00 each time, we can simplify the calculation by multiplying £41.00 by the sum of the discount factors, i.e.

$$£41.00 \times \left(\frac{1}{1.10^1} + \frac{1}{1.10^2} + \frac{1}{1.10^3}\right)$$

$$= £41.00 \times 2.48685$$

$$= £101.96 \text{ as before}$$

The discount factor of 2.48685 is termed the **three-year annuity discount factor** at 10%.

This annuity discount factor for cash flows arising from Time 1 to Time n can be calculated using the following formula

Formula to learn

$$\text{Annuity discount factor for Time 1 to Time n} = \frac{1}{r}\left(1 - \frac{1}{(1+r)^n}\right)$$

where r is the rate of interest per annum expressed as a decimal which must be constant throughout the period.

Using this formula

Wherever we pay or receive a level stream of payments over a period of time, e.g. a regular coupon from a bond assuming constant interest rates, we can use this formula to calculate their present value.

Example

Using this formula to calculate the three-year annuity discount factor at 10% gives

Annuity discount factor for Time 1 to Time n = $\frac{1}{0.10}\left(1-\frac{1}{1.10^3}\right)$

$$=\frac{1}{0.10}\left(1-\frac{1}{1.10^3}\right)$$

$$=\frac{1}{0.10}(1-0.751315)$$

$$=\frac{1}{0.10}(0.248685)$$

$$=2.48685$$

Tutor tip

> Note: people often have difficulty in entering this into the calculator. What you must remember is that
>
> $$\frac{1}{0.10}\left(1-\frac{1}{1.10^3}\right)=\frac{1}{0.10}\times\left(1-\frac{1}{1.10^3}\right)$$
>
> and when inputting this to the calculator we must remember to enter the multiplication function before the brackets. The calculator keystrokes needed are as follows
>
> 1 [÷] 0.10 [×] [(] 1 [−] 1 [÷] 1.10 [$x^{\square}$] 3 [=]

Solution

Using this approach, we could calculate the net present value of Investment A above (which we earlier calculated as £1.96) as follows.

Time	Cash Flow £	Discount Factor	Present Value £
0	(100.00)	1	(100.00)
1-3	41.00	$\frac{1}{0.10}\left(1-\frac{1}{1.10^3}\right)$	101.96
Net present value at t_0			£1.96

This approach can lead to significant time savings as the annuity period gets longer.

4.3.3 Perpetuity discount factor

A perpetuity refers to an equal annual flow which will continue **indefinitely**.

NB: Any series of flows that continue beyond 50 years could be approximated to a perpetuity without much impact or loss of accuracy.

Clearly, it will be impossible for us to evaluate each individual cash flow going on forever. For this situation, we must have a short cut.

Example

We are going to receive £10,000 per annum in perpetuity and the interest rate (which we will now start to refer to as a required rate of return or cost of capital) is 10% per annum. How would we value this series of flows?

To get a present value, we need to know how much cash invested now at 10% per annum would provide £10,000 p.a. in perpetuity. We would be indifferent between these two things which, by definition, means that it is the present value.

Solution

If we are to receive exactly the same amount in perpetuity, then we must never add to or take out of our capital invested. We are looking for an income of exactly £10,000 per annum.

Since our interest rate is 10% per annum, we can achieve this level of income by investing £100,000, the relationship being £100,000 × 10% = £10,000.

Now, we know that £10,000 × Perpetuity discount factor = £100,000 (the present value), hence the perpetuity discount factor in this case is $\frac{1}{0.10}$.

NB: What we have found is the discount factor for a stream of cash flows starting in one year, i.e. at Time1.

The general discount factor formula for a level perpetuity stream of cash flows starting at Time 1 is

Formula to learn

Perpetuity discount factor for Time 1 to $\infty = \frac{1}{r}$

where r is the rate of interest per annum expressed as a decimal.

4.3.4 Continuous Discount Factor

If, but only if, we are told that the rates are continuously compounding then the corresponding discount rate that can be used to determine present values is

$$\frac{1}{1+R} = \frac{1}{1+\left(e^{rt}-1\right)} = \frac{1}{e^{rt}} = e^{-rt}$$

This method of establishing a discount rate is used in options valuation.

Example

Calculate the present value of £100 received 30 weeks into the year when the continuous rate to apply is 6%

Solution

$$PV = 100 \times \frac{1}{e^{0.06 \times 30/52}} = £96.60$$

Tutor tip

The key strokes for this calculation are

100 [×] 1 [÷] [$e^{\square}$] 0.06 [×] 30 [÷] 52 [=]

4.4 Annuities and perpetuities not starting at Time 1

4.4.1 Introduction

As we noted in the calculation of the annuity or perpetuity discount factor, the first cash flow always arises at the end of the first time period (at Time 1). However, there will be situations when this will not be the case.

Example

An investment pays £41 at the end of Years 3, 4 and 5. Calculate the present value of the receipts assuming a 10% required rate of return.

Solution

Time	Cash Flow £	Discount Factor	Present Value £
3	41.00	$\frac{1}{1.10^3}$	30.8039
4	41.00	$\frac{1}{1.10^4}$	28.0036
5	41.00	$\frac{1}{1.10^5}$	25.4578
Present value at t_0			£84.2653

4.4.2 Alternative approaches

There are two alternative approaches that we could have adopted to calculate this, which could prove very useful in longer annuity or perpetuity situations.

Deducting unwanted years

We could view this cash stream as a normal five-year annuity (Time 1 to Time 5), but assume we must repay the Time 1 and Time 2 cash flows (hence not receive them).

Example

An investment pays £41 at the end of Years 3, 4 and 5. Calculate the present value of the receipts assuming a 10% required rate of return.

Solution

Time	Cash Flow £	Annuity Discount Factor (ADF)	Present Value £
1-5	41.00	$\frac{1}{0.10}\left(1-\frac{1}{1.10^5}\right)$	155.4224
1-2	(41.00)	$\frac{1}{0.10}\left(1-\frac{1}{1.10^2}\right)$	(71.1571)
Present value at t_0			£84.2653

Discounting back

The alternative approach is to recognise that this is a three-year annuity, which starts to pay at Time 3 rather than Time 1, i.e. two years later than a standard annuity which starts at Time 1. If all of the cash flows are two years later than in a normal annuity or perpetuity, they must be discounted back a further two years. Hence

$$\text{ADF (3-5)} = \text{ADF (1-3)} \times \frac{1}{(1+r)^2}$$

Example

An investment pays £41 at the end of Years 3, 4 and 5. Calculate the present value of the receipts assuming a 10% required rate of return.

Solution

Time	Cash Flow £	Discount Factor	Present Value £
3-5	(41.00)	$\frac{1}{0.10}\left(1-\frac{1}{1.10^3}\right)\times\frac{1}{1.10^2}$	£84.2653

Conclusion

There are three alternative approaches.

- Evaluate each separate cash flow.
- Calculate by deducting the unwanted years.
- Calculate by discounting back.

All approaches will give the same answer, and you may choose whichever approach you prefer.

4.5 Relationship between present and terminal values

One final point to note is that there is a direct relationship between present and terminal values, either gross or net. If we take the present or net present value of any investment and compound it up for the appropriate number of years, we will get the corresponding terminal or net terminal value as we can see from our sample investments.

Solution

Earlier, we calculated the terminal value, net terminal value, present value and net present value of two investments (A and B), A paying £41.00 each year for three years and B paying £134 at the end of the third year. Comparing the net present values and net terminal values we calculated earlier based on a required rate of return of 10%, we get

	Net Present Value £	Compound Factor	Net Terminal Value £
Investment A	1.96	1.10^3	2.61
Investment B	0.68	1.10^3	0.90

We can use this idea to determine the terminal value or net terminal value of anything for which we can calculate a present value or net present value (other than a perpetuity). That is, we can calculate the present value of the cash flows, then compound them up to give the corresponding terminal value.

4.6 Repayment mortgage instalments

Learning objective

26.6.3 Calculate equal instalments on a repayment mortgage given the present value of the borrowing, the fixed mortgage rate and the term of the mortgage.

A fixed rate, fixed term repayment mortgage is an example of an annuity, the question is how do we calculate the regular payments to make on such a loan?

Thinking practically, at the end of the mortgage term the borrower will want the mortgage to be exactly paid off, ie when assessing all of the relevant cash flows there should be a zero net terminal value (nothing outstanding at the end).

Based on what we have just covered, however, if there is a zero net terminal value there will be a zero net present value. That is, the present value of the payments must equal the present value of the borrowings (the value of the loan outstanding). So, if ADF is the annuity discount factor for the given borrowing period and rate we must have.

PV of borrowing = PV of repayments

Or

PV of borrowing = Regular repayment × ADF

And hence

$$\text{Regular repayment} = \frac{\text{PV of borrowing}}{\text{ADF}}$$

Example

Calculate the annual repayment required on a £100,000 25-year mortgage if the interest rate is 8%.

Solution

$$\text{ADF}(1-25) = \frac{1}{0.08}\left(1-\frac{1}{1.08^{25}}\right) = 10.6748$$

$$\text{Annual payment} = \frac{100,000}{10.6748} = £9,367.88$$

5 INTERNAL RATE OF RETURN

5.1 Definition

The **Internal Rate of Return (IRR)** is defined as follows.

IRR = The rate of interest that discounts the investment flows to a net present value of zero.

5.2 Use of the IRR

Learning objective

26.7.2 **Calculate** and interpret an internal rate of return.

The IRR may be used as a method for assessing the total return from an investment or a portfolio, and you will find this approach necessary in calculating the gross redemption yield for a bond or the money-weighted return for portfolio performance.

Example

An investment is bought for £100 and sold one year later for £110. Calculate the return realised.

Solution

Here we are making a £10 gain on a £100 investment, corresponding to a 10% return.

Clearly, with this very simple investment it was very easy to assess the return without recourse to DCF. However, if we were to discount this investment's cash flows at different rates we would find the following.

Time	Cash Flow £	Discount Factor (5%)	Present Value £	Discount Factor (10%)	Present Value £	Discount Factor (15%)	Present Value £
0	(100.00)	1	(100.00)	1	(100.00)	1	(100.00)
1	110.00	$\frac{1}{1.05^1}$	104.76	$\frac{1}{1.10^1}$	100.00	$\frac{1}{1.15^1}$	95.65
Net present values			£4.76		£0.00		(£4.35)

What we can see here is that there is an inverse relationship between NPVs and required rates of return; as rates rise, NPVs fall, and appreciating this relationship is the key to understanding the examination approach to these questions.

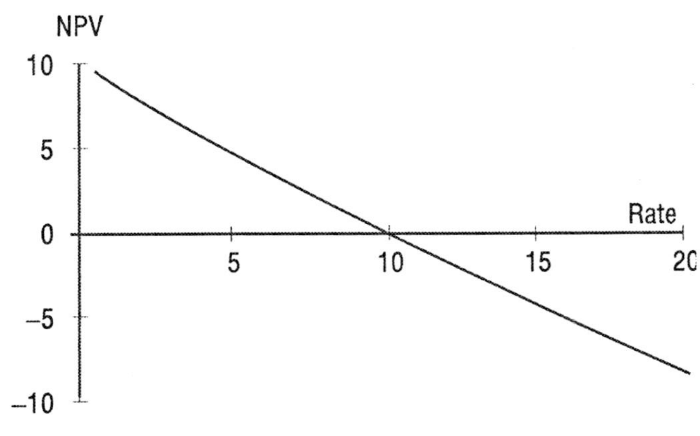

What we can also see in this example is that the IRR is 10% (the rate corresponding to a zero NPV), telling us that this investment is returning 10%. Clearly, we already knew the return from this very simple security was 10%, however the strength of this IRR approach is that it can be applied to investments that provide a much more complicated series of cash returns.

5.3 Assessment

An approximation to the IRR can be determined through a process called **interpolation**, though a trial and error approach is really the only way of finding the exact IRR. Through knowledge of the inverse relationship, however, the number of trials and errors can be minimised in a multiple choice exam where four alternative rates are offered.

5.3.1 Steps

Calculate the NPV of the various cash flows using the second highest rate, which will give rise to three possibilities.

- If the NPV is zero, then the correct rate has been selected first time.
- If the NPV is positive, then the selected rate is too low and the IRR is a higher rate. Since the second highest rate was originally selected, the correct answer must be the highest rate offered.
- If the NPV is negative, then the selected rate was too high and the IRR is one of the two lower rates offered in the question. One of these two lower rates will need to be tried to determine which it is.

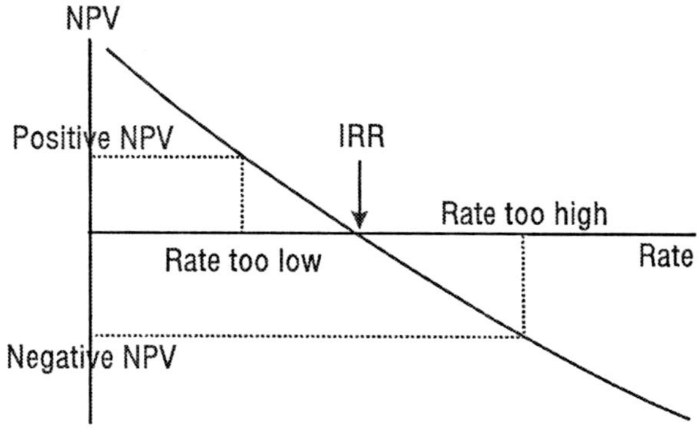

Example

An investment is bought for £88.33. It returns £6 each year for the next five years and is then sold for £100. Calculate the return realised on this investment.

A 8.7%
B 9.0%
C 9.3%
D 9.5%

Solution

Trying the Second Highest Rate of 9.3%

Time	Cash Flow £	Discount Factor	Present Value £
0	(88.33)	1	(88.33)
1-5	6.00	$\frac{1}{0.093}\left(1-\frac{1}{1.093^5}\right)$	23.16
5	100.00	$\frac{1}{1.093^5}$	64.11
Net present value at t_0			(£1.06)

Since this is negative, the rate we have selected is too high, so the correct answer must be either 8.7% or 9.0%.

Try 9.0%

Time	Cash Flow £	Discount Factor	Present Value £
0	(88.33)	1	(88.33)
1-5	6.00	$\frac{1}{0.090}\left(1-\frac{1}{1.090^5}\right)$	23.34
5	100.00	$\frac{1}{1.090^5}$	64.99
Net present value at t_0			£0.00

The NPV is zero, hence the rate of return (the IRR) is 9.0%.

6 Securities Evaluation and DCF

6.1 Introduction

The Dividend Valuation Model (DVM) is the basis for all our calculations relating to the market value of any investment.

In order to raise finance, a company must attract investors, i.e. the investors must believe that they will receive a return sufficient to match their requirements. If they do not believe this, they will not invest.

As a result, the market value of a security at any point in time is determined by two factors.

- The returns (dividends/interest/capital growth) that the investors expect.
- The rate of return that the investors require.

The dividend valuation model states that the

Market Value =	Present value of the future expected receipts discounted at the investor's required rate of return.

That is, we assume investors rationally evaluate the returns in order to determine what they are willing to pay. Though we may be cynical about particular investors, in the UK we can be fairly sure that the majority of dealing is rationally assessed.

Alternatively, the investor's required rate of return can be calculated as the IRR of the current market value and subsequent repayments (dividends, interest, capital, etc.).

NB: These comments relate equally to **all** investments.

6.2 Illustration

We will see the application of this idea to various types of securities in the following sections, but the following is included for illustration.

Example

A bond pays an annual coupon of £9 and is to be redeemed at £100 in three years. The required return on the bond (prevailing interest rate) is 8%. What will be the market value?

Solution

The market value can be established by calculating the present value of the associated cash flows at the required rate of 8%. The cash flows from the bond will be a £9.00 coupon at the end of each year, and £100 capital redemption at the end of the third year, i.e. £109 is received in total at that time.

The market value can, therefore, be calculated as

Time	Cash Flow £	Discount Factor	Present Value £
1	9.00	$\frac{1}{1.08^1}$	8.33
2	9.00	$\frac{1}{1.08^2}$	7.72
3	109.00	$\frac{1}{1.08^3}$	86.53
Market value			£102.58

7 Assumptions Underlying the IRR and NPV Approaches

7.1 Introduction

Learning objectives

26.7.3 Explain how NPVs and IRRs can be used in investment decision making.

26.7.4 Explain the limitations of each technique (NPVs and IRRs).

26.7.5 Explain why decisions using each technique may conflict.

26.7.6 Explain the scenarios in which multiple IRRs may occur.

At this stage, it is worthwhile to consider the assumptions we have implicitly been making in all of the NPV and IRR calculations made to date.

7.1.1 Using NPV and IRR for decision making

The IRR is quite an intuitive method for assessing an investment. If the IRR (its yield) is, say, 12% when borrowing costs are 10% then it should be accepted.

The idea of the NPV is intuitively more awkward though the conclusion is that an investment with a positive NPV should be accepted.

Difficulties arise on comparing alternatives and in this situation the NPV is the superior tool as a consequence of the assumptions and limitations underlying the IRR calculation discussed below.

7.1.2 The basic assumptions

- The cash flows expected to accrue from any investment can be considered in isolation, and are independent of decisions relating to any other investment.
- The cash flows are known with certainty.
- No firm or individual has sufficient funds to affect the price of funds.
- Investors have a time preference for money and make rational decisions accordingly.

7.1.3 The assumptions as to reinvestment rates

The fundamental difference between NPV and IRR is the assumption made about reinvestment rates. Under NPV, we are implicitly assuming that any surplus funds generated can be reinvested to earn a return equal to the required rate of return.

However, the IRR calculation assumes that surplus funds will be reinvested to earn a return equal to the IRR, that the time value placed on money is this rate.

Conceptually, NPV is superior because, regardless of the actual investment that is generating the cash flows, we always assume the flows can be reinvested at the same rate. There is no real justification for saying that returns from one investment can be reinvested to earn a return in excess of the returns earned from any other investment, as assumed with the IRR.

7.1.4 Multiple IRRs

If there are multiple sign changes in the series of cash flows, e.g. (Outflow – Inflow – Outflow – Inflow), there may be multiple IRRs for a single project. This means the IRR decision rule may be impossible to implement. Examples of this type of project would be nuclear power plants where there is usually a large cash outflow at the end of the project to clean up the site.

CHAPTER ROUNDUP

Interest rates

- Simple interest is where interest is received on an original capital sum only. **Compounding** occurs when interest is earned on reinvested interest.
- Given the same nominal or flat rate, the more frequent the compounding the greater the return, continuous compounding represents the limit to this.
- $(1+\text{APR})=\left(1+\frac{r}{n}\right)^n$

  Where r = annual flat rate
  n = number of compounding periods pa
- Continuously compounded interest rate

  $R=e^{rt}-1$

Discounted cash flow

- To calculate a present or terminal value there are three relevant factors.
  - Cash flow – value to be multiplied by the relevant compound or discount factor.
  - Timing – determines which factor to use, basic, annuity, perpetuity.
  - Rate – determines the rate r for that factor.
- A **terminal value** or **future value** considers the cash flows of an investment and the timing of the cash flows to calculate the value of a deposit/investment at the end of a period.
- Compound factors
  - Basic

    Compound factor with n years to run $=(1+r)^n$
  - Annuities – calculate the PV of the annuity then compound to the terminal date.
- Depreciation

  $D_n=D_0(1+r)^n$ where r is negative
- A **present value** calculation considers the cash flows of an investment and the timing of the cash flows and discounts these to calculate a value at the present time. Present value calculations are fundamental to valuation of many financial investments.
- Present value calculations may take the form of single cash flows, annuities and perpetuities.
- Net present value calculations may be used as a form of investment appraisal.
- Discount factors
  - basic

    $$\frac{1}{(1+r)^n}$$

- Annuity

  $$\frac{1}{r}\left(1-\frac{1}{(1+r)^n}\right)$$

- Perpetuity

  $$\frac{1}{r}$$

- continuous compounded basic discount factor

  $$\frac{1}{e^{rt}}$$

- Repayment mortgages

  $$\text{Regular repayment} = \frac{\text{PV of borrowing}}{\text{ADF}}$$

Internal rate of return

- The IRR is the rate of interest that discounts the investment flows to a net present value of zero.
- IRR is established for this exam through trial and error,
- NPV is a better decision tool than IRR due to the IRRs limitations of
  - assuming reinvestments can be made at the IRR,
  - multiple yields (where cash flows reverse twice),

TEST YOUR KNOWLEDGE

Check your knowledge of the chapter here, without referring back to the text.

1. Calculate the terminal value of an investment of £10,000 today for 10 years with a compound interest rate of 9%.

2. Calculate the present value of £1,000 to be received in eight years with a discount rate of 6%.

3. Write out the formula for calculating the present value of an annuity.

4. Define the Internal Rate of Return (IRR).

5. What assumption does the IRR make concerning reinvestment rates?

   A That surplus funds can be reinvested at a return higher than the IRR
   B That surplus funds can be reinvested at a return lower than the IRR
   C That surplus funds can be reinvested at a return equal to the IRR
   D That the reinvestment of surplus funds can never be reinvested

6. What is the terminal value of £1,000 invested now for six years at 8% p.a.?

7. What is the terminal value of £1,000 invested now for three years at 8% followed by three years at 7%?

8. An asset is purchased for £50. Over the next four quarters, it has returns of 4%, 5%, 2% and –3%. what will be the value of the asset at the end of the year?

9. An investment rises in value from £12,000 to £18,000 over four years. What is its constant annual rate of appreciation?

10. What is the present value of £1,000 received in nine years' time at 5% p.a.?

11. What is the present value of £10,000 to be received seven years from now if the annual interest rate is 6%?

12. What is the present value of receiving £1,000 p.a. for twelve years starting in one year's time at 4% p.a.?

13. The rate of interest for a repayment mortgage of £200,000 over 25 years is 6%. What is the annual repayment required at the end of each year?

14. A repayment mortgage of £150,000 is taken out over 20 years at a rate of interest of 5%. What is the annual repayment required at the end of each year?

15. What is the value of a bond with an infinite life that pays £20 per annum when the required rate of return is 6%?

16. What is the present value of receiving £1,000 p.a. in perpetuity at 6% p.a. starting now?

17. What is the continuously compounded rate of interest for 100 days given an annual rate of 8%?

18. What is the terminal value of £10,000 invested at 8% for 150 days continuously compounded?

19. What is the present value of £10,000 received in 200 days at 9% p.a. continuously compounded?

20. An investor invests in some shares at a price at £15.76. It pays dividends of 50p, 56p and 60p at the end of each of the next three years before he sells the shares at £17.44 what is the IRR of this investment ?

A 6.15
B 6.36
C 6.57
D 6.82

Test Your Knowledge: Answers

1. £23,673.64

   £10,000 × 1.09^{10} = £23,673.639

   (See Section 3)

2. £627.41

   $$\frac{1{,}000}{1.06^8} = £627.41$$

   (See Section 4)

3. $$\frac{1}{r}\left(1-\frac{1}{(1+r)^n}\right)$$

   (See Section 4.3.2)

4. The rate of interest that discounts the investment flows to a net present value of zero.

   (See Section 5)

5. C

   (See Section 7.1.2)

6.

Time	Cash Flow (£)	Compound Factor (8%)	Terminal Value (£)
0	1,000	1.08^6	1,587

(See Section 3.2)

7.

Time	Cash Flow (£)	Compound Factor	Terminal Value (£)
0	1,000	$1.08^3 \times 1.07^3$	1,543

(See Section 3.2)

8.

Time	Cash Flow (£)	Compound Factor	Terminal Value (£)
0	50	1.04 × 1.05 × 1.02 × 0.97	54.02

(See Section 3.2)

9.

Time	Cash Flow (£)	Compound Factor	Terminal Value (£)
0	12,000	$(l + r)^4$	18,000

$12{,}000 \times (1 + r)^4 = 18{,}000$

$(1 + r)^4 = \dfrac{18{,}000}{12{,}000}$

$1 + r = \sqrt[4]{\dfrac{18{,}000}{12{,}000}} = 1.1067$

r = 0.1067 or 10.67%

(See Section 3.2)

10.

Time	Cash Flow (£)	Discount Factor (5%)	Present Value (£)
8	1,000	$\dfrac{1}{1.05^9}$	645

(See Section 4.2)

11.

Time	Cash Flow (£)	Discount Factor (9%)	Present Value (£)
8	10,000	$\dfrac{1}{1.06^7}$	6,651

(See Section 4.2)

12. Using the annuity formula gives

Time	Cash Flow (£)	Discount Factor (4%)	Present Value (£)
1–6	1,000	$\dfrac{1}{0.04}\left(1 - \dfrac{1}{0.04^{12}}\right)$	9,385

(See Section 4.2)

13. Annual payment = $\dfrac{\text{Net borrowing}}{\text{ADF}}$

Annual payment = $\dfrac{200{,}000}{\text{ADF(1-25)}}$

Now

$$\text{ADF(1-25)} = \frac{1}{0.06}\left(1 - \frac{1}{1.06^{25}}\right) = 12.783$$

Annual payment = $\dfrac{£200{,}000}{12.783} = £15{,}645$

(See Section 4.6)

14. Annual payment = $\frac{\text{Net borrowing}}{\text{ADF}}$

$$\text{ADF(1-20@5\%)} = \frac{1}{0.05}\left(1-\frac{1}{1.05^{20}}\right) = 12.462$$

$$\text{Annual payment} = \frac{£150{,}000}{12.462} = £12{,}036$$

(See Section 4.6)

15.

Time	Cash Flow (£)	Discount Factor (6%)	Present Value (£)
1–∞	20	$\frac{1}{0.06}$	333

(See Section 4.3)

16.

Time	Cash Flow (£)	Discount Factor (6%)	Present Value (£)
0	1,000	1	1,000
1–∞	1,000	$\frac{1}{0.08}$	1,000
			17,667

(See Section 4.4)

17. $r = 0.08$ $t = 100/365 = 0.274$

Continuously compounded rate

$R = e^{rt} - 1 = e^{0.08 \times 0.274} - 1 = 0.02216 = 2.216\%$

(See Section 2.3)

18. $r = 0.08$ $t = 150/365 = 0.411$

The terminal value

$£10{,}000 \times e^{rt} = £10{,}000 \times e^{0.08 \times 0.411} = £10{,}000 \times 1.0334 = £10{,}334$

(See Section 2.3)

19. $r = 0.09$ $t = 200/365 = 0.548$

The present value equals

$$£10{,}000 \times e^{\frac{1}{rt}} = £10{,}000 \times e^{\frac{1}{0.09 \times 0.548}} = £10{,}000 \times 0.9519 = £9{,}519$$

(See Section 2.3)

20. Using trial and error gives answer D

Time	Cash Flow (£)	DF (6.82%)	PV (6.82%) (£)
0	(15.76)	1	(15.76)
1	0.50	$\frac{1}{1.0682}$	0.47
2	0.56	$\frac{1}{1.0682^2}$	0.49
3	18.04	$\frac{1}{1.0682^3}$	14.80
			0.00

(See Section 5.3)

5 Risk and Return

INTRODUCTION

Investment risk may be computed using standard deviation. The total risk of an investment may be subdivided into systematic risk and unsystematic risk.

Portfolio theory has shown that unsystematic risk may be largely eliminated through buying a diversified portfolio of investments. However, even if diversification is undertaken, an investor investing in risky assets will still be left with systematic risk.

CAPM assumes investors are well diversified and creates a measure of systematic risk known as Beta. Beta can then be used to identify a required level of return for an investor given a required level of risk. CAPM is a single factor model where returns only depend on the investments sensitivity to the market

APT is a multi-factor model where an investments return may be sensitive to several factors

CHAPTER CONTENTS

Chapter Learning Objectives

21 Investment Theories and Models

Demonstrate an understanding of the merits and limitations of the main investment theories

21.1 Risk and return and the importance of diversification

21.1.1 **Explain** this 'normal' trade off between risk and return and the concept at 'dominance' between investment strategies.

21.1.2 **Explain** the implications of assuming returns are normally distributed.

21.1.3 **Explain** the importance of risk-measurement in the analysis of investments and why ex-ante and ex-post measures of risk may be very different.

21.1.4 **Identify** the commonly used measures of risk in investment analysis and fund management.

21.1.5 **Explain** the shortfalls of standard deviation as a measure of investment risk.

21.1.6 **Explain** the meaning of drawdown as a measure of risk.

21.1.7 **Understand** the impact on changing levels of price volatility over time and how this affects predictions such as tracking error and downside risk.

21.1.8 **Understand** the importance of correlation in constructing efficient portfolios and the difficulties, limitations and meaning of correlation coefficients.

21.1.9 **Calculate** correlation coefficients from standard deviation/covariance of two investments.

21.1.10 **Explain** diversification and its role in constructing efficient portfolios and its limitations during extreme market conditions.

21.1.11 **Explain** the meaning of Value at Risk (VaR) and its advantages and disadvantages for risk management.

21.1.12 **Analyse** and explain other types of investment risk including inflation, currency, interest rate, fraud and counterparty risk.

21.2 Models of return and risk

21.2.1 **Explain** the concept of investments being exposed to a number of common factors which partially explain their return and risk profile ('Arbitrage Pricing Theory').

21.2.2 **Identify** the assumptions behind the single factor Capital Asset Pricing Model (CAPM) and other factors in common use.

21.2.3 **Explain** the limitations of the CAPM model.

21.2.4 **Define** the segmentation of risk into systematic (factor) risk and unsystematic (investment specific risk).

21.2.5 **Calculate** the total risk given some systematic and unsystematic components.

21.2.6 **Calculate** the expected return on a security by applying the CAPM through interpreting the beta of security.

21.2.7 **Explain** how the beta may be derived from a scatter chart of historic returns.

21.2.8 **Calculate** the beta of an investment given the systematic risk of the investment and the risk of the market.

21.2.9 **Calculate** the beta of an investment given the variance of the market return, and the covariance of the investment return with the market return.

21.2.10 **Calculate** the beta of a portfolio given the component betas and the investment weightings.

23 Investment performance measurement

Demonstrate an understanding of the principles of investment performance measurement

23.4 Performance measurement including risk adjusted returns

23.4.5 **Explain** the tracking error and its limitations.

26 Statistics and financial mathematics

Demonstrate an ability to apply statistical and financial mathematics techniques

26.2 Summary data

26.2.5 **Explain** the notion of probability distributions and identify the properties of the normal distribution.

26.2.6 **Explain** the notion of statistical significance in the context of investment decisions.

26.3 Correlation and bivariate linear regression

26.3.7 **Explain** the concept of autocorrelation and appreciate the impact of extreme events on correlation.

1 Introduction

Learning objective

21.1.3 Explain the importance of risk-measurement in the analysis of investments and why ex-ante and ex-post measures to risk may be different.

In a certain world, the return from an investment would always be exactly as expected and there would be no risk. The investor would merely have to compare the returns available on different investments and choose those which offered the highest returns.

Unfortunately, the existence of uncertainty means that the returns from investments are not always as expected – there is some risk involved.

In our analysis, so far, we have largely avoided the problem of risk. We have assumed that we know with certainty the future expected cash flows and required rates of return. Clearly, this is unrealistic.

Almost all investment opportunities involve a risk. All securities quoted on the Stock Exchange are subject to risk. Different types of security will have different kinds of risk associated with them, for example, UK government securities do not suffer the risk of default, but are vulnerable to changes in interest rates. However, the effect of all these different kinds of risk is the same, that is, the actual returns achieved (the ex-post returns) may differ from those originally expected by the investor (ex-ante returns). In addition, the actual risk experienced (ex-post risk) may differ markedly from what was originally anticipated (ex-ante risk). The riskier the investment, the more likely it is that the hoped-for return will not be reached or the greater the shortfall from the expected return.

One of the fundamental assumptions of investment appraisal is that investors are rational and risk averse, i.e. they will demand a higher return if they are to face a higher risk, or the return that investors demand will be commensurate with the risk that they face.

But how can we use this idea to rationally appraise any investment alternatives?

If we are to undertake a systematic appraisal of an investment opportunity, we must be able to incorporate all relevant factors. In order to incorporate these factors into our analysis, we must be able to answer the following questions.

- What causes risk?
- How can we measure/quantify risk?
- Can risk be avoided?
- How can we relate risk and return?

2 Causes of Risk

Learning objective	21.1.12 **Analyse** and explain other types of investment risk including inflation, currency, interest rate, fraud and counterparty risk.

2.1 Introduction

There are several different factors that give rise to risk, ie lead to variability in the return on an investment. Some investments, such as gilts, will have few risks associated with them, whereas company shares will be subject to many possible reasons for fluctuations in return. Factors contributing to risk in investment returns include:

- Interest rate risk
- Income risk
- Inflation risk
- Shortfall risk
- Capital risk
- Market risk
- Investment specific or business risk
- Credit risk
- Fraud
- Currency risk
- Liquidity risk
- Institutional risk
- Political risk
- Regulatory risk
- Systemic risk
- Settlement or counterparty risk
- Event risk

2.1.1 Interest rate risk and income risk

The possible future movement of interest rates affects borrowers and savers in conversely different ways.

The following cases are examples of **interest rate risk** (which you may find called **interest risk** in an exam question).

- A rise in interest rates is a risk for a **borrower** who is borrowing at a **variable** rate.
- A **saver** with a **variable** rate account faces the risk that interest rates will fall in the future.

A borrower who locks into a fixed rate mortgage rate is protected against a rise in rates of interest for the fixed period. However, the possibility that the fixed rate he locks into could be higher than prevailing variable rates, if rates fall in the future, could be seen as a 'risk' he takes on if he locks into the fixed rate deal.

Conversely, a saver who locks into a fixed rate account without instant access, or one carrying penalties for withdrawals, may be worse off than he might have been with a variable rate account, if interest rates rise during the period of the investment.

2.1.2 Income risk

The term '**income risk**' can be used to refer to the possibility that the **income from a fund** will fluctuate due to **changes in interest rates**. Another use of the term 'income risk' concerns the risk carried by individuals that their salary or wages will fall.

It has been estimated that for someone in the UK with a gross household income of £400 per week, their income is likely to be above £620 or below £260 per week for approximately 10% of the time. This illustrates the **income risk** that an average household carries. An example of the types of circumstance causing this is that the individual may have a period with no wages, when between jobs. Most self-employed people will experience fluctuating incomes throughout their self-employed career. Although some protection products can reduce the adverse effects of redundancy or having to stop work due to ill-health or disability, to some extent labour income risk will be an uninsurable risk.

Total **income risk** is found to be lower for older individuals and is slightly less for women than men. Better-off individuals are likely to have lower **income risk** than those at the lower part of the income distribution.

2.1.3 Inflation risk

Rising prices can reduce the purchasing power of an amount of capital, or income. By investing money, the investor may be risking loss in purchasing power during the period of the investment.

We discussed in the first chapter of this Study Text how **inflation in prices** erodes the purchasing power of money.

Imagine also the situation of an economy with **deflation in prices**, as has affected Japan in recent years. If prices are deflating, one could say that buying goods now bears the 'risk' that the same goods could have been bought for less later. There is then a strong incentive for people to save, since the purchasing power of cash, even if no interest were being earned, would increase through time. This is one reason why deflation can be an economic problem: if people have a strong incentive to save, demand for goods and services may be weak.

2.1.4 Shortfall risk

Shortfall risk is the risk that an amount invested will not reach a target financial goal at some time in the future. For example, a couple might start a savings plan to support the future education expenses of a child. There could be a risk that the plan does not grow enough to pay these expenses. Another example is that of a holder of an interest-only mortgage who has an investment that is intended to pay off the full amount of the mortgage at the end of its term. There is a shortfall risk that the investment will have generated insufficient returns to pay off the full target amount at the intended date.

Choosing riskier investments is likely to increase the shortfall risk. If reaching a particular target level is important to the investor, then the shortfall risk can be reduced by choosing lower risk investments. However, choosing lower risk investments is likely to mean a higher probability that returns will be relatively low, and so more may need to be invested than might have been required with more risky investments, assuming that such investments had produced higher returns.

2.1.5 Capital risk/market risk/business risk/credit risk/fraud

Capital risk is the possibility of loss of some or all of the original capital invested. This can be a very significant form of risk, with potentially devastating results to the unwary investor. Capital risk has a number of sub-components:

- Market risk
- Investment specific or business risk
- Credit risk
- Fraud

Holding **equities** presents a **capital risk** even in a well-diversified portfolio. General market falls will reduce capital values and this risk may be referred to as **market risk**.

With purchases of individual shares, there is the risk that the value of the investment will fall, and it could be totally wiped out. This can be particularly so for shares in newer smaller companies without a track record and without a full Stock Exchange listing. A company might be set up to develop a new product, such as a new type of hydraulic pump, with no revenues expected for four to five years after the company was established. If revenues fail to materialise and the company is liquidated, all of investors' capital could be lost. If an investor had invested half of his savings in the company, the personal effect on that investor would be great. This is an example of **investment specific** or **business risk**.

Especially for **derivative** investments, such as futures contracts, options or contracts for differences (CFDs), it is possible to lose **more** than the original capital invested. Such investments can be **geared** so that they offer the prospect of magnified gains, but also carry the risk of magnified losses.

Credit risk is the risk of default of a fixed income investment. This is where a bond fails to pay its coupon or principal when it falls due. Credit risk also includes the risk of a credit downgrade that will reduce bond values.

The final category of capital risk to consider is **fraud**.

Fraud is a financial loss that occurs as a result of financial crime. Though it shall not be regarded as a normal risk it is one that investors should always be aware of.

2.1.6 Currency risk

Currency risk is the risk arising from fluctuations in the value of currencies against each other. A UK resident (that is, someone whose home currency is sterling) who buys stocks or bonds in other currencies, for example the euro or the US dollar, faces currency risk.

Suppose that a UK investor buys shares in a US company which does most of its trading in the US. The share price in US dollars fluctuates on the US stock market. Additionally, the value of sterling fluctuates against the US dollar. Therefore, the sterling value of the investment will fluctuate in time as a result of two effects: the changing dollar share price, and the changing US dollar / sterling exchange rate.

Exposure to currency risk is not totally avoided by investing within the UK. Many UK companies do much of their business abroad. This means that their earnings will be affected by exchange rate fluctuations. If a UK company manufactures goods in the UK using domestically sourced raw materials, and exports much of its products to the European 'Eurozone' countries, then it is exposed to a rise in the value of sterling against the euro. If sterling rises in value, the euro-priced receipts from the company's Eurozone sales will buy fewer pounds sterling than before.

Some companies **hedge** their foreign exchange earnings or their foreign raw materials costs, to give them greater certainty about future earnings and to reduce currency risks. This may be done, for example, by entering forward currency contracts, fixing the value of future transactions of the company in advance.

Some larger **multinational** companies have costs and revenues in many different countries, and they may also have shareholders in many different countries. Since shareholders will be based in various currency areas, there may be no currency hedging strategy that serves all shareholders equally. In general, a company may seek to hedge currency exposures in such a way that currency risks between input (raw materials) costs and the income from that production are hedged. Then, each production unit should have a chance of meeting its profit targets without being affected too much by exchange rate fluctuations.

2.1.7 Liquidity risk

An investor in **property** suffers from the risk associated with **illiquidity**. A sale can only be made if a buyer can be found and this can prove a great problem. During the early 1990s, with a stagnant housing and property market few buyers of residential property could be found and prices fell. Many homeowners had negative equity: the value of their house fell to below the value of their debt (mortgage). If a client invests in property via the medium of a property unit trust or investment bond he may suffer similar, although not such acute, illiquidity. Under the terms of these investments the proceeds of a sale may be delayed for up to six months to allow the managers to realise assets to pay the investor.

2.1.8 Institutional risk

In a financial market, there are different types of investor and participant, often including both individuals and financial institutions. There are regulations and laws that aim to make information freely available to all potential participants, in many markets. In practice, and particularly in overseas markets for example, it may be difficult for 'outsiders' to become fully aware of the institutional structure.

There may be '**institutional risks**' arising from the fact that a market is relatively immature (as with so-called **emerging markets**) or with other institutional factors such as market liquidity (How easy is it to buy and sell the investment?), regulation and the availability of information.

2.1.9 Political risk

Political risk describes the risk that unexpected action by the government in the country where the investment is located may devalue an investment. This might occur, for example, if the government introduces new currency controls or new taxes, or if it nationalises assets.

2.1.10 Regulatory risk

The term **regulatory risk** can be defined as the risk associated with the potential for laws related to a given industry, country, or type of security to change and impact relevant investments. There is clearly a degree of overlap among regulatory risk and institutional and political risk. However, regulatory risk is present within any economy, affecting all domestic investments: regulations may change, affecting how an investment performs. Taxation and other laws may change, possibly to close a 'loophole' that some investments have set out to exploit.

Clearly, some degree of regulation is a positive thing for the investor. However, a government that minimises the amount of unexpected change to regulation may be able to create a more attractive environment for investors.

2.1.11 Systemic risk

Systemic risk is the risk of the failure or collapse of the entire financial system. This could be caused by extraneous events such as natural disasters or failures in a part of the system that could cause a cascading effect on other parts of the system. Systemic risk is a function of:

- **Events risk** – the risk that a security may default due to unexpected events such as natural disasters, takeovers or regulatory change

- **Settlement or counterparty risk** – the risk that a counterparty may default on a transaction

2.2 Return and risk measurement and return distribution

2.2.1 Introduction

Learning objectives

21.1.2 Explain the implications of assuming returns are normally distributed.

21.1.4 Identify the commonly used measures of risk in investment analysis and fund management.

26.2.5 Explain the notion of probability distributions and identify the properties of the normal distribution

26.3.7 Explain the concept of autocorrelation and appreciate the impact of extreme events on correlation.

Having identified the different factors contributing to the risk which exists and realised that they are the result of the possibility of different states of the world occurring in the future, how can we quantify the risk and return of any investment?

One way we may achieve this is by technical analysis of past price movements from which, as we saw earlier, we can calculate

- An expected return – the **mean**.
- A measure of risk – the **standard deviation**.

2.2.2 Normal distribution

Central to many investment management theories is the assumption that security returns are

- **Normally distributed**
- **Independent through time** – ie the return in any one period is completely unconnected with that of any other period. The correlation of the returns from one period to the next is known as **autocorrelation**.

and it is the first of these that we are examining here.

A normal distribution is a symmetrical distribution of, in this context, possible security returns that is uniquely defined by a mean and a standard deviation. Graphically the normal distribution appears as follows.

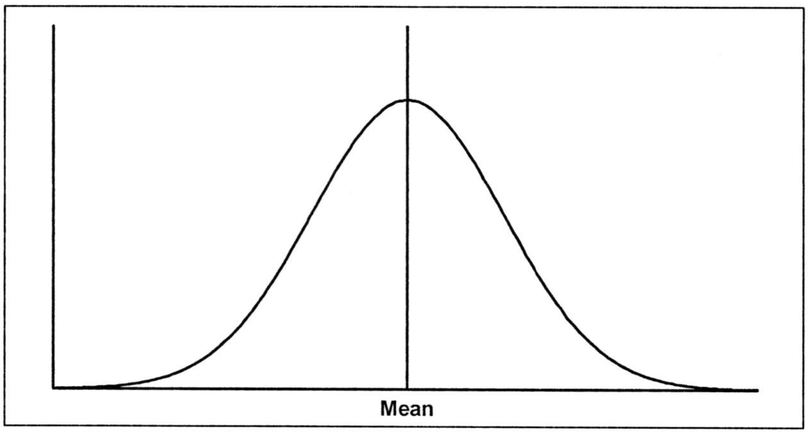

The important characteristics of normal distributions in the context of security and portfolio returns are that

- The distribution of returns is symmetrical.

- The possible returns follow a bell-shaped distribution where more central values are most likely to be observed and the more extreme the movement the less likely it is to occur.
- The distribution has a single standard deviation across the entire range of possible values and through time.

This last point is key to the use of this distribution for the analysis of risk and return. For example:

- 68.26% of all possible values fall within 1 standard deviation from the mean.
- 95% of all possible returns lie within 1.96 standard deviations from the mean.
- 99% of all possible returns lie within 3 standard deviations from the mean.

Example

An investment's returns are normally distributed with a mean of 10% and a standard deviation at 6%.

(a) Quote the range spanning 68% of all possible returns.
(b) Quote the range spanning 95% of all possible returns.

Solution

(a) 68% of values fall within one standard deviation from the mean, ie in the range:

$10\% \pm 1 \times 6\%$

ie 4% to 16%

(b) 95% of values fall within 1.96 standard deviations, ie in the range:

$10\% \pm 1.96 \times 6\%$

ie – 1.76% to 21.76%

The assumption that security returns are normally distributed is, as we have noted, central to many investment management theories such as CAPM and VAR (see later), however is this assumption supported by real life observation?

One of the assumptions of a normal distribution is that the probability of a gain will be equal to that of an equivalent loss, the distribution is symmetrical. However, empirical observation of security returns reveal that the distribution is not symmetrical, rather it is skewed, and that upside and downside risk will be misstated when a normal distribution is used.

Another assumption of the normal distribution is that more extreme movements become increasingly unlikely (the distribution has thin tails), whereas observations show that this may not be the case in extreme circumstances and that the true distribution is leptokurtic (has fat tails) especially on the downside.

A further assumption underlying a normal distribution is that the standard deviation takes just one value, ie risk is constant. Once more, this is not supported by observation that reveals that

- The risk of individual securities varies over time which means that the risk anticipated before the event (the ex-ante risk) will most probably differ from the actual risk observed after the event (ex-post risk).
- The correlation between securities and the diversification benefit that arises from that (see below) varies over time.

With risks and correlations in extreme market conditions being substantially different from those in normal market circumstances.

2.2.3 Statistical significance

Learning objective	**26.2.5 Explain** the notion of statistical significance in the context of investment decisions.

In statistics, a result is called significant if it is unlikely to have occurred by chance. It simply means there is statistical evidence there is a difference. It does not mean the difference is necessarily large, important or significant in the usual sense of the word.

Based on what we noted above, 95% of all possible values lie within 1.96 standard deviations from the mean in a normal distribution. Looking at this in another way, there is only a 5% chance that something would lie beyond 1.96 standard deviations from the mean, and a value observed in this range may be regarded as statistically significant.

This number can be reflected as a margin of error, or it can be indicated by a confidence level ("If this performance analysis were repeated, there is a probability of ninety-five percent that our conclusions would be substantiated").

2.3 Avoiding risk

Learning objective	**21.1.10 Explain** diversification and its role in constructing efficient portfolios and its limitations during extreme market conditions.

Tutor tip

Diversification is key to the ideas of investment management and the following areas should be studied closely.

2.3.1 Diversification

There is an old adage: 'do not put all your eggs in one basket'. This means that by spreading the risk of holding something, we can minimise our potential losses without necessarily reducing the value of our holding.

Though a simple and reasonably obvious idea in the context of the farmyard, it is equally applicable in the context of investment management. By spreading the total investment fund over several securities which offer the desired level of return, we get the same return that any one of them can offer, but face a much lower risk since, though one may become worthless, it is unlikely that they all will simultaneously. Hence, there is a chance of losing all our money if it is all invested in just one share, but this possibility is vastly reduced when we hold a number of shares. Obviously, the more shares we hold, the more the risk is reduced. Hence, **diversification reduces risk without necessarily reducing returns**.

Here, we have considered only default risk, the risk of losing all our money. The same principle applies, however, to other forms of risk, such as fluctuations in earnings.

If we invest all our cash in one share, then our income will vary as the company profits, hence returns from that share will vary. However, it is unlikely that returns from all shares will move in exactly the same way. Therefore, if we invest in a range of shares, it is likely that as the returns from some are falling, the returns from others are stable or rising. The result will be that we will realise a steadier overall return when we hold a spread of securities, with the losses on one being cancelled by profits on another.

This offsetting effect is, however, unlikely to arise in, say, a market crash when all securities are falling. Diversification may have significant benefits in normal circumstances but offers less benefits in extreme markets.

2.3.2 Correlation

Learning objectives

21.1.8 Understand the importance of correlation in constructing efficient portfolios and the difficulties, limitations and meaning of correlation coefficients.

21.1.9 Calculate correlation coefficients from standard deviation/covariance of two investments.

The effectiveness of this cancellation will depend on the degree of correlation between the movements of the returns. Correlation is a measure of how two variable factors move in relation to each other. A correlation coefficient will have any value between +1 and –1. The meaning of the correlation coefficient can best be understood by considering the extremes.

Perfect positive correlation – (correlation coefficient = +1)

If the returns from two securities are perfectly positively correlated, then they move up and down together in proportion. The consequence of this is that if they were combined in a portfolio, we would not get the cancelling effect that we were looking for.

Perfect negative correlation – (correlation coefficient = –1)

If the returns from two securities are perfectly negatively correlated, then they move up and down in exact opposition and in proportion. As a result, if we were to combine two such securities in a portfolio, we could achieve an exact offset of profits from one against losses from the other.

Uncorrelated – (correlation coefficient = 0)

If the returns from two securities are uncorrelated, then they move independently of each other, i.e. if one goes up, the other may go up or down or not move at all. As a result, if we were to combine two such securities in a portfolio, we would expect to see cancellation of profits and losses on some occasions, but not on others. However, this is still a better position than investing in just one share where there is no cancellation of gains and losses at all.

Limitations of correlation coefficient

Correlation coefficients may not always be a reliable measure when outliers are present. These are small numbers of observations at the extremes of a sample of data. The analyst must decide whether it is better to include or exclude outliers on a case-by-case basis.

Furthermore, a correlation between two variables may reflect a chance relationship in a particular set of data, or may arise because the two variables are themselves correlated to a third variable. For example bee stings may be positively correlated to ice cream consumption, but the underlying relationships are between sunshine and bee stings, and sunshine and ice cream consumption.

Finally, correlation coefficients are susceptible to change in times of market turbulence. A portfolio may be thought of as risk averse with a basket of uncorrelated equities, only to find the correlation between the securities becomes increasingly positive in times of market turmoil, removing many of the diversification benefits which previously existed.

Conclusion

The sign of the correlation coefficient tells us the relative direction of movement.

A positive correlation implies that returns move up and down together, negative correlation means that they move in opposition. The value of the figure, ignoring the sign, gives an indication of the strength of the relationship. The closer to a value of 1, the stronger the relationship.

The effectiveness of the diversification will depend on the degree of correlation between the returns on the securities. In practice, we are unlikely to encounter perfect positive or perfect negative correlation (though we may get close with certain derivative instruments). Most shares show a small degree of correlation in practice, and hence we see some benefit from diversification.

The correlation coefficient between the returns of two securities x and y can be calculated as

Formula to learn

$$Cor_{xy} = \frac{Covariance(x,y)}{\sigma_x \sigma_y}$$

We have already seen how to calculate variances and standard deviations σ_x and σ_y. A covariance can be calculated in a very similar tabular manner to a variance, though for the purposes of this exam it will either be a given value in a question or something to solve using this equation or another one we will see later.

2.3.3 Nature of risk

Learning objectives

21.2.4 Define the segmentation of risk into systematic ('factor') risk and unsystematic ('investment') risk.

21.2.5 Calculate the total risk given some systematic and unsystematic components.

Tutor tip

The segmentation of risk is regularly examined and should be studied closely.

Our conclusion above was that diversification reduces risk and that the more shares we hold, the greater the risk reduction.

Does this mean that we can completely eliminate the risk of investing in shares by diversifying as broadly as possible?

The answer to this can most easily be seen when we suffer a stock market crash. In these circumstances, even the most highly diversified portfolios suffer a loss in value – the market as a whole collapses.

Thus, it would appear that we can analyse the total risk of an investment into two subcategories as follows.

Total Risk of Investment

σ_i

Systematic/Market Risk

σ_s

Potential variability in the returns offered by a security caused by general market influences, e.g.

- Interest rate changes.
- Inflation rate changes.
- Tax rate changes.
- State of the economy.

Cannot be eliminated through diversification

Unsystematic/Idiosyncratic/ Specific Risk

σ_u

Potential variability in the returns offered by a security as a result of factors specific to the company, e.g.

- Quality of management.
- Susceptibility to demands of suppliers and customers.
- Profitability margins and levels.

Can be eliminated through diversification

As we note, the unsystematic risk can be eliminated through diversification. This arises as a result of the trade between companies. If one company makes a mistake and undertakes a bad deal (loses money), then its trading partner will be making a corresponding amount of money. Hence, by investing in both companies, we can eliminate this variability from our overall portfolio returns. We get the combined return regardless of which company generates it.

The systematic or market risk is something that impacts on the economy in general, which all companies are part of, hence this is the type of risk that cannot be eliminated.

2.3.4 Consequences

An **undiversified investor**, i.e. one who has most/all of his money invested in the shares of one company, will **face the full risk** of that investment, σ_i. He will therefore look for a return commensurate with this full level.

A **diversified investor** will have eliminated, through diversification, the unsystematic risk inherent in the individual securities in his portfolio and **face just the systematic risk**, σ_S. Hence, he will seek a return commensurate with the level of systematic risk only.

2.3.5 Decomposition of risk

In order to undertake calculations, we may need to decompose this total risk into its two subcomponents, which can be achieved using the relationship

Formula to learn

$$\sigma_i^2 = \sigma_s^2 + \sigma_u^2$$

NB: Risks are combined by adding variances (the square of the standard deviation).

2.4 Relating risk and return

Learning objective

21.1.1 **Explain** the 'normal' trade-off between risk and return and the concept of 'dominance' between investment strategies.

2.4.1 Risk return profile

Consider an investor comparing a number of possible investment opportunities. For each investment, the expected return and risk (standard deviation) could be measured, but we would still need a way of finding out the best combination of risk and return for that investor.

One way we could achieve this is to plot the risk-return profiles of the investments under review.

Example

Consider an investor who has the following choices of mutually exclusive investments which offer the following returns from an investment of £100.

Investment	Return ($\bar{r}$)		Risk (σ)	
	£	%	£	%
A	10	10	6	6
B	11	11	5	5
C	19	19	11	11
D	20	20	10	10

Assuming that our investor is rational and risk averse, which one will he choose?

Solution

We can represent the alternatives we have on the following diagram.

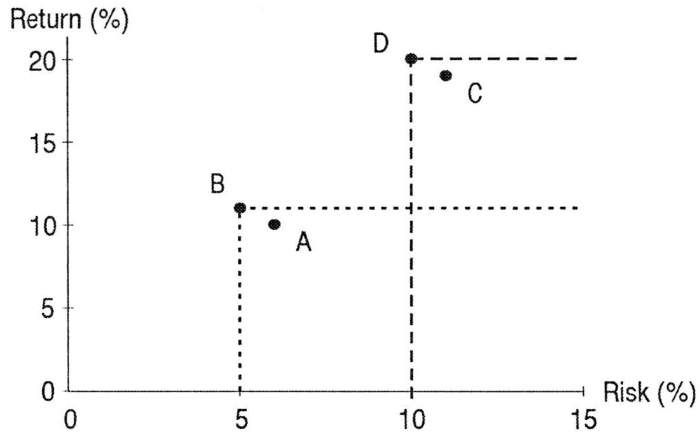

Comparing investments in turn

A and B

Comparing A and B, it is clear that B is preferable, as it has a higher return for a lower level of risk. In fact, B dominates all investments in the rectangle shown (with B in the top left-hand corner).

C and D

Similarly, D will dominate C and any others in its rectangle.

B and D

But which of B and D is preferable? Whilst D offers the higher return, it does so at a higher risk than B. Which combination of return and risk is preferable to the investor?

2.4.2 Relating risk and return

Our remaining question, then, is how do we equate the required levels of return to the risk to enable us to decide between these two, or indeed any number, investments? The Capital Asset Pricing Model (CAPM) provides such a method which is suitable for the management of **diversified portfolios** where we face only the systematic risk.

2.4.3 The efficient frontier

If rather than considering just two alternative investments we consider the risk-return profiles of all possible risky investments and all possible portfolios that can be constructed from those investments then we would obtain something called the opportunity set that would look something like this.

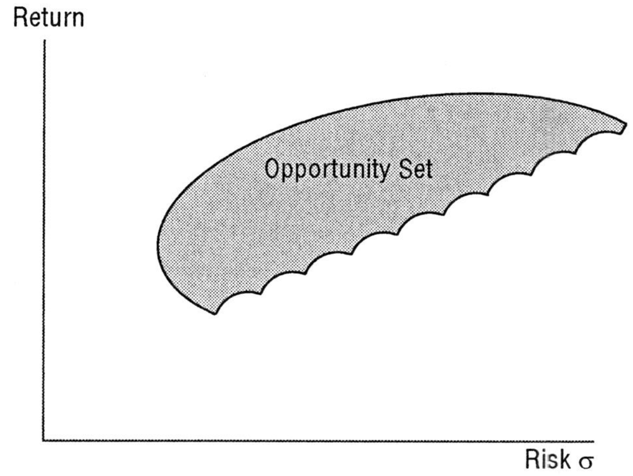

You will note that the maximum return from this opportunity set declines at the highest levels of risk. At these higher levels we have fewer available portfolios (as a result of diversification) until, ultimately, there is only one single investment at the maximum level of risk that is not necessarily the highest returning one. Though in theory risk and return go hand in hand, there is no guarantee that a higher risk investment will definitely produce a higher return.

Which of the possible portfolios would investors actually select? Applying the dominance logic from above

- An investor will look to maximise his return for any given level of risk
- An investor will only take on extra risk if it can be expected to result in a greater return

We can, therefore, rule out all portfolios except those falling on the upper edge of the opportunity set between points X (the minimum risk portfolio) and Y (the maximum return portfolio) below. This line is called the **efficient frontier** because investments/portfolios on this line dominate all other alternatives.

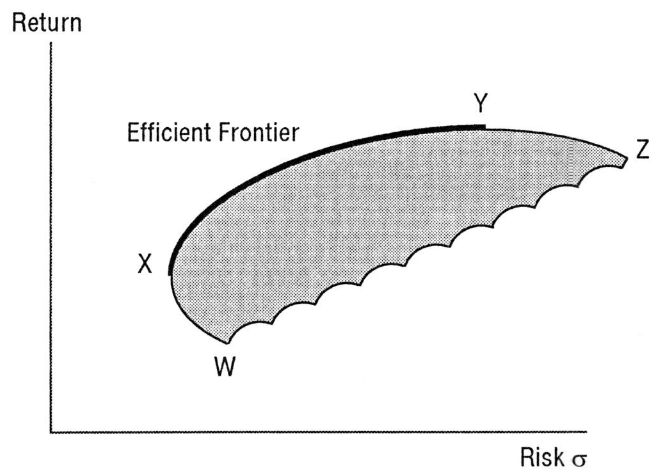

If we are looking to assess a client's attitude to risk and return we should only ask them to consider investments on the efficient frontier.

2.5 VAR

Learning objective	**21.1.11 Explain** the meaning of Value at Risk (VAR) and its advantages and disadvantages for risk management.

Definition

Value at risk (VAR) is defined as the amount by which the value of an investment or portfolio may fall over a given period of time at a given level of probability.

For example, if VAR is £1m at a probability level of 5% for one week, this indicates that there is a 95% probability that the value will not fall by more than £1m and a 5% probability that the value of a portfolio will fall by £1m or more over the next week.

We could view this as indicating that you could lose more than £1m 5% of the time, or that you will not lose more than £1m 95% of the time – it gives an indication of the expected shortfall. Importantly, VAR does not indicate the maximum loss that could happen.

Attractions and limitations of VAR

Attractions of VAR are as follows.

- It is a useful summary measure of risk, simplifying everything down to one number.
- It is easy to understand.
- It is used by regulators for risk control and capital adequacy purposes.
- It can be used by companies to measure capital at risk. This can then be used to assess divisions/traders etc. on a risk-adjusted return basis (see the next chapter for more details on this).

Limitations of VAR are as follows.

- Use of poor assumptions (e.g. ignoring non normal distributions may mean that VAR is understated).
- VAR only focuses on downside, not upside. It does not give a complete description of risk, as a result.
- It is difficult to calculate VAR for large complex portfolios, e.g. identifying VAR for an international bank with exposures in different instruments and currencies over the world.
- It can give a false sense of security, with managers believing that risk is being well controlled, even though this is not the case

2.6 Alternative measures of risk

Learning objectives

21.1.5 Explain the shortfalls of standard deviation as a measure of investment risk.

21.1.6 Explain the meaning of drawdown as a measure at risk.

21.1.7 Understand the impact of changing levels of price volatility over time and how this affects predictions such as tracking error and downside risk.

23.4.5 Explain tracking error and its limitations.

There are various ways in which risk can be measured.

- Dispersion.
  - Standard deviation and variance.
- Tracking error
- Downside risk.
  - Target semi-variance.
  - Shortfall risk.

- Value at risk.
- Drawdown

- Duration (addressed in the Fixed Income Securities chapter).

2.6.1 Dispersion

As previously discussed, the standard deviation/variance is only one possible measure of risk. In brief, the standard deviation measures the average dispersion of variables around their mean. One shortfall of standard deviation is the assumption it makes of the underlying data being normally distributed. Whilst this does not undermine its usage, it is an important consideration when looking at certain asset claimed returns which do not always exhibit a normally distributed form (such as certain types of hedge funds).

2.6.2 Tracking error

Tracking error is a relative risk measure that is most relevant to funds that are designed to track a specified index – tracker funds. Tracking error is the standard deviation of the difference between the returns of the tracking fund and the index being tracked. If a fund perfectly tracks its index it will have a zero tracking error, the less accurately it tracks the greater the tracking error.

2.6.3 Downside risk

Target semi-variance

Instead of looking at dispersion around both sides of the mean, it is possible to analyse risk by reference to returns below a specified level, such as the average return over a specific period.

The target semi-variance is based on the squared deviations below the specified target return.

Where the target return is the mean of the distribution, the target semi-variance is referred to as the **semi-variance**.

Shortfall risk

The risk of shortfall is the probability that the observation will have a value lower than the specified return. For example, a shortfall risk of 40% would indicate a 40% probability that you will earn a return less than the specified return. If the specified return is zero, this is referred to as the risk of loss.

The problem with shortfall risk is that there is no indication of how great the loss might be.

Drawdown

Drawdown is a measure of the amount by which the value of an investment has fallen from its all-time historical peak. As such, drawdown reflects the scale of historical losses that have been suffered since this peak.

Drawdown has the advantage of being easy to understand, however there are limitations in using it to compare investment risks. For example, a share that mirrors the market will, following a 20% market fall from its all-time high, show a drawdown of 20%. A share in a newly listed enterprise will show a zero drawdown since it has no price history. Considering drawdown in isolation may, therefore, lead the investor to consider this new security to have a lower risk when the reality is that new companies tend to be riskier than old established ones.

2.6.4 Impact of changing volatility levels

One problem with all of these measures is that volatility levels are not constant, so a historical average may not be relevant to the current or future circumstances. As a result, it may be difficult to determine the current required return from a security based on its historical risk, irrespective of how that risk has been assessed.

3 The Capital Asset Pricing Model

3.1 Introduction

Let us consider a highly diversified investor who has spread his funds across the full stock market, with some also invested in risk-free investments. What returns will he achieve and what risk will he face?

If

r_m = returns expected from investing in the **market portfolio** (a portfolio representative of the whole stock market, e.g. a tracker fund)

r_f = returns from risk-free investments

β = proportion of his funds invested in the market portfolio

then, considering the returns he can expect to receive and the risks he will face, we have the following.

3.1.1 Return

Learning objective

21.2.6 **Calculate** the expected return on a security by applying the CAPM through interpreting the beta of security.

The proportion of his money invested in the market portfolio β will return r_m, and the remainder invested risk free (1 – β) will generate r_f. Hence, his full portfolio will generate the sum of these amounts, i.e.

$$r = \beta r_m + (1 - \beta) r_f$$

which can be algebraically rearranged, giving

$$r = \beta r_m + r_f - \beta r_f$$

$$r = r_f + \beta(r_m - r_f)$$

3.1.2 Risk

The risk that he will face (only systematic risk since he is diversified) will only be in relation to the proportion of funds he has invested in the market portfolio, since his other investment is risk free. This level of systematic risk he faces will therefore be

$$\sigma_s = \beta \sigma_m$$

where

σ_s = the systematic risk in the portfolio

σ_m = the risk (systematic) in the market portfolio

NB: So far, we have talked about β as the proportion of funds invested in the market portfolio. It can also be more usefully viewed as the proportion of **market portfolio risk** that we are willing to face, since a simple rearrangement of the above equation gives

Formula to learn

$$\beta = \frac{\sigma_s}{\sigma_m}$$

It is this latter way of viewing β, as the proportion of the market portfolio risk, that is going to give us the relationship we need between risk and return.

3.2 The model

Considering the above equations, for any given level of risk in relation to the market portfolio $\left(\beta = \frac{\sigma_s}{\sigma_m}\right)$, the return an investor can achieve by a broad investment in the stock market and risk-free investments is given by

$$r = r_f + \beta(r_m - r_f)$$

As a result, he would only consider an alternative investment opportunity with the same level of systematic risk if it offered a higher return. Hence, this relationship gives the minimum acceptable return for an investment based on its level of systematic risk.

Plotting this relationship on a graph gives the Securities Market Line (SML) as follows, which clearly shows the relationship between relative levels of risk (β) and corresponding expected returns.

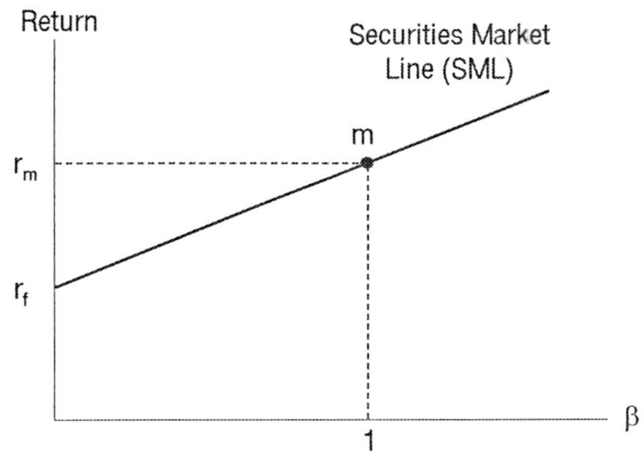

3.3 Conclusion

Thus, for an investment whose risk relative to the market portfolio is given by β, the required return is given by the Capital Asset Pricing Model (CAPM) formula

Formula to learn

$$r = r_f + \beta(r_m - r_f)$$

where

r_m = the return expected from the market portfolio
r_f = the return offered by a risk-free security
β = the risk of the investment opportunity relative to that of the market portfolio (systematic risk only)

That is, the investor can expect to achieve the risk-free return (r_f) plus a proportion of the **market risk premium** ($r_m - r_f$) based on the levels of relative risk (β) he is willing to face.

Example

For example, suppose that the risk-free rate of return is 6%, and the market is expected to return 14%, what return would a diversified investor require from an investment with a β of

- 0
- 0.5
- 1
- 1.5

Solution

Using

$$r = r_f + \beta(r_m - r_f)$$

gives

β = **0**	r = 6% + 0 × (14% – 6%) = 6%
β = **0.5**	r = 6% + 0.5 × (14% – 6%) = 10%
β = **1**	r = 6% + 1 × (14% – 6%) = 14%
β = **1.5**	r = 6% + 1.5 × (14% – 6%) = 18%

3.4 Investment appraisal under CAPM

Investment appraisal under CAPM amounts to plotting investments' expected returns and betas on the SML graph as follows.

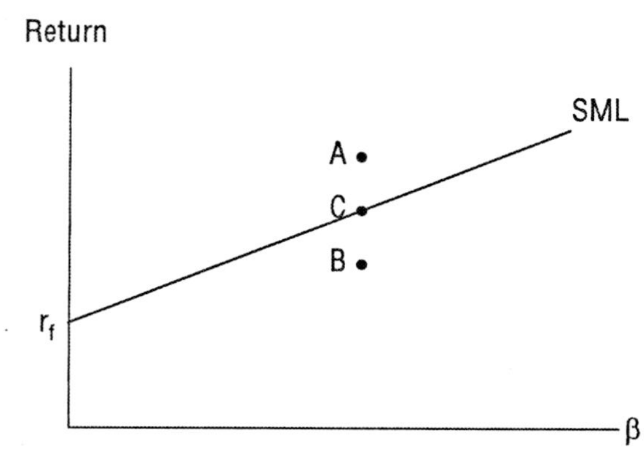

Investment A, lying above the SML, would be accepted by an investor as it is offering a return higher than that required for its level of risk, i.e. it is **undervalued**.

Investment B, lying beneath the SML, would be rejected as its current return is too low, i.e. it is **overvalued**.

Investment C, lying on the SML, is currently correctly priced in the market. An investor should be indifferent to the choice between buying it or not.

3.5 Forming portfolios using CAPM

We can use the CAPM to assist in the formation of portfolios where we have determined the degree of risk that the client is willing to face.

An individual seeking a high return would need to take on more risk. Thus, we would need to construct a portfolio with a high β. A portfolio with a β greater than 1 could be expected to give returns greater than those of the market, but at a correspondingly enhanced level of risk.

A young pension fund may be prepared to undertake a similar investment strategy with the view that there will be long-term benefits.

A mature pension fund, on the other hand, is liable to be seeking a safer portfolio and would, therefore, prefer a portfolio with a β less than 1. Clearly, as the proportion of risk-free investments is increased in our portfolio (and the proportion of equities reduced), the portfolio β reduces towards 0.

4 Betas

4.1 Introduction

4.1.1 What it means

The beta of an investment is a relative measure of the **systematic risk** of that investment.

In general terms

- The sign of the beta (+/–) indicates whether, on average, the investment's returns move with (+) the market, rising and falling when it does, or in the opposite direction (–) to the market.
- The scale or value of the beta indicates the relative volatility.

A beta of 0.5 (or –0.5) for instance, would indicate that, on average, the investment's returns move one half as much as the market's do in the same (or opposite) direction. If the market fell by 6%, we would expect the investment to fall (or rise) by 3%; if the market rose by 8%, we would expect the investment's returns to rise (or fall) by 4%, etc.

4.1.2 Summary

$\beta > 1$

On average, the investment's returns will move in the same direction as the market's returns but to a greater extent.

$\beta = 1$

On average, the investment's returns will move in the same direction as the market's returns and to the same extent.

$0 < \beta < 1$

On average, the investment's returns will move in the same direction as the market's returns but to a lesser extent.

$\beta = 0$

The investment's returns are uncorrelated with those of the market. This would be the case if the investment were risk free but, more generally, this situation will arise when all of the investment's risk is unsystematic.

$\beta < 0$

On average, the investment's returns will move in the opposite direction to the market, to a lesser extent if $\beta > -1$, to the same extent if $\beta = -1$ and to a greater extent if $\beta < -1$.

4.2 Use of betas

We can use the β for an investment to establish, from the CAPM formula, what the appropriate risk-adjusted required rate of return is in order to appraise the investment.

Example

A new one-year investment opportunity requires an initial investment of £1m and is expected to give a return of £1.2m at the end of the year.

The current market return is 14%, and risk-free return is 6%.

The investment's beta has been estimated at 1.5.

Assuming investors are well diversified, should the investment be accepted and what value would we place on the investment?

Solution

Required rate of return

The required return given by the CAPM would be

$$r = r_f + \beta(r_m - r_f)$$

$$r = 6\% + 1.5(14\% - 6\%)$$

$$r = 6\% + 12\% = 18\%$$

Investment's return and appraisal

The return on the investment will be 20% (£1.2m return from a £1.0m investment), hence it should be accepted. It is offering a better level of return for its level of (systematic) risk than can currently be obtained elsewhere on the market.

Value of investment

To value the investment, the investors will use the required rate given by the CAPM as a risk-adjusted discount rate to find the present value of its future returns (the usual market value approach) giving

Time	Cash Flow £'000	Discount Factor	Present Value £'000
0	(1,000)	1	(1,000)
1	1,200	$\frac{1}{1.18^1}$	1,017
Net present value at t_0			£17

The £1.017m is the value of the investment's returns to well-diversified investors (hence, the market value of the investment). It is the maximum price that they should be prepared to pay for such returns. The investment is accepted because it is worth £17,000 more than it costs.

If capital markets are efficient, then all quoted shares should be correctly valued (any share which was undervalued would be the subject of buying pressure, which would force its price up to the fair value). CAPM shows that a share's market value should be that which equates the actual return with the expected return given the share's beta.

4.3 Calculation of betas

Learning objective

21.2.8 Calculate the beta of an investment given the systematic risk of the investment and the risk of the market.

4.3.1 Systematic risk

To get a beta, we need to know the systematic risk element of the investment we are considering (σ_s).

We have said that systematic risk is that part of the total risk that is related to movements in the market portfolio. The correlation coefficient between two investment opportunities is a measure of this relationship, hence

Formula to learn

$$\sigma_s = \sigma_i Cor_{im}$$

where

σ_s = the investment's systematic risk

σ_i = the investment's total risk (systematic and unsystematic)

Cor_{im} = correlation coefficient between the returns of the investment and those of the market portfolios

For instance, if an investment was perfectly correlated with the market, so that all its fluctuations could be fully explained by fluctuations in the market, then all of its risk would be systematic $\sigma_s = \sigma_i$.

If an investment was uncorrelated to the market, then its systematic risk would be zero and all its risk would be unsystematic.

Between those extremes come varying proportions of systematic and unsystematic risk.

Note that as we have already stated, the relationship between these risks (total, systematic and unsystematic) is

Formula to learn

$$\sigma_i^2 = \sigma_s^2 + \sigma_u^2$$

where

σ_i = the investment's total risk (standard deviation)

σ_s = the investment's systematic risk

σ_u = the investment's unsystematic risk

That is, the investment's total variance is the sum of its systematic and unsystematic variances.

4.3.2 The Beta coefficient

Learning objective

21.2.9 Calculate the beta of an investment given the variance of the market return, and the covariance of the investment return with the market return.

Remember that beta is a relative measure or index number showing the level of systematic risk of an investment relative to the market portfolio, i.e.

$$\beta = \frac{\sigma_s}{\sigma_m}$$

and from $\sigma_s = \sigma_i Cor_{im}$ above, we can establish

$$\beta = \frac{\sigma_s}{\sigma_m} = \frac{\sigma_i Cor_{im}}{\sigma_m} = \left[\frac{\sigma_i \sigma_m Cor_{im}}{\sigma_m^2}\right] = \frac{\text{Covariance}(i,m)}{\text{Variance of the market}}$$

The term in brackets being included here as a stepping stone to the final formula.

If the covariance or correlation coefficient between the investment and the market can be established (or is given), the beta can be calculated. Alternatively, if we establish the systematic risk, we can establish the beta.

We saw in the Location and Dispersion section how to calculate standard deviations using the formula

$$\sigma = \sqrt{\frac{\sum(i-\bar{i})^2}{n}}$$

and that variances can be calculated as the square of the standard deviation, i.e.

$$\text{Variance} = \sigma^2 = \frac{\sum(i-\bar{i})^2}{n}$$

The covariance can calculated in a very similar fashion using the equation

$$\text{Covariance} = \frac{\sum(i-\bar{i})(m-\bar{m})}{n}$$

where

i = the return on investment i

m = the return offered by the market portfolio

Please note that this covariance equation is provided for information only and is not needed for this exam.

Learning objective **21.2.7 Explain** how the beta may be derived from a scatter chart of historic returns.

4.3.3 Calculation of beta coefficients in practice

Beta factors are calculated in practice for quoted shares and are available from various information services.

The method of calculation is largely based on the above ideas regarding the average variability of the returns from investments relative to those of the market, involving the use of linear regression analysis. If the historical return on the market index is plotted on a scatter diagram against the corresponding returns of a security i, then the following might be observed.

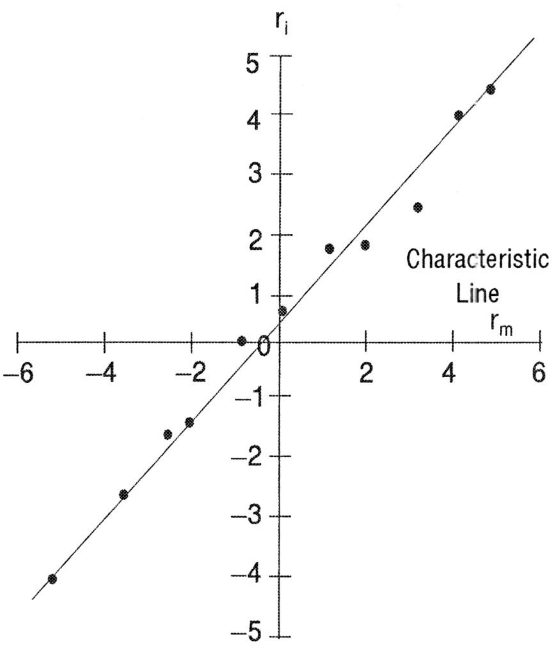

If the linear regression line of best fit is found, it will show the average relationship between the two sets of returns. This line is known as the security's **characteristic line**.

The results of a regression analysis give the terms for the linear regression equation

$$r_i = \alpha + \beta r_m$$

Looking at each of these terms

- β indicates the volatility of i's return relative to the market returns. If the slope is greater than 45%, i.e. greater than 1, then i's returns tend to be more volatile than those of the market. This is exactly how we have defined an investment's beta factor earlier in the chapter. Hence, **the slope of the regression line estimates beta**.
- α (alpha) is the intercept on the vertical axis and equals $\overline{r}_i - \beta\,\overline{r}_m$. We will see more on this in the Performance Measurement chapter.

Note that the estimated β will depend on the **time interval** and the **market proxy** used in the above process. For example, calculating a β based on monthly observations over five years will give a different answer from that based on weekly observations over one year. Using the S&P 500 as a market proxy will give a different answer from a proxy based on all NYSE quoted stocks.

4.4 Betas for portfolios of investments

Learning objective

21.2.10 Calculate the beta of a portfolio given the component betas and the investment weightings.

Although any investment must be appraised purely on the basis of its own expected return and beta (without reference, in particular, to the current portfolio), it is possible to work out the impact of accepting the investment on the portfolio's overall beta.

When two investments are combined, their combination will have a beta equal to the weighted average (by market values) of the individual betas.

Example

A portfolio has a current market value of £22m, and a beta of 0.8. We are considering an additional investment of £2m to be funded by scaling down the current portfolio. The new investment is expected to yield a net cash inflow of £2.36m in one year, the inflows having a beta of 1.5. The expected return from the market is 14% and the risk-free rate is 6%.

Should the investment be accepted and what will be the new β of the portfolio, assuming that the current portfolio is fairly priced and at equilibrium?

Solution

Required rate of return

From the CAPM formula, we can work out that the appropriate risk-adjusted discount rate to apply to the new investment is

$$r = r_f + \beta(r_m - r_f)$$

$$r = 6\% + 1.5(14\% - 6\%)$$

$$r = 6\% + 12\% = 18\%$$

Investment's return and appraisal

The return on the investment will be 18% (£2.36m return on a £2m investment), hence it is fairly valued and should be accepted. It is offering a fair level of return for its level of (systematic) risk.

New Beta

Of the total market value of £22m, £20m is the market value of flows with a beta of 0.8, while £2m is the market value of flows having a beta of 1.5.

The new overall beta will be the weighted average of 0.8 and 1.5, i.e.

$$0.8 \times \frac{£20m}{£22m} + 1.5 \times \frac{£2m}{£22m} = 0.864$$

5 Assumptions and Limitations of CAPM

5.1 The assumptions

Learning objectives	
	21.2.2 Identify the assumptions behind the single factor Capital Asset Pricing Model (CAPM).
	21.2.3 Explain the limitations of the CAPM model.

CAPM is based on a number of assumptions.

- Investors are rational and risk averse.
- Investors are diversified and, hence, are only concerned with a security's expected return and its systematic risk.
- The capital market is perfect and in equilibrium, which means in particular
  - It is not dominated by any individual investors.
  - There are no transaction costs, for instance commissions or taxes, or other imperfections.
  - All securities are fairly valued, hence r_m is a realistic return.

- All investors have the same expectations regarding the probability distributions of returns from each security.
- There exists a risk-free rate at which all investors may borrow or lend without limit.

The realism and relevance of many of these assumptions may be questioned. The first two are probably not too far-fetched, but the others are clearly invalid. The question is – are the effects of these invalid assumptions significant enough to invalidate the whole theory, or do they just produce minor distortions that can be dealt with separately?

It is worth noting that extensions made to CAPM which seek to relax these basic assumptions give results which are still broadly in line with the basic theory.

Much research has been carried out over the years to try to establish to what extent CAPM is valid. The model has proved surprisingly resilient to such testing, and it seems that β is a valid and fairly complete measure of risk.

5.2 The limitations

Aside from the limitations stemming from the CAPM's assumptions, the following limitations are worth considering.

5.2.1 Single-period (one year) model

The required rate of return derived from the model is only valid as long as the inputs (r_m, r_f, β) are valid. As a result of annual budgets, which tend to effect tax rates and interest rates (through the PSNCR), we can expect that one or more of these factors will change over a year. As such, the returns that we consider when using CAPM are the holding period returns over that time, which we cover later.

Few investment opportunities last for one year only; however, we can extend the model to more than one time period if we assume that all relevant factors (such as risk-free rate and market rate) remain constant over the period covered.

5.2.2 Only applicable to diversified portfolios

The model assumes that the overall portfolio held is diversified and equates to the market as a whole. If we were dealing with a small, undiversified portfolio, then this approach would not be appropriate. We would need to consider **Modern Portfolio Theory,** from which CAPM was developed but which is outside of the syllabus for this exam.

5.2.3 Difficult to estimate the beta factor for an investment

To calculate a beta factor for an investment, we need to estimate the future returns under different economic conditions. Obviously, this will be extremely difficult to achieve in practice. One solution could be to look at a similar investment that had been accepted in the past and calculate its β factor with the benefit of hindsight.

6 Arbitrage Pricing Theory

6.1 Introduction

Learning objective	**21.2.1 Explain** the concept of investment being exposed to a number of common factors which partially explain their return and risk profile ('Arbitrage Price Theory').

Arbitrage Pricing Theory (APT) represents an alternative pricing model to CAPM in which the expected return from a security is determined as a function of several influential factors rather than simply a function of the market risk premium. Like CAPM, APT is for diversified investors who have eliminated the unsystematic risk of their portfolios and are only concerned with the systematic risk.

APT also provides a basis for portfolio strategies where the portfolio is only sensitive to certain of those factors.

In common with CAPM, APT may also be used as a basis for performance measurement.

6.2 Returns

As noted above, APT gives the expected return from a security and it is useful to compare the two ideas.

CAPM

Using CAPM, the expected return from a security is given by

$$r = r_f + \beta(r_m - r_f)$$

where

r_f = risk-free rate
$(r_m - r_f)$ = market risk premium, i.e. the premium return available from market investment
β = beta factor or sensitivity to market movements

That is, CAPM suggests that a security or portfolio is sensitive to just a single factor, the market, and to determine the expected return we need to know how sensitive we are to this factor (the β) and the premium return associated with this factor $(r_m - r_f)$. We could restate CAPM as

Formula to learn

$$r = r_f + \beta F$$

where

r_f = risk-free rate

F = the factor to which we are sensitive, or more particularly the premium return on the factor to which we are sensitive, i.e. $(r_m - r_f)$

β = beta or sensitivity to that factor

CAPM can, therefore, be viewed as a single factor model.

APT

APT gives the expected return from a security as

Formula to learn

$$r = r_f + b_1F_1 + b_2F_2 + b_3F_3 + ...$$

where

r_f = risk-free rate

F_1, F_2, F_3 = the factors to which we are sensitive, or more particularly the premium return on those factors which, ideally, should be uncorrelated

b_1, b_2, b_3 = beta or sensitivity measures to those factors

6.3 Factors

One of the limitations of APT is that it does not specify the factors to which the investment is sensitive. However, examples of factors to which a security is sensitive may include the following.

Factors	
Equities	**Bonds**
Market returns	Market returns
Sector returns	Duration
Inflation rates	Default risk
GDP growth	Liquidity risk
Tax rates	Conversion options
Economic growth	Issuer options
Dividend yield	etc.
etc.	

6.4 The theory

APT suggests that, based on the various possible securities available and their factor sensitivities, it should be possible to construct a Pure Factor portfolio, i.e. a portfolio with unit sensitivity to just a single factor. For example, a pure factor 1 portfolio would have an expected return of

$$r = r_f + F_1$$

By combining such pure factor portfolios, it will be possible to construct a new portfolio with any level of sensitivity to each of the factors. In particular, we will be able to construct a portfolio with the same sensitivity to each factor as any selected security.

If this is achieved, then given that the portfolio and the security have the same risks, they should offer the same returns, otherwise an arbitrage opportunity would exist. As a result, the model gives the expected return from that security for the given risk.

APT also suggests that it may be possible to construct a portfolio with zero sensitivity to any of the factors, in which case we have constructed a risk-free substitute.

6.5 Use of APT

Based on APT, then, we can

- Construct portfolios with selected sensitivities to certain of the factors.
- Manage the fund to our strengths, optimising the sensitivity to factors that we can predict.
- Immunise the portfolio against uncontrollable/unpredictable factors.

6.6 Assumption and limitations

6.6.1 Assumptions of APT

The assumptions of APT are that

- Investors are rational and risk averse.
- Markets are efficient; free of transaction costs to permit arbitrage.
- The factors that are sensitive are uncorrelated.

6.6.2 Limitations of APT

The limitations of APT are

- APT does not specify the factors to use.
- The problem of determining the relevant beta factors for any security and the stability of those factors.
- The possibility that pure factor portfolios, or a risk-free substitute, may in fact be impossible to construct from the securities available.

Chapter Roundup

Risk

- Many different factors give rise to risk when investing, ranging from factors affecting the economy as a whole such as interest rates, inflation, exchange rates and tax rates, through to items more specific to the individual investment such as default and liquidity risk.
- The normal trade-off between risk and return is a higher risk results in a higher required return.
- Investment theories usually assume investment returns are
  - normally distributed.
  - independent through time (no autocorrelation).
- Characteristics (limitations) of a normal distribution
  - Symmetrical, ie probability of a gain is equal to the probability of an equivalent loss (not observed in practice).
  - Gets thinner into the tails, ie more extreme movements are increasingly likely (not observed in practice, especially on downside).
  - Has a single constant standard deviation, ie assumes investment risk is constant (again, not observed in practice, volatility can increase dramatically in extreme market conditions).
- Diversification of portfolios aims to reduce risk without necessarily reducing returns.
- The effectiveness of any diversification depends on the correlation between securities

  $$Cor_{xy} = \frac{\text{Covariance}(x,y)}{\sigma_x \sigma_y}$$

  - Securities with high positive correlation offer little diversification potential.
  - Securities with a high value negative correlation offer a great diversification potential.
- Diversification benefits reduce dramatically in extreme markets as correlation coefficients become strongly positive (all securities fall together).
- Risk can be decomposed into a systematic and an unsystematic component. Systematic (market) risk is non-diversifiable whilst unsystematic (specific/idiosyncratic) risk can be eliminated through diversification.

  $$\sigma_i^2 = \sigma_s^2 + \sigma_u^2$$

- Other risk measures
  - VAR = Amount by which the value of a portfolio may fall over a given period at time to a given level of risk.
  - Tracking error = Standard deviation of the difference between the returns on a tracker fund and the returns of the index it is tracking.
  - Semi-variance/Semi-deviation = Variance /standard deviation at below average returns only.
  - Drawdown = Amount by which an investment has fallen from its all-time high.

- Something is statistically significant if its observed value is constantly outside of the range of normal probabilities.

CAPM

- The capital asset pricing model (CAPM) assumes investors are well diversified and uses beta as a measure of systematic risk. It is based on a number of assumptions.
- CAPM calculates a discount rate (required return) for a fully diversified investor to use when discounting future expected cash flows as follows.

  $r = r_f + \beta(r_m - r_f)$

  Where

  $$\beta = \frac{\sigma_s}{\sigma_m} = \frac{\sigma_i Cor_{im}}{\sigma_m} = \left[\frac{\sigma_i \sigma_m Cor_{im}}{\sigma_m^2}\right] = \frac{\text{Co variance}(i,m)}{\text{Variance of the market}}$$

- Beta can be calculated by applying linear regression to a scaller chart of historical movements, this will be the historically observed beta based on historical risks.
- The beta of a portfolio is the weighted average of the underlying betas.

APT

- CAPM is a single factor model that could be written as

  $r = r_f + \beta F$

- APT is a multi-factor model where the expected return is dependent on the sensitively to factors, ie

  $r = r_f + b_1F_1 + b_2F_2 + b_3F_3 + ...$

TEST YOUR KNOWLEDGE

Check your knowledge of the chapter here, without referring back to the text.

1. What sort of risk can be eliminated through diversification?

2. The covariance of two investments is 240, the risk of x is 15 and the risk of y is 22. Calculate the correlation coefficient.

3. The beta of an investment is 1.2 and the risk in the market portfolio is 15%. Calculate the systematic risk of the investment.

4. A beta of +0.7 indicates a share is

   A More sensitive to systematic risk factors than the market
   B Less sensitive to systematic risk factors than the market
   C Perfectly positively correlated with the market
   D Perfectly negatively correlated with the market

5. If a security has a total risk of 13% and a systematic risk of 12% (both in standard deviation terms), what is the security's non-systematic risk, expressed in standard deviation terms?

6. An investment has systematic risk of 15% and specific risk of 20%. What is its total risk?

7. The total risk of an investment is 17%. Its unsystematic risk is 8%. What is the market risk?

8. A stock has a beta of 0.7 and the risk-free return is 4%. If the market return was 7% what would the expected return of the stock be?

9. The market risk on an investment is 8%, the risk of the market portfolio is 10%, the risk-free return is 5% and market risk premium is 3%. What is the expected return on the investment?

10. An investment's total risk is 26% and its specific risk is 10%. The market portfolio risk is 20% and return is 9%. The risk-free return is 6%. What is the expected return?

11. An investment has a beta of 0.8. Market risk is 16%, risk premium is 3% and the risk-free rate is 5%. What is the expected return?

12. An investment is expected to return 8% when the market is returning 10%. Its beta is 0.5. What is the risk-free rate?

13. Given the following information.

Share	Beta (β)	Specific Risk (σu)
A	1.2	10%
B	0.8	8%
C	1.4	16%
D	0.9	18%

Market return	= 18%
Market standards deviation	= 10%
Risk-free rate	= 8%

(a) Calculate the expected return for each of the above using the security market line.

(b) Calculate market risk (σ_s) and total risk (σ_j) for each of the above.

(c) Assuming you have 20% of your money invested in each of A and B and 30% of your money invested in each of C and D calculate your portfolio beta.

---

14. The market return is 18% and the risk-free return 8%. We are going to invest 70% of our money in A with a beta of 1.3 and 30% in B with a beta of 0.75.

(a) What will be the expected return from each investment?

(b) What will be the expected return on the two share portfolio?

(c) What will be the beta of the portfolio?

TEST YOUR KNOWLEDGE: ANSWERS

1. Unsystematic/specific risk

   (See Section 2.3.3)

2. 0.73

   $$\frac{240}{(15 \times 22)} = 0.73$$

   (See Section 4.3.2)

3. 18%

   $1.2 \times 15 = 18\%$

   (See Section 4.3.2)

4. B

   (See Section 4.1.1)

5. $\sigma_i^2 = \sigma_s^2 + \sigma_u^2$
   $13^2 = 12^2 + \sigma_u^2$
   $\sigma_u^2 = 25$
   $\sigma_u = 5\%$

   (See Section 2.3.5)

6. $\sigma_i^2 = \sigma_s^2 + \sigma_u^2$
   $= 15^2 + 20^2 = 625$
   $\sigma_i = \sqrt{625} = 25\%$

   (See Section 2.3.5)

7. $\sigma_i^2 = \sigma_s^2 + \sigma_u^2$
   $17^2 = \sigma_s^2 + 8^2$
   $\sigma_s^2 = 225$
   $\sigma_s = 15\%$

   (See Section 2.3.5)

8. $r = r_f + \beta(r_m - r_f) = 4 + 0.7(7 - 4) = 6.1\%$

   (See Section 3.3)

9. $$\beta = \frac{\sigma_s}{\sigma_m} = \frac{8}{10} = 0.8$$

   $r = r_f + \beta(r_m - r_f) = 5 + 0.8 \times 3 = 7.4\%$

   (See Section 4.3.2)

10. $\sigma_i^2 = \sigma_s^2 + \sigma_u^2$

$26^2 = \sigma_s^2 + 10^2$

$\sigma_s^2 = 576$

$\sigma_s = 24\%$

$\beta = \frac{\sigma_s}{\sigma_m} = \frac{24}{20} = 1.2$

$r = r_f + \beta(r_m - r_f) = 6 + 1.2(9 - 6) = 9.6\%$

(See Sections 2.3.5 and 4.3.2)

11. $r = r_f + \beta(r_m - r_f) = 5\% + 0.8 \times 3\% = 7.4\%$

(See Section 3.3)

12. $r = r_f + \beta(r_m - r_f)$

$8 = r_f + 0.5(10 - r_f)$

$8 = r_f + 5 - 0.5\ r_f$

$0.5\ r_f = 3$

$r_f = 6\%$

(See Section 3.3)

13. (a) Expected return, $r = r_f + \beta(r_m - r_f)$

A $r_a = 8 + 1.2\ (18 - 8) = 20\%$

B $r_b = 8 + 0.8\ (18 - 8) = 16\%$

C $r_c = 8 + 1.4\ (18 - 8) = 22\%$

D $r_d = 8 + 0.9\ (18 - 8) = 17\%$

(b) $\sigma_s = \beta\sigma_m$

$\sigma_i = \sqrt{\sigma_s^2 + \sigma_u^2}$

A $\sigma_s = 1.2 \times 10\% = 12\%$

$\sigma_i = \sqrt{12^2 + 10^2} = 15.6\%$

B $\sigma_s = 0.8 \times 10\% = 8\%$

$\sigma_i = \sqrt{8^2 + 8^2} = 11.3\%$

C $\sigma_s = 1.4 \times 10\% = 14\%$

$\sigma_i = \sqrt{14^2 + 16^2} = 21.3\%$

D $\sigma_s = 0.9 \times 10\% = 9\%$

$\sigma_i = \sqrt{9^2 + 18^2} = 20.1\%$

(c)

Share	Weight(w_i)	β_i	$w_i\beta_i$
A	0.2	1.2	0.24
B	0.2	0.8	0.16
C	0.3	1.4	0.42
D	0.3	0.9	0.27
			1.09

Beta = 1.09

(See Sections 2.3.5 and 4.3.2)

14. $r = r_f + \beta(r_m - r_f)$

(a) **Share A**

$r_a = 8 + 1.3(18 - 8) = 21\%$

Share B

$r_b = 8 + 0.75(18 - 8) = 15.5\%$

(b) The overall expected return

$r = (0.7 \times 21.0) + (0.3 \times 15.5) = 19.35\%$

(c) $\beta = (0.7 \times 1.3) + (0.3 \times 0.75) = 1.135$

Alternative

$19.35 = 8 + \beta(18 - 8)$

$$\beta = \frac{19.358.00}{18.008.00} = 1.135$$

(See Sections 3.3 and 4.4)

6 Economic Theories and Theories of Market Behaviour

INTRODUCTION

Economics studies how the scarce resources of land, labour and capital are allocated throughout society.

Microeconomics studies activities at the level of the firm and puts forward proposals on how best to maximise profitability in different types of business. Time is spent looking at theories of revenue and cost structures. We also examine methods for assessing industries and companies.

CHAPTER CONTENTS

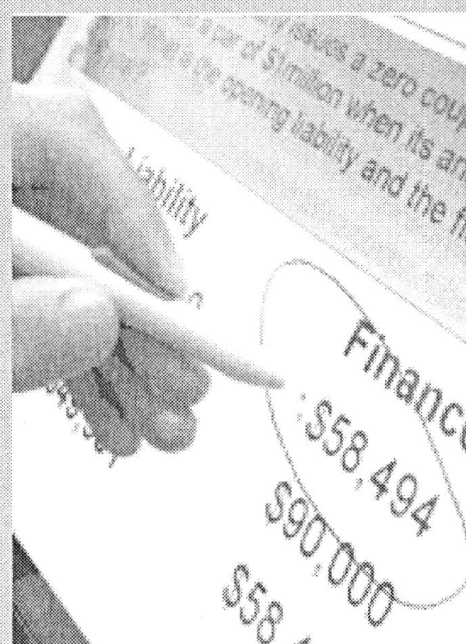

Chapter Learning Objectives

21 Investment Theories and Models

Demonstrate an understanding of the merits and limitations of the main investment theories

21.3 The Efficient Markets Hypothesis (EMH) and Behavioural Finance

21.3.1 **Explain** the key concepts of the EMH.

21.3.2 **Explain** the limitations of the EMH.

21.3.3 **Explain** the basic concepts of the behavioural finance school of thought including heuristics and framing.

21.3.4 **Evaluate** the evidence on market anomalies in relation to both EMH and behavioural finance interpretations.

21.3.5 **Examine** the concept of 'financial amnesia' and the role of behavioural factors in its promotion.

21.3.6 **Explain** the notion of 'bubbles' in financial markets.

24 The Macroeconomic Environment

Demonstrate an understanding of the macro-economic environment and its impact on investment.

24.1 The macroeconomic environment

24.1.1 **Identify** the main long term UK and global socio-economic trends.

24.1.2 **Identify** key economic indicators and explain their trends.

24.1.3 **Understand** the relationship between and importance of the main World economies.

24.1.4 **Explain** economic and financial cycles including their predictability and regional differences.

24.1.5 **Identify** international differences in consumption, credit and savings.

24.2 Determination of National Income, the circular flow of income, consumption, the multiplier, the paradox of thrift, foreign trade and income determination

24.2.1 **Distinguish** between GDP and GNP.

24.2.2 **Explain** the difference between real and nominal GDP.

24.2.3 **Explain** the components of the circular flow of income.

24.2.4 **Distinguish** between injections into, and withdrawals from ('leakages') the circular flow.

24.2.5 **Distinguish** between national income and GNP.

24.2.6 **Distinguish** between classical economics and the Keynesian and Monetarist schools of thought.

24.2.7 **Explain** the major components of the Keynesian model.

24.2.8 **Explain** Keynesian equilibrium.

24.2.9 **Calculate** the Keynesian multiplier given the marginal propensity to consume (mpc) or propensities to withdraw (tax, import and save).

24.2.10 **Explain** the paradox of thrift.

24.3 Inflation, Unemployment, Fiscal and Monetary Policy and the role of Central Banks

24.3.1 **Describe** fiscal policy and its influence on aggregate demand.

24.3.2 **Explain** the role of debt in the business cycle.

24.3.3 **Explain** the problems associated with fiscal policy.

24.3.4 **Define** money supply (from 'narrow' through to 'wide').

24.3.5 **Describe** the fractional reserve banking system.

24.3.6 **Define** the money multiplier and identify its determinants.

24.3.7 **Calculate** the potential money multiplier given a cash reserve ratio.

24.3.8 **Explain** the transmission mechanism whereby monetary policy influences economic aggregates.

24.3.9 **Define** inflation and explain how it is measured in the UK.

24.3.10 **Define** unemployment and explain how it is measured in the UK.

24.3.11 **Explain** the relationship between inflation and unemployment.

24.3.12 **Explain** how inflation targeting operates in the UK.

24.3.13 **Distinguish** between the different approaches to the control of inflation taken by the major central banks.

24.3.14 **Explain** the other tools (including Quantitative Easing (QE)) used by central banks to manage the economy and in particular inflation.

24.3.15 **Explain** the impact of bank capital and liquidity requirements and the move towards macroprudential regulation on the macro-economy.

24.3.16 **Explain** the role of securitisation on credit growth and the wider macro-economy.

24.4 The foreign exchange market, government policy and exchange rates, fixed floating and managed exchange rates, and the balance of payments

24.4.1 **Explain** how changes in supply and demand for a currency will affect its value on the foreign exchange markets.

24.4.2 **Identify** the key components of the balance of payments.

24.4.3 **Explain** the relationship between the supply and demand for a currency and the underlying transactions represented in the balance of payments.

24.4.4 **Distinguish** between a fixed, floating and a managed exchange rate ('dirty-floating' regime).

24.4.5 **Explain** the economic benefits and costs of a fixed exchange rate mechanism.

24.4.6 **Explain** an optimal currency area (OCA) and identify the advantages and disadvantages of implementing a single currency in an OCA

24.4.7 **Explain** the implications of persistent global imbalances of trade and capital.

24.4.9 **Explain** the effectiveness of monetary and fiscal policy in fixed and floating exchange rate regimes.

25 Microeconomics

Demonstrate an understanding at microeconomics

25.1 Demand and supply

25.1.1 **Explain** the laws of supply and demand.

25.1.2 **Distinguish** between movements along demand and supply schedules and shifts thereof.

25.1.3 **Identify** the factors that cause a demand or supply schedule to shift.

25.1.4 **Describe**, calculate and interpret own price elasticity of demand and its impact on total revenues.

25.1.5 **Identify** the factors that determine own price elasticity of demand.

25.1.6 **Explain**, calculate and interpret the concept of cross elasticity of demand (as applied to substitute and complementary goods).

25.1.7 **Explain**, calculate and interpret elasticity of supply and its dependence on the flexibility of factors of production.

25.2 The cost of production; marginal costs, average costs and total costs

25.2.1 **Distinguish** between explicit (accounting) costs and opportunity (economic) costs.

25.2.2 **Explain** the concept of normal, supernormal and sub-normal levels of profit.

25.2.3 **Define** fixed costs, variable costs, marginal costs, total costs and average costs.

25.2.4 **Explain** the shapes of the short-run marginal cost, average variable cost, average fixed cost, and average total cost curves.

25.2.5 **Explain** the law of diminishing marginal returns and its impact on the shape of short-run cost curves.

25.2.6 **Explain** the relationship between total revenue, average revenue and marginal revenues for a normal demand schedule.

25.2.7 **Explain** the relationship between marginal cost and marginal revenue and how this determines the profit maximising level of output for a firm.

25.3 Short and long run costs, economics and diseconomies of scale

25.3.1 **Define** short-run and long-run in the context of cost behaviour.

25.3.2 **Explain** the notions of economies of scale, a minimum efficient scale and diseconomies of scale and their impact on the shape of the long-run average cost curve.

25.3.3 **Explain** the relationship between long run marginal costs and long run average costs and explain how this determines the level of output for productive efficiency to arise.

25.4 Perfect competition and monopoly

25.4.1 **Identify** the conditions that characterise a perfectly competitive ('price-taker') market.

25.4.2 **Explain** the conditions of long-run equilibrium for a price-taker.

25.4.3 **Explain** the market mechanics through which only normal levels of profit can be earned by price takers in the long-run.

25.4.4 **Explain** the relationship between short run supply and marginal cost for a price-taker.

25.4.5 **Describe** the shape of the long run supply curve for a perfectly competitive industry.

25.4.6 **Explain** the decision by a price taker facing economic losses to either continue to operate or shut down.

25.4.7 **Identify** the conditions that characterise a pure monopoly.

25.4.8 **Explain** the conditions of long run equilibrium for a monopoly.

25.4.9 **Distinguish** between the equilibrium price, output levels, and productive efficiency of a monopoly compared to a perfectly competitive firm.

25.4.10 **Explain** price discrimination and the conditions under which it will prevail.

25.5 Commonly used methods of assessing industries/companies

25.5.1 **Understand** how business cycles may affect relative industry performance.

25.5.2 **Explain** Porter's five competitive forces that drive industry competition.

25.5.3 **Explain** the product life cycle and the characteristics of each phase (introduction, growth, maturity and decline).

25.5.4 **Explain** the concept of strengths, weaknesses, opportunities and threats (SWOT) analysis and its role in corporate evaluation.

25.5.5 **Explain** the 4Ps marketing mix (product, price, promotion and place) in the context of analysing competitive advantage and threats.

"The ideas of economists and political philosophers, both when they are right and when they are wrong, are more powerful than is commonly understood. Indeed, the world is ruled by little else. Practical men, who believe themselves to be quite exempt from any intellectual influences, are usually the slaves of some defunct economists. Madmen in authority, who hear voices in the air, are distilling their frenzy from some academic scribbler of a few years back."

J.M. Keynes

1 Introduction

Economics is the study of the **allocation of scarce resources** amongst competing claims. Whilst this is a far from perfect explanation of the subject, it will suffice for our purposes.

The objective of economic policy is generally perceived to be the maximisation of the output of the economy's product, thereby increasing the overall economic welfare of the participants.

Production Possibility Frontier

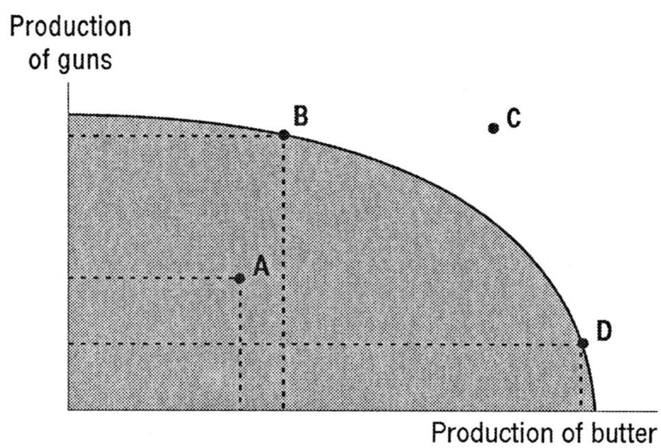

The **production possibility frontier** represents the range of possibilities from employing the resources of the economy.

Within the overall constraint of the production possibility frontier, any combinations beneath the curve represent potential production combinations of guns and butter. Option C is not possible given the current resources of the economy. However, options B and D represent combinations where the overall resources of the economy are being used to their fullest extent. Consequently, either is preferable to the option of point A, which under-utilises the resources of the economy.

The questions are, how do we get to optimal utilisation and which is the preferable alternative, B or D? It is at this point that the philosophic argument begins. Many would argue that the only option is to leave the allocation of resources to the **free market**. This should ensure that the assets are fully utilised in the most appropriate combination, reflecting the preferences of consumers for, in our example, guns or butter.

The opposite extreme to the free market is the **command economy**, where asset allocation and production decisions are taken by a central authority, immune from market forces.

In reality, there are very few economies that conform to either of these two extremes. Most economies are referred to as **mixed**, combining free markets with an element of intervention. In operation, some are biased more towards one extreme than the other.

The study of economics is divided into two elements.

- **Microeconomics** is the study of the reaction of individuals and firms to economic stimuli
- **Macroeconomics** is the study of the economy as a whole and concerns itself with the 'big picture' issues, such as unemployment and growth.

2 The Theory of Supply and Demand

2.1 Introduction

At the heart of microeconomics is the theory of **supply and demand**.

Learning objectives

25.1.1 Explain the laws of supply and demand.

25.1.2 Distinguish between movements along demand and supply schedules and shifts thereof.

25.1.3 Identify the factors that cause a demand or supply schedule to shift.

In the classical (free market) economist's world, there are two forces which dominate. These are supply and demand – the 'market forces'.

2.2 Demand

Demand represents the quantity that individuals will buy at a given price. In this context, we are talking about **effective demand**, that is to say, a want which the consumer has the resources to satisfy.

The Demand Curve

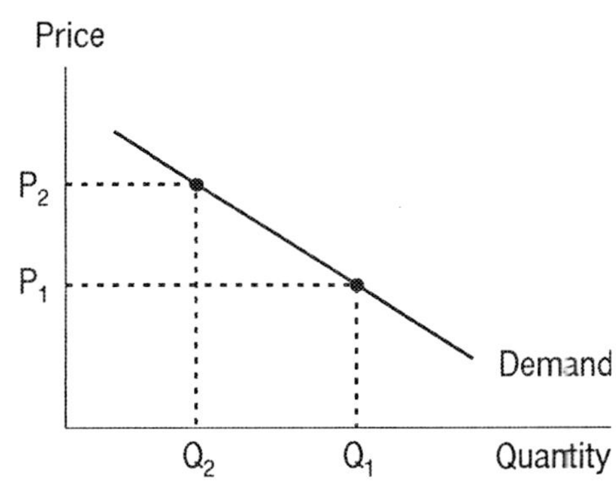

2.3 The factors behind demand

The price of the good – this gives rise to the slope of the demand curve, since as the price of a good falls, the rational consumer will demand an increased quantity of the product. Equally, as prices rise from P_1 to P_2, the quantity demanded falls from Q_1 to Q_2. A change in price generates a movement **along an existing demand curve**.

The other factors that shape demand will generate a change in the position of the demand curve.

Shifts of the Demand Curve

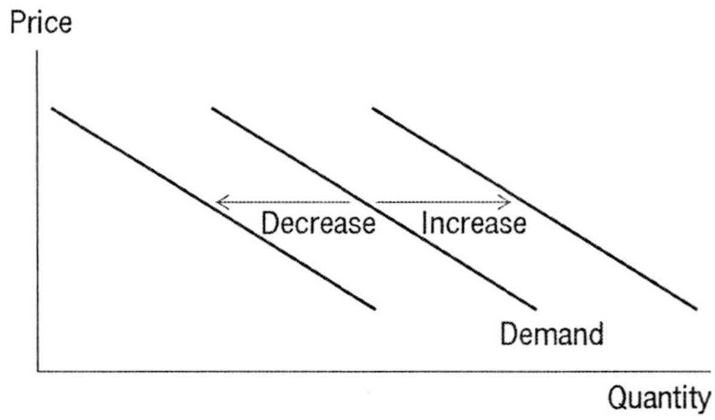

The price of other goods – the demand for one good will, in part, be determined by the price of other goods.

- **Substitutes** are goods that may be consumed as an alternative to the first good, for example, tea and coffee. If the price of coffee rises, then the demand for tea will increase, as it now represents a lower cost alternative to coffee.
- **Complements** are goods which are normally consumed in combination, for example, cars and petrol. As the price of cars falls, the demand for cars will rise and, as a consequence, so will the demand for petrol.

Tastes – as a good becomes fashionable, demand for it rises.

Incomes – if an individual's income increases then, in the case of a normal good, this is likely to increase the quantity of that good demanded. For example, if an individual's income doubled, then his/her demand for convenience food is likely to rise. There are, however, certain goods where as income rises the demand actually falls. These goods are referred to as **inferior goods**. As incomes rise, the demand for supermarket 'value' products will decrease, as consumers use their extra income to buy higher quality food products.

Other factors – advertising and marketing can increase the demand by encouraging consumers to purchase additional goods.

2.4 Supply

Supply represents the amount of a good that producers are prepared to supply to the market at a given price.

The Supply Curve

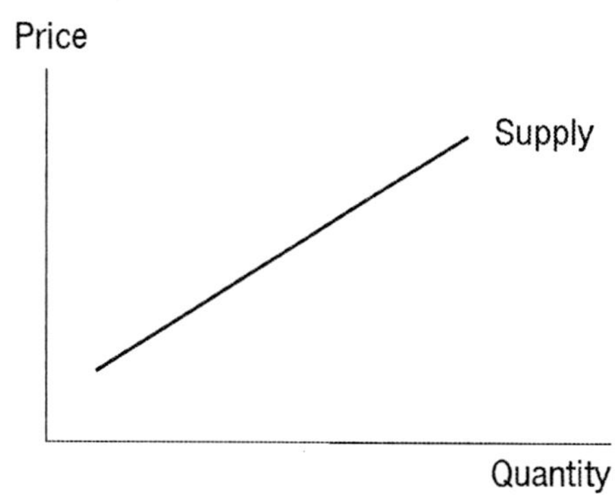

Supply is an upward-sloping function. Again, the logic behind this is that as the price rises, producers will be prepared to supply more of that particular good. As we will see later, the supply function is determined by the costs of the company.

Shifts of the Supply Curve

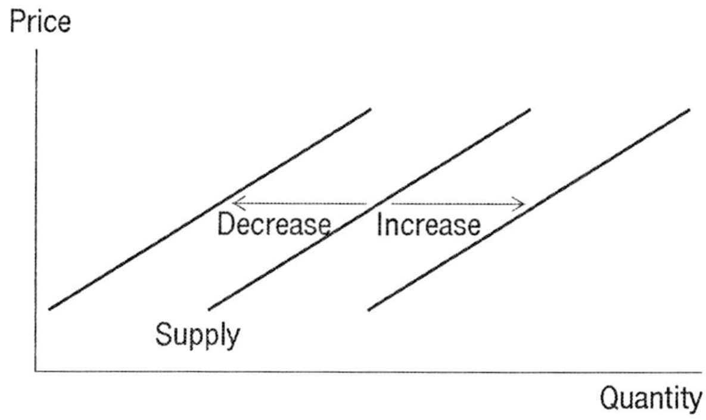

A shift in supply to the left indicates that costs have increased and the amount supplied at any given price will decrease. A shift in supply to the right indicates that costs have fallen and the amount supplied at a given price will increase.

Reasons for shifts include changes in technology (most likely causing a reduction in costs and a shift to the right) and natural factors (i.e. drought would cause a shift to the left of agricultural goods).

2.5 Equilibrium

It is the combination of these two forces – supply and demand – which generates the point of equilibrium.

The Market Equilibrium

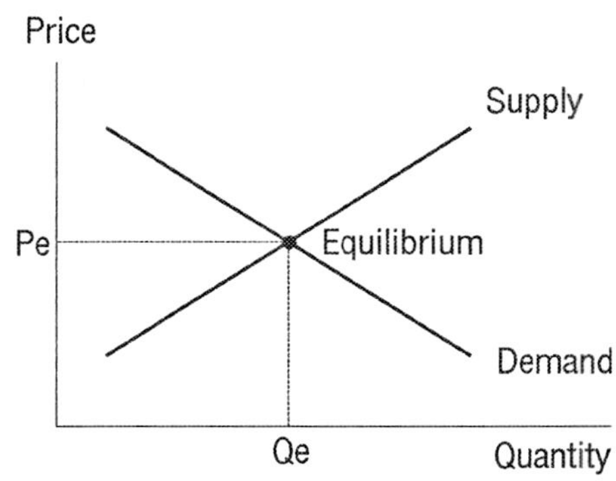

There is one price and one level of output at which supply and demand are in balance. This is the point of **equilibrium**. At this point and at this price, the amount which consumers are prepared to demand and the amount which the producers supply are in balance.

If the price were too low, then demand would be greater than supply. Those consumers who wanted the goods in question would force the price up, thereby reducing the level of demand and increasing the level of supply. This pressure would continue until the equilibrium point was reached.

Conversely, if the price were set too high, then supply would be greater than demand. Whenever there is oversupply of any good, the price of that good falls. The price will continue to fall until it reaches the equilibrium point, where supply and demand are in balance.

3 Sensitivity of Demand – Elasticity

3.1 Introduction

Learning objectives

25.1.4 Describe, calculate and **interpret** own price elasticity of demand and its impact on total revenues.

25.1.5 Identify the factors that determine own price elasticity of demand.

Returning to our demand function, we can see that demand is a function of

- Price.
- Prices of other goods.
- Tastes.
- Incomes.
- Other factors, such as advertising, etc.

Elasticity is the concept that economists use to explain the degree of sensitivity demand exhibits in respect of these factors.

Formula to learn

$$\text{Elasticity} = \frac{\text{Percentage change in quantity demanded}}{\text{Percentage change in demand factor}}$$

3.2 Price elasticity of demand (PED)

The price elasticity of demand reflects the sensitivity of demand with regard to changes in the price of the good.

Formula to learn

$$\text{Price elasticity of demand} = \frac{\text{Percentage change in quantity demanded}}{\text{Percentage change in price}}$$

Given the inverse relationship between quantity demanded and price, the price elasticity of demand (PED) will always be negative. The size of the value reflects the degree of responsiveness. If the PED is between –1 and $-\infty$, the demand is referred to as **elastic** with a PED of $-\infty$ being *perfect elasticity* – a horizontal demand curve. If PED is elastic, it means that the demand is more than proportionately responsive to changes in price.

If PED lies between –1 and 0, the demand is referred to as **inelastic** and is less than proportionately responsive to changes in price with a PED of 0 being *perfectly inelastic* – a vertical line. Where PED is exactly –1, this is referred to as **unit elasticity** and reflects the point where a fall in price is matched by a proportionate rise in quantity. For example, a 1% fall in price leads to a 1% rise in quantity demanded.

Example

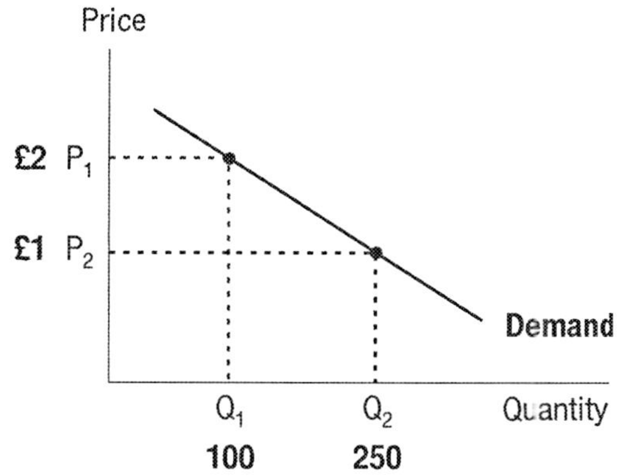

As price falls from P_1 to P_2, quantity rises from Q_1 to Q_2. The price elasticity of demand is

$$\text{PED} = \frac{\frac{Q_2 - Q_1}{Q_1}}{\frac{P_2 - P_1}{P_1}}$$

Note that the calculation of the percentage change of both quantity and price is done by **dividing the change by the starting price or quantity value**. Using the values in the example

$$\text{PED} = \frac{\frac{250-100}{100}}{\frac{£1-£2}{£2}} = -3 \text{ (elastic)}$$

The relationship between elasticity and revenue

Learning objective

25.2.6 Explain the relationship between total revenue, average revenue and marginal revenues for a normal demand schedule.

There are three important measures of revenue.

Formula to learn

$$\text{Total revenue} = \text{Quantity} \times \text{Price}$$

Formula to learn

$$\text{Average revenue} = \frac{\text{Total revenue}}{\text{Quantity}}$$

Formula to learn

Marginal revenue = The change in total revenue which results from an increase or decrease of one unit of sales.

The Revenue Curves

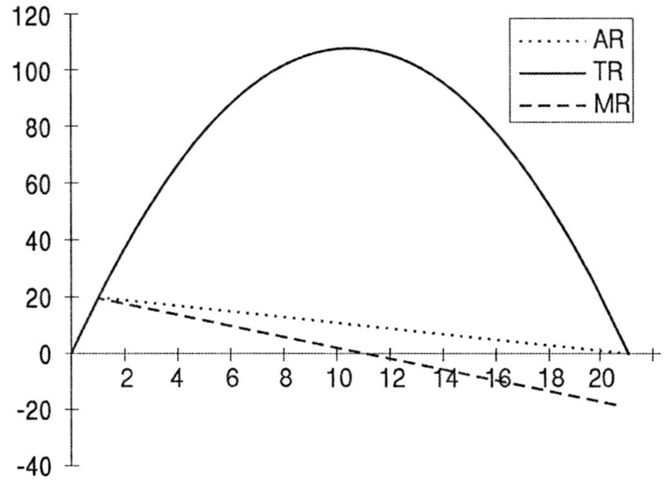

It will be noticed from the diagram below that the elasticity of demand is not constant along the demand curve. This is because it is a proportionate rather than an absolute value. PED ranges from minus infinity at the top end of the demand curve to zero as the demand curve touches the quantity axis. The logic behind this relationship, as shown in the diagram below, is quite simple. At the top end of the demand curve, if prices move by a relatively small amount (ΔP_1), quantity will rise by a proportionately greater amount (ΔQ_1). At the bottom end of the demand curve, a dramatic decrease in price (ΔP_2) will only increase quantity by a small proportion (ΔQ_2).

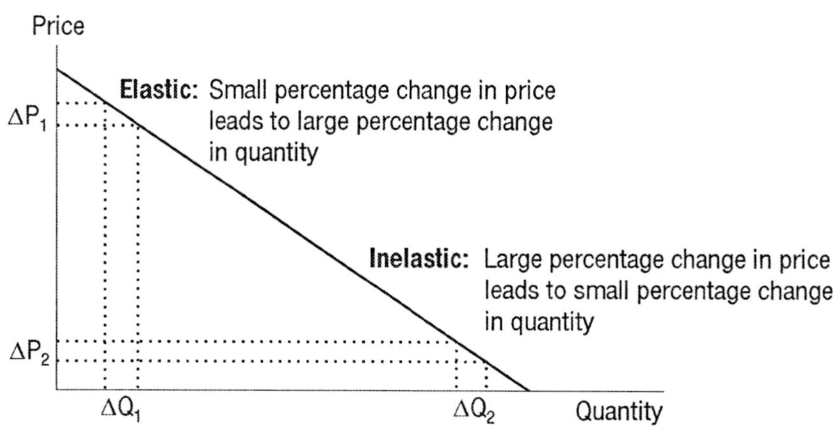

Consequently, each demand curve has both an elastic and an inelastic portion. The top of the demand curve is the elastic portion ranging from minus infinity down to **unit elasticity** of –1. The lower half of the demand curve is the inelastic portion as elasticity ranges from –1 to 0.

This links to the shape of the total revenue curve. In the elastic portion of the demand curve, if prices are reduced by, let us say 2% ΔP_1, quantity demanded will increase by more than 2% ΔQ_1. Consequently, total revenue, which is simply price times quantity, will increase.

Conversely, on the inelastic portion of the demand curve, if prices fall by 2%, quantity demanded will rise by proportionately less than 2%. The impact of a price fall on the inelastic portion of the demand curve will be that total revenue itself will fall. Therefore, on the elastic portion, total revenue is rising. On the inelastic portion, total revenue is falling. Total revenue must peak at the point of unit elasticity.

The marginal revenue schedule simply measures the impact on total revenue of one additional unit of sales. The initial impact is strong, as small price decreases lead to large quantity increases. The rate of increase in total revenue, however, slows as we approach unit elasticity. Beyond the point of unit elasticity, total revenue falls and therefore, the marginal revenue is negative. Consequently, the marginal revenue line lies below the average revenue line and cuts the horizontal axis immediately below the point of unit elasticity.

We will return to these revenue curves later on in our studies when we review the theories of the firm, for it is in the interplay between costs and revenue that output decisions will be made.

3.3 Income elasticity demand (YED)

So far in our analysis, we have looked at the price elasticity of demand, the responsiveness of the quantity demanded to the change in price of the good. An alternative formulation would be to look at the responsiveness of quantity demanded to changes in income.

Formula to learn

$$\text{Income elasticity of demand} = \frac{\text{Percentage change in quantity demanded}}{\text{Percentage change in income}}$$

Here, it is the **sign of the relationship which is important** rather than its overall magnitude. If the income elasticity demand (YED) is positive, this means that the quantity demanded increases as income increases. This would indicate that the good is a normal good. In the case of inferior goods, the quantity demanded would fall as incomes rise. The classic example of an inferior good would be supermarket 'value' products. As incomes rise, consumers do not simply buy more supermarket 'value' products, they move on to a higher consumption plane and buy higher quality food products.

There are certain goods, referred to as **Giffen goods**, which are staples of diet. Here, as income decreases, consumption will increase reflecting the fact that as incomes are contracted, the consumer has to retreat to the staples in order to keep themselves alive.

However, it is not true to say that all inferior goods are Giffen goods.

3.4 Cross-elasticity demand (XED)

Learning objective

25.1.6 Explain, calculate and **interpret** the concept of cross elasticity of demand (as applied to substitute and complementary goods).

The cross-elasticity demand measures the relationship between the quantity demanded and a change in the price of another good. Again, it is the sign which is important.

Formula to learn

$$\text{Cross-elasticity of demand} = \frac{\text{Percentage change in quantity demanded}}{\text{Percentage change in price of other goods}}$$

If the relationship is **positive**, this means that the quantity demanded of the good is rising as the price of that other good is itself rising. This would tend to indicate that the relationship between the two goods is that of **substitutes**. For example, if the price of tea rises, then the quantity demanded of coffee would also rise as consumers switch between the two drinks.

If the relationship between the two items is **negative**, then this would tend to indicate that the goods are **complements** (goods which are bought together). Here, as the price of the other good increases, the demand for the complementary good will decrease, leading to an overall negative effect.

4 The Theory of Costs

4.1 Introduction

Learning objectives

25.2.1 Distinguish between explicit (accounting) costs and opportunity (economic) costs.

25.2.2 Explain the concept of normal, supernormal and sub-normal levels of profit.

25.2.3 Define fixed costs, variable costs, marginal costs, total costs and average costs.

25.3.1 Define short-run and long-run in the context of cost behaviour.

So far, we have concentrated on the demand curve and the revenue side of the business. As mentioned above, the theory of the firm will combine revenues with costs to determine the appropriate output condition. Let us now turn our attention to cost behaviour.

In economics, it is important to remember that we are not simply considering the financial costs but, more appropriately, the **opportunity cost**: the cost that we incur by losing the opportunity of undertaking other courses of action. Consequently, the cost of undertaking a certain course of action is the return that we would have generated by undertaking the next best alternative.

Economists also regard profit as being part of the cost of a business rather than, as accountants would see it, the simple result of revenue minus expenditure. The rationale behind this view is that the entrepreneur will only remain committed to the business if it generates sufficient profits to cover his or her expected return. These profits, referred to as **normal profits**, are a compensation to the entrepreneur for

- The loss of income which they would otherwise have earned.
- The cost in terms of interest lost on the capital injected into the business.
- The risk they have undertaken starting their own business as opposed to working for somebody else.

These profits represent a **fixed cost** of the business, and if they are not met, then the entrepreneur will logically close the business down.

In economics, it is conventional to break cost behaviour down into the short-run and the long-run. There is no strict definition of what short-run is, other than it is the period in which your operations are constrained by, for example, the capital stock of the business. The long-run, by definition, is the period in which all factors of production are totally flexible.

In the short-run, the entrepreneur is restricted by the size of the factory. In the long-run, they have the ability to expand the size of the factory, the plant and the machinery within it in order to cope with increased demand. The short-run constraint is the current factory size. This is not a problem in the long-run.

Let us first look at cost behaviour in the short-run.

4.2 Short-run costs

Learning objectives

25.2.4 Explain the shapes of the short-run marginal cost, average variable cost, average fixed cost, and average total cost curves.

25.2.5 Explain the law of diminishing marginal returns and its impact on the shape of short-run cost curves.

In the short-run, the behaviour of costs is determined by the law of **increasing and then decreasing returns to a factor**. This law states that given a fixed capital stock, it will be possible, by injecting more labour, to gradually increase production until that capital stock (the factory and machinery) is operating at its optimal level. Beyond this point, each additional unit of labour which is added to the factory will produce less, hence increasing, then decreasing returns to the factor (labour).

It is conventional in economic analysis to look at the behaviour of average costs in the short-run. The following diagram summarises the behaviour of average total cost, variable cost and fixed cost. The difference between fixed and variable costs is that fixed costs, as their name suggests, are fixed for the short-run; these are costs which cannot be avoided. The variable costs will vary in line with the level of production.

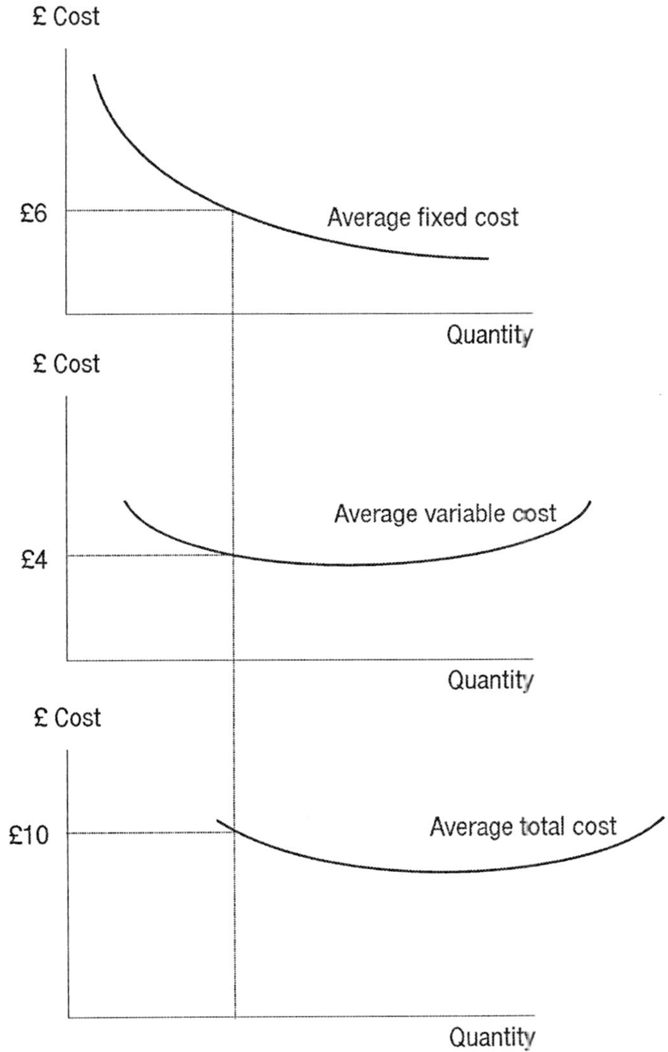

Average fixed costs decline as the total fixed cost is divided over a progressively greater quantity of output. **Average variable costs initially decline** as the company benefits from increasing returns to the factor (labour). However, eventually, decreasing returns set in and at this point, **average variable costs begin to rise**. Average total costs simply reflect the addition of the two schedules together. Initially, the increase in average variable costs after the point of optimal output is offset by the continuing fall in average fixed costs. Progressively, however, the rise in average variable costs strengthens and eventually outweighs the average fixed cost decrease.

The fourth, and perhaps most important cost curve, is the **marginal cost curve**. As with the marginal revenue curve, this measures the **impact on total costs of one additional unit of production**.

Initially, total costs rise but at a slower rate, reflecting the increasing returns to the factor (labour). However, as diminishing returns to the factor set in, then costs begin to rise at a faster rate.

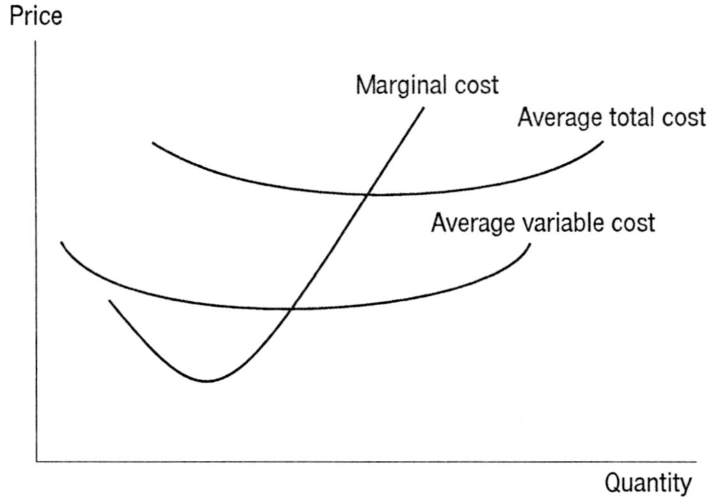

One important point to note is that the **marginal cost curve cuts both the average variable cost and the average total cost at their minimum points**. The logic behind this is, hopefully, reasonably clear.

If the marginal cost of producing an additional item is lower than the average total cost, then the production of that item must in turn reduce average costs.

Example

If the total cost for producing 100 units is £3,000, the average total cost is £30. The marginal cost, the impact on total cost, for the 101st unit is £20. The average total cost is now £3,020 ÷ 101 = £29.90. Therefore, average total cost has fallen.

Conversely, if the marginal cost of producing an item is greater than the average total cost, then the production of this item will increase the average total cost.

Therefore, if marginal cost is below average cost, average cost must be falling. If marginal cost is above average cost, then average cost must be rising. The point at which marginal cost cuts average cost must be the point at which average cost is neither rising nor falling, therefore the **minimum point** on the schedule. This logic applies both to the average variable cost and the average total cost schedule.

4.3 Long-run costs

Learning objective	**25.3.2 Explain** the notions of economies of scale, a minimum efficient scale and diseconomies of scale and their impact on the shape of the long-run average cost curve.

In the short-run, we are constrained by one of the factors of production being fixed. It is conventional to view this as being the capital stock. In the long-run, however, if the company wishes to, it can increase its capital stock and therefore, there is no limit to the level of production.

However, once a new level of production is established then, effectively, the firm is joining or entering a new short-run constraint. Consequently, economists view the long-run as being simply an **envelope (combination) of all the short-run possibilities**.

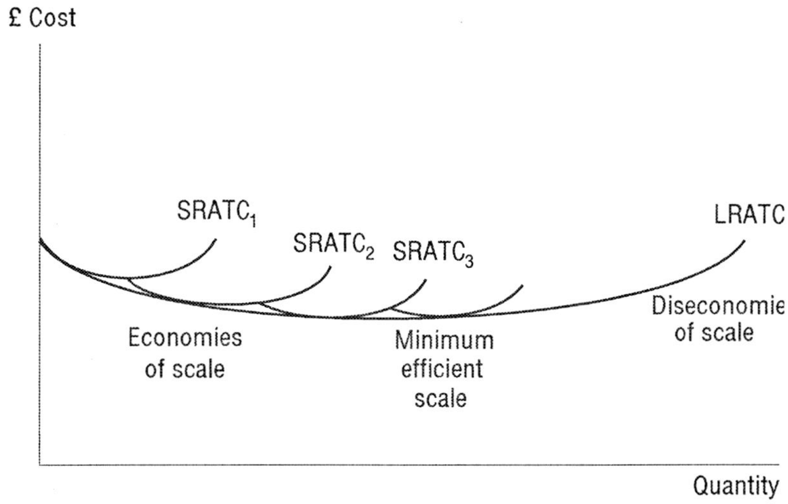

The term envelope, in this context, refers to the fact that the long-run is simply a relationship derived from the combination of any possible short-run position.

With regard to the overall shape of the long-run average total cost curve, most economists believe that, initially, it is downward sloping. For the first stage, this reflects the fact that there is probably a minimum productive size which can be used and, consequently, a minimum capital stock. If you wish to produce less than this minimum stocks optimal output, the firm will be operating at a non-optimal level on the short-run cost curve for that plant.

Moving on from this, the general belief is that long-run average costs decline, reflecting that as the size of an operation increases, it is possible to benefit from **economies of scale**. Economists have tried to measure the output level at which further economies of scale become unimportant, i.e. the point at which the long-run average total cost curve becomes horizontal. This output level is referred to as the **Minimum Efficient Scale (MES)**. Perhaps slightly more controversially, many economists believe that long-run costs, after a certain level of production has been reached, begin to increase reflecting not economies, but **diseconomies of scale**. The most obvious example of this would be perhaps a loss of control by a central management team of a large conglomerate.

The key thing to remember is this central divide between long-run and short-run costs. **In the short-run, there is constraint; in the long-run, flexibility**.

These concepts of cost and revenue are brought together in the theories of the firm.

5 The Theories of the Firm

5.1 Perfect competition

Learning objectives

25.2.2 Explain the concept of normal, supernormal and sub-normal levels of profit.

25.2.7 Explain the relationship between marginal cost and marginal revenue and how this determines the profit maximising level of output for a firm.

25.3.3 Explain the relationship between long run marginal costs and long run average costs and explain how this determines the level of output for productive efficiency to arise.

25.4.1 Identify the conditions that characterise a perfectly competitive ('price-taker') market.

25.4.2 Explain the conditions of long-run equilibrium for a price-taker.

25.4.5 Describe the shape of the long run supply curve for a perfectly competitive industry.

5.1.1 Equilibrium position – normal profits

The simplest theory of the firm is perfect competition. In this model, we make a number of assumptions and create a fairly unrealistic market place. The key assumptions in the model are as follows.

- There are an **infinite number of buyers and sellers** in the market place, and no one buyer or seller is large enough to influence price.
- All products are **homogenous**, there is no differentiation between the products of one company and those of another.
- All consumers act **rationally** in order to maximise the utility (satisfaction) that they receive from consumption of a limited income. Equally, all producers are profit maximisers.

It is a basic profit maximisation rule that in order to maximise profits, the firm should produce at the point where **marginal cost cuts marginal revenue (marginal cost cutting from below)**.

The Profit-Maximising Condition

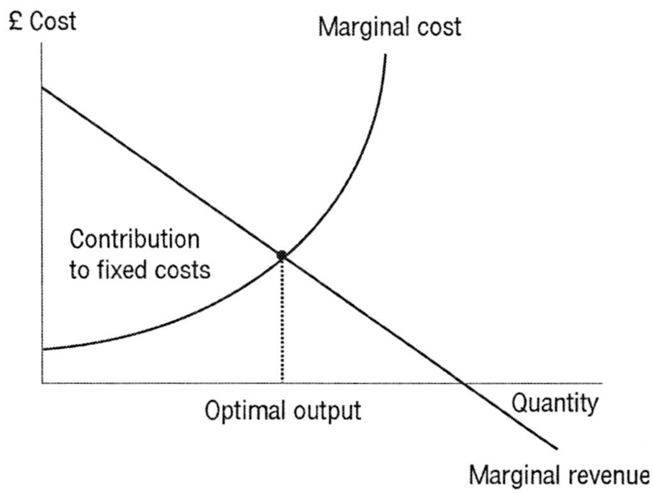

For any level of output up to the optimal output, the marginal revenue (the impact on total revenue) is greater than the marginal cost (the impact on total cost) and, consequently, it is worth producing any of these units. This does not mean that the company will be making profits because here we are talking about marginal cost and marginal revenue, and these concepts only deal with variable elements and in particular, the variable costs.

The fixed costs of the business will be incurred whatever the level of output and therefore are irrelevant in the decision-making process. These costs which are fixed in the short-run are referred to as the **sunk costs** of the business. What we are in effect maximising here is the contribution that the business makes towards its fixed costs.

It clearly makes no sense for the company to produce beyond the optimal output because every unit produced beyond this point would represent a drain on that contribution, since all units are costing more than they generate in terms of revenue.

- There is **perfect information** – all consumers and producers have perfect, instant and free information as to prices and goods available.
- There are no barriers to entry or exit from the market.
- There is **no economic friction** (transactional costs) involved in the consumer's decision to buy from one producer rather than another.

In effect, what we have by using these assumptions is a market which is perfectly free.

Supply and demand in the market place will establish a price. As far as each individual firm is concerned, this is the price at which they can sell goods. However, because there is an infinite market and they are a very small part of it, at that price, they can sell as many goods as they want.

The Firm's Demand Curve in Perfect Competition

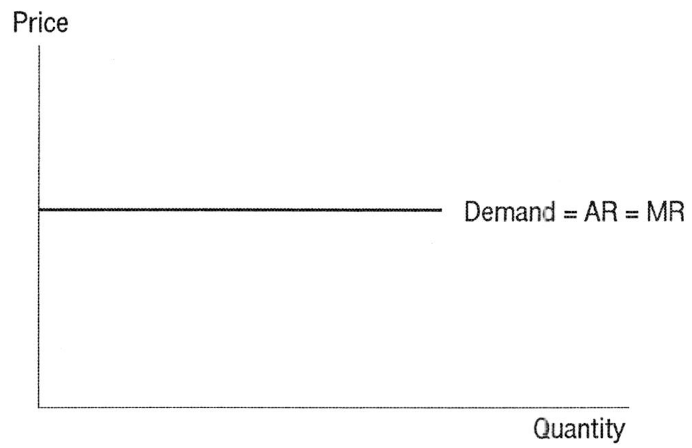

Effectively, as far as they are concerned, the firm is facing a horizontal demand curve. Not only does demand equal average revenue, but it also equals marginal revenue, since there is no need to reduce price in order to sell additional items.

On top of this, we superimpose the company's cost schedules which will be common to all companies in that industry. We can now arrive at the point of optimal output, Q_E.

Equilibrium in Perfect Competition

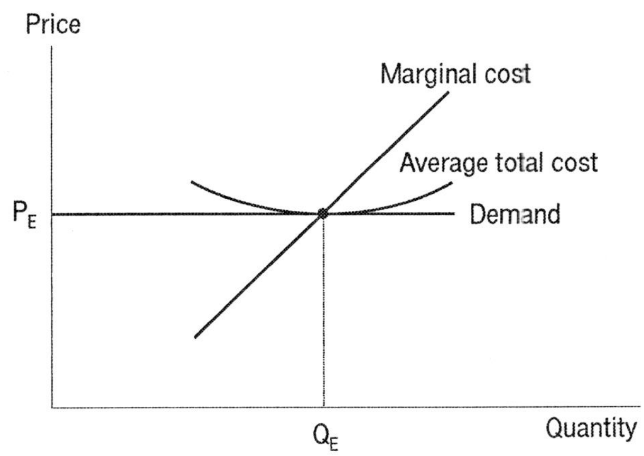

Q_E maximises the profitability of the business since, at that point, marginal cost cuts marginal revenue (marginal cost cutting from below). It also represents the point at which marginal cost cuts average total cost, therefore the price charged covers total costs. Remember that total costs also include profit (the normal profit) and, therefore, the firm is in breakeven with no factors giving rise to change.

5.1.2 Disequilibrium – supernormal profit

Learning objectives

25.1.7 Explain, calculate and **interpret** elasticity of supply and its dependence on the flexibility of factors of production.

25.4.3 Explain the market mechanics through which only normal levels of profit can be earned by price takers in the long-run.

25.4.4 Explain the relationship between short run supply and marginal cost for a price-taker.

25.4.6 Explain the decision by a price taker facing economic losses to either continue to operate or shut down.

If, for some reason, the price rises (perhaps, an increase in the level of demand in the market), then the price will rise to P_2. At this point, the price P_2 is charged and the quantity produced is established at the point where price, and therefore marginal revenue, equates to marginal cost (Q_2). However, at this point, the price more than compensates for the average total cost. The area P_2ABC represents what is referred to as **supernormal profit**.

Disequilibrium – Supernormal Profits

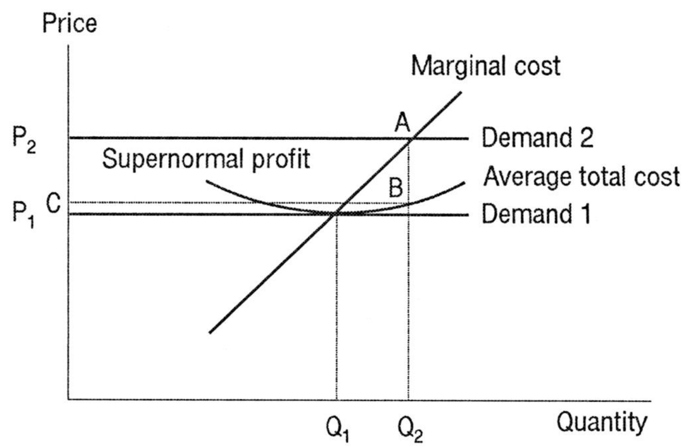

We can assess the business sensitivity to this change by considering its elasticity of supply that is calculated in a very similar manner to elasticity of demand, specifically

Formula to learn

$$\text{Elasticity of supply} = \frac{\text{Percentage change in quantity sold}}{\text{Percentage change in price}}$$

Due to the freely available information that exists in this market, other players will be aware of the availability of these supernormal profits and will be attracted into the market. In terms of the overall supply and demand in the market, this will lead to an increase in supply, and the supply curve will shift to the right. The consequence of this will be for price to fall. Price will continue to fall until the supernormal profits are eroded away and the market moves back to balance at a point where marginal cost cuts marginal revenue and average total costs are at their minimum.

Taking the opposite scenario, if prices were to fall, then the producer would face one of two options.

Disequilibrium – Prices Below Breakeven

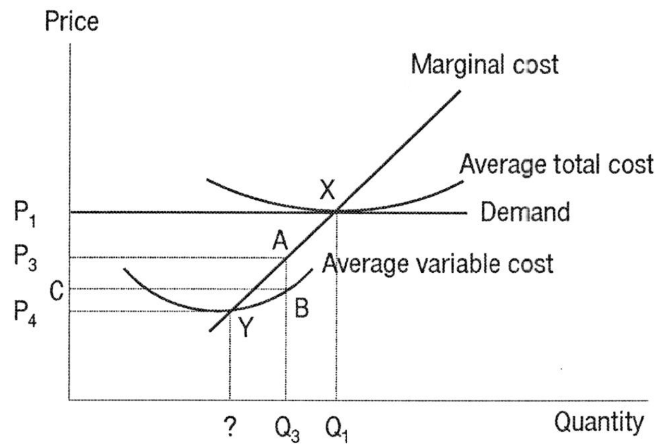

If prices were to fall to the level P_3, then the optimal quantity of output would be Q_3, for at that point, marginal cost cuts marginal revenue (marginal cost cutting from below). However, at that level of output, the firm is not covering its total costs. It is, however, making the **contribution** P_3 ABC towards its fixed costs and consequently would continue to produce in the short-run until it was able to avoid the longer run fixed costs.

However, if price were to fall to P_4, then not only would the company not be covering its fixed cost, it would also be operating **below its average variable costs**. There would be no sense in the business continuing at this level and so, consequently, at P_4 the rational producer would cease production immediately.

In summary, if price falls to any level between point X and point Y, then the business will continue to produce in the short-run, but in the long-run will withdraw from the market. If the price falls to a level below point Y, the firm will immediately shut down.

The impact of both of these moves will be to reduce the level of supply in the market place. As supply is reduced, the supply curve for the overall market gradually shifts to the left. Consequently, price will rise from P_1 to P_2.

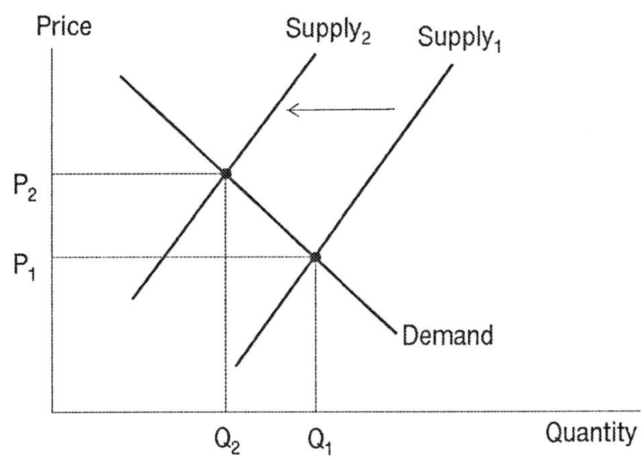

Once again, this process of change will continue until the firm returns to its point of equilibrium at which marginal cost cuts marginal revenue at the lowest point on the average total cost curve.

Overall, this system reflects a **self-balancing model** which moves to optimum level of output and reflects the efficiency of free markets.

It can also be used to prove the shape of the supply curve. Supply is simply the relationship between the price and the quantity produced. In the case of a profit-maximising firm, the decision as to the quantity to produce will be determined by the objective of profit maximisation, **MC = MR**. Given that the MR line is a horizontal line at price, then MC above the AVC equals the supply function.

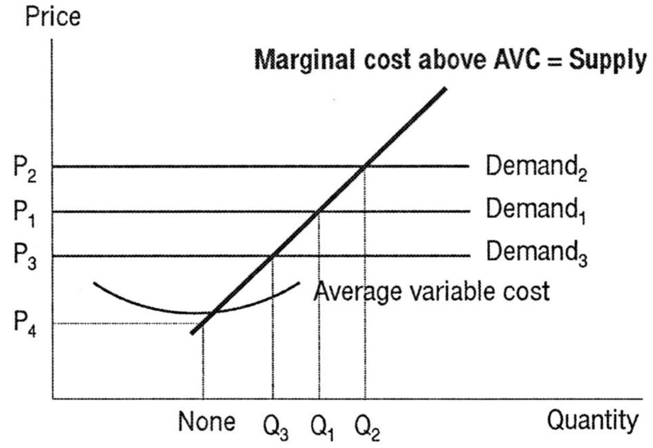

5.2 Monopoly

Learning objectives

25.4.7 Identify the conditions that characterise a pure monopoly.

25.4.8 Explain the conditions of long run equilibrium for a monopoly.

25.4.9 Distinguish between the equilibrium price, output levels, and productive efficiency of a monopoly compared to a perfectly competitive firm.

25.4.10 Explain price discrimination and the conditions under which it will prevail.

If perfect competition is a model based on an infinite number of buyers and sellers, then monopoly is the other extreme where there is only **one seller**.

In theories of monopoly, the monopolist does not face a horizontal demand curve acting as a **price taker** (as in the case of perfect competition), but rather the monopolist faces the demand curve of the whole market. It is a downward-sloping demand curve and it is the monopolist who sets the price.

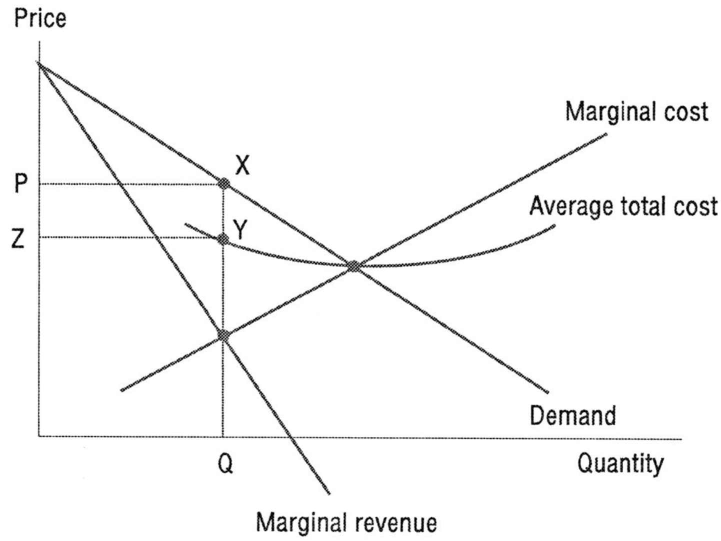

The monopolist is assumed to be a profit maximiser and, consequently, sets output at the level where marginal cost cuts marginal revenue (marginal cost-cutting from below) establishing a level of output of

Q. From the demand curve, this quantity Q can be sold at price P. This price, however, is more than is required to cover the average total costs of the business, and the area PXYZ represents supernormal profits. Unlike the situation in a perfectly competitive world, the monopoly is able to **preserve supernormal profits**.

Note that in the case of a monopoly, there is **no supply curve**, just a single point at which they are prepared to supply. This point will always be on the elastic part of the demand curve, as only then would marginal revenue be positive.

This is one of the essential ingredients for a monopoly, in some way, to be able to preserve their status. The factors which may lead to ongoing monopoly are as follows.

- **Legal protection** through patent rights, etc.
- A **natural monopoly**, where the rise of the company concerned prevents any new rivals entering the market place. For example, if a company, perhaps initially through a legal right, was able to create a monopoly, they might be able to grow during the period of protection under the patent, to such a size that it would be impossible for any rivals to enter the market place. Competition on costs would not be possible, since the larger operation would be benefiting from the economies of scale.

Equally, the monopoly might use the supernormal profits generated to acquire other business that are part of the productive chain and thereby prevent any competition from entering the market. This process is referred to as **integration**. In our example below, we consider a brewer who may expand into other areas in order to preserve the monopoly power that they start with.

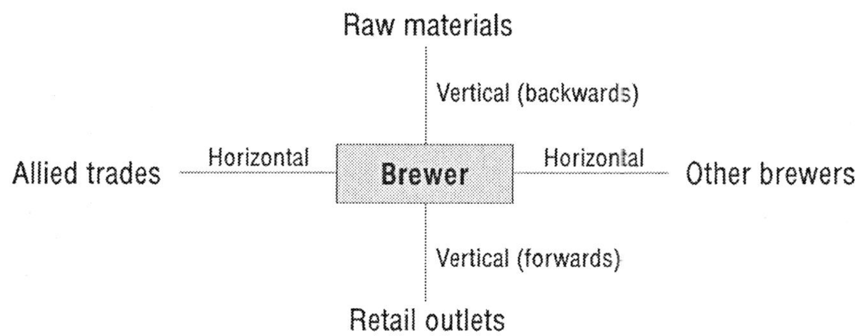

It is possible to compare the outcomes under a monopoly and perfect competition and therefore judge which is the most appropriate for society.

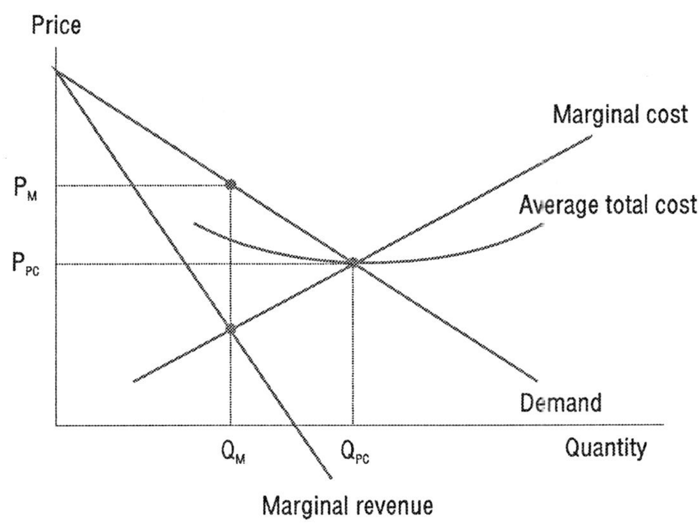

A monopolist would have an output level of P_M, producing quantity Q_M, and earn supernormal profits. It will be noticed at this point that the monopolist is not operating at the minimum point on the average total cost curve and therefore is inefficient.

The perfectly competitive firm would be operating at the point where supply and demand are in balance. Demand is the average revenue line – the downward-sloping demand curve. Supply is the marginal cost curve (assuming that the combined cost curve of the perfectly competitive firms is the same as that of the monopolist).

Consequently, the perfectly competitive firm will be producing at the level $P_{PC}Q_{PC}$, producing a greater quantity at a lower price and operating on the most efficient point on the average total cost curve. Overall, many economists would argue that monopolies represent an inefficiency, the price of which will be paid for by ordinary consumers.

However, this argument does ignore the fact that monopolies by virtue of their size may well be able to command a lower overall cost and, therefore, whilst taking supernormal profits, may actually provide consumers with a lower price.

A further criticism of monopoly power is that a monopoly is able to abuse its position through **price discrimination**.

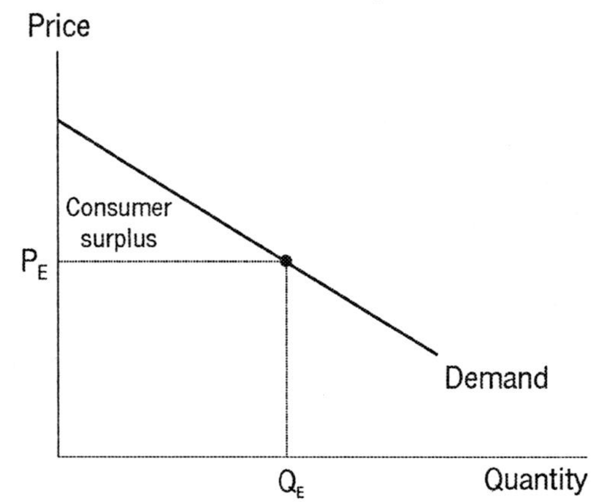

At the equilibrium price, the consumer is paying P_E for quantity Q_E. However, the demand curve tells us that because the first good that they consumed gave them a greater level of satisfaction, they were prepared to pay a higher price. This is referred to as the **consumer surplus**. Monopolies have the ability to exploit this surplus through differential pricing. For example, charging a higher price for the first units consumed or, alternatively, where the market demand for a good is made up of several sources, e.g. rail travel charging a higher price for commuter travel as opposed to the price for off-peak fares. Price discrimination will only be possible where there is no possibility of leakage between the two markets. Hence, it is most appropriate for markets such as rail travel, where the good is a personal service.

The most extreme case of price discrimination is where each customer is charged a different price. This is known as perfect price discrimination. In this situation, marginal revenue and price will be identical, as the overall price will not fall for all items if an additional unit is sold.

5.3 Other industrial structures

In the previous two sections we have discussed two extreme economic structures, perfect competition and a monopoly. In reality most businesses operate somewhere between these two extremes and there are four structures to be aware of that, in descending order of competition, are

- **Perfect competition** – discussed in detail earlier
- **Monopolistic competition** – where there are a number of competing firms with varying degrees of product differentiation
- **Oligopoly** – Where there are only a few competing producers acting as a collective monopoly
- **Monopoly** – discussed in detail earlier.

6 Assessing Industries and Companies

6.1 The business cycle

Learning objective | **25.5.1 Understand** how business cycles may affect relative industry performance.

The business cycle could be defined as fluctuations in the general level of economic activity. It has been an observed phenomenon in economies for a long period of time. This can be seen from observing a fairly typical pattern of boom and bust exhibited by the US economy.

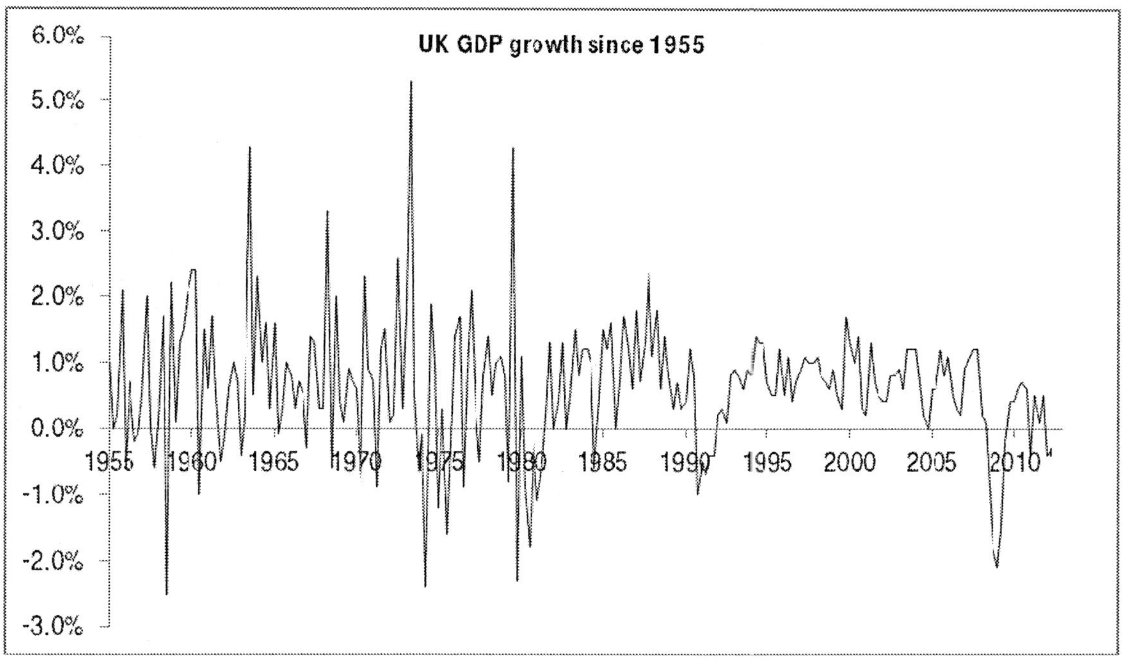

The business cycle is made up of an **expansion** phase that culminates in a **peak or boom** period, when GDP grows rapidly and there are high levels of activity.

The economy then **contracts**, GDP grows at a slower rate (or even contracts) and unemployment increases. The bottom of the contraction phase is referred to as the recessionary trough. If GDP contracts for two consecutive quarters and unemployment rises, this will be referred to as a **recession**. Where a recession continues for a prolonged period of time, this would be referred to as a depression.

Generally, there is an upward trend to the GDP through time.

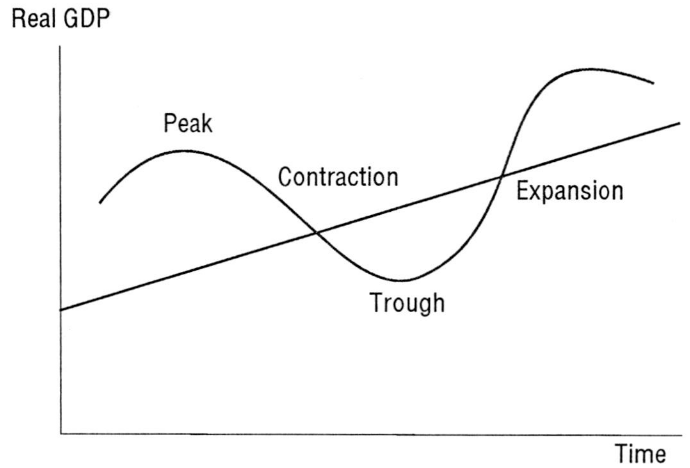

The level of economic activity is measured by variables such as the rate of unemployment and changes in real GDP (Real GDP measures the real change in output after allowing for inflation). Economic cycles typically have a term of six to twelve years but do not follow a perfectly regular pattern, so governments and businesses look out for key economic indicators (see later) to track where they are within the cycle. It has also been suggested that there is a longer term (49-50 year) cycle, the Kondratiev wave, that is a function of technological changes and developments.

6.2 Product life cycle

Learning objective	**25.5.3 Explain** the product life cycle and the characteristics of each phase (introduction, growth, maturity and decline).

6.2.1 Introduction

The product life cycle expresses the pattern of growth, maturity, stability and/or decay experienced in many industries. It can be useful in estimating growth in industry sales and profitability.

The life cycle can be illustrated as follows.

Life Cycle of Activity

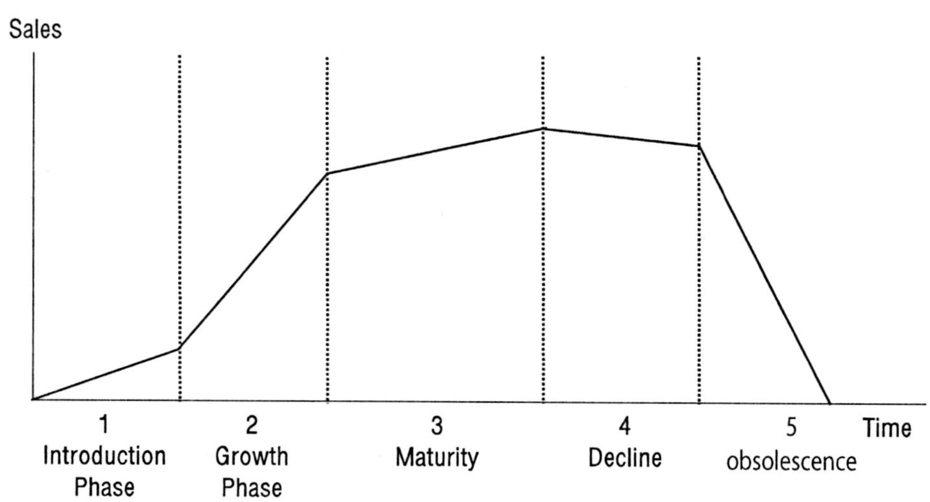

6.2.2 Introduction phase

- **Introduction Phase** – the start-up phase of a new product when sales and sales growth are fairly low due to consumer uncertainty, high prices and other related factors. Profit margins are low due to high start-up costs and low demand.

6.2.3 Growth phase

- **Rapid accelerating growth** – the market develops and demand expands substantially, giving high growth in sales. Profit margins are high due to lack of industry capacity. New entrants will have to work hard to develop their own niches and to differentiate their product from that of the pioneer in the market.

6.2.4 Maturity

- **Mature growth** – initial demand for the product has been satisfied and growth levels in sales decline. Profit margins decline as competition continues to enter the market. Competition becomes based more on price rather than product differentiation.
- **Market maturity** – sales grow in line with the economy, profit margins move towards a normal level due to competition. The emphasis shifts away from product innovation towards cost efficiency due to price-based competition becoming more important.

6.2.5 Decline

- **Deceleration of growth and decline** – shifts of demand, growth in substitute products, etc. cause demand to decline. Profit margins fall as companies compete for falling demand and capital moves to other more profitable areas of the economy.

6.2.6 Obsolescence

Where the product has reached the end of its life due to technical or regulatory changes and developments, with demand falling to zero and profit potential being extinguished.

6.2.7 Implications for investment decisions

It is, of course, easy to classify the stages of growth in the above way. The difficulty lies in identifying how long each phase will last and the expected level of change of sales as a result. Nevertheless, the approach offers a useful analytical framework.

Generally, investors will find that growing industries will offer higher growth in dividends. However, the higher risk levels implicit in such industries increase the required rate of return, reducing the present value of the dividends. The key is to find the companies with the highest returns relative to the risks involved.

6.3 Competitive strategy and industry structure

Learning objective	**25.5.2 Explain** Porter's five competitive forces that drive industry competition.

6.3.1 The five competitive forces

When analysing an industry, it is vital to understand the competitive forces that are driving that industry. Competitive forces make an industry more or less attractive to companies. In addition, the way a company responds to competitive forces will determine its profitability. A major reference work in this area is that of Porter, who developed a 'five forces model'.

In his analysis, Porter considers five key influences on industry structure at any point in time.

- New entrants.
- Industry competitors.
- Substitutes.
- Suppliers.
- Buyers.

The relative effect of each of these forces will change over time as the industry develops. The five forces will affect the ability of a company to create value and capture this value for itself, rather than passing the value on to its customers through lower sales prices, or to its suppliers through higher input prices.

The Five Competitive Forces

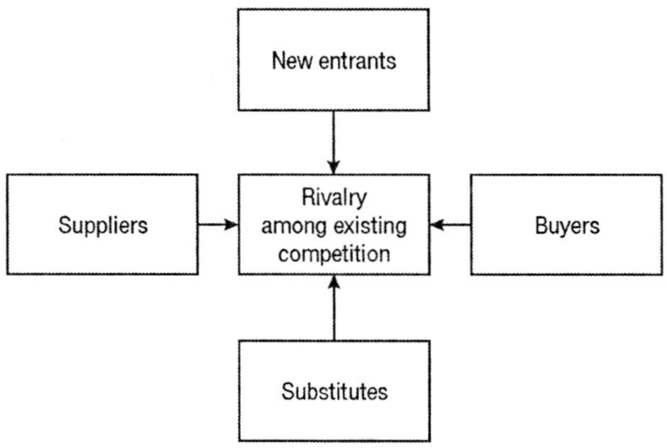

Source: Porter

6.3.2 New entrants

The inability to prevent new entrants from joining the market means that any firm currently operating with supernormal profits in an industry will see those profits eroded over time.

The key driver of longer term profitability will be the ability of the firms currently in the industry to construct effective barriers to entry to prevent new competition entering the market.

Examples of entry barriers are as follows.

- Low prices relative to costs.
- The need to invest large amounts of financial resources to compete.
- The availability of capital to invest in the market.
- Economies of scale meaning new entrants will not be able to produce goods or services as cheaply as existing companies.
- Distribution channels controlled by existing companies in the market.
- High costs for customers to switch from one supplier to another.
- Government policy and regulation.

6.3.3 Industry rivalry

There are a number of factors that will affect the competitive rivalry within the industry. The more intense the rivalry, the lower the potential for profit.

Factors affecting industry rivalry are as follows.

- The number of firms competing in the industry.
- The relative size of the competing firms. Firms of equal size will be more serious rivals to each other.
- The rate of sales growth. Slow rates of growth in industry sales means more competition for market share.
- Fixed costs. Companies with high fixed costs are more likely to compete aggressively for sales, since the revenue will flow straight through to profit.
- The level of exit barriers. If it is hard to leave an industry, rivalry will be greater, since companies have no choice but to stay in the industry.

6.3.4 Substitute goods

Analogous to the entry of new firms into the market, the presence of potential substitutes will have an impact on the profitability of an industry. The existence of good substitute products will put a ceiling on the price that the industry can charge for its products. The closer the substitute is in terms of performance, the greater the pressure.

6.3.5 Supplier power

The power of both suppliers and consumers will have an important impact on the competitive structure of an industry and its resultant profitability.

Factors affecting the bargaining power of the industry versus its suppliers are as follows.

- The number of suppliers. If there are only a few, they have more power.
- The importance of the good supplied to the industry.
- The availability of substitute products for that currently being supplied.

6.3.6 The power of buyers

The final element of the industry structure is the relationship between the industry and the buyers or the consumers of the good. This is very much the same as the position facing suppliers and it will be a matter of the balance between relative bargaining power which determines whether the industry has the ability to exploit the buyers or whether the industry is itself exploited.

Factors affecting the bargaining power of buyers are as follows.

- The proportion of sales bought by one buyer.
- The importance of the product to the buyer.
- The proportion of the buyer's total costs that the product represents. Products that are relatively minor to the buyer will be able to increase prices more easily than products that represent a major proportion of the buyer's budget.
- The degree of cost pressure the buyer is suffering from its own customers.

6.4 SWOT analysis

earning objective	**25.5.4 Explain** the concept of strengths, weaknesses, opportunities and threats (SWOT) analysis and its role in corporate evaluation.

A popular form of analysis to assess a firm's position involves its Strengths, Weaknesses, Opportunities and Threats (SWOT). Strengths and weaknesses are firm specific while opportunities and threats arise from the external environment.

- **Strengths** will include answers to the following questions: what is the firm good at? What specific skills does the firm possess? What intellectual property does the firm possess? Is the firm in a strong position with suppliers and other parties?
- **Weakness** will point to outdated products, shortcomings in the workforce and related practices, a weak financial position and missing links in business relationships.
- **Opportunities** will focus on new markets and technologies, competitor weaknesses and changes in the external environment which can be exploited.
- **Threats** could include social and legislative changes, adverse macro-economic conditions and competitor actions.

SWOT analysis is a useful way of looking at the business environment and a firm's place within it.

6.5 The four 'P's of marketing

Learning objective

25.5.5 Explain the 4Ps marketing mix (product, price, promotion and place) in the context of analysing competitive advantage and threats.

Tutor tip

This area is regularly examined by way of definitions.

In understanding the processes influencing competitive advantage and threats, marketing specialists focus on the four 'P's when studying a firm's products. These are Product, Place, Promotion and Price.

- **Product** emphasises that any product should be exactly what the consumers expect to get and to do the task for which it is bought.
- **Place** requires that the product should be available from wherever the target customers find it easiest to shop, which could be the high street, mail order catalogues or the internet.
- **Promotion** should involve advertising, selling and other forms of communication appropriate for the particular group of customers targeted for that product.
- **Price** needs to be at that level which represents good value for money to customers.

There are, however, three additional 'P's. These reflect the services provided by businesses. These three 'P's are People, Process and Physical Evidence.

- **People** are the actual staff members providing the service.
- **Process** is with regard to how that service is delivered to the consumer.
- **Physical evidence** relates to the actual element of the service.

7 Theories of the Markets

Learning objectives

21.3.1 Explain the key concepts of the EMH

21.3.2 Explain the limitations of the EMH

21.3.3 Explain the basic concepts of the behavioural finance school of thought including heuristics and framing

21.3.4 Evaluate the evidence on market anomalies in relation to both EMH and behavioural finance interpretations

7.1 Perfect capital markets

In addition to the assumptions inherent in the DVM itself, we are assuming that we have perfect capital markets, i.e. that there is perfect competition within these markets providing finance. The implications and requirements for this assumption are that

- Capital is freely available, should a company wish to raise it. If it were not, then the cost of obtaining it is liable to be higher than anticipated.
- There are a large number of small investors, none of whom can influence the market, hence the share price will be set by investors in general.
- There are no transaction costs that may deter investors from selling immediately if a share becomes overvalued.
- There is perfect information, i.e. all investors are basing their rational investment decisions on the same data and hence drawing the same rational conclusions.

7.2 The Efficient Markets Hypothesis (EMH)

7.2.1 Introduction

A question that now arises is: what is the information upon which shareholders base their expectations, and how rapidly is this information assimilated into the share price? The answer to this depends, in theory, on the efficiency of the capital markets.

The Efficient Market Hypothesis (EMH) has several implications for the management of investment portfolios. The efficiency referred to is with regard to 'informational' efficiency. The EMH suggests that because these markets are informationally efficient, it is very difficult, if not impossible, for investors to outperform the market's return through active fund management.

Markets can be termed informationally efficient when the market price of a security 'instantaneously and fully reflects all relevant available information'. The EMH suggests that three forms of market efficiency exist.

- Weak form.
- Semi-strong form.
- Strong form.

7.2.2 Weak form efficiency

The weak form of EMH suggests that all historical share price information and patterns of share price changes are fully reflected in the current share price. This means that an investor who analyses past share price movements and trading volumes to speculate on future share prices will not be able to profit from it.

The implication is that investors will be unable to earn excess returns by using technical analysis methods such as charting, analysis of volume indicators and moving averages.

It also follows that nothing in the past returns of a share or market can enhance the ability to predict anything about future returns.

7.2.3 Semi-strong form efficiency

The semi-strong form of EMH believes that prices reflect all historical and publicly available information. This implies that as soon as any information is released, it will be immediately incorporated into the share price. As a consequence investors will be unable to consistently make excess returns by buying (or selling) on the announcement of new information.

The implication for investors is that fundamental analysis of corporate accounts and published data will reveal no new price sensitive information and will, in such a market, be a fruitless exercise.

7.2.4 Strong form efficiency

The strong form of EMH states that all historical, publicly and privately accessible information is fully reflected in the share price. It suggests that even with inside information, an investor will not be able to profit from it because the market would already have reacted to it.

7.2.5 Summary

The efficient market hypothesis is probably only applicable to large developed stock markets such as the equity markets in the UK and in the US that are commonly regarded as semi-strong efficient for the major stocks, as few fund managers of stocks consistently outperform the market.

The market for smaller stocks and other emerging markets, however, may not be informationally efficient, which means that it may be possible for active fund management to generate returns in excess of the market.

Tests that have been undertaken in many markets to determine the level of market efficiency the have. Despite this, however a number of anomalies have been noted, such as

- **Seasonal Effects**
  - **Monday Effect** – returns on Mondays have been observed to be consistently lower than on other days.
  - **January Effect** – returns have been observed to be consistently higher in January than in any other month.
- **Small Companies Effect** – returns from smaller companies have consistently been higher than those of larger companies.
- **Index Effect** – the prices of shares that are taken into an index have been observed to rise. Under EMH, joining an index does not provide any justification for such a price movement.
- **Stock Market Crash** – crashes tend to follow bubbles. How can these be reconciled with EMH?
- **Weather** – observations have shown that there is a correlation between the weather and market returns, the market tending to perform well when the weather is good and less well when the weather is poor.

In conclusion, though there may be some recognisable patterns in the behaviour of share prices (predictability of returns). It is very difficult, if not impossible, to develop a worthwhile strategy to take advantage of these effects as a result of the dealing costs involved.

What EMH perhaps misses is that investors do not always react rationally and irrational behaviour can lead to pricing anomalies.

7.3 Behavioural finance

7.3.1 Introduction

One of the fundamental assumptions of modern finance theory is that investors are rational and risk-averse. The results and anomalies of some EMH studies lead us to consider whether investors do always act in a rational manner, leading into the whole area of behavioural finance.

Behavioural finance is an evolving field that is not presently well defined. However, the following points serve as a broad description of its aims.

- Behavioural finance involves the integration of classical economics and finance with psychology and the decision-making sciences.
- Behavioural finance is an attempt to explain what causes some of the anomalies that have been observed and reported in financial literature.
- Behavioural finance is the study of how investors systematically make errors in judgement, or 'mental mistakes'.

The field of behavioural finance is not new, and many investors have long considered that psychology plays a key role in determining the behaviour of markets. However, it is only in recent times that a series of concerted formal studies have been undertaken in this area, and the results of these studies have been at variance with the rational, self-interested decision maker postulated by traditional finance theory.

Behavioural finance argues that many facts about asset prices, investor behaviour, and managerial behaviour are best understood in models where at least some elements are irrational, being subject to what psychologists describe as cognitive illusions. These can be grouped in two broad classifications.

- Heuristic decision processes.
- Framing bias.

7.3.2 Heuristic decision processes

Heuristics refer to rules of thumb which humans use to make decisions in complex, uncertain environments. The decision-making process is not a strictly rational one where all relevant information is collected and objectively evaluated. Rather, the decision maker takes mental shortcuts in the process.

There may be good practical reasons for adopting a heuristic decision process, particularly when time available for decision making is limited. However, heuristic decision processes may result in poorer decision outcomes. Typical examples of misconceptions resulting from the use of heuristics include

- Sample size neglect and representativeness.
- Overconfidence.
- Memory bias.
- Conservation bias.

Sample size neglect representativeness

Representativeness refers to the tendency of decision makers to see patterns where perhaps none exist. For example, it arises when investors assume that recent events will continue into the future. This may be compounded by sample size neglect when the results of observing a small sample are then extrapolated over the market as a whole. In financial markets, this can manifest itself when investors seek to buy 'hot' stocks and to avoid stocks which have performed poorly in the recent past. This behaviour could provide an explanation for investor overreaction experienced around stock market crashes.

Overconfidence

Overconfidence leads investors to overestimate their predictive skills and believe they can 'time' the market. Studies have shown that one side effect of investor overconfidence is excessive trading.

Overconfidence is by no means limited to individual investors. There is evidence that financial analysts are slow to revise their previous assessment of a company's likely future performance, even when there is notable evidence that their existing assessment is incorrect.

Overconfidence will potentially lead to poor investment decisions as a result of an analysts excess belief in their own ability. This may manifest itself in the guise of earnings surprises, overinvestment or overtrading.

Memory bias

Memory bias arises when a value scale is fixed or anchored by recent observations. This can lead investors to expect a share to continue to trade in a defined range or to expect a company's earnings to be in line with historical trends, leading to possible under-reaction to trend changes.

Conservation bias

Conservation bias refers to the situation where investors are slow to update their investment view in the face of new economic/financial evidence. This underreaction may contribute to stocks having momentum.

7.3.3 Framing bias

The second group of illusions which can impact on decision processes can be grouped as the adoption of mental frames, or prospect theory. This idea proposes a framework for the way people make decisions under conditions of risk and uncertainty. It describes several states of mind that can be expected to influence an individual's decision-making processes. The key concepts addressed by the theory include

- Regret avoidance.
- Mental accounting..

Regret avoidance

Regret avoidance arises from the desire to avoid feeling the pain of regret resulting from a poor investment decision. Regret avoidance embodies more than just the pain of financial loss, it includes the pain of feeling responsible for the decision which gave rise to the loss.

If investors suffer from regret avoidance, they may be reluctant to realise losses. This avoidance can encourage investors to hold poorly performing shares, since avoiding their sale also avoids the recognition of the associated loss. The wish to avoid regret may bias new investment decisions, as they may be less willing to invest new sums in investments or markets which have performed poorly in the recent past.

Mental accounting

Mental accounting is the name given to the propensity of individuals to organise their world into separate 'mental accounts'. Investors tend to treat each element of their investment portfolio separately. This can lead to inefficient decision making.

It has been noted that people are often not consistent in making their investment decisions. For example, an individual may borrow at a high interest rate to buy a consumer item whilst simultaneously saving at lower interest rates for retirement.

Impact

Although the above examples of cognitive illusions are widely observed, behavioural finance does not claim that all investors will suffer from the same illusion simultaneously. The susceptibility of an individual investor to a particular illusion is likely to be a function of several variables.

If the tenets of behavioural finance are correct, several implications may arise regarding possible behavioural patterns in financial markets. There may be

- Over or under-reaction to price changes or news.
- Extrapolation of past trends into the future.
- Lack of attention to fundamentals underlying a stock.
- Focus on popular stocks.
- Seasonal price cycles.

If such patterns exist, there may be scope for investors to exploit the resulting pricing anomalies in order to obtain superior risk-adjusted returns. On a theoretical level, if exploitable pricing anomalies exist, the credibility of the EMH is undermined.

By considering that investors may not always act in a wealth maximising manner and that investors may have biased expectations, behavioural finance may be able to explain some of the observed anomalies of the EMH.

7.4 Financial amnesia and stock market bubbles

A stock market bubble occurs when market participants drive stock prices far above their fundamental fair value. Such bubbles tend to arise in times of changing business, political or economic circumstances where market participants lose sight of the business fundamentals and get caught up in the euphoria of the potential for spectacular returns from new developments. Bubbles are characterised by a period of low volatility and rapidly rising profits leading to accelerating growth in share prices, followed by a sudden price crash when the bubble bursts.

Bubbles have been a characteristic of capital markets for centuries. Two early examples were the South Sea bubble in England and the Mississippi Scheme in France, both of which ended abruptly in 1720 bankrupting many investors. More recent examples were the roaring 20s leading up to the Wall Street crash of 1929, and more recently the dot-com bubble in the 1990s that ended spectacularly at the turn of the 21st century. The 1920s crash was based on industrial change and development through the development of production line technology and corresponding increases in industrial efficiency. The dot-com bubble was driven by the emergence and development of the internet and web-based commerce. At the time of all of these bubbles there was a belief that the development was going to fundamentally alter the commercial landscape and that investors simply couldn't lose.

Behavioural finance theory suggests that these stock market bubbles arise as a result of cognitive biases that lead to group thinking and a herding behaviour. They are characterised by a belief that potentially spectacular returns will arise for investors and a loss of the consideration of the potential risks involved. Rather than being scared by potential risks, investors become scared of missing out on an opportunity and more money pours in to the market, driving prices ever higher until a first shock appears, an appreciation of risk and rationality returns and prices fall rapidly to more realistic levels. A market adage suggests that when the average man on the street who doesn't normally invest in shares starts to invest in the stock market there is a strong probability that a bubble is developing.

Given that history is littered with examples of stock market crashes it may be surprising that they continue to arise and the phrase financial amnesia has been coined to describe this occurrence. Financial amnesia arises when market participants forget or choose to ignore the financial lessons of the past. It is difficult to explain why this may be the case, however one likely contributor is that each generation certainly believes itself to be more intelligent and financially sophisticated than previous generations and appears to naively believe it will not make the same mistakes or misjudgements, only to discover how wrong it is – the behavioural finance idea of overconfidence. Strangely, this naivety doesn't just apply to investors, it also seems to apply to regulators.

The three key lessons that participants seem to forget are:

- **Innovation offers new benefits but brings with it new risks** – While innovation may well lead to improved returns there is always a limit. The belief of participants in their own financial sophistication appears to lead to a belief that they won't be fooled again, creating an illusion of safety and opportunity way beyond the reality of the situation.
- **Regulation does not remove wrongdoing or risk** – Increasing regulation leads participants to believe that businesses will behave correctly as they are being policed and that if they do not the regulators will ensure they do. History shows us, however, that whilst regulation may lead to a degree of market discipline/self-discipline it never eradicates wrongdoings.

- **Regulation is often inefficient and also often fails** – Regulators often focus on symptoms of failures rather than the underlying causes, especially where the underlying cause is their own failure to act.

Guarding against bubbles and financial amnesia is virtually impossible as successful market participants are naturally very confident, arguably overconfident, individuals and this confidence may, of itself, be the catalyst for what follows.

7.5 Contrarian investors

A contrarian investor is one who invests in a manner that differs from the consensus view when they believe that consensus view to be incorrect. A contrarian believes that irrationality exists among investors that can lead to mispricings of securities offering the opportunity for gains.

For example, contrarians take the view that, due to the herding effect, markets tend to overreact to extreme market movements, rising too far in bull markets and falling too far in bear markets. The contrarian can benefit by

- Bull market – shorting overvalued shares, buying them back once markets have settled at a more realistic level
- Bear market – buying oversold shares and selling them once their values have reached a fair level

This approach can apply to individual investment, an industry sector, or an entire market.

A contrarian does not always take the opposite view to the market consensus, rather he looks to benefit by making the opposite investment decisions to that of the majority of the market when he believes that irrational trading, and correspondingly pricing, has occurred.

7.6 Conclusion

Whilst behavioural factors undoubtedly play a role in the decision-making processes of individual investors, the big unanswered question that remains is whether they play a significant role in the market as a whole. Unfortunately, it will be difficult to decide the matter definitively, given the tools currently available for econometric studies and the difficulties of testing EMH.

8 Macroeconomic Environment

8.1 Economic indicators and trends

Learning objectives	
	24.1.1 Identify the main long term UK and global socio-economic trends. **24.1.2 Identify** the key economic indicators and explain their trends.

Investment management is not undertaken in a vacuum, rather it is undertaken subject to certain economic circumstances in order to achieve the objectives of the clients who represent a (significant) proportion of the population of that economy.

It is, therefore, vital that we are familiar with

- The key economic indicators that may influence investment decisions
- The socio-economic trends that may be influencing client demand

8.1.1 Key economic indicators

We will be examining many different types of investment as we proceed through this Study Text and will be examining the factors that may influence their values and returns. When looking at the economy at large, however, the key economic indicators that may indicate where we are in the business economic cycle discussed earlier, and hence which investments may be preferable, include

- Inflation rates
- Unemployment rates
- GDP growth rates
- Interest rates
- Capital expenditure
- Money supply
- Yield curve shifts and shapes
- Consumer confidence

and we will see how these impact in later sections.

Governments generally seek to make adjustments in order to stabilise the economic system, trying to avoid the distortions of a widely fluctuating trade cycle. In practice, this is no easy task and, of course, business cycles persist.

Forecasting the pattern of the business cycle is very difficult in practice. The cycle is affected by such things as **oil prices** and **international political stability**, all of which are themselves difficult to predict.

Businesses must try to identify those measures which tend to give **advance warning** of movements in the business cycle such as **leading indicators** that include share prices, house building actively, money supply, credit growth and interest rates.

There are also **coincident indicators** such as levels of personal income that change at the same time as the overall economy, confirming its current status. Finally there are **lagging indicators** that change after the overall economy such as the unemployment rate, labour costs, business spending, outstanding bank loans. Clearly, coincident and lagging indicators are of minimal use as predictive tools.

The above definitions of economic indicators (leading, coincident, lagging) represent a classing of economic indicators by time (before, during, after). We may alternatively classify economic indicators by their direction of movement.

Procyclic indicators move in the same direction as the economy, increasing when the economy is in the recovery/boom phase and decrease when it is moving into recession. Gross Domestic Product (GDP) is a procyclic indicator.

Counter cyclic indicators move in the opposite direction to the economy, falling when economic output is rising and rising when economic performance is declining. The unemployment rate is an example of a counter cyclic indicator.

Acyclic indicators are those with little or no correlation to the business cycle, they may rise or fall when the general economy is doing well, and may rise or fall when it is not doing well. They appear to be unconnected to the position the economy is in within the business cycle and are, therefore, of little use as an economic tool.

8.1.2 Socio-economic trends

With respect to socio-economic trends, the UK population is expanding steadily, the population now exceeding 60m and has grown by 61% since the start of the 20th century. It is also ageing, ie the average age is rising. This aspect reflects both medical advances and changes in the major industries and working environment. Levels of personal wealth are also increasing due to economic development.

Generally, the working population creates the countries wealth. With more people of retirement age, the proportion of the population that is working will be lower and the proportion that is not working and that is dependent on the working population will be higher. This puts an extra burden on the working population which must pay through taxes for expenditure on state pensions, state health care.

On a worldwide basis the increase in population is even more dramatic with the current world population being over 4 times that at the beginning of the 20th century. The greatest rates of population growth are being experienced in emerging economies with growth rates in the developed world more closely matching those of the UK. In addition, there are some substantial concentrations of population with the populations of China and India currently represent almost 40% of the total world population. China is currently the most populous country, though the population of India is expected to surpass that of China by 2025.

8.2 Economic development

Learning objectives

24.1.2 Identify key economic indicators and explain their trends.
24.1.5 Identify international differences in consumption, credit and savings.

8.2.1 Assessing economic development

We often read in the papers about something that affects developed countries/economies or developing economies but what is a developed economy or a developing economy and how do we classify any other economies.

The reality is that there is no firm definition of a developed/developing economy, however there are certain characteristics that may be considered in determining the development status of any economy that we may classify under three main headings

- **Demographic factors**
  - Total population – The number of people who live in a country.
  - Life expectancy – The average age a person lives to in a country.
  - Birth rate – The number of children born per 1,000 of the population per year.
  - Death rate – The number of people who die per 1,000 of the population per year.
- **Economic factors**
  - GDP per capita – Gross Domestic Produce per person, a measure of wealth per person.
  - Unemployment rate – The percentage of the population of working age who do not have a job.
- **Social factors**
  - Access to education – The percentage of children attending schools.
  - Adult literacy – The percentage of people in a country who can read and write.
  - Population per doctor – The number of people per doctor.

The UN has developed the Human Development Index (HDI) based on the above data in order to determine the level of development.

A country is generally considered to be developed if it is industrialised with a high GDP per capita, low unemployment, high life expectancy and high education standards. These economies are also characterised by high levels of consumption, credit and savings.

A developing economy is generally one that is becoming industrialised with low but increasing GDP per capita, high GDP growth and falling unemployment. From a social perspective, the increase I wealth would be giving rise to improving educational standards and life expectancy. Such economies are often subcategorised into less developed countries (LDCs), least economically developed countries (LEDCs). These economies tend to have low but increasing levels of consumption, credit and savings.

Underdeveloped or third world countries would be largely unindustrialised economies with low GDP per capita, low GDP growth and high unemployment. Such economies tend to have relatively poor life expectancies and levels of education. These economies tend to have very low levels of consumption, credit and savings that are showing little growth.

8.2.2 Access to education

Access to education is one of the cornerstones of economic development. Whilst the first phases of industrialisation in an economy may be undertaken by companies outside of the economy itself this is unlikely to be sufficient to change an economy from undeveloped to developed. For an economy to become developed it is necessary for the indigenous population to be setting up and running successful businesses, employing the local population and contributing to the wealth of the economy as a whole. This cannot be successfully achieved unless there is an adequate level of education and adult literacy within the economy.

Though access to education is taken for granted in most Western economies, it is very highly regarded in many East Asian economies where it has only relatively recently become the norm.

8.2.3 Growth of developing economies

The UK moved from a largely rural economy to a largely industrialised economy over the 18th and 19th centuries and claims to be the home of the industrial revolution. In contrast, there are many economies that are trying to make this move from rural to industrialised within one generation.

The economies of India and China in particular (the two most populous countries in the world) are developing very rapidly. While developed countries such as the UK may demonstrate an average annual GDP growth rate of around 2% the GDP growth rates of these two economies have been 8% pa and more over recent years.

Based simply on GDP alone, China is already the third largest economy in the world and India is the 11th. When we look at GDP per capita, however, they are ranked 98th and 139th respectively so they may be regarded as far from fully economically developed. It is forecast that as these countries continue to develop rapidly, China will be the largest economy in the world by 2030 and India will be the second largest by 2050 with, by then, Brazil as the fourth largest economy.

8.3 Globalisation

Learning objectives	**24.1.3 Understand** the relationship between and importance of the main world economies. **24.1.4 Explain** economic and financial cycles including their predictability and regional differences.

8.3.1 The process of globalisation

Companies are tending more and more to take a global view of business. The process of **globalisation** in various areas has been accelerated by improvements in communications, including the expansion and falling cost of air travel; the development of Internet based systems; and improvements in telecommunications generally.

Production facilities for multinational operations may be located in particular countries for a variety of reasons.

- To give access to markets protected by tariffs
- To reduce transport costs
- To exploit national or regional differences in demand for goods
- To take advantage of low labour costs

Centralisation of production can bring important **economies of scale**. Economies of scale are reductions in costs resulting from larger-scale production. These must be balanced against transport costs and **barriers to trade**, such as tariffs (taxes on imports) and other restrictions imposed by one country against trade from another country.

The expansion of some industries and the contraction of others can reflect both **economic and technological progress** and the trend towards globalisation. **'Sunrise' industries** include information technology and genetics, whose importance is increasing worldwide. **'Sunset' industries** in the more developed Western economies include steel and shipbuilding whose prices have been undercut by more efficient producers in the Pacific Basin.

Capital markets of various countries have become internationally integrated – 'globalised'. The process of integration is facilitated by improved telecommunications and the deregulation of markets in many countries. Securities issued in one country can now be traded in capital markets around the world. This trend can only increase as stock exchanges are linked electronically.

8.3.2 Multinational enterprises

A **multinational** company is one that has production or service facilities in more than one country. Multinational enterprises range from medium-sized companies having only a few facilities (or subsidiaries or 'affiliates') abroad to giant companies having an annual turnover larger than the gross national product (GNP) of some smaller countries of the world. Indeed the largest four US multinationals have reported turnover larger than the GNPs of all but 14 countries of the world.

The size and significance of multinationals is increasing. Many companies in middle-income countries such as Singapore are now becoming multinationals, and the annual growth in output of existing multinationals is in the range 10-15%.

8.3.3 Market failures

As a result of the process of globalisation, almost all markets are interconnected in some way and what happens in one market will almost always have an impact on others.
One of the adverse consequences of globalisation is what has become known as **financial contagion**. Financial contagion is the transmission of an economic shock occurring in one economy out to other economies. This financial contagion is primarily a consequence of trading links, financial links, exchange rate implications of the economic shock along with the herding effect of international investors.
The stock market crash of 1987, the Russian Debt crisis of 1998 allied to the failure of LTCM (a major highly geared hedge fund) in the same year, and the credit crunch of 2007/2008 are, perhaps, the most significant of the recent financial contagions that have resulted in significant economic disruption outside of their country of origin.

8.3.4 International business cycles

We examined the business cycle earlier in this chapter, the point to raise here is that through the interconnections between economies the cycles of the major trading nations at least tend to be closely correlated. The larger economies tend to be the major drivers of the cycle with the smaller economies following in their wake.

A downturn or economic shock in the US (the largest economy in the world) tends to ripple out around the world. If the US suffers a downturn then US businesses import less and exporting nations begin to suffer, moving into a downturn themselves.

This effect is not so pronounced in the less economically developed economies that are more based on internal trade than on exports.

Predicting the position of an economy within the business cycle is notoriously difficult. Indications can be gained from changes in the growth rate of economic output measures such as GBP (see later) but the lag in obtaining such data and the inaccuracies in of the data make it difficult, if not impossible, to be precise.

9 Macroeconomic Theories

9.1 National income and the circular flow of income

earning objectives

24.2.3 Explain the components of the circular flow of income.
24.2.4 Distinguish between injections into, and withdrawals from ('leakages') the circular flow.
24.2.10 Explain the paradox of thrift.

9.1.1 A closed economy

Individuals supply firms with the productive resources of the economy (factors of production) – land, labour and capital – and firms must pay households for these factors. In return households must pay firms for goods and services provide by the firms, the income of firms is the sales revenue from the sales of goods and services.

This creates a **circular flow** of income and expenditure: income and output are different sides of the same coin.

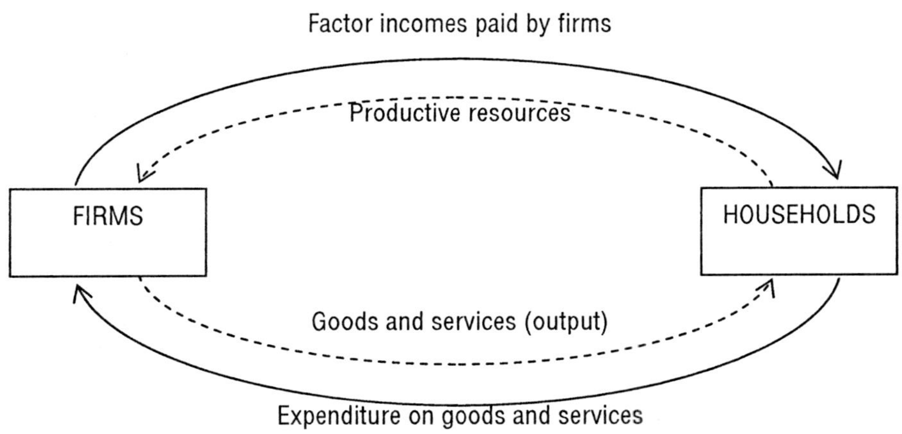

Circular flow of income

The diagram above assumes a 'closed' economy, a little later below we add further elements to the model. For this system to be in a state of equilibrium the flows must equate, ie

Output = Expenditure = Income

Example

A simple example will serve to explain why these flows must be in balance. The economy produces £1,000 worth of goods, £1,000 worth of labour is input and £1,000 worth of income is received back.

If one household decides that rather than spending their entire income, they will save £100, then £100 leaks from the system. Expenditure will now be £900 and goods worth £900 will be given back to the households. This leaves the households with net savings of £100 and firms with surplus goods also valued at £100. On the assumption that the firms do not wish to hold this increased level of stock, they will respond in the next period by reducing their requirement for labour.

In the next period, the firm might demand £800 worth of labour to produce £800 worth of goods. The income will go back to the households who will receive £800. The firm's belief must be that the £100 worth of saving during the previous period will now be used up, demanding £900 worth of goods and, thus, completely exhausting this period's production and also absorbing the stock which has built up in the previous period.

If, however, the households persisted in saving money, then demand in this period will be even lower, at the level of, let us say, £750. Once again, the household's full income is not being spent and, once again, the firms are left with surplus goods on their books. This process of reduction in output will continue until the firms are left with the stock levels they require.

From this example, it can be seen that savings in this simple system result in a decrease in the overall level of output. This phenomenon of savings leading to a decrease in output is referred to as the **paradox of thrift**.

9.1.2 Injections and withdrawals – an open economy

Savings would not be a problem in this system if they were somehow funnelled back into the flow. For example, using the numbers above, if the savings of £100 in the first period were placed with a bank, who were then to lend the money to a consumer who wished to spend more than his/her income, the system would retain its balance at an output level of £1,000.

Thus, the leakage of £100 in the form of savings is matched by the injection of a further £100 of expenditure by the second consumer. In economics, we would refer to this second consumer's expenditure as **investment**. The system will then be in balance when savings equal investment (S=I), i.e. when **leakages equal injections**. The key issue is whether actual and planned savings coincide.

A second leakage is **taxation**. The government removes income from consumers before they can spend it. If the government was simply to sit on this money and do nothing with it, this too would contract the economy, representing a leakage. However, in reality, governments use the money they raise through taxation to finance their **expenditure** and, consequently, the money finds its way back into the system. Once again, so long as **leakages and injections** are in balance (G=T), the economy will remain stable.

The final leakage or injection from our system would be **trade**. The purchase of overseas goods by individuals within our economy is a leakage, as demand, which could otherwise have been spent on our own goods, leaks into another economy. Conversely, demand from other economies met by our own production – exports – are injections into our economic cycle. As we will see later when we look at the exchange rate, economists believe that in a perfectly free world, the exchange rate itself will ensure that these two flows are in balance, once again ensuring that leakages equal injections.

Our circular flow will now appear as follows with withdrawals/leakages being removed and injections being inserted.

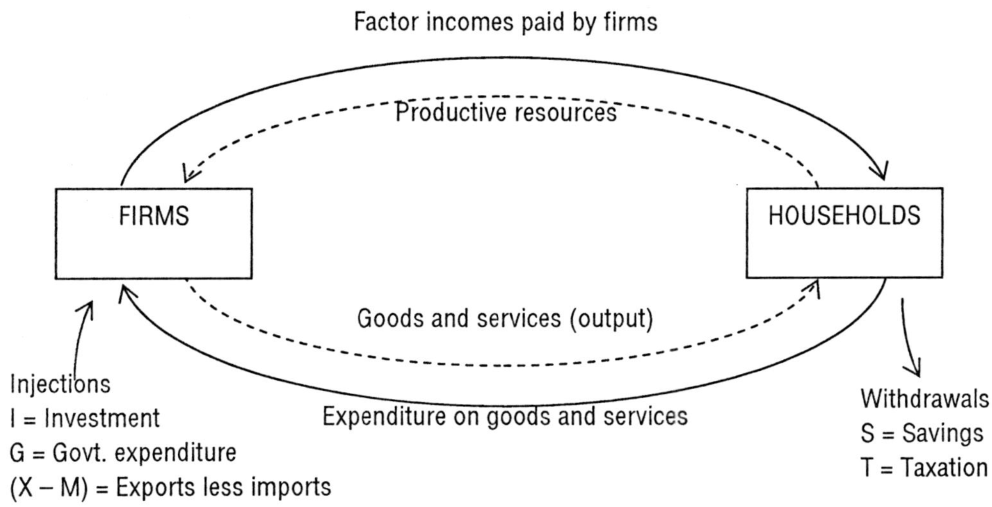

To assess national income in the economy we could measure the total factor incomes, however, an alternative would be to measure the total expenditure, the total paid to firms.

Total spending, consists of **consumer spending**, **government spending**, **investment spending**, and **net exports**, ie. spending by foreigners on our goods and services minus spending by UK residents on foreign goods and services.

This can be symbolised as

National income = C + I + G + (X – M)

where:

C = consumer expenditure
I = investment expenditure
G = government expenditure
X = expenditure on our exports by foreigners
M = expenditure by us on imports

9.2 Measuring economic activity

9.2.1 Introduction

Learning objectives

24.2.1 Distinguish between GDP and GNP.
24.2.2 Explain the difference between real and nominal GDP.
24.2.5 Distinguish between national income and GDP.

Economic activity can be measured in different ways, depending on which aspect of the circular flow is captured by the particular measure being used.

Three key measures of economic activity are:

- National income
- Gross domestic product (GDP)
- Gross national product (GNP)

9.2.2 National income

UK **national income** is the sum of all incomes of residents in the UK which arise as a result of economic activity, that is from the production of goods and services. Such incomes, which include rent, employment income and profit, are known as factor incomes because they are earned by the so-called factors of production: land, labour and capital' *(Office for National Statistics)*.

National income is also called net national product. As noted above, the terms 'income' and 'product' are two different aspects of the same circular flow of income around the economy. The term 'net' means 'after deducting an amount for capital consumption or depreciation of fixed assets' from the gross figure.

Although technically national income has a particular definition, generally you will find all of the three measures given above (NI, GNP and GDP) loosely referred to as '**national income**'.

Calculating the national income serves several purposes:

- **Measuring** the **standard** of **living** in a country (national income per head)
- **Comparing** the **wealth** of different countries
- **Measuring** the **change** in **national wealth** and the standard of living
- **Ascertaining long-term trends**
- **Assisting central government** in its **economic planning**

9.2.3 Gross domestic product (GDP)

Most UK national income is derived from economic activity **within the UK** referred to as total **domestic income** or **domestic product**. It is measured **gross,** ie before deducting an amount for capital consumption or depreciation of fixed assets, to give the **gross domestic product (GDP)**. GDP is a measure of the total value of income/production from economic activity within the UK regardless of who it belongs to. It would, therefore, include the value of cars produced at a Japanese car plant in the UK but not the value of products made in America by a UK company.

Nominal GDP refers to the actual money value of GDP. Economists also calculate real GDP which strips out the impact of inflation from the figure and shows the real output increase.

9.2.4 Gross national product

Some national income arises from overseas investments while some of the income generated within the UK is earned by non-residents. Gross national product is the value of output of the participants in the economy (UK nationals) and therefore includes net property income from abroad.

9.2.5 GDP, GNP and national income

The relationship between nominal GDP, GNP and national income is therefore as follows.

	GDP
plus	Net property income from abroad
equals	GNP
minus	Capital consumption
equals	National income (net)

GDP, GNP and national income figures are used as measures of growth in the economy. The rate of growth indicates the position the economy is in within the economic cycle and, therefore, in part predicts what action the government will take, whether expansionary or contractionary, depending on the governmental stance.

9.3 Classical economics

Learning objective | **24.2.6 Distinguish** between classical economics and the Keynesian and Monetarist schools of thought.

Classical economists believe that there is no difference between an individual market and the economy acting as a whole. In their view, individual markets will always 'clear' – that is, they will always find their equilibrium where supply equals demand. If individual markets always clear, then the economy as a whole must always move to a point of balance.

One of the key elements of classical economics is **Say's Law**. Say's Law states that **supply will create its own demand**. In effect, this is saying that where there is an excess of supply, price will fall, thereby creating demand. The result of this is that the economy will always move to a point of equilibrium and that point of equilibrium, or balance, will always be the full employment level of activity in the economy. If this were not the case, then those resources that were unemployed would reduce their price so as to ensure that they did find employment.

Classical economists therefore believe that in the long-run, the economy will always be operating at its full employment level of activity. This is a simple result of market forces and there is nothing that a government can do to alter that process.

9.4 Keynesian economics

9.4.1 Introduction

Learning objectives | **24.2.6 Distinguish** between classical economics and the Keynesian and monetarist schools of thought.
24.2.7 Explain the major components of the Keynesian model.

In the 1920s and 1930s, the UK economy underwent a period of sustained depression. Unemployment did not fall below 10% from 1920 to 1941. The conventional wisdom of the time was wrapped up with classical economics, which suggested that the only cure for unemployment was for wages to fall. The government of the 1920s and 1930s did everything it could to ensure that wages did come down, yet unemployment did not seem to change.

This phenomenon of unemployment not responding to falls in wages was not merely an aspect of the UK's economic history, but was reflected in all of the major industrial economies. It was against this background that John Maynard Keynes developed a different way of looking at the operations of the economic system.

Keynes could see that the resources in the economy were present. There were empty factories and unemployed labourers, yet the market did not seem to be operating to bring supply and demand into balance. It was at this point that Keynes made a divide in economics between micro and macroeconomics. Microeconomics looks at function of individual markets. Macroeconomics is the study of the economy as a whole. It was Keynes' belief that individual markets may clear, but the whole economy may, for a number of reasons, stick to a particular level of output.

Keynes moved on to think about the prime motivator of the economic cycle as the level of economic activity. In his view, it was the absence of this motive power that left the economy stagnating, and more power would need to be injected into the economy to ensure that activity would begin to rise.

Keynes believed that the **key power in the economy was the level of demand**. This level of demand in the economy determined the level of output, employment and income. If demand were insufficient, the economy would be underperforming. If demand were excessive, the economy would overheat. However, it would only be purely by chance that the economy might operate at a point where full employment was achieved without excessive strain.

Having identified demand as the key motivator of the economy, Keynes then moved on to consider the components of demand and how they might be manipulated.

9.4.2 The nature of demand

From our simple model of the circular flow that we considered earlier, we can see that demand arises in a number of ways. There is the demand that the consumers have for goods and services. There is the demand for investment goods and for government expenditure and, finally, there is the net demand generated by international trade. Keynes considered each of these types of demand, looking at the ways in which they were composed and the influences on them.

9.4.3 Consumption

The simple assumption of the classical model had been that households receive the income which they then spend. Keynes perceived that it was slightly different, in that the level of expenditure that you incurred was very much related to the level of income you received.

Keynes believed that the consumer's demand for goods is made up of two elements. The first element is their base or **autonomous consumption** – the level of goods they must consume to stay alive. The second element is the household's discretionary consumption which he believed to be linearly related to their income. The logic behind this is that as income increases, consumers will demand more in the way of goods and services.

Keynes therefore believed that for the economy as a whole, consumption could be described by the following function.

Formula to learn

$$C = a + bY$$

Where

a = level of autonomous consumption

b = **marginal propensity to consume**, the proportion of any increase in income, which results in increased expenditure.

Y = national income

The Keynesian Consumption Function

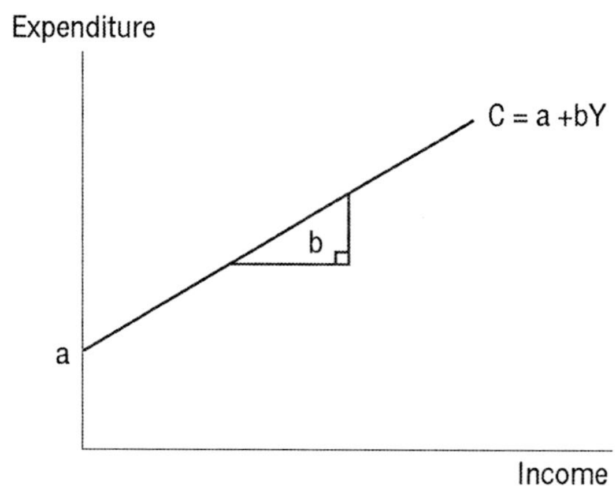

If, as Keynes suggested, demand is the key motivator of the economy, and demand is determined by the income of the individual, then the classical cure for unemployment of reducing wages, and therefore reducing income, is unlikely to work, since rather than enhancing demand, it effectively decreases it.

So far, our model of consumption simply links in a linear form the level of income and expenditure of a consumer. This is, perhaps, a trifle simplistic and a variety of alternatives have been developed.

One of these alternatives is the **Permanent Income Hypothesis**, advanced by Milton Friedman, which suggests that consumers only react to permanent changes in their level of income. If incomes rise, consumers will wait in order to establish the permanence of the change before they alter their consumption patterns.

Another, though linked, view is the **Life Cycle Hypothesis**, which links consumers' expenditure to their future expected earnings rather than simply considering the current position. People estimate their future earnings and spending plans, and base their consumption decisions on these.

In Keynes view, if we wish to alter demand then, since the level of autonomous consumption is fixed, we will need to alter people's marginal propensity to consume.

If individuals' propensity to consume alters, then this will be reflected in the slope of the consumption function.

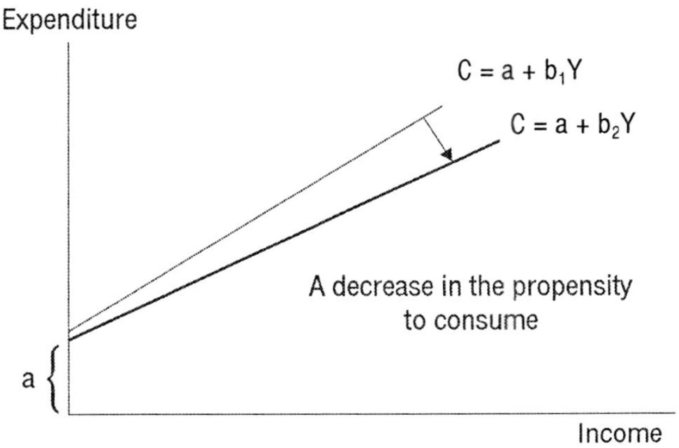

9.4.4 Investment and interest rates

In economics, the term investment means the purchase of goods without the aim of consuming them. Investment can therefore cover a number of things, including the purchase of plant and machinery and the build-up of stocks, both of which are goods that are purchased without being consumed in this period. Within our simple model, investment is the flow which balances the savings leakage. For Keynes, it is an important source of demand.

The level of investment demand is determined by the interest rate. If interest rates are low, then it will be profitable to finance an increasing number of projects. Consequently, an increasing number of projects will be undertaken. Therefore, in order to stimulate investment demand, the government needs to ensure that interest rates are low.

In the Keynesian model, interest rates are determined by interplay between money supply (a fixed value set by the government) and the money demand.

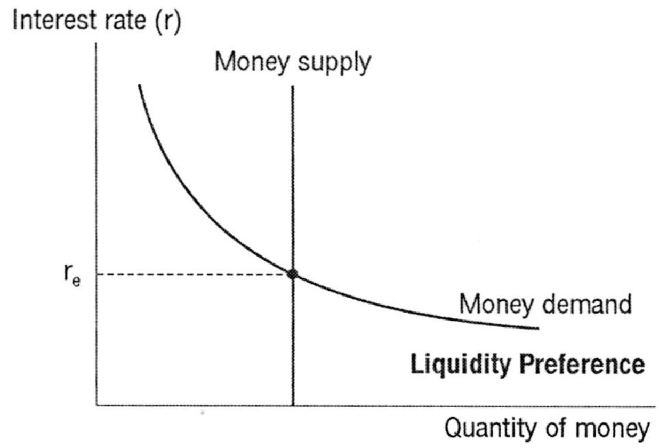

Once the equilibrium interest rate has been established, then this determines the quantity of investment activity that is undertaken. Keynes believed that there are only a limited number of investment projects which are possible. Some projects are more profitable than others and will be profitable even if the interest rate, finance cost, is high. Others are less profitable and are only profitable if the interest rate is low. The relationship between the interest rate and the demand for investment is referred to as the **marginal efficiency of investment**.

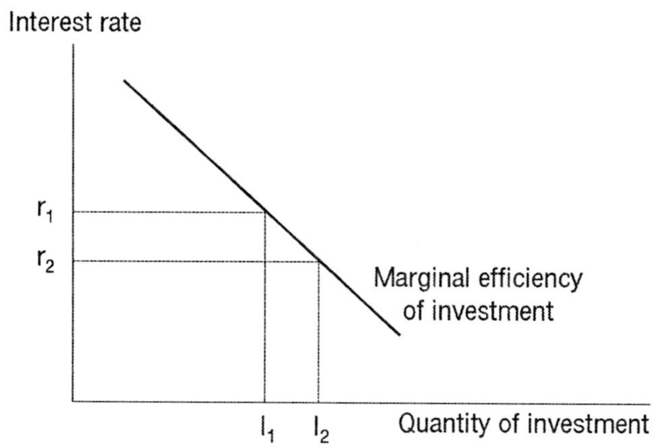

As the interest rate falls to r_2, then the quantity of investment undertaken rises. The fall in interest rates could have arisen from a variety of sources, but the most obvious would be an increase in the supply of money.

Overall demand is now made up of two elements: consumers' demand and investment.

Formula to learn

Aggregate Demand (AD) = C + I

Diagrammatically, this can be portrayed as

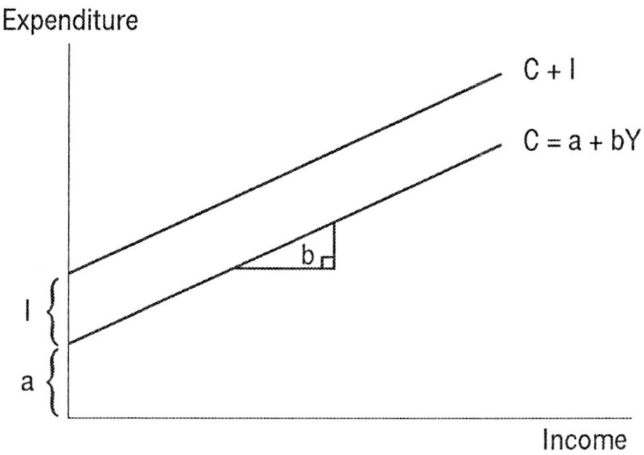

There is no change in the slope of the aggregate demand function, since investment is not conditional on the level of income but is determined by the interest rate.

In reality, Keynesians believe that it is **often difficult to control the interest rate**. Even if it were possible, the benefits might be far from obvious because experience has shown, in the UK at least, that the MEI tends to be rather steep **(inelastic)**, consequently limiting the impact of any increase in the rate of interest. This has tended to make Keynesians focus away from the interest rate and monetary policy and towards fiscal policy and the role of government.

9.4.5 Government

The third important source of demand in the economy is the government. The government raises revenue by way of taxation and then spends this money. An alternative to simply raising money through taxation would be either to borrow it or, more simply, to print it. Using either of these two routes, the government could expand its expenditure and therefore increase the overall level of demand in the economy with the following resultant demand.

Formula to learn

$$\text{Aggregate Demand (AD)} = C(1 - \text{Tax Rate}) + I + G$$

Initially, the impact of government will be to reduce the level of consumers' demand by reducing their **personal disposable income** (income less direct taxes) as it raises revenue in the form of taxes. Then, as the government spends, the level of aggregate demand will shift up. Once again, this level of demand will not be determined by income, as there is no real constraint on the government spending more than it raises in taxation. Even if the government operates a **balanced budget** (Expenditure = Revenue), this should increase the overall level of demand, since it takes money from the consumers and then spends it. This expenditure, in turn, becomes the incomes of consumers in the economy and thereby returns into the cycle.

9.4.6 International trade

So far, we have considered a closed economy. As we noted earlier, a fuller model of the economy would introduce the idea of trade flows. Demand is injected into the system through exports of goods (X), and leaks from the system are due to our own imports of overseas produce (M). As we will see later, the theories of the exchange rate predict that in the long term, imports and exports **will be in balance**. However, it may be possible for the government, in the short term, to create an imbalance, therefore forcing a higher level of demand into the economy. When we incorporate this final element into the Keynesian analysis we get

Formula to learn

$$\text{Aggregate Demand (AD)} = C(1 - \text{Tax rate}) + I + G + (X - M)$$

9.4.7 Equilibrium levels of demand

Learning objective **24.2.8 Explain** Keynesian equilibrium.

As we saw from the simple model of circular flow, for the economy to be in equilibrium

Formula to learn

Output = Expenditure = Income

In terms of the diagrammatic approach we have developed, this means

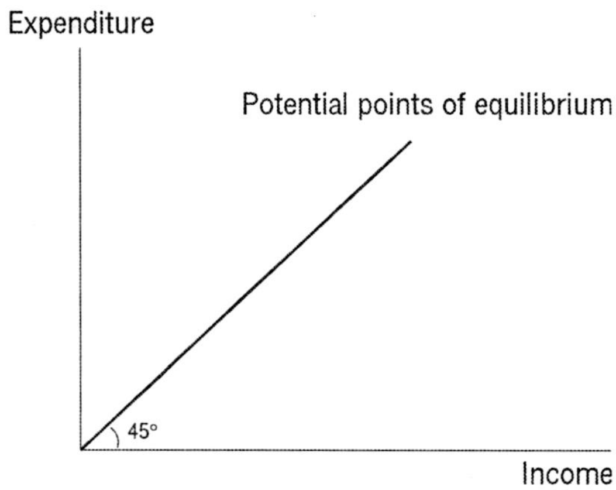

Keynes believed that the **equilibrium level of output is determined by demand.**

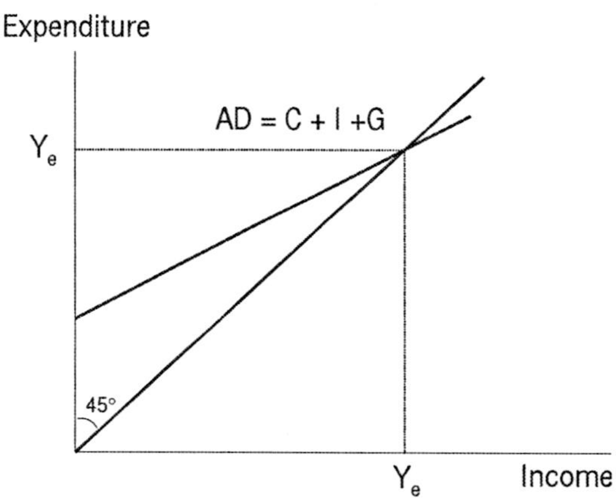

At the point Y_e, the economy is in balance. However, Keynes believed that there was no reason to believe that this was necessarily the full employment level of the economy.

Keynes' overall belief is that for the economy to be in balance at full employment, the level of demand must be right. He further believed that the economy will not automatically achieve, using Say's Law, the right level of demand and supply. In short, the economy may stick at a suboptimal position. The solution, as far as Keynes was concerned, was simple: to manipulate demand to ensure that the demand met the right level for the economy's resources.

The classical economists believed that the price of labour would fall, automatically bringing the economy back into balance. In Keynes' view, prices are sticky and it is possible for the economy to stick at a suboptimal level, explaining the experience of the UK in the inter-war period.

9.4.8 How to manipulate this demand

The easiest of the four sources of demand for a government to control was seen to be government expenditure, and Keynesian economics has, since the 1930s, focused very much on a manipulation of **fiscal policy** – that is, **government expenditure and taxation**.

One important feature that Keynes noted was that it is not essential for the government to inject exactly the right amount of demand into the economy to push demand up to the full employment level. By simply injecting a smaller amount of demand into the economy, it can kick-start or **'pump prime'** the economy, and enable it to reach full employment. This injection of a smaller amount of demand than is required overall relies upon a concept referred to as **the multiplier**.

9.4.9 The multiplier effect

earning objective | **24.2.9 Calculate** the Keynesian multiplier given the marginal propensity to consume (mpc) or propensities to withdraw (tax, import and save).

The multiplier looks at the way in which an increase in the level of demand is transmitted through the economy.

The government might decide to embark upon a new road-building project, which will cost £10m. The government pays £10m to the contractors to build the road. The contractors then spend this sum, partly on the wages of their employees, and partly on raw materials and profits.

All of these represent income to other groups in the economy. As we saw from Keynes' view of consumption, consumption is based upon level of income, and so as the workers who were previously unemployed receive wages for building the road, they in turn will spend a proportion of this money. As the workers spend the money, it becomes the income of another participant in the economy, and so on.

The beneficiaries of this increased spending by the newly employed workers have also had their income increased and, in turn, they will spend a proportion of this money. The multiplier effect continues to work through the economy until the flows become immaterial.

It can be seen from the multiplier effect that the injection of government demand is simply the catalyst which sets off a chain reaction of individuals' demand. By injecting £10 million worth of additional demand into the economy, the government may be able to achieve a much greater impact on the overall level of demand.

It is possible to express the multiplier relationship mathematically.

Formula to learn

$$\text{Simple multiplier} = \frac{1}{1 - \text{Marginal propensity to consume (MPC)}}$$

Which can be adjusted for personal tax as follows

Formula to learn

$$\text{Adjusted for tax} = \frac{1}{1 - [\text{MPC}(1 - \text{tax rate})]}$$

The impact of taxes is to reduce the consumers' disposable income and therefore weaken the multiplier.

With the open-economy multiplier, the formula acknowledges that any increase in demand will, to a certain extent (determined by the marginal prosperity to import (MPM)), leak out of the economy, thereby reducing the overall effect on demand, giving the following.

Formula to learn

$$\text{Open-economy multiplier} = \frac{1}{1-[\text{MPC}(1-\text{tax rate})]+\text{MPM}}$$

It should, however, be remembered that the multiplier effect works in both ways. If the government were to remove £10 million worth of demand, the economy would contract substantially.

9.4.10 Automatic stabilisers

Income tax, VAT and unemployment benefits can be referred to as 'automatic stabilisers'. If income and output fall, government spending on benefits will increase and government tax receipts will fall. The reason for this is that unemployment benefit will act as a floor for incomes, ensuring that the full impact of negative movement is not felt by the economy.

The role of taxation is that this, as we saw in our study of the multiplier, dampens the multiplier effect. Likewise, in an open economy, imports will similarly dampen the multiplier. The results of this will be that a given change in aggregate demand will have a less significant effect on income and expenditure.

9.4.11 Monetary policy

Keynesian economics is firmly linked with fiscal policy. Monetary policy, which involves the use of interest rates to manipulate the economy, is seen as less relevant to Keynesian economists. There are a number of reasons for this. First, Keynesians believe it is very difficult to control monetary policy correctly. They also believe that the effects may be varied and difficult to monitor.

The only area where monetary policy could be used within the Keynesian framework to manipulate demand would be in influencing investment expenditure directly, and consumer expenditure in a more indirect fashion.

With regard to the manipulation of investment expenditure, as mentioned above, Keynesians believe that investment is only slightly linked to the level of interest rates and, therefore, any impact of a reduction in interest rates may be minimal or non-existent.

Consequently, monetary policy has a very low profile within Keynesian economics. The emphasis is much more upon fiscal policy.

9.5 Monetarist economics

Monetarism is fundamentally a restatement of classical economic doctrine. It is based firmly on the belief that free markets are the only solution to economic problems. However, within this, it is not as dogmatic as classical economics, believing that markets will not automatically work. It recommends a number of pragmatic steps to achieve long-run equilibrium.

In particular, monetarism **focuses on the impact of inflation** as a distorting influence in the market. Inflation must be eradicated before any other economic problems can be solved. Monetarism is not a new doctrine. It is based upon the **Fisher equation of money**, which was developed in the early twentieth century. However, monetarism is new, in that it builds this into a coherent structure of an explanation of the way in which the economy operates.

We examine monetarism later when we consider inflation and unemployment.

9.6 Monetarism and Keynesianism

The two basic theoretical prescriptions are widely at odds. **Keynesianism is an interventionist approach**, believing that the government can intervene to clear markets which fail to work on their own account.

Where the classical approach considers that wages and prices are fully flexible, the Keynesian approach assumes wages and prices are downwardly inflexible or 'sticky'.

Monetarism is a free market non-interventionist economy policy, relying on market forces, where the only role for government is to ensure that market forces are free to operate without intervention in a stable, non-inflationary environment. Many monetarists argue that the only theoretical justification for the Keynesian model is the fact that Keynes assume that the labour market will stick and that wags will either not fall or have no effect on the level of demand for workers.

10 The Role of Government

10.1 Economic policy aims

As well as providing a legal and regulatory framework for economic activity, the government plays a role in managing the economy. Among the aims of a government's **economic policy** may be the following.

- To achieve **sustainable growth** in national income per head of the population. Growth implies an increase in national income in real terms. National income grows through expansion of economic activity: more goods and services become available for people to consume. The idea of sustainable growth implies that the fluctuations of the business cycle are avoided and that output grows on a steady upward trend. This is generally seen as the most important goal of a government's economic policy.
- To **control inflation** in prices. This has become a central objective of economic policy in many countries in recent years.
- To achieve **full employment.** Full employment does not mean that everyone who wants a job has one all the time, but it does mean that unemployment levels are low, and involuntary unemployment is short-term.
- To achieve a **trade balance** – that is, a balance between exports and imports. The wealth of a country relative to others, a country's creditworthiness as a borrower, and the goodwill between countries in international relations might all depend on the achievement of an external balance over time. Deficits in external trade, with imports exceeding exports, might also be damaging for the prospects of economic growth.

It should be noted that some of these are conflicting aims. Where aggregate demand in the economy exceeds the available resources we will experience inflation with full employment. Where aggregate demand is below the available resources we will experience unemployment and, consequently, little inflation. Under normal circumstances, inflation and unemployment are negatively correlated with one being high when the other is low.

The day-to-day economic management role is undertaken by the Treasury, a government department that acts on behalf of, and is accountable to, Parliament. The Treasury has responsibility for:

- Day-to-day economic management
- UK financial regulation (delegated to the FSA – see below)
- Negotiating EC economic directives

10.2 The changing emphasis of economic policy

The **emphasis on different policy objectives** has changed over time in line with political, social and economic events. The objective of full employment was central to policy in developed countries following the Second World War. Later, other macro economic objectives came to the fore. Explicit policy commitments have been made by governments at different times in different countries to the objectives of low inflation, balance of payments equilibrium and sustainable development of the economy.

Sustainable development describes a pattern of economic growth at a local or a national level which is stable over the long term and is unlikely to be a victim of its own success. Sustainability implies that there will always be sufficient natural, financial and human resources available to meet future growth. Sustainable development has been particularly used to describe growth which does not destroy the natural resources which are vital to further production.

10.3 Economic policy actions

10.3.1 Aggregate demand

If a government is planning its economic policy and wishes to increase the country's GDP and GNP, it might wish to turn its attention to any of these items, by:

- Trying to increase consumer spending, C
- Trying to increase private investment, I
- Deciding to increase government spending, G
- Trying to improve the balance of payments on overseas trade, (X – M)

These are the four components of aggregate demand for goods and services in the economy and can be used to determine the aggregate demand curve.

Aggregate demand is the total demand for goods and services in an economy based on general price levels. When prices are high the quantity demanded will be low, firms output will be low and hence National Income will be low. Conversely when general prices are low demand, output and National Income will be high. The aggregate demand curve will be downward sloping, as follows

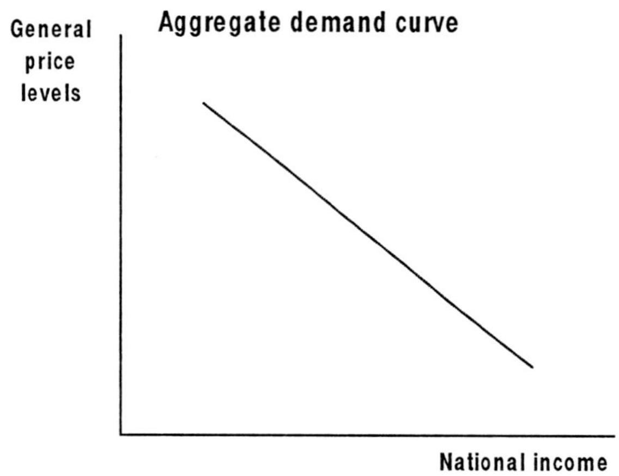

An increase in any of the four components will have the effect of shifting the aggregate demand curve to the right

10.3.2 Aggregate supply

Aggregate supply is the total of goods and services that firms are prepared to supply in an economy, however we need to distinguish between long run and short run supply.

The short-run supply refers to a time frame during which firms can change the amount of labour used but not capital (buildings, factories etc.). In the short run, unless the economy is already operating at full capacity firms will be able to increase output levels through, say, overtime and shift work, giving rise to an upward sloping aggregate supply firm.

Long-run supply refers to a time frame over which firms all factors of production may be varied, which should result in the full and optimal use of all productive factors. The long-run supply curve will, therefore, be inelastic (vertical).

Aggregate supply curve

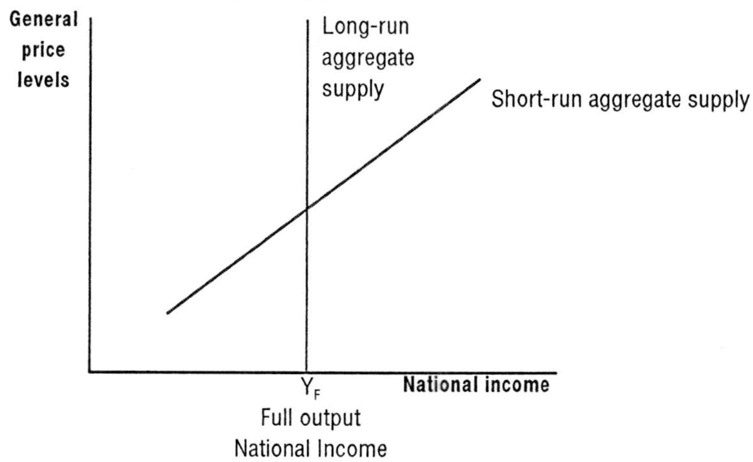

The interaction of aggregate demand and long-run aggregate supply occurs when the economy has an **internal balance** and gives the economies equilibrium full employment output and price levels, however the economy may operate in disequilibrium in the short-term.

To try to achieve its intermediate and overall objectives, a government will use a number of different **policy tools** or **policy instruments.** These policy tools are not mutually exclusive and a government might adopt a **mix of policies** to achieve its economic objectives. Conflicts may arise between different objectives, meaning that choices have to be made. Two main areas of policy are **fiscal policy** and **monetary policy**.

10.4 Fiscal policy

Learning objectives	**24.3.1 Describe** fiscal policy and its influence on aggregate demand. **24.3.2 Explain** the role of debt in the business cycle. **24.3.3 Explain** the problems associated with fiscal policy.

10.4.1 Introduction

Fiscal policy is government policy on taxation, public borrowing and public spending and Keynesian economics is almost exclusively tied in to fiscal intervention. Taxation may be either:

- **Direct taxation** is taxation of incomes.
- **Indirect taxation** is taxation of products and services, for example value added tax.

The amount that the government must borrow each year is now known as the **Public Sector Net Cash Requirement** (PSNCR) in the UK. The public sector net cash requirement (PSNCR) is the annual excess of spending over income for the entire public sector – not just the central government.

A government might intervene in the economy by:

- **Spending more money** and financing this expenditure by borrowing
- **Collecting more in taxes** without increasing spending
- **Collecting more in taxes** in order to **increase spending**, thus diverting income from one part of the economy to another

10.4.2 Fiscal policy consequences

A government's '**fiscal stance**' may be **neutral, expansionary** or **contractionary**, according to its overall effect on national income.

- **Spending more money** than it is raising in taxes and financing this expenditure by borrowing (running a **budget deficit**) would indicate an expansionary fiscal stance. Expenditure in the economy will increase and so national income will tend to rise, either in real terms, or partly in terms of price levels only: the increase in national income might be real, or simply inflationary. This may be referred to as **fiscal easing**.
- **Collecting more in taxes** without increasing spending (running a **budget deficit**) would indicate a contractionary fiscal stance.
  A government might deliberately raise taxation to take inflationary pressures out of the economy
- **Collecting more in taxes in order to increase spending**, thus diverting income from one part of the economy to another would indicate a broadly neutral fiscal stance.

If a government raises taxes and spending by the same amount so that the government's overall budget remains in balance, there will be an **increase in aggregate demand**. This is because taxpayers would have saved some of the money they pay in increased tax and the government spends all of it within the economy. (This effect is called the **balanced budget multiplier**.)

Since government spending or tax reductions might be inflationary, and higher domestic prices make imports relatively cheaper and exports less competitive in foreign markets, fiscal policy has possible implications for the **balance of payments** (discussed later).

Fiscal policy could be used in an attempt to reduce unemployment and provide jobs. For example:

- More government spending on capital projects
- Government-funded training schemes
- Taxation of companies on the basis of the numbers and pay levels of employees

Government spending, however, might create inflationary pressures, and inflation tends to create more unemployment. Fiscal policy must therefore be used with care, even to create new jobs.

The impact of changes in fiscal policy is not always certain, and fiscal policy to pursue one aim (eg lower inflation) might for a while create barriers to the pursuit of other aims (eg employment).

10.4.3 Fiscal policy problems

The three practical problems of fiscal policy are

- **Time lags** – the time between recognising an issue and seeing the effects of any formulated fiscal response can be quite significant. If a response is formulated at one stage in the business cycle but takes effect in another this can be destabilising and may lead to what has become known as **stop-go** economics where the correct intervention cannot be achieved.
- **Political manipulation** – governments have, historically, tried to manipulate the economy to achieve a boom just before an election. This is, in truth, economic mismanagement.
- **Crowding out** – If an expansionary is conducted that is financed by borrowing, this increased borrowing may increase interest rates resulting in a reduction in consumer spending or business investment. The policy may, therefore, have the opposite net effect to that desired.
- **Higher future tax rates** – If an expansionary is conducted that is financed by borrowing then future tax rates may need to rise to obtain the funds to repay this debt. An expansionary policy today may, therefore, result in a contractionary policy in the future.

Government planners need to consider how fiscal policy can affect **savers, investors** and **companies**.

- The tax regime as it affects different savings instruments or property ownership, for example, will affect **investors'** decisions.
- **Companies** will be affected by tax rules on dividends and profits, and they may take these rules into account when deciding on dividend policy or on whether to raise finance through **debt** (loans) or **equities** (by issuing shares).

Until the 1970s fiscal policy was used as the cornerstone of government economic policy, the policy being used to balance the effect of inflation and unemployment. The occurrence of stagflation in the 1970s, characterised by both high inflation and high unemployment along with economic stagnation brought about a rethink in economic policy and the adoption of monetary as well as fiscal control.

10.4.4 Fiscal policy and the Budget

A feature of fiscal policy is that a government must **plan** what it wants to spend, and so how much it needs to raise in income or by borrowing. It needs to make a plan in order to establish how much taxation there should be, what form the taxes should take and so which sectors of the economy (firms or households, high income earners or low income earners) the money should come from.

This formal planning of fiscal policy usually follows an annual cycle. In the UK, the most important statement is **the Budget**, which takes place in the spring of each year. The Chancellor of the Exchequer also delivers a Pre-Budget Report each autumn. The Pre-Budget Report formally makes available for scrutiny the government's overall spending plans.

Because of the annual planning cycle of government finances, fiscal policy cannot be very responsive to shorter-term developments in the economy. For shorter-term fine-tuning of the economy, the government may need to use **monetary policy**.

10.5 Monetary policy

Learning objectives

24.3.4 Define money supply (from 'narrow' through to 'wide').
24.3.5 Describe the fractional reserve banking system.
24.3.6 Define the money multiplier and identify its determinants.
24.3.7 Calculate the potential money multiplier given a cash reserve ratio.
24.3.15 Explain the impact of bank capital and liquidity requirements and the move towards macroprudential regulation on the macro-economy.
24.3.16 Explain the role of securitisation on credit growth and the wider macro-economy.

10.5.1 Introduction

Monetary policy is the area of government economic policy making that is concerned with changes in

- the **amount of money** in circulation – the **money supply**
- the **amount of money available** – the ability of the banks to lend as a consequence of their reserve requirements (see below)
- changes in the **price of money** – **interest rates**. These variables are linked with **inflation** in prices generally (hence indirectly to unemployment), and also with **exchange rates** – the price of the domestic currency in terms of other currencies. Tight control of the money supply should keep inflation low with the unfortunate trade-off of high unemployment.

10.5.2 Money supply

Narrow money and broad money

How much money is there in the economy? It is not always easy to decide whether a particular financial asset, for example a bank deposit, is money or not, and we can distinguish between **narrow money** and **broad money** when we try to measure the stock of money in the economy. (The **money stock** is an alternative term for the money supply.)

Financial assets must have a high degree of liquidity to be regarded as **narrow money**. A definition of narrow money is 'money balances which are readily available to finance current spending, that is to say for transactions purposes' *(Economic Progress Report).*

Broad money, in contrast, includes financial assets which are relatively liquid, but not as liquid as narrow money items. A financial asset which would be regarded as narrow money would also fall within the definition of broad money; but broad money, as its name implies, extends the range of assets which are regarded as money.

Broad money is 'money held for transactions purposes and money held as a form of saving. It provides an indicator of the private sector's holdings of relatively liquid assets – assets which could be converted with relative ease and without capital loss into spending on goods and services' *(Economic Progress Report).*

Narrow money can be defined in different ways, depending on how narrowly 'liquidity' is defined; similarly, broad money can be defined in a variety of ways. Even the broadest definition of money will exclude some financial assets. There will never be a clear dividing line between what is narrow money, what is broad money, and what is not money at all.

Monetary aggregates

Money supply measures are called **monetary aggregates**, the two main measures being M0 and M4

(a) M0 is the 'narrowest' definition of money, the great majority of which is made up of **notes and coin** in circulation outside the Bank of England. This is the formal definition:

M0 = notes and coins in circulation outside the Bank of England + Banks' operational deposits at the Bank of England

(b) M4 is a 'broad' definition of money, including deposits held for **savings** as well as **spending** purposes. The Bank of England also now publishes statistics for various 'liquid assets outside M4' for the benefit of those who are interested in a still broader definition of the money stock. The formal definition of M4 comprises:

M4 = Private sector holdings of Notes and coins
+ Banks' retail deposits
+ Building Society retail shares and deposits
+ Other interest bearing deposits (including Certificate of Deposits)

M4 itself contains some comparatively illiquid elements. For example, M4 contains deposits of any maturity with banks and building societies and certain paper and other capital market instruments of not more than five years' original maturity, although in practice the bulk of M4 is of under three months' residual maturity.

As you may be able to surmise, there are a number of other measures between M0 and M4 that are related as follows

M0 = Notes and coins in circulation

M1 = M0 + private instant access account deposits

M2 = M1 + private term deposits and CDs

M3 = M2 + institutional term deposits and CDs

M4 = M3 + private holdings of building society retail shares and deposits

Fractional reserve banking and the money multiplier

The difference between these measures arises as a result of the effect of credit creation and the money multiplier. Banks do not need to retain 100% of the cash deposited with them, rather they only retain a small fraction to cover day-to-day withdrawals, the **reserve ratio**, and lend out the remainder. This is known as **fractional reserve banking**.

If, for example, the government increases the monetary base by £10 and spend this money then the recipient will deposit this £10 in his account. If the reserve ratio is 10% then the bank will retain just £1 and lend the other £9 to someone for them to buy something. The recipient of that £9 will deposit it with the bank who will retain 90p and lend out the remaining £8.10.

This process will continue until the full £10 must be retained by the bank to cover its reserve requirements on the total effect of this money supply increase. With our numbers the money supply must, therefore have risen by £100. As a result of this fractional reserve banking a £10 increase in the monetary base has caused a £100 increase in the money supply – a money multiplier at 10×. More generally the relationship is

$$\text{Money multiplier} = \frac{1}{\text{Reserve ratio}}$$

In order to ensure the prudent operation of banks and to protect against a banking failure, international agreements (Basel II) have been developed limiting how much capital banks need to put aside to guard against the types of financial and operational risks they face. The Basel accord places constraints on bank capital and liquidity requirements that influences more than just the banks as through their impact on the reserve ratio they influence the money multiplier.

Despite these controls, however, the process of securitisation has had the effect of causing a significant increase in the money supply. Securitisation is where a bank packages up certain debts, such as mortgages, and sells them to a special purpose vehicle (SPV) that raises finance by issuing debt securities. Within the SPV, the mortgage payments received service the required debt payments making the debt an attractive secured investment. For the bank, the mortgage debts are removed from their accounts and replaced by cash that they can now lend out. Through this process the banks have effectively lent the same money out twice and could continue to securitise and lend. Such securitisation has contributed significantly to the growth in credit, increasing the money supply in a manner that is more difficult for the government to control.

10.5.3 Monetary policy objectives

Although the control of inflation has remained the main objective for some time, the UK current monetary policy framework has evolved from changing circumstances in recent decades.

Up to the 1970s, monetary policy included direct **controls** on the amount of **lending** that banks were allowed to undertake. In the 1980s, the framework of monetary policy involved trying to control the overall supply of money in the economy. Targets were set for the growth of money (notes, coins, bank deposits) and interest rates were varied accordingly. However, measures of the amount of money in the economy did not always prove to be a reliable guide to demand and inflation. As a result, by the mid-1980s monetary policy came to be based on an assessment of a wider range of economic indicators rather than a single measure of money supply growth.

One aspect of this was that there were exchange rate targets, with the object of linking monetary policy and inflation in one country with that of another or others. For a period in the late 1980s, the target exchange rate was three Deutsche Marks to one pound (DM3 = £1). In 1990, the UK entered the **European Exchange Rate Mechanism (ERM)**. Monetary policy had to be set so that the pound would not strengthen or weaken by more than a certain amount against other ERM currencies.

In 1992, differing economic conditions across Europe created tensions between setting interest rates to maintain the exchange rate target and the exchange rate required for the domestic economy. There was strong growth and inflationary pressure in Germany, following its reunification. This made German interest rates high. On the other hand, the UK, was emerging from a recession, with slow growth and falling inflation. Maintaining sterling's position in the ERM limited the scope for reducing interest rates below the German levels to a rate that would have been better for the UK economy. Investors lost confidence in UK policy and did not want to hold sterling. Downward pressure on sterling led to a **suspension of ERM membership** on 16 September 1992 and a sharp depreciation of the sterling exchange rate.

After sterling's exit from the ERM, the UK Government adopted an **explicit target for inflation** for the first time. Instead of targeting the exchange rate or some other variable as a means of controlling inflation, a rate for inflation itself was targeted. Interest rates were to be set to ensure demand in the economy was kept at a level consistent with a certain level of inflation over time. If interest rates are increased consumers have less cash available to spend, weakening consumer demand and asset prices. If rates are decreased it will have the opposite effects.

10.5.4 Monetary policy effects

Learning objectives	**24.3.8 Explain** the transmission mechanism whereby monetary policy influences economic aggregates. **24.3.14 Explain** the other tools (including quantitative easing (QE)) used by central banks to manage the economy and in particular inflation.

Introduction

UK monetary policy is currently based on an explicit inflation target of 2% or less for the Consumer Prices Index.

The Bank of England **reducing** interest rates is an **easing** of monetary policy.

- Loans will be cheaper, and so consumers may increase levels of debt and spend more. Demand will tend to rise and companies may have improved levels of sales. Companies will find it cheaper to borrow: their lower interest costs will boost bottom-line profits.
- Mortgage loans will be cheaper and so there will be upward pressure on property prices.
- Other asset values will also rise. Investors will be willing to pay higher prices for gilts (government stock) because they do not require such a high yield from them as before the interest rate reduction.
- Interest rates on cash deposits will fall. Those who are dependant on income from cash deposits will be worse off than before.
- Businesses will find it cheaper to borrow, and will find investment in expansion new business opportunities more attractive.

The Bank of England **increasing** interest rates is a **tightening** of monetary policy.

- Loans will cost more, and demand from consumers, especially for less essential 'cyclical' goods and services, may fall. Companies will find it more expensive to borrow money and this could eat into profits, on top of any effect from reducing demand.
- Mortgage loans will cost more and so there will be a dampening effect on property prices.
- Asset prices generally will tend to fall. Investors will require a higher return than before and so they will pay less for fixed interest stocks such as gilts.
- Interest rates on cash deposits will rise, and those reliant on cash deposits for income will be better off.
- Businesses' borrowing costs will rise, and this may reduce company profits and act as a disincentive to make investments.

The interest rates on financial instruments with longer periods to maturity – such as the yield on long government stocks (**gilts**) – will be influenced by changing expectations in the markets of future levels of interest rates. The short-term rates set by the Bank of England do not change direction frequently. Consequently, the first rise in short-term rates for a period can be taken as a signal by the markets that more rises can be expected in the future. The Bank must be careful about the signals it gives to the markets, since the effect of expectations can be strong.

Quantitative easing

Normally, a Central Bank seeks to control the economy through the management of interest rates. If an economy is booming and inflationary pressures are coming to the fore then the Bank will raise rates. Alternatively, if an economy experiencing recessionary conditions, the Bank may seek to stimulate the economy by lowering interest rates. If, however, interest rates are already very low (at or around zero) so there is no further scope for a rate reduction, the Bank may seek to stimulate the economy through quantitative easing.

Quantitative easing is a process by which the Bank attempts to inject cash into the economy with the aim of, through the effects of the bank multiplier, increasing the overall money supply. This is achieved by the Bank purchasing financial assets, mainly short-term government and corporate bonds, from financial institutions (such as banks) using money it has created. Quantitative easing is sometimes described as 'printing money', although the central bank actually creates it electronically 'out of nothing' by increasing the credit in its own bank account.

One further aim of quantitative easing is to create mild inflation. Inflation with very low interest rates should encourage consumers to spend now rather than save, thereby again providing a boost to the economy.

The intention is that this new money in the hands of the banks can now be lent to customers to be invested, thereby stimulating the economy. There are risks associated with such an approach however, hence it needs to be carefully managed. If, for example, inter-bank confidence is too low then the amount of money needed to achieve the Bank's objectives may prove to be beyond its scope. Alternatively, in difficult economic circumstances the banks may still be reluctant to lend to customers despite the increase in their deposits. They may prefer to pay down debt and improve their balance sheets rather than lend to customers. Consequently, the hoped for economic stimulus may not materialise.

10.5.5 Monetary policy problems

The practical problems associated with monetary policy are

1. **Controlling the money supply** – Although in theory this should be easily achieved by managing interest rates and the bank reserve ratio, the effects of securitisation (banks securitising and selling off loan books) can circumvent this.

2. **Velocity of circulation** – Controlling the money supply does not necessarily control demand and spending, it may simply result in the available money circulating more rapidly in the economy as spending continues.

3. **Time lags** – as with fiscal policy the time between recognising an issue and seeing the effects of any formulated monetary response can be significant, though monetary effects tend to have a more immediate impact that fiscal effects.

11 The Role of Central Banks

Learning objectives

24.3.12 Explain how inflation targeting operates in the UK.

24.3.13 Distinguish between the different approaches to the control of inflation taken by the major central banks.

11.1 Central banks

A **central bank** is a bank which acts on behalf of government. You will probably also have heard, for example, of the **Federal Reserve Bank** – the central bank of the USA – and the **European Central Bank** – the central bank of the Euro currency zone. The central bank for the United Kingdom is the **Bank of England.**

11.2 The Bank of England

The Bank of England ('the Bank') is a nationalised corporation run by a Court of Directors, consisting of the Governor, Deputy Governor, and some Executive Directors and part-time Directors.

The following are functions of the Bank of England.

- It acts as **banker to the central government** and holds the 'public deposits'. Public deposits include the National Loans Fund, the Consolidated Fund and the account of the Paymaster General, which in turn includes the Exchange Equalisation Account.
- It is the **central note-issuing authority** in the UK – the Treasury is responsible for issuing bank notes in England.
- It is the manager of the Exchange Equalisation Account (ie the UK's **foreign currency reserves**).
- It acts as adviser to the government on **monetary policy** and, through its **Monetary Policy Committee**, manages interest rates in the light of the Government's inflation target. Since May 1997, it has had operational responsibility for **setting interest rates** at the level it considers appropriate in order to meet the Government's inflation target.
- It acts as a **banker to the commercial banks**, who keep accounts with the Bank of England.
- It acts as the **lender of last resort to the banking system**. When the banking system is short of money, the Bank of England will provide the money the banks need – at a suitable rate of interest.

Supervision of the banking system is now the responsibility of the Financial Services Authority – not of the Bank of England. Similarly, the Bank is no longer the **manager of the National Debt** as this role has been taken over by the Treasury – ie the Treasury deals with long-term and short-term borrowing by the central government and the repayment of central government debt.

11.3 The central bank as lender of last resort

In the UK, the **short-term money market** provides a link between the banking system and the government (Bank of England). Normally, if one bank needs to bank needs to borrow money it borrows it from another bank that has surplus funds at **LIBOR (London Inter-Bank Offered Rate)**. When such surplus funds are not available the Bank of England lends money to the banking system. The Bank thus acts as the **lender of last resort**.

- The Bank will supply cash to the banking system on days when the banks have a cash shortage. It does this by buying eligible bills and other short-term financial investments from approved financial institutions in exchange for cash.
- The Bank will remove excess cash from the banking system on days when the banks have a cash surplus. It does this by selling bills to institutions, so that the short-term money markets obtain interest-bearing bills in place of the cash that they do not want.

The process whereby this is done currently is known as **open market operations** by the Bank. This describes the buying and selling of eligible bills (government bills and certain other securities) and other short-term assets between the Bank and the short-term money market.

11.4 Setting interest rates

Since 1997, the most important aspect of monetary policy in the UK has been the influence over interest rates exerted by the **Bank of England**, the **central bank** of the UK. The **Monetary Policy Committee (MPC)** of the Bank of England is charged with the responsibility of setting the **base rate** of interest with the aim of meeting the government's **inflation target of 2%** based on the **Consumer Prices Index (CPI)**, sometimes known by the name Harmonised Index of Consumer Prices (HICP).

If the inflation target is missed by more than 1 percentage point on either side – in other words, if the annual CPI inflation rate were to be more than 3% or less than 1 % – the Governor of the Bank, as Chairman of the MPC, must write an open letter to the Chancellor explaining the reasons why inflation has increased or fallen to such an extent and what the Bank proposes to do to ensure inflation comes back to the target.

The MPC influences interest rates by deciding the short-term benchmark 'repo' rate at which the Bank of England deals in the money markets. This will tend to be followed by financial institutions generally in setting interest rates for different financial instruments. However, a government does not have an unlimited ability to have interest rates set how it wishes. It must take into account what rates the overall market will bear, so that the benchmark rate it chooses can be maintained.

The monthly minutes of the MPC are published. This arrangement is intended to remove the possibility of direct political influence over the interest rate decision.

The **UK inflation objective** was formalised in the 1998 Bank of England Act. That Act states that the Bank of England is expected 'to maintain price stability, and, subject to that, to support the economic policy of HM Government including its objectives for growth and employment' (Bank of England Act 1998).

11.5 Role of central banks

Internationally, there is considerable variation between different central banks as far as the functions they fulfil. A summary of the main central banks is included below.

	Name	Sets Interest Rate Independently	Manage Govt Debt	Banking Supervision
Europe	European Central Bank (ECB)	✓*	×	×
UK	Bank of England	✓	×	×
Japan	Bank of Japan	✓	×	✓**
US	Federal Reserve	✓	×	✓***
Canada	Bank of Canada	✓	×	×
Russia	Central Bank of the Russian Federation	✓	×	✓

All the above central banks provide some degree of financial stability regulation.

* The European Central Bank (ECB) has responsibility for setting interest rates for the Eurozone countries, participating in the single currency, the euro., with the rate of maintaining inflation close to but below 2% on the medium term, with the rate of maintaining inflation close to but below 2% of the medium term.

** Proposals have emerged following the 2010 general election that banking supervision may be passed to the Bank of England but to date (July 2010) no such legislation has been enacted

*** The Bank of Japan has partial responsibility for banking supervision

None of the above central banks are responsible for managing government debt.

12 Inflation and Unemployment

Learning objective

24.3.9 **Define** inflation and **explain** how it is measured in the UK.

12.1 The nature of inflation

The price of something is the amount of money for which something of economic value is or might be exchanged. **Inflation** is the name given to a general increase in price levels.

Another way of describing a general rise in prices is as a decline in the **purchasing power of money**. Inflation is an important concern for investors, as well as for borrowers. However, just as there are many different prices, there are also many different things that a person might purchase with money. People spend money on goods for consumption, but they may also buy assets that are not for immediate consumption, such as a house. They may purchase investments, deferring consumption until a later date when the investment is sold or may provide an income.

12.2 Measuring inflation

Consumer price indices may be used for several purposes, for example as an indicator of inflationary pressures in the economy, as a benchmark for wage negotiations and to determine annual increases in government benefits payments. Countries commonly have more than one consumer price index because one composite index may be considered too wide a grouping for different purposes.

The **Retail Prices Index (RPI)** measures the percentage changes month by month in the average level of prices (including VAT and other duties) of the commodities and services, including housing and mortgage costs, purchased by the great majority of households in the UK. The items of expenditure within the RPI are intended to be a representative list of items, current prices for which are collected at regular intervals. Two further measure are

- RPIX – that excludes mortgage interest payments
- RPIY – that excludes mortgage interest and VAT

In December 2003, it was confirmed that the standardised European inflation measure, the Harmonised Index of Consumer Prices (HICP), was to be used as the basis for the **UK's inflation target** of 2%. The UK HICP is called the **Consumer Prices Index (CPI)**. The CPI excludes most housing costs such as mortgages. However, pensions and benefits and index-linked gilts continue to be calculated on the same basis as previously, using the RPI.

One final inflation measure to note is the **producer price index (PPI)** which measure the increase in 'factory gate' prices.

If a prices index was 182.6 in October 2003 and rises to 185.1 in October 2004, what is the annual percentage rate of inflation to October 2004, to one decimal place?

185.1 / 182.6	= 1.0137
$(1.0137 - 1) \times 100$	= 1.37%

After rounding, this gives an annual inflation rate of 1.4% to one decimal place.

Here are some past values for the **UK Retail Prices Index**.

October 1983	86.7
October 1993	141.8
October 2003	182.6

How has inflation eroded the purchasing power of money over the ten years and twenty years up to 2003?

£1 in October 2003 bought as much as £1 × 86.7/182.6 = 47.5p would have bought twenty years earlier.

£1 in October 2003 bought as much as £1 × 141.8/182.6 = 77.7p would have bought ten years earlier.

Savings of £1,000 held for the 20 years up to 2003 would need to have grown to £100 x 182.6/86.7 = £2,106 to preserve their purchasing power over the period.

12.3 Inflation, deflation and disinflation

Historically, there have been very few periods when inflation has not been present. High rates of inflation are generally considered to be harmful. However, **deflation** (falling prices, for a sustained period) is normally associated with low rates of growth and even **recession** (two or more consecutive quarters of falling real GDP). This is because falling prices could encourage companies to reduce output, as they will find that anticipated prices are less likely to cover their input costs. Reduced output may lead to rising unemployment, which will tend to depress demand and, in turn, production. The decline brought about may thus be self-perpetuating.

The causes of deflation are:

- Decline in output and demand for goods and services
- Delays in investment and purchasing of assets/goods and services

Deflation can be countered by:

- Creating demand for goods and services by maintaining higher prices
- Maintaining wage settlements at higher levels
- Reducing interest rates

Disinflation refers to a situation in which there is a **reducing rate of inflation**. Prices are still rising, but at a reducing rate. If inflation is at too high a rate, a government will want a period of disinflation to bring it back to an acceptable range. Policymakers do not generally want to have a situation of deflation however, since this can produce the kind of problems we have mentioned above.

Factors affecting inflation

The outlook for inflation is affected by several factors:

- World economic conditions; whether global demand is rising or falling
- State of the real domestic economy; when output is above capacity inflation will tend to rise
- Commodity prices, especially the price of oil as this will put pressure on higher wages
- Asset prices such as housing: although housing costs are not included in the inflation measure the increased housing costs will create demand for higher wages
- Investor expectations are vital in determining an investor's behaviour and need to be considered when forming economic policy. Expectations for future inflation can have a strong impact on wage growth demands and hence impact on future inflation

12.4 Why is inflation a problem?

An economic policy objective which now has a central place in the policy approaches of the governments of many developed countries is that of stable prices. It would seem that a healthy economy may require some inflation. This is implicitly recognised in the UK inflation target of 2% or less for the CPI (the same target as that of the European Central Bank, for the euro zone). Certainly, if an economy is to grow, the money supply must expand, and the presence of a low level of inflation can help to ensure that growth is not hampered by a shortage of liquid funds.

Inflation leads to a **redistribution of income and wealth** in ways that may be undesirable. Redistribution of wealth might take place from creditors (eg, lenders) to debtors (borrowers). This is because debts lose 'real' value with inflation. For example, if you owed £1,000, and prices then doubled, you would still owe £1,000, but the **real value** of your debt would have been halved. In general, in times of inflation those with economic power tend to gain at the expense of the weak, particularly those on fixed incomes such as many elderly people.

Also, there can be **balance of payments** effects. If a country has a higher rate of inflation than its major trading partners, its **exports** will become relatively expensive and **imports** relatively cheap. As a result, the balance of trade between imports and exports will suffer, affecting employment in exporting industries and in industries producing import-substitutes. Eventually, exchange rates between currencies will be affected.

Once the rate of inflation has begun to increase, there is a danger of **expectations** making it worse. This means, regardless of whether the factors that have caused inflation are still persistent or not, there will arise a generally held view of what inflation is likely to be, and so to protect future income, wages and prices will be raised now by the expected amount of future inflation. This can lead to the vicious circle known as the **wage-price spiral**, in which inflation becomes a relatively permanent feature because of people's expectations that it will occur.

12.5 Inflation and unemployment

Learning objectives	**24.3.10 Define** unemployment and explain how it is measured in the UK. **24.3.11 Explain** the relationship between inflation and unemployment.

This last point highlights the crucial of inflation and that is its relationship to unemployment. Unemployment can be defined as the number of people of working age that are registered as available to work but failing to find employment at the current wage rate.

The possible causes of unemployment include

- **Classical unemployment** – the effects of supply and demand. If wage demands are too high employment will fall.
- **Structural unemployment** – resulting from structural changes in the economy such as industry closures.
- **Seasonal unemployment** – Unemployment resulting from certain jobs only being available at certain times of the year, eg harvest time in the agricultural industry
- **Frictional unemployment** – people between jobs or incapable of being employed due to disability.
- **Keynesian unemployment** – structural unemployment on a national scale as a result a drop in aggregate demand causing unemployment in manufacturing and service suppliers.

It is generally assumed that there is a **natural rate of unemployment** that will exist even if jobs are available for full employment. This may occur mainly as a consequence of seasonal and frictional effects, though all causes may contribute to this natural rate. Since jobs are available for everyone natural unemployment may be regarded as voluntary.

12.6 Economic theories of inflation and unemployment

12.6.1 Classical unemployment

For the classical economists, **unemployment is simply a supply and demand phenomenon** taken, in this case, from the labour markets. Unemployment represents the position where the supply of a good – labour – is greater than the demand for that good. This excess of supply over demand represents the unemployed. In very simple terms, the only reason that workers are unemployed is that the price they are charging for wages is too high. If the price were allowed to fall, then more workers would be demanded and unemployment would be cured.

In essence, the classical view is that workers who are without a job are **voluntarily unemployed** in that it is their choice to work at a given wage. If they are prepared to reduce their wage, then they will be able to obtain employment.

Classical Unemployment

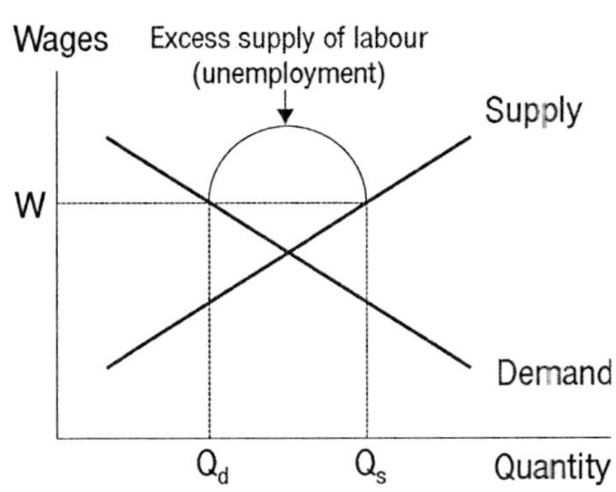

The classical view of inflation is the other side of this. Under the classical view, inflation arises when wages are too low and demand exceeds supply at that level. This excess demand drives up the price of labour (wages) with the result that firms face rising input prices. In order to stay in business the firms need to pass on these price increases to customers creating **cost-push inflation**. This may, in turn, cause consumers to demand higher wages to cover the extra costs, potentially leading to an inflationary spiral.

12.6.2 Keynesian theory of unemployment and inflation

If inflation is expected to rise more than is acceptable the government should tighten fiscal policy by raising tax rates.

In the event of unemployment, Keynesian theory suggests that the government should resort to fiscal policy, ie reduce taxation and increase its own expenditure in order to boost demand in the economy. This type of activity designed to restore full employment can be referred to as stabilisation policy.

For example, if an economy is at equilibrium at the point Y_1 that is below the point of full employment (Y_f), then to move towards full employment the government needs to inject sufficient demand to raise aggregate demand to AD_2. This will close what nay be referred to as the **deflationary gap** and bring the economy to full employment.

Unemployment – The Deflationary Gap

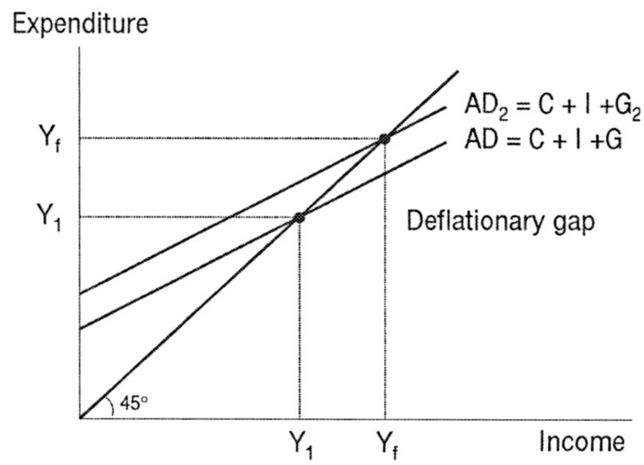

The effect of such a fiscal policy is twofold. Firstly, government expenditure increases and, following the multiplier effect from above, this will increase the incomes of participants within the economy. Secondly, by reducing the rate of tax, individuals will have a greater disposable income and therefore will consume more. The result of this is that overall demand will increase substantially.

Keynesian theory suggests that fiscal policy can also be used where the government is dealing with an economy which is overheated. In an economy where demand is greater than the available resources, the result will be **inflation**. This may be referred to as **demand pull inflation**. Put simply, **'too much money chasing too few goods'**. In this environment, the government should adopt exactly the opposite policy – spending less and taxing more. This will have the effect of reducing demand to a sustainable level.

This time the economy is trading above the full employment level and the government is obliged to reduce the level of aggregate demand back to AD_2.

The Inflationary Gap

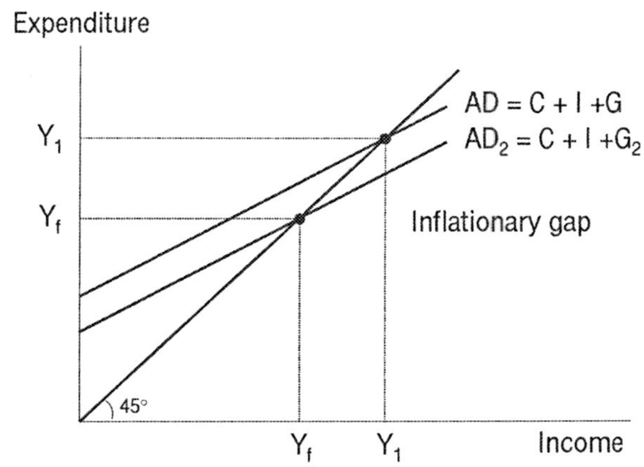

Unemployment and inflation – the Phillips Curve

In the 1960s, a Keynesian economist, Phillips, plotted the relationship between unemployment and inflation in the UK.

The Phillips Curve

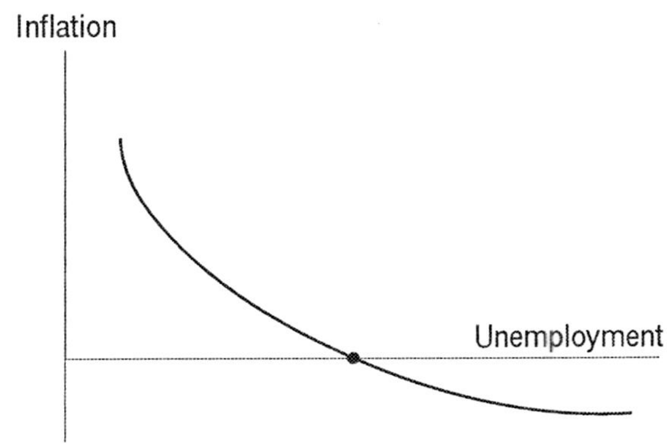

This relationship seems to indicate that a trade-off between the level of inflation and unemployment exists.

This would tend to support the main Keynesian contention that unemployment and inflation are both demand features. The main policy prescription was that if the government wishes to, it will be able to reduce unemployment by stimulating demand, but at the price of a slightly higher level of inflation.

The Expectations Augmented Phillips Curve

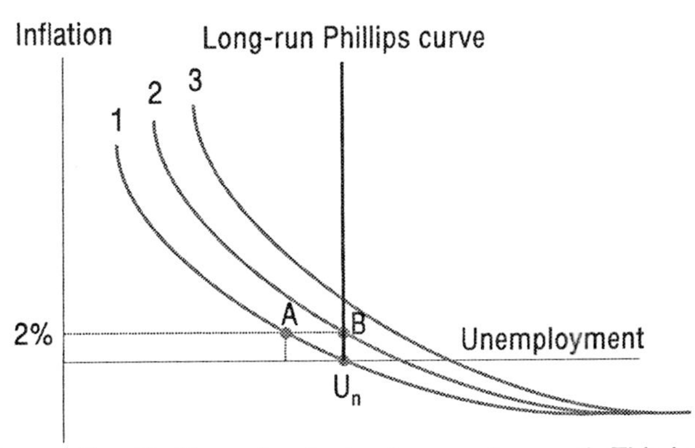

The economy starts at the position U_n (the natural rate of unemployment). This is sometimes referred to as NAIRU, the non-accelerating inflation rate of unemployment. If the government wishes to reduce unemployment below U_n, then it will have to, following Keynesian policies, inject demand into the economy. This increase in demand will stimulate the employers into demanding more workers. In order to encourage more workers back into the labour market, a higher wage will have to be offered.

The higher wages attract those workers who, at this stage, can be viewed as voluntarily unemployed. However, the employer will have to increase their prices in order to compensate for the higher wage costs (moving to point A on the diagram). As the general level of prices begins to rise to, let us say, 2%, then the workers who have been enticed back into the labour market will see the real value of their pay packets diminish.

They will, at this point, decide that there is no point in their continuing in employment as the real value of their pay packet has been eroded. Indeed, they were only enticed to rejoin the labour market by a form of **money illusion**. The economy now moves to point B, where unemployment is still at the **natural rate** but inflationary expectations have been introduced into the system. All other workers are now making all of their decisions on the assumption that there will be inflation of 2% in the system.

We have now moved on to a higher Phillips curve reflecting inflationary expectation, but with no improvement in unemployment. If the government persists in its attempt to reduce unemployment below the natural rate, then the only result will be to accelerate expectations of inflation with only short-run reductions in the level of unemployment.

The impact on the market

Keynesian economics had as its guiding objective the cure for unemployment. It was accepted during the 1950s and 1960s that this may involve a minor level of inflation, but that this was a price well worth paying for full employment.

Throughout the period, this led to a gradual increase in the background level of inflation, which obviously had an impact on bond yields, particularly at the long end of the yield curve.

The use of fiscal policy has another impact on bond markets. In particular, the level of the government deficit tends to vary in line with the economic cycle quite substantially, as governments spend heavily in recessions and operate a budget surplus in periods of boom. However, provided that the cycles and the economy are not too wide, this impact will not be dramatic.

The Keynesian economics consensus dominated government economic policy, in all of the G7 nations, right through the 1950s, 1960s and early 1970s. The relationship between unemployment and inflation broke down in the early 1970s when governments around the world were faced with a phenomenon which Keynesian economics could not explain: the existence of both unemployment and inflation at the same time (known as **stagflation**).

At this stage, it was felt that Keynesian economics had failed and a change was called for.

12.6.3 Monetarist theory of inflation and unemployment

Inflation

Monetarist economists have argued that **inflation** is caused by **increases in the supply of money**, hence inflation can be brought under control by reducing the rate of growth of the money supply. There is considerable debate as to whether increases in the money supply are a cause of inflation or are a symptom of inflation, however the monetarist views have some strong support.

Monetarists argue that since money is a direct substitute for all other assets, an increase in the money supply, given a fairly stable velocity of circulation, will have a direct effect on demand for other assets because there will be more money to spend on those assets. If the total output of the economy is fixed, then an increase in the money supply will lead directly to higher prices.

This can be referred to as the **quantitative theory of money** can be expressed through the **Fisher equation**:

$$MV = PY$$

Where:

- M = Money supply
- V = Velocity of circulation of money in the economy
- P = Price levels of goods traded
- Y = A real output in the economy, ie the number of transactions undertaken

Based on this, a rise in the money supply will lead to a rise in prices and probably also to a rise in money incomes. In the short run, monetarists argue that an increase in the money supply might cause some increase in real economic output and so an increase in employment. In the long run, however, all increases in the money supply will be reflected in higher prices unless there is longer-term growth in the economy.

However, if the government controls the money supply without telling anyone what its planned targets of growth are, then people's **expectations** of inflation will run ahead of the growth in the money supply. Wage demands will remain at levels in keeping with these expectations **creating cost push inflation**. If the government succeeds in its aim of limiting the growth of the money supply, but wages rise at a faster rate, then higher wages will mean less real income and less real output. In other words, the economy will slump even further.

It is for this reason that the government must announce its targets for inflation and the growth in the money supply. Some economists argue that an **incomes policy** should also be imposed by the government to prevent wage rises in excess of government targets

Monetarists point to the high inflation of the mid-1970s as evidence in support of their views since very rapid monetary growth preceded the price inflation experienced at that time. Later research suggested that soaring oil and commodity prices may have been the culprits and that falling commodity prices subsequently helped to reduce inflation.

Unemployment

The monetarists accept that, because of the squeeze in government finances initially required to remove surplus money from the economy, unemployment will result from their policies. However, their assertion is that unemployment would be there anyway, and the choice is between either unemployment as a side effect of inflation, or unemployment as part of the cure for inflation.

Fundamentally, their **views on unemployment are similar to the classical view** that in part, unemployment is a voluntary phenomenon created by workers pricing themselves out of jobs by demanding too high a wage rate. Added to this, monetarists do believe there is a core of unemployment – referred to as **natural unemployment** – which represents, perhaps, longer structural changes taking place in the economy.

The reason for the persistence of unemployment in the long term is the inability of the markets to clear. Inflation is regarded as being one of the key reasons for this inability, in that it establishes a form of static interference which prevents market mechanisms from understanding the messages that are being given to them. The monetarists believe that once inflation is cured, market forces will be able to work more effectively and unemployment will be resolved by the power of the invisible hand.

Often allied with this, monetarists have asserted that there should be **supply-side economic policies**. Supply-side economic policies are designed to free the market and ensure that it is able to respond quickly to market forces. Supply-side economic policies include the removal of union powers, privatisation, reduction of unemployment benefit, retraining schemes, relocation grants and a general increase in the provision of information available to the unemployed.

Monetarists argue that the combination of a low inflation environment and supply-side policies will ensure that market forces work efficiently and effectively to remove unemployment, and that the economy moves to full employment equilibrium.

12.7 Impact on inflation on investment return

12.7.1 Nominal returns and real returns

The quoted rate of interest or return on a deposit or other investment is sometimes called the **nominal rate of interest**.

If the return on deposits exceeds the rate of inflation, then there is a **positive real rate of return**. For example, if deposits earn 3.8% while the general rate of inflation is 2.3%, then the real rate of return is roughly 1.5%. £1,000 placed on deposit over one year will gain 1.5% in purchasing power during the year. Compared with one year earlier, 1.5% more in goods in services can be bought with the money.

If the rate of inflation exceeds the return on deposits, then there is a **negative real rate of return**. For example, if deposits earn 2.8% while inflation is 4.8%, there is a negative real rate of return of approximately 2%. £1,000 placed on deposit over one year will lose 2% of its purchasing power during the year. Significantly negative real rates of return can discourage saving, since the purchasing power of money will be eroded through time.

The true link between nominal returns, real return and inflation rates is

$$(1 + \text{Nominal return}) = (1 + \text{Real return}) \times (1 + \text{Inflation rate})$$

This can be approximated by

$$\text{Nominal rate} = \text{Real rate} + \text{Inflation rate}$$

which is what we have used in the above illustrations.

12.7.2 Inflation and deposits

Deposits, for example in retail bank and building society accounts, have generally yielded a positive rate of return in recent years while the rate of inflation has been low. During past periods of higher inflation, for example during the 1970s and 1980s, there were negative real rates of return.

Protection against erosion of purchasing power is provided by the **Index-Linked Savings Certificates** offered by the government agency **National Savings & Investments (NS&I)**.

12.7.3 Inflation and fixed interest securities

With fixed income **government securities ('gilts')** and fixed interest **corporate bonds** issued by companies, an investor receives the same income whatever the rate of inflation. If inflation rises, the purchasing power of the income will fall.

The prices of fixed interest securities will be influenced by expectations of inflation as well as by actual movements in inflation. If higher future inflation is expected, the prices of fixed interest securities will tend to fall, and *vice versa*.

Index-linked government securities can protect against inflation, if they are held to redemption. If held over a shorter term and sold before redemption, the degree of protection offered is less certain because the price of the gilt will fluctuate in the market.

12.7.4 Inflation and returns on equities

Equities are seen as a good hedge against inflation because dividends and capital values tend to grow in line with the economy in money terms.

Over the longer term, shares in companies (**equities**) have generally provided returns **in excess of inflation**. Ultimately, equity returns depend upon **company earnings** (profits), which have tended to rise by more than the rate of inflation, as levels of economic activity and productivity have grown over time.

At any time, it is **expectations of future earnings** can have as much effect on equity market sentiment as current or recently reported earnings. Expectations are subject to rapid changes in sentiment, and may be swayed one way or another by the flow of news on economic prospects and company prospects.

Rising company earnings are paid out in the form of dividends to shareholders or are retained in the business for future investment.

- Over the **long term**, the capital value of shares may rise, offering a return additional to the dividends received.
- Over **shorter periods**, the values of equities can fall or fluctuate quite dramatically, as sentiment changes. For this reason, equities are best seen as a long-term investment.

12.8 Inflation in prices and earnings

The earnings of those in jobs (**average earnings**) tend to increase by more than prices over the longer term. This is because of economic growth: more goods are produced over time, and people have an increased purchasing power arising from that extra production.

13 Exchange Rates and the Balance of Payments

13.1 What is an exchange rate?

13.1.1 Introduction

Learning objectives

24.4.1 Explain how changes in supply and demand for a currency will affect its value on the foreign exchange markets.

24.4.3 Explain the relationship between the supply and demand for a currency and the underlying transactions represented in the balance of payments.
24.4.4 Distinguish between a fixed, floating and a managed exchange rate ('dirty-floating' regime).
24.4.5 Explain the economic benefits and costs of a fixed exchange rate mechanism.

24.4.9 Explain the effectiveness of monetary and fiscal policy in fixed and floating exchange rate regimes.

An **exchange rate** is the price of one currency in terms of another. Dealers in currencies, such as banks, make their profit by buying currency at one exchange rate and selling it at a different rate. This means that there is a selling rate and a buying rate for deals between any two tradeable currencies. So, of course, no tradeable currency has only a single exchange rate.

13.1.2 Exchange rate regimes

From 1946 to 1972, the UK operated within an environment of **fixed exchange rates**, with sterling pegged to the dollar. This was not an absolute link and sterling was devalued twice, in 1950 and 1967.

In 1972, the sterling rate was allowed to float, and supply and demand set the rate. This was a **dirty float**, where the Bank of England intervened in order to establish a government set floor, or ceiling, to the exchange rate.

Even when sterling joined the ERM in 1990, the rate was not fixed but merely stabilised around a level (the parity with the DM). Since the UK's exit from the ERM in 1992, sterling has again floated against the other currencies.

Fixed exchange rates

Use of monetary policy may well be undermined by the establishment of fixed exchange rates, which effectively act as a constraint on interest rates. Consequently, the objectives of monetary policy may not be achievable within the rate target. Effectively, the government has a choice. It can attempt to control the exchange rate or the money supply, and hence interest rates, **but not both**.

With regard to fiscal policy, one of the prime constraints on policy, the risk of **crowding out**, is no longer a problem in the open economy. This is because, assuming that there is full capital mobility, funds will flow in from overseas in order to ensure that the interest rate remains in line with overseas interest rates. There is no restriction on the flow of capital in terms of the fear of exchange rate risk, since rates are fixed.

A balance of payments surplus or deficit will have an effect on the money supply under fixed exchange rates, as government will be obliged to buy or sell currency to maintain that fixed rate. The process by which such changes in the money supply are offset by the exchange by government of domestic currency for bonds is known as **sterilisation**.

Floating exchange rates

Within floating rates, therefore, the exchange rate is no longer a constraint on monetary policy and consequently, providing that the government is prepared to abide by the consequences in terms of the exchange rate, there is no longer a policy problem.

In terms of fiscal policy, the problem of crowding out returns, since overseas investors will be concerned about the risk of exchange depreciation. As the government attempts fiscal expansion, this crowds out domestic consumption and puts an upward pressure on interest rates. In addition, the increase in interest rates will lead to an appreciation of the exchange rate, thereby reducing the demand for the economy's exports and increasing the level of imports.

13.2 Factors influencing exchange rates

A currency may have a fixed exchange rate meaning that its value is pegged to that of another currency. Alternatively a currency may have a floating exchange rate which is the case for the currencies of most major developed economies.

The exchange rate between two floating currencies is determined primarily by **supply and demand** in the foreign exchange markets. Demand comes from individuals, firms and governments who want to buy a currency, for example sterling is demanded by overseas individuals to pay for UK exports to them. Supply comes from those who want to sell the currency, for example to buy a foreign currency to pay for imports. The exchange rates of a currency are subject to a number of influences.

The Short-Term Determination of the Exchange Rate

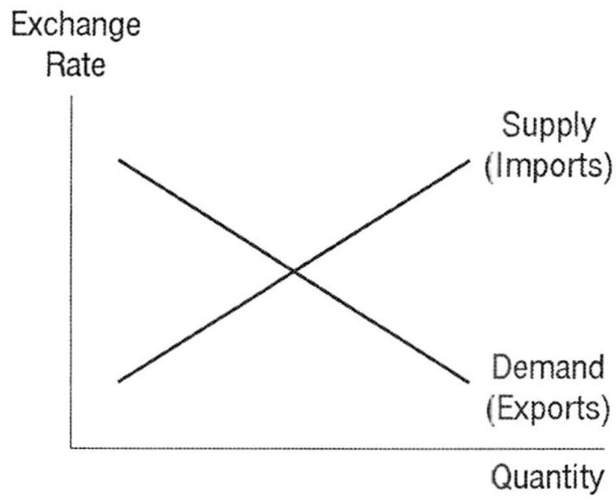

These supply and demand factors should bring the market to an equilibrium rate and this rate should ensure that the trade flows are in balance.

Levels of **inflation**, compared with the rate of inflation in other countries, have an influence. A country with a high level of inflation will tend to have a depreciating currency: if it did not, its exports would start to become uncompetitively priced in world markets. **Purchasing power parity (PPP)** (see later in this Study Text) theory predicts that, over the long run at least, exchange rates should move in line with prices so that an amount of money will buy the same goods and services, whichever currency it is changed into.

Real exchange rates can be calculated by adjusting exchange rates to take account of changes in relative prices levels between countries. How the adjustment is made would depend on the use to which the rates were to be put.

Interest rates compared with interest rates in other countries affect exchange rates. Higher interest rates will attract investment flows into a currency. Here it is the real level of interest that is important: a currency with high inflation as well as high interest rates is less attractive for investment than a currency with relatively low inflation and high interest rates.

Levels of imports and exports will affect exchange rates. If a country imports much more than it exports, it must attract investment flows to balance its excess payments for imports. This may only happen up to a point. If the deficit persists, the currency may decline in value if investors become less willing to invest. As commented earlier, the USA currently runs a significant balance of trade deficit, and some commentators take the view that this may lead to a further decline in the value of the US dollar against other currencies.

Government policy on intervention can influence the exchange rate. Governments over some periods commit themselves, either publicly or without announcement, to maintaining a particular exchange rate or exchange rate range for their currencies. Governments may intervene by buying and selling currencies although most governments' currency reserves are too small to have much effect in this way. Another action that governments can take is to adjust interest rates to defend the desired exchange rate. In 1992, the UK Government sought to defend the value of the pound in order to keep it within its bands as specified in the European Exchange Rate Mechanism (ERM), a precursor to the single European currency (the euro). Interest rates in the UK were increased to 15% but a wave of selling by speculators forced the Government to abandon its attempt, and the pound was removed from the ERM.

Speculation can have an influence, particularly over a shorter-term period, and speculators may be particularly strong influence if a government is seeking to maintain a particular exchange rate, as in the ERM example just mentioned.

13.3 Foreign currency and international trade

The benefits of international trade include

- **Increased competition** – improving the choice and prices to the consumer
- **Specialisation** – international trade allows economies to specialise in areas where they have some unique resources. According to a theory called comparative advantage, all economies should operate in the areas where they have the greatest comparative advantage, then exchange (trade internationally) for their mutual benefit. Through collectively producing things most efficiently and minimising the opportunity costs of global production the both individual and global economies should benefit.

Despite these benefits, many countries engage in protectionism or erect trade barriers to protect domestic industries that are not (on an international comparison) efficiently run. Such protectionism tends to result in trade retaliation, the ultimate effect being detrimental to all involved.

The General Agreement on Tariffs and Trade (GATT) of 1948 was intended to promote free trade. It resulted in the creation the World Trade Organisation (WTO) who have succeeded in gradually reducing the barriers to free trade.

Whenever there is international trade, there is generally a need for foreign currency for at least one of the parties to the transaction.

- If a UK exporter sells goods to a US buyer, and charges the buyer £20,000, the US buyer must somehow obtain the sterling in order to pay the UK supplier. The US buyer will do this by using some of his US dollars to buy the £20,000 sterling, probably from a bank in the USA.
- If a UK importer buys goods from Germany, he might be invoiced in euros, say €100,000. He must obtain this foreign currency to pay his debt, and he will do so by purchasing the euros from a UK bank in exchange for sterling.
- If a UK investor wishes to invest in US capital bonds, he would have to pay for them in US dollars, and so he would have to sell sterling to obtain the dollars.

Thus **capital outflows**, such as investing overseas, not just payments for imports, cause a demand to sell the domestic currency and buy foreign currencies. On the other hand, exports and capital inflows to a country cause a demand to buy the domestic currency in exchange for foreign currencies.

Exporters might want to sell foreign currency earnings to a bank in exchange for domestic currency, and importers may want to buy foreign currency from a bank in order to pay a foreign supplier.

13.4 Effects of a strengthening or a weakening currency

If the domestic currency strengthens (ie 'appreciates') in value against the currencies of a country's major trading partners, there will be the following effects.

- **Imports** will become cheaper. This can help companies that import raw materials although, if more goods, including consumer goods, are imported, the balance of trade may suffer.
- **Exports** will become more difficult for companies to sell at a profit. Exporters must either increase prices on world markets, which may mean that buyers go elsewhere, or they must hold their prices in foreign currency terms and thus receive less in the domestic currency. These effects may lead to the **share prices** of exporters suffering when the currency strengthens. Some larger companies may have 'hedged' against these effects, by using financial instruments that reduce the risks arising from currency fluctuations.

This may lead to a short-term deterioration in the balance of payments as the sterling cost of any foreign goods bought on credit will rise immediately. However as the longer term benefits of the changes in imports and exports varies the balance of payments should improve

13.5 Optimal currency area

Learning objective

24.4.6 Explain an optimal currency area (OCA) and identify the advantages and disadvantages of implementing a single currency in an OCA.

An optimum currency area (OCA) is a geographical region in which overall economic efficiency will be maximised through the use of a single currency.

Historically, each country developed its own currency that ensured internal economic efficiency as historically the majority of trade in a country was internal. In such an economy it simply makes sense that household income and household expenses are all denominated in a single currency for everyone operating in that country or economy.

Trade is, however, becoming increasingly international and the issue of overall economic efficiency needs to be considered more broadly between major trading partners. Perhaps the most obvious illustration of the idea of an optimal currency area has been the adoption of the Euro across much of Europe that removes currency risk and eliminated foreign exchange costs on international trade within the Eurozone.

To achieve and maintain a common currency requires, as an absolute minimum, the harmonisation of monetary policy across the region. It is likely that it also requires fiscal policy union as the fall-out of the 2008 credit crunch seems to be indicating.

Of course, we can see some of the dangers of such a policy and there is currently a distinct possibility that some members may need to withdraw from the Euro as the impact of the necessary monetary policy is having adverse impacts on some countries.

Whilst it is possible that an optimal currency area may span several countries whose businesses, trade and economies are closely linked, it is equally true that an optimal currency area could be smaller than a country. Some economists have argued that certain regions of the US do not fit into an optimal currency area with the rest of the country.

Certain criteria must be satisfied for any currency union to be successful, specifically

- **Mobility of labour and wage flexibility** – Workers must be able to travel and work anywhere in the region and there should be no barriers to this movement.
- **Mobility of capital and price flexibility** – Market forces of supply and demand must automatically distribute money, goods and services to where they are needed.
- **Common business cycles** – If the participant countries are so economically linked they will have similar business cycles, if this is not the case then this weakens the argument that it belongs in an optimal currency area.
- **System of risk sharing** – A system by which the poorer regions are supported by the wealthier ones, as has always been the case internally within any country.

The Eurozone scores well on the mobility of capital, the harmonisation of business cycles and labour mobility (though this is currently lower than in the US). However current rules restrict risk-sharing and this situation is unlikely to change unless and until there is fiscal union alongside the monetary union an citizens of one country are unlikely to be prepared to pay higher taxes to support another country where citizens are taxed at a lower level.

13.6 The balance of payments

Learning objective	24.4.2 **Identify** the key components of the balance of payments.

13.6.1 Introduction

The total pattern of all flows of funds into and out of a country is recorded in the country's **balance of payments**. The **balance of payments** is the statistical accounting record of all of a country's external transactions in a given period.

In balance of payments statistics, **current account** transactions are sub-divided into four parts.

- Trade in goods
- Trade in services
- Income
- Transfers

Before 1996, the term **visibles** was used in official statistics for trade in goods and the term **invisibles** was used for the rest (services, effects of tourism etc). These terms have now been dropped in order to give more emphasis to the balances for trade in goods and services, although you may still find them mentioned.

These items equate to (X – M) in our earlier discussion of National Income. Exports are assumed to be independent of the level of UK National Income since they arise from overseas demand. Imports will, however, be dependent on UK National Income levels and the marginal propensity to import (MAN) as they are a product of UK demand that cannot be satisfied from within the UK.

Income is divided into two parts.

- Income from employment of UK residents by overseas firms
- Income from capital investment overseas

Transfers are also divided into two parts:

- Public sector payments to and receipts from overseas bodies such as the EU. Typically these are interest payments
- Non-government sector payments to and receipts from bodies such as the EU

The **capital account** balance is made up of public sector flows of **capital** into and out of the country, such as government loans to other countries.

The balance on the financial account is made up of flows of capital to and from the non-government sector, such as direct investment in overseas facilities; portfolio investment (in shares, bonds and so on); and speculative flows of currency. Long-term capital flows from are encoring to another may be referred to as **foreign direct investment (FDI)**. Movements on government foreign currency reserves are also included under this heading.

A **balancing item** appears in the balance of payments accounts because of errors and omissions in collecting statistics for the accounts (for example, sampling errors for items such as foreign investment and tourist expenditure and omissions from the data gathered about exports or imports).

The sum of the balance of payments accounts must always be **zero** (ignoring statistical errors in collecting the figures). This is for the same reason that a balance.

13.6.2 The UK balance of payments accounts

A UK balance of payment account at a particular point in time is summarised below.

UK balance of payments accounts

	£ billions
Current account	
Trade in goods	(92,877)
Trade in services	54,479
Income	26,940
Transfers	(13,610)
Current balance	(25,068)
Capital account	3,393
Financial account	18,121
Net errors and omissions	3,554
	0

Given that the balance of payments in principle sums to zero, you may wonder what is meant by a surplus or deficit on the balance of payments. When journalists or economists speak of the balance of payments they are usually referring to the deficit or surplus on the **current account**, or possibly to the surplus or deficit on trade in goods only (this is also known as the **balance of trade** or **external balance**).

Overall, all of the flows making up the balance of payments must balance, but if we take out flows such as investment flows and transfers between international institutions, we can calculate a **balance of trade**. The balance of trade includes all of a country's **imports** and **exports** of goods and services.

13.7 The balance of trade

The overall figure for the **balance of trade** or the **'current account'** shows us the difference between a country's imports and its exports of goods and services.

A problem arises for a country's balance of payments when the country has a deficit on current account (a **trade deficit**) year after year, although there can be problems too for a country which enjoys a continual current account **surplus**.

The problems of a **deficit** on the current account are probably the more obvious. When a country is continually in deficit, it is importing more goods and services that it is exporting. This leads to two possible consequences.

- The country may borrow more and more from abroad, to build up external liabilities which match the deficit on current account, for example encouraging foreign investors to lend more by purchasing the government's gilt-edged securities.
- The country may sell more and more of its assets. This has been happening recently in the USA, for example, where a large deficit on the US current account has been offset by large purchases of shares in US companies by foreign firms.

If a country has a **surplus** on its current account year after year, it might invest the surplus abroad or add it to official reserves. The balance of payments position would be strong. There is the problem, however, that if one country which is a major trading nation has a continuous surplus on its balance of payments current account, other countries must be in continual deficit. These other countries can run down their official reserves, perhaps to nothing, and borrow as much as they can to meet the payments overseas, but eventually, they will run out of money entirely and be unable even to pay their debts. Political pressure might therefore build up within the importing countries to impose tariffs or import quotas.

13.8 How can a government rectify a current account deficit?

Learning objective	24.4.7 **Explain** the implications of persistent global imbalances of trade and capital.

The government of a country with a balance of payments deficit will usually be expected to take measures to reduce or eliminate the deficit. A deficit on current account may be rectified by one or more of the following measures.

- A depreciation of the currency (called **devaluation** when deliberately instigated by the government, for example by changing the value of the currency within a controlled exchange rate system).
- Direct measures to restrict imports, such as tariffs or import quotas or exchange control regulations.
- Domestic deflation to reduce aggregate demand in the domestic economy.

The first two are **expenditure switching** policies, which transfer resources and expenditure away from imports and towards domestic products while the last is an **expenditure reducing** policy.

Problems with a trade deficit include the following.

- **Effect on growth**

  Since a trade **deficit represents a leakage** of income from the national economy, there is a danger that **economic growth diminishes** unless internally generated growth can compensate for this.

- **Exchange rates**

  A persistent trade deficit is likely to put **downward pressure** on the **exchange rate** as confidence in the currency is weakened and as demand for it, relative to other currencies in general, falls.

- **Domestic consequences**

  A depreciating exchange rate will mean that the **price of imports** in domestic terms will be **rising**, putting pressure on **domestic inflation** with consequent knock-on effects for wage demands and unemployment.

Problems can emerge with persistent surpluses.

- **Overheating**

  A trade surplus represents an injection into the national economy which may result in an **overheating** of the economy if domestic production is already at full capacity. Overheating will tend to reflect itself in **upward pressure on prices** as total demand for goods (domestic and foreign) exceeds total domestic supply.

- **Exchange rates**

  Surpluses are likely to put **upward pressure** on the **exchange rate** which will push up the price of exported goods in foreign countries. This gives rise to the possibility that the surplus will decline.

Where trade is out of balance, governments can take a number of measures, including the following, to restore the balance.

- **Transport restrictions**

  Governments can discourage imports through **quotas**, controls or taxes (although this would doubtless lead to retaliatory action). Some argue that the imposition of product standards testing is a form of control. It might be illegal under EU rules or other treaty obligations (eg WTO).

- **Giving support to exporters**

  This may take a number of forms such as export monopolies, advice (as provided by the government). Export credit insurance reduces the risk, and hence the return that might have to be earned.

- **Devaluing the currency**

  Devaluation makes **exports** cheaper and increases their value.

- **General fiscal and monetary policy**

  Economic policy can reduce the overall level of activity in the economy. While (a), (b) and (c) are **expenditure switching** policies, which transfer resources and expenditure away from imports and towards domestic products, this is an **expenditure reducing** policy.

- **Rising interest rates**

  This will **increase** the value of the currency, to make imports cheaper.

- **Supply side measures**

  In the long term, supply side measures on the 'supply side' – that is, to improve competition and the free up markets – can encourage exports.

Chapter Roundup

Microeconomics

- Microeconomics is the study of the reaction of individuals and firms to economic stimuli.

Demand and Supply

- A demand curve shows the quantity demanded for a good at any given price. A supply curve shows the amount the market is willing to supply at any given price level.
- Equilibrium occurs when supply = demand.
- Demand may be affected by
  - substitutes.
  - complements.

  An increase in demand moving the demand or supply curve to the right, a decrease moving it to the left.
- An increase in supply shifts the supply curve to the right moving the equilibrium point along the demand curve.
- Elasticity measures the sensitivity of demand or supply to changes in factors such as price (price elasticity) and income (income elasticity).

$$\text{Elasticity} = \frac{\text{Percentage change in quantity demanded}}{\text{Percentage change in demand factor}} = \frac{\frac{Q_2 - Q_1}{Q_1}}{\frac{P_2 - P_1}{P_1}}$$

$$\text{Price elasticity of demand} = \frac{\text{Percentage change in quantity demanded}}{\text{Percentage change in price}}$$

$$\text{Income elasticity of demand} = \frac{\text{Percentage change in quantity demanded}}{\text{Percentage change in income}}$$

$$\text{Cross-elasticity of demand} = \frac{\text{Percentage change in quantity demanded}}{\text{Percentage change in price of other goods}}$$

$$\text{Elasticity of supply} = \frac{\text{Percentage change in quantity sold}}{\text{Percentage change in price}}$$

Cost

- Microeconomics considers opportunity costs = costs incurred by losing the opportunity of undertaking an alternative course of action.
- Average cost curves illustrate the relationship between quantity and prices.
- In the short run some factors of production (land, labour, capital) are fixed. Average variable costs decline at first due to more efficient used of resources then rise due to diminishing marginal returns. The marginal cost curve cuts the average variable cost and average total cost curves at their lowest points.
- In the long run all factors can be varied and total cost may become lower at first due to economies of scale, but rise later due to diseconomies.

Firms

- Theories of the firm include 'perfect competition' and 'monopolies'.
- Firms will produce at the point where profits are maximised ie MC = MR.
- Perfect competition = many small price taking firms that all generate normal profits when at equilibrium.
- Monopolistic competition = a number of competing firms with varying degrees of product differentiation
- Oligopoly = only a few competing producers acting as a collective monopoly
- Monopoly = one firm that sets the price and can earn supernormal profits.

Assessing industries and companies

- Business cycle is characterised by four stages
  - Expansion.
  - Boom/peak.
  - Deceleration/contraction.
  - Though recession (recession = two or more consecutive quarters of falling real GDP).
- Product life cycle, typically four phases
  - Introduction.
  - Growth.
  - Maturity.
  - Decline.
  - Obsolescence.
- Porter's five competition forces include the threat of new entrants, level of industry competition, presence of substitute goods, and the power of both suppliers and buyers.
- SWOT analysis considers strengths, weaknesses, opportunities, threats.
- The 4P's of marketing are product, place, promotion and price.

Market theories

- EMH has three forms
  - Weak = all information in past price movements has been incorporated in the current price (therefore technical analysis cannot make superior gains as it reveals no new information).
  - Semi-strong = all information from past price movements and from published data has been incorporated in the current price (therefore fundamental analysis cannot make superior gains as it reveals no new information).
  - Strong = all information (public and private) is reflected in the price (therefore no one can make superior gains except through luck).
- Behavioural finance
  - Heuristics = rules of thumb people use to make decisions (eg representatives, over confidence, anchoring, gamblers fallacy, availability bias).
  - Mental frames = a framework for how individuals make decisions (eg loss aversion, regret aversion, metal accounting, self-control).
- Bubbles and financial amnesia
  - Bubble = irrational behaviour by market participants driving stock prices far above their fundamental fair value.

- Financial amnesia = where participants forget/choose to ignore errors of the past, believing their modern financial sophistication will prevent a recurrence of past mistakes.

Macroeconomic environment

- Key economic indicators include
  - Inflation tares
  - Unemployment rates
  - GDP growth rates
  - Interest rates
  - Money supply
  - Yield curve shape and shifts
- The UK population is growing slowly, the average age is increasing as is the average level of wealth.
- The worldwide population is growing rapidly with increasing life expectancy and wealth.
- The process of globalisation has resulted in many linkages between the developed economies, one downside of which is financial contagion.

Macroeconomic theory

- Macroeconomics is the study of the economy as a whole.
- Gross Domestic Product (GDP) is a measure of the total value of economic output within a country.
- The relationship between nominal GDP, GNP and national income is therefore as follows.

	GDP
plus	Net property income from abroad
equals	GNP
minus	Capital consumption
equals	National income (net)

- Economic growth – growth in national output – is a central objective of governments. National output (or national income – another way of looking at the level of economic activity) is found to vary over a period of years in what is called the business cycle or the trade cycle.
- In an open economy

  $Y = C + I + G + (X - M)$

Keynesian theory

- The driver of the economy is demand and governments should use fiscal policy to manage this.
- Consumption = autonomous and discretionary based on income levels and the marginal propensity to consume, ie

  $C = a + bY$
- Demand can be managed by altering the marginal propensity to consume.
- The effect of any increase/decrease in government expenditure is amplified by the multiplier.

$$\text{Simple multiplier} = \frac{1}{1 - \text{Marginal propensity to consume (MPC)}}$$

Monetarist theory

- Governments should control inflation to remove its distorting effect and allow the economy to operate normally.

Role of government

- Fiscal policy = policy towards taxation and government expenditure to manage the economy (central to Keynesian views).
- Where a government
  - spends more than it raises in tax it runs a deficit financed by borrowing.
  - spends less that it receives in tax it runs a surplus allowing it to repay borrowings.
- The difficulties of fiscal policies are time lags, political manipulation, crowding out, future tax rates.
- Monetary policy = control of money supply and interest rates to manage economic effects.
- Money supply measures
  - M0 = Notes and coins in circulation (Narrow money)
  - M1 = M0 + private instant access account deposits
  - M2 = M1 + private term deposits and CDs
  - M3 = M2 + institutional term deposits and CDs
  - M4 = M3 + private holdings of building society retail shares and deposits
- M4 = Broad money = MO + Bank retail deposits + Building society retail shares/deposits + Other interest bearing deposits.
- Money multiplier = $\frac{1}{\text{Reserve ratio}}$

Role of central banks

	Name	Sets Interest Rate Independently	Manage Govt Debt	Banking Supervision
Europe	European Central Bank (ECB)	✓*	×	×
UK	Bank of England	✓	×	×**
Japan	Bank of Japan	✓	×	✓***
US	Federal Reserve	✓	×	✓
Canada	Bank of Canada	✓	×	×
Russia	Central Bank of the Russian Federation	✓	×	✓

All the above central banks provide some degree of financial stability regulation.

* The European Central Bank (ECB) has responsibility for setting interest rates for the Eurozone countries, participating in the single currency, the euro., with the rate of maintaining inflation close to but below 2% on the medium term, with the rate of maintaining inflation close to but below 2% of the medium term.

** Proposals have emerged following the 2010 general election that banking supervision may be passed to the Bank of England but to date (July 2010) no such legislation has been enacted.

*** The Bank of Japan has partial responsibility for Banking Supervision

Inflation and unemployment

- The Retail Prices Index (RPI) and the new Consumer Prices Index (CPI) measure the general level of consumer prices. Unlike the RPI, the CPI excludes most housing costs. Inflation creates problems for economic decision makers, and for those on fixed incomes, and expectations of inflation can lead to a wage-price spiral which is difficult to stop.
- Disinflation describes a situation of falling inflation. Deflation is a term for negative inflation (falling prices). Deflation can be bad for economic welfare because companies may cut back on output if they anticipate prices falling, as they may not be able to cover their costs and make profits.
- The UK government targets a range for the inflation rate, using interest rate changes as its main policy instrument. An earlier policy approach was to target a level of money supply growth, but money supply growth was found to be an unreliable guide to the level of consumer demand and inflation.
- Possible causes of inflation
  - Cost push (classical view).
  - Demand pull (Keynesian view).
  - Increase in money supply (monetarist view)
    MV = PY
- Possible causes of unemployment
  - Classical.
  - Structural.
  - Seasonal.
  - Frictional.
  - Keynesian.
- There is a natural rate of unemployment so full employment never exists.
- Phillips curve shows the relationship between inflation and unemployment.
- Inflation
  - Erodes the real value of nominal assets (cash, bonds).
  - Results in price increases for real assets (index linked bonds, equities, property).

Exchange rates and balance of trade

- Exchange rates are the prices of a currency in terms of other currencies. As with all markets, supply and demand factors determine prices.
- Purchasing power parity theory predicts that, over the long run, exchange rates should move into line with prices, so that an amount of money can buy the same goods and services in different currencies.
- Optimum currency area = a geographical region in which overall economic efficiency will be maximised through the use of a single currency.
- The balance of payments records transactions between a national economy and the rest of the world, including investment flows (capital account), as well as trading transactions (current account).
- When people talk of a balance of payments deficit, or surplus, they are generally referring to the balance of a country's trade between imports and exports of goods (visibles) and services. The financial services sector and tourism help to give the UK a surplus on its trade in services (invisibles).

TEST YOUR KNOWLEDGE

Check your knowledge of the chapter here, without referring back to the text.

1. What factors could cause the demand curve to shift to the right?

2. An increase in supply has what effect on demand

3. A good with a price elasticity of demand of between 0 and –1 is referred to as

   A Inelastic
   B Elastic
   C Sensitive
   D Insensitive

4. If when prices rise 5% quantity demanded falls 4%, what is the price elasticity demand of demand?

5. What does marginal revenue measure?

6. Where does the marginal cost curve cut through the average total cost curve?

7. Why does the short run average total cost curve have a U shave

8. Why does the long run average total cost curve have a U shape and what is its minimum point called

9. 'Perfect competition' assumes all consumers act rationally. *True or false?*

10. What are the conditions for perfect competition

11. Contrast perfect competition with a monopoly

12. What are the phases of the business cycle

13. What are the steps in the product life cycle?

14. Which of the following is not one of the P's of marketing?

    A Product
    B Promotion
    C Price
    D Perception

15. What are the three forms of EMH and their relevance to analysts

16. What is the difference between GDP and GNP?

17. Distinguish between 'narrow money' and 'broad money'.

18. Outline the possible effects of a tightening of monetary policy.

19. What is measured in the M0 money supply?

20. Which inflation measure is used for the UK Government's inflation target?

21. How is 'recession' usually defined?

22. Distinguish between the current account and the capital account of the balance of payments.

23. What is the difference between deflation and disinflation?

Test Your Knowledge: Answers

1. Increase in the price of a substitute, decrease in the price of a complement, rise in incomes, increased advertising and marketing, change in tastes.

   (See Section 2.3)

2. The demand curve is unaltered but the equilibrium quantity increases as the supply curve moves to the right.

   (See Section 2.3)

3. A

   (See Section 3.2)

4. $$\text{PED} = \frac{\text{Percentage change in quantity}}{\text{Percentage change in price}} = \frac{-4\%}{+5\%} = -0.8$$

   (See Section 3.2)

5. The change in total revenue that results from an increase or decrease of one unit of sales.

   (See Section 3.2)

6. At the lowest/minimum point.

   (See Section 4.2)

7. Short run average total costs fall at first due to the more efficient use of the factors of production (land, labour, capital) then rise due to decreasing returns to factors.

   (See Section 4.2)

8. Long run average total costs fall then risk due to economies of scale then rise due to diseconomies of scale. The minimum point is called the minimum efficient scale.

   (See Section 4.3)

9. True

   (See Section 5.1)

10. - Consumers are rational
    - Many buyers and sellers none of whom can influence the market
    - Products are homogeneous
    - There is perfect information
    - There are no barriers to entry or exit
    - There is no economic friction

    (See Section 5.1)

11.

	Perfect competition	Monopoly
Degree of concentration	Infinite number of small firms	One firm
Profit maximisation condition	MC = MR	MC = MR
Homogeneity of product	Homogeneous	Differentiated
Demand curve faced by firm	Horizontal, a very small part of total demand	The full demand curve
Ability to earn supernormal profits	Short term only if demands rises	Long term

(See Sections 5.2 and 5.3)

12.
- Expansion
- Boom/peak
- Contraction
- Trough/recession

(See Section 6.1)

13. Introduction – Growth – Maturity – Decline

(See Section 6.2)

14. D

(See Section 6.5)

15.

EMH Form	Relevance to analysts
Weak	Technical analysis fruitless as it reveals no new information
Semi-strong	Fundamental analysis fruitless as it reveals no new information
Strong form	Even insider dealers would only make gains through luck

(See Section 7.2)

16.

	GDP
plus	Net property income from abroad
	GNP
minus	Capital consumption
	National income (net)

(See Section 9.2)

17. Narrow money is money balances readily available to finance current spending. Broad money includes financial assets that are relatively illiquid.

(See Section 10.5)

18. Notes and coins in circulation.

    (See Section 10.5)

19. Notes and coins + Banks operational deposits at the Bank of England.

    (See Section 10.5)

20. CPI – the inflation target being 2% or less.

    (See Section 12.4)

21. Two or more successive quarters of falling real GDP.

    (See Section 12.3)

22. The current account is the result of trade flows of goods and services. The capital account reflects capital flows into and out of a country.

    (See Section 13.5)

23. Deflation is falling prices, disinflation is reducing inflation.

    (See Section 12.3)

7 Cash Deposits and Money Market Instruments

INTRODUCTION

Money market investments are those with a maturity of less than 12 months. This includes investments such as T-bills, commercial paper and certificates of deposit.

The money markets are a predominantly institutional market for investors looking to make investments for short periods of time, retail investors primarily using cash deposits for the same purpose. Cash deposits and money market investments are both stable in price and have little in the way of credit risk.

The Bank of England controls interest rates through the issuance and redemption of T-Bills and acts as the lender of last resort to the institutions involved.

CHAPTER CONTENTS

CHAPTER LEARNING OBJECTIVES

18 Asset classes

Demonstrate an ability to evaluate the characteristics, inherent risks, behaviour and correlation of asset classes.

18.10 Cash and cash equivalents

18.10.1 **Explain** the main characteristics and risks associated with cash deposits and money market instruments (Treasury Bills, CDs, CPs, FRNs).

18.10.2 **Calculate** the discount and quoted yield on a UK Treasury Bill.

1 CASH DEPOSITS

Learning objective

18.10.1 Explain the main characteristics and risks associated with cash deposits and money market instruments (Treasury Bills, CDs, CP, FRNs).

1.1 Types of account

1.1.1 Cheque-based accounts

The purpose of these is to enable settlement of transactions. They will often pay interest but at a very low level. It is possible to earn higher rates of interest, but the bank or building society will usually require a higher minimum balance to compensate.

The problem with cheque accounts is the level of charges that can be levied. Although many banks and building societies offer free banking while a customer is in credit, this is compensated for in various ways.

- Very low interest rates on cash balances, resulting in an opportunity cost on money not earning deposit rates.
- High charges when a customer becomes overdrawn, even for a small period of time.
- High interest rates on overdrafts.

1.1.2 Deposit accounts

Deposit accounts may be on call or for a set notice period. The level of interest received increases the longer the cash is tied up and the larger the amount of cash placed on deposit. The risk of investing all your cash in one account for a long period of time is twofold.

- The bank may go under.
- You may need the money quickly.

Top quality banks and building societies will offer lower rates than riskier banks. The risk of investing in a fringe bank to obtain a higher rate of interest is that it may become insolvent, meaning that part of your money might be lost.

Under the **FSA's Financial Services Compensation Scheme (FSCS)**, if a bank or building society goes under, the maximum compensation paid to investors with bank or building society accounts is £85,000 calculated as follows.

100% of the first £85,000 of the money deposited per person per separately authorised deposit taker

Some banks and building societies offer higher rates of interest because of their low cost base – telephone and postal-based organisations do not have the high cost of a branch network. The disadvantage can be the lack of face-to-face contact and, with postal-based services, slow response time.

1.1.3 Money market deposits

Some banks will place large amounts on deposit in the money markets for their customers, earning higher rates of interest. This may be useful if the investor has a large sum of money available for the short term. However, it is unlikely to be a sensible investment alternative for the long term.

1.1.4 Other accounts

Banks and building societies offer a range of different accounts targeted at different investors, such as children's accounts, and there is also a variety of cash deposit accounts that could be held through the National Savings and Investments (previously known as simply National Savings).

1.1.5 Offshore accounts

It is possible to invest in offshore deposits accounts in places such as the Channel Islands and the Isle of Man. These may pay higher interest and interest is received gross (but is taxable). Unless the investor is either not ordinarily resident or not domiciled in the UK, tax is due in the year in which the interest is credited, not when it is remitted to the UK. The level of protection may be lower than for UK-based deposits, depending on the location of the deposit and the status of the bank concerned.

Offshore accounts can be useful for tax-free investors and people living overseas who are classed as non-resident for tax purposes.

2 The Nature of the Money Market

The money markets are the focus for trading in short-dated (conventionally with maturities of under one year) interest-bearing products and hedging instruments. Note, however, that though the majority of money market instruments are very short term, money market instruments are not limited to products with maturities of less than one year. The maturity of the instrument is not the factor that determines where it is traded, rather it is the pricing mechanics, price stability and risk of the instrument involved. Instruments traded on the money markets are those with a low credit risk that are priced by reference to prevailing money market rates giving them very low price volatility and, for coupon paying instruments, a price close to par. The market itself is a complex intermeshed structure with a wide variety of instruments and is generally used by **wholesale investors**.

The London money market is a complex market where banks balance their liquidity requirements and the Bank of England attempts to control the interest rate.

2.1 An overview of the market

The London Money Market

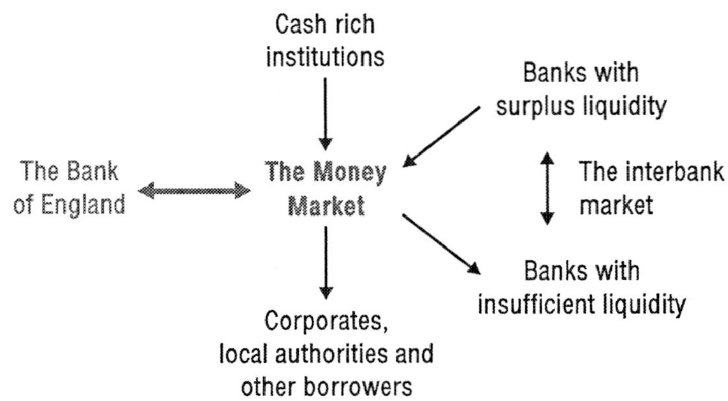

The Bank of England is a key player in the market. The Bank's role is focused on the implementation of policy rather than the raising of finance (which is the responsibility of the Debt Management Office of the Treasury). It is through the money markets that the Monetary Policy Committee is able to dictate the direction of interest rates and monetary policy.

The Bank of England's final role in the market is as the **'Lender of the Last Resort'**, whereby the Bank ensures that the market will not fail to meet its obligations. As the credit crisis Of 2008/09 showed, this is not a blank cheque to the industry. The Bank will, however, step in where there is a 'systemic' risk to the market.

The principal users of the market are the banks. Banks make their money by taking in deposits from individuals and lending them out at a higher rate to borrowers. In doing so, the bank always has to ensure that they have enough liquid assets to meet the demands by their investors for cash. The bank will achieve this by carrying a proportion of the money invested in the form of cash and will also put other money on deposit at very short notice. The remainder of their liquidity will be held in the form of short-term investments such as gilts that are easily convertible into cash.

Banks can also manage their liquidity via the interbank markets. Those banks with surplus funds can earn a return by passing them to banks short of funds. The average rate at which funds can be raised is **LIBOR (London Interbank Offered Rate)** and the average rate earned on deposits is **LIBID (London Interbank Bid Rate)**. Secured lending and borrowing also takes place via the repo market, which is discussed later.

Other participants include cash-rich institutions that use the money markets as a safe channel to earn returns on their liquid assets. Larger corporates may use the money markets as a source of short-term flexible finance and in order to hedge interest rate risk.

2.2 Settlement of money market instruments

In September 2003, money market instruments were introduced into CREST, part of Euroclear. The existing CREST settlement system for gilts and equities was to be integrated, to allow for the settlement of **money market instruments (MMIs)**. Previously, the issue, transfer and settlement of certain MMIs was carried out through the Central Moneymarkets Office (CMO). The CMO ceased operations in October 2003.

Money market instruments are traditionally short-term transferable securities, with maturities of up to one year. They include securities such as Treasury bills (T-bills), Certificates of Deposit (CDs), local authority bills, bank bills and Commercial Paper (CP). MMIs are also traditionally **bearer** instruments.

The electronic settlement system of CREST required the creation of an **'eligible debt security' (EDS)**, which is the dematerialised equivalent of the MMI. These EDSs are the same, in economic terms, as the underlying MMI. However, an EDS may only be held and transferred in the dematerialised form within CREST. These EDSs are registered securities, which are settled using CREST settlement functionality, with the registration details maintained by CREST. There are no such materialised EDSs. However, banks may still issue certificated MMIs outside of CREST.

3 Money Market Instruments

earning objective

18.10.1 Explain the main characteristics and risks associated with cash deposits and money market instruments (Treasury Bills, CDs, CP, FRNs).

As mentioned above, the normal definition of a money market instrument encompasses any instrument with a maturity of under one year. However, in reality, longer dated instruments can come under the aegis of the market. Given the short maturities of the instruments, there is a tendency for them to be **discount securities**, issued at a discount to par rather than carrying a coupon. However, some securities with a maturity of over one year pay annual coupons.

Whilst it is possible for some of the securities to be in registered form, the conventional approach is for these securities to be in **bearer form**. The security problems that this raises are now normally dealt with through the use of computerised book entry systems.

3.1 Deposits

The simplest of all money market instruments is cash itself. In the deposits market, banks simply take and lay off deposits from each other.

The market is liquid over a wide range of maturities, although primarily less than one year. Interbank deposits are **unsecured** and usually have a **minimum size of £500,000.**

Interest is computed on a simple basis, i.e. no compounding. For example, for a £1m deposit for three months (91 days) the interest at 10% would be

$$£1{,}000{,}000 \times \frac{10}{100} \times \frac{91}{365} = £24{,}931.51$$

We must also take care to apply the correct money market conventions for the market concerned, ie

- the **UK and Commonwealth countries** use the day count convention of **Actual/365**
- the **US, EU and Japan** use the convention of **Actual/360**.

Note this is often at variance with the accrued interest convention in use in the bond markets.

3.2 Treasury Bills

earning objective

18.10.2 Calculate the discount and quoted yield on a UK Treasury bill.

A Treasury bill (T-bill) is a promise to repay (**a promissory note**) a set sum of money by the Treasury (via the Debt Management Office) at a specified date in the future, normally not longer than **91 calendar days (three months)**. Usually, the minimum block size for trading would be **£25,000** though prices are stated per £100 of principal.

T-bills are issued by way of a **weekly auction** when bids are made on a **yield basis** and then trade at a discount to their face value. The Bank's T-bill issues are not part of the government's funding programme per se, but are much more an instrument of monetary policy.

The principal measures used to evaluate T-bills are as follows.

Formula to learn

$$\text{Discount rate} = \frac{100 - \text{Discounted value}}{100} \times \frac{365}{\text{Days}}$$

Formula to learn

$$\text{Interest rate or yield} = \frac{100 - \text{Discounted value}}{\text{Discounted value}} \times \frac{365}{\text{Days}}$$

Whilst this may be the quoted annualised yield it is not the return an investor could expect per annum as their returns would be reinvested and compounded every three months. Using DCF ideas the compound annual return (r) could be calculated using

Formula to learn

$$(1+r) = \left(\frac{100}{\text{Purchase price}}\right)^{\frac{365}{\text{Days}}}$$

Example

91-day T-bill issued at £98.

Discount rate

$$\frac{£100 - £98}{£100} \times \frac{365}{91} = 0.0802 \text{ or } 8.02\%$$

Interest rate or yield

$$\frac{£100 - £98}{£98} \times \frac{365}{91} = 0.0818 \text{ or } 8.18\%$$

Compound annual return

$$(1+r) = \left(\frac{100}{98}\right)^{\frac{365}{91}} = 1.0844$$

r = 0.0844 or 8.44%

Local authorities may also raise short term finance by using **local authority bills** that have characteristics very similar to Treasury bills.

It is conventional for bills to **trade on the discount rate**, ie it is the discount rate that is quoted rather than the price or yield, and this requires the holder to convert to the yield in order to compare with other investments.

3.3 Bills of Exchange

A Bill of Exchange is an instrument which is drawn and issued by the seller of goods to the buyer, specifying an amount to be paid either immediately or at some particular date in the future. Once the bill has been accepted by the buyer (by stamping and signing the reverse), i.e. the buyer formally acknowledges the obligation to pay the amount stated, the bearer of the bill is entitled to the proceeds at maturity. The accepted bill may then be discounted provided the purchaser is willing to take on the credit risk of the bill's acceptor, which is the promise of repayment.

A bank may add its **acceptance** to a bill in which case it becomes a **bank bill**. This service to their clients is effectively a guarantee of the repayment. If the accepting bank is one of a list of approximately 51 'eligible' banks, maintained by the **Bank of England**, then it becomes an **eligible bill**.

A further condition imposed on a trade bill in the UK is that it must have an underlying commercial substance. The idea behind this is that the bills must not be used as financing instruments, other than for working capital. For example, the FSA is prepared for bills to be 'secured' against the receipt of a cash flow under a particular contract. Bills can now be drawn against contracts in general, but not used as a means of creating pure finance for long-term acquisitions.

3.4 Commercial Paper

In the same way that governments issue short dated money market instruments, so too do companies. **Commercial Paper (CP)** has the following characteristics.

- Unsecured.
- Trades at a discount to par value.
- Maturity periods are normally less than 12 months.

The return investor's demand for buying commercial paper will be dependant on the risk of the company issuing it. The higher the risk, the higher the required return and the greater the discount to par value when the paper is issued.

Credit agencies, such as Moody's and Standard & Poor's (covered further in the Fixed Income Securities Chapter), provide credit ratings on short-term debt. This guides investors on the risk of the underlying issuer.

Short-term credit rating

Moody's	Standard and Poor's
P – 1	A – 1+ A – 1
P – 2	A – 2
P – 3	A – 3

3.5 Certificates of Deposit

A Certificate of Deposit (CD) is in effect a securitised bank deposit, issued by commercial banks and building societies. Ideally, banks would like to be able to take deposits from customers on the understanding that these deposits would not be repayable within the short term. However, investors are either unwilling to commit their funds for specified time periods (time deposits) or demand too high a premium.

The resolution to this dilemma came in the 1960s with the creation of certificates of a bank deposit that was committed for a period of time. Such certificates carry a fixed coupon rate and have a maturity of up to five years, more normally one year or less. Like any other security, the certificate can be traded, enabling the deposit holder to realise the deposit through the sales proceeds and not by withdrawal.

Conventionally, CDs are issued by highly rated banks and other financial organisations and therefore carry a limited credit risk. Unlike the other money market instruments, they do carry a coupon, which is only paid on maturity.

Once issued, CDs **trade on a yield basis**. That is to say, the amount that is to be paid for the CD means that, given the fixed coupon, the new purchaser will generate the yield at which it is trading. The minimum denomination for a CD is usually £100,000; they then trade in increments of £10,000 above this.

3.6 The repo market

From 1996, an open repo market in gilts has been allowed to develop. This represents a modernisation of the gilt market, making it more in line with other major government debt markets.

A repo is a **sale and repurchase agreement at an agreed price.** The basis of the transaction is that the holder of a bond is able to sell his holding of a particular bond in order to raise cash. Simultaneous to the sale, the holder enters into an agreement to repurchase the bond at a date in the future, at the same price plus interest.

Example

Leg one

£200,000 worth of bonds are sold for £180,000. The size of this 'haircut' (the difference between the amount advanced by a lender and the market value of collateral securing the loan, i.e. £200,000) will depend on the repo securities and the duration of the loan. The repo rate will be set at this point, let us say 6% for a 90-day repo.

Leg two

The bonds are repurchased for £180,000 plus interest. The interest is worked out on a simple basis using the following formula.

$$\text{Interest} = \text{Principal amount} \times \text{Repo rate} \times \frac{\text{Days}}{365}$$

$$\text{Interest} = £180{,}000 \times 0.06 \times \frac{90}{365} = £2{,}663$$

Therefore, the sum due on repayment is £182,663. In return for this, the original holder will receive back the bond, their collateral. This therefore represents an effective way for the firm to finance its holding of the bond. The initial position taken would otherwise represent a cash drain on the business. The repo allows the holder to raise cheap cash on the back of the bond. The cash raised in this fashion can then be used to take additional positions, thereby gearing up the initial capital of the investor, allowing larger positions to be entered into.

The end result is, in effect, a secured loan where one party borrows money on the surety of the gilts that they own. Given the security of the loan, the rates will be below LIBOR (London Interbank Offer Rate).

3.7 Floating rate notes and other debt

Other forms of 'low risk' debt will also be traded through the money markets, including short-dated gilts, local authority issues and highly rated corporate issues. The market will tend to prefer those issued by banks and building societies, since these will obviously carry very limited credit risk.

Floating rate notes are bonds where the coupon is periodically reset (usually every six months) by reference to some measure of the market rate of interest (commonly LIBOR – London Inter Bank Offered Rates or LIMEAN – the average of the offered and bid rates) and consequently tend to trade close to their par value.

As a result of the link to money market rates and their (close to) par values, FRNs are considered by the markets to be money market instruments and are traded on the money markets rather than the bond markets.

FRNs tend to be issued with a minimum term of three years though the majority of issues would be classified as medium to long term. Historically there were two floating rate gilts in issue that both traded on the money markets rather than the bond markets, though no such gilts exist at present.

The coupon on these bonds comprises two elements. Firstly, the reference or index rate, for example LIBOR, and secondly, a quoted margin, the rate above LIBOR that must be paid. An example might be a five-year bond with a coupon of LIBOR (the index rate) plus 25bp (the quoted margin). The quoted margin is established at the outset of the deal and reflects the borrower's credit rating and the size of the issue, along with the market conditions at the time.

As a consequence of this resetting of coupons FRNs are always paying a fair return hence they always tend to trade close to their par value and have very little volatility, i.e. virtually zero duration (see Fixed Income Securities chapter).

CHAPTER ROUNDUP

Cash deposits

- Bank deposit offering low returns and having low volatility.
- FSCS pays 100% of the first £85,000 of money deposited per person per separately authorised deposit taker.

Money Markets

- Markets for trading shot-term liquidity primarily used by banks and institutional investors.
- Bank of England influences interest rates via the money markets through its weekly treasury bill auctions.
- Interest rates
  - Base rate = rate set by Bank of England.
  - LIBOR = London interbank offered rate.
  - LIBID = London Inter-bank bid rate.
- The Bank of England acts as lender of last resort to the money markets.

Money market instruments

- The money market is where banks, companies and institutional investors trade investments of a short maturity.
- Money market investments include Treasury bills, local authority bills, Bills of Exchange (Banks bills and eligible bills), Commercial Paper and Certificates of Deposit.
- Short term credit ratings are provided by rating agencies.
- Treasury bills are issued by the DMO and may be described by their discount rate or their interest rate/ yield. They normally have a maximum term of 91 days and a minimum block size of £25,000. They trade on a yield basis (the yield is quoted).

$$\text{Discount rate} = \frac{100 - \text{Discounted value}}{100} \times \frac{365}{\text{Days}}$$

$$\text{Interest rate or yield} = \frac{100 - \text{Discounted value}}{\text{Discounted value}} \times \frac{365}{\text{Days}}$$

$$\text{Compound annual return (r): } (1+r) = \left(\frac{100}{\text{Purchase price}}\right)^{\frac{365}{\text{Days}}}$$

- Bill of exchange is an acknowledgeable of an obligation to pay a specified sum at a given maturity date. If it is accepted by a bank it becomes a bank bill and is tradeable, if the bank is on the list of eligible banks it becomes an eligible bill.
- Commercial paper is the corporate equivalent of a treasury bill. It is unsecured, has a maturity <12 months and is unsecured.
- CDs are securitised bank deposits that pay a regular coupon. They have maturities up to five years and trade on a yield basis (the yield is quoted). The minimum denomination is usually £100,000 going up in steps of £10,000 above this level.

- Repo = sale and repurchase agreement that is effectively a securitised loan. A bond is 'sold' but it is agreed to be 'repurchased' later, the price difference being the interest on the loan.

  $$\text{Interest} = \text{Principal amount} \times \text{Repo rate} \times \frac{\text{Days}}{365}$$

- FRNs pay coupons linked to LIBOR.
- Settlement of most money market investments takes place on CREST if they have been dematerialised as EDSs.

Test Your Knowledge

Check your knowledge of the chapter here, without referring back to the text.

1. What is the cover provided for cash deposits under the Financial Services Compensation Scheme?

2. What is the primary risk for a cash deposit?

3. What roles does the Bank of England have in the money markets?

4. What are the interest rates at which banks borrow and lend between each other?

5. What is an eligible debt security?

6. Who issues Treasury bills?

7. What is the discount rate, the interest yield and the compound annual return on a Treasury bill that is priced at £99.30 and has 32 days to maturity.

8. What is an eligible bill?

9. What are the normal characteristics of commercial paper?

10. What is the highest short-term credit rating obtainable from Moody's?

11. How do CDs trade?

12. A repo is a sale and repurchase agreement at an agreed price. *True or False?*

13. What is a FRN?

Test Your Knowledge: Answers

1. 100% at the first £85,000 of money deposit per person per separately authorised deposit taker

   (See Section 1.1.2)

2. That the deposit taker will become insolvent when the deposit exceeds the FSCS limit

   (See Section 1.1.2)

3. The Bank of England

   – Sets interest rates
   – Acts as lender of last resort

   (See Section 2.1)

4. LIBOR and LIBID

   (See Section 2.1)

5. A dematerialised money market deposit

   (See Section 2.2)

6. The DMO

   (See Section 3.2)

7. Discount rate = $\frac{100.00 - 99.30}{100.00} \times \frac{365}{32} = 0.0798$ or 7.98%

   Yield = $\frac{100.00 - 99.30}{99.30} \times \frac{365}{32} = 0.0804$ or 8.04%

   Compound annual return: $(1+r) = \left(\frac{100.00}{99.30}\right)^{\frac{365}{32}} = 1.08342$

   r = 0.08342 or 8.342%

   (See Section 3.2)

8. A bill of exchange that has been accepted by an eligible bank

   (See Section 3.3)

9. Unsecured, maturity < 12 months, trade at a discount

   (See Section 3.4)

10. P-1

    (See Section 3.4)

11. CDs trade on a yield basis

    (See Section 3.5)

12. True

    (See Section 3.6)

13. Floating rate note, an instrument whose coupon is linked to money market rates

    (See Section 3.7)

8 Fixed Income Securities

INTRODUCTION

There are many different types of fixed income securities, including government and corporate bonds. Government bonds issued by the UK government are known as gilts and are issued to finance the governments expenditure over and above receipts from taxation.

Discounted cash flow techniques are central to identifying the value and interest rate risk of a bond.

To ensure that investors pay the correct amount of tax there is a system for calculating interest that has accrued within a bonds value.

Yield calculations identify expected returns from investing into bonds. The flat yield measures income return, and the gross redemption yield the total return. Gross redemption yields for a particular issuers different maturity bonds may be plotted onto a graph to form a yield curve.

Corporate bonds may be secured or unsecured against the assets of the firm. Bonds which are unsecured will be required to offer a high return to investors to compensate them for the additional risk.

CHAPTER CONTENTS

Chapter Learning Objectives

18 Financial instruments and other investments

Demonstrate an ability to evaluate the characteristics, inherent risks, behaviour and correlation of asset classes

18.5 Fixed interest securities – characteristics

- **18.5.1** **Explain** the structure and characteristics of the various types of fixed income instruments issued in the UK including government bonds, index linked bonds, corporate bonds and Eurobonds.
- **18.5.2** **Understand** the rationale for and risk to the issuer and holder of a convertible, callable or putable bond.
- **18.5.3** **Explain** clean (quoted) and dirty pricing.
- **18.5.4** **Understand** the valuation methodology for fixed income securities.
- **18.5.5** **Calculate** the price of a fixed income security given its maturity, coupon and yield.

18.6 Fixed interest securities – risk and return

- **18.6.1** **Identify** the components of return of fixed income securities.
- **18.6.2** **Explain** the main risks faced by bond holders and how these risks can be addressed.
- **18.6.3** **Explain** the two components of interest rate risk (price and reinvestment risk).
- **18.6.4** **Explain** the nature of the relationship between yield and price.
- **18.6.5** **Analyse** the factors that affect the sensitivity of a bond's price to a change in required yield.
- **18.6.6** **Define** and calculate the (Macaulay) duration of a bond.
- **18.6.7** **Define** and calculate the modified duration of a bond.
- **18.6.8** **Calculate,** given the duration of a bond, the change in price given a change in required yield.
- **18.6.9** **Explain** the convexity error that arises from using duration to estimate a change in bond price using duration.
- **18.6.10** **Define** credit risk as it affects bonds.
- **18.6.11** **Explain** the role of the major credit rating agencies.
- **18.6.12** **Interpret** the key classes of rating on the scales published by the major rating agencies.
- **18.6.13** **Explain** the concept of debt seniority.
- **18.6.14** **Identify** key features and financial ratios considered by credit rating agencies in conducting a corporate rating.

18.7 Fixed interest securities – yields and the yield curve

18.7.1 **Define** and calculate

- Flat yield.
- Gross redemption yield (GRY).
- Net redemption yield (NRY).
- Grossed-up NRY.

18.7.2 **Explain** when each of the above measures may be appropriate to use.

18.7.3 **Define** the yield curve.

18.7.4 **Explain** the theories that contribute to explaining the shape of the yield curve.

18.7.5 **Define** forward and spot interest rates.

18.7.6 **Explain** the relationship between forward rates, spot rates and the GRY.

18.8 Fixed income securities – transaction costs

18.8.1 **Explain** and identify transaction costs associated with dealing in UK fixed interest securities.

18.8.2 **Calculate** the total transaction costs for a fixed interest security transaction, given the appropriate data.

18.8.3 **Contrast** the trading methods for fixed interest securities with equities and examine the impact on trading costs.

21 Investment theories and models

Demonstrate an understanding of the merits and limitations of the main investment theories

21.2 Models of return and risk

21.2.11 **Explain** how different asset class returns may be related for example Merton models relating fixed income risk to equity.

1 What is a Bond?

Learning objective

18.5.1 Explain the structure and characteristics of the various types of fixed income instruments issued in the UK including government bonds, index linked bonds, corporate bonds and Eurobonds.

1.1 Definition and development

A bond may be defined as a negotiable debt instrument for a fixed principal amount issued by a borrower for a specific period of time, making a regular payment of interest/coupon to the holder until it is redeemed at maturity, when the principal amount is repaid.

Historically, bonds began as very simple negotiable debt instruments, paying a fixed coupon for a specified period, then being redeemed at face value – a 'straight bond'. In the 1960s and 1970s, bond markets were seen as being investment vehicles for 'widows and orphans'. They were thought to be dull markets with predictable returns and very little in the way of gains to be made from trading.

The bond markets emerged from this shadow during the mid-1970s, when both interest rates and currencies became substantially more volatile. Bonds have emerged since then to be much more complex investments, and there are now a significant number of variations on the basic theme.

Whilst it is perhaps easy to be confused by the variety of 'bells and whistles' which have been introduced into the market in recent years, one should always bear in mind that the vast majority of issues are still straight bonds. The reason for this is that investors are wary of buying investments which they do not fully understand. If an issue is too complex, it will be difficult to market.

1.2 Who issues bonds and why?

Bonds are used by a number of 'individuals' as a means of raising finance. Major bond issuers include the following.

- **Sovereign governments** – who need to raise finance to help them cover any national debt or budget shortfall.
- **Local authorities** – who need to raise finance to help them cover any local budget shortfall.
- **Companies** – who need to raise cash to help them finance business requirements.

Regardless of who the issuer is, there are a number of general characteristics that any bond is likely to have which we will examine next.

1.3 General characteristics

Examining the above definition in a little more detail reveals the general characteristics that a bond may have.

1.3.1 Negotiable instrument

Negotiability means that it is a piece of paper which can be bought and sold. For certain types of bonds, this is easier than for others. Government bonds tend to be highly liquid, i.e. very easy to buy or sell, whereas certain corporate bonds are almost illiquid and are usually held to maturity by the initial buyer.

1.3.2 Nominal value

As we noted above, all bonds are issued for a fixed principal amount or nominal value, which historically represented the amount invested. On UK bonds, it is normal to have a bond nominal value of £100, and bond prices are quoted on this basis. This nominal value serves two important purposes.

- Determining the scale of the coupon payments.
- Determining the value of the redemption proceeds.

We discuss both of these purposes below.

1.3.3 Maturity

Initially, all bonds were redeemable at a specific maturity date, which determines when the principal is due for repayment. However, there are now a number of variations we will need to consider. We can subcategorise bonds between

- Redeemable Bonds.
- Irredeemable/Perpetual Bonds.

Redeemable bonds

The majority of bonds fall into this category, though there are some subsets we will need to consider.

- **Single-dated bonds** – bonds which mature at a pre-set date only.
- **Double-dated bonds** – bonds that can be redeemed by the issuer between the specified dates. On a double-dated bond, the earlier date specifies when the issuer may redeem, the later date specifies when the bond must be redeemed.
- **Callable bonds** – where the issuer of the bond is able to redeem the bond at an earlier date, should they wish to do so. Double-dated bonds may be considered as a subset of callable bonds, though callable bonds may have many other features (e.g. call premiums) and may be callable throughout their lives.
- **Putable bonds** – a more recent innovation which gives the holder the ability to sell the bond back to the issuer at a premium over the face value.

Irredeemable bonds

On irredeemable or perpetual or undated bonds, there is no maturity date and the issuer is under no obligation to redeem the principal sum, though he may have the right to do so if he wishes. On these bonds, the coupon will be paid into perpetuity.

1.3.4 Coupon

The basis for the determination of the coupon on a bond is set before issue, though this does not mean that the value is known at that date. Whilst the vast majority of bonds issued are straights (i.e. a fixed coupon), there are a number of variants on this theme. In addition, there are bonds whose coupons vary with economic factors. We may, therefore, categorise bond coupons between

- Pre-determined; and
- Variable.

However the amount is calculated, the full coupon for the period will be paid to the holder of the bond on the ex-dividend date.

Pre-determined coupons

This category would include, as we have already stated, the vast majority of bonds. On these bonds, the gross annual coupon (i.e. the amount due to be paid in a one-year period, irrespective of the frequency of payment) is specified as a percentage of the nominal value of the bond. Sub-classes here would include

- **Straight/Fixed coupon bonds** – where the coupon is at a set level for the entire life of the bond.
- **Stepped coupon bonds** – where the coupon increases in steps to pre-specified amounts as the bond moves through its life.
- **Zero-coupon bonds** – bonds that carry no coupon and simply redeem at face value at maturity. With such bonds, the investors realise a return since they pay only a fraction of the face value on issue.

Variable coupons

This category would include

- **Floating rate bonds** – where the coupon varies as interest rates vary.
- **Index-linked bonds** – where the coupon and redemption proceeds figures get scaled for the effects of inflation.

1.3.5 Coupon frequency

The frequency of the payment of the coupons is predetermined before issue, normally following the local market conventions. As a result, all investors will be (or should be) aware of those dates.

Conventions regarding the frequency of payment differ between the various bond markets. Some markets have a convention of paying semi-annual coupons, as is the case in the UK and the US, whereas other markets, in particular the Eurobond market, France and Germany, pay coupons on an annual basis.

1.3.6 Recipient

The norm is that the holder of the bond receives all of the asset flows from that bond throughout its life to the maturity date. There are, however, some markets where it is possible to strip the coupons and the bond apart so that the holder of the underlying bond may receive the redemption proceeds, whilst the coupons (the 'tint') are paid to another party.

1.3.7 Redemption at maturity

As we noted above, it is possible for bonds to be issued which will not redeem at maturity, known as irredeemables. Most bonds are, however, redeemed though, once again, there are a few variations to be aware of. The primary consideration here is the form that the redemption proceeds takes which may be either

- Cash; or
- Other assets.

Cash redemption proceeds

Once more, the vast majority of bonds fall into this category whereby the bonds are redeemed in cash at maturity. This redemption may be

- **At par value** – redeemed at the nominal value of the bond at the redemption date.
- **At a premium** – redeemed at a specified premium above the nominal value of the bond at the redemption date.

Other assets

Instead of obliging the issuer to repay cash at maturity, the bond may offer the holder the choice between normal cash redemption proceeds and some other asset, such as

- An alternative bond of a later maturity.
- Shares issued by a corporation.

1.4 UK Government Bonds – Gilts

1.4.1 Characteristics

Governments, as a rule, spend more money in a year than they raise in revenue. Consequently, they are obliged to borrow money to cover the deficit. Due to their high credit rating, they are able to borrow substantial sums with a wide range of maturities. The combination of this high credit rating and the size of the issues attracts investors. Government debt markets are the largest markets in the world in terms of activity.

1.4.2 Gilts

Gilts are UK Government bonds. Historically, they were issued and managed by the Bank of England on behalf of the government. However, this role is now undertaken by the Debt Management Office (DMO).

Let us take a typical issue and examine the key features.

Treasury	12½%	2015-17	@	£126.56
I	I	I		I
Name	**Coupon**	**Maturity**		**Price**

Name

Each stock bears a title. Treasury, Exchequer, Funding, Conversion, Consolidated (Consols) and War Loan are names used to indicate the government department that issued the debt. The names are irrelevant, since all debt is the government's debt and ranks equally.

Coupon

This is the rate of interest that will be paid each year based on the nominal value of the stock. In the UK, the convention is for this coupon to be paid on a semi-annual basis, in equal instalments. However, the **2½% Consolidated stock pays on a quarterly basis**.

Maturity

This is the date on which the government has agreed to repay the debt. In this case, the government has issued debt with two dates. The government has reserved its right to redeem the debt from 2015, but must redeem the stock by 2017. The decision on redemption will be taken with reference to the coupon. If the government is able to replace the borrowing at a cheaper rate, then it will redeem the stock on the earlier of the two dates. Gilt-edged stocks are classified with respect to their maturity dates. The official Debt Management Office definitions are

- **Shorts** – gilts with **7 years or less** to run.
- **Mediums** – gilts with **between 7 and 15 years** until redemption.
- **Longs** – gilts with **over 15 years** until redemption.

Double-dated stocks are normally classified using the later of the two dates, since this is the point on which redemption has to take place.

In the past, the government has been able to issue some bonds without specifying a date on which redemption will take place. These **undated stocks** are all redeemable from a certain date. For example, the Treasury 3% '66 Aft has been redeemable since (**or after**) 1966, however, unlike double-dated stocks, there is no date by which the issue must be redeemed.

Price

This is quoted in terms of the amount that an investor would have to pay in order to buy £100 nominal of the stock. Technically, an investor can buy as much as they want of a gilt. The market simply adopts this as a convention for the quote. The price is quoted in pounds and pence (decimal terms) and can be found in the Financial Times or the DMO website.

Yield

In the *Financial Times*, both the Flat and Gross Redemption Yield are published. By convention, the yield figures shown for gilts is twice the six-monthly yield, **not** the six-monthly yield compounded.

1.4.3 Types of gilts

Straight gilts

Our example above represents a straight gilt paying a fixed coupon at 12½% p.a. until maturity. The market value of such straight bonds may vary significantly as interest rates vary, as we will see later. This may however be expected since, as interest rates rise and fall, this coupon rate will become less or more attractive.

Variable coupon gilts

The advantage of a floating rate bond is that the coupon rate is always at a fair level regardless of interest rate movements, hence the price remains at or around par. Thus, a floating rate bond protects the nominal value of the investment. In 1994 and 1996, the government issued floating rate gilts into the domestic market, however these issues have now matured and there are currently **no variable coupon gilts in issue**. Due to their low credit risk and low price volatility these gifts were traded as money market instruments rather than bonds.

Index-linked stocks

Whilst a floating rate gilt may protect the nominal value of the investment, it cannot protect against the effects of inflation which, over time, reduces the value in real terms. This protection can, however, be achieved with index-linked bonds.

As inflation increases, the return demanded by investors, the yield, will also increase in order to maintain the real rate of return. Because inflation in the UK became an issue in the 1970s, the government has issued a number of index-linked gilts (ILGs) which automatically compensate the investor for the impact of inflation. **This compensation for inflation is applied to both the coupon and the capital repayment.**

For example, the coupon is scaled up by the increase in the **Retail Prices Index (RPI)** from the issue reference date to the payment reference date.

For all ILGS there needs to be a reference date for measuring the RPIs used. That reference was historically 8 months prior to the related cash flow but for issues since September 2005 this has been reduced to three months, ie depending on the original issue date

- The issue reference date is 3 months/8 months prior to issue
- The reference date for any coupon is 3 months/8 months prior to the coupon
- The reference date for the redemption proceeds is 3 months/8 months prior to redemption

Example

2½% index-linked stock issued in March 1985. This is before June 2005 so this ILG will have 8 month lag.

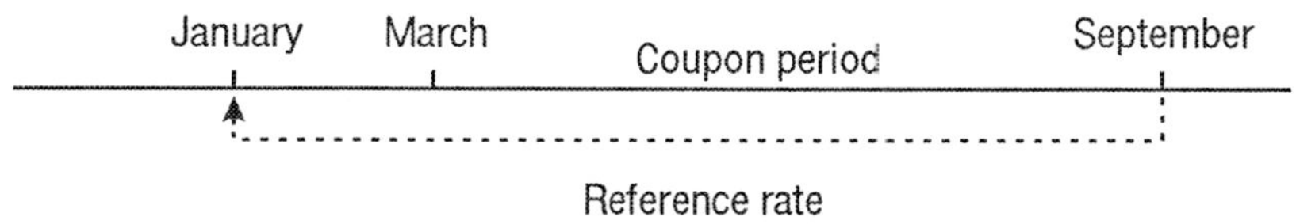

The bond has payment dates in March and September. The September coupon will be half the annual coupon uplifted by the RPI eight months prior to the coupon date (January = 374) compared with the RPI eight months prior to the issue date (July 1984 = 240).

$$£1.25 \times \frac{374}{240} = £1.948$$

Another difference between the 3 month and 8 month issues is how the reference RPIs are assessed bearing in mind that RPI statistics are published monthly.

With the 8 month issues, the RPI is taken as the RPI eight months prior to the month in which the relevant coupon is paid, i.e. an October (month 10) coupon would be referenced to the February (month 2) RPI.

With the 3 month issues, the calculation is not simply done based on the month that a coupon is paid but based on the exact date. For example, a coupon paid on 16 July will need an RPI for that specific date. To determine this, with the three month time lag the reference RPI for a month is deemed to relate to the first of that month, ie April's RPI is the reference for 1st July, May's RPI is the reference for 1st August, and we must interpolate to five decimal places to get the reference RPI for a specific date in the month.

One further difference is how prices are quoted. The price of the 8-month ILGs are quoted in nominal terms, i.e. the price that needs to be paid. The price of the 3-month ILGs are quoted in real terms and the price that is paid needs to be determined by multiplying the real price by the RPI inflation factor.

Convertible gilts

Convertible gilts are issued with an option to convert at a future date (or dates) into longer dated issues. The alternative course of action open to the holder is to allow the bond to mature and receive the redemption proceeds. There are currently no outstanding issues of convertible gilts.

Foreign currency debt issues

Over recent years, the government has been obliged to issue some foreign currency gilts. The main purpose of these loans has been to finance the foreign currency reserves at the Bank of England. There are outstanding bonds in **US$** (straight) and **€**.

These bonds are not like ordinary gilts and trade like Eurobonds with the same conventions for accrued interest.

1.4.4 New issues of gilts – the primary market

Role of the Debt Management Office (DMO)

The prime responsibility of the DMO is to ensure that the government is able to borrow the money it requires to fund the Public Sector Net Cash Requirement (PSNCR). The most important source of financing open to the government is the gilts market.

The DMO controls the issue of gilts into the market place and uses a variety of methods depending upon the circumstances it faces at any time.

Types of issue

Issues by the DMO may be of an entirely new gilt with a coupon/maturity dissimilar to existing issues. Currently, the DMO believes that the range of issues in the market is, if anything, too large and may lead to excessive fragmentation of supply and demand.

In order to avoid the problem above, the DMO may issue a **tranche** of an existing stock. This entails issuing a given amount of nominal value on exactly similar terms to an existing gilt. The DMO refers to this as 'opening up an existing gilt'. The advantages of tranches are that they avoid adding further complexity to the gilt market and increase the liquidity of current issues. When a tranche is issued, it may be identified by the letter 'A' in order to indicate that when the tranche is issued, a full coupon may not be paid on the next payment date to reflect the fact that the gilt has only been an issue for part of the coupon period.

A small tranche may be referred to as a **tranchette**.

Methods of issue

Tenders

Until 1987, gilts were primarily issued by means of tenders, also referred to as Dutch Auctions. In a tender, investors communicate to the DMO both the desired quantity and the price that they are willing to pay. The DMO accepts the applications at the highest prices sufficient to account for the nominal value being issued. All successful bidders receive the gilts at a common price: the lowest accepted bid price. In response to the credit crisis, in October 2008 the DMO used a series of mini-tenders to supplement the pre-announced auctions. The use of mini-tenders was extended to the first quarter of 2009.

Auctions

From 1987, the primary issuance method became the competitive auctions system.

In a competitive auction investors apply for gilts at a price they are prepared to pay. The DMO issues the gilts to those investors who apply at the highest prices. The key difference to a tender is that all successful applicants pay the price for which they bid. Thus, in an auction, all successful candidates do not pay the same price.

Currently, issuance by auction is the DMO's primary funding method. Either new issues or tranches of existing stock can be sold by way of an auction.

Running alongside each competitive auction are non-competitive bids where investors can apply for up to **£500,000 of nominal value for all gilts**. Applicants through non-competitive bids will receive the gilts they applied for at a weighted average of accepted prices in the auction. The smaller investors can participate in the primary market for gilts, whilst avoiding the necessity of determining an appropriate price.

Taps

The government's current principal method of funding is through regular competitive auctions. However, the government may still wish to issue smaller quantities of stock to improve liquidity or improve market efficiency. In such situations, the DMO will sell smaller quantities of stock to investors via the gilt-edged market makers.

When tapping stock into secondary markets in this way, it will often be a tranche of existing stock, or a tranchette if a relatively small amount. Alternatively, it could be as a result of a failed auction where the DMO has not received application sufficient to account for nominal value on offer. In such a situation, the remaining stock will be available on tap from the DMO.

If a particular gilt is to be tapped into the secondary market, the *Financial Times* will indicate this by marking the gilt with a '•' symbol. The last top issue took place in August 1999.

Strips

Strip stands for Separately Traded Registered Interest and Principal of Securities, and a strips market was introduced for gilts from late 1997. This market facilitates the trading of individual gilt cash flows rather than the whole bond. Thus, each coupon payment and the final redemption proceeds can be traded as if they were individual government-backed zero-coupon bonds.

For example, a four-year gilt will have eight semi-annual coupons and the redemption proceeds can be separated into nine strips.

This stripping of gilts is undertaken by financial institutions that buy a quantity of conventional gilts and strip them by selling off the rights to the component cash flows.

1.4.5 The secondary market

arning objectives

18.8.1 Explain and identify transaction costs associated with dealing in UK fixed interest securities.

18.8.2 Calculate the total transaction costs for a fixed interest security transaction, given the appropriate data.

18.8.3 Contrast the trading methods for fixed interest securities with equities and examine the impact on trading costs.

As with the equities market, gilts used to be traded on the floor of the Exchange, however, in 1986, they moved to a telephone-driven market supported by market makers.

The Debt Management Office (DMO)

The DMO is the lead regulator in the gilts market. Its objective is to ensure that the gilts market remains solvent, liquid and, above all, fair. The reason for this commitment is that the DMO is obliged to issue, on the government's behalf, gilts to fund the Public Sector Net Cash Requirement (PSNCR). In order to do this, the DMO must have access to the markets. It is the DMO which allows participants to enter the gilts market and thereafter, it is the DMO or the FSA that monitors their capital adequacy **on a daily basis**.

Gilt-Edged Market Makers (GEMMs)

The GEMMs are the focus of the market place. Their role is to ensure that two-way quotes exist at all times for all gilts. GEMMs are allowed to enter the market by the DMO. Once accepted as a gilt-edged market maker, the firm is obliged to make a market in **all conventional gilts** at a size deemed appropriate by the DMO. For index-linked stocks, because the market is less liquid, the DMO has authorised a more limited list of market makers.

Inter-Dealer Brokers (IDBs)

The IDBs act as an escape valve for GEMMs. If a GEMM were to build up a large position in a particular stock and then decide to unwind it, this might be difficult to achieve without revealing to the rest of the market that he was long or short of a stock. This is obviously a dangerous position and would discourage GEMMs from taking substantial positions. The IDBs provide an anonymous dealing service, allowing GEMMs to unwind positions. IDBs are only accessible to market makers in the gilts market.

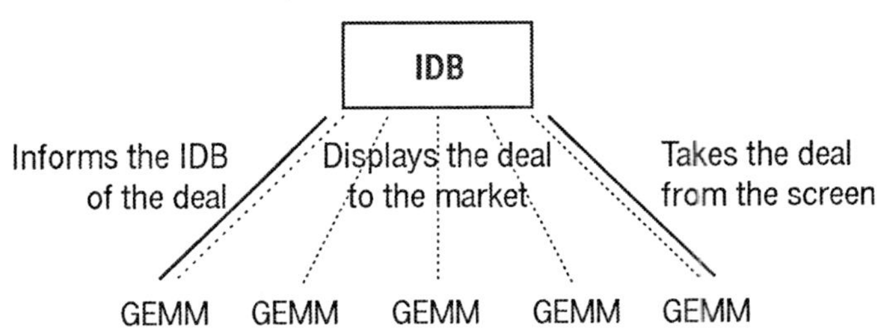

Stock Borrowing and Lending Intermediaries (SBLIs)

If market makers wish to take a short position in a stock, i.e. sell more than they currently have on their books, they will need to have stock in order to settle the trade. The SBLIs provide access to large pools of unused stock. The institutional investors in the UK buy large blocks of gilt-edged securities and often hold these blocks for a number of years, possibly to redemption. The SBLIs borrow stock on behalf of market makers from these dormant positions. The stock is passed to the market maker who uses it to settle the trade and, in effect, to go short.

Eventually, the market maker will be obliged to buy stock to cover the short position, and this stock will then be passed back to the institutional investor. The SBLI charges commission on the trade of around ½%. This commission is split between the intermediaries and the institution. This is a facility available to all market participants and provides them with vital access to stock positions enabling them to go short. Since the introduction of the gilt repo market in 1996, activity of SBLIs in the gilts market has been minimal.

The SBLIs also act as a focus for surplus cash, enabling those who are long of funds to deposit money, and market makers who need to borrow money to obtain finance.

Dealing and settlement

The predominant form of trading in UK bond markets is based around the bond dealer, though gilt investors also have the option of dealing through Computershare, the DMO's Gilt Purchase and Sale Service.

Dealers trade with clients either on a bilateral basis or, increasingly in some market segments, via multi-dealer trading platforms. There is also significant inter-dealer trading, either directly or, more commonly, through interdealer brokers, who provide dealers with anonymity. Institutional investors normally trade directly with dealers, whereas retail investors typically buy and sell bonds through a broker in the same way as they buy and sell equities.

As a reflection of the liquidity characteristics of most bonds (high average trade size and relatively low trading frequency) market making has remained the preferred trading structure. The transaction costs faced by investors will, therefore, be

- Dealers bid-offer spread (not a feature of an order-book system)
- Broker's commission for retail investors, commission rates are negotiable and are typically 0.5% to 1% for trades below £5,000 falling to zero on trades over £1m

Note that in contrast with equity markets, there is no stamp duty reserve tax (SDRT) payable on gilts, corporate bonds or Eurobonds.

The LSE has traditionally provided the principal organised marketplace for securities trading in the UK. The gilt market, in particular, operates largely under LSE rules, with all Gilt-Edged Market Makers (GEMMs) obliged to make quotes on request and to deal. The LSE also provides a marketplace for corporate bonds that also operates on the basis of bilateral trading and market maker obligations.

These facilities were expanded on 1 February 2010 when the LSE launched its electronic Order book for Retail Bonds (ORB) offering, for the first time, continuous two-way pricing for trading in UK gilts and retail-size corporate bonds on-exchange. Minimum trading sizes on this system are £1 for gilts and £1,000 for corporate bonds.

To be traded on this new system, bond issuers must request that their bonds be admitted to the electronic order book as their default location.

Despite the existence of these facilities, most corporate bond trading takes place off-exchange. As such, there is no formal market place in the UK for trading bonds and dealing continues to take place by telephone, though an increasing number of dealers also provide electronic, bilateral order-execution facilities. These operate either through proprietary systems or through arrangements with third party providers, such as data vendors. The market is regulated by the **International Capital Markets Association (ICMA)**, which operates rules regulating the conduct of dealers in relation to gilts, corporate bonds and eurobonds.

Gilt settlement occurs on the business day following the transaction **(T + 1)**. Market professionals such as GEMMs or IDBs would settle electronically through CREST.

1.5 Foreign government bonds

Other government bonds share similar features to gilts. Below is a summary of the major foreign government bonds and their key features.

	Japan (JGB)	US T-Bond	French OAT***	German Bund	Eurobonds	UK Corporates	Italian BTP	UK Gilt
Coupon Frequency	Semi-annual	Semi-annual	Annual	Annual	Annual	Annual	Semi-annual	Semi-annual
Settlement	3 business days	Same/ Next day	3 business days	3 business days	3 business days	3 business days	3 business days	Same/ Next day
Registered or bearer	R or B	R	B	B	B	R	B	R
Normal life	10 years, some super longs with life of 40 years	Life of over 10 years	Issued with lives of between 6 and 30 years	Mostly 10 years	Varied		Usually 5-7 years, but have been as long as 10 years	Varied
Withholding tax	25%, but bilateral agreement reduces to 10%	None	None	None	None	20%	12.5%	None
Medium-term debt	–	T-Note life of 2 to 10 years**	BTAN life of 2 to 5 years	BOBLs with lives of up to 5 years and Schatz with lives of 2 to 6 years	–	–	CTOs with lives of up to 6 years	–
Settlement agencies	Japanese Government Bond Clearing Corporation (JGBCC)	Federal Reserve	Relit, Euroclear and Clearstream	Euroclear and Clearstream	Euroclear and Clearstream	CREST	Bank of Italy, Euroclear and Clearstream	CREST, Clearstream, Euroclear and Bank of New York
Accrued interest convention	$\frac{\text{Actual}}{365}$	$\frac{\text{Actual}}{\text{Actual}}$	$\frac{\text{Actual}}{\text{Actual}}$	$\frac{\text{Actual}}{\text{Actual}}$	$\frac{\text{Actual}}{\text{Actual}}$	$\frac{\text{Actual}}{\text{Actual}}$	$\frac{\text{Actual}}{\text{Actual}}$	$\frac{\text{Actual}}{\text{Actual}}$

** **All types of US Government bond are issued by Dutch Auction.**

*** The French government bond is known as the OAT. In addition to this, there is also an inflation-linked bond, known as the OATi. The BTAN settles T + 1, whereas the OAT settles T + 3.

Tutor tip

> Historically the main examination areas for overseas bonds have been names (OAT, BTP), coupon frequencies, accrued interest conventions and whether they are registered or bearer instruments. For UK bonds and gilts all details are examinable.

1.6 Domestic corporate bonds

1.6.1 Debentures/loan stock

Debentures and loan stock are written acknowledgement of debt which, as such, can often be traded. The word debenture is used when the lender is being furnished with some security by the borrower; when there is no security being provided, the stock is referred to as loan stock or unsecured loan stock (ULS).

There is no obligation for a company to give security on any loan. However, the consequence of not giving security will be that the coupon it is obliged to pay will be higher. Many companies have issued unsecured loan stock in the UK markets, but they tend to be only those companies with, in general, a high credit rating or status.

1.6.2 Choice of market

The corporate borrower has a choice as to which market to issue into. Large multinational firms with high credit ratings are able to access the Eurobond or international market. Smaller companies will be constrained to use the less active domestic corporate bond market.

A **Eurobond** could be defined as an international bond issue, underwritten by a syndicate of banks, and sold principally in countries other than that of the currency of denomination.

However, the instruments are essentially the same, the only difference being that the pace of innovation is greater in the Euromarkets. The basic terms of any issue will be contained in the **indenture**.

1.6.3 Legal form

Most Eurobonds issued are in bearer form, whereas domestic issues are obliged to be in registered form.

1.6.4 Security

Companies have the ability to issue debt which is secured against the company's assets. There are two types of legal charge that a company can issue over its assets.

Fixed charge

A fixed charge is a charge over an identifiable asset of the company; the debenture deed will note the specific asset in question. Typically, a specific fixed asset such as land or a freehold building will be used for this purpose, as it can be readily identified and should not deteriorate substantially in value over the term of the debenture. This is normally referred to as a **mortgage bond**, as the bond is secured against specific collateral, such as a building.

The commercial impact of having a fixed charge is that the company cannot sell the asset in question unless the debenture holder releases the charge. The debenture holder is unlikely to do this unless he is offered some equally good asset over which he can have an alternative charge.

If the company falls into arrears with its interest payment or defaults on its capital repayment, then the debenture holder can either

- Appoint a receiver and obtain income from the assets held under charge; or

- Take possession of the asset and sell it, using the proceeds to repay the debentures in full. Any excess proceeds will be returned to the company; any shortfall will become an unsecured liability of the company.

Floating charge

A floating charge is secured against the assets in general rather than against specific assets. A floating charge has no effect until the company defaults on a loan. At this stage, the holder of a floating charge has the right to appoint a receiver to take over the running of the company. The receiver will then manage the company and any money coming in will be used to repay the bondholder's debt.

Unlike a fixed charge, where the company loses the right to dispose of an asset covered by a charge, here the company has full rights over the assets of the business until there is an event of default. At that stage, and at that stage only, does the charge crystallise.

Relevance – priority on liquidation of a company

earning objective | **18.6.13 Explain** the concept of debt seniority.

Fixed charges are legally superior to floating charges. This is demonstrated by looking at the order of payout on the liquidation of a company. The process of liquidation is one in which the company is wound up by a liquidator. The company is turned into its liquid asset – cash. Assets are sold, money is collected and then used to pay out, in a specific order, the obligations of the company.

The liquidator's task is to convert the company into cash as quickly and efficiently as possible. The order of payout is determined by the Insolvency Act and the Enterprise Act 2002, and is as follows.

Priority on Liquidation
1. The Liquidator's Fees
2. Fixed Charge Holders
3. Preferential Creditors
4. Floating Charge Holders
5. Unsecured Creditors
6. Subordinated Creditors
7. Preference Shareholders
8. Ordinary Shareholders

The liquidator will pay out each category in full before moving on to the next. Since liquidations may be the result of insolvency, there may be insufficient funds left to pay out all debts. The order of liquidation is an attempt to reward those who have some form of security first before moving on to the unsecured creditors.

Please note that **warrant** holders will receive nothing on a winding up; they have a right to buy a share in a company which is now defunct.

The priority on liquidation may be referred to as seniority. Bonds would therefore rank as follows.

- Senior secured.
- Senior unsecured.
- Subordinated.

1.6.5 Redemption

Corporate bonds can have a variety of redemption terms.

Bullets

The vast majority of bonds issued are still in the form of bullets. A bullet issue has a single redemption date. There has been a tendency to issue callable bonds, or indeed putable bonds, where the holder has the right to call for early redemption, but the complications involved in analysing these issues often dissuade investors from purchasing them. This shift away from unorthodox redemption patterns is particularly true for the next two potential repayment schemes that are now rarely used.

Sinking funds or sinkers

This is a process whereby a proportion of the bonds in issue are redeemed each year. The bonds to be redeemed in each year are selected by the process of 'drawing' the serial numbers. The serial numbers of the bonds drawn in this way are then published and the holders submit the bonds to the paying agent for redemption at par. The final repayment is normally larger than the others and is referred to as the balance or balloon repayment.

Sinking funds tend to come into operation towards the end of the bond's life and rarely start to redeem from the first coupon date.

Purchase fund

A purchase fund buys back the bonds in the secondary market, and not at par. The obligation to repay is triggered by a condition specified in the offer document, normally the bond trading below par.

Serial notes

A serial note is one where a proportion of the capital is repaid each year along with the interest.

Optional redemption

The option to redeem a bond can be given to either side of the deal. A call right would give the issuer the right to seek an earlier redemption; for example, the double-dated gilts in the UK market, where the government has the right to redeem from the earlier of the two dates, but must redeem by the later date.

1.6.6 Coupons

Zero coupon

Bonds may be issued with zero or a very small dividend. Such bonds would be issued at a discount to their redemption value to provide an acceptable gross redemption yield.

Discounted bonds will be subject to a specific tax regime if their discount exceeds either 0.5% for each year of life or 15% in total. Bonds that exceed these criteria may be referred to as deep discount bonds and the owner will pay income tax on the excess received over cost when realised by sale or redemption.

Most bonds are issued with a fixed coupon. However, a number of variations are possible.

Stepped coupons

A stepped coupon rises over the life of the bond.

Year 1	4%
Year 2	6%
Year 3	8%
Year 4 to Year 10	10%

The advantage to the issuer is that it will not be burdened by the full interest cost in the early years of the debt. However, overall the issuer will be paying a higher coupon rate. It is also possible to issue a reversed stepped coupon with the coupon rate declining progressively over the life of the bond.

Floating Rate Notes (FRNs)

FRNs are bonds that have a variable coupon that is linked to a money market reference rate such as LIBOR and therefore tend to trade close to par. As a result of the link to money market rates and their (close to) par values, FRNs are considered by the markets to be money market instruments and are traded on the money markets.

Floating rate notes were discussed in detail in the Money Markets chapter but are revisited here to introduce some additional characteristics that may be experienced with corporate issues.

A corporate FRN may be a **drop lock** where the coupon is allowed to float but once it reaches its set minimum, the bond locks into being a fixed coupon bond at that minimum interest rate.

This is obviously a fairly rigid structure and a more flexible alternative would be a floor where the bond's coupon level cannot fall below a certain point. For example, the floor of a bond might be 5%. If the index rate and the quoted margin gradually floated down to this level then, at the point of 5%, the coupon will be locked. However, as the index rate began to pick up, then the coupon could increase beyond 5% unlike with a drop lock where, of course, once it touches the floor, the bond is locked until redemption.

The minimum rate or floor is obviously a protection for the investor purchasing the floating rate note. It is possible for the issuer also to take up protection in the form of a ceiling or a cap whereby as interest rates rise, the coupon on the FRN also rises, but not beyond this pre-set ceiling.

It has been common for corporate issuers to offset the costs of establishing a ceiling by including a floor value (**minimax bonds**), which in effect **collars** the interest rate available on the floating rate note.

1.6.7 Currency

There is no need for the currency of the coupon and that of redemption to be the same; it is entirely possible for the two to be different – **dual currency bonds**. For example, a bond may pay coupons in dollars whilst be redeemed in sterling. The rate of exchange can either be established at the outset or be the spot rate at the time of the transaction.

Bonds have also been issued which contain an option to use a variety of currencies, either at the issuer or holder's choice.

1.6.8 Convertible bonds

earning objective	**18.5.2 Understand** the rationale for and risk to the issuer and holder at a convertible, callable or putable bond.

A conversion right gives the bondholder the right, at a specified date or dates in the future, to convert their bond into shares of the company. The rate of conversion will be fixed at the time of issue and represents an option to purchase the shares at a given price.

Depending on the movement in the underlying share price, this conversion right or option may be very valuable indeed. The trade-off in this sort of issue is that the coupon will often be much lower than the market would otherwise expect on a bond from that particular company.

1.6.9 Callable and putable bonds

Callable bonds

Callable bonds are where the issuer has the right to redeem the bonds at an agreed price prior to its maturity. This price may be above the normal redemption price and the extra price paid is referred to as the call premium.

The call provision is valuable to the issuer, but is a disadvantage to the investor, since the issuer will only exercise the call if it suits the issuer to do so. As a result, the price at which a callable bond can be issued will be lower than for a comparable straight bond, and the interest rate it will need to pay will consequently be higher.

A call provision will reduce the expected time to maturity of the bond, since there is a possibility that the bond will be retired early as a result of the call provision being exercised.

Call provisions will be exercised when the issuer can refinance the issue at a cheaper cost due to interest rates having fallen. For example, if a bond were issued when interest rates were 15% and interest rates have now fallen to 5%, the issuer could issue a new bond at the currently low i/r and use the proceeds to call back the higher coupon bond.

Putable bonds

This is where the investor has a **put option** on the bond, giving him the right to sell the bond back to the company at a specified price (the put price). The put price is typically around par, given that the bond was issued at par.

The benefit to the investor is that if interest rates rise after the bond is issued, they can sell the bond at a fixed price and reinvest the proceeds at a higher interest rate. As a result of the benefit to investors, putable bonds are issued at higher prices or lower coupons than comparable non-putable bonds.

1.6.10 Covenants

Covenants are terms and conditions attached to a bond issue.

The negative pledge

The negative pledge clause specifically relates to Euromarkets. Most Eurobonds are not secured in any way against the underlying assets of the borrower. A negative pledge clause is where the borrower undertakes to refrain from raising other finance on which it grants a better security. In effect, this means that any borrower who raises funds through the Euromarkets is normally then prevented from raising money through the domestic markets since, in general, domestic investors will require some form of security.

Cross default clause

A cross default clause is included in most loan agreements and states that if the borrower defaults on any one of its loans, then this will constitute a default of this borrowing as well.

The important consequence of this is that the borrower may default on one loan due to, perhaps, overly strenuous covenants which the lender is prepared to waive, but that will still constitute a default for any other borrowing which has a cross default clause in existence.

Pari Passu

A pari passu clause ensures that any lender is granted the same level of security as given to any new lenders.

Restrictive financial covenants

It is possible to include within the loan documentation a number of key ratios that the borrower must not exceed. These normally include some measure of the ability to pay interest and may state an express limit on the overall level of borrowing that can be undertaken. These forms of covenant are notoriously difficult to enforce and are frequently strongly resisted by the borrower.

New owner

New Owner Clause is included to allow the lender the right of repayment, should the ownership of the corporate borrower change.

Nature of business

This is linked to the New Owner Clause. Should the nature of the company's business change dramatically, then this will again affect the rights of the holders of the bonds, and may give the right to request a redemption of the bond.

Events of default

A breach of the covenants or the failure to pay the coupon or principal on the due dates are events of default. Whilst within the agreement there may be allowance for 'grace periods', if the borrower remains in default, then the loan is immediately repayable.

Most bonds are constituted in such a way that there is a trustee who is responsible for ensuring that the bondholder's interests are protected. Where there is no trustee, the bondholder is obliged to seek redress directly from the company.

1.6.11 Corporate bond issuance

Placing

In the domestic market, the most common form of issuance is via a placing. In the Euromarkets, a more structured approach is required in order to cope with the size of the issues involved.

New Issues in the Corporate Bond Market

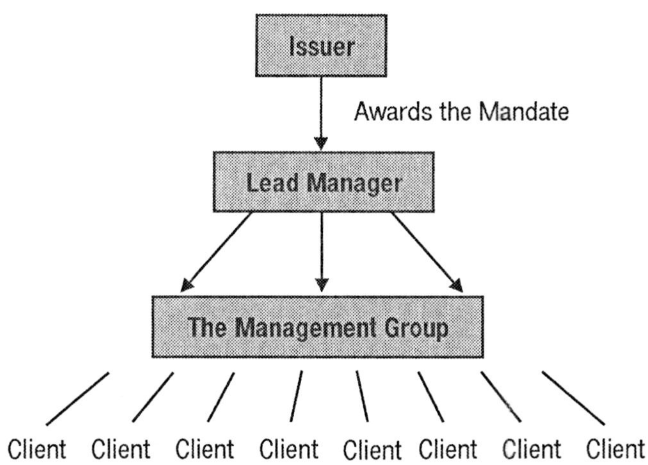

As noted above, most common form of issue used in the domestic corporate bond market is a **placing**Error! Bookmark not defined.. A traditional method of issuing a corporate bond is for an issuer to appoint a lead manager and award them the mandate. The mandate gives the lead manager the power and responsibility to issue the bond on the issuer's behalf.

A **bought deal** is where the lead manager agrees detailed terms with the issuer, including the coupon and the maturity. In normal issues, the lead manager has the ability to amend the terms of the issue as market conditions dictate.

The lead manager may then create a management group of other issuing houses. Each house receives a portion of the deal and places it with its client base. Alternatively, the lead manager may elect to run the entire book alone, and omit the other members of the management group.

There are a number of variations on this method of issue. Under a **fixed price re-offer**, the members of the management group are prohibited from selling the bonds in the secondary market at below the issue price until the syndicate has been broken. The syndicate will break when the lead manager believes the bulk of the issue has been placed.

LSE Order book for Retail Bonds (ORB)

Under the Prospectus Directive, the EU regulation that governs the documentation published when a bond is listed and brought to a market such as the London Stock Exchange, the regulatory regime distinguishes between wholesale and retail bonds. Wholesale bonds are tradeable in units of £50,000 or greater, whereas retail bonds are tradeable in smaller size, often in denominations of £1,000 for example.

Until recently, most of bonds issued in the UK were wholesale bonds and are therefore not accessible to many private investors because of the large size of the denominations in which they must be traded. However, following the success of Borsa Italiana's highly successful MOT retail bond market, the London Stock Exchange (LSE) launched its own retail bond market, the Order book for Retail Bonds (ORB).

As noted earlier, the LSE launched ORB in February 2010 in response to increasing demand from retail investors for access to the bond market. The ORB is an electronic trading platform similar to SETSqx for equities, a market supported by dedicated market makers that seeks to offer investors a cost effective, transparent and efficient trading for retail investors in corporate bonds and gilts. Investors can see prices on-screen, and can trade in increments as low as £1 for gilts and £1,000 for corporate bonds (though some are tradable in increments of £5,000 or £10,000), in a process similar to share dealing.

At launch ORB had, 49 gilts and ten corporate bonds listed for trading. All securities admitted to trading ORB are London-listed securities admitted to the EU-Regulated Main Market, ensuring a high level of regulatory oversight and offering the benefits of the transparency afforded by the Financial Services Authority's disclosure and continuing obligations regimes.

1.6.12 The secondary market

The secondary market for all bond trading was described under gilts above. In both the domestic and Euromarkets, there is only a limited secondary market, the majority of issues are never actively traded. Consequently, as noted earlier, the market is not particularly structured with very little involvement of market makers. Settlement of any domestic bond trades is based on a **three-business-day (T + 3)** settlement system.

1.7 Eurobonds

1.7.1 The market

The Eurobond market is in effect an international market in debt. Companies issuing debt in the Eurobond market have their securities traded all around the world and are not limited to one domestic market place.

The market only accepts highly rated companies, since Eurobonds themselves are unsecured debt.

1.7.2 The instrument

In essence, a Eurobond is simply a debt instrument issued by a borrower (typically, a government or a large company) normally or predominantly outside of the country in whose currency it is denominated. For example, a US dollar Eurobond could be issued anywhere in the world, except for the US. As such, a better name for it might be an 'international bond'. As mentioned above, Eurobonds frequently carry no security other than the high name and credit rating of the issuer. Another important feature of bonds issued in this market is that, for the most part, they are issued in **bearer form**, with no formal register of ownership held by the company.

It should be noted that for a number of pragmatic reasons, the clearing houses in the Euromarkets do maintain a form of register of ownership, but that this register is not normally open either to government or tax authorities. Combined with the feature of being bearer documents, a vital aspect of the Eurobond is that, unlike most Government bonds, it does not attract withholding tax. **Eurobonds pay coupons gross** and usually **annually**.

Most Eurobonds are issued in **bullet form**, redeemed at one specified date in the future. However, a number of issues have alternative redemption patterns. Some bonds are redeemed over a number of years with a proportion of the issue being redeemed each year. Whilst Eurobonds are not issued in registered form, each will have an identifying number. A **drawing** of numbers is made every year from the pool of bonds in issue, the numbers drawn are published, and the bonds are called in and redeemed. This redemption process is known as a drawing on a Eurobond.

1.7.3 Settlement

The secondary market for all bond trading was discussed under gilts earlier. Settlement in the Eurobond market is based on a **three-business-day (T + 3)** settlement system. Once again, the important feature about the registers maintained by the two clearing houses is that they are not normally available to any governmental authority, thereby preserving the bearer nature of the documents.

1.7.4 Eurobond issuance

The methods of Eurobond issuance are identical to those of corporate bond issues in the domestic markets.

New Issues in the Eurobond Market

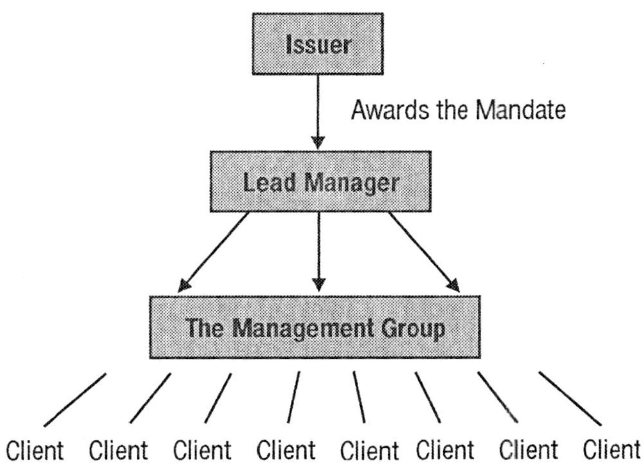

As for domestic corporate bonds, the most common form of issue used in the Eurobond market is a **placing**.

2 Pricing Bonds

2.1 Introduction

Since the cash flow values and timings from a bond are known with such certainty, at least for a straight bond, the application of DCF evaluation techniques is clearly appropriate.

There are, however, two pricing aspects to consider.

- DCF evaluation
- Clean and dirty bond pricing

The first of these ideas is the method that we will primarily use to evaluate a bond, the second of these is relevant for determining the correct tax treatment.

2.2 Discounted cash flow valuation of straight bonds

Learning objectives

18.5.4 Understand the valuation methodology for fixed income securities.

18.5.5 Calculate the price of a fixed income security given its maturity, coupon and yield.

2.2.1 Redeemables

A straight redeemable bond pays a coupon to the maturity date, then pays the redemption proceeds at that date. If we know the required return to the bondholders, we can, using DCF, evaluate this bond. If the bond is of a fairly short maturity, we may consider each cash flow separately. If, however, the bond is longer dated, it would be more convenient to apply the idea and calculation of an annuity.

Example

A bond pays an annual coupon of 9% and is redeemable at par in three years. Evaluate this bond if interest rates are

- 8%
- 9%
- 10%

Solution

Interest rate at 8%

Time	Cash Flow £	DF (8%)	Present Value £
1	9.00	$\frac{1}{1.08}$	8.33
2	9.00	$\frac{1}{1.08^2}$	7.72
3	109.00 (100.00 + 9.00)	$\frac{1}{1.08^3}$	86.53
			£102.58

Interest rate at 9%

Time	Cash Flow £	DF (9%)	Present Value £
1	9.00	$\frac{1}{1.09}$	8.26
2	9.00	$\frac{1}{1.09^2}$	7.58
3	109.00	$\frac{1}{1.09^3}$	84.16
			£100.00

Interest rate at 10%

Time	Cash Flow £	DF (10%)	Present Value £
1	9.00	$\frac{1}{1.10}$	8.18
2	9.00	$\frac{1}{1.10^2}$	7.44
3	109.00	$\frac{1}{1.10^3}$	81.89
			£97.51

Conclusion

This example illustrates two important features about bonds, specifically

- There is an **inverse relationship between bond prices and interest rates**, i.e. as interest rates rise, market values fall (and vice versa).
- When the coupon rate on the bond is equal to the prevailing interest rate, the bond will be valued at par, as illustrated above, when interest rates are 9%.

It is vital that you are aware of, and comfortable with, these two conclusions. Their appreciation is essential for the effective appraisal of a bond investment or the management of a bond portfolio.

This calculation may be expressed mathematically as follows.

Formula to learn

$$\text{Redeemable straight bond price} = \frac{C_1}{1+r} + \frac{C_2}{(1+r)^2} + \frac{C_3}{(1+r)^3} + \cdots + \frac{C_n + R}{(1+r)^n}$$

where r = investor's required return

We shall refer to this formula from time to time. However, the above tabular approach to the calculation is probably most convenient.

Example

Calculate the value of the above bond at 10%, assuming it matures in eight years.

Solution

This bond will pay its coupon for the next eight years and then be redeemed. Its value will, therefore, be

Time	Cash Flow £	DF (10%)	Present Value £
1-8	9.00	$\frac{1}{0.10}\left(1-\frac{1}{1.10^8}\right)$	48.01
8	100.00	$\frac{1}{1.10^8}$	46.65
			£94.66

2.2.2 Irredeemables

When we have an irredeemable bond, we are evaluating a perpetuity stream of cash flows.

Example

Evaluate a 9% irredeemable, assuming interest rates are 10%.

Solution

Time	Cash Flow £	DF (10%)	Present Value £
1-∞	9.00	$\frac{1}{0.10}$	90.00
			£90.00

This calculation may be expressed mathematically as follows.

Formula to learn

$$\text{Irredeemable straight bond price} = \frac{\text{Coupon}}{r}$$

where r = investor's required return

2.3 Clean and dirty prices

Learning objective

18.5.3 Explain clean (quoted) and dirty pricing.

2.3.1 Introduction

A further pricing aspect is clean and dirty pricing, the distinction being made for tax purposes as income and capital gains may be taxed differently on bonds.

The value of a bond has two elements, the underlying capital value of the bond itself (the **clean price** which is quoted) and the coupon that it is accruing over time (**accrued interest**). Periodically, this coupon is distributed as income to the holders or, more specifically, the individual who was the registered holder on the ex-dividend date (normally **seven business days** prior to payment date).

The **dirty price** calculated above using DCF is the price that is paid for a bond, which combines these two elements. Consequently, ignoring all other factors that might affect the price, a dirty price will rise gradually as the coupon builds up and then fall back as the stock is marked either ex-dividend or pays the dividend.

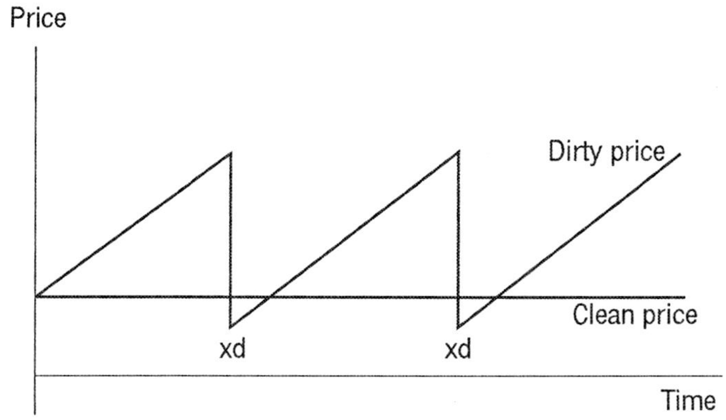

The advantage that this offered investors in the past was that rather than claiming the dividend, they could sell the bond at the high price just prior to the payment of the dividend, and this gain would be free of tax. This process was known as **bond washing**. In February 1986, the UK moved to a system of clean pricing which separates the two elements.

Under clean pricing, whenever an investor buys or sells a bond, the dirty price they pay/receive is split into the **clean price** (capital value) component and the **accrued interest** (income) component, allowing these two components (income and gain) to be taxed separately.

2.3.2 Cum dividend bargains

A purchase made before the ex-dividend date is referred to as a cum dividend bargain. In this situation, the buyer of the bond will be the holder on the next ex-div date and will, therefore, receive the full coupon for the period. The seller, however, has held the bond for part of this period and is therefore entitled to a part of that coupon. To account for this, the purchaser of the bond must compensate the seller for the dividend which he has earned.

Example

In this example, the purchaser will pay the clean price plus the interest from the last payment date up to the purchase. On the next payment date, the holder will receive the whole of the interest for the six months. However, on a net basis, they will only have received the interest for the period of ownership.

The formula used by the DMO in the gilts market is

Formula to learn

$$\text{Dirty price} = \text{Clean price} + \text{Period coupon} \times \frac{\text{Days}}{\text{Days in period}}$$

$$\text{Paid} = \text{Quoted} + \text{Accrued interest from period start}$$

where

Days = number of days from the **last coupon payment date** up to and including the calendar **day before the settlement** day (next business day following the trade)

Days in period = number of days from the **last coupon payment date** up to and including the calendar **day before the next coupon** (**Note** that for this exam this is taken as 182.5 days irrespective of the actual period involved)

Thus, the period coupon is spread over the number of days in the period, giving a coupon per day, then allocated to the relevant holder on a daily basis.

Example

Coupons are paid on 1 April and 1 October. On 10 July, an investor buys £10,000 nominal of Treasury 8% @ £101.50 for settlement on 11 July. How much is paid?

Solution

The 8% gilt pays a 4% coupon each period (half year) giving

		£
Clean Price	£10,000 @ £101.50	10,150.00
Accrued Interest	$(£10{,}000 \times 4\% = £400) \times \frac{101}{182.5}$	221.37
Dirty Price		£10,371.37

the number of days having been calculated as follows.

Month		**Days**
April	From last coupon (inclusive)	30
May		31
June		30
July	To day before settlement	10
		101

2.3.3 Ex-dividend bargains

An ex-div bargain is one occurring after the ex-div date, but before the coupon is paid. Gilt-edged stocks, for example, are usually marked ex-div **seven business days** prior to the payment day in order to allow the DMO to ensure that the dividend is paid to the appropriate party. Any person buying the stock after it has been marked ex will not, therefore, be entitled to the interest. Consequently, the pricing must reflect this.

Example

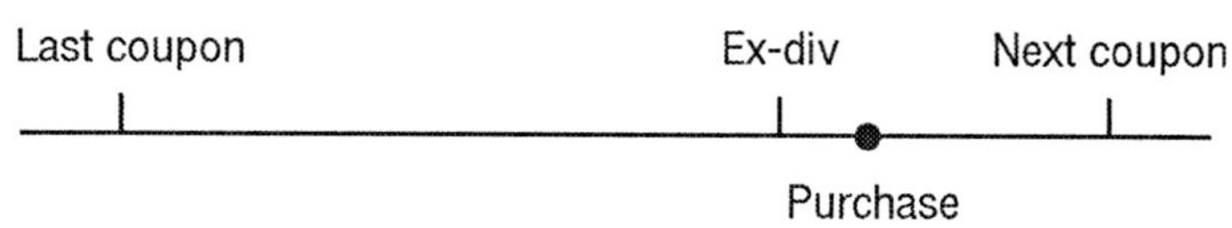

In this example, the buyer of the bond will be entitled to the coupon for the last few days of the period, but will receive nothing, as this will all go to the seller who held at the ex-div date. He will, therefore, require this to be adjusted in the price.

Accordingly, he pays the clean price as determined by the market less the number of days' worth of interest that he is not receiving.

The formula used in this situation by the DMO in the gilts market is

Formula to learn

$$\text{Dirty price} = \text{Clean price} - \text{Period coupon} \times \frac{\text{Days}}{\text{Days in period}}$$

$$\text{Paid} = \text{Quoted} - \text{Accrued interest from period start}$$

where

Days	=	number of days from the **settlement day** (next business day) to the calendar **day before the next coupon payment date** (inclusive)
Days in period	=	number of days from the **last coupon payment date** up to and including the calendar **day before the next coupon** (Again, for this examination this is approximated to 182.5 days for a 365 day year irrespective of the actual period involved)

3 Returns Measures – The Yield

Learning objectives

18.6.1 Identify the components of return of fixed income securities.

18.6.4 Explain the nature of the relationship between yield and price.

18.7.1 Define and calculate: Flat yield; Gross redemption yield (GRY); Net redemption yield (NRY) and Grossed-up NRY.

18.7.2 Explain when each of the above measures may be appropriate to use.

The value of any investment will depend on the return that it generates and the risks inherent in those returns. In bond markets, the single most important measure of return is the yield. There are, however, several different yield measures that we may wish to calculate, each having its own uses and limitations. For each of these measures, we need to know

- How it is calculated.
- Its uses.
- Its limitations.

In basic terms, however

Total return = Income + Gain

and the various yield measures assess either one or both of these components.

3.1 The flat yield

3.1.1 Calculation

The simplest measure of the return used in the market is the flat (interest or running) yield. This measure looks at the annual cash return (coupon) generated by an investment as a percentage of the cash price. In simple terms, what is the regular annual income that you generate on the money that you invest?

$$\text{Flat Yield} = \frac{\text{Annual coupon rate}}{\text{Market price}}$$

Example

We hold 10% Loan stock (annual coupon) redeemable at par in four years. The current market price is £97.25. Calculate the flat yield.

Solution

The flat yield for the above would be

$$\text{Flat yield} = \frac{£10.00}{£97.25} = 0.10283 \text{ or } 10.283\%$$

3.1.2 Uses

This measure assesses the **annual income return** only and is most appropriate when either

- We are dealing with **irredeemables**, which pay no return other than income into perpetuity; or
- Our priority is the short-term cash returns that the investment will generate.

3.1.3 Limitations

This measure, while of some use (particularly in the short term), has three important drawbacks for the investment markets.

- In addition to the coupon flows, bonds may have returns in the form of the redemption moneys. Where the bond has been purchased at a price away from par, this will give rise to potential gains and losses which are excluded from this calculation.
- The calculation completely ignores the timing of any cash flows and the time value of money.
- With some bonds (floating rate notes – FRNs), the return in any one period will vary with interest rates. If the coupon is not constant, then this measure is only of historic value unless the predicted return is used.

These limitations combine to make the flat yield of only marginal use.

3.2 The Japanese gross redemption yield

3.2.1 Calculation

The idea behind the Japanese gross redemption yield (GRY) calculation is to overcome the first of the limitations of the flat yield noted above, specifically that any gains or losses to redemption are ignored. This measure recognises that the total return in any period is a combination of both income and capital components, i.e. the coupon received plus any gain (minus any loss) for the period.

The Japanese method for calculating the GRY is to take the flat yield and then add the average annual capital gain (or deduct the average annual loss) to redemption, stated as a percentage of the current market price. Thus, we can state the Japanese GRY as follows.

Formula to learn

$$\text{GRY} = \frac{\text{Annual coupon rate}}{\text{Market price}} + \frac{\text{Average annual capital gain to redemption}}{\text{Market price}}$$

or

$$\text{GRY} = \frac{\text{Annual coupon rate}}{\text{Market price}} + \frac{\dfrac{\text{Redemption price - Market price}}{\text{Years to redemption}}}{\text{Market price}}$$

Example

We hold 10% Loan stock (annual coupon) redeemable at par in four years. The current market price is £97.25. Calculate the Japanese GRY.

Solution

The Japanese GRY for the above would be

$$\text{Japanese GRY} = \frac{£10.00}{£97.25} + \frac{\frac{£100.00 - £97.25}{4}}{£97.25}$$

$$= \frac{£10.00}{£97.25} + \frac{£0.6875}{£97.25}$$

$$= 0.10283 + 0.00707 = 0.10990 \text{ or } 10.99\%$$

3.2.2 Uses

The main use of this method is to provide a quick and easy way of assessing the GRY, which assesses the **total return**, income and gain.

It should be noted that it is not an absolutely accurate measure of return, since it assumes linear capital growth rather than the more realistic compound growth. As a result, it is liable to overstate the effects of any capital gain or loss. Furthermore, this inaccuracy increases the further away a bond is from maturity.

3.2.3 Limitations

Whilst this method does overcome the first limitation of the flat yield, i.e. its failure to account for any capital gains or losses to redemption, it does not overcome the other noted drawbacks, specifically

- The calculation completely ignores the timing of any cash flows and the time value of money.
- With some bonds (floating rate notes – FRNs), the return in any one period will vary with interest rates. If the coupon is not constant, then this measure is only of historic value unless the predicted return is used.

The first of these limitations can only be overcome through the use of discounted cash flow techniques as illustrated below. The second is a valid limitation of all yield measures.

3.3 Gross redemption yield

3.3.1 Calculation

Introduction

The gross redemption yield (GRY) resolves the issue of the redemption values and the time value of money by using discounted cash flow techniques.

The gross redemption yield is the internal rate of return (IRR) of

- The dirty price paid to buy the bond.
- The gross coupons received **to redemption**.
- The final redemption proceeds.

Mathematical formulation

This could be expressed mathematically as follows.

When GRY = r, then

$$\text{Price} = \sum \frac{C_t}{(1+r)^t} + \frac{R}{(1+r)^n}$$

Alternatively, this may be expressed as

$$\text{Price} = \frac{C_1}{1+r} + \frac{C_2}{(1+r)^2} + \frac{C_3}{(1+r)^3} + \cdots + \frac{C_n + R}{(1+r)^n}$$

It should be noted that these formulae **cannot** be algebraically solved (except in very rare circumstances) and must be found through trial and error.

3.3.2 Uses

This measure overcomes the major deficiencies highlighted in relation to the flat yield and the Japanese GRY. It considers all cash returns and exactly when they occur.

As a result, the GRY represents a realistic measure of the expected overall future return from a bond at any point in time.

3.3.3 Limitations

As a measure of predicted return, the yield is limited, since it **assumes that interest rates remain constant throughout the period and hence, that any coupon receipts may be reinvested at the same rate as the yield**. If this is the case, then the GRY does represent the return achieved. If rates vary, however, the return achieved will differ from the GRY.

If the bond is not held to redemption, but sold at some earlier date, then the return achieved will be a function of the price of the bond (hence, interest rates) at the disposal date.

Even if the bond is held to redemption, the terminal value will differ, as the reinvested coupons will grow at a different rate, altering the ultimate return achieved.

3.4 The net redemption yield

3.4.1 Calculation

The GRY measures the gross return before the effects of taxation. The net redemption yield (NRY) is the return that the investor can expect net of taxation.

The NRY is most appropriate for individual investors to help them assess their after-tax returns. As each individual has a different tax position, the NRY will obviously be different for different individuals. The market convention is to compute the NRY at assumed levels of personal tax such as 40%.

In the UK, the taxation treatment of the income and gain elements differs for individual investors. The coupon income is subject to income tax, however the capital gain (or loss) on gilts and sterling non-convertible debt is tax free.

The net redemption yield can, therefore, be calculated as the internal rate of return (IRR) of

- The dirty price paid to buy the bond.
- The **net** coupons received **to redemption** (net of the appropriate rate of tax).
- The final redemption proceeds.

3.4.2 Uses

Since it is based on discounted cash flow techniques, as is the GRY, this measure overcomes the major deficiencies highlighted in relation to the flat yield and the Japanese GRY. It considers all cash returns and exactly when they occur and their tax implications for the investor.

The NRY therefore represents a realistic measure of the expected overall return to the investor at any point in time net of taxes.

3.4.3 Limitations

The limitations of the NRY are as for the GRY, specifically it only represents the net return that will be achieved if interest rates to maturity remain constant throughout the holding period.

3.5 Gross equivalent yield or grossed-up NRY

3.5.1 Calculation

As we noted earlier, the tax status for individual investors holding gilts or sterling non-convertible debt is that coupons are taxed, but any capital gain is not. This may be contrasted with an investment in shares where both income and capital are subject to tax.

The Gross Equivalent Yield (GEY) calculates the gross return required from a fully taxed source of income in order to produce the same after-tax return as a particular bond.

The approach to the calculation is to measure the after-tax return that the bond is providing using the NRY calculation, which the fully taxed source of income will need to match, then gross this up for the appropriate tax rate to see what gross return is required from that source. The calculation is

Formula to learn

$$GEY = \frac{NRY}{1 - T_p}$$

where

T_p = the personal tax rate upon which the NRY was calculated

Example

We hold 10% Loan stock (annual coupon) redeemable at par in four years. The current market price is £97.25 based on a GRY of 10.8842% and an NRY of 6.8084% for a 40% taxpayer. Calculate the GEY.

Solution

The flat yield for the above would be

$$GEY = \frac{6.8084}{0.60} = 11.3473\%$$

If the bond is valued below par it will generate a tax-free gain to maturity. Any fully taxed alternative would need to match this gain **after tax** and hence requires a higher return before tax. As a result the GEY will exceed the GRY.

Conversely, if the bond is valued above par, then the capital loss it will suffer to maturity would **not** attract tax relief, whereas it would on the fully taxed alternative. As a result, a much higher capital loss could be sustained on the fully taxed alternative whilst still having the same effect net of tax. The result is that the GEY will be lower than the GRY in this situation.

If a bond is valued at par, then the two measures will be identical as there will be no capital gain or loss, hence the tax treatment will be the same.

3.5.2 Uses

The use of this measure is to enable comparison of the returns of alternatives regardless of their tax treatment.

It does **not** represent the pre-tax return the bond will offer that is given as accurately as can be by the GRY. Instead, it provides a benchmark for appraising alternatives that are fully taxed.

3.5.3 Limitations

Since it is based on the NRY, its limitations are as for that measure, specifically it only represents the gross return required from the alternative if interest rates to maturity remain constant throughout the holding period.

In addition, the calculation only caters for one tax rate, hence we must assume that this will also be constant to over the period.

3.6 Relating the yield measures

The flat yield, Japanese GRY and GRY are all pre-tax measures assessing

- Flat Yield – the annual gross income generated.
- GRY – the annual total return (Income + Gain) generated.
- Japanese GRY – an approximation of the annual total return (Income + Gain) generated, which overstates any gain (or loss).

Since the majority of the return from a bond comes in the form of income, we would expect these three measures to be fairly similar, being related as follows.

Bond Value	Relationship
Above Par (loss to redemption)	Flat Yield > GRY > Japanese GRY
At Par	Flat Yield = GRY = Japanese GRY
Below Par (gain to redemption)	Flat Yield < GRY < Japanese GRY

The NRY is a post-tax measure, and as a result would be considerably lower than any of the three pre-tax alternatives for normal straight bonds.

The relationship between the GEY, GRY and the flat yield could be summarised as follows.

Bond Value	Relationship
Above par (loss to redemption)	Flat yield > GRY > GEY
At par	Flat yield = GRY = GEY
Below par (gain to redemption)	Flat yield < GRY < GEY

You will notice that the relationship between the flat yield, GRY and Japanese GRY is the same as that between the flat yield, GRY and GEY.

The relationship between the GEY and the Japanese GRY, however, depends on the tax rate involved, the coupon rate and the term to maturity and cannot, therefore, be generalised.

4 Yield Curve and Term Structure of Interest Rates

4.1 Introduction

In all of our evaluation exercises so far, we have applied the same interest rate in discounting the cash flows regardless of when they arise. The question is: is this reasonable?

Example

What will be the market values of two zero-coupon bonds which are identical in all respects, except that one matures in one year and the other in five years, if the interest rate is 10%? How will these values change if interest rates fall to 9%?

Solution

Maturity	10%	9%	Change
1 year	$MV = \frac{£100}{1.10} = £90.91$	$MV = \frac{£100}{1.09} = £91.74$	£0.83 or 0.913%
5 years	$MV = \frac{£100}{1.10^5} = £62.09$	$MV = \frac{£100}{1.09^5} = £64.99$	£2.90 or 4.671%

In both absolute and relative terms, the five-year bond shows significantly more price volatility, hence we may conclude that the five-year bond is a more risky investment.

One of the fundamental precepts of investment appraisal is that if an investor faces a higher risk, then he will demand a higher return. On the basis of this, it is unreasonable to be applying the same required return to these two bonds; the required return on a longer dated bond should be at some premium over that of a shorter dated bond to reflect the additional risk.

Thus, there should be a term structure to interest rates and bond yields, which we would normally expect to rise as we consider investment cash flows further and further into the future.

4.2 The yield curve

Learning objective	**18.7.3 Define** the yield curve.

4.2.1 Introduction

The yield curve demonstrates the relationship between bond yields and their maturities.

Normal yield curve

The normal shape of the yield curve is illustrated below.

The Normal Yield Curve

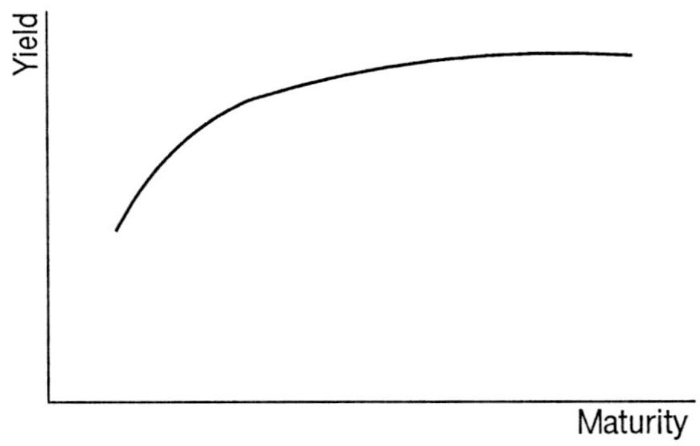

This curve clearly demonstrates the point made above, i.e. longer maturity results in higher risk which, in turn, results in higher returns or yields.

Problem with these ideas

Unfortunately, the yield curve does not always follow the shape described above, indeed occasionally it becomes inverted with short-term yields exceeding longer term ones as shown below.

The Inverted Yield Curve

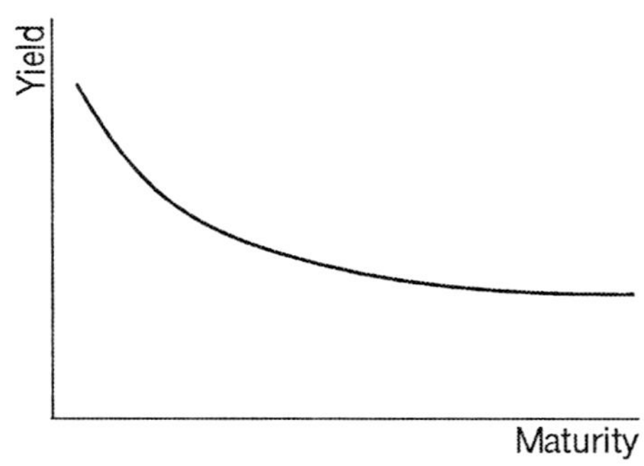

This appears to contradict our fundamental ideas of higher risk means higher return, one of the cornerstones of investment theory and hence we need to consider what factors determine the shape of this curve. There are clearly some other forces at work here in addition to the simple risk return relationship that we have considered so far.

4.3 Shape of the yield curve

Learning objective	**18.7.4 Explain** the theories that contribute to explaining the shape of the yield curve.

4.3.1 Introduction

What, then, determines the shape of the yield curve? The risk/return relationship is one factor at work here but, as we noted earlier, there must be other, perhaps more significant factors, otherwise we would never see an inverted yield curve.

A number of theories have been advanced to explain the shape of the yield curve which we outline below.

4.3.2 Liquidity preference

This theory states that if an investor's money is invested in longer term (and therefore riskier) stocks, then they will require a greater return or **risk premia**. Short-term liquid stock carry a lower risk and therefore require a lower return.

This risk premium gives rise to the normal upward sloping yield curve.

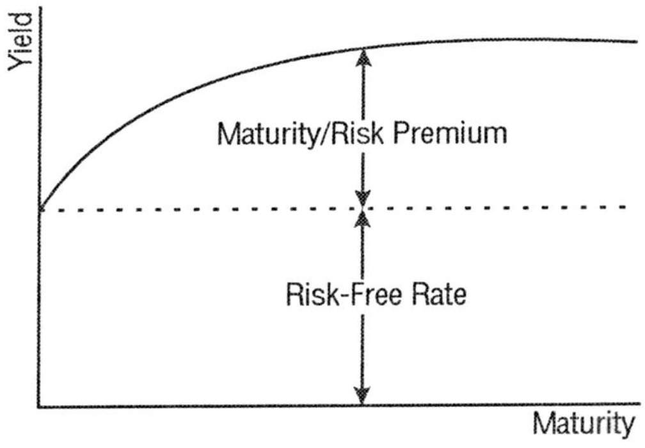

4.3.3 Expectations theory

Expectations theory states that the yield curve is a reflection of the market's expectation of future interest rates. If the market believes that the yield at the long end of the yield curve is high and is likely to fall, then, in order to profit from the increase in prices that this will create, it will buy long-dated stocks. As a result, the demand for these stocks will rise and this demand pressure will force the price to rise. As a consequence, the yield will fall reflecting the expectation of a fall.

On the other hand, if the market believes that rates will have to rise, then the forces will work in the opposite direction and this will lead to a fall in the price and a rise in the yield.

The expectations of the market can clearly be seen in an inverted yield curve.

The Inverted Yield Curve

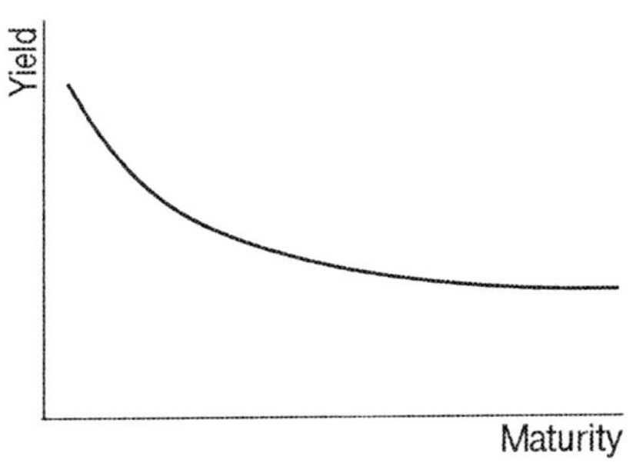

Here, the short-term rates are high, but the market anticipates that this cannot last for long and the longer end of the market has anticipated this change by forcing yields down. This can lead to the anomalous situation where the long end of the market, because it has anticipated change, remains constant and the short end (which is technically the least volatile) exhibits all of the movement.

Another key element of the market's expectations will be the **expectation of inflation**. If the market believes that inflation will rise in the future, then the yields on the longer dated stocks will have to rise in order to compensate investors for the fall in the real value of their money. The expectation of inflation is much more of a problem with the long end rather than the short end.

4.3.4 Preferred habitat and market segmentation – demand effects

This is not a theory to explain the full shape of the yield curve as such. Rather, it should be viewed as an addendum to the above two theories to help explain certain other features observed in the markets, such as humped yield curves in relation to the liquidity preference theory.

Certain maturity ranges are appropriate to particular types of investors. In the UK, the short end of the market is dominated by the financial sector and general insurance companies maintaining a proportion of their assets in liquid investments, whereas the long end is dominated by institutional investors such as pension funds and life assurance companies.

In effect, this gives rise to two markets concentrated at different ends of the yield curve. The impact of this concentrated demand at these two ends is that prices are driven up and hence, yields fall below those that may otherwise have been expected at these points. This may result in a discontinuity or hump in the yield curve.

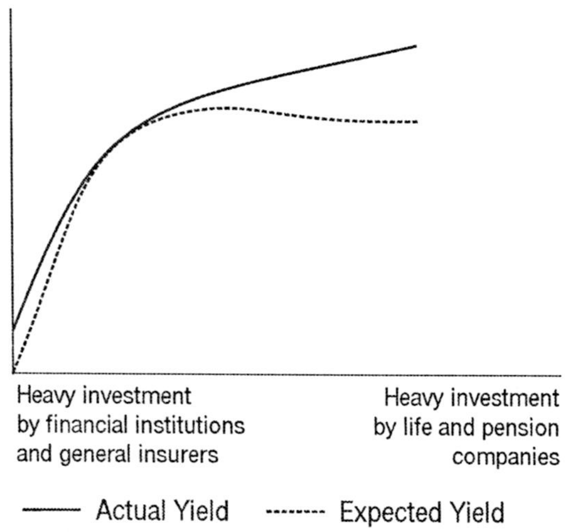

4.3.5 Supply-side factors

The availability of stocks in certain maturity ranges may lead to either an excess or shortage of stock and consequently, an anomalous yield on some stocks. This is more often a problem at the long end of the yield curve where governments may be priced out of the issuance market.

4.4 Spot rates and forward rates

Learning objectives

18.7.5 Define forward and spot interest rates.

18.7.6 Explain the relationship between forward rates, spot rates and the GRY.

4.4.1 Spot rates

Introduction

If the cash flows from a one-year bond should be discounted at the yield for one-year bonds, then why should the first year coupon from a five-year bond (received on the same day) be discounted at a different rate (the yield on the five-year bond)? Both represent cash in one year, hence both represent equal risk to an investor.

What we should have are various rates of interest which are appropriate for cash flows at certain dates, regardless of whether they are from a one-year bond or a five-year bond. These are the spot rates.

The spot rate is the rate of interest that the market demands for money from now to a specific future time, i.e. the rate for one-month money or one-year money or five-year money. If we wished to price a bond, then strictly we should do this using spot rates.

Example

A bond pays an annual coupon of 9% and is redeemable at par in three years. Evaluate this bond if spot rates of interest are

- 1 year – 7%
- 2 year – 8%
- 3 year – 9%

Solution

Time	Cash Flow £	DF (spot rate)	Present Value £
1	9.00	$\frac{1}{1.07}$	8.41
2	9.00	$\frac{1}{1.08^2}$	7.72
3	109.00 (100.00 + 9.00)	$\frac{1}{1.09^3}$	84.17
			£100.30

Link to GRY

Based on the above data a one year bond will have a 7% GRY (since its only cash flow would be discounted at the one year spot rate). This three year bond has a GRY at 8.88% ie we have on upward sloping relationship.

We can see, however, that the GRY on the three year bond (8.88%) is below the three year spot rate (9%). This is because the GRY is a single rate that discounts all the bonds cash flows to the same £100.30 present value so it must be a form of weighted average of the spot rates used for pricing.

4.4.2 Forward rates

Introduction

Whereas a **spot** rate is a rate of interest that can be agreed today for a deposit or borrowing from today for a fixed period, a **forward** rate is a rate of interest that can be agreed today for a deposit or borrowing from one future date to another.

A forward rate can be determined using DCF ideas as

$$(1 + r_2)^2 = (1 + r_1)(1 + {}_1f_2)$$

Where

r_1 = one year spot rate
r_2 = two year spot rate
${}_1f_2$ = one year forward rate beginning in one years' time

Example

Calculate the forward rate from time 1 to time 2 and from time 2 to time 3 based on the above spot rate example

Solution

Forward rate from time 1 to time 2

$(1 + r_2)^2 = (1 + r_1)(1 + {}_1f_2)$

$1.08^2 = 1.07 \times (1 + {}_1f_2)$

$$(1 + {}_1f_2) = \frac{1.08^2}{1.07} = 1.0901$$

${}_1f_2 = 0.0901$ or 9.01%

Forward rate from time 2 to time 3

$(1 + r_3)^3 = (1 + r_2)^2 \times (1 + {}_2f_3)$

$1.09^3 = 1.08^2 \times (1 + {}_2f_3)$

$$(1 + {}_2f_3) = \frac{1.09^3}{1.08^2} = 1.1103$$

${}_2f_3 = 0.1103$ or 11.03%

Link between spot rate, forward rate and GRY

From the forward rate calculation we can see that the spot rate is the geometric mean of forward rates. As such, their movements lag behind those of forward rates. Similarly, the yield is a weighted average of the spot rates and hence demonstrate less movement still.

When rates are rising, at first we see that forward rates rise rapidly, with spot rates next, closely followed by yield curves. In a normal rising term structure environment, we would therefore expect to see the following relationships between yields, spots (the term structure of interest rates or zero-coupon curve) and forwards.

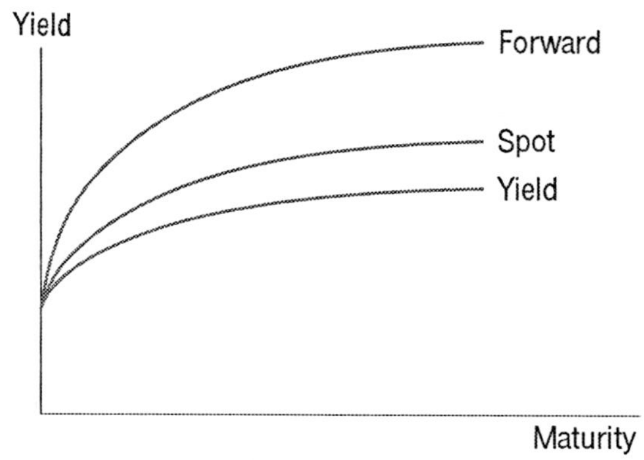

We can see that the increase in forward rates rapidly outpaces that of spot rates and yields.

Note that if the yield curve was inverted then forward rates would be below spot rates which, in turn, would be below yields.

5 The Risks of Holding a Bond

5.1 Introduction

Learning objective

18.6.2 **Explain** the main risks faced by bond holders and how these risks can be addressed.

An investor in a fixed income security is exposed to a number of different risks, and any complete assessment of a bond must include consideration of these factors. These risks include the following.

5.1.1 Interest rate risk

This is probably the most important risk because of the powerful relationship between interest rates and bond prices. Duration and modified duration (volatility) are the means of measuring this risk. Convexity is the measure that is used to explain the variation away from the predicted return.

5.1.2 Credit and default risk

Credit and default risk is the risk of the issuer defaulting on its obligations to pay coupons and repay the principal. The ratings by commercial rating companies can be used to help assess this risk.

5.1.3 Inflation risk

Inflation risk is linked to interest rate risk, as interest rates rise to compensate bondholders for inflation.

5.1.4 Liquidity and marketability risk

This has to do with the ease with which an issue can be sold in the market. Smaller issues especially are subject to this risk. In certain markets, the volume of trading tends to concentrate into the 'benchmark' stocks, thereby rendering most other issues illiquid. Other bonds become subject to 'seasoning' as the initial liquidity dries up and the bonds are purchased by investors who wish to hold them to maturity.

5.1.5 Issue specific risk

There may be factors specific to the issue, which tend to either increase or decrease the risk, e.g. issuer options such as the right to call for early redemption or possibly, holder options.

5.1.6 Fiscal risk

Fiscal risk represents risk that withholding taxes will be increased. For foreign bonds, there would also be the risk of the imposition of capital controls locking your money into the market.

5.1.7 Currency risk

For any investor purchasing overseas or international bonds, then there is obviously also the risk of currency movements.

5.2 Interest rate risk

Learning objectives	18.6.3 **Explain** the two components of interest rate risk (price and reinvestment risk). 18.6.5 **Analyse** the factors that affect the sensitivity of a bond's price to a change in required yield.

5.2.1 Introduction

The most predictable of these risks is the interest rate risk. Within bond markets, this is sometimes referred to, somewhat confusingly, as the **volatility**. The sensitivity of any bond to movements in the interest rate will be determined by a number of factors.

Sensitivity to maturity

Longer dated bonds will be more sensitive to changes in the interest rate than shorter dated stocks as illustrated by these prices for three 12% bonds of differing maturity subject to differing GRYs.

Coupon %	Maturity (Years)	Price for a GRY of		
		8%	10%	12%
12	4	£113.24	£106.34	£100.00
12	7	£120.83	£109.74	£100.00
12	26	£143.23	£118.32	£100.00

In this example, it is the price of the 26-year bond that exhibits the greatest range as the yield alters (moving from £143.23 to par). The logic behind this is that the longer dated bond is more exposed to the movements of the yield, since it has longer to go to maturity.

Sensitivity to coupon

With regard to the level of coupon, it is the lower coupon stocks that demonstrate the greatest level of sensitivity to the yield.

Coupon %	Maturity (Years)	Price for a GRY of		
		9%	10%	11%
5	15	£67.75	£61.97	£56.85
10	15	£108.00	£100.00	£92.81
15	15	£148.30	£138.03	£128.76

In this example, the price of the 5% bond moves from £61.97 when the GRY is 10%, to £67.75 if GRY drops to 9% (a rise of 9.3%) and to £56.85 if GRY rises to 11% (a fall of 8.2%). The other bonds whilst exhibiting the same overall relationship are not as responsive to the alteration in the GRY. The 10% bond rises by 8% and falls by 7.2%.

It should be noted that the relationship between the coupon and maturity and the price are not symmetrical (equal for both a rise or a fall in GRY). This is a relationship that we will return to later and is known as **convexity.**

The logic behind this relationship is that the lower coupon bonds have more of their value tied up in the terminal value. The ultimate low-coupon bond is, after all, the zero-coupon bond where the entire value is in the final payment.

The impact of the yield

If yields are particularly high, then the flows in the future are worth relatively little and the sensitivity is diminished. Conversely, if the yield is low, then the present value of flows in the future is enhanced and the bond is more sensitive to the changing GRY.

Summary

Long Dated	>	Short Dated
Low Coupon	>	High Coupon
Low Yields	>	High Yields

Whilst these simple maxims are good indicators of the likely sensitivity to fluctuations in the rate of interest, they do not allow for two bonds to be compared.

For example, which of the following is likely to be the most sensitive to a rise in interest rates – a high-coupon long-dated stock or a low-coupon short-dated stock? It was for this reason that in the 1930s a composite measure of interest rate risk was devised: the **duration**.

5.2.2 Reinvestment risk

An investor in bonds will usually receive coupons over the life of the bond, unless it is a zero-coupon bond. These coupons will often need to be reinvested. If interest rates have fallen since the bond was issued, the interest rate earned on reinvested coupons will be lower than previously expected. This will reduce the investor's return compared to what he expected when buying the bond originally.

5.2.3 Macaulay's duration

Learning objective

18.6.6 Define and **calculate** the (Macaulay) duration of a bond.

Introduction

This calculation gives each bond an overall risk weighting, which allows two bonds to be compared. In simple terms, it is a composite measure of the risk expressed in years.

Duration is the weighted average length of time to the receipt of a bond's benefits (coupon and redemption value), the weights being the present value of the benefits involved.

This concept can be shown diagrammatically

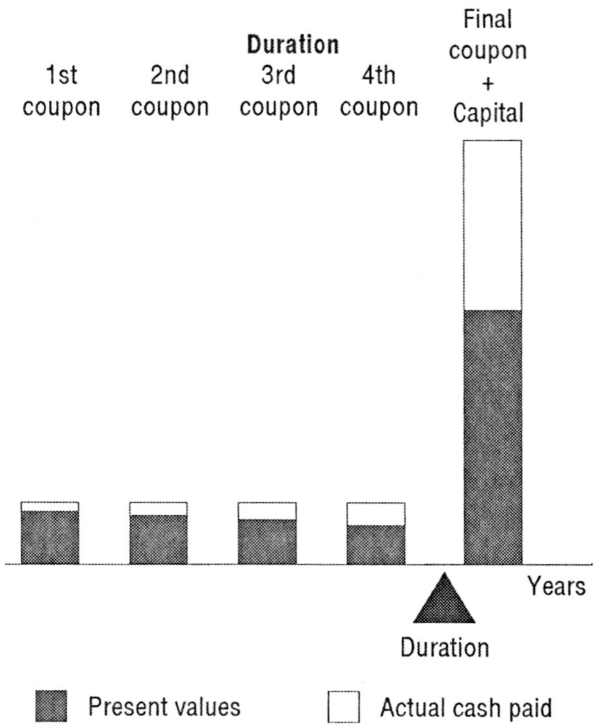

where the fulcrum or point of balance represents the duration of the bond.

Calculation

Mathematically, duration can be expressed using the following formulae.

Formula to learn

$$\text{Macaulay's Duration (D)} = \frac{\sum(t \times PV_t)}{\text{Price}}$$

or

$$\text{Macaulay's Duration (D)} = \frac{(1 \times PV_1) + (2 \times PV_2) + (3 \times PV_3) + \cdots + (n \times PV_n)}{\text{Price}}$$

where

PV_t = present value of cash flow in period t (discounted using the redemption yield)

n = number of periods to maturity

This may look difficult, but can be easily calculated in a normal DCF pricing table which simply adds one column next to the one used for valuation.

Example

A bond pays an annual coupon of 9% and is redeemable at par in three years. Calculate the duration of the bond if interest rates are 8%.

Solution

Time	Cash Flow £	DF (8%)	PV £	t × PV £
1	9.00	$\frac{1}{1.08}$	8.33	8.33
2	9.00	$\frac{1}{1.08^2}$	7.72	15.44
3	109.00 (100.00 + 9.00)	$\frac{1}{1.08^3}$	86.53	259.59
			£102.58	£283.36

Using the above, the duration is

$$\text{Duration} = \frac{£283.36}{£102.58} = 2.7623 \text{ years}$$

Macaulay's duration can also be referred to as the **economic life of a bond**.

Properties of duration

The basic features of sensitivity to interest rate risk are all mirrored in the duration calculation.

- **Longer dated bonds** will have longer durations.
- **Lower coupon bonds** will have longer durations. The ultimate low-coupon bond is a zero-coupon bond where the duration will be the maturity.
- **Lower yields** will give higher durations. In this case, the present value of flows in the future will fall if the yield increases, moving the point of balance towards the present day, therefore shortening the duration.

The duration of a bond will shorten as the lifespan of the bond decays. However, the rate of their decay will not be the same. In our example above, a three-year bond has a duration of 2.7623 years. In one year's time, the bond will have a remaining life of two years, and a duration based on the same GRY of 1.9182 years. The lifespan has decayed by a full year, but the duration by only 0.8441 of a year.

5.2.4 Modified duration/volatility

Learning objectives	
	18.6.7 Define and **calculate** the modified duration of a bond.
	18.6.8 Calculate, given the duration of a bond, the change in price given a change in required yield.

Introduction

At the same time as the Macaulay's duration was being promoted as a means of expressing the sensitivity of a bond to movements in the interest rate, Hicks was developing a formula to explain the impact of yield changes on price. Not surprisingly, the two measures are linked.

Hick's basic proposition was that the change in yield multiplied by this sensitivity measure would give the resultant percentage change in the bonds price, i.e. the volatility gives the percentage change in price per unit change in yield.

Calculation and use

The modified duration formula may be derived through the use of calculus, specifically differentiation of the price equation with respect to interest rates. Fortunately, there is an easier definition, specifically

Formula to learn

$$\text{Modified duration/Volatility} = \frac{\text{Macaulay's Duration}}{1+\text{GRY}}$$

Example

Calculate the change in price of the above bond and the new resulting price in yields

- Fall by 0.5%
- Rise by 1%

Solution

From the above example

$$\text{Modified duration} = \frac{2.7623}{1.08} = 2.5577$$

Hence, the price will move by 2.56% for every one percentage point change in the yield. **NB:** bear in mind the inverse relationship.

Given that the current price is £102.58, then this will be a price movement of £2.62 (£102.58 × 2.5577%).

Yields fall 0.5%

If yields **fall** 0.5%
then prices will **rise** £1.31 (£2.62 × 0.5)
to £103.59 (£102.58 + £1.31)

Yields rise 1%

If yields **rise** 1%
then prices will **fall** £2.62 (£2.62 × 1)
to £99.96 (£102.58 – £2.62)

This can be generalised as

Percentage change in price = −MD × change in yields

The minus sign giving the negative relationship between prices and yields. In turn this may be expressed as

$\%\Delta P = -MD \times \Delta Y$

and to get the actual change in price we apply this percentage move to the price itself, ie

Price change = $-MD \times \Delta Y \times \text{Price}$

Or

$\Delta P = -MD \times \Delta Y \times P$

Properties of modified duration

As the modified duration is derived from the Macaulay's duration, it shares the same properties.

- Longer dated bonds will have higher modified durations.
- Lower coupon bonds will have higher modified durations.
- Lower yields will give higher modified durations.

The higher the modified duration, then the greater the sensitivity of that bond to a change in the yield.

5.2.5 Convexity

Learning objective	**18.6.9 Explain** the convexity error that arises from using duration to estimate a change in bond price using duration.

Introduction

Modified duration predicts a linear relationship between yields and prices. If the modified duration is 2, then if yields rise by 1%, the price will fall by 2%. If the rise in yields had been 3%, then the fall in price would have been 6%.

The Price/Yield Relationship Predicted by the Modified Duration

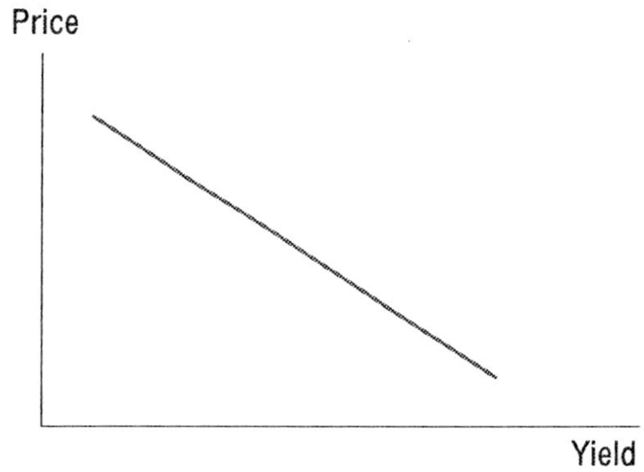

The slope of the line is the modified duration.

However, as the yield changes, then so will the duration and consequently, the modified duration. It is this which gives rise to the concept of convexity.

The Impact of Changing Yields on the Modified Duration

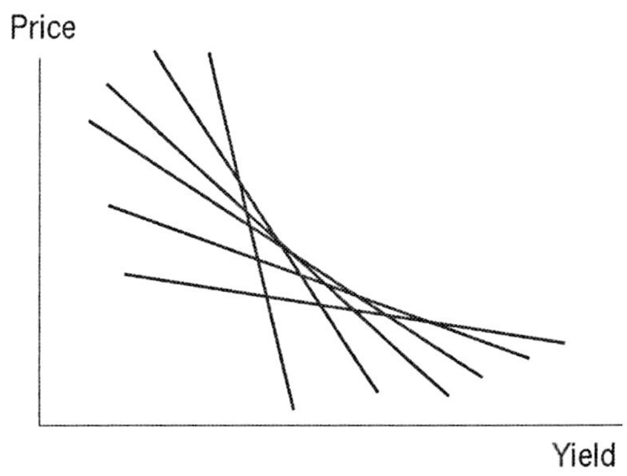

As the yield falls, the duration will increase and therefore, so will the modified duration. As modified duration increases, the line will steepen.

The actual relationship between the yield and price is given by the convex function that these individual linear relationships describe. We are after all aware that the relationship between bond prices and interest rates is not linear. The actual relationship between prices and yields is curved, with increases in yields resulting in prices falling, but at a reducing rate, as illustrated by the example at the start of this session.

The actual convex relationship and the linear one predicted by the modified duration formula are illustrated below.

Modified duration and Convexity

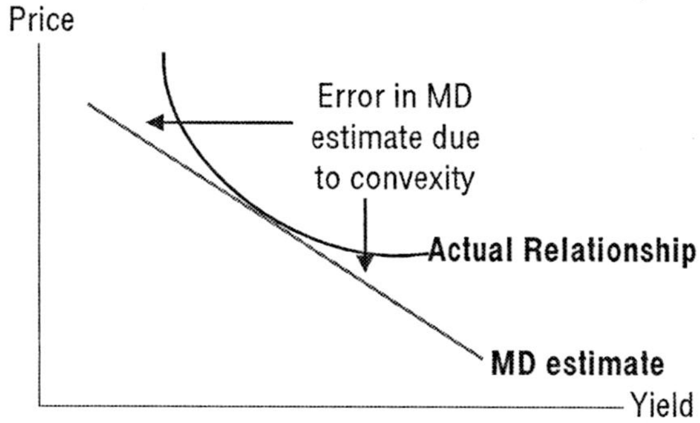

The impact of convexity will be that the modified duration will tend to **overstate the fall in a bond's price and understate the rise**. However, for relatively small movements in the yield, the modified duration will be a good estimate; the problem of convexity only becomes an issue with more substantial fluctuations in the yield.

5.3 Credit and Default Risk

Learning objectives

18.6.10 Define credit risk as it affects bonds.

18.6.11 Explain the role of the major credit rating agencies.

18.6.12 Interpret the key classes of rating on the scales published by the major rating agencies.

18.6.14 Identify key features and financial ratios considered by credit rating agencies in conducting a corporate rating

21.2.11 Explain how different asset class returns may be related, for example Merton Models relating fixed income to equity.

5.3.1 Credit risk

Corporate bonds are exposed to a greater degree of credit risk than gilts. Credit risk covers the risk that the issuer will default on his obligations to pay interest and capital, and is measured by the rating agencies.

5.3.2 Rating agencies

The credit risk of bonds is assessed by the various rating agencies, such as Moody's and Standard & Poor's who ascribe bonds with a credit rating. They are independent of the bond issues hence their ratings are considered to be very relevant and reliable to investors. Should they decide to downgrade this rating, the return investors' demand will increase (the discount rate), causing the price to fall. Alternatively, a rating upgrade will reduce the required return of investors causing the price to rise.

5.3.3 Credit ratings

The purpose of credit ratings is credit risk evaluation, i.e. identifying the probability of default by an issuer. It is not a recommendation to take investment actions, since it does not take into account factors such as price and the preferred investment characteristics of the investor. Ratings are usually assigned to individual issues and hence do not serve as a general purpose of rating the issuer.

Credit ratings are calculated from financial history and current assets and liabilities. Rating agencies focus on various accounting ratios such as interest cover, in order to identify the probability of the subject being able to pay back the loan.

It is conventional for issuers in the Euromarkets to have a credit rating. Whilst this does not in itself make the company any more secure, it will mean that potential investors have a clearer perception of quality. Credit ratings are sub-categorised between prime/investment grade and junk/non-investment grade, and we need to be aware of the cut-off points between these gradings.

Standard & Poor's	Moody's	Meaning
	Investment Grade (Prime)	
AAA	Aaa	Highest quality
AA+	Aa1	
AA	Aa2	High quality
AA–	Aa3	
A+	A1	
A	A2	Strong quality
A–	A3	
BBB+	Baa1	
BBB	Baa2	Adequate quality
BBB–	**Baa3**	
	Non-Investment Grade (Non-Prime or Junk)	
BB+	**Ba1**	Capacity to pay uncertain
BB	Ba2	
BB–	Ba3	
B+	B1	
B	B2	High risk
B–	B3	
CCC	Caa	
CC	Ca	Vulnerable to default
C	C	
D		Already in default

5.3.4 Credit spreads

In practical terms, the credit rating will affect the required yield on any bond and hence its price. We are aware that risk and required return are related with a higher risk resulting in a higher required return. A lower credit rating implies a higher risk, hence a higher required return and hence, for the same coupon, a lower price.

The credit spread or yield spread or yield-yield spread is a measurement of the extra yield demanded over that of a gilt of the same maturity. The spread is influenced by a number of factors including

- **Credit rating** – the lower the rating the wider the spread.
- **Maturity** – in general, the higher the maturity the greater the spread.
- **Economic and market circumstances** – the more uncertain the market/economic circumstances the greater the spread.

It should be noted that credit spreads are not, themselves, stable, rather they are quite volatile and widened enormously during the credit crunch of 2008/09.

Both credit spreads and probability of default tend to be relatively low for investment grade bonds but as ratings fall further through the non-investment grades, spreads and risks of default increase exponentially.

5.3.5 Credit analysis

The objective of credit analysis is to assess the ability of a borrower to service and repay its loan obligations. In evaluating credit risk there are three key issues to be borne in mind.

- How probable is it that a default will take place
- How severe will the loss be if there is a default
- When will any default take place (near term/far term)

It is the answers to these three questions that allow rating agencies to fully appraise the credit risk of the bond.

Factors that will be considered in undertaking such an assessment will include

- **Economic cyclicality** – The responsiveness of an industry to cyclical factors should be considered. Industries may closely track GDP growth (e.g. retailers). Alternatively, they may be defensive stocks with relatively slow growth (e.g. utilities).
- **Growth** – A company's growth should be compared to the growth trend of its own industry and any differences should be analysed and explained.
- **Competition** – Increasing competition will reduce prices and increase costs, increasing credit risk.
- **Sources of supply** – Companies with guaranteed stable, low-cost sources of supply will be favourably placed compared to companies without such sources. For example, paper companies need a readily available cheap source of wood pulp, i.e. forest lands.
- **Regulation** – Regulation itself is not a credit problem, however, the credit analyst will need to look at regulation and see whether it is resulting in excessive costs for the industry, highly restricted prices and restrictions on the company making good business decisions.
- **Management** – Acting agencies will consider the quality of management of the business in question. A well-managed business with an experienced team is liable to be regarded more highly than a less well managed/less experienced team.
- **Labour** – More labour-intensive industries will give greater cause for concern than less labour-intensive industries. A heavily unionised industry that is highly militant is going to increase credit risks. The historical occurrence of strikes, the likelihood of future strikes, the relative power of the unions and related factors should be considered.

- **Financial analysis** – Obviously one key source of information in determining the viability of a company will be the financial statements. The key issues considered will be the level of assets, liabilities, profits and cash flow generation, all of which are discussed in detail later in this Study Text. The key ratios that will be considered (also covered later in this Study Text) will be
  - Debt to equity
  - Interest cover
  - Asset cover
  - Current ratio
  - Quick ratio
- **Bond security and covenants**

5.3.6 Merton model

The Merton model provides a method of determining the credit and default risk on a company's debt. Where a company has bonds in issue it will need to realise certain assets in the future to repay these bonds when they falls due. If the assets have insufficient value at the repayment date there will be a default, whereas any excess asset value will belong to the shareholders.

The Merton model views the value of the equity as a call option on the value of the assets of the company with an exercise date being the bond repayment date and an exercise price equal to the bond redemption value, and uses options pricing methods to determine the default probability and equity value.

The inputs to the Merton model are the current equity value, the value and volatility of the company's assets and the value and maturity of any outstanding debt. Based on these inputs, the model can be used to estimate either the probability that the company will default or the credit spread on the debt.

Chapter Roundup

Characteristics

- A bond is a negotiable debt instrument for a fixed principal amount issued by a borrower for a specific period of time and typically making a regular payment of interest.
- The interest payment is known as the coupon and it is based on the nominal value of the bond. The nominal value also refers to how much capital shall be paid on maturity.
- Bonds may be issued by governments and companies. Bonds issued by the UK government are known as **Gilts**.
- Index linked gilt coupons and redemption proceeds are linked to the RPI with either a 3 month (post September 2005) or 8 month (pre September 2005) lag.
- 8 month ILG prices are quoted in nominal terms and the inflation uplift to the cash flows is based on the IRP for the month that is 8 months prior to the relevant cash flow date.
- 3 month ILG prices are quoted real and the nominal amount paid is scaled up for inflation to the exact cash flow date. The RPI figure needs to be for the exact payment date. The RPI reference for the 1st of any month is the RPI from three months earlier, we must interpolate to get the RPI for the specified date. E.g. the July RPI is the reference for 1 October, the August RPI is the reference for 1 November, The RPI for a coupon paid on 20 October would be obtained by interpolating these reference figures.
- The DMO has responsibility for issuing gilts at regular gilt auctions to finance the PSNCR.
- Gilt-edged market makers (GEMMs) have an obligation to create a liquid market in gilts during the mandatory quote period.
- Corporate bonds may be issued with a wide variety of different structures and different levels of security and payment benefits. Secondary trading is limited but is primarily off exchange.
- Dealing costs are
  - Bid-offer spread.
  - Brokers commission for retail investors.

Pricing

- Bond pricing is based on the principals of discounted cash flow.
- Market convention for gilts
  - Quoted yield = 2× semi-annual yield.
  - Quoted price = clean price.
- Clean and dirty pricing conventions are designed to ensure investors pay the correct amount of tax on their accrued interest.
  - Cum div

    $$\text{Dirty price} = \text{Clean price} + \text{Periods coupon} \times \frac{\text{Days}}{\text{Days in period}}$$

  - Ex div

    $$\text{Dirty price} = \text{Clean price} - \text{Periods coupon} \times \frac{\text{Days}}{\text{Days in period}}$$

  - To simplify for this exam the denominator, Days in period, is taken on 182.5 days

Yields

- The flat yield represents the income return to an investor. The gross redemption yield represents the total return to an investor, on the assumption the investment will be held to maturity.
  - $\text{Flat yield} = \dfrac{\text{Annual coupon}}{\text{Market price}}$
  - $\text{Japanese GRY} = \dfrac{\text{Annual coupon}}{\text{Market price}} + \dfrac{\dfrac{\text{Redemption price} - \text{Market price}}{\text{Years to redemption}}}{\text{Market price}}$
  - GRY = IRR calculation
  - NRY = IRR if after tax returns (NB: only coupon taxed)
  - $\text{GEY} = \dfrac{\text{NRY}}{1 - T_p}$
- Relationships

Bond Value	Relationship
Above Par (loss to redemption)	Flat Yield > GRY > Japanese GRY/GEY
At Par	Flat Yield = GRY = Japanese GRY/GEY
Below Par (gain to redemption)	Flat Yield < GRY < Japanese GRY/GEY

- Yield curves represent the gross redemption yield on bonds issued by a particular issuer.
- The normal yield curve is upward sloping though an inverted yield curve if markets expect interest rates will fall.
- A spot rate is the rate of interest from now to a given future date.
- A forward rate is the rate of interest from one future date to another.

Risk

- Macaulay's duration measures the sensitivity of a bond to changes in interest rates and is measured in **years**.
  - $\text{Macaulay duration (D)} = \dfrac{\sum(t \times PV_t)}{\text{Price}}$
- Modified duration indicates the percentage change in a bond's price given a 1% change in yields.
  - $\text{Modified Duration/Volatility} = -\dfrac{\text{Macaulay duration}}{1 + \text{GRY}}$
- Forecasting price changes
  - $\%\Delta P = -MD \times \Delta Y$
    $\Delta P = -MD \times \Delta Y \times P$
- Convexity is a measure of the curvature in the true relationship between prices and yields.
- Rating agencies provide credit ratings on individual bonds based on the credit quality of the bond and its overall risk of default.

Test Your Knowledge

Check your knowledge of the chapter here, without referring back to the text.

1. Define a callable bond.

2. What inflation rate are index-linked gilts tied into?

3. What is an FRN?

   A Fixed Rate Note
   B Fixed Rate Notification
   C Floating Rate Note
   D Floating Rate Notification

4. Calculate the price of a two-year annual 6% coupon bond with a discount rate of 5.5% and a nominal value of £100.

5. An 8% Treasury is redeemable in four years. Calculate its price if rates are 7%

6. 8% Treasury stock was quoted at 97.3125 on Friday 10 November. Interest payment dates are 15 May and 15 November. Calculate the following as on 10 November.

   (a) Flat yield per annum.
   (b) Price paid for £100 nominal.

7. Conversion 10¼% stock was quoted at £104.91 on Tuesday 23 February. Interest payment dates are 22 May and 22 November.

   (a) What was the flat yield on 23 February?
   (b) What would a purchaser on 23 February pay for £100 nominal?

8. Exchequer 13½% stock was quoted at 117.875 on Friday 16 September. Interest payment dates are 22 March and 22 September.

   Calculate

   (a) The flat yield on 16 September.

   (b) You buy £1,000 nominal on Friday 16 September, how much would you pay excluding transaction costs?

9. You buy £10,000 nominal of 3½% War Loan on Tuesday 2 September cum div and pay £3,915.10 excluding transaction costs. Interest payment dates are 1 June and 1 December.

   Calculate

   (a) The quoted price per £100 nominal on 2 September.
   (b) The flat yield on 2 September.

10. A bond is bought for £92.40 with six full years to maturity and paying a 4% annual coupon. What is its GRY

A 5.37%
B 5.52%
C 5.74%
D 5.91%

---

11. A £100 bond is priced at £105.47 with an 8% coupon payable at the end of each of the next twelve years, and is then redeemable at par. What is its yield to maturity?

A 7.00%
B 7.10%
C 7.20%
D 7.30%

---

12. A bond has three years before being redeemed at par at maturity and pays a 6% coupon at the end of each of the three years. Spot interest rates (payable at the end of each year) are 8% in the first year, 7% in the second year and 6% in the third year. Calculate the price of this bond.

---

13. A bond with a life of two years will pay a 5% coupon at the end of each of the two years. The bond will be redeemed at par. If spot rates are 6% in the first year and 7% in the second year (payable at the end of each year), what is the price of this bond?

---

14. List the different risks of investing in a bond.

---

15. A bond pays an annual coupon of 6% and has three years to redemption. If it is yielding 7%, what is its duration?

---

18. If a bond has three years to redemption and pays a 7% annual coupon, with interest rates at 10%, what is the duration of the bond?

---

17. If the coupon rate on a bond increases, what will be the impact on its duration?

---

18. A 10% bond is redeemable in exactly three years and pays interest annually. Calculate the duration if its yield is 9%

---

19. A bond has three years to redemption at par and pays an 8% coupon at the end of each of the three years. If its yield is 7.5%, what is the duration of this bond?

---

20. A bond is priced at £103.47 and has a modified duration of 4.64. If yields rise by ½%, what will the new price of the bond be?

---

21. What is convexity?

TEST YOUR KNOWLEDGE: ANSWERS

1. A bond where the issuer has the right to redeem the bond early.

   (See Section 1.6.9)

2. Retail Price Index

   (See Section 1.4.3)

3. C

   (See Section 1.6.6)

4. £100.93

   $$\frac{6}{1.055}+\frac{106}{1.055^2}=5.69+95.24=100.93$$

   (See Section 2.2)

5. **Price**

Time	Cash Flow (£)	DF (7%)	PV (£)
1–4	8	$\frac{1}{0.07}\left(1-\frac{1}{1.07^4}\right)=3.387$	27.10
4	100	$\frac{1}{1.07^4}$	76.29
			103.39

   (See Section 2.2)

6. (a) Flat yield $=\frac{\text{Annual coupon}}{\text{Market (clean) price}}=\frac{8.00}{97.3125}=0.08221$ or 8.221%

   (b) With the deal date of Friday 10 November, settlement is Monday 13 November, hence the accrued interest days equals 13 November to 14 November inclusive, i.e. two days. The coupon period runs from 15 May to 14 November, a period of 184 days.

	(£)
Quoted clean price	97.3125
Less: Accrued interest $\frac{2}{184}\times 4$	(0.0435)
Price paid per £100 nominal	97.2690

   (See Sections 2.3 and 3.1)

7. (a) Flat yield = $\frac{\text{Annual coupon}}{\text{Market (clean) price}} = \frac{10.25}{104.91} = 0.0977$ or 9.77%

(b) Accrued interest is from 22 November (last coupon date) to 23 February (day before settlement day) inclusive, i.e.

		Accrued	Coupon
Days	November	9	9
	December	31	31
	January	31	31
	February	23	28
	March		31
	April		30
	May		21
Dirty price paid		94	181

	(£)
Quoted clean price	104.91
Add: accrued interest $\frac{94}{181} \times 5.125$	2.66
Dirty price paid	107.57

A purchaser on 23 February would pay £107.57 for £100 nominal.

(See Sections 2.3 and 3.1)

8. (a) Flat yield = $\frac{\text{Annual coupon}}{\text{Market (clean) price}} = \frac{13.50}{117.875} = 0.1145$ or 11.45%.

(b) Settlement will take place on Monday 19 September, hence the accrued interest is calculated from 19 September to 21 September inclusive, i.e. three days. The coupon period runs from 22 March to 21 September, a period of 184 days.

	(£)
Quoted clean price	117.875
Less: Accrued interest $\frac{3}{184} \times 6.75$	(0.110)
Price paid per £100 nominal	117.765

The price paid on 16 September for £1,000 nominal equals 10 × £117.765 equals £1,177.65

(See Sections 2.3 and 3.1)

9. (a) Accrued interest is for the period 1 June (last coupon date) to 2 September (day before settlement date) inclusive, hence

	Accrued	Coupon
June	30	30
July	31	31
August	31	31
September	2	30
October		31
November		30
	94	183

Accrued interest equals $\frac{94}{183} \times 1.75 = £0.899$

	(£)
Price paid (dirty price) per £100 nominal = £3,915.10 ÷ 100	39.151
Less: Accrued interest	(0.899)
Quoted (clean) price	38.252

(b) Flat yield = $\frac{\text{Annual coupon}}{\text{Market (clean) price}} = \frac{3.50}{38.252} = 0.0915$ or 9.15%

(See Sections 2.3 and 3.1)

10. Through trial and error

Time	Cash Flow (£)	DF (5.52%)	PV (£)
0	(92.40)	1	(92.40)
1–6	4.00	$\frac{1}{0.0552}\left(1-\frac{1}{1.0552^6}\right)$	19.96
6	100.00	$\frac{1}{1.0552^6}$	72.44
			0.00

(See Section 3.3)

11. Through trial and error

Time	Cash Flow (£)	DF (7.3%)	PV (£)
0	(105.47)	1	(105.47)
1–12	8.00	$\frac{1}{0.073}\left(1-\frac{1}{1.073^{12}}\right)$	62.54
12	100.00	$\frac{1}{1.073^{12}}$	42.93
			0.00

(See Section 3.3)

12.

Time	Cash Flow (£)	DF	PV (£)
1	6	$\frac{1}{1.08}$	5.56
2	6	$\frac{1}{1.07^2}$	5.24
3	106	$\frac{1}{1.06^3}$	89.00
			99.80

(See Section 4.4)

13.

Time	Cash Flow (£)	DF	PV (£)
1	5	$\frac{1}{1.06}$	4.72
2	105	$\frac{1}{1.07^2}$	91.71
			96.43

(See Section 4.4)

14. Interest rate risk, credit/default risk, inflation risk, liquidity risk, issue specific risk, fiscal risk and currency risk.

(See Section 5.1)

15.

Time	Cash Flow £	DF (7%)	PV £	tPV £
1	6	$\frac{1}{1.07}$	5.61	5.61
2	6	$\frac{1}{1.07^2}$	5.24	10.48
3	106	$\frac{1}{1.07^3}$	86.53	259.59
			97.38	275.68

$$\text{Duration} = \frac{275.68}{97.38} = 2.83 \text{ years}$$

(See Section 5.2.3)

18.

Time	Cash Flow £	DF (10%)	PV £	tPV £
1	7.00	$\frac{1}{1.10}$	6.36	6.39
2	7.00	$\frac{1}{1.10^2}$	5.79	11.58
3	107.00	$\frac{1}{1.10^3}$	80.39	241.17
			92.54	259.11

$$\text{Duration} = \frac{259.11}{92.54} = 2.80 \text{ years}$$

(See Section 5.2.3)

17. Low-coupon bonds are more sensitive to interest rates than higher coupon bonds and therefore have higher durations. If the coupon increases the duration decreases.

(See Section 5.2.3)

18.

Time	Cash Flow (£)	DF (9 %)	PV (£)	tPV (£)
1	10	$\frac{1}{1.09}$	9.17	9.17
2	10	$\frac{1}{1.09^2}$	8.42	18.84
3	110	$\frac{1}{1.09^3}$	84.94	254.82
			102.53	280.83

$$\text{Duration} = \frac{280.83}{102.53} = 2.74 \text{ years}$$

(See Section 5.2.3)

19.

Time	Cash Flow (£)	DF (7.5%)	PV (£)	tPV (£)
1	8.00	$\frac{1}{1.075}$	7.44	7.44
2	8.00	$\frac{1}{1.075^2}$	6.92	13.84
3	108.00	$\frac{1}{1.075^3}$	86.94	260.82
			101.30	282.10

$$\text{Duration} = \frac{282.10}{101.30} = 2.78 \text{ years}$$

(See Section 5.2.3)

20. Proportionate change in price = MD × ΔY = –4.64 × 0.005 = –0.0232 or –2.32%

This is a negative figure, hence prices will fall by 2.32% or £2.40 (£103.47 × 2.32%) to £101.07 (£103.47 – £2.40).

(See Section 5.2.4)

21. Convexity represents the error in modified duration, due to modified duration overstating price falls and understating price rises.

(See Section 5.2.5)

9 Equities

INTRODUCTION

Equities offer a form of long-term financing to companies. There are various different types of shares that a company may issue, the most common being referred to as ordinary shares.

There is an active primary market in the UK that enables companies to issue new shares to investors. Furthermore, the London Stock Exchange offers a developed secondary market to allow investors to sell and buy shares.

Various ratios may be used to evaluate whether or not a share in a company is worth buying.

CHAPTER CONTENTS

Chapter Learning Objectives

18 Asset classes

Demonstrate an ability to evaluate the characteristics, inherent risks, behaviour and correlation of asset classes.

18.1 Equity capital characteristics

18.1.1 **Identify** the characteristics, and the risks to the investor, of the various classes of share capital.

18.1.2 **Explain** the reasons for issuance of preference shares and the implications to the investor.

18.1.3 **Explain** the characteristics of Global and American Depository Receipts.

18.2 Equity issuance

18.2.1 **Distinguish** between primary and secondary share issuance.

18.2.2 **Explain** the key features of the following equity issuance methods.

- Placing.
- Intermediaries offer.
- Offer for sale.
- Offer for sale by subscription.

18.2.3 **Define** and **explain** the purpose of a rights issue, a scrip issue and a stock split.

18.2.4 **Calculate** the theoretical ex-rights price and the value of the right (nil-paid) given the cum-rights price, the issuance ratio and the subscription price.

18.2.5 **Calculate** the theoretical ex-scrip price given the scrip ratio and the cum-scrip price.

18.2.6 **Evaluate** the options open to an investor in response to a rights offer and explain the effect on the investor's wealth.

18.2.7 **Explain** the motivations behind a company buying back its own shares.

18.3 Equity valuation

18.3.1 **Calculate** a holding period return for an ordinary share, comprising capital gain and dividend income.

18.3.2 **Explain** the components, assumptions and limitations of the dividend discount model (Gordon's growth model).

18.3.3 **Calculate** the present value of a share using the dividend discount model.

18.3.4 **Calculate** an estimated growth rate for dividends using historic data or using return on equity and a retained earnings ratio.

18.3.5 **Explain** the reasons for a company's chosen dividend policy.

18.3.6 **Explain** the practical constraints on companies paying dividends.

18.3.7 **Explain** the importance of the dividend yield and dividend cover in stock analysis.

18.3.8 **Calculate** dividend yield and dividend cover.

18.3.9 **Distinguish** between and evaluate the merits of relative valuation models and absolute valuation models and between historic and prospective measures of value.

18.3.10 **Calculate** a basic earnings per share.

18.3.11 **Explain** what is meant by diluted earnings per share.

18.3.12 **Explain** the rationale for the use of the following ratios in equity valuation: price-earnings, price to book, price to sales, price to cash flows, Enterprise Value (EV) to earnings before interest tax, depreciation and amortisation (EBITDA).

18.3.14 **Apply** the company ratios to the valuation of another given company.

18.3.15 **Explain** the possible shortfalls of using each of these price multiples in corporate valuation.

18.3.16 **Explain** the basics of Free cash-flow based valuation methods (FCFF, FCFE) and Residual Income Valuation methods.

18.3.17 **Define** (financial) gearing and evaluate the effect on required equity returns and this dividend valuations.

18.4 Equity transaction costs

18.4.1 **Explain and identify** transaction costs associated with dealing in UK equities.

18.4.2 **Calculate** the total transaction costs for an equity transaction, given appropriate data.

18.4.3 **Evaluate** the impact of alternative trading platforms, facilitated by MiFID, on transaction costs associated with equity dealing.

1 THE NATURE OF A SHARE

earning objective

18.1.1 Identify the characteristics, and the risks to the investor, of the various classes of share capital.

The shareholders of a company are the owners of the company. Initially, businesses were so small that one individual could finance the whole enterprise. As businesses became larger, it was difficult for an individual to provide sufficient finance for the operation. Companies allow a large number of individuals to pool their capital into one organisation, thereby facilitating the formation of larger companies.

Each original owner (shareholder) provides capital and receives shares. The more the individual contributes, the greater the allotment of shares. As owners, the shareholders take the greatest risks. If the company does badly, they will lose their money. However, they normally have only a **limited liability**, i.e. limited to the amount that they agreed to contribute.

On the other hand, if the company prospers, then the shareholders will reap the rewards. However, regardless of the company's fortunes, the return to debt will solely be interest and repayment. In contrast, shares do not normally have a fixed return and consequently participate fully in the remaining profits of the business. These profits may be distributed by way of a dividend, or can be retained within the operation in order to increase the potential for future profit. This is often paid in two instalments: the first known as the interim dividend and the second as the final dividend.

1.1 Equity shares

Ordinary shares are often referred to as **equity shares**. Here, the term equity means that they have an equal right to share in profits. For example, if a company has 10,000 ordinary shares in issue, each share is entitled to $^1/_{10,000}$ of the profits made during any period.

UK companies have to ascribe a nominal or par value to each share. This represents

- The **minimum value at which shares can be issued**. The company is not allowed to issue fully paid shares at a price below nominal value. A company can, however, issue partly paid shares where only a portion of the nominal value is required to be paid immediately. On such shares the company can demand the payment to the remainder of the nominal value at a later date, making them **fully paid**.
- The **limits of the liability of the shareholder**. If the company becomes insolvent, shareholders' liability is limited to any unpaid element of this nominal value. Where the share is a fully paid share, the shareholder has no more liability.

With respect to share capital it is, therefore, important to understand the distinction between

- **Authorised share capital** – the maximum number/nominal value of shares that the company can issue as specified in its formation documents. A company does not have to issue all of its authorised share capital, this simply represents a maximum.
- **Issued share capital** – the number/nominal value of shares that have been issued.
- **Called up share capital** – the amount of the issued share capital that the company has asked shareholders to pay for. Shares can be issued partly paid and the called up share capital is the part of the issued share capital where payment has been demanded.
- **Paid up share capital** – the amount of the issued share capital for which payment has been received.

For the vast majority of companies, all the shares that have been issued are fully paid and for these companies the issued share capital, called up share capital and paid up share capital are identical, representing the total nominal value of shares in issue at the year end. In our example, the company had issued 100,000 shares, each with a nominal value of £1.00 that had been paid in full, giving £100,000 issued, called up and paid up share capital.

1.1.1 Ordinary shares

The rights of ordinary shares are detailed in the company's constitutional documents and in particular, the **Articles of Association**. However, it is normal for ordinary shares to **possess a vote**. This means that the holder of any ordinary shares may attend and vote at any meetings held by the company. Whilst the day-to-day control of the company is passed into the hands of the directors and managers, the shareholders must have the right to decide upon the most important issues that affect the business, such as

- Corporate policy.
- Mergers and takeovers.
- Appointment and removal of directors.
- Raising further share capital.

1.1.2 Deferred shares

Some entrepreneurs find themselves in a difficult position. Their business has reached the stage where they need to obtain additional finance, but if they go to the stock market, they will have to relinquish control of the business. One method of avoiding this is by the issue of deferred shares to the original owner. Deferred shares normally carry greater voting rights, for example, they may have ten votes per share. To compensate the other shareholders for this benefit, deferred shares will often not receive a dividend for the first few years of issue.

It is possible for a company to specify any number of terms for each different type of share capital it issues, and it is possible to see 'A' and 'B' ordinary shares. The difference between A and B ordinary shares is often related to the voting rights, one set having enhanced voting rights or, potentially, no votes at all.

1.2 Preference shares

Learning objective

18.1.2 **Explain** the reasons for issuance of preference shares and the implications to the investor.

As mentioned above, ordinary shares carry the full risks and rewards of ownership. Another type of share which a company can issue is a **preference share** which takes on **debt-like characteristics** and offers only limited risks and returns.

1.2.1 The normal terms

A preference share is preferred in two basic forms.

- The preference share **dividend must be paid out before any ordinary dividend can be paid**. It is conventional for preference shares to be cumulative and if the dividend is not paid in any one year, the arrears and the current year's dividend must be paid before any ordinary dividend can be paid in the future. The assumption is that preference shares are cumulative unless they are stated not to be so.
- The second form of preferencing is on the order of pay out on a winding-up (liquidation). Preference shares will be paid prior to ordinary shares.

In order to receive these benefits, preference shareholders have to give up a number of rights normally attached to shares. First, the dividend on preference shares is **normally a fixed dividend** expressed as a percentage of the nominal value. For example, 7% £1 preference shares would pay a dividend each year of 7p per share. The quoted rate on a preference share is the **net** figure (for individuals assumed to be net of a 10% tax credit).

In addition, on liquidation the preference shareholders will **only ever receive the nominal value**. Using the above example, the preference shareholders would receive the £1 nominal they had contributed. This is not the case for ordinary or equity shares. Equity shares would receive anything that remains.

It is conventional for preference shares to carry **no voting rights**. However, most company constitutions contain a clause which states that if the preference dividend has not been paid **for five years**, preference shareholders will receive the right to attend and vote at general meetings of the company. It should be remembered that, as with all dividends, the payment is at the discretion of the directors and no shareholder may sue for a dividend.

1.2.2 Preference shares as investments

As we can see, preference shares offer the rewards one would normally see attached to debt – a fixed return with no voting rights. However, they carry greater risk, since they are in effect at the bottom of the table (above only ordinary shares) in the event of a winding-up. Since they share many of the features of debt, preference shares are sometimes described as quasi-debt capital.

There are, however, a number of special features that can be added to preference shares to enhance their attractiveness.

Preference shares may be attractive to institutional investors, since dividends would be classed as **franked investment income** and not subject to corporation tax.

1.2.3 Special features of preference shares

Some preference shares can be specified as **participating shares**. A participating share has a right, when profits reach certain levels, to take a share of those profits as opposed to simply receiving a fixed return. This participation right may also apply to the proceeds on a winding-up (liquidation).

Preference shares may also be issued with **conversion rights**. These rights will allow the preference shares to be converted into ordinary shares at specified rates in the future. As such, the preference share in this instance is more like a convertible bond than a share.

Finally, preference shares may be given specified **redemption dates**. For the most part, shares are not seen to be redeemable, but preference shares frequently carry a redemption date, making them seem, once again, more like debt than shares.

1.3 Depository receipts

Learning objective 18.1.3 **Explain** the characteristics of Global and American Depository Receipts.

1.3.1 American depository receipt

American Depository Receipts (ADRs) are the conventional form of trading UK shares in the US on the NYSE or NASDAQ, enabling UK firms to gain access to the funds available in the US; enabling UK forms to gain access to the funds available in the US. In order to encourage US investors to buy UK shares, the shares are lodged with an American bank which then issues a receipt for the shares. This receipt is in bearer form and denominated in dollars.

It is usual for each ADR to represent a number of shares to bring its value in line with US norms. For example, the average price of a share in the FTSE 100 is less than £10 whereas the average price of a share in the Dow Jones index and in the S&P 500 index is over $40.

It is possible to trade ADRs in what is known as **pre-release form**. Here, the holding bank releases the receipt to the dealer prior to the deposit of shares in its vaults. The dealer may then sell the ADRs in the market. However, the cash raised through this trade must then be lodged with a holding bank as collateral for the deal. This situation may exist for a maximum of three months, at the end of which the broker must purchase shares in the cash market and deposit them with the holding bank which then releases the collateral.

ADRs, whilst being designated for the American market, also trade in London. These securities are traded in the normal way through the International Order Book. In line with the domestic American markets, settlement for ADRs takes place in three business days.

The ADR holder has all the transferability of the American form document with no stamp duty, other than a one-off fee on creation of 1½%. Dividends are received by the bank which holds the shares. They are then converted into dollars and paid to the holders. The holder of the ADR has the right to vote at the company's meeting in the same way as an ordinary shareholder.

The only right which they do not possess is that of participation in rights or bonus issues. In the case of such an issue, the bank holding the shares will sell the bonus shares or rights nil paid and distribute the cash proceeds to the ADR holders. Any ADR holder who wishes to participate in the rights issue will have to convert their ADR back into share form.

1.3.2 GDR

A Global Depositary Receipt (GDR) is very similar to an ADR. Like an ADR, a GDR is a security, which bundles together a number of shares of a company listed in another country. It is a term used to describe a security primarily used to raise dollar-denominated capital either in the US or European markets.

The name GDR is a generic term describing structures deployed to raise capital either in dollars and/or euros. Like ADRs in the UK, GDRs trade through the LSEs International Order Book.

2 The Primary and Secondary Markets

Learning objective | 18.2.1 **Distinguish** between primary and secondary share issuance.

The primary market is the new issuance market. The secondary markets (markets in second-hand securities) exist to enable those investors who purchased investments to realise their investments. It is vital to ensure that the primary market is selective. A poor quality primary market will undermine the liquidity of the secondary market.

2.1 New issues of equities

When a company is formed, the shareholders have a choice as to the type of company that is created. The initial choice is between a Private Limited Company (Ltd) or a Public Limited Company (plc). The difference between these two legal forms is that only a plc may issue its shares or securities to the public. One important point to note is that even though a company may be a plc, it is in no way obliged to issue securities to the general public. In fact, the majority of plcs do not take this route for finance.

At this stage, the firm's management faces a second choice – whether or not to raise finance through the London Stock Exchange (LSE). The LSE is a company that runs a market place for securities. It should be noted that it has no monopoly powers over the running of the market place, and other operations may compete against it.

If a plc decides to issue shares, there is no obligation to use the LSE. However, without the ability to trade on the LSE, it is very difficult to encourage investors to buy shares. The LSE provides them with the 'guarantee' that they will be able to sell their shares in a secondary market.

Not all companies will be allowed to be listed on the exchange. The first process any company that wishes to have its shares traded on the LSE will have to go through is a rigorous vetting procedure.

2.2 Issue methods

Learning objective | 18.2.2 **Explain** the key features of the following equity issuance methods: placing; intermediaries offer; offer for sale and offer for sale by subscription.

Not only does the LSE limit who can enter the market, it also limits the way in which access to the market place is gained. There are five permitted issue methods.

- An offer for subscription.
- An offer for sale.
- An offer for tender.
- A placing.
- An intermediaries offer.
- An introduction.

The first four of these methods are described as **marketing operations**. A marketing operation is one in which the company raises cash. The fifth method – the introduction – does not raise additional finance for the company, it merely allows the company's shares to be traded on the market place.

2.2.1 Offer for subscription

Offer for Subscription

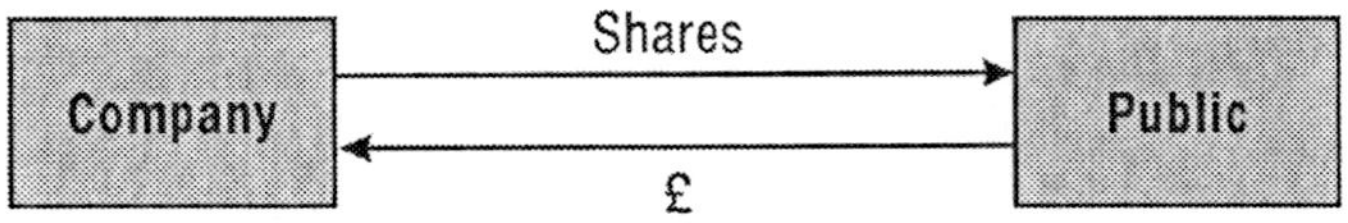

An offer for subscription is where the company issues new shares directly to the public. Most companies are not capable of organising and running an issue themselves, or do not wish to spend management time in doing so. Consequently, there are very few offers for subscription. More commonly, companies appoint an agent to act on their behalf. This is described as an offer for sale.

2.2.2 Offer for sale

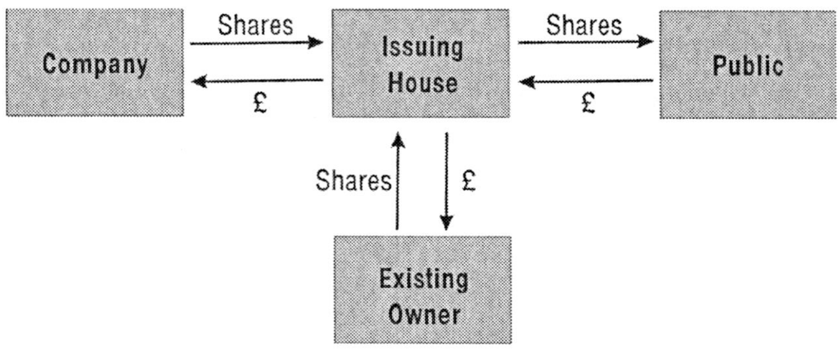

With an offer for sale, the company appoints an issuing house to deal with the public on its behalf. The issuing house advertises the security, obtains acceptances from the public, processes and allots shares and then sends the money to the company after the deduction of a fee. An offer for sale need not revolve around the issue of new securities; it can equally be used by a large shareholder selling a stake into the market place. Privatisations launched by the government have been offers for sale where a broking house has acted on the government's behalf to sell a large block of the shares in a company.

With both offers for sale and offers for subscription, there is the problem of knowing how to price the issue. There are two main solutions.

- A fixed price offer.
- A tender offer.

Fixed price offer

Under a fixed price offer, the issuing house establishes a fair price for the security. This price is frequently based on the price of similar company securities already trading in the market. Once the price has been arrived at, the offer is made to the public on the basis that potential purchasers state the number of shares they wish to buy at the fixed price. In the event of over-subscription, allocations are dealt with on a pro rata basis in line with the terms contained in the offer document.

It is frequently the intention of the company that the offer price should be artificially low so that potential purchasers can foresee an immediate rise in the share price. It is hoped that this will generate goodwill amongst purchasers which, in future, guarantees the company's access to new finance. Investors who purchase shares in a new issue in the belief that the share will rise due to its underpricing are called **stags**.

Tender offer

Under a tender offer, the potential purchasers are asked to divulge the number of shares they wish to buy and the price they are prepared to pay. The issuing house then receives their application forms that are ranked in order of the prices purchasers are prepared to pay – highest first.

Example

A company wishes to issue 20 million shares and states that there is a minimum price of £1.00. Bids are received from potential shareholders in the following sequence.

1 million @ £1.50

3 million @ £1.45

7 million @ £1.40

11 million @ £1.35

10 million @ £1.30

17 million @ £1.25

Progressing down the list, the offer can be filled at the point where the price is £1.35, since there are more than 20 million applicants. However, a company will frequently establish the price at a lower value, say £1.30, as this will again encourage the market to rise on issue, ensuring both profit and investor goodwill. Note that within this structure, all the shareholders applying for shares pay the common strike price set by the company, be it £1.35 or £1.30. Even those applicants who entered at £1.45 will only pay the common strike price.

The tender method is by far the more complicated of the two methods available and, consequently, the tendency is for the fixed price offer to be the dominant issue method.

2.2.3 Placing

By far the cheapest route open to a company is to elect for a placing. Under a placing, the company sells its shares to a particular broker who then sells the securities to its client base. This removes most of the requirement for advertising, and is also the most efficient method of issuing shares. A placing must be carried out in such a way to **ensure marketability**.

Placing

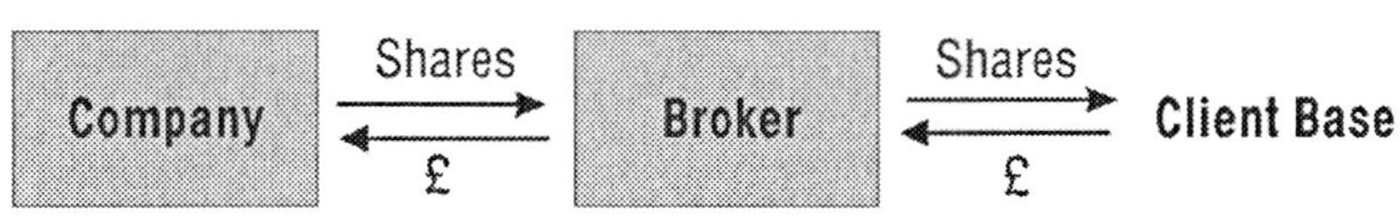

Where a number of brokers are involved in placing an issue with their own clients, widening the investor base, it is known as an **intermediaries offer**.

2.2.4 Intermediaries offer

An **intermediaries offer** is where financial intermediaries, such as stockbrokers, apply to the company's issuing house to subscribe for shares on behalf of their own clients. It is clearly cheaper and administratively simpler for the issuer than an offer for sale, but gives more opportunity for the public to participate than with a placing. It can be represented diagrammatically as follows.

Intermediaries Offer

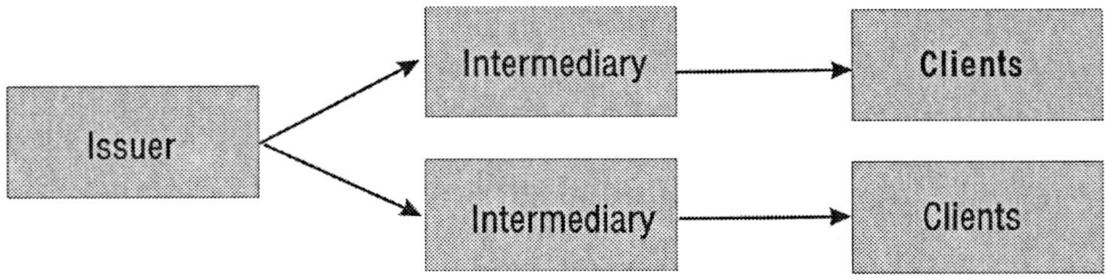

2.2.5 Introductions

As mentioned above, offers for subscription, offers for sales and placings are all marketing operations in that they raise cash for the company. An introduction is not a marketing operation, it merely brings the shares already held by shareholders into the market place.

2.3 Underwriting

Underwriting is, in effect, an **insurance policy** taken out by an issuing company to protect themselves against the risk that the issue may fail. Under the agreement, the underwriters guarantee to purchase the shares if insufficient applications are received from the public. The price paid by the issuing company for this underwriting is a small commission. This commission is payable to the underwriters whether they are required or not.

If the stock is issued at a deep discount, to ensure that issue will be successful, there is normally no requirement for an underwriter.

2.4 Subsequent issues

Learning objectives

18.2.3 Define and **explain** the purpose of a rights issue, a scrip issue and a stock split.

18.2.4 Calculate the theoretical ex-rights price and the value of the right (nil-paid) given the cum-rights price, the issuance ratio and the subscription price.

18.2.5 Calculate the theoretical ex-scrip price given the scrip ratio and the cum-scrip price.

18.2.6 Explain the options open to an investor in response to a rights offer and explain the effect on the investor's wealth.

2.4.1 Pre-emption rights

There is an obligation contained within the Companies Act to ensure that whenever a company issues shares for cash, those shares are first offered to the existing shareholders. This is the right of pre-emption and gives rise to rights issues.

2.4.2 Rights issues

Rights issues are simply a way of raising new finance from existing investors. Shares are normally offered at a discount to their price prior to the rights issue being announced. The effect this has is two-fold.

- It will dilute the value of the existing shares in the market place. We will look to calculate this price, known as the theoretical ex-rights price (TERP).
- An investor receiving a rights issue is, in effect, receiving a certificate giving them the right to buy a share in the company. This right is itself tradable on the market. Given that it will be giving the right

to buy a share below its current market value, there will probably be a value attributable to the 'nil paid right'. We will look to calculate this nil-paid value.

Shareholders who receive a rights letter have four possible courses of action. They may:

- Let the rights lapse, in which case the company can sell them nil paid.
- Exercise the rights, buy and hold the shares.
- Exercise the rights, buy then sell the shares.
- Sell the rights nil paid.

The latest date for taking up rights in a rights issue is called the **Last Acceptance Payment Date (LAPD)**, that is at least 21 calendar days after issue. The rights letter itself is a **temporary document of title** to the underlying shares evidencing entitlement to them.

Theoretical ex-rights prices

It is important to be able to determine the amount the purchaser pays for the rights nil paid.

Example

One for three rights issue at £4.00 when market price is £5.00

	Number	Price	Value
		£	£
Holding before issue	3	5.00	15.00
Rights issue	1	4.00	4.00
Holding after issue	4		19.00

As a result of the rights issue, the shareholder has four indistinguishable (fungible) shares with a total value of £19.00.

Therefore, each share now has a value of $\frac{£19.00}{4}$ = **£4.75**

As a result of the rights issue, the share price will, theoretically, fall from its current market level of £5.00 to £4.75. This price of £4.75 is referred to as the theoretical ex-rights price. This reflects the dilution aspect of issuing one new share at £4.00 when the existing market price of shares is £5.00.

The deeper the discount on the issue of shares, then the less likely is the need for underwriting.

Nil paid values

If the new share price is £4.75, then the maximum price that anybody would be prepared to pay for the rights letter, which gives the right to buy the shares at £4.00, would be **75p**. As the shares after the rights issue will be theoretically priced at £4.75, it would be irrational to pay what amounts to more than this for a share.

In reality, prices will reflect other factors, which will contribute to share prices rising and falling by different amounts.

2.4.3 Bonus issues

Bonus issues are also referred to as **scrip issues**, capitalisation issues, cap issues and free issues. Here, the company issues new shares, but does not require a payment for them from the shareholder. The main use of bonus issues is to dilute the price of the share in the marketplace by spreading it over a larger number of securities. This is felt to be important in the UK markets, since shares with too high a value may discourage activity, and therefore liquidity, in a stock.

Example

One for three bonus/scrip issue when market price is £5.00.

	Number	Price	Value
		£	£
Holding before issue	3	5.00	15.00
Bonus issue	1	0.00	0.00
Holding after issue	4		15.00

As a result, each share now has a diluted value of $\frac{£15.00}{4}$ = £3.75.

Many companies in the UK have historically offered the shareholders the right to receive their dividend in the form of shares rather than in the form of cash. This is referred to as a **scrip dividend.**

2.4.4 Stock split

Like a scrip issue, a stock split increases the number of shares in issue. There are some slight differences however.

- A 2 for 1 stock split will offer investors two new shares for every one old share held. In other words, the investor will hand back one share and receive two new shares (whereas with a bonus issue investors keep hold of their existing shares).
- As well as reducing the share price, the stock split will reduce the nominal value of shares in issue.

2.4.5 Share buybacks

Learning objective | **18.2.7 Explain** the motivations behind a company buying back its own shares.

Instead of using profits to pay a dividend to shareholders, a company can use the cash to buy back its own shares. The implications of doing so are a potential increase in EPS, ROCE and financial gearing, as the equity in the business is reduced (see the Analysis of financial statements chapter). Share buy backs tend to occur when a company has surplus funds it cannot profitably invest and when the share price is low.

Before 2003, any shares repurchased had to be cancelled by the company, however since that date companies have been allowed to hold shares as treasury shares, an asset on their balance sheet that they can sell later.

2.5 Secondary markets

2.5.1 The role of the London Stock Exchange

The London Stock Exchange is, above all else, a business. Its primary objective is to establish and run a market place in securities. In any economy there are savers and borrowers. The exchange acts as a place in which they can meet.

Initially, the companies (the borrowers) issue shares to the investing public (the savers). This is known as the **primary market**. Investors would not be willing to invest their money unless they could see some way of releasing it in the future.

Consequently, the exchange must also offer a **secondary market** trading in second-hand shares, this allows the investor to convert the shares into cash.

Overview of the Exchange's Activities

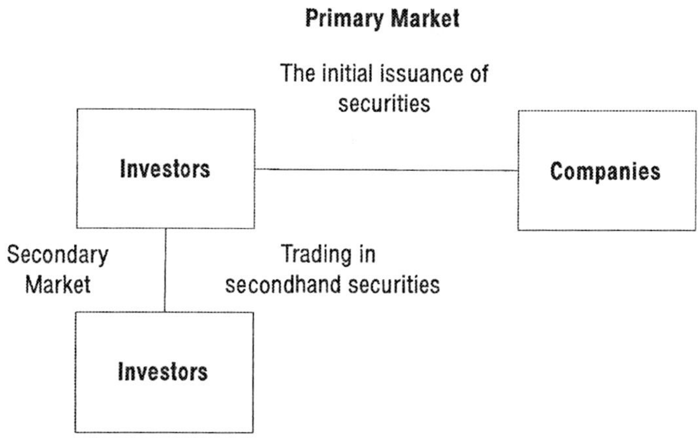

2.5.2 Dealing costs

arning objectives

18.4.1 Explain and **identify** transaction costs associated with dealing in UK equities.

18.4.2 Calculate the total transaction costs for an equity or gilt transaction, given the appropriate data.

18.4.3 Evaluate the impact of alternative trading platforms, facilitated by MiFID, on transaction costs associated with equity dealing.

Introduction

Dealing costs fall into one of two categories

- **Explicit dealing costs** – those dealing costs that will be reflected on the contract note for the deal.
- **Implicit dealing costs** – other potential consequences of the trade that the investor should be aware of.

Explicit dealing costs

When dealing in UK shares commission will be charged. This will be negotiable and dependent upon the level of service being provided by the broker, but for institutional traders it will be around 0.1% – 0.2%. Smaller institutional trades are likely to be nearer 1% – 1.5%. There is also a levy on all UK equity trades where the consideration **exceeds £10,000**. This levy funds the Panel on Takeovers and Mergers (POTAM/PTM) and is currently set at a flat **£1** on both buyer and seller.

When dealing in gilts, commission will also be charged in a similar way. Commission rates vary, but can be up to 1% of the value of the transaction, where the value is £5,000 or less. Normally, any transaction with a value of more than £1,000,000 would have no commission charged on it.

In addition to the above, a purchaser of UK shares must also pay **stamp duty** or **stamp duty reserve tax (SDRT)** to the Inland Revenue. Stamp duty is payable on the transfer of certificated shares which is now very uncommon, SDRT is payable on electronically registered or dematerialised transfers that have become the norm. The current rate of stamp duty is **0.5%** on the consideration, rounded up to the next £5. The current rate of SDRT is 0.5% on the consideration, rounded up/down to the nearest 1p.

Certain securities are exempt from stamp duty and SDRT. Most notably, gilts are **exempt**, as well as corporate loan stock, foreign securities, bearer securities and traded options on NYSE Liffe.

In addition to these securities being exempt, **market makers** are also **exempt** from paying SDRT as well as the PTM levy.

Implicit dealing costs

In addition to these explicit costs, other costs that may be faced include

- **Bid-offer spread** – Although trading on SETS does not involve a spread, relying instead on matching buy and sell prices, the dealer may add a spread to cover their own costs of processing the order and generate a profit. The less liquid the stock, the larger this spread is likely to be.
- **Scale and price impact of trade** – The price of a share in the market is determined by the balance of supply and demand for that share. If an unusually large sell or buy order is placed this may alter this balance and cause the share price to move. Market makers are aware of this and their price quotes are only fixed up to a certain deal size. The implicit cost of such a large trade can be determined as the difference between the actual price achieved and the volume-weighted average price of the transactions around the trade (the weighted average price of normal sized transactions occurring around the same time).
- **Opportunity costs** – The cost of delaying a trade or spreading a large trade over a number of days in order to avoid the potential adverse price effects discussed above. The share price will tend to move each day and delaying or spreading a trade may result in the sale being completed at an inferior price.

2.5.3 Impact of MiFID

The Markets in Financial Instruments Directive (MiFID), the Europe wide regulatory framework for dealing in financial instruments, paved the way for equity transactions to be undertaken off-exchange.

Historically all equities trades had to be undertaken through a stock exchange. MiFID has allowed investment banks to trade shares bilaterally, off-exchange, though they are required to publish prices. MiFID also introduced the concept of a multilateral trading facility (MTF) that allows off-exchange trades between multiple counterparties. It is anticipated that direct bilateral trading will result in lower transaction costs and higher trading volumes.

The main trading costs incurred by brokers are the costs of the

- **Trading platform** – The costs of order receipt and matching through the chosen trading platform. Historically, the main UK trading platform has been the LSE, however alternative platforms now include **BATS**, **Chi-X** and **Turquoise**.
- **Central counterparty (CCP)** – The costs of clearing the trade for settlement, ie netting transactions, dealing with settlement instructions and dealing with failed trades. The main clearing counterparty for UK shares has historically been **LCH.Clearnet** however alternative platforms now include **EMCF** and **EuroCCP**.
- **Central securities depository (CSD)** – The costs of settling the transaction once cleared by the CCP. This involves ensuring the buyer has the requisite funds, the completion of the transaction through the transfer of those funds and the transfer of ownership. For UK shares the CDS is CREST.

A recent study by Oxera consultants (May 2010) has shown that the average explicit cost per transaction by the various routes are as follows

	LSE/LCH.Clearnet	BATS/EMCF	Chi-X/EMCF
	p	p	p
Trading platform	23.8	3.0	3.0
Central counterparty	4.2	3.8	3.8
Central security depository	0.6	0.4	0.4
	27.6	7.2	7.2

Though we should note that the implicit costs of the larger LSE platform are liable to be lower making this comparison somewhat incomplete.

3 Evaluating Equity

3.1 Introduction

Learning objective

18.3.9 Distinguish between and evaluate the merits of relative valuation models and absolute valuation models and between historic and prospective measures of value.

The valuation of a company's shares could never be considered an exact science – there is simply no single right answer. There are, however, a number of possible bases that we could use to try to determine a value of equity that can be divided between absolute valuation methods and relative valuation methods. An absolute valuation method is an approach that determines the value of a business or the shares of the business without reference to any other business. A relative valuation method relies on some statistic derived from another business in order to evaluate the business in question. The methods we need to consider are

- Asset-based valuations – an absolute measure.
- Dividend valuation model – an absolute measure.
- Dividend yield-based valuations – a relative measure.
- Earnings-based valuations – a relative measure.

We examine each of these possible bases below.

3.2 Asset-based valuations

3.2.1 Introduction

A business can be seen as a collection of individual assets. As a result, the value of the business could be calculated as the value of those assets, or what those assets would realise if sold off separately.

The value of the company's equity will be the value of the business assets as a whole, less the value of the debt that must be repaid from those assets – an absolute valuation method.

3.2.2 Net realisable value of assets

The minimum selling price for a vendor

The net realisable value of the assets is of relevance to existing shareholders, since it represents the minimum sum for which they should be prepared to sell the shares. There is no point in accepting £1m for a business if the assets could have been sold off separately for £3m.

Establishing realisable values

In calculating realisable values, care needs to be taken in assessing the values of fixed assets and stocks. If the break-up of the company is occurring over a rapid timescale, or as a result of a forced sale, then values will be lower than if the business were run down in an orderly fashion over a period of time.

In addition, we also need to consider any selling costs and tax consequences that may arise as a result of the sale.

3.2.3 Use of asset-based valuations

Asset-based valuations will be appropriate for investment trusts, property companies and capital based industries, e.g. manufacturing businesses, where a large amount of the value of the business is tied up in the value of the assets owned. Asset-based valuations will be less useful for service industries, where their value is largely tied up in the value of the intangibles.

An asset-based valuation is **not** relevant for a minority investor who owns shares in a company which is a going concern, except perhaps for investment trusts and property companies. Since the company is not going to be wound up, the asset value will never be realised.

3.3 Dividend-based valuations

Learning objectives

18.3.2 Explain the components, assumptions and limitations of the dividend discount model (Gordon's growth model).

18.3.3 Calculate the present value of a share using the dividend discount model.

18.3.17 Define (financial) gearing and evaluate the effect on required equity returns and this dividend valuations.

3.3.1 Introduction

Whereas an asset-based valuation relies on the assumption that the assets can or will be realised, the dividend-based approach assumes that a company is a **going concern** and values the company according to its **dividend flows**. It is of most use to a minority investor who has little influence over a company's affairs and just receives a regular dividend payment.

There are two methods that we could apply to establish the value of equity based on dividend information. These are

- The dividend valuation models – an absolute valuation method.
- Dividend yields – a relative valuation method.

3.3.2 The dividend valuation model

The dividend valuation model states that the market value of a security is equal to the present value of the future expected receipts discounted at the investor's required rate of return. For equity, we can establish formulae to help with these calculations in two circumstances, where we have

- A **constant dividend**, as in the case of preference shares.
- A **constant growth rate for the dividend** (or constant after a certain time), which may be suitable for ordinary shares.

We can only utilise these formulae for non-redeemable shares. When dealing with redeemable securities, we are likely to need to resort to first principles.

Relevant cash flows

The cash flows involved are

Time	Inflow/(Outflow)
0	Market value ex-div
1-∞	(Dividends paid)

Notes

- The outflow at t_0 is the ex-div market value that must be paid to acquire the shares, since we are assuming that the first dividend will be received at t_1.
- If the shares currently in issue are presently cum div, then we must calculate the ex-div value using the equation

Formula to learn

$$E_{ex\text{-}div} = E_{cum\ div} - d_0$$

where

$E_{ex\text{-}div}$ = the ex-div market value of the shares

$E_{cum\ div}$ = the cum div market value of the shares

d_0 = the dividend about to be paid now

3.3.3 Constant dividend

Market value

The investor will be looking for a return to satisfy his required return. If his required rate of return is r_e and the annual perpetuity dividend payment is d, then he will be willing to pay and hence, the ex-div market value (assuming that the first dividend will be paid in one year's time and, therefore, we can correctly apply the perpetuity discount factor) will be

Formula to learn

$$E_{ex\text{-}div} = \frac{d_1}{r_e}$$

That is, the market value is determined by the investor, based on his expectations of future returns and his own required rate of return.

Example

If shareholders require the return on their investment in a certain share to be 10% and they expect the share to yield a dividend of 10p per annum in perpetuity, what will be the market value of the shares?

Solution

The ex-div market value of the share will be determined by shareholders to be

$$E_{ex\text{-}div} = \frac{d_1}{r_e}$$

$$E_{ex\text{-}div} = \frac{10p}{0.10}$$

$$= £1.00$$

This may appear to be over-simplistic, and you may feel that, in practice, there are many other factors that influence share price. However, the above is an illustration of the dividend valuation model, which provides a good starting point for any analysis.

Required rate of return

This equation can be fairly simply rearranged to give the investor's required rate of return as

Formula to learn

$$r_e = \frac{d_1}{E_{ex\text{-}div}}$$

3.3.4 Constant growth in dividends

Introduction

For ordinary share capital, it is unrealistic to expect a dividend to remain constant. It is more likely that dividends would grow in the future. If we were to assume a constant rate of growth at the rate of g per annum, then

Gordon's Growth Model

Formula to learn

$$E_{ex\text{-}div} = \frac{d_1}{r_e - g}$$

where

$E_{ex\text{-}div}$ = the ex-div market value of the shares which may need to be calculated using

- $E_{ex\text{-}div}$ = $E_{cum\ div} - d_0$
- $E_{cum\ div}$ = the cum div market value of the shares
- d_0 = the dividend about to be paid now if we are cum div

d_1 = the expected dividend in one year's time which may need to be calculated as $d_1 = d_0 \times (1 + g)$

r_e = the investors' required rate of return

g = the expected annual growth rate of the dividends

Investors' required rate of return

This formula can be rearranged to solve for the investors' required rate of return as follows.

$$r_e - g = \frac{d_1}{E_{ex\text{-}div}}$$

Formula to learn

$$r_e = \frac{d_1}{E_{ex\text{-}div}} + g$$

Example

A company is about to pay a dividend of 10p on its £1.00 ordinary shares. The shares are currently quoted at £2.30. The dividend is expected to grow at the rate of 10% per annum. Calculate the investors' required rate of return.

Solution

Since we are about to pay the dividend, we will assume that the share is currently cum div. Hence, since we need the ex-div value, we must use the expression

$$E_{ex\text{-}div} = E_{cum\ div} - d_0$$

to calculate the ex-div price as

$$E_{ex\text{-}div} = £2.30 - 10p = £2.20$$

Then, using the above formula for the required return to equity, we get

$$r_e = \frac{d_1}{E_{ex\text{-}div}} + g$$

$$r_e = \frac{10p \times 1.10}{£2.20} + 10\%$$

$$r_e = \frac{11p}{£2.20} + 10\%$$

$$r_e = 5\% + 10\% = 15\% \text{ p.a.}$$

3.3.5 Estimating required rate of return – r_e

Introduction

If we wish to apply Gordon's growth model to value the shares of a company we will need to determine the required return, r_e. This may be achieved either by

- Inter-company comparison
- Applying CAPM

Inter-company comparison

The required rate of return can be found by using published information on comparable companies. One method would be to select a company and identify its anticipated dividend growth and prospective dividend from brokers' forecasts and similar publications. These two figures and the company's share price can be slotted into the dividend valuation formula above.

$$r_e = \frac{d_1}{E_{ex\text{-}div}} + g$$

The company's required return can be used as an estimate for our company's required rate of return.

One further factor to consider will be the financial structure of the business. The risk of an all-equity financed business is a function of its business risk only, ie the risk inherent in the market it trades in and the way it trades.

A geared business, however, exposes its shareholders to an additional risk. Since debt demands a fixed return, the interest payment, that must be deducted from profits, gearing amplifies the volatility of returns experienced by shareholders. In the extreme, if profits are insufficient to cover the debt payments the business may go into liquidation – a situation that would not be the case in an equivalent all-equity financed business.

As a consequence, the return required by shareholders in a geared company will be higher than those required by shareholders in an equivalent ungeared company in order to compensate for this extra risk.

CAPM

Alternatively the Capital Asset Pricing Model (CAPM) can be used. A comparable company's beta and other relevant information can be found from published sources. After adjusting the β for our company's level of gearing, this can be inserted into the CAPM formula

$$r = r_f + \beta(r_m - r_f)$$

to determine the shareholder's required return r_e.

3.3.6 Calculating the dividend growth rate – 'g'

Learning objective

18.3.4 Calculate an estimated growth rate for dividends using historic data or using return on equity and a retained earnings ratio.

One problem that we have currently left unanswered is how we establish the investors' expectations regarding the dividend growth rate. There are two approaches we can take to tackling this.

- Look at the past dividend growth rates.
- Consider what causes growth.

Past dividends

Shareholders' expectations of future dividend growth will be based on many factors, but perhaps the most obvious indicator is the rate of past dividend growth.

If dividends have been growing at the rate of 5% p.a. for a number of years, it will be reasonable (in the absence of any further information) to assume that this rate of growth will continue in the future. Since past dividend information will be available we will be able to ascertain this compound growth rate by using the formula

Formula to learn

Dividend this year = Dividend n years ago × $(1 + g)^n$

Example

The dividend paid by a company in 2011 was £12,634. In 2016, they are proposing to pay a dividend of £22,265. Estimate the growth rate for the dividends.

Solution

Each year, the dividends grow by a factor of (1 + g) and hence, over the five years in question, the dividends will have grown by $(1 + g)^5$. Thus

$$£22{,}265 = £12{,}634 \times (1 + g)^5$$

or

$$(1 + g) = \sqrt[5]{\frac{£22{,}265}{£12{,}634}}$$

$$(1 + g) = \sqrt[5]{1.7623}$$

$$(1 + g) = 1.12$$

g = 0.12 or 12% p.a.

Causes of growth – reinvestment

When looking at growth rates it is important to consider what causes growth in dividends, or may cause growth in the future, since it is investors' expectations of the future that we are concerned with.

If a company fully distributes all of its profits this year, then at the end of the year (start of next year) it will be in exactly the same position as it was at the start of this year i.e. it will not have grown.

Long-term growth results from retaining a portion of earnings and reinvesting them to generate higher earnings and higher dividends in the future.

This leads to the expression that we could have used to calculate the growth rate directly.

Formula to learn

$$g = r \times b$$

where

r = rate of return on reinvested capital
b = proportion of profits retained and reinvested

3.3.7 Dividend policy

arning objectives

18.3.5 Explain the reasons for a company's chosen dividend policy.

18.3.6 Explain the practical constraints on companies paying dividends

Reasons for setting a dividend policy

Dividend policy is a strategy developed by a company's directors for the level of dividends they will pay each year. Dividend policy may be expressed in terms of a desired growth rate, e.g. 5% annual growth in real terms. It may also be expressed as a cover ratio, e.g. dividends will be covered by a ratio of at least 2× when compared to earnings for the year. Whatever way they do it, the directors will have some target dividend rate.

The reason that directors set a dividend policy for their company is that they believe stockholders like to have a stable or steadily growing dividend each year. Typically, they will look at past dividend growth, this year's earnings and expected future earnings levels and from these three factors aim to set an acceptable level of dividend this year which will grow at a roughly constant rate in the future.

Constraints on dividend policy

In order to pay a dividend a company needs just two things

- Cash
- Retained earnings

Note that it is not necessary for any dividends to be financed from this years profits, companies can pay dividends from historically retained earnings. Having said that, for dividends to be sustainable in the long term they cannot exceed normal annual profit levels.

3.4 Dividend yield

arning objectives

18.3.7 Explain the importance of the dividend yield and dividend cover in stock analysis.

18.3.8 Calculate dividend yield and dividend cover.

3.4.1 Basic ratio

The dividend yield of a company is calculated as

Formula to learn

$$\text{Dividend Yield} = \frac{d}{E_{ex\text{-}div}}$$

where

d = the net dividend paid

$E_{ex\text{-}div}$ = the current share price

3.4.2 Comparable company information

The dividend yield for a comparable company can be found from published sources. This can then be used as a surrogate for the required dividend yield for the company in question and inserted into the formula together with our company's own dividend. The required equity valuation will then fall out as the missing figure.

3.4.3 Ensuring consistency of information

It is important to ensure that the dividend yield calculation is being done on the same basis for both the companies.

Typically, published dividend yields are done on a net basis, ie calculated based on the net dividend paid to the shareholders. The net dividend is the amount paid by the company and is considered to be net at 10% tax, satisfying a basic rate taxpayers tax liability.

In addition, dividend yields may be historic or prospective, i.e. based on last year's actual dividend or on next year's expected dividend.

3.5 Dividend cover

On the last point of expected growth rates of dividends, one measure that we can look to is the dividend cover.

3.5.1 Basic ratio

Dividend cover is used as an attempt to assess the likelihood of the existing dividend being maintained. The dividend cover is calculated as follows

Formula to learn

$$\text{Dividend cover} = \frac{\text{Earnings per share}}{\text{Net dividend per share}}$$

3.5.2 Considerations

An unusually high dividend cover implies that the company is retaining the majority of its earnings, presumably with the intention of reinvesting to generate growth.

3.6 Earnings-based valuations

earning objective

18.3.12 Explain the rationale for the use of the following ratios in equity valuation: price-earnings; price to book; price to sales; price to cash flow; enterprise value (EV) to earnings before interest tax, depreciation and amortisation (EBITDA).
18.3.14 Apply the company ratios to the valuation of another given company.
18.3.15 Explain the possible shortfalls of using each of these price multiples in corporate valuation.

3.6.1 Price to earnings ratio

The typical method of valuing a company based on its earnings levels is to use price to earnings (P/E) ratio, calculated as

Formula to learn

$$P/E = \frac{E_{ex\text{-}div} \text{ per share}}{EPS}$$

where

EPS = earnings per share

$E_{ex\text{-}div}$ per share = current share price

The P/E ratio expresses the number of years' earnings represented by the current market price.

The P/E ratio for a similar company can be inserted into the formula along with the earnings per share of our company. The required valuation will fall out as the missing figure.

The significance of a P/E ratio can only be judged in relation to the ratios of other companies in the same type of business. If the median P/E ratio for an industry sector was eight, then a ratio of 12 for a particular company would suggest that the shares of that company were in great demand, possibly because a rapid growth of earnings was expected. A low ratio, say four for example, would indicate a company not greatly favoured by investors which probably has poor growth prospects.

Clearly, central to this valuation method is the calculation of the earnings per share.

3.6.2 Earnings per share

Earnings per share (EPS) is the one ratio for which there are some professional accounting rules regarding the calculation. These are laid out in FRS 14 (Financial Reporting Standard) which basically defines the EPS as

Formula to learn

$$EPS = \frac{\text{Earnings attributable to ordinary shareholders}}{\text{Number of ordinary shares}}$$

Under this accounting standard, earnings are defined as consolidated profit after tax, after minority interest, after extraordinary items and after preference dividends, i.e. earnings represent the profit available to pay out to the ordinary shareholders.

The standard defines each of these terms and the adjustments that should be made to them under certain circumstances, such as the issue of shares during the year. It also details disclosure requirements.

Example

A company has 100 million ordinary shares in issue and its reported profits for the year are as below. Calculate the EPS.

Income Statement Extract

	£'000
Profit before tax	8,500
Tax	(1,890)
Profit after tax	6,610
Dividend	(4,960)
Retained profit	1,650

Solution

Assuming no changes in capital and taking the figures directly from the accounts, the EPS is

$$EPS = \frac{£6.61m}{100m\ shares}$$

$$EPS = 6.61p$$

3.6.3 Fully diluted earnings per share

The objective of the fully diluted earnings per share figure is to warn shareholders of the company's possible future deterioration in the earnings per share figure, as a result of an obligation to issue new shares. There are a number of reasons why earnings could be diluted in the future.

- Convertible loan stock in issue.
- Convertible preference shares in issue.
- Options issued by and exercisable on the company.
- Warrants in issue.

Each of these circumstances may result in more shares being issued in future years. These would be taken into account when calculating the fully diluted earnings per share.

Fully diluted earnings per share is calculated on the basis that conversion of the debentures/preference shares or the exercise of warrants/options has already occurred. The impact of the notional conversion/exercise on earnings per share is calculated, and the result is fully diluted earnings per share.

3.6.4 Accounting ratio based valuations

One of the most commonly used methods for pricing a business is to use accounting ratios such as

- Price to earnings
- Price to book
- Price to sales
- Dividend yield etc

Imagine that we wished to value a particular company based on dividend yield. The dividend yield for a comparable company can be found from published sources that can then be used as a surrogate for the required dividend yield for the company in question and inserted into the formula together with our company's own dividend. The required equity valuation will then fall out as the missing figure – a dividend yield based valuation. The same approach could be applied for any accounting ratio involving the share price.

For the resultant value to be of any practical use it is important to ensure that the dividend yield calculation is being done on the same basis for both of the companies. In addition, for the valuations to be realistic it will be essential to apply ratios derived from very similar businesses, ie businesses

- Of a similar size
- Operating in the same sector, hence subject to the same business risk
- With a similar financial structure, hence subject to the same financial risk
- Experiencing similar profits and growth

ie a company experiencing very similar returns and risks.

3.7 Free cash flow-based valuations

Learning objective

18.3.16 Explain the basics of Free cash-flow based valuation methods (FCFF, FCFE) and Residual Income Valuation methods.

3.7.1 The advantages of a free cash flow-based valuation

Discounted cash flow-based valuations are theoretically superior to other valuation methods, since they are based on the fundamental determinant of corporate value, ie. Cash. We have already seen examples of cash-based valuations in the dividend valuation model and the asset-based valuation. The first was based on cash dividends and the second assumed that the company would be liquidated.

Earnings-based valuations are often used as an alternative because historically, earnings information has been easier to obtain for companies and therefore, earnings valuations are easier and quicker to apply.

3.7.2 The use of free cash flow-based valuations

The dividend valuation method valued a company on the basis of its cash dividends. As such, it was particularly appropriate to minority investors who only get the dividends determined by the direct ors. The cash valuation used here focuses on the cash that the business generates before investors have received their returns. It is of use to a **controlling shareholder** who can decide whether to reinvest this **free cash flow** or to pay it out as a dividend.

3.7.3 Estimating free cash flows

Free cash flow

In order to produce a cash flow-based valuation of a company, it is first necessary to estimate the cash flows the business can generate from its operations.

This is often referred to as 'free cash flow' or 'net operating cash flow' and it can be calculated at two different levels.

- Free cash flow to the firm (FCFF) – that can be used to value the business as a whole.
- Free cash flow to equity (FCFE) – that can be used to value the equity shares of the business.

Both of these free cash flow measures can be assessed as follows

Items	**(£)**
Profits before interest and tax	X
Add: Depreciation charged	X
Less: Tax payments	(X)
Less: Capital expenditure	(X)
Less/Add: (Increase)/Decrease in working capital	(X)/X
Free cash flow (to the firm (FCFF)	X
Less: Debt interest paid net of tax relief	(X)
Add: Net new debt	X
Free cash flow to equity (FCFE)	X

The free cash flow for the firm is the total amount the company could pay out to all of its investors (debt and equity) after funding capital expenditure and any required increases in working capital. Free cash flow to equity is the total that could be paid to shareholders.

The forecasting period

The valuer will need to forecast cash flows for a period of between five and ten years. The longer the period used, the more sophisticated the final valuation but the less reliable the forecasts are likely to be.

3.7.4 Discounting the free cash flows and terminal/residual values

The present value of the free cash flow

Having established the cash flows the company is capable of generating and distributing to investors, these need to be discounted to a present value. The discount rate used will reflect the risk of the business. Methods used to identify an appropriate discount rate have already been referred to in connection with the dividend valuation model, i.e. comparable returns or the use of CAPM.

To establish the value of the business a s a whole we would discount the free cash flow to the firm (FCFF) at the weighted average cost of capital (WACC) a composite rate reflecting the financing of the business that is possibly part equity and part is debt.

To establish the value of the equity we would discount the free cash flow to equity (FCFE) at a suitable required equity return.

In order to calculate the value correctly, it is necessary to rake account of all its expected future cash flows. One way to do this would be to forecast the flows into the future for an extremely long period of time. The problem with this is that it would be very time consuming and the figures will probably not be very accurate.

An alternative approach is to forecast the cash flows for a limited number of years into the future and then ascribe a value to the business at that date. This value, known as the **residual value** or terminal value, reflects the sale proceeds that would be received for the business as a whole (FCFF value) or by the equity holders (FCFE value) if the business were sold at the date of the terminal value. It would need to be discounted to its present value at the appropriate rate and added to the value of the relevant free cash flows.

There is no single way to arrive at a terminal value. Possibilities include assuming a nil terminal value or using a P/E ratio applied to forecast profits at that date.

Example

A company is expected to generate free cash flow to the firm of around £500,000 p.a. for the next five years. In five years' time, its profits after tax are forecast to be £600,000. The valuer believes that a discount rate of 20% is appropriate for the area of business and assumes that an appropriate P/E ratio to use for the terminal value is 13. Calculate the value of the company.

Solution

Interest rate at 8%

Time	Narrative	Cash Flow (£'000)	Discount Factor at 20%	Present Value (£'000)
1-5	Cash flow	500	2.99	1,495
5	Terminal value (600 × 13)	7,800	$\frac{1}{1.20^5}$	3,135
				4,630

The discount factor for Times 1 to 5 at 20% has been calculated using the formula

$$\frac{1}{r}\left(1-\frac{1}{(1+r)^n}\right) = \frac{1}{0.20}\left(1-\frac{1}{1.20^5}\right) = 2.99$$

3.8 Holding period return

Learning objective

18.3.1 Calculate a holding period return for an ordinary share, comprising capital gain and dividend income.

3.8.1 Introduction

When deciding on which investments he wishes to hold in his portfolio, an investor must be able to compare them directly. We have seen in our consideration of DCF that one measure of the return from an investment would be the IRR. An alternative, sometimes used, is the holding period return.

3.8.2 Basic calculation

Calculating the percentage holding period return for the investment avoids the problem of comparing different sized investments. This return is simply the gain during the period held (money received less cost) divided by the initial cost, i.e.

Formula to learn

$$r = \frac{(d_1 + E_1) - E_0}{E_0}$$

where

r = the holding period return

d_1 = any returns paid out during the period

E_1 = the value of the investment at the end of the holding period

E_0 = the cost

Example

Suppose an investment costs £50, is held for one year and then sold for £60, having paid a dividend of £4.00. What was the holding period return?

Solution

Using this equation the holding period return for the investment is

$$r = \frac{(d_1 + E_1) - E_0}{E_0} \times 100\%$$

$$r = \frac{(£4 + £60) - £50}{£50} \times 100\% = 28\%$$

This can also be rearranged to identify a projected price at a future point given an expected return

$$(E_1 + d_1) = (1 + r) \times E_0$$

Chapter Roundup

Characteristics

- The shareholders of the company are the owners of the company. As the owners they have a right to vote and to dividend payments when they are distributed.
- UK companies may be either public companies (who can issue shares to the public), or private companies (who cannot issue shares to the public).
- The majority of shares are 'ordinary' shares with equal rights to votes and to share in the profits.
- Preference shares pay a fixed dividend which must be paid before the company can pay out an ordinary dividend. They also have priority over ordinary shareholders in the event of a company winding up. They have no voting rights unless there is five years dividend arrears. Sub classes include
  - Redeemable.
  - Convertible.
  - Participating.
- ADRs allow UK shares to trade in the US, GDRs allow shares listed in one country to be traded in another.
- There are several ways of issuing new shares to investors. These include an offer for subscription, an offer for sale, a placing and an intermediaries offer.
- The Companies Acts provide existing shareholders with first rights over any new shares that are issued (pre-emption rights).
- Bonus issues and stock splits are methods of cosmetically reducing the share price to increase liquidity in the shares, they do not raise finance.
- Rights issues are issue to current shareholders at a discount to the current share price. They do raise finance.
- You must be able to calculate the theoretical price after an issue.

Transaction costs

Cost	Purchase transaction	Sale transaction
Commission	Yes – negotiable	Yes – negotiable
Stamp duty/SDRT*	0.5%	N/A
PTM Levy	£1.00 Transactions > £10,000	

* Stamp duty is payable on certificated transfers and is *rounded up* to the nearest £5. SDRT is payable on electronically registered transfers and is rounded to the *nearest* 1p.

- MTF = Multi-lateral trading facility introduced by MiFID that is expected to reduce equity transaction costs.

Valuation

- The dividend valuation model is one approach to valuing equity. Other methods include asset based and earnings based valuations.
- Asset based valuation is relevant to a capital intensive business and
  - Minimum price to seller = realisable value of net assets.
  - Maximum price to buy = replacement cost of net assets.

- Dividend valuation model

  $$E_{ex\text{-}div} = \frac{d_1}{r_e - g}$$

  $$E_{ex\text{-}div} = E_{cum\ div} - d_0$$

  Growth estimated based on

  – Past dividend growth

    Dividend this year = Dividend n years ago × $(1 + g)^n$

  – Causes of growth

    $$g = r \times b$$

    where

    r = rate of return on reinvested capital
    b = proportion of profits retained and reinvested

- Dividend yield based valuation and dividend cover

  $$\text{Dividend Yield} = \frac{d}{E_{ex\text{-}div}}$$

  $$\text{Dividend cover} = \frac{\text{Earnings per share}}{\text{Net dividend per share}}$$

- Earnings based valuation based on P/E ratio

  $$P/E = \frac{E_{ex\text{-}div}\ \text{per share}}{\text{EPS}}$$

- Similar calculations can be undertaken based on other ratios such as

  – price to book.
  – price to sales.
  – price to cashflows.

- To get a reasonable assessment based on accounting ratios it is essential to base them on a similar business, ie similar size operating in the same sector with a similar financial structure.

- Free cash flow

Profit before interest and tax	X	
Add: depreciation charged	X	
Less: tax on operating profit	(X)	
Less: capital expenditure	(X)	
Less increase/Add decrease in working capital	(X)	
Free cash flow to the firm (FCFF)	X →	Discount at WACC = Value of firm as a whole
Less: Debt interest paid net of tax relief	(X)	
Add: Net new debt	X	
Free cash flow to equity (FCFE)	X →	Discount at cost of equity = Value of shares

- Companies adopt a dividend policy to satisfy shareholder demands for steady returns

Equity returns

- Holding period return

  $$r = \frac{(d_1 + E_1) - E_0}{E_0}$$

TEST YOUR KNOWLEDGE

Check your knowledge of the chapter here, without referring back to the text.

1. Name three special types of preference share.

2. What is an ADR?

3. An introduction is a method of raising finance. *True or false?*

4. A company does a 1 for 4 bonus issue. The share price is £1.00 prior to the issue, what is the theoretical price after the issue?

5. A company does a 1 for 4 rights issue at a subscription price of £0.90. The price prior to the issue is £1.00; what is the theoretical price after the issue?

6. An investor holds 100,000 shares in a company which announces a rights issue to raise £30 million by issuing one 25p ordinary share at 240p for every eight 25p ordinary shares held. The middle market price of the shares on announcement of the rights issue and project was 294. calculate
   (a) The ex-rights price.
   (b) The value of nil paid rights per old share.
   (c) The value of nil paid rights per new share.

7. (a) A company has paid a constant dividend of 10p per share for many years. If the required rate of return is 8% p.a., what is the ex-div and cum-div market value of the share?
   (b) A company is about to pay a dividend of 10p which is expected to grow at 5% p.a. What is the ex-div and cum-div market value of the share if the required rate of return is 8% p.a.?

8. A company has just paid a dividend of 16.1p which has risen from 10p five years ago. If the required rate of return is 15%, what is the ex-div market value of the share.

9. A company has just paid a dividend of 25p. It pays out 80% of its earnings each year as dividends and earns 20% on the earnings reinvested. Calculate the ex-div market value of its shares if shareholders require a 15% return.

10. What is the ex-div market value of a 9% preference share when investors are requiring a compound return of 10% p.a. and it pays coupon
    (a) Annually?
    (b) Quarterly?

11. The price to earnings ratio measures the share price/EPS. *True or false?*

12. What is the holding period return for a share whose market value now is 160p, is expected to be 185p in one year and to have paid a dividend of 11p at the end of the year?

13. 20,000 shares are bought in A plc at a price of 56p and 4,000 are sold in B plc at a price of £3.20. If the broker charges 0.2% commission what is the total cost and net revenue from each transaction.

Test Your Knowledge: Answers

1. Participating, conversion and redemption.

   (See Section 1.2.3)

2. American Depository Receipt.

   (See Section 1.3)

3. False. An introduction merely allows a company's shares to be traded on the market.

   (See Section 2.2.5)

4.

	Number	Price (£)	Value (£)
Before	4	1.00	4.00
Issue	1	0.00	0.00
After	5		4.00

Theoretical price after $= \frac{£4.00}{5} = 0.80$

(See Section 2.4.3)

5.

	Number	Price (£)	Value (£)
Before	4	1.00	4.00
Issue	1	0.90	0.90
After	5		4.90

Theoretical price after $= \frac{£4.90}{5} = 0.98$

(See Section 2.4.2)

6. (a)

	Number	Price (£)	Value (£)
Before	8	2.94	23.52
Issue	1	2.40	2.40
After	9		25.92

$$\text{Theoretical price after} = \frac{£25.92}{9} = £2.88$$

(b) The value of the nil paid rights per old share is the theoretical loss in value of each old share following the issue, i.e.

294 – 288 = 6p

(c) The value of the nil paid rights per new share is the theoretical gain to the new shareholder having acquired a new share at the subscription price, i.e.

288 – 240 = 48p

(See Section 2.4.2)

7. (a) $E_{ex\ div} = \frac{d}{r_e} = \frac{10}{0.08} = 125p$

$E_{cum\ div} = E_{ex\ div} + d_0 = 125 + 10 = 135p$

(b) $E_{ex\ div} = \frac{d_1}{r_e - g} = \frac{d_0(1+g)}{r_e - g} = \frac{10 \times 1.05}{0.08 - 0.05} = 350p$

$E_{cum\ div} = E_{ex\ div} + d_0 = 350 + 10 = 360p$

(See Section 3.3)

8. $10 \times (1 + g)^5 = 16.1$

$(1 + g)^5 = \frac{16.1}{10.0}$

$1 + g = \sqrt[5]{\frac{16.1}{10.0}}$

Growth rate $g = \sqrt[5]{\frac{16.1}{10.0}} - 1 = 0.10$

$E_{ex\ div} = \frac{d_1}{r_e - g} = \frac{d_0(1+g)}{r_e - g} = \frac{16.1 \times 1.10}{0.15 - 0.10} = 354.2p$

(See Section 3.3)

9. $b = 0.2$ $r = 20\%$ $g = rb = 0.04$ or 4%

$E_{ex\ div} = \frac{d_1}{r_e - g} = \frac{d_0(1+g)}{r_e - g} = \frac{25 \times 1.04}{0.15 - 0.04} = 236.4p$

(See Section 3.3)

10. (a) Annual Cash Flows - £9 p.a.

$$E_{ex\ div} = \frac{d}{r_e} = \frac{9}{0.10} = £90.00$$

(b) Quarterly Cash Flows - £2.25 per quarter

$1 + r_e = (1 + R)^n = 1.10^{1/4}$

$r_e = 1.10^{1/4} - 1$

$$E_{ex\ div} = \frac{d}{r_e} = \frac{2.25}{1.10^{1/4} - 1} = £93.31$$

(See Section 3.3)

11. True

(See Section 3.6.1)

12. The holding period return equals

$$\frac{(185 + 11) - 160}{160} = 0.225 \text{ or } 22.5\%$$

(See Section 3.7)

13. **A plc**

		£
Cost of shares (20,000 × 56p)		11,200.00
Add:	Broker fee (11,200 × 0.2%)	22.40
	SDRT (11,200 × 0.5%)	56.00
	PTM Levy	1.00
Total cost		11,279.40

		£
B plc		
Sale proceeds (4,000 × £3.20)		12,800.00
Less:	Brokers fees paid (12,800 × 0.2%)	(25.60)
	PTM Levy	(1.00)
Net proceeds after deducting costs		12,773.40

(See Section 2.5.2)

10 Property

INTRODUCTION

Property has very many similar characteristics to shares as an investment class. Over the long term the value of property tends to rise and the income an investor could derive from it (rent) also rises, just like the capital value and income from shares.

There are, however, a number of distinguishing characteristics of property that impact on their suitability as an investment vehicle. We need to be aware of the advantages and disadvantages of investing in property, be aware of the methods available for making property investments and techniques for appraising and valuing property investments.

CHAPTER CONTENTS

CHAPTER LEARNING OBJECTIVES

18 Asset classes

Demonstrate an ability to evaluate the characteristics, inherent risks, behaviours and correlation of asset classes

18.9 Property

18.9.1 **Distinguish** between the commercial and residential property markets.

18.9.2 **Understand** the rational for investing in property.

18.9.3 **Identify** the main investors in the commercial property market and the characteristics of the principal commercial property sectors.

18.9.4 **Explain** how the direct commercial property market works with regard to

- Ownership and lease structure.
- Buying and selling.
- Cost, the valuation of property and investment performance measurement.

18.9.5 **Identify** the risks associated property investment both direct and indirect.

18.9.6 **Explain** the routes to indirect property investment.

18.9.7 **Identify** the transaction costs associated with property investment.

1 CHARACTERISTICS

1.1 Introduction

Property is another form of investment and, as for equities, returns are realised by investors as a combination of income and gains. However, there are certain characteristics of property which distinguish it from other investments. For many other types of investment, we have assumed that the markets are perfect, i.e. that there is a perfect competition within those markets. Competition in the **property market** is far from perfect. Imperfections include the immobility of the product and the possibility of a low number of buyers and sellers. In extreme circumstances, there may be only one potential purchaser. Invariably for any property, there will only be one seller who has almost monopolistic powers. Even if relatively identical units of property exist, they will not necessarily be offered for sale simultaneously, causing imperfections in this particular market.

1.2 Commercial and residential property

Learning objectives

18.9.1 Distinguish between commercial and residential property markets.

18.9.2 Understand the rational for investing in property.

18.9.3 Identify the main investors in the commercial property market and the characteristics of the principal commercial property sectors.

1.2.1 Commercially property

Commercially property is used for business purposes and may be subcategorised into a number of different types, including

- Shops
- Offices
- Industrial
- Agricultural
- Special (eg public houses)

The market in **commercial property** in the past has tended to be dominated by insurance companies and pension funds. These institutions may act as property developer and, once the property is built, the landlord. More recently, more private investors have been making direct investment in commercial property. Some have made investments via Self-Invested Personal Pension Plans (SIPPs).

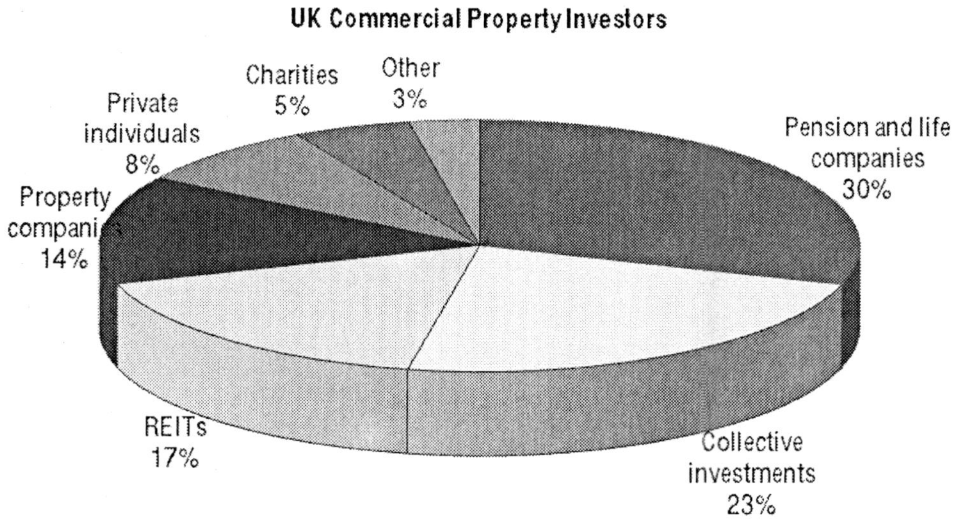

1.2.2 Residential property

Residential property is property used by individuals as homes.

The UK has a relatively high level of **owner-occupation** of **residential property**. Home ownership has been promoted by tax incentives, including exemption from capital gains tax for the taxpayer's own principal private residence.

The rented sector has seen the rise of '**buy-to-let**' ownership of property by many new private landlords during the 1990s and early 2000s. More easily obtainable mortgage finance for buy-to-let and rising house prices have fuelled the buy-to-let boom. By 2003, almost 5% of total mortgages outstanding were buy-to-let loans, up from under 1% five years earlier. The expansion in buy-to-let could make residential property values more volatile, as buy-to-let landlords may be more likely sellers than owner-occupiers in a housing market downturn.

1.2.3 Distinction between residential and commercial property

Through in principle, any property could theoretically be used for either commercial or residential purposes, planning and building control regulations make it difficult to change this categorisations.

As a result, the commercial and the residential property markets should be viewed as quite distinct. Distinguishing characteristics between these markets include.

- In the UK, the majority at residential property is owned by the occupier, whereas the majority of commercial property is rented
- Residential property tends to be rented for short periods, e.g. 1 year renewable lease, whereas commercial property leases tend to be longer term, typically 10-15 years with 5 year rent reviews
- Residential leases tend to be landlord repairing, commercial leases tend to be tenant repairing
- Commercial property rents tend to be fixed for a number of years, whereas residential property rents move each year with house prices. As a general rule, the less frequently the rent is reset the higher it tends to be, and hence the greater the proportion of total return that is made up of income. Commercial property landlords are, therefore, primarily benefiting from a source of income whereas residential property landlords benefit more from gains. Similarly industrial property rents tend to be larger than retail properties rents.

The key differences between residential and commercial property are summarised below

	Residential	Commercial
Investment	A wide range of properties throughout the UK from very small investments to very substantial	The range of investments is even wider, from small corner shops to major office buildings and factories.
Investors	Mainly private individuals but also a number of institutions	Due to the sums involved the more substantial properties are only held by institutions
Tenancy	Usually short-term, typically less than one year	Medium to long-term, typically 5 to 10 years
Repairs	Landlord's responsibility	Tenants responsibility
Returns	Mainly the gain from price appreciation low net yields (rent income less costs)	Mainly income returns

1.3 Long-term returns

1.3.1 Introduction

Research shows that, over the long run, investment in property has provided real returns ahead of the returns on cash and gilts and slightly below that of equities. The annualised total return for commercial property was 12.2% over the last 36 years (IPD estimates) with income yields of 4.9%. Returns from equities were 13.6% over the same period with income yields of 3.2%. The **commercial property** market has undergone 'crashes' from time to time: between 1989 and 1992, following a period of significant levels of speculative development in London, some office rent levels halved. Property yields are currently looking attractive on income grounds relative to the low yields from government bonds.

The **residential property** market tends to move in cycles different from those of the commercial property market, and it is influenced by economic factors such as disposable incomes and interest rates. A major slump in the residential market followed substantial rises in interest rates in the years following 1989.

A shortage of building land and planning restrictions contributes to rising prices in some areas, particularly the South of England.

In early 2007, many commentators believed that residential property was significantly overvalued in the market and that a correction was likely at some stage. The credit crunch that arose in late 2007 resulted in significant falls in the value of residential property and some commentators now believe it to be undervalued in many areas.

Over the long run, a fairly stable relationship between real incomes and house prices can be expected: this implies that, as the economy grows, positive long-term real returns are likely. Over shorter periods, expectations and buyer psychology play a part: a widespread belief that property prices will continue to rise can become a self-fulfilling prophecy over shorter-term periods as buyers pile in to the market.

1.3.2 Advantages of property investment

There are various **advantages** in owning **property**.

Security

Many investors participate in residential property ownership by owning the home in which they live. One of the attractions of **owner-occupation** is psychological: most owner-occupiers like the security of a permanent home they own, even if it is subject to a mortgage.

Capital appreciation

Over the long term, UK residential and commercial property values have out-stripped general price inflation, although the property market is susceptible to cyclical fluctuations.

Income generation

If the owner cannot live in a residential property for a period, for example when working abroad, the property can be let and used to create an income. Similarly, if a client owns a holiday home, this can be let for part of the year. The rental income will, hopefully, offset general running expenses.

Income stream

Tenants in property must continue to pay their rent even if they are unemployed (residential) or making trading losses (commercial). The characteristic of the **rental income** stream is more like that from fixed interest securities than from shares (equities). This insulates the landlord from some cyclical economic changes, provided the property does not fall vacant.

Increasing income

Property can produce an **increasing rental income** if good tenants can be found and maintained and as capital value rises.

Buy-to-let

'Buy-to-let' investment – discussed further below – offers the prospect of rental yield plus a potential capital gain.

Collateral

Residential and commercial property can be used as collateral security for a loan or mortgage. This borrowing capacity is more easily accessible on a property than on many other assets.

Diversification

Including property as an asset class provides diversification for the investor who also has investments in other asset classes such as fixed interest securities, equities and different property classes. The **capital value** of commercial property does not follow the residential property market.

Downsizing

It is possible to use a property as part of an investor's retirement fund. He or she can decide to sell a large house, moving to a smaller one on retirement and using the surplus funds to invest and create income.

1.3.3 Returns summary

Generally speaking then, property can be viewed as a higher yielding real asset. It is a real asset as, in the long term, values move with inflation, like shares. However, the income yield from property relatively high and stable, more like the income from bonds. In addition, for an investor seeking real returns, property markets offer the potential for diversification away from equities, thereby potentially reducing portfolio risk.

To appreciate the risks inherent in these property investments, and hence the factors affecting their values, it is essential to appreciate the features that distinguish property from other types of investment.

1.4 Distinguishing features/risk of property investment

Learning objective	**18.9.5 Identify** the risks associated with direct property investment, both direct and indirect.

1.4.1 Heterogeneity

Unlike Stock Exchange investments, property investments tend to be unique or **heterogeneous in terms of location, design, condition, size, etc.** Although there may be similar or close substitutes, especially in the case of say, housing, there is frequently a limited amount of supply available. In certain extreme cases, the opportunity to buy property may be absolutely unique, such as the opportunity to acquire a historical location or a location of national interest.

1.4.2 Indivisibility

Property is frequently indivisible, which is also true for single shares in companies. However, the cost of each individual, indivisible unit is significantly higher. As a result, property is often unattainable as an investment medium for the small investor, except through acquiring shares in property companies or through property bonds or other indirect means.

1.4.3 Costs and time of transfer

The costs of dealing directly in property are relatively high, compared to those of other types of investment. Investigation of title, the need for formal contracts and the frequent need to create a mortgage are reasons for employing a solicitor, significantly adding to any **transaction costs**.

In addition, dealing is often a long and protracted event with sales usually taking months, sometimes even years.

1.4.4 Management cost considerations

There are a number of legal and economic problems associated with property management which may consume a considerable amount of time and money on the part of the investor. For example, where the **repair and maintenance** liabilities fall upon the landlord (the investor), he will need to investigate the repairs that are required, obtain quotes, hire workers and see the work through to completion, which is all very time consuming. This is dramatically different compared to gilt-edged stock where no such management problems are encountered.

1.4.5 Decentralised market

Unlike the LSE, property is not sold on a central market. Property is normally bought and sold through agents in a particular location. Occasionally, major firms operate nationally, and even internationally, in the purchase or sale of investments for major clients. However, this is not true of the general property market which is highly **decentralised**.

1.4.6 Liquidity

Unlike securities, it may not always be possible to arrange a sale when required. However, other possibilities exist for the property investor who requires capital. The property could be **mortgaged** or alternatively a **sale and leaseback** arranged.

1.4.7 Volatility

From time to time, there will be **slumps** in the property market and these may be protracted and may adversely affect both capital values and yields.

1.4.8 Quality of tenants

If a property is leased out, there may be times when a suitable tenant cannot be found. In addition there are charges involved in letting property. A letting agent may be needed to vet suitable tenants establish suitable rental agreements, collect rents and oversee the upkeep of the property.

1.4.9 Occupancy levels

Occupancy levels can never be guaranteed and if a property is unoccupied (a **void period**) maintenance costs will still be incurred but no income generated to cover them rendering the investment a drain on income rather than a source.

1.4.10 Government intervention

Legal controls

There is great political significance attached to property. After all, countries are defined by the area that they own. It is a government's responsibility to look after the resources of their country as they best see fit, and property is simply one of those resources. As a result, **regulation in the property market is rife**, including

- Rent control and security of tenure.
- Discriminatory taxation and relief from taxation.
- Control of land use and control of the construction, maintenance and use of buildings enforced under the Housing Acts.
- Compulsory purchase and public development.

Security of tenure

Perhaps the most relevant legislation in the context of property investments relates to **security of tenure** in the private and commercial sectors. The governing regulations are

- Rent Act 1977 in relation to residential properties.
- Landlord and Tenants Act 1954 Part Two in relation to commercial properties.

Security of tenure means that lessees may apply for a new lease at the expiration of the old one at a rent that ignores the effect of any qualifying improvements they have carried out or goodwill they have established. If the landlord has grounds for obtaining possession, the tenant may be entitled to some compensation for disturbance under this Act.

The effect of this government intervention has caused most investing institutions to avoid purchasing property where tenants are covered by such regulations.

Taxation

Taxation legislation operates selectively towards different classes of investor. Different classes of investor may be subject to different rates of tax according to their circumstances, and certain classes, such as insurance companies, charities and pension funds, may be treated favourably or even be exempt.

1.4.11 Specific factors affecting property values

As a result of this special nature of property, there are a number of general market supply and demand features and risks associated with its ownership as an investment which may impact on the **supply and demand** of property, and hence its value. These include the following.

Supply features

- The **price inelasticity of supply** and vulnerability to changes in the economic conditions.
- Government (local or national) may limit the supply of land for the specific purpose through **planning constraints**.
- **Geographical immobility** may further restrict supply. Surplus office space in London cannot be transferred to other cities where demand may exist.

Demand features

- Fashion, local demand and changes in the demographic structure.
- Individual property features, e.g. state of repair, services, development potential, etc.
- Communications and accessibility.
- The degree of government intervention, impacting on returns, taxation and values of the property.
- Physical risks, such as fire, earthquakes, flooding, etc.

Risks

- Imperfect knowledge regarding the details of transactions undertaken.
- Legal liability to third parties due to defective premises.
- Economic risk that a property will become obsolete in terms of design or purpose – a price that seems high at the commencement of a development scheme may be just about right by the time the scheme is completed and may seem ridiculously low a year or two later.

Due to the inelasticity of the supply of property, **the major short to medium-term influence on property prices is demand**.

1.5 Direct investment

Learning objective

18.9.4 Explain how the direct commercial property market works with regard to; ownership and lease structure; buying and selling; costs, the valuation of property and investment performance measurement.
18.9.7 Identify the transaction costs associated with property investment

1.5.1 Freehold

The highest form of property ownership in England and Wales is the 'fee simple', or more generally termed, freehold interest. A **freeholder** is said to hold the property absolutely and in perpetuity. He may be in possession of the property or he may have forgone the right to possession (occupation) by letting it as an investment. In the latter case, he will be entitled to possession on the expiry of the tenancy and this is described as the landlord's reversion. The ability to gain reversion may be affected by legislation.

One particular version of this form of ownership is **sale and leaseback,** where the owner sells the freehold to a new owner then rents it back. This provides the old owner with a positive injection of cash and clearly provides the new owner with a guaranteed income stream from his investment.

Although the freehold is the most powerful direct interest, it is nevertheless subject to some restrictions, such as the use to which the land or buildings may be put and the liability to compulsory purchase.

1.5.2 Leasehold

A leasehold interest is created from a freehold interest, and is therefore, of necessity, less powerful than the freehold interest. It is of limited duration and is subject to covenants which may be of a positive or negative nature. The consideration paid to acquire a leasehold interest may take one of two forms (or both).

- A premium or single capital payment.
- Ground rent relating to the site or rack rent relating to the land and buildings.

The leaseholder may in turn create a lesser interest or sublease, in which event he becomes known as the head lessee paying a head rent. This process may continue down the line and a whole train of interests may be built up.

The lease terms and the quality of the tenant are important in assessing the merits of an investment. In addition, the duration of the lease may also be critical. For the purposes of evaluating property, a **lease term of 999 years would certainly be treated as freehold**.

A lease contract will normally specify who is liable to pay for repairs, insurances, etc., which may be either the freeholder or the leaseholder. These factors are obviously important from the point of view of making such an investment.

1.5.3 Life interests

It is possible to create an interest in property for the duration of the life of a person or persons. It is also possible to make such an interest commence after the life of one or more persons, possibly contingent upon some other event. Such an interest is known as a life interest.

1.5.4 Dealing costs

The main transaction costs in property deals are

- **Estate agent fees** – paid from the sale proceeds by the seller. Agents fees are negotiable but are often around 2% of the sale price
- **Legal fees** – Negotiable, paid by both the buyer and the seller

- **Stamp duty land tax (SDLT)** – a tax payable by the buyer at rates that depend on whether the property is residential or commercial and based on the property value. The rates for 2012/13 are shown below, with SDLT payable is rounded down to the next multiple of £1.

Residential property	Residential property in disadvantageous areas	Commercial property	Rate
Up to £125,000	Up to £150,000	Up to £150,000	Nil
£125,001 – £250,000	£150,001 – £250,000	£150,001 – £250,000	1%
£250,001 – £500,000	£250,001 – £500,000	£250,001 – £500,000	3%
£500,001 – £1,000,000	£500,001 – £1,000,000	>£500,000	4%
£1,000,000 – £2,000,000	£1,000,000 – £2,000,000	N/A	5%
>£2,000,000	>£2,000,000	N/A	7%*

*The rate of 15% is applied to property sold for over £2,000,000 to a non-natural person (eg a company or trust).

The commercial property rates apply whether or not the property is in a designated Disadvantaged Area.

No SDLT is chargeable for transfers on divorce or for transfers to charities if the land is to be used for charitable purposes.

1.6 Indirect investment

Learning objective	**18.9.6 Explain** the routes of indirect property investment.

1.6.1 Indirect investment through property funds

Investors may choose to invest directly in property and personally manage their portfolio, or they may choose to invest in a professionally managed property fund.

There are many advantages to collective investments including professional management, greater diversification, lower dealing costs and the general advantages and disadvantages of collective investments are dealt with in that chapter.

1.6.2 Real Estate Investment Trusts

The Finance Act 2006 allowed for the creation of Real Estate Investment Trusts (REITs). These are companies that own income generating property in both the residential and commercial property markets.

There are tax advantages of being incorporated as a REIT rather than as a normal company in that the income and gains generated by the underlying portfolio of properties are not subject to corporation tax. Instead the income is subject to income tax and is ultimately paid by the underlying investor as the REIT deducts basic rate tax from income distributions paid. In addition, gains are only taxed when the investor sells their holding. As a result, the tax treatment more closely mirrors that of a direct investment in property.

In order to qualify as a REIT the company must meet certain conditions:

- UK resident closed-ended company
- Obtain a listing on a UK or overseas recognised stock exchange such as the LSE Main Market or AIM.
- The shares in the company must not be closely held, which means that no one person (individual or corporate) should hold more than 10% of the shares

- The property letting business, which will be tax exempt, must be effectively ring-fenced from any other activities and should comprise of at least 75% of the overall profits
- Furthermore, of the funds' assets, at least 75% must be held for the tax-exempt property letting business
- Pay out at least 90% of its ring-fenced property net profits to investors
- Withhold basic rate tax on the distribution of property income
- Own at least three properties, with no single property making up more than 40% of the portfolio
- Subject to an interest cover test to ensure it is not too highly geared

Ultimately REITs also offer many of the advantages of an investment trust in that they are diversified, professionally managed, and offer liquidity. Many large listed property companies have now converted into REITs.

1.6.3 Property shares

The purchase of shares in property companies offers the small investor, who may not have sufficient resources to actually involve himself in property development directly, the chance to share in the involvement in property.

1.6.4 Property bonds

A property bond is an investment opportunity where an investor pays a premium to a life company, part of which provides for insurance and the remainder of which is invested in the shares of property companies. In this way, they are very similar to linked insurance with the premiums and dividends being linked to the value of the underlying value and income received from the property.

Property bond schemes operate through insurance companies selling units to smaller, tax-paying investors in order for them to participate in larger commercial ventures. The price of the units is governed by the valuation of the properties. When the bondholder wishes to dispose of his units, they are bought back by the managing company which usually quotes a spread between bid and offer prices to cover management charges.

The underlying fund is liable to corporation tax on income and on chargeable gains. Depending on the investor's personal taxation position, he may be liable to pay higher rates of income tax in respect of any gain over and above his initial investment.

1.6.5 Property unit trusts and OEICs

Originally, unit trusts were prohibited from directly investing in property and could only invest indirectly via property shares. This has now changed and unit trust and Open-Ended Investment Company (OEIC) managers can invest directly into commercial property. At the launch of such a fund, the manager must be confident that he will attract sufficient funds to make adequate property purchases to establish a well spread portfolio.

There are, however, restrictions on the proportion of the fund that can be invested in leases with less than 60 years to run, or in unoccupied property. There are also restrictions on holding mortgaged property, which limit gearing. No more than 15% in value of the fund assets can be invested in a single property.

Additionally, there are unit trusts and OEICs that invest in property company shares.

As with unit trusts and OEICs generally, the investment will be redeemed at net asset value. However, if many investors choose to sell at one time, the unit trust or OEIC may need to invoke its right to postpone encashment of units/shares until property can be sold. This makes property funds potentially illiquid.

1.6.6 Property investment trusts

Property investment trusts are pooled property investments but they are only allowed to invest in shares and securities of property companies, not in property directly. They are permitted to borrow in order to increase their exposure to property investments. While property is performing strongly, this will enhance returns as the returns from the extra property will cover the borrowing costs. However when property is performing poorly the returns may be insufficient to cover the costs of the associated borrowings resulting in losses for the investors. As a result, this gearing increases the risk to the investor as well as the possible return.

The share price of the trust will fluctuate with supply and demand for the shares of the trust, and may be at a discount or premium to net asset value.

1.6.7 Pension funds

As a long-term real returning asset, property is a highly suitable investment class for a pension fund. Investors with a Self-Invested Personal Pension (SIPP) may invest their pension fund in commercial property, though not residential property.

1.6.8 Limited liability partnership

A limited liability partnership is a business structure that is governed by the Limited Liability Partnership Act 2004. Limited liability partnerships are popular with institutional investors as they offer tax advantages over other structures and can be geared. The disadvantage is their exposure to stamp duty that is not a cost in other structures.

1.6.9 Derivatives

Property derivatives are available based on certain property indices published by the Investment Property Databank (IPD) such as the UK IPD Index and IPD index swaps.

2 Valuation

Learning objective

18.9.4 Explain how the direct commercial property market works with regard to; ownership and lease structure; buying and selling; costs, the valuation of property and investment performance measurement.

2.1 Introduction

There are several conventional methods of valuation which include

- The comparative method.
- The investment method.
- The profits method.

Of these, the comparative and investment methods are considered the most important, though we will consider each in turn.

2.1.1 Comparative method

This is probably the most widely used method and even if one of the other methods is used by the valuer, he will still almost inevitably have recourse to comparison as well. The method entails making a valuation by directly **comparing** the property under consideration **with similar properties that have been sold**, finding its value from these past transactions.

2.1.2 Investment method

This method is used for valuing properties which are normally held as income-producing investments. We can view it as being the **same as a fixed income security** (assuming the rent is fixed). Freehold properties may be used to produce perpetual income for valuation purposes, hence, this approach may be suitable for this property.

2.1.3 Profits method

Where comparables are not available, as with certain types of property such as theatres, restaurants and hotels, the valuation may have to be made purely by reference to the profits which a tenant of reasonable business acumen could make from occupation of the property, ie its **value in use**. If this valuation method reveals a higher value than the other methods, the difference is known as the **consumer surplus**.

Chapter Roundup

Characteristics

- Some of the key differences between residential and commercial property are summarised below.

	Residential	Commercial
Investment	A wide range of properties throughout the UK from very small investments to very substantial	The range of investments is even wider, from small corner shops to major office buildings and factories.
Investors	Mainly private individuals but also a number of institutions	Due to the sums involved the more substantial properties are only held by institutions
Tenancy	Usually short-term, typically less than one year	Medium to long-term, typically 5 to 10 years
Repairs	Landlord's responsibility	Tenants responsibility
Returns	Mainly the gain from price appreciation low net yields (rent income less costs)	Mainly income returns

Direct investment

- Direct investment may be made by investment in freeholds and leaseholds.
- The main transaction costs in property deals are
  - **Estate agent fees** – negotiable, paid by the seller.
  - **Legal fees** – Negotiable, paid by both the buyer and the seller.
  - **Stamp duty land tax (SDLT)** – a tax payable by the buyer at the following rates (rounded down to the next multiple of £1).

Residential property	Residential property in disadvantageous areas	Commercial property	Rate
Up to £125,000	Up to £150,000	Up to £150,000	Nil
£125,001 – £250,000	£150,001 – £250,000	£150,001 – £250,000	1%
£250,001 – £500,000	£250,001 – £500,000	£250,001 – £500,000	3%
£500,001 – £1,000,000	£500,001 – £1,000,000	>£500,000	4%
£1,000,000 – £2,000,000	£1,000,000 – £2,000,000	N/A	5%
>£2,000,000	>£2,000,000	N/A	7% or 15%

Indirect investment

- Real Estate Investment Trust (REIT).
- Property shares.
- Property bonds.
- Property unit trusts and OEICs.
- Property investment trusts.
- Pension funds.
- Limited liability partnership.
- Derivatives (eg IPD Index swaps).

Risk characteristics

- Supply features
  - Heterogeneity.
  - Indivisibility.
  - Inelasticity of supply/
- Demand features
  - Cost of transfer.
  - Problems of management.
  - Imperfect knowledge.
  - Government intervention.
  - Geographical features/

Valuation

- Comparative method.
- Investment method.
- Profits method.

Test Your Knowledge

Check your knowledge of the chapter here, without referring back to the text.

1. What is the difference between the typical term of a residential and a commercial lease
2. Who are the three main property investor categories
3. List four distinguishing features of property.
4. What factors affect the demand for property?
5. What are the routes of direct property investment?
6. Name the conventional methods for valuing a property.

Test Your Knowledge: Answers

1. Residential leases are usually for one year at a time, commercial leases are typically 10-15 years

   (See Section 1.2)

2. Pension and life companies

   Direct investment

   Property funds

   (See Section 1.2)

3. The lack of liquidity, high transaction costs, heterogeneity, and the decentralised nature of the market means it has very different characteristics from, say, share trading on the London Stock Exchange.

   (See Section 1.4)

4. Fashion, changes in demographics, accessibility, government intervention, physical risks of fire, earthquakes etc.

   (See Section 1.4.11)

5. Freehold, leasehold and life interest

   (See Section 1.5)

6. The comparative method; the investment method; the profits method

   (See Section 2)

11 Commodities and Alternative Investments

INTRODUCTION

Previously we have examined what may be regarded as normal investments. There are, however, two final investment classes for us to consider commodities and alternative investments which we consider in this section.

Commodities is the generic term for physical resources that are of some value. They are assets (i.e. they have some value) as a result of their rarity, usefulness and characteristics.

In the main, physical commodities only have a real value to their user, e.g. the manufacturer who needs the raw material and they frequently deteriorate in value over time (e.g. foodstuffs). As such, commodities, are rarely appropriate as an asset class for most types of fund, though speculators may look to gain from any price changes they exhibit. Most of this speculative trade in commodities is achieved through the use of derivatives which are covered in a separate chapter.

CHAPTER CONTENTS

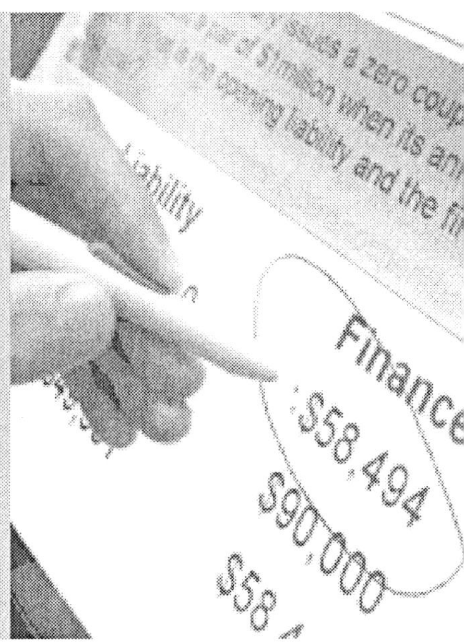

Chapter Learning Objectives

18 Asset classes

Demonstrate the ability to evaluate the characteristics, inherent risks, behaviour and correlation of asset classes

18.11 Alternative investments

18.11.3 **Explain** how commodity exposure can be viewed as a hedge against inflation and 'event' risk.

18.11.5 **Explain** the advantages and risks at investing in 'alternative' investments including gold and antiques.

1 Commodities

Learning objective	18.11.3 **Explain** how commodity exposure can be viewed as a hedge against inflation and 'events' risk.

1.1 Introduction

Commodities for investment purposes are essentially raw materials that can be bought and sold easily in large quantities on organised markets. They fall into one of three categories.

- **Energy commodities:** oil, natural gas, coal, bio fuels
- **Hard commodities**: metals (gold, copper, lead, tin, etc.) and diamonds.
- **Soft commodities**: mostly foodstuffs, such as cocoa, coffee, soya, sugar, etc.

The prices of these commodities are, as for all assets, driven by the influences of supply and demand and can, therefore, be significantly affected by factors such as

- Good/poor harvests;
- Exceptionally good/bad weather;
- Political unrest in the producing country.

As a result, commodities have the following general characteristics

- They generally produce no income
- Values can change dramatically in response to economic change, natural disasters and other economic stocks
- Prices are normally negatively correlated to equities and bonds
- Commodities may be expensive to store
- Commodities may be subject to deterioration over time, especially softs

In relations to the second of these points, natural disasters and other economic shocks often lead to a shortage of supply in essential commodities, leading to significant price rises. Commodities can therefore, be viewed as a hedge against such events.

Investors can buy and sell commodities in two ways.

1.1.1 Cash market

Trade on the cash market is for immediate delivery, known as trading **physicals** or **actuals**, with the price paid being the **spot price**. Payment must be made immediately and charges are made for storage and insurance. There is a standard contract size, 25 tonnes for copper for example, to aid the smooth running of the market.

1.1.2 Derivatives market

Trade on derivatives markets is for delivery at an agreed future date. There are rules about how far in advance such derivatives contracts can be arranged (up to three months for copper for example). The advantages of dealing in derivatives are the absence of storage costs and the effect of gearing – only a small margin being required to gain exposure to a large asset value.

Major commodity derivatives exchanges include

- Chicago Mercantile Exchange (CME) group (which includes CME, Chicago Board of Trade (CBOT) and the New York Mercantile Exchange (NYMEX)) – trades in all commodities
- London Metal Exchange (LME) – the major exchange for metals trading
- ICE Futures Europe – trades in oil

1.2 Investment in commodities

1.2.1 Direct investment

Physicals

An investor can buy and sell commodities directly through a commodity broker, or invest in a commodities fund. Dealing in physical commodities is not a practical proposition for most investors because of the minimum quantities that must be traded and the risk of deterioration in quality. The cash market is primarily for users of that raw material/agricultural product, rather than the investor.

For non-deteriorating commodities such as metals, however, it is possible and practical to take a direct holding in the commodity, which will be stored in a London Metal Exchange (LME) approved warehouse. The investor should consider the storage costs, etc. involved with this option.

Derivatives

Derivatives do, however, provide a useful investment vehicle for the purposes of diversifying and hedging as we discuss in the chapter on derivative products later in this Study Text.

Advantages of direct investment

Direct investment offers the following advantages over indirect investment.

- Commodity consumers will want to be able to acquire the commodity possibly in advance of needing it if prices are favourable.
- There will be lower risks (counterparty risk, political risk).

1.2.2 Indirect investment

Shares of commodity companies

One approach to indirect investment would be to acquire shares in a commodity producing company, e.g. mines. As commodity prices rise, we could anticipate that the company's revenue, and correspondingly, the share price will rise. The extent of this relationship, however, also depends on how the costs may fluctuate.

Although all producers will face the same selling price, they will not all face the same cost pressures and hence, though we may expect share prices to move with the underlying commodity prices, the correlation will not be perfect.

Commodity funds

The choice for most investors is a sterling commodities fund. Authorised unit trusts are not allowed to invest in commodities; hence, if the investor wishes to have a professionally managed fund, he must look offshore. A variety of funds deal in commodities, differing in their areas of specialisation, permitted levels of gearing and ability to go short. Most funds use both the cash and futures markets, hence the fund performance may not exactly correspond to the underlying commodities.

These funds are of interest to an investor who is interested in real assets as a hedge against inflation and is also looking more towards capital growth than income.

In addition to these more normal funds, exposure may be gained to commodities through certain hedge funds, and through Exchange Traded Commodities (ETCs), a variation of ETFs where a number of competing products have been issued.

Like ETFs, ETCs are asset-backed open-ended investments that track the performance of the underlying commodity/index. They are traded and settled like shares and have the support of a market maker to ensure liquidity and are available on single commodities (eg gold) or on commodity indices (eg energy or precious metals).

Advantages of indirect investment

The advantages of indirect investment are as follows.

- The shares will probably pay a dividend unlike any direct investment.
- Lower holding/storage costs.
- Lower minimal dealing size.

2 Collectibles

Learning objective

18.11.5 Explain the advantages and risk at investing in 'alternative' investments including gold and antiques.

2.1 Introduction

A collectible is a physical asset that appreciates in value over time as a result of its rarity, desirability or simply as a result of inflation.

The objectives of investing in collectibles may vary considerably depending on the particular investor and collectible in question. Collectibles offer no guarantee of price appreciation and any growth that does arise may be very slow.

There are no strict rules as to what is or is not a collectible, however the following are types of investment that could be called 'collectibles'.

Works of art	Wine	Race horses	Comic books
Antiques	Limited edition books	Books	Toys
Coins	Diamonds	Autographs	Memorabilia
Stamps	Gold items	Posters	
Veteran cars	Jewellery	Celebrity photos	

Collectibles have the following general features.

- They generally produce **no income**.
- They can be **difficult to value**, particularly for unique items.
- **Values can change** with changes in fashion or, for commodities like gold, with inflation.
- Collectibles are **expensive to keep** because they are vulnerable to atmospheric change, burglary and so on. There can be additional costs of custodianship, possibly in a bank, and heavy insurance premiums.
- The **cost of buying and selling** collectibles can be high, with dealers' margins or commissions being substantial.
- Collectibles may have low **marketability**. An item may be difficult to sell in a hurry and the price raised may be a great disappointment.
- **Specialist knowledge** is required in the selection of the item.
- The less knowledgeable **investor may be vulnerable** to the unscrupulous expert.

2.2 Collectibles in a portfolio

Investment advisers will not often be called upon to recommend an alternative investment. The client will normally already have an interest in whatever the collectible item may be. The pleasure provided by the activity of collecting items will often be an important aspect.

Collectibles may be of particular use to a higher rate taxpayer who has no intention of disposing of the items during his lifetime. As the artefacts generate no income, the collector will suffer no tax whilst he holds them. There will be no CGT on death. Inheritance tax will be avoided if the item is given for national purposes or the public good.

Collectables tend to provide a good hedge against inflation and demonstrate low correlation to other asset classes, offering a significant diversification benefit to any fund seeking long term real returns.

There are, however, several disadvantages of collectible investments

- Can be difficult to sell quickly
- Valuation can be problematic
- Subject to trends and fashion
- Storage costs
- Insurance costs
- Dealer's charges
- No regulation
- Lack of income
- Risk of forgery
- High sale costs through auction etc.

Chapter Roundup

Commodities

- Commodities are essentially raw materials that can be easily bought and sole in large quantities on organised markets.
- They fall into one of three categories
  - **Energy commodities:** oil, natural gas, coal, bio fuels.
  - **Hard commodities**: metals (gold, copper, lead, tin, etc.) and diamonds.
  - **Soft commodities**: mostly foodstuffs, such as cocoa, coffee, soya, sugar, etc.
- Characteristics
  - Pay no income.
  - Volatile values heavily influenced by natural disasters and economic shocks (price rises in these events make commodities a good hedge against them).
  - Prices normally negatively correlated to equities and bonds.
  - Expensive to store.
  - May deteriorate over time (especially softs).
- Direct trading
  - Cash market – dominated by producers and users of commodities.
  - Derivatives market.
- Indirect
  - Share in commodity companies.
  - Commodity funds (ETCs, offshore funds).

Collectibles

- Collectibles such as art or antiques can be a part of a portfolio of investments, and this will usually be where the investor has a particular interest in the items collected.
- Characteristics/risks
  - Pay no income.
  - Difficult to value, value is volatile and fashion driven.
  - Expensive to hold/store.
  - High dealing costs.
  - Low marketability.
  - Specialist knowledge required for dealing and management.

Test Your Knowledge

1. What are the three categories of commodities?

2. List the characteristics of commodities and explain why they may provide a good hedge against natural disasters and economic stocks.

3. What is an ETC?

4. Identify the features of collectibles which are relevant to the investor.

5. Which investors should consider investing in collectibles?

Test Your Knowledge: Answers

1. **Energy commodities**: oil, natural gas, coal, bio fuels

   Hard commodities: metals (gold, copper, lead, tin, etc.) and diamonds.

   Soft commodities: mostly foodstuffs, such as cocoa, coffee, soya, sugar, etc.

   (See Section 1.1)

2. Characteristics

   - Pay no income
   - Volatile values that respond to natural disasters and economic shocks
   - Prices normally negatively correlated to shares/bonds
   - Expensive to store
   - May deteriorate over time (esp softs)

   Commodity prices rise sharply if there is any anticipation of increased demand or limited supply that tends to occur when we experience natural disasters and economic shocks.

   (See Section 1.1)

3. Exchange traded commodity, the commodity equivalent of ETF. Like ETFs, ETCs are asset-backed open-ended investments that track the performance of the underlying commodity/index. They are traded and settled like shares and have the support of a market maker to ensure liquidity and are available on single commodities (eg gold) or on commodity indices (eg energy or precious metals).

   (See Section 1.2.2)

4. Characteristics

   - No income
   - Difficult to value as values are volatile
   - Expensive to hold
   - High trading costs
   - Low marketability
   - Specialist knowledge required to avoid vulnerability

   (See Section 2.1)

5. Investors who invest in collectibles/hard commodities

   - require no income
   - are seeking a long-term real return
   - wish to diversify their portfolios

   (See Section 2.1)

12 Derivative Products

INTRODUCTION

Derivatives are investments whose value is derived from some underlying asset or security.

The two main types of exchange traded derivatives are futures and options. Futures are agreements to buy or sell a specified asset at a future date, whilst options give the right to buy or sell an asset at a future specified date.

Futures and options may be packaged together to create trading strategies such as straddles and strangles.

Companies may also enter into swap transactions such as interest rate swaps when managing their financing. These are a form of over the counter derivative (OTC) and not traded on formal derivative exchanges.

CHAPTER CONTENTS

Chapter Learning Objectives

18 Asset classes

Demonstrate the ability to evaluate the characteristics, inherent risks, behaviour and correlation of asset classes

18.11 Alternative investments

18.11.1 **Explain** the characteristics of the main commodity derivatives, including

- Energy.
- Softs.
- Biofuel.
- Metals.
- Emissions.
- Weather.

18.11.4 **Understand the role at the investment property database indices in the market.**

20 Derivatives and other instruments

Demonstrate an ability to analyse the characteristics, inherent risks of derivatives and other instruments

20.1 Derivatives and other instruments

20.1.1 **Distinguish** between forwards, futures and options.

20.1.2 **Explain** the nature, trading and settlement of exchange traded derivatives.

20.1.3 **Understand** the motive for using a futures contract rather than a trade in the underlying asset.

20.1.4 **Explain** the nature of, and reasoning behind, a contango and backwardation market.

20.1.5 **Define** the 'basis' of a futures contract.

20.1.6 **Know** the contract specifications of the following NYSE Liffe contracts.

- Short-term interest rate (STIR) futures.
- Long Gilt futures.
- FTSE 100 futures.

20.1.7 **Explain** the possible uses of the above contracts in an investment management context.

20.1.8 **Understand** the concept of index arbitrage.

20.1.9 **Distinguish** between American style and European style options.

20.1.10 **Explain** time value and intrinsic value relating to an option premium.

20.1.11 **Identify** when an option is in-the-money, out-of-the-money, or at-the-money.

20.1.12 **Calculate** the time value of an option given the premium, strike price and current market value.

20.1.13 **Explain** the factors that determine the premium of an option.

20.1.14 **Calculate** the maximum profit, maximum loss and the motivation behind the following option strategies.

- Long and short call.
- Long and short put.
- Long and short straddle.
- Long and short strangle.
- Long and short butterfly.
- Covered call and protective put.

20.1.15 **Explain the use of futures and options in hedging an equity portfolio.**

20.1.16 **Calculate the number of FTSE 100** futures or options contracts required to hedge a portfolio with a specified beta value.

20.2 Selling short, stock lending and contracts for differences (swaps)

20.2.1 **Explain the mechanics and uses of short selling.**

20.2.2 **Explain the role of stock lending in the markets, and the benefits to the participants.**

20.2.3 **Explain** the nature of contracts for differences.

20.2.4 **Explain the nature of, and motivations behind**

- Interest rate swaps.
- Currency swaps.
- Equity swaps.
- Inflation swaps.

20.3 Convertibles and warrants

20.3.1 **Explain** the nature of convertible bonds and convertible preference shares.

20.3.2 **Calculate** a conversion price, value and premium.

20.3.3 **Explain** the component parts of the valuation of a convertible bond, all namely

- straight land value.
- call option value.
- dilution effect.
- conversion ratio.

20.3.4 **Define a warrant.**

20.3.5 **Distinguish between a warrant and a call option.**

20.3.6 **Explain the key features of covered warrants.**

20.4 Credit derivatives

20.4.1 **Explain** the purpose, mechanics and implications of a credit default swap (CDS).

20.4.2 **Explain** the risks to the financial system resulting from the proliferation of credit derivatives.

1 Derivatives

1.1 Introduction

In the minds of the general public, and indeed those of many people involved in the financial services industry, derivative products such as futures and options, warrants and swaps are thought of as very complicated. They are also thought of as having little to do with the real world. Television coverage, showing pictures of young traders in brightly coloured jackets shouting at each other in an apparent frenzy, makes it difficult to imagine that what they are engaged in may be of enormous value to the smooth functioning of the economy.

At the heart of these products is the concept of deferred delivery. The instruments allow you, albeit in slightly different ways, to agree **today** the price at which you will buy or sell an asset at some time in the future. This is unlike normal everyday transactions. When we go to a supermarket, we pay our money and take immediate delivery of our goods. Why would someone wish to agree today a price for delivery at some time in the future? The answer is **certainty**.

Imagine a farmer growing a crop of wheat. To grow such a crop costs money; money for seed, labour, fertiliser and so on. All this expenditure takes place with no certainty that, when the crop is eventually harvested, the price at which the wheat is sold will cover these costs. This is obviously a risky thing to do and many farmers are unwilling to take on this burden. How can this uncertainty be avoided?

By using derivatives, the farmer is able to agree **today** a price at which the crop will ultimately be sold, in maybe four or six months' time. This enables the farmer to achieve a minimum sale price for his crop. He is no longer subject to fluctuations in wheat prices. He knows what price his wheat will bring and can thus plan his business accordingly.

From their origins in the agricultural world, derivative products have become available on a wide range of other assets, from metals and crude oil to bonds and equities. To understand these instruments properly requires some application. There is much terminology to master, and definitions to be understood but, essentially, they are really quite simple. They are products that allow you to fix today the price at which assets may be bought or sold at a future date.

1.2 Advantages of derivatives

Derivatives allow investors to very speedily and efficiently take a view on the value of an asset such as a bond, equity, commodity or property, or on some other financial measure such as interest rates and even on other measures such as weather. The advantages of dealing in derivatives rather than the underlying asset or measure are

- Transactions can be executed more rapidly – especially for the less liquid assets such as property
- Contracts are more liquid than the underlying asset – again especially for the less liquid assets such as property
- Transaction costs tend to be much lower – for example there is no stamp duty on a derivatives trade
- Investors can easily establish a short position allowing them to gain if the asset price falls
- Exposure can be gained at a lower cost – the up-front cost of a derivative is always much lower than the cost of the asset.

2 Futures

Learning objectives	20.1.1 **Distinguish** between forwards, futures and options. 20.1.2 **Explain** the nature, trading and settlement of exchange traded derivatives.

2.1 Definition of a future

A future is an agreement to buy or sell a standard quantity of a specified asset on a fixed future date at a price agreed today.

There are two parties to a futures contract, a buyer and a seller whose obligations are as follows.

- The buyer of a future enters into an **obligation** to buy on a specified date.
- The seller of a future is under an **obligation** to sell on a future date.

These obligations relate to a **standard quantity** of a **specified** asset on a **fixed future date** at a **price agreed today**.

2.1.1 Standard quantity

Exchange-traded futures are traded in standardised parcels known as **contracts**.

For example, a futures contract on a gilt is to be for **£100,000 nominal of a 4% gilt**, or an interest rate future might be for £0.5m nominal value. The purpose of this standardisation is that buyers and sellers are clear about the quantity that will be delivered. If you sold one gilt future, you would know that you were obligated to sell £100,000 nominal of gilts.

Futures are only traded in whole numbers of contracts. So, if you wished to buy £200,000 nominal of gilts, you would buy two gilt futures.

2.1.2 Specified asset

Imagine that you entered into a futures contract on a car. Let us say you buy a car futures contract that gives you the obligation to buy a car at a fixed price of £15,000, with delivery taking place in December.

It is obvious that something very important is missing from the contract – namely any detail about what type of car you are to buy. Most of us would be happy to pay £15,000 for a Porsche, but would be rather less happy if all our £15,000 bought was a Gee Whiz.

All futures contracts are governed by their **contract specifications**. These legal documents set out in great detail the size of each contract, when delivery is to take place, and what exactly is to be delivered.

2.1.3 Fixed futures date

The delivery of futures contracts takes place on a specified date(s) known as **delivery day(s)**. This is when buyers exchange money for goods with sellers. Futures have finite lifespans so that, once the **last trading day** is past, it is impossible to trade the futures for that date.

At any one time, a range of delivery months may be traded (for example most NYSE Liffe contracts have **March**, **June**, **September** and **December** delivery months) and as one delivery day passes, a new date is introduced.

In many cases, a physical delivery does not actually occur on the delivery day. Rather, the exchange calculates how much has been lost, or gained, by the parties to a futures contract. It is only this monetary gain or loss that changes hands, not the underlying asset. The **NYSE Liffe gilt future** is an example of a **physically settled contract**, whereas the FTSE 100 Index future is **cash settled**.

2.1.4 Price agreed today

The final phrase in the definition is the most important of all. The reason why so many people, from farmers to fund managers, like using futures is, as was explained in the introduction to this chapter, that they introduce certainty.

Imagine a farmer growing a crop of wheat. In the absence of a futures market, he has no idea whether he will make a profit or a loss when he plants the seeds in the ground. By the time he harvests his crop, the price of wheat may be so low that he will not be able to cover his costs. However, with a futures contract, he can fix a price for his wheat many months before harvest. If, six months before the harvest, he sells a wheat future, he enters into an obligation to sell wheat at that price on the stipulated delivery day. In other words, he knows what price his goods will fetch.

You might think that this is all well and good, but what happens if there is a drought or a frost that makes it impossible for the farmer to deliver his wheat?

Futures can be traded, so although the contract obligates the buyer to buy and the seller to sell, these obligations can be **offset** (closed out) by undertaking an equal and opposite trade in the market.

Example

Let us suppose a farmer has sold 1 September wheat future at £120 per tonne. If, subsequently, the farmer decides he does not wish to sell his wheat, but would prefer to use the grain to feed his cattle, he simply buys 1 September future at the then prevailing price. His original sold position is now offset by a bought position, leaving him with no outstanding delivery obligations.

This offsetting is common in future markets; very few contracts run through to delivery.

2.1.5 Futures v Forwards

A **forward** is an agreement to buy or sell a specified quantity of a specified asset on a specified future date at a price agreed today.

From the above definition you can see they have many of the same characteristics as futures. However, there are some key differences that can best be summarised in the following table.

Attribute	Futures	Forward Contracts
Traded	Exchange traded	OTC
Quality and Quantity	Standardised by the exchange for all products	Specified in the contract
Delivery Dates	Standard fixed dates	Specified in the contract
Liquidity/Ability to Close Out	Generally good liquidity/easy to close out	May be limited
Counterparty Risk	None due to the workings of the clearing and settlement system	Default risk exists
Costs/Margin	Relatively low initial costs (margin)	Costs specifically agreed, may be high. Margin not normally required
Regulation	Significant regulation and investor protection	Less regulated

2.2 Using futures

Learning objective

20.1.3 Understand the motive for using a futures contract rather than a trade in the underlying asset

All sorts of people use futures. Some may use them to reduce risk, others to seek high returns – and for this, they must be willing to take high risks. Futures markets are, in fact, wholesale markets in risk – markets in which risks are transferred from the cautious to those with more adventurous (or reckless) spirits. The users fall into one of three categories; the **hedger**, the **speculator** and the **arbitrageur** whose motivations are as follows.

- **Hedger** – someone seeking to reduce risk.
- **Speculator** – a risk-taker seeking large profits.
- **Arbitrageur** – seeks riskless profits from exploiting market inefficiencies (mispricing).

In this section, we will look at the first two types of user, starting with the speculator.

2.2.1 The speculator – Buying a future or forward

Introduction

A transaction in which a future is purchased to open a position is known as a **long futures position**. Thus, the purchase of the oil future would be described as **going long of the future** or simply **long**.

The purpose of undertaking such a transaction is to open the investor to the risks and rewards of ownership of the underlying asset by an alternative route.

Example

On 1 May, a speculator thinks that the situation in the Middle East is becoming more dangerous and that war is imminent. If war takes place, he would expect oil supplies to become restricted and the price of oil to rise.

The current cash price of oil is $119.00 per barrel, and the futures price is $120.50. The speculator does not have the facilities to store the oil at present.

How can he use the futures market to buy in anticipation of this price rise, and what will his position be if the price rise does occur on 21 May (cash price becoming $135, futures price being $130)?

Solution

Action 1 May: Buy 1 July oil future at $120.50

Since he does not have the facilities to store the oil, he cannot use the cash market, hence the speculator could buy 1 July oil future at $120.50 per barrel. Thus, he is now obliged to buy one contract (here 1,000 barrels) to be delivered on 1 July.

The investor's exposure will now appear as follows.

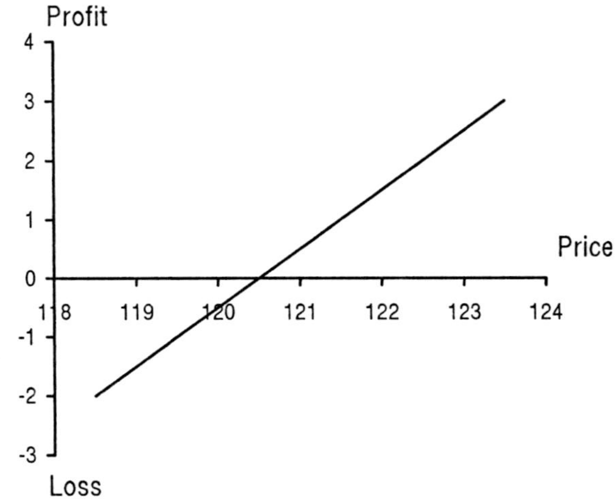

If the price remains at the current level of $120.50 the investor will simply break even. If, however, prices rise (as he anticipates) he will make a profit, though if prices fall he will incur a loss.

Action 21 May: Sell 1 July oil future at $130

Following the price rise, our speculator can now sell this contract at $130.00 per barrel, realising a profit of $9.50 per barrel or $9,500.

The reason the speculator has made a profit is that the futures market has risen in response to a rise in the cash market price of oil. Generally, futures prices can be expected to move at substantially the same rate and the same extent as cash market prices. This is a far from trivial observation. The cash market and the futures market in this example have both risen: the cash market from $119 to $135 – an increase of $16 per barrel; and the futures market from $120.50 to $130.00 – a rise of $9.50.

Summary of position

Risk	Almost unlimited – The maximum loss would occur if the future fell to zero. For our oil speculator, this would be if the July future fell from $120.50 to 0.
Reward	Unlimited – As the futures price could rise to infinity, the profit is potentially unlimited.

2.2.2 The speculator – Selling a future or forward

Introduction

A transaction in which a future is sold to open a position is known as a **short futures position**. Thus, the sale of the oil future would be described as **going short of the future** or simply **short**.

The purpose of undertaking such a transaction is to open the investor to the opposite risks and rewards of ownership of the underlying asset.

Example

On 1 July, a speculator feels that the oil market is becoming oversupplied and that oil prices will fall. On that date, the September futures contract is trading at $122.00 per barrel.

How can the speculator use the futures market to profit from this situation and what will be his profit if the price fall does occur on 14 July, when the futures price has fallen to $120.00 per barrel?

Solution

If a speculator thinks that an asset price will fall, he will seek to make a profit by selling the future at the currently high price and subsequently buying it back at a low price. This is not an activity commonly undertaken in the cash markets and therefore needs a little explanation.

There are two ways of making profits.

- Buy at a low price and sell at a high price. For example, we may buy a house at £80,000 and sell it at £100,000 making a £20,000 profit.
- In futures markets, it is equally easy to sell something at a high price and buy it back at a low price. If you thought the property market was going to fall, you could sell a house at £100,000 and buy it back at £80,000 again realising a £20,000 profit.

In the actual property market, it is not easy to go **short** of a house, but in the futures market, in which deliveries are at some future date, it is straightforward.

Action 1 July: Sell 1 September Oil Future at $122

The speculator is committing himself to delivering an asset he does not own on 1 September.

The investor's exposure will now appear as follows.

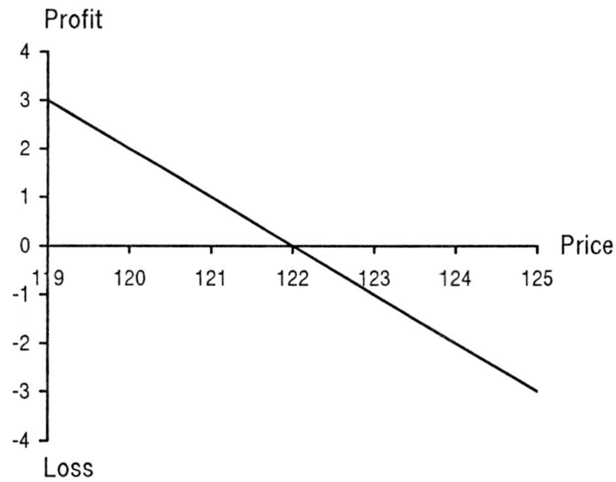

If the price remains at the current level of $122 the investor will simply break even. If, however, prices fall (as he anticipates) he will make a profit, though if prices rise he will incur a loss.

Action 14 July: Buy 1 September Oil Future at $120.00

By 14 July, the future price has fallen and the speculator **buys back** his short futures position, thus extinguishing any delivery obligations. The profit can be calculated again as $2.00 per barrel or $2,000 in total.

Summary of position

Risk	Unlimited.
Reward	Limited, but large. The future can only fall to zero.

2.2.3 The hedger – Protecting against a fall

Learning objective **20.1.15 Explain the use of futures and options in hedging an equity portfolio.**

Speculators use futures to take on risks in the hope of large profits. Hedgers use futures to reduce the risk of existing cash market positions. They are motivated by a need for certainty and security.

Let us think about the position of an oil producer. The producer's profitability will be determined largely by the price of crude oil. When times are good, and the demand for oil is high, he will make good profits. However, if oil prices fall, he may find that the market price for oil is so low that the price does not cover the costs of extracting the oil from the ground. It is in helping people such as this that futures have their most important application.

The following graph shows the oil producer's exposure to the price of oil.

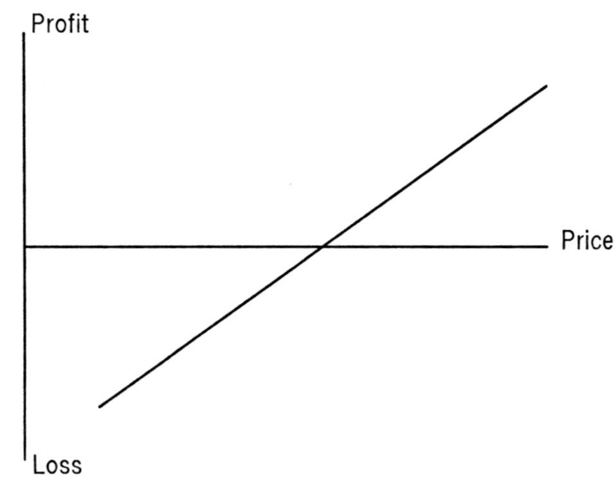

This shows that if prices go up, so do profits; if the price falls below a certain level, losses will emerge. This position is described as a **long position**.

How can the risk from a fall in price be reduced?

This can be done by selling futures and thereby entering into a contract that will obligate the futures seller to deliver oil at some time in the future at a price agreed today.

Through this mechanism, the oil producer can establish a sale price for his, say, July production of oil some time in advance, without having to wait until July when the price may be much lower. When futures are sold to hedge a long cash market position, it is known as a **short hedge**.

The theory of futures **hedging** is based on the future's position, producing profits or losses to offset the losses or profits in the cash market.

Example

An oil producer will have 100,000 barrels of crude oil available for delivery in July. He is nervous about the price of oil and expects it to fall sharply. On 1 May, the cash market price of oil is $122 a barrel, and the July future is trading at $123.

How can he use the futures market to hedge his position and minimise the risk of owning the asset (note, one contract is 1,000 barrels), and what will his position be if by 15 June the price has fallen to $118 in the cash market and $119 in the futures market?

Solution

Action 1 May: Sell 100 July oil futures at $123

(100 because each contract represents 1,000 barrels, and the producer is hedging 100,000 barrels.)

The oil producer is now long in the physical market (that is, he has 100,000 barrels for July delivery). He is also short 100,000 barrels in the futures market.

Action 15 June: Buy 100 July oil futures at $119

The profit from the futures trade should, if we have constructed the hedge properly, compensate the producer for the fall in oil prices. Let us see if this is true by first calculating the futures profit and then calculating the oil market loss.

Futures Profit

Profit per barrel = $4.00 per barrel ($123.00 – $119.00)
Total profit = $400,000 ($4.00 × 100,000 barrels)

Cash Market Loss

Loss per barrel = $4.00 per barrel ($118.00 – $122.00)
Total loss = $400,000 ($4.00 × 100,000 barrels)

As can be seen, the profit and loss net each other out, demonstrating that the fall in oil prices did not hurt the producer.

It can be shown on a graph as follows.

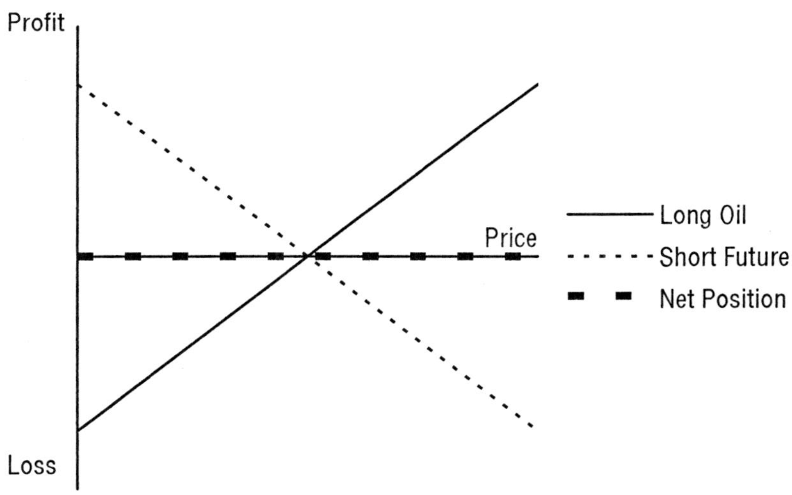

Whether the price of oil goes up or down, the producer need not worry as he has, by selling futures, **locked in** a sale price for his oil.

The numbers in this example are slightly unrealistic, as there is a perfect offset between cash and futures markets. In the real world, futures do not always move precisely in line with the cash market. This point will be examined in more detail later on.

In the example above, we have seen how futures can be used to protect the oil producer against a price fall with a short hedge.

Short hedge: Protects against price fall.

2.2.4 The hedger – Protecting against a rise

The scenario that we are considering here is that an investor wishes to acquire an asset at some time in the future when cash is available, but is concerned that the current price may rise making the asset unaffordable. He therefore wishes to protect against this price rise.

Example

A chemical company, whose principal raw material is crude oil, is becoming nervous about a rise in oil prices.

The current cash price of crude oil is $118.00, and the November future trades at $118.50 per barrel.

How can the company use the futures market to hedge against any price rise and what will their position be if the cash price rises to $124.00 and the futures price to $124.50 on 10 October?

Solution

To protect itself against the possibility of a rise, the company could agree today the price it will pay for oil to be delivered in November. To guarantee the purchase price, all the company need do is buy or go long in the futures contract.

Action 20 September: Buy 10 November oil futures at $118.50

(To hedge its requirement for 10,000 barrels)

Action 10 October: Sell 10 November oil futures at $124.50

Has the hedge worked?

Cash market loss

To find out, let us see how the price rise would have affected the cost of purchasing the physical oil.

	£
Cash price on 10 October	124.00
Cash price on 20 September	118.00
Cost increase per barrel	6.00

For the quantity required by the chemical manufacturer (10,000 barrels), this movement would have increased its costs by $60,000 ($6 × 10,000).

This increased cost should, in whole or in part, be offset by the futures profit.

Futures profit

	£
Futures price on 10 October	124.50
Futures price on 20 September	118.50
Futures profit per barrel	6.00

Hence, the total profit on the futures contract is $60,000, which covers the price increase.

Thus, whilst the physical oil will now cost more to acquire, the extra cost of purchase will in fact be covered by the futures profit.

	£
Cash price of 10,000 barrels of oil at 10 October	240,000
Less futures profit	(60,000)
Net cost	180,000

This equates to $118 per barrel, the cash price on 20 September.

This is an example of a long hedge, which protects against a rise.

Long hedge: Protects against a rise.

2.2.5 Summary

In short hedges, you sell futures to protect an existing holding.

In long hedges, you buy futures to protect an anticipated holding.

2.3 Some specific contracts and their uses

Learning objectives

20.1.6 Know the contract specifications of the following NYSE Liffe contracts: Short-term interest rate (STIR) futures; Long Gilt futures and FTSE 100 futures.

20.1.7 Explain the possible uses of the above contracts in an investment management context.

2.3.1 Introduction

In order to understand the use of futures to a fund manager we need to be familiar with contracts he may wish to use, how he may use them and why. We consider three futures contracts, in particular

- FTSE 100 Index Future.
- Three-Month Sterling Future.
- UK Gilt Future.

One bit of terminology we will introduce here in relation to futures is the **tick**. There are two aspects to this.

- The **tick size** is the smallest permitted quote movement on one contract.
- The **tick value** is the change in the value of one contract if there is a one-tick change in the quote.

These two factors enable us to calculate our futures dealing profit or loss by using

Formula to learn

Profit = Quote change in ticks × Tick value × Number of contracts

When we look at the Three-Month Sterling Futures contract in particular, it will be most convenient to calculate the profit this way.

2.3.2 FTSE 100 Index Future

Purpose and characteristics

The FTSE 100 Index future fixes the price at which the underlying index may be bought or sold at a specific future date.

The general characteristics of the contract are as follows.

Unit of trade

Formula to learn

Unit of trade = Index value × £10

That is, a contract can be valued by multiplying the index value by £10. If, for example, the index stood at 6,000, then one contract would have a value of 6,000 × £10 = £60,000.

What this means is that

- A speculator may gain £60,000 of exposure to the market by buying a contract.
- A hedger who already holds shares could use the contract to hedge his exposure to £60,000 of those shares.

Delivery

This contract is **cash settled**. That is, rather than the two parties exchanging the underlying asset and the pre-agreed price at the delivery date, they simply settle up by the payment from one to the other of the difference in value.

Quotation

The quote given is in index points.

Tick

The tick size, the smallest permitted quote movement, is 0.5 index points, which corresponds to a tick value of £5.00 (0.5 × £10).

Uses

As we indicated above, we may use this contract to gain exposure to, or hedge exposure against, the index, i.e. the stock market in general.

Example

We are managing a £20m pension fund portfolio and we believe that the market is about to fall. The index and the future currently stand at 6,000.

The alternatives that we have are as follows.

- Sell the portfolio and move into cash/bonds – this will avoid the market fall, but will clearly incur massive dealing costs.
- Set up a short hedge using the futures contract.

Short hedge

The future is quoted at 6,000, hence each contract will hedge £60,000 (6,000 × £10) of our exposure. To hedge the full portfolio, we will therefore need 333$^1/_3$ contracts (£20m ÷ £60,000). However, we can only deal in whole contracts, therefore we will sell 333 contracts (the closest whole number).

Let us now consider what our position is if the market (and the futures contract) fall 200 points.

Cash position

	£
Old portfolio value	20,000,000
New portfolio value = £20m × $\frac{5,800}{6,000}$	19,333,333
Loss	(666,667)

Futures position

	Points
Sold index at	6,000
Bought index to close position at	5,800
Gain	200 = 400 ticks

Hence, the total profit on our 333 contracts will be

Profit = Ticks × Tick value × Number of contracts
= 400 × £5.00 × 333 = £666,000

As we can see, our futures profit almost exactly cancels the loss on the portfolio and hence represents a good hedging strategy.

Hedge ratio

Learning objective

20.1.16 Calculate the number of FTSE 100 futures or options contracts required to hedge a portfolio with a specified beta value.

One assumption we have made here is that our portfolio is as volatile as the index, i.e. it has $\beta = 1$. If this is not the case, then we may need to sell more or less contracts to achieve the hedge. The important determinant is the relative volatility.

By definition, the futures contract has a $\beta = 1$. If the portfolio has a $\beta = 1.2$, then a 1% change in the index will cause a 1% change in the value of a future but a 1.2% change in the portfolio value. We will therefore need 1.2 times as many futures contracts to provide sufficient profit to cancel any losses suffered in the portfolio. When we hedge with futures, we should use

$$\text{Number of contracts} = \frac{\text{Portfolio value}}{\text{Futures value}^{*}} \times \beta$$

* To determine the futures value for the denominator it is necessary to consider the period for which the hedge is being established. If the hedge is being established for an anticipated almost immediate change in price then we would use

Futures value = Futures quote × £10

Alternatively, if a hedge is being established that will be maintained to the maturity date of the contract then we should use

Futures value = Cash market quote × £10

The reason for this difference is due to futures pricing and basis (covered later). For an immediate change in price the basis on the future will be largely unaltered and the change in value of the futures position will be based on the change in the futures quote. When hedging to the futures maturity date, however, we will necessarily experience convergence – the fact that the futures price converges to the cash price at the delivery date. Since we know the futures price will be equal to the cash price at delivery we must use this cash price as the basis.

Please note that this is a rather technical and very subtle point that is unlikely to be a key feature in an exam question, however it has been introduced to deal with the locked-in value issue below. For the exam, if you are asked to calculate the number of contracts required to hedge a position, use the first calculation only (Futures quote × £10) and select the closest answer.

Example

A fund manager wishes to hedge a portfolio with a value of £30m and a beta of 1.27. How many FTSE 100 futures contracts will be required to hedge (assuming the cash index is at 4000 and the future is at 4050)?

Solution

Hedging against an immediate price movement – Normal examination calculation

Futures value = Futures quote × £10

$$\text{Number at contracts} = \frac{£30\text{m}}{(4050 \times £10)} \times 1.27 = 940.74$$

To hedge, sell 941 contracts.

Hedging to maturity

Futures value = Cash market quote × £10

$$\text{Number of contracts} = \frac{£30\text{m}}{(4000 \times £10)} \times 1.27 = 952.5$$

To hedge to maturity sell 953 contracts

Note that beta hedging applies equally to hedging a portfolio with index options.

Hedge efficiency

The futures contracts utilised in a hedge will not necessarily move exactly in parallel with the portfolio being hedged.

The following ratio could be utilised to assess the efficiency of a futures hedge.

Formula to learn

$$\%\ \text{Hedge efficiency} = \frac{\text{Absolute loss/gain on futures}}{\text{Absolute gain/loss on cash market}}$$

A value of 100% indicates a perfect hedge. A value of less than or greater than 100% indicates that a level of residual exposure remains.

Locked-in value

If a hedge has been established, the question may arise as to what will be the value of the hedged position if we hold the contract to maturity – what is the locked-in value of the hedged portfolio?

This can be most easily established by assuming that the underlying index does not change in which case

- The assets in the portfolio will have the same value as at present
- The futures price will have converged to the asset price generating a corresponding gain or loss

In determining the locked-in value assume that fractions of contracts can be purchased, allowing a perfect hedge to be established.

Example

Determine the locked-in value for the above £30m fund assuming the index itself is standing at 4000 when the hedge is established.

Solution

Futures position

Assuming the index stays at 4000

	Points	
Sold index at	4050	
Bought index to close at maturity at	4000	
Gain	50	= 100 ticks

Hence the total profit on 952.5 contracts will be

Profit = Ticks × Tick value × Number of contracts

100 × £5.00 × 952.5 = £476,250

Portfolio position

Assuming the index stays at 4000 we have

	£
Portfolio value	30,000,000
Futures gain	476,250
Locked-in value	30,476,250

This locked-in value

- assumes the contract is held to maturity
- assumes the beta of the portfolio remains stable
- ignores the fact that we have needed to round the number of contracts and so do not, in fact, have a perfect hedge
- ignores any income that the assets may have generated and that may be reinvested

When viewed in this way we can see that the locked in value is the portfolio value plus the futures gain on a hedge to maturity where the cash index will be used as the basis. These ideas can be combined together into a single formula as follows

$$\text{Locked-in value} = \text{Portfolio value} \times \left(1 + \left(\frac{\text{Futures quote} - \text{Cash quote}}{\text{Cash quote}} \times \beta\right)\right)$$

Solution

Based on the above example this formula gives

$$\text{Locked-in value} = £30\text{m} \times \left(1 + \left(\frac{4050 - 4000}{4000} \times 1.27\right)\right)$$

$$= £30\text{m} \times (1 + (0.0125 \times 1.27))$$

$$= £30\text{m} \times (1 + 0.015875) = £30{,}476{,}250$$

as above.

For exam purposes either approach may be used.

2.3.3 Three-month sterling future

Purpose and characteristics

The purpose of the three-month sterling contract is to provide a means to gain or hedge interest rate exposure for a period of three months from a given future date.

The general characteristics of the contract are as follows.

Unit of trade

The unit of trade = £500,000, i.e. the contract measures the effects on the total interest costs of interest rate changes on a notional borrowing of £500,000 for three months.

Note. The £500,000 does not change hands, just the interest effect.

Delivery

This contract is **cash settled**, that is the two parties simply settle up by the payment from one to the other of the difference in value between the interest bill for three months at the rate agreed when the contract was traded and the actual rate that arises.

Quotation

Formula to learn

Quotation = 100 – Rate of interest

where the rate of interest is the **forward rate** for the three months from the delivery date. Hence, if three-month forward rates from the delivery date are 8%, the contract will be quoted at 92 (100 – 8).

Considering more interest rates we could find.

Implied Interest Rate	Futures Quote
7%	93.00
8%	92.00
9%	91.00
10%	90.00

This method of quotation means that as interest rates rise, futures prices fall, and vice versa. This is done so that short-term interest rate futures follow the normal **inverse relationship** that is found in bond markets.

Tick

The tick size, the smallest permitted quote movement, is 0.01, i.e. one basis point, which corresponds to a tick value of £12.50 (£500,000 × 0.01% × $\frac{3}{12}$).

Uses

As we indicated above, we may use this contract to gain exposure to, or hedge exposure against, interest rate movements.

Example

If a speculator believes interest rates will, say, rise, then he will know that this contract will fall in value. He could then open his position by selling now at a high price and buying to close his position later, realising a profit if his view turns out to be correct.

Three-month forward rates from June are currently quoted as 8.26%. The speculator sells 107 contracts now (January) and closes out his position in May when the three-month forward rates from June have moved to 9.14%. What gain does he make?

Solution

	Forward Rate (%)	Quote
Sell in January	8.26	91.74
Buy in May	9.14	90.86
		0.88 = 88 ticks

Hence, the total profit on the 107 contracts will be

Profit = Ticks × Tick value × Number of contracts
= 88 × £12.50 × 107 = £117,700

Example

An investor wants to borrow £5m for three months from June, but is worried that interest rates will rise from their current levels. The forward rate for three months from June is currently quoted as 7.23%.

What action should the borrower take now?

If the rate has risen to 8.8% by June, what position will he be in?

Solution

Action now

If the borrower is correct that interest rates are rising, then he will suffer a higher interest burden than at present. He therefore needs a futures position that will yield profits when interest rates rise to offset this loss. Hence, as for our speculator above, he should sell futures contracts, and in particular sell ten contracts, since each one will hedge £500,000 of the loan.

Final position

Cash position

	£
Interest actually paid on loan £5m × 8.80% × $^3/_{12}$	110,000
Interest due at original rate £5m × 7.23% × $^3/_{12}$	90,375
Extra interest suffered	19,625

Futures position

	Forward Rate (%)	Quote
Sell in January	7.23	92.77
Buy in June	8.80	91.20
		1.57 = 157 ticks

Hence, the total profit on the 10 contracts will be

Profit = Ticks × Tick value × Number of contracts
= 157 × £12.50 × 10 = £19,625

and will exactly offset the extra interest suffered.

In conclusion we have

Borrowers sell futures to hedge.

Lenders or depositors of money suffer if rates fall, but gain if rates rise. Thus, to fix their deposit rates they buy futures.

Depositors buy futures to hedge.

2.3.4 UK Gilt future

Purpose and characteristics

The purpose of UK Gilt futures contract is to provide a means to gain or hedge exposure to UK gilts. It can be considered as similar to the FTSE Index futures in that it can be used in the management of bond funds to hedge or gain exposure. It effectively represents a bond index contract.

The general characteristics of the contract are as follows.

Unit of trade

The unit of trade = £100,000 nominal of a notional 4% gilt, i.e. gilts with a nominal value of £100,000.

Delivery

This contract is **physically settled**, that is the seller of the future must deliver gilts and the buyer must pay the pre-agreed price. Clearly, however, there is a problem here with the contract being based on a notional gilt. To overcome this difficulty the exchange specify a range of eligible deliverable gilts for each delivery date that the seller may choose to satisfy delivery, and the seller decides which gilts he delivers. The decision is always to deliver whichever is cheapest at the delivery date, referred to as the cheapest to deliver (CTD).

2.4 Contract specification summary

Futures are exchange-traded contracts and are standardised. The syllabus requires you to be aware of the following contracts, some of which have been mentioned in our previous examples.

FTSE 100 Index futures

Unit of Trading	Contract valued at £10 per index point
Quotation	Index points and half index points
Minimum Price Movement (Tick Value)	0.5 point (£5.00)
Settlement	**Cash**

Long gilt future

Contract Size	4% coupon, 10 years to average maturity £100,000 nominal value (NV)
Quotation	Per £100 NV
Tick Size and Value	Tick size = 0.01; $\frac{1}{100^{th}}$ of a point Tick value = £10
Settlement	**Physical**

Three-month (short) sterling interest rate future

Unit of Trading	£500,000
Quotation	100.00 minus rate of interest
Minimum Price Movement (Tick Size & Value)	Tick size = 0.01% = 1 basis point Tick value = £12.50
Settlement	**Cash**

2.5 Futures pricing

Learning objectives

20.1.4 Explain the nature of, and reasoning behind, a contango and backwardation market.

20.1.5 Define the 'basis' of a futures contract.

Basis is the term used to describe the numerical difference between a cash price and a futures price. Basis is normally quoted as the futures price minus the cash price.

Formula to learn

Basis = Futures Price – Cash Price

Let us look at the following example.

Cash price = £120

Price of July future = £125

The basis is therefore

£125 – £120 = £5

Although cash and futures prices generally move broadly in line with one another, the basis is not constant. During some periods, cash prices move faster than futures. At other times, futures outpace the cash market. For this reason, futures hedges are sometimes less than perfect.

This movement in basis is brought about by a variety of factors. Most important is the relationship between supply and demand. Under normal conditions, futures prices, at least those of physical commodities, are higher than cash prices. Where this occurs, the market is said to be in **contango**.

However, this normal or contango situation in which futures prices are higher than cash prices can be radically altered if there is some short-term lack of supply. If, for example there is very little zinc available for delivery, the price demanded for what little is available can be very high indeed. Markets in which futures prices are lower than cash prices are said to be in **backwardation**. The terms 'contango' and 'backwardation' are not used in all markets. Sometimes, when futures are higher than cash prices, the market is said to be at a **premium**; when futures are lower than cash, it is said to be at a **discount**.

A Contango Market

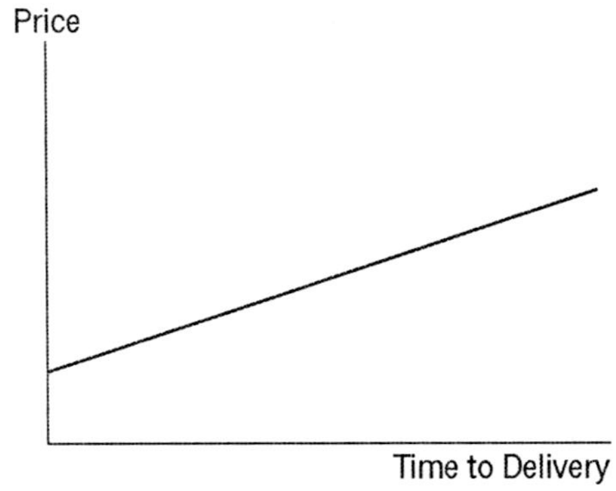

A Backwardation Market

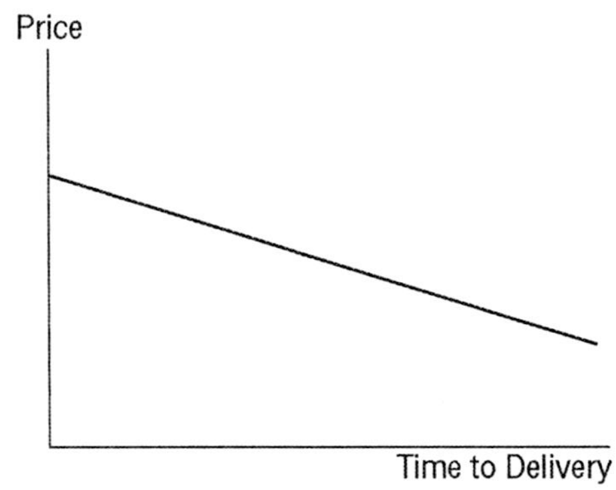

2.6 Arbitrage and index arbitrage

Learning objectives

20.1.2 Explain the nature, trading and settlement of exchange traded derivatives.

20.1.8 Understand the concept of index arbitrage.

It is unnecessary for our purposes to discuss how, theoretically, futures prices are arrived at. However, the link between cash markets and futures markets is ensured by arbitrage activity. An arbitrageur is someone who looks to exploit pricing anomalies between markets.

We have just noted that the price of a future is related to (derived from) the price of an underlying asset. If a future trade is below its theoretical or fair value, it will be bought driving its price up, whilst if it trades above its fair value, it will be sold driving its price down. In this way, the cash and futures markets are tied together. This activity can be undertaken on an individual stock or on an index (index arbitrage)

A final point: there is only one time when a future's price must be the same as the cash price. This happens on the final day of a future's life when the future itself becomes a contract for immediate delivery and, consequently, must have the same price as the cash market.

2.7 Futures settlement

The London derivative markets are cleared by **LCH.Clearnet** (previously known as the **London Clearing House (LCH)**) that, under FSMA 2000, is a Recognised Clearing House (RCH). LCH.Clearnet is owned by the exchanges which clear through it and their members.

Amongst the roles fulfilled by the clearing house are those of registrar and guarantor.

Clearing houses act as registrars or bookkeepers to the market place by recording details of all matched trades.

At the moment of registration, an important change in the legal character of all derivative contracts takes place. Prior to registration the contracts are bilateral undertakings between the buyer and seller with the attendant risk of counterparty default. However, from the instant of registration, the clearing house becomes the buyer to every seller and the seller to every buyer and thus the counterparty to every contract. This legal change is known as **novation** and eliminates counterparty risk for the original counterparties.

Aside from acting as registrar, the clearing house also acts as guarantor. This is a natural follow-on from novation and simply means that, even if the original counterparty were to go into liquidation or default, the clearing house will honour all contractual obligations. The existence of the guarantee is fundamental to maintaining confidence in the markets.

2.8 Margin on futures

To avoid ever having to honour its guarantee, LCH.Clearnet calls sureties from those with futures positions; this is called margin. LCH.Clearnet calls two types of margin on those with either long or short futures positions.

On the opening of a position, an **initial** margin is called. This margin relates to the worst probable one-day loss.

Secondly, a **variation** margin is calculated on a daily basis. The variation margin represents the profit/loss on that trading day. The process by which positions are revalued each day is known as **marking to market**. Variation margin thus turns 'paper' profits and losses into cash flows.

Variation margins that are due are paid in **cash** to the clearing house the following morning, each day. Initial margins can be supplied in cash or with other approved non-cash assets.

Example

An investor sells 10 FTSE futures contracts at 4000.

His initial margin requirement would be

Initial margin specified × No. of contracts per contract

= £3,000 × 10

= £30,000 initial margin

NB: The £30,000 per contract is a figure calculated by LCH.Clearnet. The amount can be varied at the discretion of the clearing house as market volatility changes.

Imagine that, by the end of the trading day, the future has moved up to 4010. The short position will show a loss of

(The tick size is 0.5, value is £5.00)

Ticks	×	**Tick value**	×	**No. of contracts**
20	×	5.00	×	10

= £1,000 variation margin loss

The variation margin will be paid to the clearing house the next business day.

Remember, initial margin remains with the clearing house until the position is either offset or delivered.

3 Options

3.1 Definition

An **option** is a contract that confers the right, but not the obligation, to buy or sell an asset at a given price on or before a given date.

All the comments relating to standard quantities, specified assets, fixed future dates and price agreed today that we noted above for futures still apply.

3.2 Using options

3.2.1 The speculator – buying an option

Conventionally, a speculator anticipating a rise in the price of shares would simply buy the shares for immediate delivery and then hold them, hoping to sell them for a profit once the price rose. If we imagine that the price of a share is £6.00 and that the speculator buys just one share, the expenditure would be £6.00.

Another way of representing the hope of a rise in share prices would be to buy an option on a share – specifically, an option that would give the right, but not the obligation, to buy a share at a price of £6.00 for a period of three months. The purchase of this option would cost, say, 50p.

Remember that an option is a contract for a future delivery, so it would not be necessary to pay £6.00 in the first instance; the only money to be invested at this point is the 50p.

One advantage is immediately apparent. Options are cheaper than purchasing the underlying asset.

Example

If three months later, as expected, the price of the share has risen from £6.00 to £7.00, what will be the position of

- The speculator who bought the physical share?
- The speculator who bought the option on the share?

Solution

Physical Share

	£
Sale Price	7
Purchase Price	(6)
Profit	1

On an investment of £6.00, the investor has made a profit of £1.00 in just three months.

Option on Share

Now let us look at the profit for the options buyer. Three months ago, he entered into a contract that gave him the right, but not the obligation, to buy a share at £6.00. When purchased, that right cost just 50p per share. With the share now trading at £7.00, the right to buy at £6.00 must be worth at least £1.00 – the difference between the current price and the stated price in the contract.

This right to buy at £6.00 was purchased for 50p. With the market price at £7.00 at the end of the option's life, the option will now be worth £1.00, hence

	£
Sale Price	1.0
Purchase Price	(0.5)
Profit	0.5

On an investment of 50p, a 50p profit has been achieved. In percentage terms, this profit is spectacularly greater than on the conventional purchase and sale of the physical share.

One important thing to note is that options can be traded. It is not necessary for the underlying asset to be bought or sold. What more commonly occurs is that **options** are bought and sold. Thus, an option bought at 50p could be sold to the market at £1.00, realising a 100% profit with the investor never having an intention of buying the underlying asset.

At this stage, it is necessary to introduce some of the vocabulary used in the options market.

3.3 Terminology

Learning objective | **20.1.9 Distinguish** between American style and European style options.

In the definition of an option given earlier, an option was described as being the right, but not the obligation, to buy or sell. The right to buy and the right to sell are given different names.

- The right to buy is known as a **call option**.
- The right to sell is known as a **put option**.

The rights to buy (call) or sell (put) are held by the person buying the option who is known as the **holder**.

The person selling an option is known as a **writer** and is obliged to make (call) or take (put) delivery on or before the date on which an option comes to the end of its life. This date is known as its **expiry date**.

Options can also be differentiated by their exercise style. Most options are known as **American style**, which means that the holders can exercise at any time until the expiry date. A less common type of exercise is the **European style** exercise. In these types of options, the holder can only exercise on the expiry date. The exchange stipulates the type of exercise style in its contract specifications. Most option contracts traded on NYSE Liffe are American style.

The following diagram shows the relationship between holders and writers.

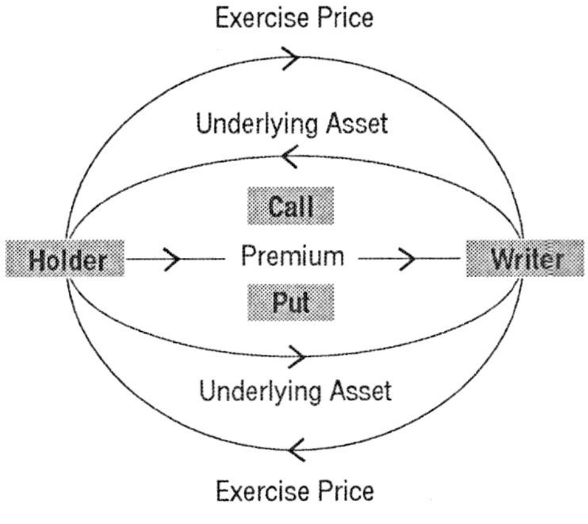

The first thing to understand is the flow of **premium**. Premium is the cost of an option. In our share example, the premium was 50p and this is paid by the holder and received by the writer.

In return for receiving premium, the writer agrees to fulfil the terms of the contract, which of course are different for calls and puts.

3.3.1 Call options

Call writers agree to deliver the asset underlying the contract if **called** upon to do so. When options holders wish to take up their rights under the contract, they are said to **exercise** the contract. For a call, this means that the writer must deliver the underlying asset for which he will receive the fixed amount of cash stipulated in the original contract.

Thus, for a share call option that gives the holder the right, but not the obligation, to buy at £6.00, this would mean that the writer would be required to deliver the share to the holder at £6.00. The option holder will only want to buy at £6.00 when it would be advantageous for him to do so, i.e. only when the real or market price is somewhat higher than £6.00. If the market price were less than £6.00, there would be no sense in paying more than the market price for the asset.

Call options writers run very considerable risks. In return for receiving the option's premium, they are committed to delivering the underlying asset at a fixed price. As the price of the asset could, in theory, rise infinitely, they could be forced to buy the underlying asset at a high price and to deliver it to the option holder at a much lower value. The price at which an options contract gives the right to buy (call) or sell (put) is known as the **exercise price** or **strike price**.

3.3.2 Put options

The dangers for put options writers are also substantial. The writer of a put is obligated to pay the exercise price for assets that are delivered to him. Put options are only exercised when it is advantageous for the holders to do so. This will be when they can use the option to sell their assets at a higher price than would be otherwise available in the market.

3.3.3 Summary

To summarise, options writers, in return for receiving a premium, run very large risks. This is similar to the role undertaken by insurance companies. For a relatively modest premium, they are willing to insure your house against fire, but if your house burns down, they will be faced with a claim for many thousands of pounds. The reasons why insurers and options writers enter into such contracts are that houses do not often burn down, and markets do not often rise or fall substantially.

If writers price options properly, they hope to make money in most instances. Options writing is not for the faint hearted, nor for those without substantial resources. This said, many conservative users do write options as part of strategies involving the holding of the underlying asset. Such strategies are **covered** (as opposed to **naked**) and much less risky. We discuss these later.

When investors buy or hold options, the risk is limited to the option's premium. If the market moves against them, they can simply decide not to exercise their options and sacrifice the premium. Remember, options holders have the right, **but not the obligation** to buy (call) or sell (put). If it does not make sense to buy or sell at the exercise price, the holder can decide to **abandon** the option.

3.4 Describing options

Another way in which options are described relates to their maturity. Options are instruments with limited life spans. The date on which an option comes to the end of its life is known as its **expiry date**. The expiry date is the last day on which the option may be exercised or traded. After this date, the option disappears and cannot be traded or exercised.

Below are quoted the prices for **call options** based on the shares of a fictitious company, XYZ plc. The options give an entitlement to buy (call) the company's shares. The **underlying price is 76**.

XYZ calls

Exercise Price	Expiry Date		
	Jan Premium	April Premium	July Premium
60	23	28	33
70	12	18	23
80	5	8	12

You will notice that there are a range of exercise prices and expiry dates available. Normally, you would expect there to be exercise prices available both below and above the underlying price.

There is also a range of expiry dates available – this allows investors a choice as to the maturity of their options. As one expiry date passes, a new expiry date is introduced, thus maintaining the choice of dates.

A similar range of exercise prices and expiry dates would be available in XYZ puts. The premiums quoted for calls and puts would, however, be different.

3.5 How much would you pay?

In our table, the premium that is quoted for the April 60 call is 28. To find out how much this would be, we must know two things: first, how the product is quoted and second, the contract size.

Options are traded on a wide variety of assets from currencies, bonds and shares to metals, oils and commodities. Each market has different conventions. For example, share option prices for UK companies are quoted in pence per share.

Governing the operation of options contracts are contract specifications that set out, amongst other things, rules specifying how they are quoted, expiry dates and when exercise prices are introduced. These documents are important because they enable everyone to understand the details of the contract. Exchange-traded options, such as futures contracts, are **standardised**, with the method of quotation and contract size being fixed. The only variable is the option's premium.

So what does a quote of 28 for the April 60 call mean? The premium for shares is quoted in pence, hence '28' means 28 pence per XYZ share.

To determine how much the option costs, we must consult the contract specification again to find out the contract size. This is given as **1,000 shares per contract**.

All options, like futures, are traded in standardised lots or contracts. It is only possible to trade in whole numbers of contracts. You could not, for example, buy 1½ April 60 calls.

We know that the quote for XYZ options is in pence per share and that the contract size is 1,000 shares. Therefore, one XYZ April 60 call would cost £280 (£0.28 × 1,000 shares).

3.6 The simple uses of options

3.6.1 Buying a call

Introduction

This strategy is motivated by a view that an asset's price will rise.

Risk – The investor's risks are limited to the premium he pays for the options. So, if the 80 call could be bought for a premium of 5, this 5 is all he risks. The premium of the call option will only be a fraction of the cost of the underlying asset, so the option can be considered less risky than buying the asset itself.

Whilst this is true, remember that the whole premium is at risk and it is easy to lose 100% of your investment, albeit a relatively small amount of money.

Reward – The rewards from buying a call are unlimited. As the contract gives the holder the right to buy at a fixed price, this right will become increasingly valuable as the asset price rises above the exercise price.

Imagine an investor who buys one XYZ call option which gives him the right, but not the obligation, to buy the XYZ asset at a fixed price of 80 between now and the option's expiry date in January. The cost of this option is 5.

If the asset price rises to 120, the right to buy at 80, i.e. the premium of the 80 call, must be worth at least 40. The net profit for the call would be 35 (40 – 5). Of course, if the price of XYZ falls below 80 at the option's expiry date, the 80 call will be worthless and 100% of the initial 5 invested will be lost. This loss occurs because no sensible person would want the right to buy at 80 if they could buy the asset more cheaply elsewhere.

Graphically

By using graphs, we can show how much an option will be worth at expiry.

On the vertical axis of the graph is profit/loss and on the horizontal axis is the asset price.

Holder of 1 XYZ January 80p Call – Premium 5p

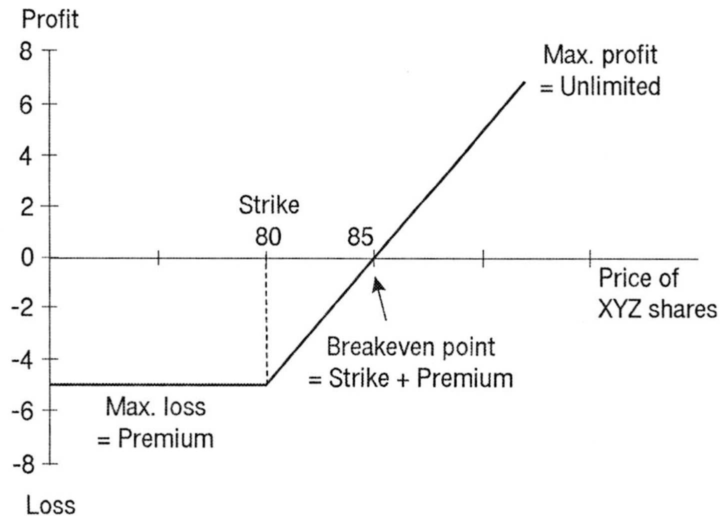

What the graph shows is that losses of 5 are made anywhere below 80, whilst profits emerge above 85. 85 which represents the **breakeven** point. This is the point at which the original investment is recouped and it is calculated by simply adding the premium to the exercise price, e.g. 80 + 5 = 85. The buying of a call to open a position is known as a 'long call'.

3.6.2 Selling a call

Introduction

Risk – The selling or writing of a call without, at the same time, being in possession of the underlying asset, is extremely risky. The risk is unlimited because the writer has a duty to deliver the asset at a fixed price regardless of the prevailing asset price. As the share price could, in theory, rise to infinity, the call writer assumes an unlimited risk. This strategy is sometimes called naked call writing and as it suggests, can leave you feeling very exposed.

Reward – You might ask why someone would assume such an unlimited risk. The answer, of course, is the hope of a profit. The maximum profit the writer can make is the premium he receives. Let us look again at an 80 call with a premium of 5. The seller of this call will receive the 5 premium, and providing the asset price at expiry is less than 80, no-one will rationally want to exercise the right to buy. The graph for selling a call is set out below. You will see that it is the equal and opposite of buying a call.

Graphically

Writer of 1 XYZ January 80p Call – Premium 5p

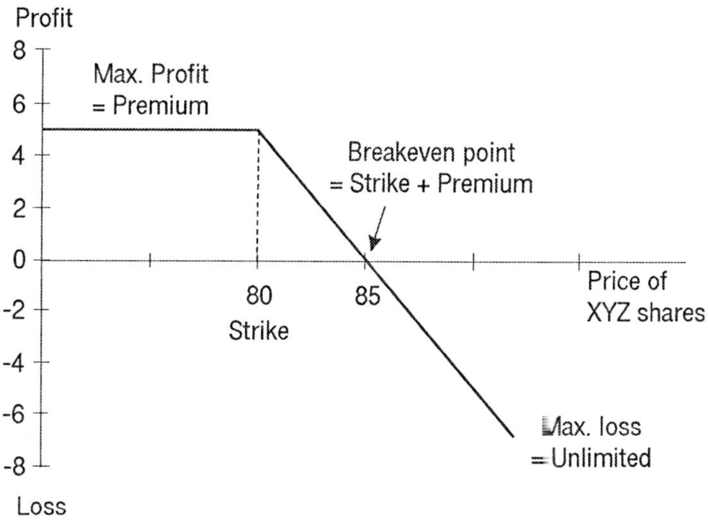

As the graph demonstrates, the call writer believes that the asset price is likely either to stay the same or fall. If this happens, the writer simply pockets the premium received and will not have to deliver the asset. The selling of a call to open a position is known as a 'short call'.

3.6.3 Buying a put

Introduction

Risk – As when buying a call, the risk is limited to the premium paid. The motivation behind buying a put will be to profit from a fall in the asset's price. The holder of a put obtains the right, but not the obligation, to sell at a fixed price. The value of this right will become increasingly valuable as the asset price falls.

Reward – The greatest profit that will arise from buying a put will be achieved if the asset price falls to zero.

Graphically

Holder of 1 XYZ July 80p Put-Premium 8p

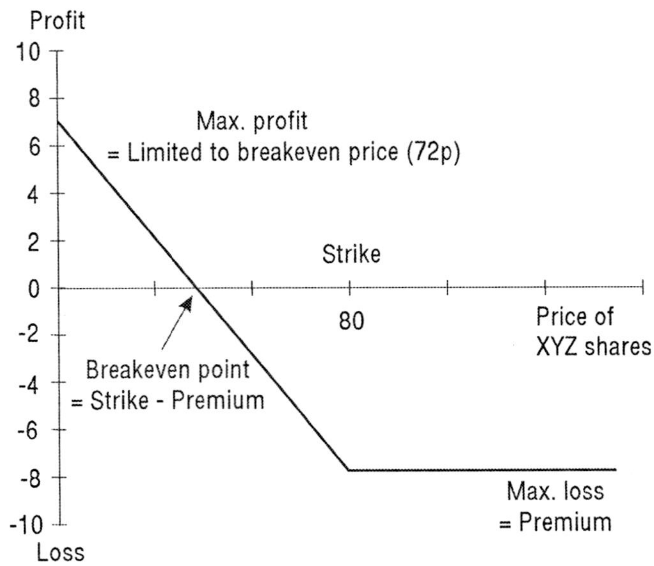

The breakeven point, and maximum profit, is calculated by deducting the premium from the exercise price, e.g. 80 – 8 = 72. Like the purchase of a call, the premium needs to be recovered before profits are made. The buying of a put to open a position is known as a 'long put'.

3.6.4 Selling a put

Introduction

Risk – The selling of a put is dangerous, as the writer enters into an obligation to purchase an asset at a fixed price. If the market price of that asset falls, the put writer will end up paying a large amount of money for what could be a valueless asset. The worst case will arise when the asset price falls to zero. If this happens, the loss will be the exercise price less the premium received.

Reward – What the put option writer hopes for is that the put will not be exercised. This will occur if the asset has a price above the exercise price at expiry. The maximum reward is the premium received. The selling of a put to open a position is known as a 'short put'.

Graphically

Writer of 1 XYZ July 80p Put -Premium 8p

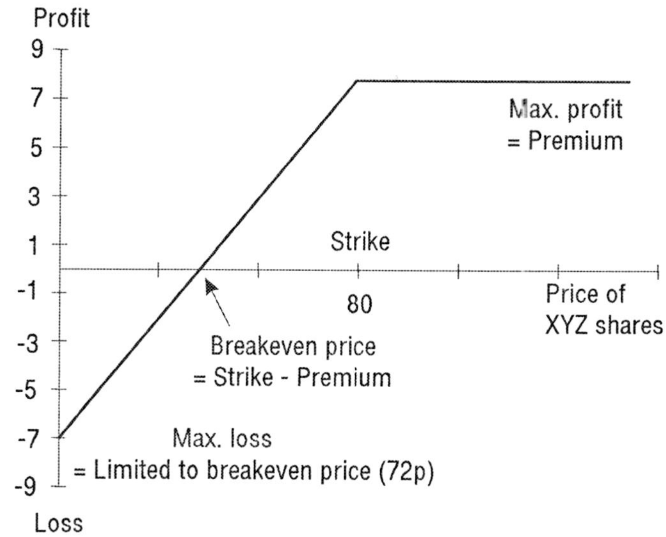

The four basic strategies outlined above form the building blocks of the more complicated option techniques. You should ensure that you are clear about three things.

- What is the motivation behind each trade?
- What are the risks associated with them?
- What are the rewards?

3.7 Options on futures

The options discussed so far have been options which, upon exercise, result in the purchase or sale of a tangible underlying security, such as a share. More common than those discussed above are options on futures, such as the NYSE Liffe UK Gilt Option. This apparently complex term merely describes particular options, the exercise of which results in a long or short futures position.

Thus, the exercise of a **long call** results in the holder establishing a **long futures** position in the same delivery month.

The exercise of a **long put** results in the holder establishing a **short futures** position in the same delivery month.

Clearly, the attributes of futures products and tangible assets are quite different. Two characteristics are worth highlighting – gearing and risk.

3.8 Option pricing

arning objectives

20.1.10 Explain time value and intrinsic value relating to an option premium.

20.1.13 Explain the factors that determine the premium of an option.

Why are some options more expensive than others? Below the prices for **call options** on a particular asset are provided. The **underlying price is 98**.

Exercise Price	Expiry Date Jan Premium	April Premium	July Premium
70	29	31	32
80	19	21	22
90	10	12	13
100	3	4	5
110	1	2	2.5
120	0	0.5	1

Two influences on options prices are readily apparent: (a) **the underlying security price** and (b) **time until expiry**.

3.8.1 Underlying security price

Learning objectives

20.1.11 Identify when an option is in-the-money, out-of-the-money, or at-the-money.

20.1.12 Calculate the time value of an option, given the premium, strike price and current market price.

Compare the value of the January 70 call and the January 90 call from the table. The 70 call is priced at 29 whilst the 90 call is priced at 10. Why?

Remember that we are looking at call options, i.e. the right to buy. The value of the 70 call is greater than the 90 call because the right to buy at a low price (70) must be more attractive than the right to buy at a high price (90).

It is also worth noting that the **call premium** will be **higher**, the **higher the price** of the **underlying asset** becomes, when compared against the exercise price, as again the call option would be more attractive.

Why is the 70 call priced at 29?

We can readily explain at least part of the premium. If we bear in mind that the underlying stock is trading at 98, the right to buy at 70 must be worth at least 28. If the 70 call was worth less than 28, it would be possible to buy the call, exercise it to acquire stock and immediately sell the stock at the market price of 98 and thereby realise a risk-free profit. Markets do not give away money. The 70 call, with an underlying stock at 98 must be worth 28. This value of 28 is known as the option's **intrinsic value**.

The option is not just valued at 28, its price is 29, so where does the 1 come from?

This part of the premium is known as **time value**. The amount of time value in an option is a function of probability of the chance of further movements in the underlying asset.

The premium of the 70 call is made up of two things – intrinsic value and time value.

Intrinsic Value	+	Time Value	=	Premium
28	+	1	=	29

Not all options have intrinsic value. If you look at the table, you will see the premium of the January 110 call is 1.

The 110 call has no intrinsic value because it gives the right to buy at a level above the current price of 98. It is, therefore, not immediately valuable. However, because things may change between now and expiry, the option has a time value of 1. The **longer** the option's **time until expiry**, the **greater the time value** and hence the **greater the premium** for **both call and put options**.

Options that have intrinsic value are described as being **in-the-money**.

Options that have only time value are described as being **out-of-the-money**.

Practitioners sometimes describe options as being **at-the-money**. This term has nothing to do with intrinsic value, it merely describes the option exercise price that is nearest to the current underlying price. Thus, the 100 call from our table, as the exercise price nearest the underlying (98), would be the 'at-the-money' option.

3.9 Volatility

Aside from time and underlying security price, the most important other factor is **volatility**.

Volatility is a measure of how much an underlying price varies. If an underlying asset varies a great deal, the risk for the options writer becomes larger and the premiums he demands rise accordingly. If, however, an option is sold on a reasonably stable asset, the premiums will be lower. At times of crisis or change, such as wars or elections, people become uncertain about the future. This uncertainty brings with it higher options premiums.

The impact of changes in volatility is quite straightforward.

If volatility rises, call and put premiums increase.

If volatility falls, call and put premiums decrease.

3.10 Interest rates

A less important influence on option prices is interest rates. The basic relationship is

Interest rate rises – call premiums rise
– put premiums fall

The reasons for these changes are related to the cost of hedging the option's position, but need not detain us here. However, it is important to recognise that interest rate changes are of only minor importance. Volatility changes are much more influential.

3.11 Sensitivity of option values

It has already been noted that there are five factors that influence the fair value of all options. They are

- Value of the underlying asset.
- Exercise price.
- Time to expiry.
- Volatility.
- Interest rates.

NB: Dividend payments will also influence the fair value of options on dividend-paying stock.

A change in any one of these factors will impact on the price of an option. A holder of an option will want to know what the exact impact is likely to be, i.e. they will wish to know how sensitive their options are to changes in these factors.

Sensitivities are named after Greek letters, as follows.

Sensitivity to	Known as
Underlying asset	Delta
Changes in delta	Gamma
Time decay	Theta
Volatility	Vega
Interest rates	Rho

3.11.1 Delta

Delta can be defined in a number of ways.

First, delta is the **rate of change of an option's premium with respect to the underlying security**. For example, an option with a delta of 0.25 can theoretically be expected to move at one quarter of the rate of the underlying. If the underlying goes up or down by 4, the option could be expected to go up or down by 1 – all other factors remaining constant.

Secondly, delta can be thought of as being the **probability** that an **option will expire in-the-money**. Thus, a delta of 0.25 or 25% means that there is only a small chance of being in-the-money; a delta of 0.9 or 90% gives an obviously higher chance.

Thirdly, delta can be thought of as the **theoretical number of futures or underlying units** of which the holder of the call option is long, or of which the holder of a put option is short. For example, if the delta of a call (put) is 0.25, the holder of a call (put) is theoretically long (short) a quarter of a futures contract. In this example, the call holder's position at this instant is equivalent to a long position in a quarter of a future, i.e. the holder will make or lose money at a quarter of the rate of a futures contract.

3.11.2 Positive and negative deltas

If you are long of a call, you have a positive delta, i.e. if the underlying asset goes up, so does the call option premium, a move to the benefit of the holder.

If, conversely, you are short of a call and the market moves up, such a move is to your disadvantage, as the option becomes more expensive – you have a negative delta.

Put holders benefit from downwards moves, but are hurt by upwards moves. They are negatively correlated with the underlying.

Finally, short puts are helped by up-moves, but hurt by down-moves; they have positive deltas.

Long Calls **Short Puts**	Positive Delta
Long Puts **Short Calls**	Negative Delta

It should be noted that the delta of the underlying asset or futures contract is **always 1. If you are long of a future you have a positive delta, if short, a negative delta of 1. Similarly, the delta of a holding of the underlying is also 1.**

3.11.3 Gamma

The **sensitivity of delta** to a change in the value of the underlying asset is known as gamma.

3.11.4 Theta

This is the measure of the change in the theoretical value of a call or put option as **time to expiry increases**.

3.11.5 Vega

This is the measure of the effect on the theoretical value a change **in volatility** will have.

3.11.6 Rho

Rho is the measure of the sensitivity of an option's theoretical value to a change in **interest rates**.

3.11.7 Phi

Phi is the measure of the sensitivity of an option's theoretical value to a change in **asset yields**.

4 Options Trading Strategies

Learning objective

20.1.14 Calculate the maximum profit, maximum loss and the motivation behind the following option strategies: long and short call; long and short put; long and short straddle; long and short strangle; long and short butterfly; covered call and protective put.

Tutor tip

Calls and puts are regularly examined in detail, straddles and strangles are regularly examined conceptually (i.e. that they are volatility grades).

4.1 Motivation

Before embarking on a detailed discussion of the attributes of the various options trades, let us first think about the reasons why they are undertaken.

The first and most obvious reason for speculating in the markets is that investors have a view on their future direction, be it up or down. These are **directional** trades and may be either **bullish** (the investor feels the market is likely to go up) or **bearish** (the investor feels the market is likely to go down). Investors may also feel the market is likely to go up or down very markedly, or only slightly. There are option trades to accommodate all views.

People also trade because they feel the market is likely to be highly volatile or remain broadly static. These investors do not know in which direction the market may move, but have opinions as to its likely variability. These types of trades are known as **volatility** trades and options are unique in allowing investors to trade in this way.

Others use options not to speculate, but for more conservative ends. These may be to reduce portfolio risks or to enhance returns. A number of the more important trades are reviewed in the pages that follow. Although the language may appear bizarre and the graphs complicated, it should be remembered that they are all built up from the four simple trades examined earlier.

STRATEGY 1	**Long Straddle**
MOTIVATION	Volatility – Undertaken to Exploit Increasing Variability.
CONSTRUCTION	Purchase of call and put with same exercise price and expiry.
COMMENTS	Straddles are bought when investors feel that the market may move considerably either up or down. They are also bought when the investor feels that option premiums do not fully reflect likely volatility. Consequently, if the perception of volatility rises, so will the premiums of the purchased options, thereby giving an opportunity to sell the purchased options at higher prices.
EXAMPLE	BUY 100 CALL @ 0.98, BUY 100 PUT @ 1.91
GRAPH	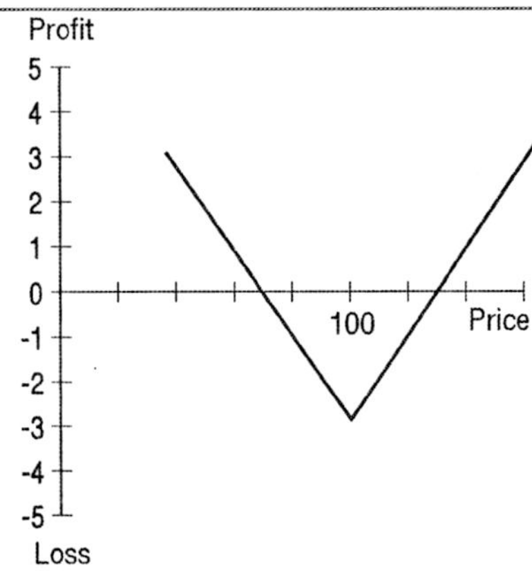

STRATEGY 2	**Short Straddle**
MOTIVATION	Volatility – Undertaken to Exploit Decreasing Variability.
CONSTRUCTION	Sale of call and put with same exercise price and expiry.
COMMENTS	This trade is undertaken by investors who believe that the market will trade within a narrow range. It is also undertaken by investors who believe options premiums to be expensive and likely to fall. As can be seen from the graph below, the risks from this trade are potentially unlimited.
EXAMPLE	SELL 100 CALL @ 0.98, SELL 100 PUT @ 1.91
GRAPH	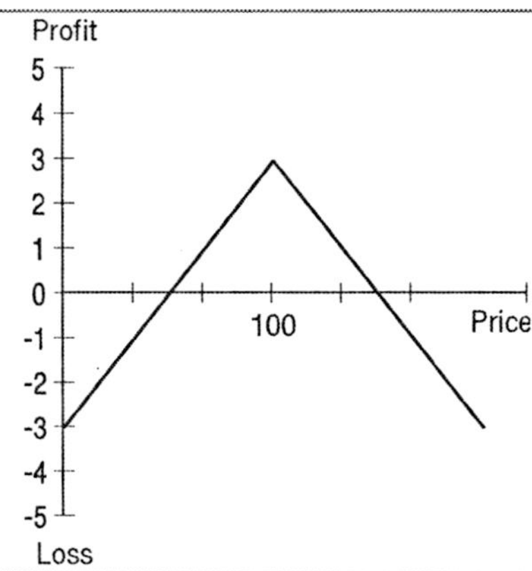

STRATEGY 3	**Long Strangle**
MOTIVATION	Volatility – Expect Large Increase in Market Variability.
CONSTRUCTION	Purchase of call and put with same expiry but different strike.
COMMENTS	Generally a lower cost alternative to a long straddle, but which requires greater movement for profitability.
EXAMPLE	BUY 101 CALL @ 0.62, BUY 99 PUT @ 1.40
GRAPH	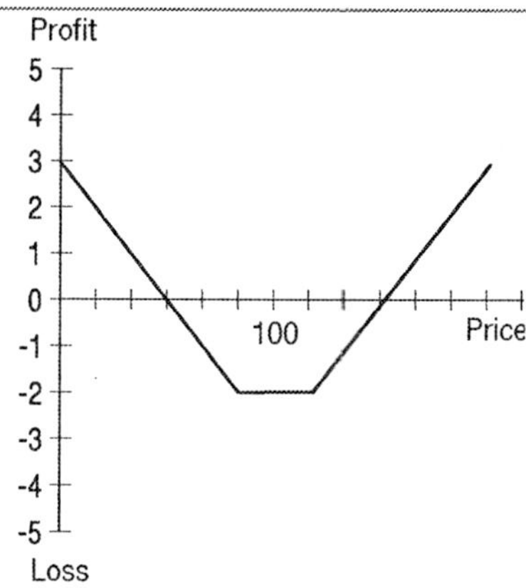

STRATEGY 4	**Short Strangle**
MOTIVATION	Volatility – Expect Large Reduction in Market Variability.
CONSTRUCTION	Sale of call and put with same expiry, but different strike.
COMMENTS	Alternative to short straddle, generally breakevens are more widely displaced and thus position is less quickly loss making.
EXAMPLE	SELL 101 CALL @ 1.47, SELL 99 PUT @ 2.55
GRAPH	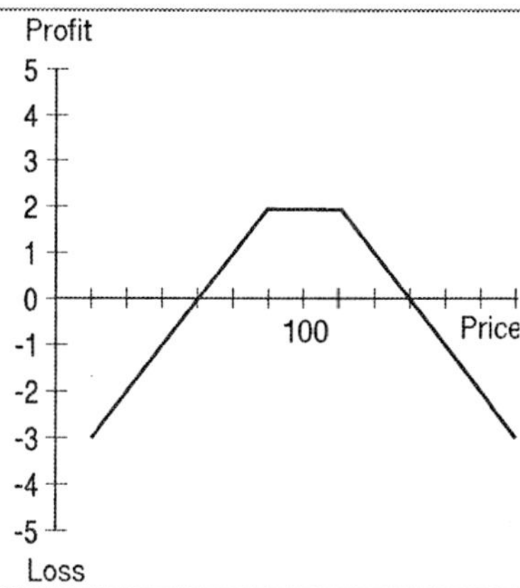

STRATEGY 5	**Short Butterfly**
MOTIVATION	Volatility – Undertaken to Exploit Increasing Variability.
CONSTRUCTION	Sale of low-strike call/put. Purchase of two mid-strike calls/puts. Sale of high-strike call/put.
COMMENTS	Alternative to long straddle/strangle. May be expensive to execute because of commissions. Note also its limited profit.
EXAMPLE	SELL 103 PUT @ 0.62, BUY 2 104 PUTS @ 1.04, SELL 1 105 PUT @ 1.63
GRAPH	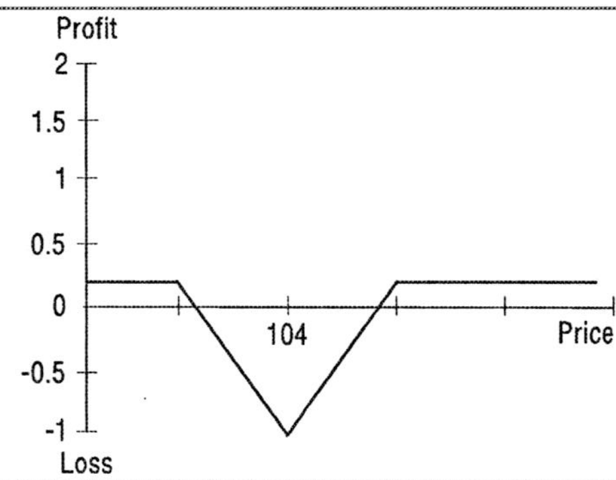

STRATEGY 6	**Long Butterfly**
MOTIVATION	Volatility – Undertaken to Exploit Reducing Variability.
CONSTRUCTION	Purchase of low-strike call/put. Sale of two mid-strike calls/puts. Purchase of high-strike call/put.
COMMENTS	Patently less risky than short straddle/strangle. But beware high commission and execution costs.
EXAMPLE	BUY 103 CALL @ 1.52, SELL 2 104 CALLS @ 0.94, BUY 1 105 CALL @ 0.53
GRAPH	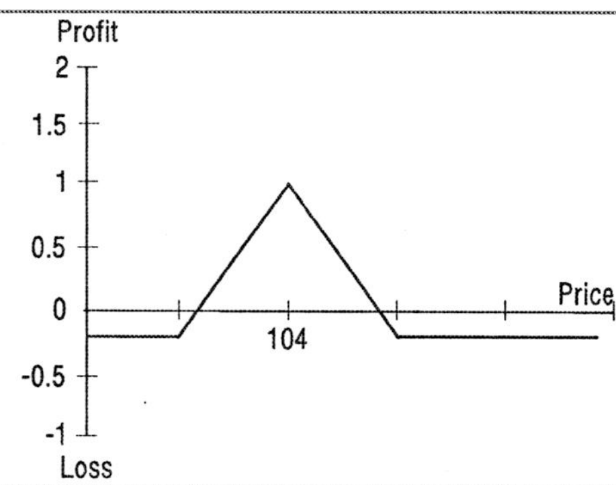

STRATEGY 7	**Covered Call**
MOTIVATION	Normally Neutral Subject to Strike.
CONSTRUCTION	Long position in stock and sale of call. If call sold is out-of-the-money, the trade is bullish; if at-the-money, call is sold, trade is neutral; if in-the-money, call is sold, trade is bearish.
COMMENTS	Very familiar investment strategy that can enhance returns in static markets, whilst also providing limited protection against falls. (Protection = Call premium). The trade is commonly used by fund managers who already hold a stock, but are neutral about the share's prospects in the short term. To enhance the returns over any dividend flows, they sell the call and thereby receive premium. In doing this, they effectively give up their opportunity to profit if the share unexpectedly rises above the exercise price.
EXAMPLE	BUY ABC STOCK @ 99.07, SELL 100 CALL @ 0.98
GRAPH	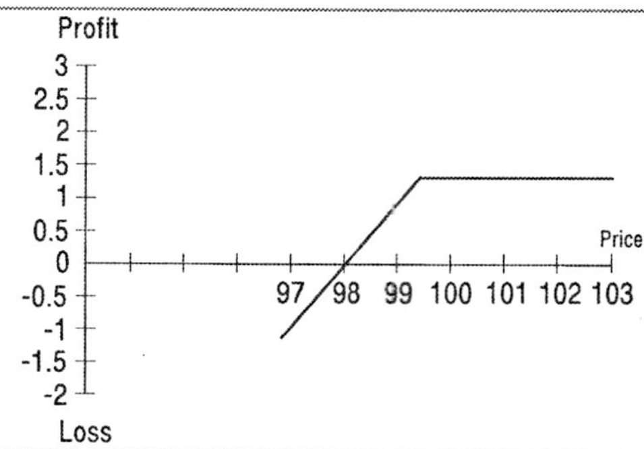

STRATEGY 8	**Protective Put**
MOTIVATION	Directional, bullish, but with limited downside risk
CONSTRUCTION	Long position in stock/future and purchase of put.
COMMENTS	Classic options hedge of long position in underlying; protects downside but allows profit if market advances. More flexible and thus more expensive than short hedge with futures. If we use an out-of-the-money put then losses will be incurred until the price falls to the strike price. Any further price falls on the asset will be offset by gains on the put, providing the desired hedge.
EXAMPLE	BUY STOCK @ 99, BUY 100 PUT @ 6
GRAPH	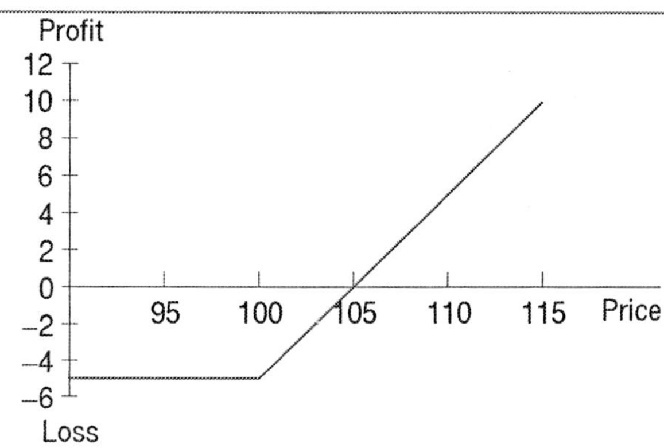

4.2 Summary

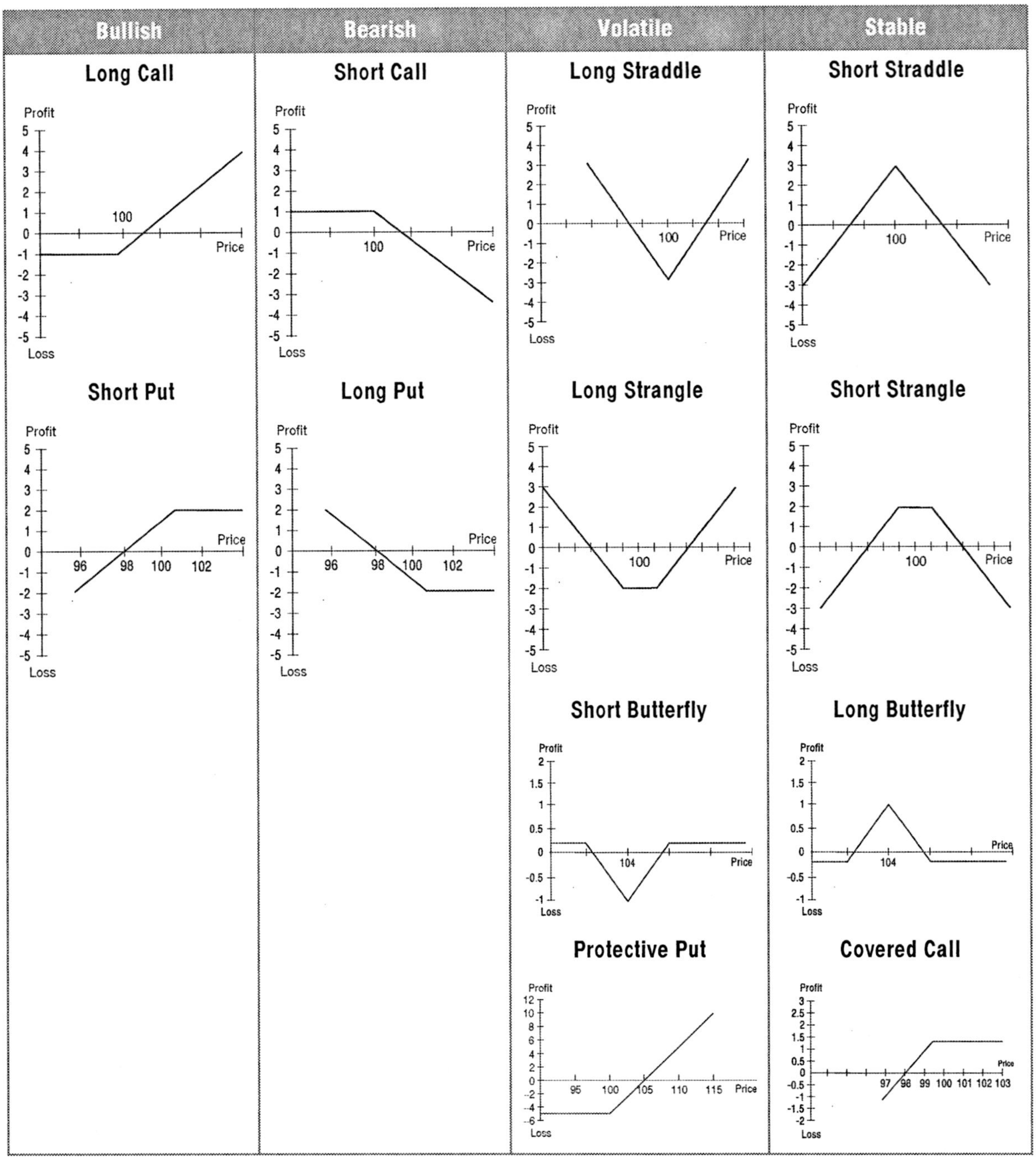

5 Contracts for Differences

Learning objective | **20.2.3 Explain** the nature of contracts for differences.

Contracts for Differences is a rather complicated term used to describe cash-settled derivatives.

In such contracts, cash passes between buyer and seller at expiry, rather than a physical asset or future. The reason why some contracts are cash settled is largely for administrative ease. Whilst it might be possible to design an equity index product, e.g. FTSE 100, that leads to the physical delivery of each of its hundred constituents (in the FTSE's case), this would be both cumbersome and expensive. Rather than do this, a cash value changes hands.

For instance, an investor buys and subsequently exercises one call option on the FTSE index. The exercise price is 4800 and the EDSP 4840.

At expiry this option has 40 points of intrinsic value and, in accordance with the contract specification, each point has a value of £10.

Following exercise, £400 (40 × £10) will be paid by the call option writer to the holder.

The contract is thus cash settled for the difference between the exercise price and the settlement price.

6 Warrants

6.1 Introduction

Learning objectives

20.3.4 Define a warrant.

20.3.5 Distinguish between a warrant and a call option.

A similar product to a call option is an equity warrant. If you own an equity warrant, it gives you the right, but not the obligation, to buy a company's shares at a fixed price before a stated expiry date. They are similar to call options, but there are some important differences.

Firstly, equity warrants are normally **long dated** when issued. The life span of an equity warrant is determined by the company, but may often be several years. This differs from exchange-traded call options, which normally have life spans of less than a year.

Secondly, the exercise of an equity warrant will **result in new shares being issued** by the company. This differs from equity options, which simply redistribute already issued shares.

Thirdly, equity warrants are **traded on stock exchanges**, whilst equity options are traded on derivative markets.

6.2 Pricing warrants

6.2.1 Warrant price

The pricing of equity warrants is like that of an option, subject to the fact that options are priced on a per-share basis whereas warrants are priced per warrant and that may cover several shares. We can, therefore, use an options pricing model to value a warrant, however, in doing so we need to consider the differences between an option and a warrant, specifically that when a warrant is exercised, new shares are issued by the company, diluting the value of the shares in existence.

The value of a warrant can therefore be established as

Formula to learn

$$\text{Warrant value} = \frac{A}{1+q} \times \text{Number of shares}$$

where

A = value of an equivalent option derived from a suitable option pricing model.

Q = percentage increase in the number of shares in issue once the warrant is exercised (expressed as a decimal).

The price of a warrant can consist of both time value and intrinsic value. In the context of warrants, the intrinsic value of the warrant is sometimes also known as the **formula value**, whereas the time value is sometimes also known as the **premium**.

Because of their longer maturities, however, pricing can be more problematic due to the difficulty in estimating volatility.

6.2.2 Warrant premium

The warrant premium is a term which must not be confused with an option's premium. The warrant premium is the price by which the warrant price plus the exercise price exceed the share price.

$$\text{Warrant premium} = \frac{\text{Warrant price + Exercise price}}{\text{Share price}} - 1$$

Though it may not be obvious, this is also the time value of the warrant expressed as a percentage of the share price, as can be demonstrated by the following algebraic rearrangement.

$$\begin{aligned}\text{Warrant premium} &= \frac{\text{Warrant price} + \text{Exercise price}}{\text{Share price}} - 1 \\ &= \frac{\text{Warrant price} + \text{Exercise price} - \text{Share price}}{\text{Share price}} \\ &= \frac{\text{Warrant price} + (\text{Exercise price} - \text{Share price})}{\text{Share price}} \\ &= \frac{\text{Warrant price} - (\text{Share price} - \text{Exercise price})}{\text{Share price}}\end{aligned}$$

Formula to learn

$$\begin{aligned}\text{Warrant premium} &= \frac{\text{Warrant price} - \text{Intrinsic value}}{\text{Share price}} \\ &= \frac{\text{Time value}}{\text{Share price}}\end{aligned}$$

6.3 Covered warrants

Learning objective

20.3.6 Explain the key features of covered warrants.

Covered warrants are instruments issued by securities houses. These are warrants over the shares of another company. Technically a warrant can only be issued by the company itself, since it gives the investor the right to buy new shares in the company. The securities house issues a long dated option into the security and this is referred to as **the covered warrant**. In order to cover its position, the securities house may own shares in the relevant company, or warrants on the company's shares.

This is a relatively new market which emerged in the late 1980s and has only recently been introduced on to the London Stock Exchange.

Covered warrants have the following characteristics.

- The original company is not the issuer.
- The issuer will be a financial institution (e.g. investment bank) which hedges its position in traded options or the underlying shares.
- The issuer bank makes a market in the covered warrants.

- Covered warrants have a future expiry date of up to five years and can **normally** be exercised at any time up to this date.
- Most are 'call' types (i.e. giving the investor the right to benefit from price increases) but 'put' types (i.e. benefit from price falls) are also available.
- Covered warrants are cash settled so stamp duty is not payable on exercise.
- Covered put warrants are a useful way to hedge exposure to an underlying share.

Comparison table

	Warrants	Covered Warrants
Issuer	The company to whom the underlying shares relate	Third party, e.g. investment bank
Maturity	Long dated	Average life of 6 to 12 months (some up to 5 years)
Trading	London Stock Exchange	London Stock Exchange
Types	Right to buy	Right to buy or sell
Stamp Duty	Yes	No
Exercise	Physical shares	Cash settled

7 CONVERTIBLES

Learning objectives

20.3.1 Explain the nature of convertible bonds and convertible preference shares.

20.3.2 Calculate a conversion price, value and premium.

20.3.3 Explain the component parts of the valuation of a convertible bond (namely straight bond value, call option value, dilution effect and conversion ratio).

A conversion right gives the preference shareholder or bondholder the right, at a specified date or dates in the future, to convert their bond into shares of the company. The rate of conversion will be fixed at the time of issue and represents an option to purchase the shares at a given price.

Depending on the movement in the underlying share price, this conversion right or option may be very valuable indeed. The trade-off in this sort of issue is that the coupon will often be much lower than the market would otherwise expect on a bond from that particular company.

There are a number of useful statistics that may be employed in the analysis of convertibles, including

- Conversion ratio
- Conversion value
- Conversion premium
- Conversion price

Conversion ratio

The conversion right can be expressed in a number of ways. By convention, the right is normally to convert the debt into the Ordinary shares of the company in a given **conversion ratio**. For example, £100 nominal is converted into 25 shares then we have a conversion ratio of 25, ie

Formula to learn

Conversion ratio = Number of shares received per bond held

Conversion value

The conversion value represents the value of the convertible if it is converted into shares today, i.e.

Formula to learn

Conversion value = Conversion ratio × Share price

Example

A bond can be converted into 25 ordinary shares. The current share price is £3.00, what is the conversion value?

Solution

Conversion value = 25 × £3.00 = £75

Conversion premium

One important measure often used in this market is to look at the premium at which the bond is trading over the market price of the share.

Formula to learn

$$\text{Premium} = \frac{\text{Conv} - \text{S}}{\text{S}}$$

where

Conv = value of the convertible on a per share basis

S = price per share

Example

A convertible bond offering the opportunity to convert into 50 shares is trading at £110. The current share price is £1.90. Calculate the conversion premium.

Solution

Value of the share on a per share basis

Conv = £110.00 ÷ 50 = £2.20

Hence the premium is

$$\text{Premium} = \frac{£2.20 - £1.90}{£1.90} = 15.8\%$$

The investor has to judge whether this premium is justifiable. Will the underlying share price move sufficiently over the life of the conversion right to bring in a profit on conversion? The investor also has to consider the coupon the bond is generating. Whilst this is likely to be low, it may be greater than the dividend on a share and it therefore makes sense to hold the bond and then to convert in the future into the share itself.

Convertible price

The asset flows from a convertible are identical to the asset flows available from a bond plus a warrant that is exercisable at the redemption proceeds. Under either alternative

- If the cash redemption proceeds are worth more than the shares, the investor will take the cash, either through not converting or through receiving the proceeds and abandoning the warrant.
- If the shares are worth more than the cash redemption proceeds, the investor will take the shares, either through conversion or through the exercise of the warrant with the redemption proceeds.

Since the asset flows experienced are the same, the values must also be the same. A general formula for valuing a convertible would be

Formula to learn

$$\text{Value of convertible} = \text{Value of straight bond} + \text{Value of warrant}$$

$$\text{Value of convertible} = \text{Value of straight bond} + \frac{A}{(1+q)} \times CR$$

where

CR = the **conversion ratio** (number of shares per £100 nominal of the bond)

A = the value of the American option on the shares of the company

q = the percentage change in the outstanding share capital of the company if the bonds are converted

The attraction of convertible bonds is that they offer a two-way bet. If the share price rises, then the conversion right itself has value. If the share price falls then, at worst, the bondholder is left with a low-coupon bond. Consequently, the minimum value of a convertible must be the value of the straight bond.

Warrants

A warrant is similar in many ways to a conversion right. The principal difference is that rather than converting a bond into shares, a bond is issued with a warrant attached to it and that warrant gives the holder the right to buy new shares at a specified price from the company at specified dates in the future. A warrant is effectively **a call option** to subscribe for new shares in the company.

The advantage to the company of issuing warrants rather than convertible bonds is that the holder of the bond may **split** the warrant off and trade both aspects of the security separately.

Time and intrinsic value

The warrant price can be split into two elements: the **intrinsic (or formula) value** and the **time value (or premium)**.

The intrinsic value is what the investor would generate if he exercised the warrant now. The time value is linked to the expectation of future gains before the end of the warrant's life. For example, if a warrant is priced at 86p and gives the right to buy a share at £1.00, the intrinsic and time value would be calculated as follows if the share on which the warrant is based trades at 112p.

Intrinsic = 112p – 100p = 12p

Time = 86p – 12p = 74p

Thus, intrinsic can be calculated by a comparison of the exercise price to the current underlying price. The time value is the warrant price less the intrinsic value.

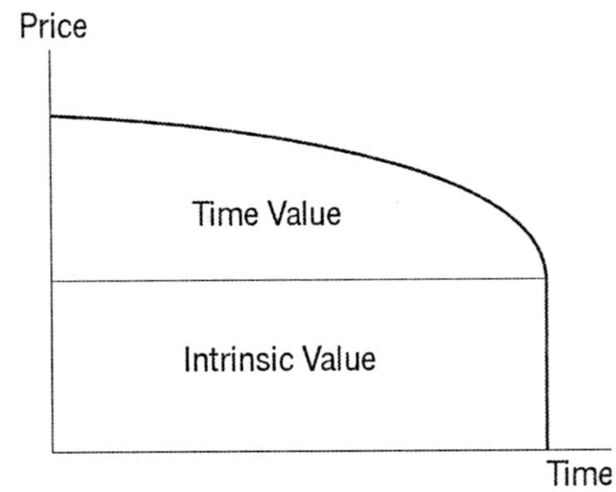

Time value declines over the life of a warrant. However, the rate of decay is not constant and increases over the warrant's life.

8 Selling Short and Stock Lending

Learning objectives

20.2.1 Explain the mechanics and uses of short selling.

20.2.2 Explain the role of stock lending in the markets, and the benefits to the participants.

When an investor buys an investment, he will have done so in the belief its price will rise in the future. Conversely, when an investor undertakes short selling (or 'goes short'), he is anticipating a decrease in share price.

A short sale is the sale of a security that isn't owned by the seller. This may at first appear somewhat confusing but it is relatively straightforward.

When you short sell a stock, you will need to borrow it first from someone. It is likely a stockbroker will facilitate in this process. The stock may come from the broker's own account, from another one of the firm's customers, or from another brokerage firm. The lender will most typically be a

- Pension fund
- Life assurance fund
- General insurance fund
- Collective investment vehicle

where the securities are passively managed and hence unlikely to be traded in the short term. Active funds may lend stocks but the risk of a recall makes them less attractive to borrowers.

The shares are then sold and the proceeds are credited to the investor's account. At some point the investor will be required to close out their position by buying back the same number of shares and returning them to the broker.

If the price drops, the investor can buy back the stock at the lower price and make a profit on the difference. If the price of the stock rises, the investor will have to buy it back at the higher price and suffer a loss as a result.

Since the investor doesn't own the stock, he has an obligation to pay the lender of the stock any dividends declared during the course of the loan. The cost to the borrower will typically be around 40 basis points for an equities trade and 5 basis points for a bond trade, though the actual cost will vary depending on the availability of the specific stock in question.

9 Swaps

Learning objective

20.2.4 Explain the nature of, and motivations behind: interest rate swaps; currency swaps, equity swaps and inflation swaps.

A swap is an agreement to exchange future cash flows for a specified period.

9.1 Interest rate swaps

9.1.1 Definition

Alongside the exponential growth of exchange-traded derivatives over the past decade, there has been a similar, if less visible, growth in **over-the-counter (OTC)** products, especially swaps. Whilst exchange-traded structures, by virtue of their standardisation, liquidity and visibility, have provided the investment community with much needed risk management tools, some attributes of these markets are particularly irksome. The limited availability of products, fixed delivery dates, standardised contract sizes, limited exercise prices and expiry dates and the strictures of exchange margining rules have all conspired to make the bespoke OTC markets particularly attractive. One significant disadvantage of over-the-counter products is their lack of a clearing house. With exchange-traded derivatives, the existence of the clearing house virtually eliminates counterparty risk. In the over-the-counter market, very considerable counterparty risks exist between buyers and sellers. In this section the most important OTC product – the interest rate swap – is examined.

An interest rate swap is a contract which commits two counterparties to exchange, over an agreed period, two streams of interest payments, each calculated using a different interest rate index, but applied to a common notional principal amount.

9.1.2 Key points

Only interest is exchanged in the swap; there is **no exchange of principal**. Swaps do not, therefore, impact on the balance sheet, only on the profit and loss account. They are, therefore, classed as 'off balance sheet instruments'.

An interest rate swap is a contract for difference and cash movements that take place at intervals during the swap's life are netted. For example, in a quarterly settled interest rate swap with a national principal of €40m in which one side is paying a fixed rate of 6% pa and the other a floating rate, such as three-month LIBOR that is 5% pa further period in question, only the cash difference of 1% pa is exchanged. The actual settlement sum will, therefore, be

Settlement sum = £40m × 1.00% × ¼ = £100,000

The last term here (¼) reflecting the fact that the swap settles quarterly.

This reduces credit risks.

An Interest Rate Swap

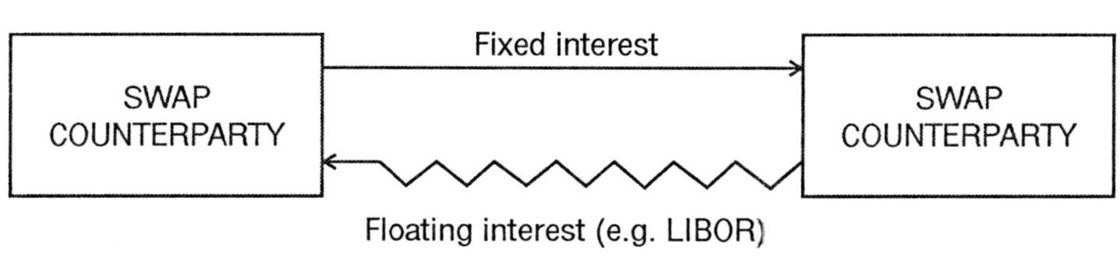

The above is an example of the most common type of interest rate swap in which a fixed rate of interest is exchanged for a floating rate of interest and is known as a coupon swap. The floating rate is normally measured by an index such as LIBOR.

9.1.3 How swaps are traded and quoted

The market in interest rate swaps is an OTC market. Trading is conducted over the telephone and price information is disseminated through quote vendor systems such as Reuters and Telerate.

In interest rate swaps, the floating rate in a coupon swap (the most common) is assumed to be six-month LIBOR. Negotiation, therefore, concentrates on the fixed rate, sometimes called the swap rate.

9.1.4 Why use interest rate swaps?

As with futures and options, there are three basic motivations – speculation, hedging and arbitrage.

9.2 Currency swaps

9.2.1 Definition

A currency swap is one in which

- Agreed principal sums of two currencies are exchanged at inception
- Interest is paid on these sums at pre-agreed rates for the term of the swap
- The principal sums are swapped back at the end of the swap

Since the cash flows being exchanged are in different currencies they cannot be netted as they are for interest rate and equity swaps. As a result, a currency swap is not a contract for difference.

9.2.2 Characteristics

Primary currency

One currency is defined as the primary currency and the nominal value of the primary currency is used to describe the national principal value of the swap.

Secondary currency

The other currency is the secondary currency and the nominal value of this will be a function of prevailing exchange rates at inception.

Interest rates

The interest rates payable in the two currencies are the fair rates for the relevant currencies and the term of the swap to make the exchange fair.

9.2.3 Buyer and seller

Terms

The terms buyer and seller are a little awkward in relation to currency dealing since each party is giving (selling) one currency and receiving (buying) the other.

The terms buyer and seller relate to these swap arrangements from the point of view of the primary currency cash flows at inception. The **buyer** is the person who, at inception, purchases the primary currency (selling the secondary currency), the **seller** is the individual who, at inception, sells the primary currency (buying the secondary currency).

Cash flows

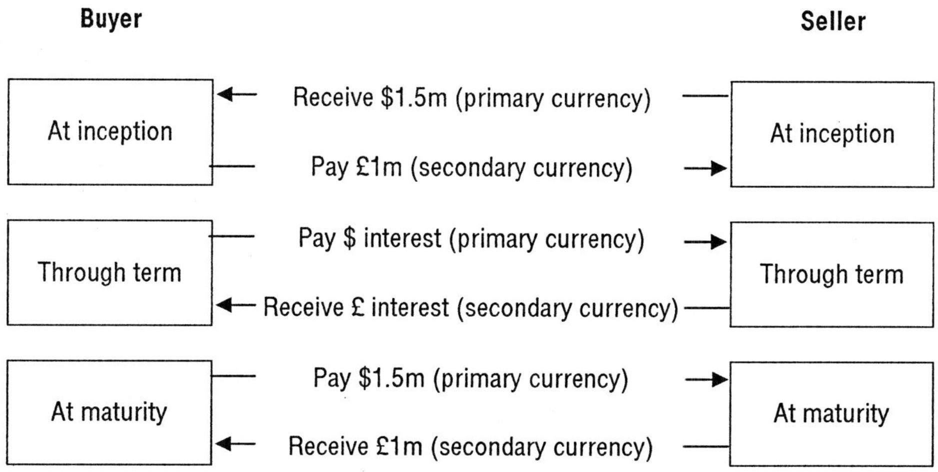

9.2.4 Dealing

The market in short-term currency swaps, as for interest rate swaps, is an OTC market. Trading is conducted over the telephone and price information is disseminated through quote vendor systems.

9.3 Equity swaps

9.3.1 Definition

Equity swaps are similar in concept to interest rate swaps. An equity swap is a contract for difference under which the buyer pays the return on a money market deposit (e.g. LIBOR) and in exchange receives the total return on an equity investment (capital gains plus dividends). The two payments are usually netted and are generally exchanged between two and four times annually. As with interest rate swaps, **no exchange of principal** is involved.

Example

A fund manager enters into a one-year FTSE 100 index swap with a notional principal amount (NPA) of £20m and quarterly reset dates.

If LIBOR is 5% pa (1.25% per quarter) and the total annualised return on the FTSE over the first quarter is 8% (i.e. 2% for the quarter) the settlement sum received by the fund manager will be

Settlement sum = £20m × (2% – 1.25%) = £20m × 0.75% = £150,000

If the FTSE has, say, fallen and underperformed LIBOR the fund manager would have to pay the difference to the counterparty.

The arrangement can be pictured as follows

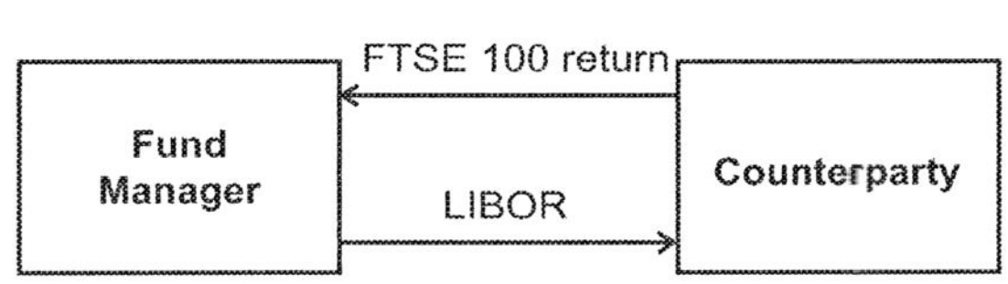

9.3.2 Uses of equity swaps

Indexation

As a route to indexation, the equity swap may hold certain advantages over either a physically constructed fund or one synthesised using futures.

Speculating and hedging

Counterparties can use swaps to either gain or hedge their own exposure to physical equities.

The opportunities for swap counterparties to run a matched book in equity swaps are limited, as whilst the index funds are naturally receivers of index returns, there are fewer people who would wish to pay equity returns other than over a short period of time (as they would for short futures).

There is therefore a fundamental disequilibrium that may limit further growth.

Arbitrage

There are opportunities for arbitrage profits where offsetting equity swaps and futures positions are taken and futures trade away from their fair value.

9.4 Inflation swaps

Investors who have traditionally wanted a return tied in with movements in inflation have targeted investments such as index-linked gilts. There is an increasing market for inflation linked solutions. Inflation swaps offer investors the opportunity to generate a return linked in to a particular inflation rate.

Inflation swaps based on ILGs are similar to interest rate swaps that are effectively based on fixed rate bonds. An interest rate swap exchanges the fixed nominal return of a bond for LIBOR, an inflation swap exchanges the nominal return of an ILG (fixed real return + inflation) for LIBOR.

9.5 Credit default swaps and collateralised debt obligations

9.5.1 Credit default swaps

Learning objectives	
	20.4.1 Explain the purpose, mechanics and implications of a credit default swap (CDS).
	20.4.2 Explain the risks to the financial system resulting from the proliferation of credit derivatives.

Credit default swaps (CDSs) are something of a misnomer. In reality, they are not swaps, but more accurately reflect insurance contracts on which the insurance premium is referred to as the credit default swap spread. One important difference, however, is that it is not necessary for the buyer of the swap to have any interest in the underlying asset, though this is the case with insurance.

At present there are a wide variety of credit derivative products available, however credit default swaps are the most widely available and tradeable products in the market.

A credit default swap may be based upon the credit status of a single reference asset. The buyer of the swap pays a periodic premium to the protection seller, with the credit swap only paying out on the occurrence of a credit event in relation to that reference asset.

A credit event would, under ISDA definitions, include

- Bankruptcy
- Obligation acceleration (where a payment becomes due early)
- Obligation default (a failure to pay)
- Restructuring – though this may be difficult to define precisely

A credit default swap as described may be referred to as a single name credit swap as it is referenced to a single asset. An alternative to this single name swap is a portfolio credit default swap where the seller is exposed to the risk of one or more constituents of a portfolio of assets.

Credit derivatives may be written of a funded or an unfunded basis, a situation similar to writing covered and uncovered options. A funded credit derivative is one where the protection seller makes an initial payment to cover any potential credit event. In an unfunded arrangement no such initial payment is made and the two counterparties face their mutual credit risk.

The credit default swap is the core credit default instrument used in financial markets. If a bank was to make a loan to a borrower the bank would be able to collect interest on the loan in return for taking on the counterparty credit risk. However, the bank may not want to take on board this credit risk and want to offset it in some way. This is where the credit default swap (CDS) comes into play.

The CDS allows the bank to find someone who is willing to take on this risk and enter into a transaction with them. Under the CDS the bank pays the investor a fee. In return the investor agrees to indemnify the bank against losses if the company fails to pay the interest on its loan or goes into bankruptcy.

The CDS is therefore enabling the transfer of default risk. The buyer of the protection (the bank) pays a fee (the **premium** or **credit default swap spread**) which is normally expressed as a number of **basis points per annum** applied to the principal covered. In the example above the asset was a loan, but it could have been a bond or even a swap. In effect a CDS is a form of insurance for the holder of the underlying asset and acts like a put option for a buyer who does not hold the asset.

Various default indices have been created to track the performance of credit default swaps. These include the Markit CDX North American investment-grade index which tracks the cost of debt insurance for a portfolio of investment grade companies in the US. There is also a Markit CDX North American Emerging Markets Diversified index, which was launched in 2005, and monitors 40 equally weighted sovereign and high quality emerging market corporates. In Europe there is a Markit iTraxx Crossover index tracking 50 European corporates, many of which are junk rated. All of these help investors gauge the relative risk within their respective markets.

Over the last decade, credit derivatives have boomed, in part because of the benefits they offer to lenders and investors. They enable lenders and investors to take the credit risks they want and largely eliminate the risks they do not want. Furthermore, they diffuse credit risks across markets and reduce risk concentration by putting such risks in the hands of those who want (and are better equipped) to take it on.

However, with the benefits come risks. In particular, a credit derivative's ability to manage risk depends on markets staying relatively liquid, even in periods of stress. Events throughout 2007 showed this will not always be the case.

9.5.2 Collateralised Debt Obligation (CDO)

A **Collateralised Debt Obligation (CDO)** is an asset-backed investment vehicle designed to remove debt assets (e.g. mortgaged, loans, credit card receivables, etc), and importantly their associated credit risk, from an originator's balance sheet in return for cash. To achieve this, the assets are sold by the originator to a special purpose vehicle (SPV) for cash, that cash having been raised by the SPV through the issue of bonds to investors, the return on those bonds being paid from the debt asset cash flows.

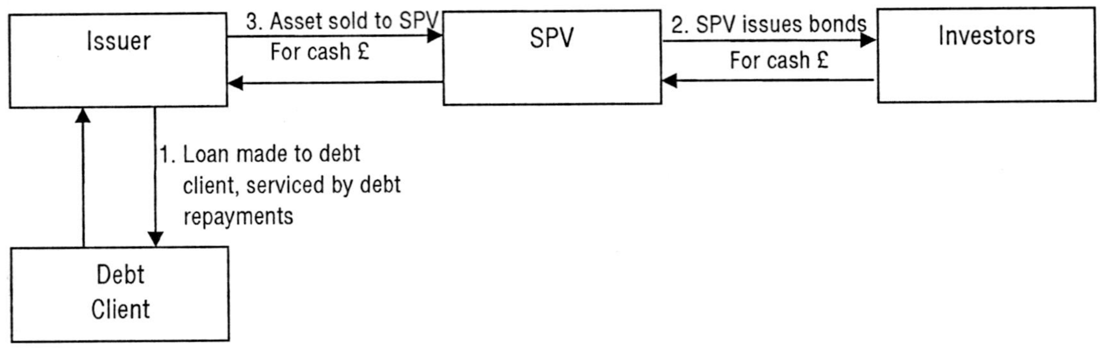

The financing structure of a CDO is designed to redistribute the risk and return from that single pool of debt assets to meet the various SPV investor needs. Usually CDOs are broken down into a number of tiers or tranches through issuing several classes of security to investors, each with different interest rate risk, credit risk and return. Thus a single pool of assets is used to back several securities, each with different levels of priority when it comes to repayment. The typical structure of a CDO would include:

- A senior tranche usually paying a floating rate coupon and representing 70%-80% of the fund
- Tranches of more junior subordinated debt with decreasing credit quality paying fixed coupons and representing 10%-15% of the fund
- An equity tranche offering a variable geared equity return, representing 10%-15% of the fund.

The primary motivation underlying a CDO is for the originator to transfer the credit risk associated with certain debt assets they own but the structure makes the vehicle of interest to various investors.

A synthetic CDO is a collateralised debt obligation (CDO) in which the underlying credit exposures of the issuer are taken on by the CDO using a credit default swap rather than through selling the debt assets to an SPV.

A synthetic CDO issues various tranches of security to investors as with a normal CDO, but then invests this cash in a high quality bond portfolio paying a safe, but low, return with minimal credit risk. They then boost this income by selling credit default swaps, thereby taking on the credit risk of the issuer's asset portfolio.

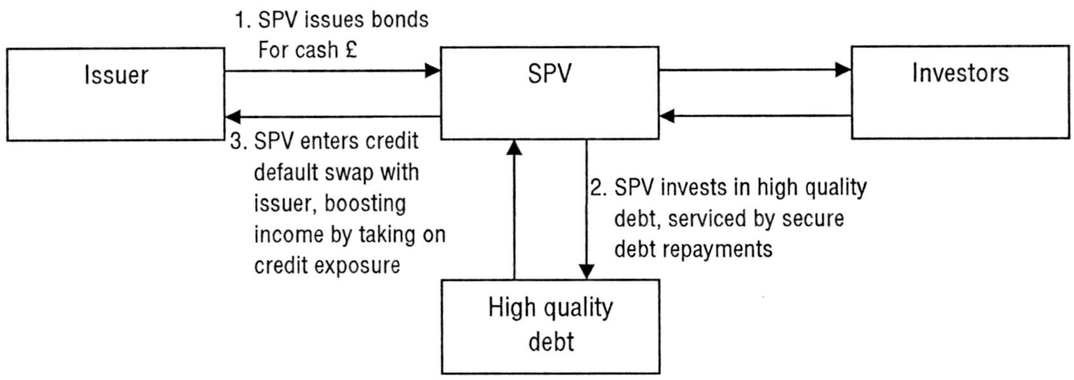

10 Commodity and Non-conventional Derivatives

Learning objective

18.11.1 Explain the characteristic of the main commodity derivatives, including, energy, softs/biofuels, metals, emissions, weather.

10.1 Introduction

Commodities may be divided into three categories

- Energy commodities – oil, natural gas and coal
- Soft commodities – agricultural
- Hard commodities – metals, diamonds

Derivatives are available on many of these products, and the pricing, trading and settlement principles of exchange traded derivatives are as described earlier under futures and options.

In addition to these commodity derivatives, non-conventional derivatives are available in relation to weather and emissions.

10.2 Energy derivatives

The main exchanges for energy derivatives are the New York Mercantile Exchange (NYMX) and ICE Futures Europe based in London, the latter settling its trades through LCH Clearnet.

In addition to exchange traded products, OTC contracts are also readily available in many products.

Energy derivatives allow investors to hedge energy costs or gain exposure to energy prices as a speculator.

10.3 Agricultural derivatives

The main exchange for agricultural derivatives is based in Chicago, the 'home' of the modern derivatives market, the Chicago Mercantile Exchange (CME).

10.4 Metal derivatives

The main exchange for metal derivatives is the London Metal Exchange.

10.5 Non-conventional derivatives

The CME trades derivatives in weather covering each of the US, Canada, Europe and Asia Pacific. These derivatives may cover temperature, snowfall, hurricanes and other potential weather events in specific regions and allow farmers to hedge against adverse weather effects.

A temperature-based derivative, for example, will pay out based on the number of 'heating degree days', ie the number of days in a specific period when the temperature falls below a certain level (usually 19°C) and the amount by which it falls below this level in the specified area.

11 Property Derivatives

Learning objective	**18.11.4 Understanding** the role of the Investment Property Database indices in the market.

11.1 Introduction

The Investment Property Databank (IPD) is a London based organisation specialising in the provision of data related to commercial property investment worldwide, and property derivatives are available based on certain IPD indices. These derivatives are primarily targeted at institutions and high net worth individuals allowing them to easily gain or hedge property market exposure.

IPD based derivatives include

- **Property income certificates (PICs)** – structured as listed Eurobonds with an embedded swap, delivering IPD returns on a quarterly basis over a specified period, commonly three years.
- **IPD Index Swaps** – where the buyer receives the total return on the IPD index in exchange for LIBOR plus a margin.
- **UK IPD Trades** – pays the total return earned by UK commercial property based on the IPD annual index less 2.8%. They are warrants listed on the LSE.

Chapter Roundup

Derivatives

- A derivative is an investment whose value is derived from the value of something else.
- Derivatives may be used by
  - Speculators = risk-taker seeking large profits.
  - Hedger = someone seeking to reduce risk.
  - Arbitrageurs = someone seeking a riskless profit.

Futures/forwards

- A future is an agreement to buy or sell a standard quantity of a specified asset on a fixed future date at a price agreed today.
- Futures are exchange tradeable, forwards are OTC equivalents of futures.
- Futures/forwards avoid the up-front cost and holding costs of trading the physical items.
- Speculator believes
  - Prices rising => Buy/long future.
  - Prices falling => Sell/short future.
- Hedger = establish a position with futures that will make a gain to offset the loss arising on the asset/interest rate movement.
  - Protect against price fall/interest rate rise = short hedge (sell futures) – Buyer/borrower hedge.
  - Protect against price rise/interest rate fall = long hedge (buy futures) – Seller/depositor hedge.
- Specific contracts

Contract	FTSE100	Long gilt	Short-term interest rate
Unit of trade	Index pts × £10	£100,000 nominal 4% notional gilt	£500,000 principal
Quote	Index pts	Price per £100 nominal	100 – Interest rate
Tick size	0.5 points	£0.01p	0.01% (1 basis point)
Tuck value	£5 (£10 per point)	£10	£12.50
Settlement	Cash	Physical	Cash

- Hedging with future

$$\text{No contracts} = \frac{\text{Portfolio value}}{\text{Futures quote} \times £10} \times \beta$$

$$\text{\% Hedge efficiency} = \frac{\text{Absolute gain/loss on future}}{\text{Absolute gain/loss on cash market}}$$

$$\text{Locked-in value} = \text{Portfolio value} \times \left(1 + \left(\frac{\text{Futures quote} - \text{Cash quote}}{\text{Cash quote}} \times \beta\right)\right)$$

- Basis = futures price – cash price, normally negative.

- Futures fair value is established by arbitrages/index arbitrage.
- Contango = futures price > cash price = Normal market circumstances.

  Backwardation = cash price > futures price = when asset is in short supply.
- Futures traded on NYSE Liffe settle on LCH.CLearnet who require
  - Initial margin = returnable deposit equal to the worst probably one day price movement paid by both the buyer and seller.
  - Variation margin = mark to market profit/loss for the previous **trading day**.

    Loss maker → LCH → gain maker

Options

- An option is a contract that confers the right but not the obligation to buy or sell an asset at a given price on or before a given date.
- A call option is a right to buy and a put option is a right to sell.
- American = can be exercised on or before the expiry date.

  European = can be exercised on at expiry only.
- In-the-money → option is worth exercising.

  Out-of-the-money → option is not worth exercising.

  At-the-money → asset price = strike price (or is close to it).
- Premium = intrinsic value + time value.

  intrinsic value = difference between asset price and exercise price if the option is in-the-money, zero if out-of-the-money.

  Time value = balance of premium.
- Factors affecting option values and sensitively measures

	Impact		
Increase in	**Call option**	**Put option**	**Sensitivity measures**
Share price	Up	Down	Delta and gamma
Exercise price	Down	Up	N/A
Volatility	Up	Down	Vega
Time of expiry	Up	Down	Theta
Interest rates	Up	Down	Rho
Asset yields	Down	Up	Phi

- Option and future positions can be combined together to form trading strategies.

Short selling/stock lending

- Sale of an asset that is not owned, achieved through stock borrowing.

Contract for difference

- A contract that is settled by a cash payment equating to the change in value of the underlying asset over the relevant period.

Warrants

- Long call option with some differences
  - Longer dated.
  - Exercise results in a new share being issued.
  - Traded on LSE.
- Warrant value = $\frac{A}{1+q}$ × Number of shares
- $= \frac{\text{Warrant price} - \text{Intrinsic value}}{\text{Share price}}$
- $= \frac{\text{Time value}}{\text{Share price}}$
- Covered warrants are issued by financial institutions to hedge their position in the underlying shares or options thereon.

Convertibles

- Give the right, but not the obligation, to convert debt/preference shares into ordinary shares.
- Statistics
  - Conversion ratio = Number of shares received per bond held.
  - Conversion value = Conversion ratio × Share price
  - Conversion premium = $\frac{\text{Conv} - \text{S}}{\text{S}}$
  - Convertible price = Value of straight bond + $\frac{A}{1+q}$ × CR

Swaps

- Swaps are a form of over-the-counter derivative (OTC). There are many different types of swaps including interest rate, currency and equity swaps.
- Interest rate swap = exchange interest flows only, no exchange of principal, used to speculate or hedge interest rates. Cash flows are netted – a contract for difference.
- Currency swap = exchange of interest and principal in different currencies used to speculate or hedge foreign currency/currency borrowings. Cash flows cannot be netted as in different currencies.
- Equity swap = exchange total return from an index for money market return, used to speculate or hedge equity exposure. No exchange of principal. Cash flows are netted – a contract for difference.
- Inflation swap = exchange inflation indexed return for a money market return, no exchange of principal. Cash flows netted – a contract for difference.
- Credit default swap (CDS) = a form of insurance that can be bought against the potential default of a specific asset or basket of assets.
- Collateralised Debt Obligation (CDO) = Securitised portfolio of assets financed by tranches with differing risk characteristics.

Commodity and property and other derivatives

- Derivatives are available on energy, hard and soft commodities as well as weather and emission.
- IPD = Investment Property Databank publishes index data, swaps are available on this index.

Test Your Knowledge

Check your knowledge of the chapter here, without referring back to the text.

1. Define a future.

2. What is the primary difference between forwards and futures?

3. An investor goes long five December FTSE 100 futures at 4523 and closes out their position at 4551. Calculate the profit or loss on the trade.

4. A portfolio with a beta of 0.9 is valued at £42m. If the FTSE-100 index future is quoted at 5,400 points how many contracts will be needed to hedge the portfolio against the market fall.

5. An investor is looking to borrow £50m for three months in three months' time and is concerned that rates may rise. Which contract should they use to hedge, how many contracts should they trade and what action should they take?

6. How much is the notional coupon, the tick size and tick value on the Long Gilt Future?

7. Define basis, contango and backwardation.

8. Define an option.

9. What is the breakeven price for a 140 put with a 8 premium?

10. A share is priced at 120. A 110 call has a premium of 15. What is the time value.

11. What factors influence the fair value of an option?

12. What is the motivation of a long straddle?

    A Increasing volatility
    B Decreasing volatility
    C Moderately bullish
    D Moderately bearish

13. Contracts options, covered warrants and warrants.

14. A convertible bond is priced at 98.20 and gives the right to convert into 20 shares. The current share price is £3.95, calculate the conversion premium.

15. Define a swap.

16. What is a CDS and a CDO?

Test Your Knowledge: Answers

1. A future is an agreement to buy or sell a standard quantity of a specified asset on a fixed future date at a price agreed today.

   (See Section 2.1)

2. Futures are exchange tradeable, forwards trade OTC

   (See Section 2.1.5)

3. £1,400 profit

   28 point × £10 × 5 contracts = £1,400 profit

   (See Section 2.2)

4. No contracts = $\frac{\text{Portfolio value}}{\text{Futures quote} \times \text{£10}} \times \beta = \frac{42{,}000{,}000}{5{,}400 \times \text{£10}} \times 0.9 = 700$ contracts

   (See Section 2.2.2)

5. The investor should use the 3-month sterling future. To cover a £50m borrowing they should sell 100 contracts.

   (See Section 2.4)

6. 6%, £0.01, £10.00

   (See Section 2.3.4)

7. - Basic = futures price – cash price, normally negative
   - Contango = futures price > cash price = Normal market circumstances
   - Backwardation = cash price > futures price = when asset is in short supply

   (See Section 2.5)

8. An option is a contract that confers the right but not the obligation to buy or sell an asset at a given price on or before a given date.

   (See Section 3.1)

9. 140 – 8 =132

   (See Section 3.6.3)

10. Intrinsic value = 120 – 110 = 10

    Premium = intrinsic value + time value

    15 = 10 + Time value

    Time value = 5

    (See Section 3.8)

11. The value of the underlying asset, exercise price, time to expiry, volatility, interest rates and asset yield.

    (See Section 3.8)

12. A A long straddle is a suitable strategy for someone who believes volatility will increase.

(See Section 4)

13.

	Option	Covered warrant	Warrant
Term	Short < 9 months	Short/medium	Long
Exercise	Existing share is transferred	Existing share is transferred	New share issued by the company
Dilution	None	None	Dilution by new shares of exercised
Pricing	Per share	Per share	Per warrant (may cover several shares)
Issuer	Anyone	Anyone	The relevant company
Settlement	Physical	Cash	Physical
Traded	NYSE Liffe	LSE	LSE
Stamp duty	No	Yes	Yes

(See Section 6)

14. Premium = $\frac{\text{Conv} - \text{S}}{\text{S}} = \frac{(98.20/20) - 3.95}{3.95} = 0.243$ or 24.3%

(See Section 7)

15. A swap is an agreement to exchange future cash flows for a specified period.

(See Section 9)

16. CDS = Credit default swap – a means of hedging credit risk, a form of insurance against default.

CDO = Collateralised debt obligation – asset backed (securitised) investment vehicle used to remove credit risk from the originator's balance sheet.

(See Section 9.5)

13 Collective Investments

INTRODUCTION

The vast majority of funds invested by UK citizens is not invested directly, rather it is pooled with the funds of many other individuals and managed on a combined basis

In this chapter we outline the major collective investment vehicles available in the UK, detailing their characteristics, structure and regulations.

We then examine some of the more specialist funds such as ETFs, hedge funds and structured products that are typically established offshore where the investment restrictions are lower and the tax position is more benign.

We also consider the various tax wrappers available to UK individuals that may allow them to make their investments in a more tax-efficient manner.

Finally we take a look at investment products provided by life assurance companies and at pension funds that are also commonly pooled.

CHAPTER CONTENTS

Chapter Learning Objectives

19 Investment products

Demonstrate an ability to analyse the characteristics, inherent risks, behaviours and relevant tax considerations of investment products

19.1.1 **Compare** and contrast investing through direct investments in securities and assets compared with investing through indirect investments.

19.1.2 **Distinguish** between open and closed ended funds.

19.1.3 **Distinguish** the features, risks and benefits of unit trusts, investment trusts and open-ended investment companies.

19.1.4 **Explain** the additional benefits and risks of investing in split capital investment trusts.

19.1.5 **Explain** the key features and objectives of Exchange Traded Funds (ETFs) and Exchange Traded Commodities (ETCs).

19.1.6 **Explain** the key features and objectives of Venture Capital Trusts and Enterprise Investment Schemes.

19.1.7 **Explain** the features and objectives of

- private client funds.
- hedge funds and funds of hedge funds.
- structured products.
- wraps and other platforms.

19.1.8 **Identify** the characteristics and advantages of Individual Savings Accounts (ISAs), Child Trust Funds (CTFs), National Savings and Investments, Life assurance based investments and Defined Contribution pension arrangements.

1 Collective Investments

Learning objective

19.1.1 Compare and contrast investing through direct investments in securities and assets compared with investing through indirect investments.

19.1.2 Distinguish between open and closed ended funds.

1.1 Introduction

A **collective** or **pooled** investment is a scheme by which the money of a large number of investors can be pooled to purchase shares or other securities. By participating in a collective investment, investors can participate in a pool of investments that would be more difficult to own directly as an individual.

1.2 Advantages and disadvantages of collective investments

There are advantages and disadvantages of collective investment, as compared with direct investment.

Advantages of indirect investments	Disadvantages of indirect investments
An individual can invest relatively small amounts, perhaps on a regular basis.	The individual can only choose baskets of investments selected by fund managers, not by himself, and this will not suit all investors.
The pooling of investments enables the fund to make purchases of securities at lower cost than would be possible for an individual.	Although the individual does not have to pick individual securities, he still has to choose the fund manager, and different managers' performance can vary widely.
The time involved in directly managing one's own portfolio is saved.	Although 'star' fund managers can have a successful track record with a fund, such 'star' managers may switch jobs, making future management of the fund less certain.
The funds are managed by professional fund managers. A fund manager with a good past performance record may be able to repeat the performance in the future.	Larger collective funds find it more difficult to invest in shares of companies with a relatively small capitalization, because of the small quantities of stock available.
A wide diversification between different shares and sectors can be achieved: this can be impractical and costly in dealing charges for a small portfolio held by an individual.	Successful collective funds investing in smaller companies can become a victim of their own success if more funds are brought in, as a greater fund size can make it more difficult for such a fund to follow their successful strategy.
Risk is reduced by exposure to a widely diversified spread of investments in the underlying portfolio.	There is a layer of charges that are payable within funds that would not be incurred through direct investment.
Specialisation in particular sectors is possible.	
The investor can gain exposure to foreign stocks, which can be costly and inconvenient for an individual who holds shares directly.	
Different funds provide for different investment objectives, such as income or growth, or a combination of both.	
There is no capital gains tax payable when the fund trades in shares, (as would be the case with direct investment), CGT only arises for the investor when the fund is sold.	

1.3 Types of collective investment

Collective funds may be either

- **Onshore funds** – where the assets are held and managed in the UK and are subject to UK regulations and UK taxes.
- **Offshore funds** – where the assets are held and managed overseas and are subject to overseas regulations and overseas taxes.

Note that we are referring above to how the fund itself is taxed on any income it generates or any gains it makes. From the individual investor's perspective, a UK investor will be subject to UK tax on any income or gains made from their investment irrespective of where a fund is located.

UK collective investments may take one of the following forms

- Unit trusts
- Open-ended investment companies (OEICs), also known as Investment Companies with Variable Capital (ICVCs)
- Investment trusts (including split level trusts)
- Private client funds
- Life assurance funds
- Pension funds

Offshore funds typically have a similar legal form to these onshore funds though the offshore regulatory and tax nature is more suitable for specialist funds such as

- Exchange traded funds (ETFs) and exchange traded commodities (ETCs)
- Hedge funds and funds of hedge funds
- Structured products

In addition to these types of collective fund there are various tax wrappers that we need to consider that may allow an investor to partly or fully shelter any income or gains from tax and particular tax wrappers we need to be aware of include

- NS&I (formerly National Savings and Investments) products
- Individual savings accounts (ISAs), junior ISAs (JISAs) and child trust funds (CTFs)
- Enterprise Investment Schemes (EISs), Seed Enterprise Investment Schemes (SEIS) and Venture Capital Trusts (VCTs)

1.4 Open-ended and closed-ended funds

Unit trusts are normally open-ended funds which means that the trust can create new units when new investors subscribe and it can cancel units when investors cash in their holdings. OEICs are similarly structured. This buying and selling causes money to flow in to these funds when individuals are investing and causes money to flow out when they are realising their investments.

In contrast investment trusts are closed-ended. Investment trust shares trade on the stock exchange just like any other listed shares and new investors buy investment trust shares from existing holders of the shares who wish to sell. Such buying and selling does not alter the funds held by the investment trust.

Open-ended funds	Closed-ended funds
▪ The price closely reflects the underlying net asset value (NAV) of the investment.	▪ The investments must be purchased from another investor. The price is subject to supply and demand and may not reflect the underlying net asset value (NAV). High demand increases the price; low demand reduces the price. ▪ Where the price is greater than the underlying value of the investment, it is said to be at a 'premium' to NAV, where it is below it is at a 'discount' to NAV.
▪ New investors can bring in new money, allowing the fund managers to invest in new opportunities.	▪ There is no new money coming in: fund managers must sell assets in order to make investments.
▪ When investors sell, assets must be sold to release cash to pay them possibly disrupting set policies and strategies.	▪ When investors sell, there is no need to sell assets as the total amount of money invested remains; the same set policies and strategies can be maintained.
▪ Unit trusts, OEICs and life assurance investments are open-ended, as are many offshore investment funds.	▪ Investment trusts and some offshore funds are closed-ended.

2 Unit Trusts

Learning objective

19.1.3 Distinguish the features, risks and benefits of unit trusts, investment trusts and open-ended investment companies.

2.1 Characteristics of unit trusts

Unit trusts are, legally, trusts, and as such their activities are monitored by **trustees**. The overall objectives of each fund are determined in advance and laid out in a **trust deed**. This states the fund investment objectives in terms of the risk/reward profile and may indicate the appropriate markets the fund may invest in. For example, it may be felt worthwhile for a fund manager to establish a unit trust investing in highly speculative emerging markets in order to maximise returns for its investors.

On the other hand, other groups of investors may wish to have their money placed into reasonably secure short-term liquid issues, e.g. short-dated gilts, generating a reasonable income flow. Each scheme will have its own particular emphasis and a selection of stocks and a strategy determined by this emphasis.

2.2 Parties involved

There are three parties involved in the operation of a unit trust:

- The unit trust manager – an authorised firm whose role is to
  - market the unit trust
  - price the unit trust
  - buy and sell units from/to investors
  - create and liquidate units
  - define the trust terms
  - appoint the trustee

- The trustee – normally a bank or insurance company who holds the unit trusts' investments on behalf of the fund and whose roles include
  - Safeguard the assets of the trust.
  - Ensure that the manager is acting in accordance with regulations
  - Ensure the fund manager invests in accordance with the investment objectives
- The fund manager who deals in the funds' assets in accordance with the terms of the trust deed

The unit trust manager and the trustee must apply jointly to the FSA for the fund to gain authorisation (see later). If the FSA refuse authorisation the applicants must refer the matter to the Financial Services and Markets Tribunal within 28 days if they wish to appeal.

2.3 Pricing and dealing in units

Unit trusts raise money by issuing **units** that are **created** by the manager when cash is subscribed. This cash forms the initial pool of funds invested by the manager for the unit holders. The manager must then act as a market maker for the units, quoting **bid** and **offer** prices based on the bid and offer values of the underlying investments and the level of his initial charge, though unit trusts may adopt single pricing that is common for OEICs.

Unit trusts are not continuously priced in the same way as shares, instead the value of the underlying fund is determined at regular intervals (normally daily) at what is called the **valuation point**. At that time the total value of the underlying assets is measured and this value is divided by the number of units in issue to give a value or price per unit.

Prices can be set on a historic or forward pricing basis.

- Where the price the investor pays is based on the previous valuation point, the pricing is described as historic. All units purchased up to the next valuation point, usually on the following day, will be at the same price.
- Where the investor pays a price based on the next valuation point, it is called forward pricing. All units purchased up to next valuation point will be at that price.

A manager using the historic pricing basis must move to a forward pricing basis if the value of the fund is believed to have changed by 2% or more since the last valuation point or if the investor requests forward pricing.

If an individual then wishes to buy/sell units, then the fund manager must accommodate him. The manager will attempt to match purchases and sales, though this may not always be possible. If the purchases exceed the sales, the fund manager will have to create new units and invest, as part of the trust property, the excess money received. If, however, the sales exceed the purchases, the fund manager will have to liquidate some units, i.e. sell some of the underlying investments of the fund and cancel the units. The creation and cancellation of units only takes place at the valuation point and all dealing, creations and cancellations are undertaken based on the value at that point.

As **open-ended** funds, unit trusts may suffer significant inflows and outflows of cash depending on whether investors are buying or selling units. As a result, unit trusts need to maintain a reasonable degree of liquidity.

To ease the trading process trust managers can keep units repurchased from unit holders to enable them to supply purchasers without creating new units, ie hold a stock of units in what is called the manager's box. This helps the manager avoid having to create and cancel units every day and saves considerable money on the acquisition and disposal costs of the underlying assets, as units are recycled rather than being created and destroyed.

2.4 Fund charges

The charges on a unit trust must be explicit in the trust deed and documentation. They should give details of the current charges and the extent to which managers can change them.

Charges need to be made to cover the following costs.

- Managing the fund
- Administration of the fund
- Marketing
- Regulation and compliance costs
- General administration
- Direct marketing costs
- Commissions for intermediaries

These charges can be taken in one or more of three ways, via an initial charge, an exit charge or through annual management charges.

When there are net purchases of units by investors and new units are created, the manager must buy securities for the fund, incurring dealing costs. Similarly, when there are net sales and units need to be liquidated, the manager must sell some of the underlying securities of the fund and, again, incur dealing costs.

Part of the purpose of the initial and exit charges is to cover these costs and normally they will simply be absorbed by the fund, however where the scale of the creation/liquidation is significant in relation to the size of the fund the manager can charge a dilution levy on those investors who have caused the fund to incur these costs in order to avoid any adverse effect on other investors.

As such, a dilution levy is a discretionary charge. In addition, it is not a charge paid to the manager, rather it is paid to the fund to cover these dealing costs. Any dilution levy charged is not reflected in the quoted price of the units, rather it is displayed as a separate explicit charge on the contract note.

Where the fund does not have a bid-offer spread but adopts single pricing this dilution issue is much more significant as any dealing in fund assets must then be borne by the unit holders

2.5 Fund distributions

Income generated by the fund must be distributed to the unit holders. Distributions from unit trusts (and OEICs) are treated in the same manner as the underlying investments. That is, distributions made by an equity fund are treated as dividends and paid net of 10% withholding tax, whereas distributions from bond and money market funds are treated as interest payments and are paid net of 20% tax.

2.6 Regulation of unit trusts and OEICs

2.6.1 Financial Services Authority

In the context of collective investments the role of the FSA is to authorise and regulate UK funds and recognise offshore funds that are subject to adequate overseas regulation. Only authorised or recognised funds can be marketed to the general public and regulated collective investments that can be marketed in this way include

- OEICs, also known as ICVC
- Authorised unit trusts
- Recognised overseas schemes

Unregulated schemes cannot be marketed to retail investors.

In respect of unit trusts the FSA controls the contents of the trust's trust deed and other key areas such as pricing of units. To be authorised a unit trust must be constituted under trust, the manager and the trustee of the scheme must be separate UK or EU companies, each with a UK place of business and each authorised to conduct regulated activity in its own right under the **Financial Services and Markets Act (FSMA) 2000**.

The FSA has the right at any stage to revoke the authorisation of any scheme if it is satisfied that

- The requirements of the authorisation order are no longer satisfied.
- It is undesirable for the interests of participants, or potential participants, in the scheme that it should continue or be authorised.
- The manager or trustee of the scheme has contravened any provision of FSMA 2000, or any rules or regulations made under it.

The FSA has the right to appoint inspectors to investigate and report on the affairs of any authorised scheme. As with the FSA's other investigative powers, all parties are obliged to supply any information or assistance required of them.

The FSA has made a number of regulations which specify the constitution and management of authorised schemes, the powers and duties of the trustees and the rights and obligations of the participants. These regulations cover

- Trust constitution
- Restrictions placed on the manager
- Scheme investment and borrowing powers
- Pricing of units
- Dealing in units
- Unit holder meetings.

The regulations covering authorised unit trusts (AUTs) and OEICs/ICVCs are found in the Collective Investment Schemes Sourcebook named '**COLL**' which came into force on **13 February 2007**.

2.6.2 Types of authorised fund

The FSA recognises three different types of scheme

- **UCITS schemes** – schemes that conform to the UCITS directive and can be marketed throughout the European Economic Area (EEA)
- **Non-UCITS retail schemes** – authorised funds capable of being marketed to retail investors but which do not fall within the scope of UCITS, perhaps as a result of the assets held. Such schemes can only be marketed in the UK
- **Qualified Investor Scheme (QIS)** – only available to experienced professional investors, not retail investors

Only the first two of these classes may be marketed to retail investors and in order to ensure the protection of retail investors, the FSA impose investment limits for these schemes. No investment limits are considered necessary for QISs.

2.6.3 Types of security

The FSA recognises two different types of security, approved securities and non-approved securities.

Approved securities consist of securities that are listed on an eligible market, ie

- Transferable securities
  - Shares
  - Debentures
  - Government and public securities
  - Warrants
  - Certificates representing certain securities (eg depository receipts)
- Approved money market instruments
- Collective investments
- Derivatives
- Deposits

Any other securities, eg unlisted securities, are non-approved.

A market in an EEA member state is automatically an eligible market. In addition, a market can be deemed to be eligible if the investment manager and the trustee decide it is appropriate which requires that it is

- Regulated
- Regularly operational
- Recognised
- Open to the public
- Liquid
- Effectively arranged to facilitate the unimpeded transmission of income and capital

2.6.4 Investment limits

Authorised fund managers of AUTs and ICVCs must ensure that, taking account of the investment objectives and policy of the authorised fund as stated in the most recently published prospectus of the fund, the scheme property of the authorised fund aims to provide a prudent spread of risk. This is achieved by setting

- **Aggregate spread limits** – limits on the proportion of the fund that may be invested in certain classes of investments
- **Individual spread limits** – limits on the proportion of the fund that may be invested in the approved securities of one body/issuer
- **Concentration limits** – limits on the maximum proportion of the securities issued by any one body that may be held by the fund

Aggregate spread limits

The following aggregate limits are placed on fund investments.

	UCITS schemes	Non-UCITS retail schemes
Transferable securities – approved – non approved	90% – 100% 10% – 0%	80% – 100% 20% – 0%
Other funds – regulated – non regulated	100% 0%	80% – 100% 20% – 0%
Money market instruments and deposits	100%	100%
OTC derivatives	100%	100%
Gold	0%	10%
Real property	0%	100%
Fund borrowing	10% (Temporarily)	10% (Permanently)

Individual spread limits

In addition to these aggregate limits, the FSA impose the following spread limits. For non-tracking funds, the maximum proportion of the fund that can be exposed to any one body (excluding government and public securities) is as follows.

	UCITS schemes	Non-UCITS retail schemes
Deposits	20%	20%
Transferable securities **or** money market instruments	10% in each of up to 4 securities, 5% thereafter	10%
Transferable securities **and** money market instruments	20%	20%
Aggregate of two or more of Transferable securities **or** money market instruments Deposits OTC derivatives	20%	20%
Government and public securities where they represent <35% of the fund >35% of the fund	 No limit 30% in any one issue + minimum six issues held in fund	 No limit 30% in any one issue + minimum six issues held in fund
Other funds Provided that the other fund's own exposure to further other funds is limited to	20% 10%	35% 15%
OTC derivatives	5% (increased to 10% if the counterparty is an approved bank)	10%
Real property	N/A	15%

For tracking funds, both UCITS and non-UCITS schemes can invest up to 20% in any one particular share, and up to 35% where justified by exceptional conditions.

Concentration limits

UCITS schemes must comply with the following concentration limits related to the proportion of the issue of any one investment that they may hold

	UCITS schemes
Non-voting shares	0%
Shares issued by one company	10%
Debt issued by one company	10%
Money market instruments issued by one body	10%
Units in a collective investment	25%

3 OEICs AND ICVCs

Learning objective

19.1.3 Distinguish the features, risks and benefits of unit trusts, investment trusts and open-ended investment companies.

3.1 The OEIC framework

Investment trusts and unit trusts have existed in the UK since the 1860s and 1930s respectively. However in January 1997 the Treasury introduced regulations in connection to OEICs that created a new type of investment product with many (the best) of the features of both unit and investment trusts.

In order to accommodate the OEICs into the system, a special company structure was introduced to allow a company to continually issue and redeem its own shares, making it **open-ended**. The aim was to make an investment product that was more flexible and more appealing to the European market.

OEICs are be able to issue both **bearer and registered** shares. Several classes of shares are possible and within each class it is possible to have both large and small denomination shares.

An OEIC must use a depositary to look after the funds, much as a unit trust uses a trustee. The depository must be independent of the OEIC and separately authorised and the assets of the OEIC are registered in the depository's name.

OEICs were originally required to adopt single pricing with no bid-offer spread, the manager levying entrance and exit charges as necessary. Since October 2008 OEICS have been permitted to use dual pricing though few do.

4 INVESTMENT TRUSTS

Learning objective

19.1.3 Distinguish the features, risks and benefits of unit trusts, investment trusts and open-ended investment companies.

19.1.4 Explain the additional benefits and risks of investing in split capital investment trusts.

4.1 Introduction

The name investment trust is, to an extent, misleading. Investment trusts are not trusts in law, rather they are **public limited companies** whose shares are listed on the Stock Exchange. As listed companies their activities are regulated by the Companies Act and the by London Stock Exchange.

In an investment trust the money is invested by the fund manager on behalf of the shareholders to generate a combination of capital growth and income in accordance with the investment trust's objectives. The aim of the investment manager is to maximise the value of the shares of the investment trust and the majority of investment trusts invest very heavily in equities, both UK and overseas, in order to achieve this objective. The fund manager will obviously charge a fee for this service, typically around 0.5% of the fund value.

Investment trusts initially raise money by issuing shares. If an individual wishes to liquidate his investment, or make a new investment, he needs to either sell the shares to someone else, or buy some shares from someone else, through the stock exchange. Other than to pay income distributions, money will not be repaid from the fund unless it is terminated.

As a result, investment trusts are not subject to inflows and outflows of capital as faced by unit trusts and OEICs so do not need much liquidity in their investments. Investment trusts are, therefore, referred to as **closed-end funds**, since the size of the fund itself is independent of the buying or selling of shares. It is a function of the initial capital subscribed and the gains generated on that capital.

If an investment trust wishes to raise new funds they can do this in the same way as any other company through either a rights issue or through borrowing and trusts are able to gear up the portfolio without being constrained by the FSA's investment and borrowing restrictions as these only apply to unit trusts and OEICs. This gives investment trusts the potential to significantly increase the risk of the fund, as well as increasing the potential for returns.

4.2 Split-capital investment trusts

The split-capital company, often called a split-level trust, was first introduced in the 1960s. In this type of investment trust company there are two or more classes of capital made up of sub-classes of ordinary shares and preference shares .

Types of share that may be issued by a split-capital trust include the following, in descending order of risk.

- **Capital shares** – Capital shares are ordinary shares that, at the end of the company's life (set as a fixed period at the inception of the investment trust), are entitled to the value of the underlying portfolio attributable to ordinary shareholders (ie after satisfying any preference shares), less the income shares' fixed right to capital represented by their nominal value. The typical life of an investment trust with such a class of capital is seven to ten years. Capital shares tend to be volatile as they accept the majority of the underlying portfolio's capital risk.
- **Income shares** – This class of capital is entitled to all the income from the underlying portfolio and a fixed entitlement to capital.
- **Preference shares** – These provide a constant dividend which is paid in any year in which dividends are paid. They also have an entitlement to a fixed nominal value on the winding up of the company. With some of the more recent preference share issues this has been as low as 1p per share. These are sometimes referred to as Annuity Income Shares as, like an annuity, they provide a high level of income in return for an initial capital investment. Indeed, since the initial investment is eroded over the life of the investment trust, the dividend yield will be very high.
- **Zero dividend preference shares (zeros)** – These offer a predetermined capital growth over the life of the investment trust, receiving only a fixed capital sum on winding up, before any capital is

returned to any other shareholders. This capital return is not certain, however, as the assets of the investment trust could be insufficient to cover this sum on a winding up if the trust performs particularly badly.

As in any company the preference shares carry a lower risk than the ordinary shares as they have priority for the payment of any dividends or capital. The zeros have the highest priority, hence the lowest risk on a winding-up, the capital shares rank last in this event and therefore carry the highest risk.

4.3 Pricing and dealing

As we noted above, investment trusts are public limited companies whose shares trade like any other equities on the London Stock Exchange and any dealing is subject to the same charges as any other shares, ie brokers fees, SDRT and the PTM levy – a feature that clearly distinguishes them from unit trusts and OEICs.

Another distinguishing feature is how they are priced. Whereas unit trust and OEICs are priced regularly (usually daily) based on the value of the underlying assets, the price of shares in investment trusts is governed by the market forces of supply and demand that may result in the price being at a premium (above) or a discount (below) the underlying portfolio value.

When share prices are rising, investment trust shares are particularly strong and at such times it is common to find shares are trading at a premium. In normal market conditions, however, investment trust shares normally trade at a discount as the fund manager's fees consume some of the fund income, thereby absorbing some of its value.

4.4 Fund distributions

Unit trusts generally distribute all their income, except in the case of accumulation trusts. Investment trust companies, like other companies, declare dividends that may or may not exhaust the available income. Most of them reinvest part of their profits, which increases the invested capital for the benefit of the Ordinary shareholders.

4.5 Regulation

As a UK collective investment an investment trust is also subject to regulatory oversight by the **Financial Services Authority**, however, the investment powers of investment trust companies is limited by their Articles of Association and LSE rules.

Under these LSE rules

- 70% of their income must be derived from investments in shares and other securities.
- No individual investment may total more than 15% of the fund to avoid over-concentration.

5 Private Client Funds

earning objective	**19.1.7 Explain** the features and objectives of: private client funds.

5.1 Types of fund

Private clients are, generally speaking, high net worth individuals who place their funds under management with a broker. As with collective investment schemes, the objectives of these individuals vary. Some customers may be looking for rapid capital appreciation with minimal income flows, whilst others may be looking for a secure portfolio with a guaranteed flow of income.

In addition, there are a number of levels of service that clients may require, specifically

- **Execution-only service** – where the broker gives no advice or recommendations to the client but simply executes the clients orders. This is most suitable where the client either has a small number of shares, perhaps from a privatisation, that they need to be able to trade in, or where the client is an experienced investor who has the time and experience to control their investments. An additional facility the broker may offer here is a limit order service where the client may instruct the broker to buy or sell an asset if it reaches a certain price.
- **Advisory dealing service** – Where, in addition to executing trades the broker offers advice about any proposed transactions if requested to do so, though the client is not obliged to follow that advice.
- **Portfolio advisory service** – Where the broker undertakes an analysis of the client's financial position and objectives and advises the client about a long-term investment strategy and portfolio construction. With such a service the broker will be free to call the client and offer advice, though, again, the client is not obliged to follow that advice.
- **Portfolio discretionary service** – Where the broker undertakes an analysis of the client's financial position and objectives, formulates a long-term investment strategy and constructs and manages a portfolio on the client's behalf. The advantage to the broker is that, when operating within agreed parameters, they do not need to contact the client before dealing.

In addition to these services it is usual for the broker to offer a **nominee service** where any shares bought for the client can be registered in that nominees name with the broker's systems keeping track of their ownership. Such a system simplifies the paperwork and eases transaction execution. Brokers may also offer a **limit order service** where the broker will only fulfil the client's order if a particular price is reached during the day.

The exact structure and holdings of a private client will be dependent on a number of factors and how the fund manager assesses this is investigated later in this Study Text.

Given the differing objectives and constraints of private clients, performance appraisal has always been an issue, though the WM Private Client Performance Indicators or the FTSE APCIMS Private Client Indices may be useful here as benchmarks. Performance appraisal is covered in depth later in this Study Text.

6 Offshore Funds

6.1 Introduction

As well as UK funds many offshore funds exist which may be either

- **Regulated** – in which case they may be marketable in the UK. Typically Exchange Traded Funds (ETFs) are a regulated offshore funds that can be marketed in the UK and have a structure not dissimilar to OEICs.
- **Unregulated** – in which case they cannot be marketed in the UK. Typically hedge funds fall into this category.

The term 'offshore fund' refers to funds run outside the UK, usually in low tax areas. These include the Channel Islands, the Isle of Man, the Cayman Islands, Hong Kong and Bermuda. In recent years, Luxembourg and Dublin have become more significant also, as 'tax havens' within the European Union.

Many offshore funds are run by companies associated with large UK unit trust groups and most of the countries involved now have their own regulatory framework. Certain offshore funds receive recognition under the Financial Services and Markets Act 2000 (FSMA 2000) and may be marketed in the UK.

Non-regulated and non-recognised funds are subject to severe marketing restrictions in the UK. Prospectuses and details can only be forwarded to investment professionals such as stockbrokers and Independent Financial Advisers (IFAs).

The reduced investment restrictions and the absence of internal fund taxation makes these offshore locations particularly attractive for more specialist funds such as

- ETFs
- Hedge funds
- Structured products
- Private client funds – especially for non-UK residents

6.2 Exchange traded funds

Learning objective

19.1.5 Explain the key features and objectives of Exchange Traded Funds (ETFs) and Exchange Traded Commodities (ETCs).

6.2.1 Introduction

Exchange Traded Funds (ETFs) are open-ended collective investment vehicles that are UCITS compliant and represent a type of type of low cost, passively managed, diversified tracker fund. ETFs are usually established offshore (UK ETFs often being registered in Dublin) and have a structure similar to an OEIC, though some ETFs are constituted more like a unit trust.

In the UK, ETFs are listed on the LSE, their shares are priced in real time, traded through the SETS order book and settle through CREST. Their lack of initial charges makes their dealing costs much lower than either unit trusts or OEICs.

ETFs allow exposure to an index through the purchase of shares which must be listed and tradable on a stock exchange. ETFs are most commonly available for various international equity and bond indices however, they are also available on property, commodities and currencies. As passive funds they tend to have very low annual management fees, typically below those of other tracker funds.

ETFs are shares that afford the legal right of ownership over part of a basket of individual assets held by the fund. Through the activities of the ETF manager discussed below the ETF shares trade at prices that very closely match their underlying assets, hence very closely match the index.

To create an ETF a fund manager firstly needs to describe precisely the composition of the ETF, usually an index whose constituents change infrequently. They then assemble the appropriate basket of stocks and send them to a custodian bank for safekeeping. This basket of securities may have been purchased by the fund manager for the purposes of establishing the ETF, alternatively they may have been borrowed from other investors such as pension funds. On receipt of the appropriate stocks, the custodian issues the appropriate number of ETF shares. The ETFs can then be freely sold into the open market and from then on they can be freely traded between investors.

Redemption of ETFs is simply the reverse of the above creation process. The manager buys a large block of ETFs on the open market and sends it to the custodian bank and in return receives back an equivalent basket of individual stocks which are then sold on the open market or returned to their lenders.

In practice only the very biggest institutional money management firms with experience in indexing tend to play the role of managing an ETF. They direct pension funds with enormous baskets of stocks in markets all over the world to loan stocks necessary for the creation process. They also create demand by lining up customers, either institutional or retail, to buy a newly introduced ETF.

Because ETFs are based on indices that tend to be quite stable, the fund management costs tend to be very low. The manager looks to make money on the bid-offer spread and from any price anomalies between the ETF and the underlying shares. Whenever there is an opportunity to earn a little by buying one and selling the other, yielding on arbitrage gain, the manager will do so. This activity will have the effect of keeping the price of the ETF in line with the price of the underlying shares since it will involve buying the relatively under-priced asset (driving its price up) and selling the relatively overpriced asset (driving its price down).

Though a little cumbersome, this process achieves transparency and liquidity at modest cost. Everyone can see what goes into an ETF, investor fees are clearly laid out, investors can be confident that they can exit at any time, and the manager's fees are guaranteed to be modest.

ETFs are available in the UK over a wide variety of indices providing an easy and low cost route to investing in the main index, in high yield stocks, in growth stocks, in value stocks etc.

ETFs are also available on commodities where they are also known as Exchange Traded Commodities (ETCs). Like ETFs, ETCs are asset-backed open-ended investments that track the performance of the underlying commodity/index. They are traded and settled like shares and have the support of a market maker to ensure liquidity and are available on single commodities (eg gold) or on commodity indices (eg energy or precious metals).

A third category to be aware of is the Exchange Traded Note (ETN) that are unsecured bonds offering a return that tracks an index, often in specialist areas such as currencies. ETNs are typically issued by banks and investors face the credit risk of the issuer.

ETFs, ETCs and ETNs allow investors to adopt an investment style even with low levels of investment.

ETFs are eligible for ISA inclusion, and no Stamp Duty Reserve Tax (SDRT) is payable on the purchase of these dematerialised securities.

6.2.2 Synthetic ETFs

Rather than buying the underlying assets it is possible for the ETF manager to create a synthetic ETF by holding the investor's funds on deposit and gaining exposure to the relevant index through the use of derivatives.

One difficulty here is that there is no regulation governing how the investor's funds that represent the underlying collateral should be held. If they are held in the form of a safe and liquid deposit and the derivatives exposure is in line with the scale of this collateral then a synthetic fund exposes the investor to the same returns and risks as a normal physical ETF. If, however, they are held in a different form, such as a basket of shares, the underlying collateral will be at risk of a significant market downturn as experienced in the 2008 credit crunch. In addition, any lack of liquidity in this underlying collateral may also cause problems if investors wish to cash-in on a downturn.

Synthetic ETFs have also come under international criticism as when they are used in relation to emerging economies it is quite possible that a large fund may represent a disproportionately large share of the actual index itself, a proportion that possibly could not be held by a physical fund. It is suggested that such funds added to the economic difficulties arising from the credit crunch.

6.2.3 Charges

The charges incurred by ETFs are the same as for unit trusts and OEICs though they are usually at a lower level with, typically, zero initial and exit charges and 0.5% annual charges.

6.3 Hedge funds and absolute return funds

Learning objective

19.1.7 Explain the features and objectives of: hedge funds and funds of hedge funds.

6.3.1 Characteristics

In a normal fund (pension fund, unit trust, etc.) the fund manager is constrained to taking long positions in assets/asset classes dictated by the trust deed/investment policy. Such funds will, therefore, gain in a rising market and lose in a falling one.

Losses in falling markets may be reduced through, if permitted

- Switching to cash.
- Hedging the fund, perhaps through the use of derivatives, though typically the manager would not be permitted to hedge more than the value of the fund

As a result, normal funds tend to either hold positive asset positions or a zero position (cash/fully hedged).

Hedge funds were originally intended to offer investments against falling markets using derivatives and short selling. However hedge funds have moved away from this and now there are many different hedge funds with a massive range of strategies. Some are geared and highly focussed, whilst others consider the macroeconomy and gamble on interest rates and currencies. The one thing that all hedge funds have in common is their desire to search for **absolute returns**.

The hedge fund manager is not concerned about performance compared to benchmarks and therefore has the freedom to try and generate high returns and hence high personal rewards. This may create the need for a risky portfolio, and therefore the name hedge fund is slightly misleading. A better name would probably be isolation fund, since the hedge fund manager looks for specific bets to try and generate high returns.

There are many different classes of hedge fund, hence it is difficult to give a general definition, however, the features of a hedge fund would generally include the following.

- The facility to take both long and short positions (i.e. no constraint to long positions only).
- The facility to gear up long or short exposure with borrowings and/or derivatives to gain a level of exposure (value at risk) significantly greater than the intrinsic value of the fund itself. The level of exposure gained
- May render arbitrage trades cost effective, that otherwise would not be.
- Produces geared performance, sometimes producing quite spectacular returns.
- The possibility of investing in any security from shares and bonds through to currencies and commodities, though many hedge funds specialise.
- Typically, a very high minimum investment level, often in excess of £1m, though this is now changing.
- Typically based offshore, where regulations and disclosure requirements are lower.

6.3.2 Regulation

Hedge funds are themselves not regulated by the FSA and so are not generally marketable investments. However, the fund managers are themselves FSA regulated firms.

6.3.3 Fees

Hedge fund managers will receive a fixed base management fee, which is a percentage (often between 1% and 2%) of the value of assets under management and an incentive fee which is related to profits. As this cannot be negative if losses are made, there will often be a clause stating that if losses are made, these losses have to be repaid in any subsequent profits before an incentive fee can be paid.

Example

A hedge fund has a base fee of 1%. The incentive fee is 25% for any returns made over and above the risk-free rate. Gross returns during the year were 38% and the risk-free rate is 6%. What is the net return?

Solution

Fee = 1% + 25% × (38% – 6%) = 9%

Net return = 38% – 9% = 29%

6.3.4 Types of hedge funds

As we have already noted, the name 'hedge fund' is a huge misnomer that is applied to many categories of fund, from very low risk to super-geared funds. These funds may be broadly classified as follows.

- **Directional Long/short funds** – These take positions in stock and are often geared. They are not normally market neutral, but instead have a long or short bias.
- **Market-neutral or relative value funds** – These take long positions in stocks that are considered undervalued and short positions in stocks that are considered overvalued. The fund is neutral, in that the value of short positions is equal to the value of long positions and the sensitivity of long and short positions is the same. Other strategies of a market neutral portfolio are to look for arbitrage opportunities in warrants or derivatives. They should therefore be relatively intuitive to changes in the underlying market.
- **Global macro or tactical trading funds** – These bet on macroeconomic variables such as currencies or interest rates. They are often highly geared and use derivatives. Subgroups of macro funds are **futures funds**, which use futures to bet on certain asset classes such as currency, fixed income and commodities and **emerging-market funds**. These can sometimes be referred to as speculative or tactical funds.
- **Event-driven funds** – These bet on events specific to a company or security. One example of this would be to invest in distressed securities or shares involved in a merger or acquisition.

Fund of funds

Fund of funds – A fund of funds is, as the name suggests, a fund that invests in a selection of hedge funds. It enables small investors to access hedge funds. The benefits of a fund of funds are as follows.

- The fund of funds will invest in a variety of hedge funds, allowing the investor to diversify.
- A fund of funds provides easy access to investors who may be otherwise unable to use hedge funds. There may also be the opportunity to invest in funds that have otherwise closed to new investors.
- The manager of the fund of funds will have more expertise than the investor. He will have better access to information and will be more experienced in the due diligence required prior to investing in a hedge fund.

There are, of course, disadvantages, primarily the fee that the fund manager will charge.

6.4 Structured Products

earning objective

19.1.7 Explain the features and objectives of: structured products.

Structured products are securities that provide investors with a full or partial capital protection plus a certain type of return. The return typically depends on underlying performance of an index, and may be achieved through the buying and selling of embedded options or other **derivatives**. Structured products are often located offshore to take advantage of the greater investment freedom available.

Structured products are available that link repayment of capital to the investor by a pre-determined formula to the performance on an index such as the FTSE 100 Index (most commonly), or to other factors or combinations of factors.

- Some funds make use of derivatives in order to make a guarantee of a return of capital to the investor (which might be in the range of 85 to 100% of the original investment, for example).
- A **fixed period** often applies to the investment. There may or may not be a secondary market in the instrument, enabling the investor to sell before redemption.

7 Tax Wrappers

earning objective

19.1.8 Identify the characteristics and advantages of Individual Savings Accounts (ISAs), Child Trust Funds (CTFs), National Savings and Investments, Life assurance based investments and Defined Contribution pension arrangements.

19.1.6 Explain the key features and objectives of Venture Capital Trusts and Enterprise Investment Schemes.

7.1 National Savings & Investments products

7.1.1 Introduction

National Savings & Investments (NS&I) was formerly called 'National Savings'. Since they are guaranteed by HM Treasury NS&I products are offered by the government and, as such, are regarded as **'risk free'** investment since they are guaranteed by HM Treasury. NS&I products are generally available through **Post Offices**.

7.1.2 Tax treatment

None of NS&I's products are subject to capital gains tax, but some products are subject to income tax.

7.1.3 NS&I product range

The NS&I product range can be divided into the following types, on which more detail is provided below.

- Savings accounts
- Income bonds
- Growth bonds
- Tax-free schemes, comprising:
  - Fixed Interest Savings Certificates
  - Index Linked Savings Certificates
  - Direct ISAs
  - Children's Bonus Bonds
  - Premium Bonds

From time to time, NS&I also issues **Guaranteed Equity Bonds**, a product linked to stock market growth.

Interest rates and terms change fairly frequently, and up-to-date information can be found at the NS&I website – **www.nsandi.com**. (Follow the link to 'IFA Centre' and see the 'Quick Guide' for the latest summary).

7.2 Individual Savings Accounts (ISAs)

7.2.1 Introduction

An ISA is an **Individual Savings Account**, a form of tax-efficient savings plan. ISAs came into existence from 6 April 1999, as a replacement for Personal Equity Plans (PEPs) and TESSAs and from 6 April 2008 PEPs and TESSAs have no longer existed, having been automatically converted into ISAs.

An **ISA manager** must have HMRC approval and in order to gain HMRC approval to offer an ISA, all ISA managers must be authorised by the FSA.

7.2.2 Eligible investors

Eligible investors include anyone who:

- Is aged **18 or over**, or **aged 16 or over in the case of a cash ISA**, and
- Is **resident and ordinarily resident** in the UK for tax purposes, or
- Is a **Crown employee working abroad** and subject to UK tax on earnings or is the **spouse** or **civil partner** of such a person, and
- Has not already subscribed to any ISA of the same type as is to be applied for, in the same tax year

If the ISA holder ceases to be resident and ordinarily resident in the UK, the ISA can remain open and retain the UK tax benefits, but no new contributions can be made. There may be tax to pay in the foreign jurisdiction to which the investor emigrates.

It is not possible to hold an ISA jointly or as a trustee for someone else.

7.2.3 Types of ISA

There are **two** possible types of ISA, namely

- **Cash ISA**
- **Stocks and shares ISA.**

and each year an individual can invest in either or both a cash ISA and a stocks and shares ISA.

The definition of a cash ISA is given below. Any ISA that does not satisfy the definition of a cash ISA is a stocks and shares ISA.

7.2.4 Investment limits

The ISA contribution limits (**2012/13**) are summarised in the Table below.

ISA	Investment limited
Cash	£5,640
Stocks and shares	£11,280 less amount invested in cash ISA

Since 6 April 2011 these limits increase annually in line with the RPI.

Once funds are withdrawn from an ISA, they cannot be paid back in without counting as a new subscription. The ISA subscription limits apply to the total **payments in** to the account during the tax year.

Shares acquired from an approved profit-share scheme, share incentive plan or all-employee share option scheme may be **transferred directly** into the stocks and shares ISA. The value of the shares at the date of transfer will count towards the normal stocks and shares annual limit. They must be transferred within 90 days of the exercise of the option or release from the profit-sharing scheme.

Other subscriptions to ISA managers must generally be in the form of cash rather than, for instance, by means of existing shares. (If an investor wants to continue to hold shares he or she currently holds, but within the ISA wrapper, it is necessary to sell the shares, and then re-purchase within the ISA. This will normally incur dealing costs, although some providers may waive some of the costs). Subscriptions can be either lump sum or via regular savings schemes.

7.2.5 Cash ISA

The following can be included in a cash ISA.

- Cash deposited with building societies, credit unions and UK or European banks. Such accounts will have interest credited gross.
- Units in a money market fund holding cash deposits, or in a qualifying 'fund or funds' which invests solely in money market funds
- Funds and (from 6 April 2005) life insurance and stakeholder products qualifying for the cash component by passing the '5% test', ie they guarantee to return at least 95% of the capital
- The National Savings & Investments cash ISA

As noted above, any ISA that does not satisfy the conditions of a cash ISA is a stocks and shares ISA.

7.2.6 Tax benefits

Individuals are permitted to invest monies into an ISA (subject to annual limits) and once invested, any resultant **income or capital gains** generated will be **tax-free** and does not need to be recorded on the investor's tax return. Note, however, that the 10% tax credit on any dividends received by a stocks and shares ISA cannot be reclaimed.

7.2.7 Fund switching

If the investor is unhappy with the ISA manager for any reason, it is permissible to transfer funds between ISA managers. When doing so, any funds in a

- Cash ISA can be transferred into either a new cash ISA or a stocks and shares ISA
- Stocks and shares ISA must be transferred into a new stocks and shares ISA

7.3 Junior ISAs and Child Trust Funds

7.3.1 Junior ISAs

The Junior ISA is a new tax efficient savings account designed for adults to save and invest on behalf of children that will be available from 1 November 2011. Junior ISAs will be open to any child who is

- resident in the UK or are the dependent of a Crown servant working overseas
- under the age of 18
- either
  - born on or after 3rd January 2011
  - does not have a Child Trust Fund account

Types of Junior ISA

As with adult ISAs there aree two different types of Junior ISA

- A Junior cash ISA – which earns interest and has the same investment permissions and restrictions as an adult cash ISA
- An Junior stocks and shares ISA – which can invest in stocks and shares and has the same investment permissions and restrictions as an adult stocks and shares ISA

and Junior ISAs become their equivalent adult ISAs on maturity.

Note, investors can take out both a Junior cash ISA and an Junior stocks and shares ISA, with either the same or different providers so long as they remain within the relevant investment limits and money may be freely switched between these two accounts.

JISA contributions

Only the parent, or someone with parental responsibility, can take out a Junior ISA on behalf of an eligible child. Once established, however, parents, family and friends can contribute up to the annual limit of £3,600 a year into a Junior ISA and this limit will increase with each year with the CPI. The investment is locked away for the child who can withdraw the proceeds when they reach 18 years.

Taxation of JISAs

No income tax or capital gains tax is payable on a JISA even when parental contributions have been made. As already noted, JISAs convert into the equivalent cash ISAs at maturity maintaining the tax benefit.

7.3.2 Child Trust Fund (CTF)

Before the advent of Junior ISAs the government aimed to promote positive attitudes to saving by funding a **Child Trust Fund (CTF)** account for each child born on or after 1 September 2002.

CTF accounts first became available from April 2005 and, up to the 31 December 2010, the CTF was initially funded by a **government contribution** of £250 at birth and another £250 at age seven. However in order to reduce UK's budget deficit no government contributions have been paid since 1 January 2011 it has not been possible to open a new CTF since that date, though existing schemes continue to operate under CTF scheme rules.

In common with JISA accounts it is possible for **friends and family** (including parents) to contribute up to £3,600 a year to the account. that may include:

- Cash accounts
- Life products
- Collective funds (unit trusts and Open Ended Investment Companies)
- Equity-based schemes, including stakeholder or non-stakeholder investments and including self-selected equities

Taxation of CTFs

No income tax or capital gains tax is payable on the CTF. This applies even if parental contributions have been made.

Once the child reaches the age of 16 they can take over the management and operation of the fund. They cannot, however, draw on the funds until they are 18 when they have complete control of the use of the fund.

7.4 Venture Capital Trusts (VCTs)

7.4.1 Introduction

Venture capital trusts (VCTs) are listed companies that invest in unquoted trading companies and meet certain conditions. The VCT scheme differs from the enterprise investment scheme (below) in that the individual investor may spread his risk over a number of higher-risk, unquoted companies. An individual aged 18 or over investing in a VCT obtains the following tax benefits.

- **Income tax relief** – A tax reduction of **30%** of the amount invested to the permitted maximum of **£200,000 (2012/13)** in the year of making the investment (was 40% tax reduction 2005/06 and earlier) though this relief is withdrawn if the shares are sold within 5 years
- **Dividend relief** – Dividends received from the VCT are exempt from further taxation within the permitted maximum of £200,000
- **Disposal relief** – Capital gains on the sale of shares in the VCT are exempt from CGT (and losses are not allowable) irrespective of the investment term
- **Deferral relief** – Deferral relief has not been available since 6 April 2004 but investments made before that date could be used to defer capital gains to later years.

In addition, capital gains which the VCT itself makes on its investments are not chargeable gains, and so are not subject to corporation tax.

7.4.2 Conditions for VCT status

In order to qualify as a VCT the following conditions must be satisfied

- At least 70% of the trust's instruments will have to be in unquoted trading companies (including AIM).
- A maximum of 15% may be invested in any company or group of companies.
- Its Ordinary share capital must be quoted on the London Stock Exchange.
- Its income must be wholly or mainly derived from shares or securities.

Distributions from VCTs and gains on disposals are exempt from tax where the investment is within the VCT limits.

Unlike other investment trusts, a VCT can distribute as dividends any gains arising on the disposal of investments.

7.5 Enterprise Investment Schemes (EISs)

7.5.1 Introduction

The Enterprise Investment Scheme (EIS) provides tax incentives as a means of encouraging individuals to invest in new and growing businesses.

7.5.2 Income tax relief

Individuals can claim a reduction in income tax payable (a tax 'reducer') amounting to the lower of:

- **30%** of the amount subscribed for qualifying EIS investments (maximum annual qualifying investments are **£1,000,000**, for the **2012/13** tax year) though this relief is withdrawn if the shares are sold within 3 years (except for the transfer to a spouse on death)
- The individual's tax liability for the year after deducting any Venture Capital Trust relief (covered above) but before deducting any other tax 'reducers'

7.5.3 Capital gains tax reliefs

Where shares qualify for income tax relief under the EIS, there are also special rules that apply to those shares for capital gains purposes.

- Where shares are disposed of after three years any gain is exempt from CGT. If the shares are disposed of within three years any gain is computed in the normal way.
- If EIS shares are disposed of at a loss at any time, the loss is allowable but the acquisition cost of the shares is reduced by the amount of EIS relief attributable to the shares, ie the original investment relief.

CGT deferral relief is also available for investors who wish to defer capital gains tax on other chargeable gains. The shares must be acquired one year before to three years after the disposal that generated the gain to be held over.

7.5.4 EIS conditions

The key points to note about the scheme are

- It must be an investment by an individual in new **equity** shares.
- The company **cannot be listed** but could be a member of AIM, since, for tax purposes, the latter is treated as unquoted.
- The company must be engaged in a 'qualifying trade'. This excludes, for example, accountancy, banking, and other financial services and property companies.
- The company must have gross assets of less than £15m before the investment and less than £16m after.
- It is possible for an investor to become a director of the company after making the investment, and not lose tax relief.

7.6 Seed Enterprise Investment Scheme (SEIS)

From 6 April 2012 a new scheme, the Seed Enterprise Investment Scheme (SEIS), has been introduced to encourage seed investment in new businesses. Individual investors who have a **stake of less than 30%** will benefit from tax relief to investors in shares issued between 6 April 2012 and 5 April 2017.

7.6.1 Tax benefits

Income tax relief is available at **50% (2012/13)** on a **new equity investment** in **qualifying companies** up to an annual limit of **£100,000** in the tax year, subject to their being an income tax liability payable. To benefit from the relief the shares must be subscribed for in cash and must be fully paid. Any unused tax relief in one year can be carried back to the previous year.

In common with EISs, dividends received from Seed EIS investments are taxable.

Where the income tax relief was received, any **disposal of shares will be exempt capital gains tax provided the shares are held 3 years**. In addition, in this first year other disposals in 2012/13 will also be exempt.

7.6.2 Scheme rules

A qualifying company is one that, at the time of investment

- **less than 2 years old**
- is **undertaking or planning to undertake a new business**
- has **≤ 25 employees**
- has **gross assets ≤ £200,000**

Any funds invested must be used by the company within three years. The company may raise further funds under the EIS or VCT schemes but only after 75% of the SEIS funds have been used.

The scheme is open to all investors, including directors and company staff, though there is a **cumulative investment limit of £150,000** to the amount that can be injected into any one business under the SEIS.

8 Comparison of Fund Types

Learning objective

19.1.3 Distinguish the features, risks and benefits of unit trusts, investment trusts and open-ended investment companies.

19.1.5 Explain the key features and objectives of Exchange Traded Funds (ETFs) and Exchange Traded Commodities (ETCs).

The following table summarises the differences between the various main types of retail collective investment scheme in the UK.

	Unit Trust	Open-Ended Investment Company	Investment Trust and Venture Capital Trust	ETF
Legal Structure	Trust	Company	Company	Company
Investors' Holdings	Units	Shares	Shares	Shares
Nature of Fund	Open-ended	Open-ended	Closed-ended	Open-ended
Pricing frequency	At valuation point	At valuation point	Real time	Real time
Pricing System	Dual price (bid/offer)	Single price (no bid/offer spread)	Single price (SETS order book)	Single price (SETS order book)
Pricing Calculation	Precise value of the underlying investments, charges calculated within spread	Precise value of the underlying investments, charges shown separately	Reflects value of underlying investments but driven by supply and demand for the shares, charges shown separately	Based on underlying investments due to arbitrage activities of ETF manager
Stock Exchange Listing	No	Listing optional	Listed	Listed
Secondary Market	None	Unlikely	As for Ordinary shares	As for Ordinary shares

9 Fund Supermarkets and Wrap Accounts

Learning objective

19.1.7 Explain the features and objectives of: wraps and other platforms.

9.1 Fund supermarkets

Fund supermarkets are a concept in internet-based financial services (**e-commerce**) that aim to keep charges low. Fund supermarkets offer funds from various different providers, particularly for holding in an **Individual Savings Account (ISA)**.

A full online fund supermarket may provide:

- The ability to **'mix and match'** funds from different providers within a single ISA or other account without incurring the extra charges normally associated with self-select ISAs. However, only **unit trusts** and **open-ended investment company** investments can be held, so that investors wanting a selection of individual shares or investment trusts will still need to choose a self-select ISA
- The facility to **deal online** by credit card or debit card in real time without the need to download and print an application form
- The facility to **track and manage** the account online
- The ability to switch between funds within the service at minimal cost

Discounts may be offered on funds' initial charges, and the fund supermarket may hope to generate revenue from ongoing trail commissions from customers who use their service. In addition, fund supermarkets hope to win customers by offering the convenience of consolidating the availability of different funds through a single agency.

With funds supermarket **consolidation services**, it is possible to invest with several different fund managers and have all transactions summarised on a single statement, electronic or paper. Distributions can be aggregated and paid by a single cheque and in many cases, regular withdrawals of capital from the whole portfolio can be automated to 'simulate' an 'income'. As well as having a wide choice of funds it is possible to switch between funds at low cost and avoid a high proportion of the initial charge.

Most fund supermarkets specialise in unit trusts and OEICs, but there are similar services for onshore and offshore life assurance funds and also pension funds.

9.2 Wrap accounts

A further development is the introduction of **'wrap' accounts**. These allow a wider range of assets to be held including:

- Unit trusts/OEICs – based on a 'supermarket'-type arrangement
- ISAs
- Pension investments from a SIPP or SSAS
- Life Assurance Bonds
- Junior ISAs
- Shares, held in a nominee account

All in a single account with a single provider and a single annual management fee, usually on a tiered basis ranging from 3% to 1% with lower charges for larger funds. Wrap accounts are designed for individual investors who wish to have a professional manager handle a their investments and usually require minimum initial investments of at least £25,000

There may be charges for transfers into the wrap account, again on a tiered basis, and charges for transferring out. Assets with tax complications or subject to heavy regulations such as pensions tend to have higher transfer charges both in and out. Against this there are typically many other cost savings such as reduced initial charges on funds through fund supermarkets.

The holdings are all shown in a single account, which can usually be accessed online. Wraps use secure internet systems to streamline investment transactions, administration and service, whilst also allowing an investor to view the value of his or her assets and asset allocation, based on up-to-the-minute data.

Investors will also receive a single consolidated tax statement for tax reporting purposes, simplifying their tax administration.

The ability to analyse all these assets from a single source allows easy management of funds under a range of different arrangements as part on a single portfolio. It allows investors to adjust their holdings as their move through various life stages without suffering the cost of changing providers.

10 Life Assurance Based Investments

Learning objective

19.1.8 Identify the characteristics and advantages of Individual Savings Accounts (ISAs), Child Trust Funds (CTFs), National Savings and Investments, Life assurance based investments and Defined Contribution pension arrangements.

10.1 Protection and investment

The term **life assurance** implies some form of protection in the event of death. There are broadly two types of life assurance contract:

- Contracts that are only for **protection** (insurance) purposes (eg term assurance, which pays out only on death and only if death occurs within a fixed term)
- Contracts with both **protection and investment** elements

Here we are primarily considering at **life assurance policies** investment products.

10.2 Types of policy

The types of policy offered by life companies varies from pure protection to almost pure investment, covering

- **Term policies** – Pure protection policies that pay out in the event of death within a specified period as long as the regular premiums have been paid
- **Whole of life policies** – A policy that runs for the whole of an individual's life and that pay out on their death, again as long as the regular premiums have been paid. This is where the term life assurance comes from as it is assured that we will all die at some time. There may be a small investment element and the policies may be capable of being realised but they are primarily for protection.
- **Endowment policies** – Regular savings vehicles with added life cover and providing a lump sum at maturity or a payout on death. A mixture of protection and investment.
- **Annuities** – A lump-sum investment products designed to pay a regular return, a pure investment product.
- **Investment bond** – A lump-sum investment product that can be fully or partially encashed at any time and that allows 5% of the initial investment to be drawn each year with no tax consequences.

10.3 Fund structures

Life funds are structured in one of two ways:

- **With profits funds** – that aim to smooth the returns. A with profits fund is set up with a basic sum assured to which bonuses are added each year and once added they cannot be taken back. The investor therefore benefits from steady growth, though this may not be spectacular.
- **Unit linked funds** – much like unit trusts with attached life insurance.

11 Pension Arrangements

Learning objective

19.1.8 Identify the characteristics and advantages of Individual Savings Accounts (ISAs), Child Trust Funds (CTFs), National Savings and Investments, Life assurance based investments and Defined Contribution pension arrangements.

11.1 Tax advantages

Pension schemes approved by HM Revenue and Customs (HMRC) represent a very tax-efficient form of investment. The reasons for this are as follows.

- **Contributions qualify for tax relief**
- **Savings grow free of tax**, except for tax deducted on share dividends
- Up to **25%** of a pension fund can be taken as a **tax-free cash lump-sum**. This applies to both personal and company schemes.
- Certain tax free payments may be made on death

It doesn't matter what type of pension arrangement is contributed to, the tax advantages are all the same. So whether a person contributes to a company scheme, a personal pension or stakeholder scheme, an additional voluntary contribution (AVC) scheme or any other variety of pension savings, he or she is still entitled to the tax relief.

11.2 Types of scheme

There are basically three types of pension scheme.

- **State pensions** provided by the government.
- **Occupational** pension schemes provided by an employer. The main HMRC limitation for a scheme to be approved for tax purposes is on benefits that can be paid.
- **Personal** pension plans have much the same tax advantages as occupational schemes. They can be utilised by persons who have additional non-pensionable income or those in an occupational scheme earning £30,000 or less. In the event of the latter, they may invest in either a personal pension or Stakeholder pension up to £3,600 gross per annum. The limitation on these schemes is applied to contributions rather than final benefits.

11.3 Scheme entitlement

11.3.1 Final salary schemes

Final salary schemes are offered by some employers and are also called defined benefit pension schemes. The level of pension benefits received by the employee is linked to their final salary and their years' service. It is the responsibility of the employer to ensure that sufficient contributions are paid into the scheme to pay the final guaranteed benefit. The risk in the scheme therefore lies largely with the employer rather than the employee.

The scheme may be contributory, in which case both the employer and employee make contributions, or non-contributory, in which case only the employer makes contributions.

11.3.2 Money purchase schemes

Money purchase schemes are also referred to as defined contribution pension schemes and may be either occupational schemes or personal schemes. In an occupational scheme, the employer agrees to make a guaranteed level of pension contributions. The pension rights will be determined by the investment performance of the scheme, the yields available on annuities at the date of retirement, and the type of pension selected by the individual. The risk therefore lies with the employee rather than the employer, since the employer has not guaranteed a particular level of pension rights.

Chapter Roundup

Collective investments

- Indirect investment provides a low cost route to a professionally managed diversified fund for small investment levels with the advantage of there being no CGT liability to the investor until the fund is sold (irrespective of the trading within the fund).
- Open-ended funds – investing/divesting increases/decreases the fund value and funds trade at or close to for value.
- Closed-ended funds – investing/divesting is achieved by buying/selling an existing share. Fund values are heavily influenced by supply and demand and may trade at a notable premium or discount to fair values.

Unit trusts and OEICs

- Unit trusts and OEICs are open-ended collective investments, and so their price closely reflects the underlying net asset value. OEICs are Investment Companies with Variable Capital (ICVCs).
- Unit trust and OEIC investments carry the risks of their underlying investment class – for example, equities or bonds – but provide a vehicle for diversification within asset classes and sectors.
- The COLL rules provide for two types of fund for retail investors: UCITS schemes – similar to existing schemes – and non-UCITS schemes – with less stringent rules. QISs – qualified investor schemes – are for institutions and expert private investors.
- There are FSA rules covering the extent of diversification of funds and maximum holdings by the fund in individual companies and securities.
- The valuation point is different for funds using historic pricing compared with those using forward pricing.
- Income from equity funds is taxed in the same way as dividends. Income from funds investing in bonds is taxed as interest. Disposals are chargeable to CGT.
- The OEIC/ICVC framework allows a fund to be marketed throughout the EEA.

Investment trusts

- Investment trusts are a form of collective investment offering diversification in various sectors and in stock markets around the world. Investment trusts are set up as listed public limited companies (plcs) that invest in securities.
- Investment trusts are closed-ended (fixed number of shares in the market) and their shares are priced according to the supply and demand for them in the market. This price may be at a discount or sometimes at a premium to the net asset value (NAV) of the trust.
- Investment trusts do not have the restrictions on investments that apply to unit trusts and OEICs. They can borrow money to increase their gearing, which in turn increases their volatility and risk for the investor.
- Investment trusts can issue different classes of share and can have a split capital structure. Zeros can provide capital growth at low risk while income shares can provide an above average yield.
- The investment trust must comply with the Companies Act and with FSA listing rules. External investment managers and firms operating savings schemes need authorisation by the FSA under FSMA 2000.
- An investor may buy shares in an investment trust through a broker or through an investment trust manager who operates a savings scheme or ISA. A financial adviser may be used.

Exchange traded funds

- ETF = open-ended exchange-traded (traded through SETs, settled through CREST in the UK).
- No actual charges, very low management fees, priced in real time.
- ETFs provide exposure to index.
- ETCs provide exposure to commodities.
- ETNs provide exposure to other assets but leave exposure to counterparty risk

Hedge funds

- Global macro funds bet on macroeconomic variables such as currencies or interest rates. They are often highly geared and use derivatives. Subgroups of macrofunds are futures funds, which use futures to bet on certain asset classes such as currency, fixed income and commodities and emerging-market funds. These can sometimes be referred to as speculative or tactical funds.
- Directional long/short funds take positions in stock and are often geared. They are not normally market neutral, but instead have a long or short bias.
- Event-driven funds bet on events specific to a company or security. One example of this would be to invest in distressed securities or shares involved in a merger or acquisition.
- Market-neutral funds take long positions in stocks that are considered undervalued and short positions in stocks that are considered overvalued. The fund is neutral, in that the value of short positions is equal to the value of long positions and the sensitivity of long and short positions is the same. Other strategies of a market neutral portfolio are to look for arbitrage opportunities in warrants or derivatives. They should therefore be relatively intuitive to changes in the underlying market.

NS&I products

- Only certain NS&I products are tax-free, specifically
  - Direct ISAs
  - Savings certificates (fixed income and index linked)
  - Children's bonus bond
  - Premium bond

ISA

- The Individual Savings Account is a tax-efficient investment vehicle for limited amounts of cash, and stocks and shares.
- Investment limits
  - Cash ISA £5,640
  - Stocks and shares ISA £11,280
- There is no tax charge for income or gains made on assets held in an ISA though the 10% tax credit on dividends received cannot be reclaimed.

JISA

- JISAs were introduced on 1 November 2011,family and friends can contribute £3,600 p.a.
- JISAs are tax-free until the child reaches the age of 18 when the child can either withdraw the funds or they automatically convert into the equivalent adult ISAs.

CTF

- CTFs were introduced in 2005 but withdrawn in 2010, though existing funds continue to operate.
- Family and friends can contribute £3,600 pa since 1 November 2011 (previously £1,200 p.a.)
- CTFs are tax-free until the child reaches the age of 18.

VCT/EIS/SEIS

	VCT	EIS	SEIS
Income tax reliefs			
Investment limit	£200,000	£1,000,000	£100,000
Income tax relief	30%	30%	50%
Clawback term	5 years	3 years	3 years
Tax-free dividends	Yes	No	No
CGT reliefs			
Tax-free gain on disposal	Yes	Yes after 3 years	Yes after 3 years
Tax relief for losses	No	Yes after 3 years	Yes after 3 years
Deferral relief if investment			
- Before gain	N/A	1 year before gain	N/A
- After gain	N/A	3 years after gain	N/A

Fund supermarket and wrap account

- Fund supermarkets allow investment in various funds through a single account.
- Wrap account allow a range of different investments (funds, shares, life bonds etc) to be held in a single account with a single fee and a single consolidated tax statement.

Life Assurance Based Investment

- Main investment products are
  - Endowment policies – Regular savings vehicles with added life cover and providing a lump sum at maturity or a payout on death. A mixture of protection and investment.
  - Annuities – A lump-sum investment products designed to pay a regular return, a pure investment product.
  - Investment bond – A lump-sum investment product that can be fully or partially encashed at any time and that allows 5% of the initial investment to be drawn each year with no tax consequences.
- Fund structures
  - With profits funds – that aim to smooth the returns through adding bonuses to basic sum assured.
  - Unit linked funds – much like unit trusts with attached life insurance.

Pension arrangements

- Tax benefits
  - Contributions qualify for tax relief
  - Savings grow free of tax, except for tax deducted on share dividends
  - Up to 25% of a pension fund can be taken as a tax-free cash lump-sum. This applies to both personal and company schemes.
  - Certain tax free payments may be made on death

- Final salary scheme – employer must fulfil obligation and faces the risk of any investment shortfall
- Money purchase scheme – employer guarantees what they will pay in but not investment returns, the individual faces the risk of any investment shortfall

Test Your Knowledge

Check your knowledge of the chapter here, without referring back to the text.

1. What are the advantages of indirect investment in terms of diversification and taxation?
2. OEICs and ETFs are both open-ended investment companies. What is the difference in their pricing?
3. Can open-ended funds trade at a premium or discount?
4. What is meant by a fund being termed 'open-ended'?
5. Outline the duties of the trustee of a unit trust.
6. In what circumstances must a fund manager who uses historic pricing switch to providing quotes on a forward pricing basis?
7. What is the 'dilution levy' in respect of an OEIC?
8. What is the significance of UCITS certification?
9. What are the FSA rules on diversification of funds?
10. What is meant by an investment trust share 'trading at a premium'?
11. What are the four classes of share in a split level trust?
12. What is the full term for a 'zero', and what is a 'zero'?
13. What are structured products?
14. What is the tax position regarding dividends on ordinary shares in a Venture Capital Trust?
15. What is the capital gains tax position regarding holdings in Venture Capital Trusts?
16. What are the two types of pension scheme

Test Your Knowledge: Answers

1. Indirect investment offers broad diversification potential even for small investment. With direct investment, CGT would be payable as a result of any trading within the fund, with an indirect investment CGT only arises when the fund is realised

   (See Section 1.2)

2. OEICs are priced at valuation points, ETFs are continuously priced.

   (See Section 8)

3. Open-ended funds are always priced on the basis of the value of the underlying fund, hence they cannot trade at a premium or discount.

   (See Section 2.3)

4. Capital of the fund can rise and fall as investors invest/divest.

   (See Section 1.4 and 2.3)

5. See list of duties

   (See Section 2.2)

6. If the price has changed by 2% or more since the last valuation point

   (See Section 2.3)

7. To protect current investors is in decline or experiencing exceptionally high volumes of net purchases or sales

   (See Section 2.4)

8. Allow funds to be marketed throughout the EEA

   (See Section 2.6.2)

9. Not more than 10% of the fund may be invested in the shares of any one company, Holdings exceeding 5% must not add up to more than 40% of the fund in aggregate

   (See Section 2.6.4)

10. Where the share price exceeds the net asset value per share

    (See Section 4.3)

11. **Split-Level Trusts**

    Types of share that may be issued by a split-capital trust include the following.

    - **Income shares** – This class of capital is entitled to all the income from the underlying portfolio and a fixed entitlement to capital.
    - **Capital shares** – At the end of the company's life (set as a fixed period at the inception of the investment trust), the capital shares are entitled to the value of the underlying portfolio, less the income shares' fixed right to capital represented by their nominal value. The typical life of an investment trust with such a class of capital is seven to ten years. Capital shares tend to be volatile as they accept the majority of the underlying portfolio's capital risk.

- **Preference shares** – These provide a constant dividend which is paid in any year in which dividends are paid. They also have an entitlement to a fixed nominal value on the winding up of the company. With some of the more recent preference share issues this has been as low as 1p per share. These are sometimes referred to as Annuity Income Shares as, like an annuity, they provide a high level of income in return for an initial capital investment. Indeed, since the initial investment is eroded over the life of the investment trust, the dividend yield will be very high.
- **Zero dividend preference shares** – These offer a predetermined capital growth over the life of the investment trust, receiving only a fixed capital sum on winding up, before any capital is returned to other shareholders. This capital return is not certain, however, as the assets of the investment trust could be insufficient to cover this sum on a winding up if the trust performs particularly badly.

(See Section 4.2)

12. Zero dividend preference share, offers a fixed return at a pre-set future date

    (See Section 4.2)

13. Funds offering a return with full or partial guarantee of capital value.

    (See Section 6.4)

14. Exempt tax within the permitted investment limit

    (See Section 7.4)

15. No chargeable gain, no allowable loss (within the permitted investment limit)

    (See Section 7.4)

16. Pension schemes may be either

    - A specific return based on the employee's salary and number of years' service with the company – a **defined benefit/final salary scheme** (liability matching to the specific return); or
    - A general increase in value of the contributions paid on behalf of the employee – **defined contribution/money purchase scheme** (liability matching and return maximisation).

    (See Section 11.3)

14 Foreign Exchange

INTRODUCTION

Currencies are traded in both a spot market for immediate currency trades, and a forward market which allows for agreements to buy and sell currencies in the future.

Forward rates are computed by banks and based on interest rate differentials. These interest rate differentials may then be applied to the spot rate to compute the forward rate.

Purchasing power parity is a method used by currency forecasters in their efforts to forecast future spot rates.

CHAPTER CONTENTS

Chapter Learning Objectives

24 The macroeconomic environment

Demonstrate an understanding of the macroeconomic environment and its impact on investment

24.4 The foreign exchange market, government policy and exchange rates, fixed, floating and managed exchange rates and the balance of payments

- **24.4.8** **Explain** the notion of purchasing power parity as a forecasting tool for exchange rates.
- **24.4.10** **Understand** the nature and basic operations of the foreign exchange market.
- **24.4.11** **Explain** the nature of exchange rate risk and how it can be managed.
- **24.4.12** **Explain** spot and forward exchange rates.
- **24.4.13** **Calculate** forward rates using interest rate parity (IRP).
- **24.4.14** **Explain** the concept of purchasing power parity (PPP).
- **24.4.15** **Distinguish** between IRP and PPP.
- **24.4.16** **Explain** the International Fisher effect.

1 Overseas Investment

Learning objective	**24.4.10 Understand** the nature and basic operations of the foreign exchange market.

1.1 Foreign exchange risk

Although overseas investment has many advantages, a number of different problems arise through such exposure.

1.2 Additional transaction costs

1.2.1 Foreign currency transactions

Dealing in overseas markets will probably have to be done in overseas currencies, incurring dealing costs.

1.2.2 Information gathering

The investor will have less knowledge about overseas markets than his domestic UK market. This represents a risk that inappropriate investment decisions will be made. In order to avoid this problem, substantial costs will need to be incurred to understand and analyse the overseas companies and markets in which the investor is interested.

1.3 Taxation

1.3.1 Local taxes

Additional tax costs can be incurred when receiving dividends from overseas companies. Initially, the company may suffer high rates of corporate taxation on its profits, reducing its level of post-tax income significantly. Secondly, when dividends are paid, withholding taxes may be deducted, further reducing the final return to investors.

1.3.2 Double taxation treaties

The cost of overseas taxation will be mitigated by double taxation treaties. These mean that, where overseas tax has already been suffered on income, additional UK tax may not be payable. Even where the UK does not have a double taxation agreement with another country, it may be the case that the UK tax authorities will give tax relief to avoid excessive taxation.

1.4 Political risk

Unexpected changes overseas can lead to major catastrophes. Nationalisation of industries without compensation, changes in government, reversals of policy and changes in tax rates will all significantly affect the returns available to investors.

1.5 Operating risk

UK companies with overseas operations and markets will find the volatility of their earnings and cash flows increases as a result of exchange rate movements. This will directly impact on returns to investors.

1.6 Changes in exchange rates

earning objective | **24.4.11 Explain** the nature of exchange rate risk and how it can be managed.

Changes in exchange rates will cause the sterling value of overseas investments to vary.

Example

We buy 1,000 shares in US Inc. for \$100 each. We hold the shares for a year and receive a dividend of \$5 a share before selling the shares for \$110 each.

The return in dollars over the year is given by

$$R_{\$} = \frac{\$5 + \$110 - \$100}{\$100} = 0.15 \text{ or } 15\%$$

The return in dollars is not, however, necessarily that relevant for us. When we originally bought the shares, we converted sterling into dollars to make the purchase. On final realisation, we will then convert the dollar receipts into sterling.

The sterling return is more relevant and this will vary depending on exchange rates. Assume that the exchange rate at the beginning of the year was \$1.50:£1 and the exchange rate at the end of the year is either \$2:£1 or \$1:£1.

Scenario 1

If the sterling dollar exchange rate moves from $1.50: £1 to $2.00:£1 this may be referred to either as

- Sterling has strengthened or appreciated – it will now buy $2.00 where previously it would only buy $1.50 so it has appreciated by $0.50 or 33.33% ($0.50/$1.50).
- The dollar has weakened – $1 will now only buy £0.50 when previously it would buy £0.6667.

Strengthening and weakening are relative terms and when one currency relatively strengthens the other relatively weakens. Considering the details given, the original cost of purchasing each share = $100 × £1/$1.50 = £66.67

Proceeds per share = $115 × £1/$2 = £57.50

$$\text{Return} = R_{£} = \frac{£57.50 - £66.67}{£66.67} = -0.14 \text{ or } -14\%$$

What we see here is that if we hold dollar assets and the dollar weakens we will incur an exchange loss.

Scenario 2

In this scenario the exchange rate moves from $1.50: £1 to $1.00:£1 this may be referred to either as

- Sterling has weakened (it will now only buy $1.00 where previously it would previously buy $1.50)
- The dollar has strengthened

Proceeds per share = $115 × £1/$1 = £115

$$\text{Return} = R_{£} = \frac{£115 - £66.67}{£66.67} = 0.72 \text{ or } 72\%$$

What we see here is that if we hold dollar assets and the dollar strengthens we will benefit from an exchange gain.

In conclusion, the sterling return on the investment is dramatically different, depending on how exchange rates move over the year.

This example is an illustration of **exchange rate risk** that increases the variability inherent in equity stock, but can also introduce variability into what would have been previously a certain return. For example, a UK investor investing in US government bonds and holding them to maturity would have a virtually guaranteed return in dollars, but the sterling return would still be uncertain.

2 Currency Rates

Learning objective	**24.4.12 Explain** spot and forward exchange rates.

In order to be able to analyse foreign currency risk in more detail, it is important to be able to perform basic foreign currency calculations.

2.1 Spot rates

The spot market is the market for **immediate currency trades**. Delivery will take place **two business days (T + 2)** after the deal is made. The market has no formal market place and trading takes place via telephones with prices being quoted on screen services.

2.1.1 Quotation of spot rates

The spot market quotes bid/offer prices (spot rates) in the form of a spread, normally using the US$ as the base though these quotes against the dollar can be used to determine the quotes between any currencies such as sterling to euro.

If we consider the sterling/euro exchange rate, this could be quoted in one of two ways

- Number of pounds per euro
- Number of euros per pound sterling

Within the UK we would describe the first of these as a direct quote. A **direct quote** is where the exchange rate is quoted as the number of units of the local currency per single unit of the foreign currency. In the UK we would describe the second version as an indirect quote. An **indirect quote** is where the exchange rate is quoted as the number of units of the foreign currency per single unit of the local currency. Where we are looking at normal exchange rate quotes against the dollar, the majority of rates are quoted as the number of units of the currency per $1, this may be referred to as a quote in **European terms**. The main exceptions to this is £:$ (known as cable) and €:$, where the convention is to quote the number of dollars per £1/€1, a quote in **American terms**.

Whichever currencies are involved, exchange rates are quoted as the number of units of one currency per single unit of another. It is common to refer to these as the variable currency and fixed currency, respectively. You may also hear them referred quoted and base – you should view these terms as interchangeable.

2.1.2 £/$ Spot rate

$1.4275-$1.4385

The $ buyers' rate	The $ sellers' rate
£1.00 will get $1.4275	$1.4385 will get £1.00

To assist in remembering which rate to use, remember that the bank **always gives you the worst rate**. For example, if you want to buy dollars with £1.00, the bank will give you the least dollars it can, i.e. $1.4275 rather than $1.4385 in return. Alternatively, if you have dollars and want to buy £1.00, then the bank will charge you the most it can, i.e. $1.4385 rather than $1.4275.

2.2 Forward rates

The forward market is a market in currencies for delivery at an agreed date in the future. The exchange rate at which delivery takes place is agreed now.

2.2.1 Quotation of forward rates

Forward rates are quoted as **premiums (pm)** or **discounts (dis)** to the spot rate. It is possible for rates to be quoted at par where the spot and forward are the same.

Example

Spot	$1.4275-$1.4385
One-month forward	0.37-0.35c pm
Three-month forward	1.00-0.97c pm

Calculate the three-month forward rate.

Solution

It is important to remember that these rates are quoted in cents, whereas the spot rate is quoted in dollars.

A premium implies that the currency is becoming more expensive (strengthening against sterling), i.e. £1.00 will buy fewer dollars. Hence, to obtain the forward rate the premium is **subtracted** from the spot rate. Similarly, the discount is **added**. This will be the rule regardless of the nature of the quote, **direct or indirect**, premiums are subtracted and discounts are added.

Based on the above figures, the three-month forward rate is

Spot rate	\$1.4275 - \$1.4385
Less premium	(\$0.0100 - \$0.0097)
	\$1.4175 - \$1.4288

2.2.2 Calculation of forward rates

One important factor to remember about this market is that it does not reflect an expectation of what the spot rate will be in three, six or nine months' time. It is simply a mathematical result of the difference in interest rates in the two countries.

Example

In the example below, three-month sterling interest rates were 10%, meaning the interest rate for the three-month period is 2.5% (10% × 3/12). Three-month dollar rates were 6%, meaning the interest rate for the three-month period is 1.5% (6% × 3/12).

Now spot rate				**Three months' time forward rate**
£1,000	→	@ 3-month £ rates at 2.5%	→	£1,025
↓				↓
@ \$1.4275				Therefore @ \$1.4135
↓				↑
\$1,427.50	→	@ 3-month \$ rates at 1.5%	→	\$1,448.91

The forward rate is simply calculated on the basis that the money is invested at the current rate of interest in the two countries. At the end of the period, the relationship between the value of the two deposits gives the forward rate.

$$\frac{\$1{,}448.91}{£1{,}025} = \$1.4135$$

If this relationship were not the case, then it would be possible to make an arbitrage profit by borrowing in one currency, converting it at today's spot rate into the other currency and placing this on deposit for, say, three months. At the same time, a forward contract could be taken out to reverse the original spot transaction, locking in a profit.

2.2.3 Interest rate parity formula

Learning objective

24.4.13 Calculate forward rates using interest rate parity (IRP).

The link between exchange rates and interest rates can be worked through using first principles as above. Alternatively, the link can be summarised by the **interest rate parity** formula, which says that

Formula to learn

$$\text{Forward rate} = \frac{1+r_V}{1+r_F} \times \text{Spot rate}$$

where

r_V = variable currency interest rate for the relevant period.

r_F = fixed currency interest rate for the relevant period.

Example (continued)

$$\text{Forward rate} = \frac{1.015}{1.025} \times \$1.4275 = \$1.4135$$

For exam purposes this is an equation with four variables, spot rate, forward rate, r_V and r_F and you may be given any three and asked to calculate the fourth. To deal with this is may be better to think of this formula as

$$\text{Spot rate} \times (1 + r_V) = \text{Forward rate} \times (1 + r_F)$$

We must also take care to apply the correct money market conventions as discussed earlier in this Study Text under money market instruments. As we noted there

- the **UK and Commonwealth countries** use the day count convention of **Actual/365**
- the **US, EU and Japan** use the convention of **Actual/360**.

When banks work out the yield they wish to pay or receive, they take this into account in their quote.

For example, if dollar interest rates for a three-month (91-day) period are 8%, the relevant value for r_V is (8% × 91/360) 2.02%. If sterling interest rates for a three-month (91-day) period are 10%, then the relevant value for r_F is (10% × 91/365) 2.49%.

3 Exchange Rate Forecasting

In order to be able to make informed decisions on currency exposure and overseas investment, it is important to appreciate the factors affecting exchange rates and the likely future direction of exchange rates.

3.1 Shorter term factors affecting exchange rates

3.1.1 Interest rates

In the short term, high interest rates will attract 'hot money' from around the world seeking high yields into a currency. This will create demand for the currency and increase the exchange rate.

Interest rate differentials are also relevant in the **International Fisher Effect**, covered later.

3.1.2 Balance of payments

If the UK has a balance of payments surplus, then it is exporting goods with a higher value than it is importing. In order to pay for these goods, overseas customers will need to purchase sterling. Demand for sterling will increase, meaning that the currency will strengthen. Alternatively, as is unfortunately more likely to be the case, if the UK has a balance of payments deficit, then UK companies will need to sell sterling to buy overseas currencies to fund their purchases. This will cause sterling to weaken.

3.1.3 Economic growth

Economic growth will stimulate demand for a currency both through capital flows into the country, due to attractive investment opportunities, and current account flows, due to increased supply and demand for the country's traded goods and services. Alternatively, a credit boom, which causes demand for overseas goods and services, will cause the currency to weaken.

3.1.4 Fiscal and monetary policies

Taxation and public spending policies have a direct impact on economic growth. Government borrowing plans will impact on interest rates, as will monetary policy, which aims to reduce or increase money supply through changes in interest rates.

3.1.5 Natural resources

The discovery or existence of valuable natural resources, such as oil, can cause a currency to strengthen dramatically.

3.1.6 Currency block membership

Some currencies are pegged to the US dollar, such as certain middle Eastern currencies. Such formal or informal relationships should be noted, since they will have a key impact on the exchange rate.

3.1.7 Political events

Central bank intervention can affect exchange rates, although experience has shown that it is sometimes the speculators who win the day rather than the central authorities. On top of this, events such as elections, public opinion polls, government ministers' statements and press releases can all affect the exchange rate.

3.2 Longer term factors – inflation and purchasing power parity

Learning objectives	
	24.4.8 Explain the notion of purchasing power as a forecasting tool for exchange rates.
	24.4.14 Explain the concept of purchasing power parity (PPP).

In the shorter-term, the exchange rate is determined by supply and demand factors and, to a greater or lesser extent, market sentiment. Longer-term exchange rates are determined by **purchasing power parity**, which is a relationship between economies and the levels of **inflation** they suffer. Purchasing power parity is best explained by way of a small example.

If a basket of goods costs £100 in London and the same basket of goods costs €200 in Paris, this predicts the exchange rate between the two countries will be £1 = €2. However, if the two economies suffer differing rates of inflation then, over time, the exchange rate will alter.

If, after a number of years, the basket of goods costs £115 in London, due to the impact of inflation on UK prices, and yet remains at €200 in Paris, this would suggest that the exchange rate between the two currencies is now £1 = €1.74 – a decline in the value of sterling. This theory of exchange rate behaviour can also be referred to as **The Law of One Price**.

Short-term supply and demand features may well mask this overall trend, but purchasing power parity gives an underlying theme to the foreign exchange markets. If one economy consistently has an inflation rate in excess of its competitors, then its currency will deteriorate against its trading partners.

3.3 The International Fisher Effect

Learning objective

24.4.15 Distinguish between IRP and PPP.

24.4.16 Explain the International Fisher effect.

We have seen above that longer term exchange rates are theoretically determined by purchasing power parity and the inflation differential between two currencies. We have also seen in relation to currency rates above that forward rates are determined by reference to interest rate differentials. These two concepts are brought together in the Fisher theorem, which links together interest rates, inflation and the foreign exchange markets.

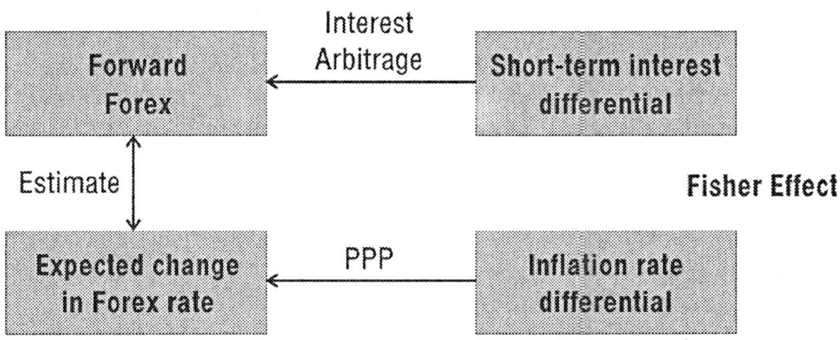

Forward foreign exchange prices are derived from the short-term interest rate differentials between two economies. The expected foreign exchange spot rate in the future is given by the purchasing power parity theorem which we developed above.

The **forward forex rate** is merely a mathematical computation, but it should represent an unbiased view of what the exchange rate will be in the future. Fisher's model links the interest rate differential to the inflation rate differential of PPP.

If short-term interest rate differentials generate the forward forex market and inflation differentials generate the expected change in forex rates, and these two are deemed to be approximately equal, then the short-term interest rates must be determined by the inflation rate differential.

Fisher states that the nominal rate of return (r) is equal to the real rate of return (R) adjusted to compensate for the effect of inflation (i).

Formula to learn

$$1+r=(1+R)(1+i)$$

Alternatively, this may be expressed as

$$\frac{1+r}{1+i}=1+R$$

On the assumption that the real rate of return should not vary between countries, then the **difference in nominal rates is generated by the differential in inflation.**

This idea can be expressed in a formula, as follows.

First, we assume that the real interest rate (R) is constant in both currencies, say dollars and sterling.

$$1+R_F = 1+R_V$$

Substituting in this equation

$$\frac{1+r_V}{1+r_F} = \frac{1+i_V}{1+i_F}$$

And using this in the interest rate parity formula gives us a model for forecasting future exchange rates as

Formula to learn

$$\text{Future rate} = \frac{1+i_V}{1+i_F} \times \text{Spot rate}$$

Thus, it should be possible to arrive at the forward foreign exchange rate from **either the interest rates or the inflation rates** in the two currencies for the period.

Once again, it may be more convenient to think of this as

Formula to learn

$$\text{Spot rate} \times (1 + i_V) = \text{Future rate} \times (1 + i_F)$$

Where $(1 + i_V)$ and $(1 + i_F)$ are the effects of accumulated compound inflation over the relevant forecast period.

Chapter Roundup

Currency markets

- There is no formal market place for foreign currency, trading takes place by phone.
- The spot market is the market for immediate currency trades, settlement is T + 2 business days.
- Direct quote = number of units of local currency per single unit of foreign currency.
- Indirect quote = number of units of foreign currency per single unit of local currency.
- American terms = number of dollars per single unit of the second currency.
- European terms = number of units of the second currency per single dollar.
- If a currency strengthens it can buy more units of the second currency.
- If a currency weakens it can buy fewer units of the second currency.
- A forward currency transaction is an agreement to buy or to sell a currency at a future date at a price agreed today.

Exchange rates

- Exchange rates are quoted with a bid-offer spread.
- Forward rates are quoted at a premium or discount to the spot rate.
- Forward rates are computed on the basis of interest rate parity.
- Forward rate $= \frac{1+r_V}{1+r_F} \times \text{Spot rate}$

  or

  Spot rate × $(1 + r_V)$ = Forward rate × $(1 + r_F)$
- Longer-term exchange rates are determined by purchasing power parity which is the relationship between economies and the level of inflation they suffer.
- Future rate = $\frac{1+i_V}{1+i_F} \times \text{Spot rate}$

  or

  Spot rate × $(1 + i_V)$ = Forward rate × $(1 + i_F)$

Test Your Knowledge

Check your knowledge of the chapter here, without referring back to the text.

1. What are the additional risks of investing overseas?

2. What is the settlement period for spot currency trades?

3. Where a forward rate is quoted at a premium to the spot rate, the premium should be

   A Deducted from the variable spot quote
   B Added to the variable spot quote
   C Deducted from the fixed spot quote
   D Added to the fixed spot quote

4. What factors drive short-term movements in exchange rates?

5. What factors drive long-term movements in exchange rates?

Test Your Knowledge: Answers

1. Additional rules
   - Higher transaction costs
   - Overseas taxation/double taxation
   - Political risk
   - Operating risk
   - Fluctuating exchange rates

   (See Section 1)

2. T + 2

   (See Section 2.1)

3. A

   (See Section 2.2)

4. Interest rates, economic growth, balance of payments, fiscal and monetary policy, natural resources, currency block membership, political events.

   (See Section 3.1)

5. Inflation and purchasing power parity.

   (See Section 3.2)

15 Introduction to Financial Statements

INTRODUCTION

The primary purpose of financial statements is to provide a medium by which the directors can report to the shareholders on the performance of the company concerned.

The financial statements are, however, frequently used by other interested parties, such as lenders, creditors, potential investors, tax authorities and the government to help them assess their returns and the risk that they may face.

This chapter explains the purpose and format of the three main financial statements, the balance sheet, the income statement (profit and loss account) and the cash flow statement.

CHAPTER CONTENTS

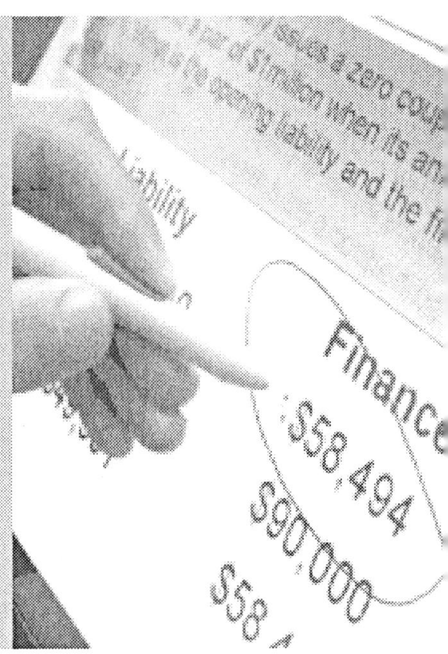

Chapter Learning Objectives

27 Accounting

Demonstrate an understanding of accounting principles

27.1 Fundamental precepts

27.1.1 **Explain** the legal requirement to prepare financial statements.

27.1.2 **Explain** the concept of a company being a separate legal entity, and the purpose of the preparation of the accounts.

27.1.3 **Define** 'small companies' for the purpose of financial statement preparation and explain the relevance of this definition.

27.1.4 **Explain** when accounts may be required to be prepared under IFRS, rather than UK GAAP.

27.1.5 **Explain** the role of the auditor.

27.1.6 **Identify**, in outline, the reasons for auditors issuing a qualified report.

27.2 The balance sheet

27.2.1 **Explain** the purpose of a balance sheet.

27.2.2 **Identify** and **explain** the key balance sheet categories and content.

27.2.3 **Distinguish** between capital and revenue expenditure.

27.2.4 **Explain** the valuation of non-current assets.

27.2.5 **Calculate** depreciation under the straight-line and reducing balance methods.

27.2.6 **Calculate** the profit or loss on disposal of a non-current asset.

27.2.7 **Explain** the principles behind the valuation of inventories.

27.2.8 **Explain** the effects of first-in-first-out and last-in-first-out valuations on inventory values and profits.

27.2.9 **Identify** the types of current and non-current liabilities that typically appear in financial statements.

27.2.10 **Explain** the concept of a provision.

27.2.11 **Explain** the treatment of contingent liabilities within financial statements.

27.2.12 **Explain** the treatment of pension costs in financial statements.

27.2.13 **Explain** what is meant by a post-balance sheet event.

27.2.14 **Distinguish** among authorised, issued, paid up and called up share capital.

27.2.15 **Explain** the effect of the following on a balance sheet

- Rights issue.
- Bonus/scrip issue.

- Stock split.
- Share repurchases.

27.2.16 **Identify** and **explain** the main types of reserve found in the balance sheet.

27.3 The accounting treatment of financial instruments

27.3.1 **Identify** the various classifications of financial instruments and outline the accounting treatment of each.

27.4 Income statement and statement of changes in equity

27.4.1 **Identify** and **explain** the classification of expenses based on nature or function.

27.4.2 **Explain** the principle of revenue recognition.

27.4.3 **Identify** the following different levels of profit and understand which classes of expenses are considered in arriving at each level.

- Gross profit.
- Trading (or operating) profit.
- Net profit.

27.4.4 **Explain** the objective of a statement of changes in equity.

27.4.5 **Identify** the information to be reported in a statement of change in equity.

27.5 The cash flow statement

27.5.1 **Explain** the purpose of a cash flow statement.

27.5.2 **Identify** the classification of cash flow activities.

27.5.3 **Calculate** net cash flow from operations given operating profit (or vice versa) and the relevant balance sheet movements.

27.6 Group accounts

27.6.1 **Define** and distinguish between corporate investments, associated companies and subsidiaries.

27.6.2 **Explain** the purpose of group accounts.

27.6.3 **Define** a minority interest and explain how it is represented in the financial statements.

27.6.4 **Explain** how goodwill arises in acquisition accounting.

27.6.5 **Explain** the treatment of goodwill and intangible assets in the group accounts, including amortisation, useful lives and the requirement for impairment review.

27.7 Major accounting ratios

27.7.6 **Explain** the effect of the following on the major accounting ratios.

- Rights issue.
- Bonus/scrip issue.
- Stock split.
- Share repurchases.

1 Purpose of Financial Statements

1.1 Introduction

Learning objective	27.1.2 **Explain** the concept of a company being a separate legal entity, and the purpose of the preparation of the accounts.

A company is a business organisation created in law that is owned by its members or shareholders but is legally distinct from them – it is a separate legal entity. A company may sue in its own name or be sued, it may even sue, or be sued by, its own shareholders.

Generally, for listed companies and larger unlisted ones, the shareholders appoint directors to manage the company on their behalf, having little involvement in the day-to-day operations of the companies themselves.

The primary purpose of annual financial statements is to provide a medium enabling the directors to report to the shareholders on the performance of the company.

The financial statements are, however, frequently used by other interested parties such as lenders, creditors, potential investors, tax authorities, the government, etc. to help them assess the returns they are receiving and the risks that they may face.

2 UK Regulation of Accounts

2.1 Introduction

As a result of the segregation of management and ownership, and the limitation of liability, strict reporting rules/regulations have been developed to ensure that the shareholders are kept fully informed to enable them to assess their risks and returns.

There are three sources of regulations in relation to a quoted company's accounts.

- Legal rules (the Companies Act).
- The UK Listing Authority (UKLA) Listing Rules.
- Professional accounting rules (International Accounting Standards or Financial Reporting Standards).

The first two are concerned with what should be disclosed in the accounts. The latter is principally concerned with the accounting methods that should be used, although the rules frequently give additional disclosure guidance as well.

2.2 Legal rules

2.2.1 Introduction

As with most UK legislation, the Companies Act rules have developed gradually over the years. The The Companies Act 2006 (CA06) consolidated the previous statutes and contains the most recent legislative developments.

2.2.2 True and fair view

One of the requirements of the Companies Act is that the accounts should give a **true and fair view** of the performance of the company for the period, and its financial position at the end of that period. The requirement to show a true and fair view **overrides all other requirements** in the preparation of accounts.

2.2.3 Formats of disclosure

In line with EU practice, UK accounts are now prepared in accordance with strict formats. Both the balance sheet and the profit and loss account are obliged to be presented in prescribed formats.

2.2.4 Other regulation

Companies may have other regulatory structures to satisfy in relation to overseas investors, for instance, the 20-F return to the US Securities and Exchange Commission.

2.3 Professional accounting rules

arning objectives	27.1.4 **Explain** when accounts may be required to be prepared under IFRS rather than UK GAAP.

2.3.1 UK accounting standards and GAAP

GAAP signifies all the rules, from whatever source, which govern accounting. In individual countries this is seen primarily as a combination of

- National company law
- National accounting standards (FRSs in the UK)
- Local stock exchange requirements

Although those sources are the basis for the GAAP of individual countries, the concept also includes the effects of what may in an individual country be non-mandatory sources such as

- International accounting standards
- Statutory requirements in other countries

In many countries, like the UK, GAAP does not have any statutory or regulatory authority or definition, unlike other countries, such as the USA. The term is rarely mentioned in legislation, and only then in fairly limited terms.

2.3.2 The International Financial Reporting Standards

International Financial Reporting Standards are being developed through an international process that involves the worldwide accountancy profession, the preparers and users of accounts and the national standard setting bodies.

Since 2005, all **UK listed companies** have been **required to apply international standards** (International Financial Reporting Standards (IFRSs) and International Accounting Standards (IASs)) to their group accounts. All non -listed companies may apply either IFRSs or UK FRSs.

3 Reporting Requirements

3.1 Responsibility for accounts preparation and audit

Learning objectives	**27.1.1 Explain** the legal requirement to prepare financial statements.

It is the **directors' legal responsibility** to prepare accounts for the shareholders that must

- Give a true and fair view.
- Comply with the requirements of the Companies Acts.

> The auditor is an independent third party appointed by the shareholders (to whom they report) to give an opinion as to whether the directors have correctly fulfilled these responsibilities.

3.2 Auditor's report

Learning objective	**27.1.5 Explain** the role of the auditor. **27.1.6 Identify**, in outline, the reasons for auditors issuing a qualified report.

3.2.1 Introduction

Under the Companies Act 2006, every company is required to appoint an auditor or auditors at each Annual General Meeting, who will hold office from the conclusion of that meeting until the conclusion of the next AGM.

3.2.2 Scope of the audit

The auditors are required to report to the members as to whether, in their opinion, the accounts of the company give a true and fair view of the state of the company's affairs and its performance to the year-end and comply with the Companies Acts. This form of audit report will be considered an **unqualified** audit report; this may also be referred to as a clean or **clear report**.

If, however, they do not feel that they can express this positive opinion, then they must give a **qualified report**.

Note: There is no need for dormant companies (those not currently trading) to have their accounts audited.

3.2.3 Reason for qualified audit reports

Qualified audit reports fall into two categories.

Limitation on the scope of the audit

Where there is uncertainty which prevents the auditor from forming an opinion on a matter, e.g. the outcome of litigation which will materially impact upon the company. In such circumstances, the auditor will issue a **disclaimer of opinion**.

Disagreement

Where an auditor's opinion on a matter conflicts with that disclosed in the financial statements, the auditor must give an **adverse opinion**.

3.2.4 Wording of qualified audit reports

Dependent upon the significance of the problem, there are **four** possible qualified audit reports, each of which will attract a slightly different wording in the auditor's report. The table below shows the form of wording that will be used when the auditor is stating his opinion.

	Limitation of Scope	Disagreement
Fundamental	**(Disclaimer of opinion)** Unable to express an opinion	**(Adverse opinion)** Do not give a true and fair view
Less significant	Generally give a true and fair view except for a few specific details	Generally give a true and fair view except for a few specific details

In all cases, the auditor will state what he is uncertain about or disagrees with.

3.3 Content and maintenance of financial statements

3.3.1 Content

Though, as we discuss later, smaller companies have reduced disclosure and audit requirements, for the financial statements for listed companies must contain

- Balance sheet (this year plus last year)
- Income statement (this year plus last year)
- Cash flow statement (this year plus last year)
- Statement of changes in equity
- Supporting notes to the above expanding on the detail they contain
- Accounting policies
- Directors' report
- Auditors' report
- Operating and financial review
- Five year summary

Note that a chairman's statement is not required.

3.3.2 Accounting records

The Companies Act requires that a plc must hold its accounting records for six years and a private limited company (Ltd) for three years.

4 Directors' Report

Under the Companies Act, the Directors' Report must contain certain key pieces of information.

- A fair review of the performance of the business during the year, together with an indication of likely future developments.
- Particulars of significant changes in fixed assets.
- The names of the directors and their share interests (beneficial and non-beneficial). This information may be contained in the notes to the accounts rather than in the Directors' Report.
- Any important events which have taken place since the balance sheet date. If these are **adjusting events** described as post-balance sheet events which relate to circumstances in existence at the year-end, then they will be adjusted for in the accounts. Non-adjusting events, which relate to new developments, will only be adjusted for if they have a bearing on the going concern concept.
- Details of any of its own shares which the company has acquired (and cancelled) during the year.

- A statement with regard to the company's policies with regard to the employment of disabled people and employee communications.
- Political and charitable contributions in excess of £200.

4.1 Fundamental accounting concepts

4.1.1 Introduction

Accounting practice has developed gradually over a matter of centuries. The procedures in common use imply the acceptance of certain concepts, which are by no means self-evident.

Some of these accounting concepts will now be considered in more detail.

4.1.2 Going concern

This concept assumes that the business will continue in operational existence for the foreseeable future. This means, in particular, that the profit and loss account and balance sheet assume no intention or necessity to liquidate or curtail significantly the scale of operations.

4.1.3 Accruals (or matching)

This concept assumes that the revenue and costs are

- Accrued, i.e. recognised as they are earned or incurred, not as money received or paid.
- Matched with one another so far as their relationship can be established or justifiably assumed.
- Dealt with in the profit and loss account of the **period to which they relate**.

NB: Where the accrual concept is inconsistent with the prudence concept (see below), **the latter prevails**.

4.1.4 Consistency

This concept assumes that there is consistency of accounting treatment of like items within each accounting period and from one period to the next.

4.1.5 Prudence

This concept assumes

- **Revenue and profits are not anticipated**, but are recognised by inclusion in the profit and loss account only when realised in the form of cash or other realisable assets.
- **Provision is made for all known liabilities** arising as a result of actions taken.

4.1.6 Historic cost

This concept means transactions are recorded at the cost when they are incurred.

4.1.7 Concept of entity

This simply means a business is considered as a separate entity from its owner.

4.1.8 UK and international accounting terminology

The learning objectives of the syllabus do not highlight whether UK or International accounting terminology will be used in the exam. We have been consistent with UKSIP and have used international terminology throughout the study book. Please be aware however that the following equivalent UK terminology could be used by the examiner:

Balance sheet

International	UK
Non-Current Assets	Fixed Assets
Property, Plant and Equipment	Tangible Assets
Non-Current Liabilities	Long Term Liabilities
Trade Receivables	Debtors
Trade Payables / Current Liabilities	Creditors
Inventory	Stock
Retained Earnings	Profit and Loss Account Reserve

Income Statement

International	UK
Revenue	Turnover
No equivalent	Exceptional items

Cash Flow Statement

International	UK
3 separate headings	8 separate headings

The balance sheet structure is also different. UK accounts typically show net assets on the top of the balance sheet and shareholders' funds on the bottom. Whereas International accounts tend to show total assets on the top, and total financing (equity and liabilities) on the bottom.

5 Balance Sheet

arning objective | 27.2.1 **Explain** the purpose of a balance sheet.

5.1 Introduction

The balance sheet is a statement of the financial position of the business at a specific point in time, such as the year-end.

It is the product of the accounting equation that, as its name suggests, must always equate or balance.

It should always be borne in mind that it is only a picture of the company at the **specific point of time**. Each transaction impacts on the accounting equation, hence the balance sheet just after the year-end may be significantly different from that at the year-end, if a company has undertaken significant transactions between the two dates.

5.2 Accounting equation

arning objective | 27.2.2 **Identify** and **explain** the key balance sheet categories and content.

5.2.1 Introduction

The **accounting equation** can be stated as

Formula to learn

Assets = Liabilities + Shareholders' funds
Or alternative
Net assets (Assets – Liabilities) = Shareholders' funds

The format usually adopted presents this equation vertically with assets above liabilities and shareholders' funds rather than horizontally where they are alongside one another. In outline, a balance sheet appears as follows.

NB: Brackets are used to denote negatives.

Balance Sheet Outline	
Net Assets	**£'000**
Assets	400
	400
Liabilities + Shareholders funds	
Share Capital	100
Reserves	150
Liabilities	150
	400

As we can see, the accounting equation holds – the balance sheet balances.

The four categories we have outlined are as follows.

5.2.2 Assets

These represent resources owned or controlled by the company and available for its use, such as inventories of goods for sale or production equipment. These can be subcategorised under two headings.

Non-current assets/ Fixed assets

Assets acquired for **continued use in the business to earn profit**, not for resale. Examples of such items would include office and production buildings, and equipment. Clearly, we intend to use these long term, not simply sell them on at a profit.

Current assets

Assets **acquired for conversion to cash** during the ordinary course of business. Examples of such assets would include stocks of goods available for sale to customers, or customers' account balances, which will be settled for cash.

5.2.3 Liabilities

Learning objective 27.2.9 **Identify** the types of current and non-current liabilities that typically appear in financial statements.

These represent **amounts owed by the company** to outside suppliers and lenders. These too are subcategorised broadly into

- Current liabilities = amounts due for payment within one year
- Non-current liabilities = amounts due for payments after more than one year.

The purpose of the above classification is to provide a clear indication of the timescales for settlement.

5.2.4 Share capital

This is **money invested in the company** by shareholders, i.e. money subscribed for shares.

5.2.5 Reserves

These generally represent **profits earned and retained by the company** since it started to trade, although there may be other types of reserves, as we will see later.

5.2.6 Illustration

The idea of the accounting equation can be illustrated with a simple example considering the first few transactions of a company, starting with its formation and the issue of shares for cash.

(1) Issue of shares for cash

If a company issued shares for cash and raised £100,000, the equation would be in balance because the two financial effects would be reflected as

	£'000
Impact on Assets	
Cash up (current asset)	+100
	+100
Impact on Liabilities + Shareholders' Funds	
Called-up share capital	+100
	+100

The impact on the balance sheet would be

	Before £'000	Issue £'000	After £'000
Assets			
Current assets			
Cash	–	+100	100
	–	+100	100
Liabilities + Shareholders' Funds			
Called-up share capital	–	+100	100
	–	+100	100

(2) Borrowing from the bank

If the company borrowed £50,000 from the bank, repayable in five years, the effect on the accounting equation would be

	£'000
Impact on Assets	
Cash up	+50
	+50
Impact on Liabilities + Shareholders' Funds	
Non-current liabilities	+50
	+50

There is, therefore, a change in the total assets and liabilities, and the balance sheet would now be

	Before £'000	Loan £'000	After £'000
Assets			
Current assets			
Cash	100	+50	150
	100	+50	150
Liabilities + Shareholders' Funds			
Called-up share capital	100	–	100
Non-current liabilities	–	+50	50
	100	+50	150

(3) Buying equipment for cash

If the company used £60,000 cash to buy machinery for long-term use, i.e. a non-current asset, the equation would be affected as follows.

	£'000
Impact on Net Assets	
Non-current assets up	+60
Cash down	–60
	–
Impact on Liabilities + Shareholders' Funds	–

This does not affect the total assets or liabilities. We are simply exchanging one asset (cash) for another (the machinery). The balance sheet would now become

	Before £'000	Buy Equip £'000	After £'000
Assets			
Non-current assets	–	+60	60
Current assets			
Cash	150	–60	90
	150	–	150
Liabilities + Shareholders' Funds			
Called-up share capital	100	–	100
Non-current liabilities	50		50
	150	–	150

(4) Buying goods for resale for cash

If the company now spends £20,000 cash to buy goods intended for resale, the equation would be affected as follows.

	£'000
Impact on Assets	
Inventories up	+20
Cash down	–20
	–
Impact on Liabilities + Shareholders' Funds	–

Once more, we are simply exchanging one asset for another, with no impact on the total assets or the liabilities. The balance sheet would now become

	Before £'000	Buy Inventories £'000	After £'000
Non-current Assets			
Non-current assets	60	–	60
Current assets			
Inventories	–	+20	20
Cash	90	–20	70
	150	–	150
Liabilities + Shareholders' Funds			
Called-up share capital	100	–	100
Non-current liabilities	50	–	50
	150	–	150

(5) Selling goods for cash

The company now sells half of these goods for £19,000, i.e. goods that had cost £10,000 are being sold for £19,000. As a result, a profit of £9,000 is being realised. The impact on the accounting equation would be

	£'000
Impact on Assets	
Inventories down	–10
Cash up	+19
	+9
Impact on Liabilities + Shareholders' Funds	
Retained earnings up	+9
	+9

The balance sheet would now become

	Before £'000	Sell Inventories £'000	After £'000
Assets			
Non-current assets	60	–	60
Current assets			
Inventories	20	–10	10
Cash	70	+19	89
	150	+9	159
Liabilities + Shareholders' Funds			
Called-up share capital	100	–	100
Retained earnings	–	+9	9
Non-current liabilities	50	–	50
	150	+9	159

(6) Selling goods on credit

If the company now sells the remaining goods (which cost £10,000) for £21,000 on credit, it generates a profit of £11,000.

NB: In accordance with the accruals concept, this revenue is recognised when earned, we do **not** wait for the cash to be received. The impact on the accounting equation would be

	£'000
Impact on Assets	
Inventories down	–10
Receivables up	+21
	+11
Impact on Liabilities + Shareholders' Funds	
Retained earnings up	+11
	+11

The balance sheet reflects this change as

	Before £'000	Sell Inventories £'000	After £'000
Assets			
Non-current assets	60	–	60
Current assets			
Inventories	10	–10	–
Receivables	–	+21	21
Cash	89	–	89
	159	+11	170
Shareholders' Funds			
Called-up share capital	100	–	100
Retained earnings	9	+11	20
Non-current liabilities	50	–	50
	159	+11	170

(7) Buying goods on credit

If the company now buys £25,000 worth of goods, obtaining credit from the supplier, the impact on the accounting equation would be

	£'000
Impact on Assets	
Inventory up	+25
	+25
Impact on Liabilities + Shareholders' Funds	–
Current liabilities up	+25
	+25

Which would be reflected in the balance sheet as

	Before £'000	Buy Inventories £'000	After £'000
Assets			
Non-current assets	60	–	60
Current assets			
Inventories	–	+25	25
Receivables	21	–	21
Cash	89	–	89
	170	+25	195
Liabilities + Shareholders' Funds			
Called-up share capital	100	–	100
Retained earnings	20	–	20
Current liabilities	–	+25	25
Non-current liabilities	50	–	50
	170	+25	195

(8) Paying for expenses

Let us say the company pays the following expenses from cash.

- Wages of £2,000.
- Rent of £4,000.
- Telephone bills of £1,000.

That is £7,000 in total. Hence, the impact on the accounting equation would be

	£'000
Impact on Assets	
Cash down	–7
	–7
Impact on Liabilities + Shareholders' Funds	
Expenses up (retained earnings down)	–7
	–7

Which would be reflected in the balance sheet as

	Before £'000	Expenses £'000	After £'000
Assets			
Non-current assets	60	–	60
Current assets			
Inventories	25	–	25
Receivables	21	–	21
Cash	89	–7	82
	195	–7	188
Liabilities + Shareholders' Funds			
Called-up share capital	100	–	100
Retained earnings	20	–7	13
Current liabilities	25	–	25
Non-current liabilities	50	–	50
	195	–7	188

Summary of accounting equation illustration

From this example, we can see that each transaction the company enters into impacts upon the balance sheet. However, the impact occurs in such a way as to keep the balance sheet in balance. At any point in time, and for each individual transaction, the **accounting equation** holds, i.e.

Formula to learn

Assets = Liabilities

5.3 Format

The general format for a balance sheet is illustrated by the following example.

XYZ plc – Balance Sheet as at 31 December 2012

	Notes	2012 £'000	2011 £'000
Non-current assets	1		
Intangible	2	877	662
Tangible	3	19,798	19,854
Investments	4	37	39
		20,712	20,555
Current assets	5		
Inventories		19,420	19,101
Receivables	7	27,882	35,980
Investments		1,487	2,116
Cash		3,923	4,804
		52,712	62,001
Total asset		**73,424**	**82,556**
Capital and reserves			
Called-up share capital	12	1,743	1,725
Share premium account reserve	13	2,237	2,182
Revaluation reserve	14	4,687	3,806
Other reserves	15	1,204	1,204
Retained earnings	16	8,557	6,875
Total shareholders' funds		18,428	15,792
Minority interests	17	1,000	800
Shareholders' funds		19,428	16,592
Non-current liabilities			
Provisions for liabilities and charges	10	1,484	2,193
Loans	11	3,695	18,553
Current liabilities	6 & 7	48,817	45,218
Total liabilities		**73,424**	**82,556**

You will notice that the balance sheet is shown for both this year-end (31 December 2012) and the previous year-end (31 December 2011) for comparison. The notes referred to above would normally provide further detailed analysis, but here they are being used to provide additional explanations of the terminology.

5.4 Terminology

5.4.1 Non-current assets

As already noted, non-current assets are assets **acquired for continued use** within the business and not for resale. As we can see, these should be sub-classified into

- Property, plant and equipment (tangible assets).
- Intangibles.
- Investments.

Depreciation

The Companies Act requires that all fixed assets that have limited useful economical lives must be depreciated, but what is **depreciation**?

Example

A company buys some production machinery at a cost of £60,000. It expects, from previous experience, that it will last five years, after which time it will be sold for £5,000. It will therefore cost the company £55,000 (£60,000 cost, less £5,000 expected sale proceeds) to use the equipment over these five years.

Applying the matching concept, this £55,000 cost should be spread over the five years, i.e. an expense of £11,000 charged against the profit each year.

Depreciation is the method by which the cost of using the asset is matched against its related benefit. On the balance sheet, fixed assets are usually stated at net book value (NBV), i.e. cost, less the accumulated depreciation provision.

Thus, at the end of each of the next five years, the fixed asset will be valued in the balance sheet as follows.

	Year 1 £'000	Year 2 £'000	Year 3 £'000	Year 4 £'000	Year 5 £'000
Cost	60	60	60	60	60
Depreciation provision	(11)	(22)	(33)	(44)	(55)
Net book value	49	38	27	16	5

As we can see, the balance sheet net book value of the equipment falls by £11,000 each year (as the amount is charged as an expense – depreciation) until, in Year 5, it has dropped to the estimated sales proceeds of £5,000.

Impairment review

The purpose for depreciating an asset is to match the cost of the asset to the benefits derived from its use on the assumption that the future benefits, alternatively referred to as the **recoverable amount**, will exceed the cost, ie the asset is to be used profitably – an essential requirement for a business to be a going concern.

If a product is late in its life cycle and demand is falling it could be that the recoverable amount for the manufacturing asset will fall below the net book value of the asset on the balance sheet – an impairment loss has occurred. When an asset has experienced such an impairment loss then, under both UK and international accounting standards, its value needs to be written down to the recoverable amount – effectively an additional depreciation charge equal to the impairment loss.

It is not necessary to check each individual non-current asset each year to determine whether it has suffered an impairment loss, rather a business can disregard this requirement unless there is an indication that impairment may have occurred, eg a fall in demand that the business itself will be well aware of.

The same principle also applies to intangible non-current assets, though for goodwill arising from an acquisition or any other intangible with an indefinite life a full impairment test needs to be undertaken each year, ie a full analysis and valuation of the recoverable amount in order to determine whether an impairment has occurred.

Disposal

When an asset is disposed of, any difference between the disposal proceeds and the net book value at the disposal date will represent a profit or loss on disposal that needs to be reflected in the income statement.

5.4.2 Intangible non-current assets

Learning objectives

27.6.4 Explain how goodwill arises in acquisition accounting.

27.6.5 Explain the treatment of goodwill and intangible assets in the group accounts including amortisation, useful lives and the requirement for impairment reviews.

Intangibles are literally assets **without physical form**. They frequently represent intellectual property rights of the company, or abilities of its staff, that enable it to operate and generate profits in a way that competitors cannot.

The types of intangible assets that most frequently appear on the balance sheet are as follows.

- Research and development expenditure.
- Patents, licences and trademarks.
- Publishing rights and titles.
- Goodwill.
- Brands.

Goodwill arises in the event of a company completing an acquisition. Where the company has paid more that the fair value of the net assets goodwill arises. For example, if Company ABC plc pays £5m to buy company XYZ plc, whose net assets are £3m, then company ABC will have purchased £2m of goodwill.

Internally generated goodwill can never appear on the balance sheet, it is permitted in the event of an acquisition since it can be objectively valued.

Depreciation of intangible fixed assets is frequently referred to as **amortisation**. Under IFRS 3, goodwill must be capitalised as an intangible fixed asset and subject to an annual impairment review. The same accounting treatment is applied in the UK under FRS 10.

5.4.3 Tangible non-current assets

These are physical assets that are used within the business over a number of years with a view to deriving some benefit from this use, e.g. through their use in the manufacture of goods for resale.

Tangible non-current assets include items such as

- Freehold land and buildings (including buildings under construction).
- Leasehold land and buildings.
- Plant and machinery.
- Motor vehicles.
- Fixtures and fittings.

5.4.4 Investments

These represent long-term ownership of shares in other companies and are usually reported in the balance sheet at historical cost. Additional reporting regulations apply to significant levels of shareholdings that have caused the investments to be classified as either a subsidiary (50%+) or an associated undertaking (20%+).

5.4.5 Current assets

Strictly speaking, these are assets other than non-current assets, although perhaps the best description is that current assets are assets held for conversion into cash in the ordinary course of business. As we can see, current assets are subcategorised into (in order of liquidity)

- **Inventories:** goods held available for sale.
- **Receivables:** amounts owed to the company, perhaps as a result of selling goods on credit. This includes **prepayments**.

  These may be

  - Raw materials – goods purchased for input into the manufacturing process
  - Work in progress – part made products
  - Finished goods – fully manufactured products
  - Prepayments are amounts paid before the balance sheet date, which relate to the period after that date. Since we have paid the money over, but not yet received the benefit due from the expenditure, we still have an asset at the balance sheet date. Prepayments are therefore shown as part of **receivables**.
- **Investments:** shares held in the short term with the intention of reselling, e.g. short-term speculative investments.
- **Cash**.

In valuing current assets, the fundamental accounting concept of **prudence** is applied, in that they are valued at the lower of

- Cost.
- Net realisable value (NRV), i.e. net cash recoverable from trading or realising the asset after taking account of all selling and recovery costs. For inventories this will be illustrated below.

Thus

- If the NRV exceeds cost, the asset is valued at cost, i.e. no profit is anticipated.
- If the NRV is less than cost, the asset is devalued down to NRV, i.e. a loss is recognised.

5.4.6 Current liabilities

Current liabilities due within one year should fully reflect all liabilities payable within 12 months of the year-end.

They include bank overdrafts and both dividends and taxation payable within one year as well as amounts owed to suppliers, known as trade payables.

Accruals

An accrual is an amount due in respect of goods and services used during the year, but not yet invoiced. Since we owe the amount, even though we have not yet been invoiced for it, we have to show it as part of our liabilities. Accruals are therefore shown as part of **current liabilities**.

5.4.7 Non-current liabilities

This will typically include such items as

- Long-term bank loans.
- Loan stock and debentures issued by the company.

Both must be repaid long term. It would also include any other known liabilities, such as trade payables, that do not require settlement within the next 12-month period.

5.4.8 Provisions and contingencies

Learning objectives

27.2.10 Explain the concept of a provision.

27.2.11 Explain the treatment of contingent liabilities within financial statements.

Definition of a provision

A provision represents an amount set aside by the company to meet probable future costs arising as a result of past events. An example of such a provision is the costs associated with the demolition and site clearance of a factory, closed down during the year.

The amounts are estimated because they are not yet known with certainty, and will not be until the process is completed sometime in the future. Their value is, therefore, less reliable than items in **non-current liabilities** such as bank loans, where it is known with certainty what is owed and when it is due to be paid.

Definition of contingencies

A contingent liability is and uncertain liability that does not meet the criteria recognising a provision and is either of the following.

- A **possible** obligation arising from past events whose existence will be confirmed only by the occurrence of one or more uncertain future events not wholly within the entity's control.
- A present obligation that arises from past events but is not recognised because it is not probable that a transfer of economic benefits will be required to settle the obligation or because the amount of the obligation cannot be measured with sufficient reliability.

Examples of contingencies would include the following.

- Outcome of litigation cases.
- Guarantees provided by the company.
- Goods sold under warranty or guarantee.
- Bills of exchange discounted with banks.

Contingent liabilities should not be recognised in the accounts. There should instead be a description of the nature of contingent liabilities in the notes to the accounts. The international standard is IAS 37 the UK GAAP accounting standard dealing with contingent liabilities is FRS12.

For each class of contingent liability the following should be disclosed.

- The nature of the contingency.
- An estimate of its financial effect.

5.4.9 Pension costs

Learning objective

27.2.12 Explain the treatment of pension costs in financial statements.

Accounting for Defined Contribution schemes is relatively straightforward. The cost to the employer is recognised as an expense in the profit and loss account, in a similar way to how salary is expensed to the profit and loss account to reduce down annual profits.

Accounting for Defined Benefit schemes is more complicated because of the uncertainty of the scheme's future assets and liabilities. The international standard, IAS 19, and its UK equivalent, FRS 17, both require the pension assets and liabilities to be shown on the balance sheet.

The overall impact is that the firm will realise a pension cost in the income statement relating to servicing the scheme. The balance sheet will show a net pension liability or pension asset. The notes to the accounts will disclose in detail the full pension asset amount, and also the full present value of the liability.

The discount rate applied to calculate the present value of the pension fund liability is that of an AA rated corporate bond of similar maturity.

Fluctuations in the stock market and actuarial adjustments can lead to significant movement in the assets and liabilities of the pension fund, and so too have a significant effect on the balance sheet.

5.4.10 Called-up share capital

earning objective — **27.2.14 Distinguish** among authorised, issued, paid up and called up share capital.

Under the Companies Act, UK companies have to ascribe a nominal or par value to each share. This represents

- The **minimum value at which shares can be issued**. The company is not allowed to issue fully paid shares at a price below nominal value. A company can, however, issue partly paid shares where only a portion of the nominal value is required to be paid immediately. On such shares the company can demand the payment to the remainder of the nominal value at a later date, making them **fully paid**.
- The **limits of the liability of the shareholder**. If the company becomes insolvent, shareholders' liability is limited to any unpaid element of this nominal value. Where the share is a fully paid share, the shareholder has no more liability.

With respect to share capital it is, therefore, important to understand the distinction between

- **Authorised share capital** – the maximum number/nominal value of shares that the company can issue as specified in its formation documents. A company does not have to issue all of its authorised share capital, this simply represents a maximum.
- **Issued share capital** – the number/nominal value of shares that have been issued.
- **Called up share capital** – the amount of the issued share capital that the company has asked shareholders to pay for. Shares can be issued partly paid and the called up share capital is the part of the issued share capital where payment has been demanded.
- **Paid up share capital** – the amount of the issued share capital for which payment has been received.

For the vast majority of companies, all the shares that have been issued are fully paid and for these companies the issued share capital, called up share capital and paid up share capital are identical, representing the total nominal value of shares in issue at the year end. In our example, the company had issued 100,000 shares, each with a nominal value of £1.00 that had been paid in full, giving £100,000 issued, called up and paid up share capital.

There are four main types of shares. In the event of the company going into liquidation, these shares will rank in a strict order of priority, as follows.

1. Preference shares.
2. Ordinary shares.
3. Deferred shares.
4. Warrants to subscribe to new shares.

5.4.11 Share premium account reserve

arning objective — **27.2.16 Identify** and **explain** the main types of reserve found in the balance sheet.

If a company trades profitably and retains those profits to finance expansion, then its value will grow. As a result, it will be able to raise cash in later years by issuing more shares at a price in **excess of their nominal value**, i.e. at a premium.

Example

A company could raise £20,000 by issuing 5,000 new £1.00 ordinary shares at a price of £4.00 each, then there is a premium of £3.00 on each share (full price of £4.00 less nominal value of £1.00).

Under the Companies Act, the company must record the issue of these shares by increasing the called-up share capital by only the nominal value of the shares issued, i.e. £5,000. The premium of £15,000 must be added to the share premium account. The impact on the accounting equation is

	£'000
Impact on Assets	
Cash up	+20
	+20
Impact on Liabilities and shareholders' funds	
Share capital up	+5
Share premium account up	+15
	+20

Having been created, the share premium account can only subsequently be reduced in **five** circumstances without the court's permission.

(a) To issue **bonus shares**. Bonus shares are issued by a company when it feels that the share price has gone too high. A bonus issue, like a rights issue, is made to the existing shareholders and gives them a number of free shares proportionate to their existing holding.

A two for four bonus issue, with the share price at £9.00, would give the owner of four shares two new shares.

The impact on the share price is as follows.

	Number	Price £		Value £
Existing holding	4 shares	@ £9	=	£36
Bonus shares	2 shares	@ £0	=	0
Final holding	6 shares		=	£36 or **£6 per share**

In terms of the balance sheet, the effect is

Impact on Net Assets	None
Impact on Shareholders' Funds	Share capital up Share premium account down Any surplus over the value of the share premium would have to go to other reserves

A bonus issue can be financed out of any reserve, not solely from a share premium account.

(b) To write off **preliminary expenses** of forming a company.

(c) To write off **expenses of issue** of shares or debentures.

(d) To charge the **premium on repayment of debentures**.

(e) To charge the **discount on issue of debentures**.

The share premium account can **never be reduced to pay dividends** to the shareholders. It is one of the company's non-distributable reserves.

5.4.12 Revaluation reserve

UK companies are permitted by the Companies Act to revalue all assets, other than goodwill upwards, increasing net assets and shareholders' funds.

Where a company does revalue its fixed assets upwards, it would be imprudent to treat this increase in shareholders' funds as part of the company's realised profits for the year. It has not been generated by the operational performance of the company and it is certainly not represented by cash. It is therefore considered unrealised and **non-distributable**, i.e. the company cannot use the revaluation reserve to pay a dividend.

In this situation, the increase in the net book value of the assets is reflected within shareholders' funds in the revaluation reserve.

Impact on Net Assets	Non-current assets up
Impact on Shareholders' Funds	Revaluation reserve up

If there is a significant difference between the market value and balance sheet value, the Companies Act requires a statement of this fact if a revaluation is not carried out.

5.4.13 Other reserves

Any other reserves generally represent an apportionment or allocation from retained earnings. This is frequently done for the following reasons.

- To indicate that a certain element of profit is being retained for a specific reason.
- To indicate that a portion of profits will never be paid out as a dividend.
- To account for the treatment of unusual terms, such as goodwill, written off.

5.4.14 Retained earnings

The retained earnings balance on the balance sheet represents the **accumulated profits made by the company since it started to trade**, which have **not been paid out as dividends** or transferred to other reserves. As such, it is a **distributable reserve** under the Companies Act rules, i.e. it can be used to cover the payment of dividends to shareholders.

The separate **income statement** details the impact of this year's trading activities on this accumulated figure. Any profits retained this year which are detailed in the separate income statement will be added to the accumulated retained earnings (or reserves) brought forward, giving the accumulated position at the end of the year. This could be viewed like a bank statement, where the statement only shows the movements for the month, but these are added to the opening cash balance to arrive at the closing one.

Ensure that you can distinguish the balance sheet retained earnings and the income statement in your mind, i.e.

- The balance sheet figure represents the accumulated position since the company started trading.
- The income statement (covered next) details the movements for the year.

Please note that the various reserves discussed above can be reduced by various transactions occurring. These scenarios that will lead to a reduction include the following.

- Losses sustained during the year.
- Issue and redemption expenses.
- A revaluation of an asset in a downward direction.
- An impairment of goodwill.

5.4.15 Minority interests

Minority interests arise when a company has a partly owned subsidiary company. For example, XYZ plc may own 80% of ABC Limited. The balance of the shares in ABC Limited are owned by other shareholders, referred to as the minority interest.

When XYZ plc prepares its consolidated accounts, it will include all the assets and liabilities of ABC Limited on the top half of its balance sheet as being part of the group's assets and liabilities. The reason that it does this is that it controls all of ABC Limited's assets, since it has a majority of voting rights.

However, it only owns 80% of ABC Limited's net assets, with the other 20% being owned by the minority interest. XYZ plc recognises this fact by analysing out total shareholder financing into group shareholders' funds and minority interest. The minority interest shows how much of the net assets belong to the minority shareholders in ABC Limited.

5.4.16 The impact of rights issues, bonus (scrip issues), stock splits and share repurchases on the balances sheet

Learning objectives

27.2.15 Explain the effect of the following on a balance sheet: rights issue; bonus/scrip issue; stock split and share repurchases.

27.7.6 Explain the effect of the following on major accounting ratios: rights issue; bonus/scrip issue; stock split and share repurchases.

Bonus issues

Bonus issues result in new shares being created and given free to existing shareholders pro-rata to their existing holdings. The balance sheet impact will be a transfer from the share premium account to the share capital account. No new finance has been raised so there is no adjustment to the asset half of the balance sheet. A transfer has simply been made from a reserve to the share capital account.

Stock splits

Stock splits have a similar cosmetic effect to a bonus issue in that they create more shares and so reduce the share price. Stock splits differ from bonus issues in that the nominal value of the shares is split.

For example, a company has 200,000 issued shares with a nominal value of £1. The company undertakes a 2 for 1 stock split. This implies the company will be replacing each share with two new shares. We will identify the impact on the share capital account.

Before the stock split the company had

Share Capital £200,000 (representing 200,000 £1 NV shares)

After the stock split the company will have 400,000 shares with a NV of £0.50

Share Capital £200,000 (representing 400,000 £0.50 N.V. shares)

So we can see there has been no impact on the share capital account. Nor has any cash been raised, so again there is no impact on the asset half of the balance sheet.

Rights issues

A rights issue results in additional equity finance being raised from existing shareholders. Assume a company has a £1 N.V. per share and issues 100,000 shares at £3. The impact will be:

Cash	+£300,000
Share Capital	+£100,000 (£1 NV × 100,000 shares)
Share Premium	+£200,000 (Excess over NV × 100,000 shares)

Share repurchases

Companies may repurchase their own shares for many reasons. These include

- To pay surplus cash back to shareholders as an alternative to dividends
- To increase the share price and the earnings per share
- To adjust the capital structure of the company by increasing the proportion of debt financing relative to shareholder funding

The impact of the balance sheet will be to reduce cash and to reduce shareholders funds. Here is a basic illustration.

ABC plc wishes to repurchase 200,000 £1 N.V. shares from a particular shareholder at the current share price of £3.00. The repurchase will be financed from cash balances and the shares will subsequently be cancelled. What is the impact on the balance sheet?

Cash	–£600,000
Share capital	–£200,000
Profit and loss account reserve	–£400,000

6 ASSET VALUATION

Learning objective	**27.2.4 Explain** the valuation of non-current assets.

Whilst we have covered the basics of asset valuation in the context of the fundamental accounting concepts and the review of the balance sheet, there are a number of other points that need to be considered.

6.1 Tangible non-current assets

IAS 16 and FRS 15 cover accounting for tangible non-current assets.

6.1.1 Definition and purpose

Under the accounting standards we must **depreciate** all non-current assets with finite useful lives. The purpose of this depreciation is to apply the accruals or matching concept, i.e. to match the cost of the asset against the benefits derived from its use.

When we apply depreciation, the effect on the accounting equation is

- Provision for depreciation up, hence non-current assets down (assets down).
- Depreciation charge up, hence profits down (shareholders' funds down).

NB: The purpose of depreciation is not to reflect the loss in value of the fixed asset, though it may reasonably approximate to being that. The purpose of depreciation is to spread the cost of the asset over the lifetime of the asset from the business' viewpoint.

6.1.2 Calculation

The calculation is to spread the cost, less the residual value, over the expected useful life of the asset, by the method considered most appropriate with regard to the type of asset and its use in the business. We consider two different methods below to illustrate the alternatives that the accounting professions have developed.

Firstly, however, let us look at some of the terminology involved.

6.1.3 Cost

The cost of a fixed asset is its purchase price – if acquired, or production cost – if manufactured. These terms, however, warrant further consideration.

Purchase price

Purchase price is the actual price paid, together with the incidental costs of acquisition, such as legal fees, on the acquisition of property.

Production cost

Production costs

- Must include the purchase price of all raw materials and consumables used, together with all other costs incurred, which can be directly attributable to production, such as construction wages.
- May include a reasonable proportion of overheads incurred by the company over the period of construction, including interest on capital borrowed for the purposes of financing production.

6.1.4 Residual value

The residual value represents the estimated realisable value of the asset at the end of its life, but based upon current prices, i.e. we do not try to anticipate or take account of any potential future inflation. The residual value will be the amount at which we could sell a similar asset of a similar age now, net of any disposal expenses.

6.1.5 Expected useful life

The expected useful life is the period over which the **current owner** will derive some benefit from its use, which may differ substantially from the full asset life. For example, if the company policy is to replace company cars every three years, then this represents the expected useful life of the cars to the company (and the residual value will be the value of a three-year old car), although the full life of a car (between when it is manufactured to when it arrives at the scrap yard) may be, say, ten years or more.

However, when determining the depreciation charge, it is only that portion of the life for which the asset will be used by the company that is relevant to the company. For the rest of its full life, it belongs to someone else and they must provide depreciation based on their cost, their residual value and how long they use it for.

A company must depreciate from its cost down to its residual value (at the end of its expected useful life) and it must spread that difference over its expected useful life.

With regard to determining the expected useful life, it may be

- Predetermined by the duration of a lease.
- Governed by the rate of extraction in the case of mines or quarries.
- Estimated at the outset, in which case it must be reviewed regularly and revised if necessary.

6.2 Methods of depreciation

Learning objectives	
	27.2.5 Calculate depreciation under the straight-line and reducing balance methods.
	27.2.6 Calculate the profit or loss on disposal of a non-current asset.

6.2.1 Introduction

We will illustrate each method based on the same example.

Example

A machine is bought at a cost of £100,000; it has an estimated useful life of five years and an estimated residual value of £25,000. What will be the balance sheet value and profit and loss charge each year under each of the following methods?

- Straight-line.
- Reducing balance.

6.2.2 Straight-line method

Under the straight-line method, an equal amount of depreciation is charged each year, so that the net book value of the asset diminishes steadily – on a straight line. This method assumes that we get equal use (benefit) from the asset each year, hence charge an equal cost each year. It is probably the most common method applied in practice.

Straight-line depreciation is sometimes quoted in accounts as being a percentage on cost.

The depreciation charge for the year can be calculated as follows.

Formula to learn

$$\text{Depreciation} = \frac{\text{Cost} - \text{Residual value}}{\text{Expected useful life}}$$

Solution

From our example, the depreciation charge for each year would be

$$\text{Depreciation} = \frac{£100{,}000 - £25{,}000}{5 \text{ years}} = £15{,}000 \text{ p.a.}$$

This could be quoted in the accounting policies note as depreciation at 15% (£15,000/£100,000) on cost. The balance sheet value and income statement charges are illustrated in the table below.

Items	Year 1	Year 2	Year 3	Year 4	Year 5
	£'000	£'000	£'000	£'000	£'000
Balance Sheet					
Cost	100	100	100	100	100
Depreciation provision	(15)	(30)	(45)	(60)	(75)
Net book value	85	70	55	40	25
Income statement					
Depreciation charge	15	15	15	15	15

6.2.3 Reducing balance method

The reducing balance method apportions larger amounts of depreciation to the earlier years and lower amounts to the later years. The implication of applying this method is that a greater benefit is derived from the use of the asset in the earlier years than in the later ones.

The depreciation rate may be described in the accounting policies note as being a **percentage on the opening net book value of the asset** (last year's closing net book value), compared to the straight line method where the depreciation percentage is on cost. That depreciation rate can be worked out by following the formula

Formula to learn

$$\text{Depreciation rate} = 1 - \sqrt[n]{\frac{\text{Residual value}}{\text{Cost}}}$$

Solution

On the basis of the example above, we can calculate the depreciation rate to apply as

$$\text{Depreciation rate} = 1 - \sqrt[5]{\frac{£25,000}{£100,000}} = 24.214\% \text{ p.a.}$$

Hence, our depreciation charge for any year would be 24.214% of the opening net book value for that year. Over the five-year period, the balance sheet net book values and income statement charges would appear as follows.

Items	Year 1 £'000	Year 2 £'000	Year 3 £'000	Year 4 £'000	Year 5 £'000
Balance Sheet					
Cost	100.0	100.0	100.0	100.0	100.0
Depreciation provision	(24.2)	(42.6)	(56.5)	(67.0)	(75.0)
Net book value c/f	75.8	57.4	43.5	33.0	25.0
Income statement					
Depreciation charge	24.2	18.4	13.9	10.5	8.0
	(100.0 × 24.214%)	(75.8 × 24.214%)	(57.4 × 24.214%)	(43.5 × 24.214%)	(33.0 × 24.214%)

Clearly, applying this method charges higher depreciation and thus produces lower profits in the earlier years, but against that it charges lower depreciation, hence higher profits in the later years.

If an asset is sold prior to the end of its useful expected life a profit or loss will be recognised in the income statement. If sold for more than its NBV, a profit will be realised , if for less than its NBV, a loss will be realised.

6.3 Inventories – SSAP 9/IAS 2

Learning objective **27.2.7 Explain** the principles behind the valuation of inventories.

The basic valuation rule, as we have already noted, is that inventories should be valued at the **lower of cost and net realisable value** (the amount recoverable from its use). We need to consider the strict definitions of each term in the context of inventory.

6.3.1 Valuation

Introduction

The comparison of cost and NRV should be done for each item of inventory separately, i.e. line by line. If this is impractical, we may consider groups or categories of similar inventory items on a category-by-category basis. However, the comparison should **never** be based on the totals.

Example

	Sale proceeds £	Selling costs £	NRV £	Cost £	Balance Sheet Value £
Inventory Item 1	1,570	70	1,500	1,000	1,000
Inventory Item 2	420	20	400	500	400
Inventory Item 3	825	25	800	800	800
					2,200

You will note from the above example that

- The total cost is £2,300 (£1,000 + £500 + £800).
- The total net realisable value is £2,700 (£1,500 + £400 + £800).

We do not pick the lowest of these two totals, rather we have evaluated each item separately. Therefore, for item one, the lower of cost (£1,000) and NRV (£1,500) is £1,000; for item two, it is £400; for item three, it is £800.

For a retail business that simply buys and sells units of inventory, the evaluation of costs should cause no real problem, nor should the evaluation of NRV. However, for a manufacturer, who buys in raw materials and then undertakes quite a lot of work to turn them into a finished unit that can then be sold, cost may be more difficult to ascertain for partly made or finished units. Similarly, NRV may be more difficult to ascertain for these units. We need to consider the strict definitions of both cost and NRV.

6.3.2 Cost

Cost is defined as that expenditure incurred in the normal course of business in bringing a product to its present location and condition. This cost comprises two components.

- **Cost of purchase** – The cost of purchase comprises purchase price, plus import duties, transportation and handling costs and any other directly attributable costs, less trade discounts, rebates, subsidies, i.e. the net overall amount paid to get the goods here.
- **Cost of conversion** – The cost of conversion equals manufacturing labour costs, plus production overheads, plus other overheads related to bringing the product to its current location and condition, e.g. factory heat and light, etc.

6.3.3 Allocating costs

Learning objective	27.2.8 **Explain** the effects of first-in-first-out and last-in-first-out valuations on inventory values and profits.

If a business only deals with a small number of items of inventory that are of high value, e.g. an art gallery or jewellers, it would be very easy to track the exact cost of each item individually. However, most businesses deal with a large amount of very similar or identical items. For example, a car manufacturer will probably use millions of nuts and bolts a year, and it would be very inconvenient to track the exact cost of each one separately. What we need is a practical approximation to tracking the true cost.

A variety of methods have been established to achieve this. However, in order to give a true and fair view, we must use only those methods providing a reasonable approximation to the expenditure actually incurred. The Companies Act 1985 permits the following historical cost alternatives.

- **First In First Out (FIFO).**
- **Last In First Out (LIFO).**
- **Weighted average.**
- Any other methods similar to those mentioned above.

Although LIFO is popular in the US, IAS 2 does not permit it to be used as it is considered unlikely to approximate to the actual expenditure incurred (especially in times of inflation as we will see below). For the same reason it is discouraged in the UK under SSAP 9. Furthermore, in the UK, LIFO is not a method of inventory valuation acceptable to HMRC. We will illustrate each of the possible options with a simple example.

Example

A company undertakes the following transactions in this chronological order.

Buy/Sell	Units No.	Price £	Value £
Buy	100	10	1,000
Sell	60	20	1,200
Buy	50	12	600
Sell	40	20	800
Buy	10	14	140

What is the closing value of inventory and the reported profit on these transactions?

Solution

Introduction

Regardless of how we value the inventory

- The total sales have been 100 units at £20, i.e. £2,000.
- The total number and cost of units acquired has been 160 units at £1,740.

As a result, the cost of 100 of the 160 units bought must be treated as the cost of the sales, the rest of the cost being carried forward in inventory to be matched against revenues in the future when those goods are sold. But how do we split the cost of £1,740 associated with these 160 units?

What will be the impact on our balance sheet and report profits of applying the various possible bases for evaluating this inventory?

FIFO

The First In First Out basis means literally what it says, i.e. the first units bought are the first ones sold. As a result, if we have any inventory at a particular point in time, it must represent the latest units purchased.

It can perhaps be visualised as a tube where items are put in at one end when they are bought, and taken out from the other end when they are sold. What is left in the tube will always be the last ones bought.

In our example above, we have bought 160 units and only sold 100. We therefore have 60 units left in inventory.

Under the FIFO basis, we would take these to be the last 60 purchased and evaluate them as follows.

Purchase	Units No.	Unit Price £	Total £
Last but one	50	12	600
Latest	10	14	140
	60		740

Our reported profits could now be calculated as follows.

Income Statement

	£	£
Revenue		2,000
Cost of sales		
Opening inventory	–	
Purchases (1,000 + 600 + 140)	1,740	
Less: Closing inventory	(740)	
		1,000
Profit		1,000

An obvious alternative here would be to say that the 100 units sold were the first 100 purchased and, as such, cost £1,000. This can easily be done for this short example, but would be less practical if there were many purchases and sales throughout the year. In this situation, it will be much more convenient to evaluate the few units that remain in inventory.

LIFO

The Last In First Out method assumes that the latest units bought (last in) are the first ones sold (first out).

NB: This does not mean to say that any inventory we have will be the earliest unit bought, rather that each sale will be made from the most recent purchases prior to that particular sale.

You could view LIFO as being like a bin where units when acquired are placed in the bin and units sold are taken out from the top. The level in the bin will go up and down; we may empty the bin completely at some point then refill it again, but each sale will be from the most recent purchase.

Using the LIFO method, we would match each sale against the most recent purchase that it could be from, and hence evaluate the 60 units of inventory as follows.

Buy No.	Sell No.	Balance No.	Unit Price £	Total £
100	(60)	40	10	400
50	(40)	10	12	120
10		10	14	140
		60		660

A report of profits under this basis of evaluating our inventory is

Income statement

	£	£
Revenue		2,000
Cost of sales		
Opening inventory	–	
Purchases (1,000 + 600 + 140)	1,740	
Less: Closing inventory	(660)	
		1,080
Profit		920

As already noted, this method is not considered appropriate in the UK.

Weighted average

Under the weighted average method of evaluating units of inventory, units are not distinguished. Rather

- An ongoing average is calculated after each new addition to our inventory.
- This average is the amount at which all units sold and units held are evaluated.

Under the weighted average method we would evaluate the 60 units of inventory as follows.

	Units No.	Unit Price £	Value £	Weighted Average £	Calculation of Average
Buy	100	10.00	1,000	10.00	£1,000 ÷ 100 units
Sell	(60)	10.00	(600)		
Bal.	40	10.00	400		
Buy	50	12.00	600		
Bal.	90		1,000	11.11	£1,000 ÷ 90 units
Sell	(40)	11.11	(444)		
Bal.	50	11.11	556		
Buy	10	14.00	140		
Bal.	60		696	11.60	£696 ÷ 60 units

The report of profits under this basis of evaluating our inventory is

Income statement

	£	£
Revenue		2,000
Cost of sales		
Opening inventory	–	
Purchases (1,000 + 600 + 140)	1,740	
Less: Closing inventory	(696)	
		1,044
Profit		936

Net realisable value

Net realisable value is estimated **sales proceeds, less all costs**

- That will be incurred to complete the product if it is still being built.
- To market and sell the product, and to distribute it to the ultimate customer.

Here, as in most situations, the NRV exceeds cost, since we are selling at a profit. However, a unit of inventory may suffer from a low NRV for the following reasons.

- It is obsolete/has suffered from physical deterioration.
- It is a loss leader, i.e. where a unit of inventory is being sold as a low price to encourage the sales of related higher priced products.
- An unforeseen fall in the selling price or an increase in the cost of the product, perhaps as a result of exchange rate fluctuations.
- A purchasing or production error, e.g. buying the wrong item, which proves unusable.

6.4 Receivables

In common with all other current assets, receivables should be valued at the **lower of cost and net realisable value** (see inventories above). In the context of receivables

- Cost is the amount that we have invoiced.
- NRV equals the amount that we anticipate we will receive net of all recovery costs.

As with inventory, this comparison must be done on a line-by-line (receivable-by-receivable) basis. The question that arises in a normal commercial environment is: why may what we receive be less than the amount invoiced? There are two possibilities.

- Our debtor has gone into liquidation and simply cannot pay.
- We have some dispute on the invoice, perhaps as a result of poor quality goods, and the invoice may not be paid.

Each of these is accounted for in a slightly different way.

6.4.1 Bad debts

Where a company has gone into liquidation and definitely will not pay, then there is no point whatsoever in keeping any record of amounts owed from them on the balance sheet. The amount should simply be extinguished and removed from the accounts, this bad debt is said to be written off. The effect on the accounting equation of writing off a bad debt is

- Receivables down (assets down).
- Profits down (liabilities down).

6.4.2 Doubtful debts

Where there is a dispute over an invoice, it would be **prudent** to anticipate that the disputed amount may not be recovered. However, we do not wish to write off the debt and forget the whole invoice outstanding completely, as we still do have some hopes of recovering the amount. We therefore reduce the value of the receivable down to the expected net realisable value by setting up a provision, in a similar way that setting up a depreciation provision reduces the cost of our non-current asset down to a net book value.

The impact on the accounting equation of making such a provision is

- Provision for doubtful debts up, hence receivables down (assets down).
- Bad debt expense up, hence profit down (liabilities down).

NB: The figure shown in the balance sheet will be net of this provision, the accounts will not show the total receivable less the provision as it does for non-current assets.

Example

A company has total receivables of £500,000, made up as follows.

Receivable	**Owed**
	£'000
A	30
B	70
Others	400
Total	500

Receivable A has gone into liquidation and we have been informed by the receivers that there is no chance of receiving any of the amount outstanding.

Receivable B is disputing one of the five invoices we have issued on the basis that the goods did not arrive. The value of the invoice in dispute is £15,000. None of the other invoices are in dispute, therefore, we will definitely receive the other £55,000 from this receivable, but what will happen to the £15,000 in dispute is currently uncertain.

In addition, our experience over the years has shown us that 2% of our invoices that we issue do not get paid due to the bankruptcy/insolvency of the customer. We cannot highlight which particular receivables will not pay up; it is just our practical experience that shows this. We therefore anticipate that 2% of the other receivables of £400,000 will not pay.

How would these receivables be valued on the balance sheet?

Solution

In relation to each of the receivables identified

- Write off £30,000 in relation to receivable A as a bad debt, reducing the listing of invoices outstanding down to £470,000 that we hope we can recover.
- Make provisions against the other receivables for what we may not recover, specifically
  - £15,000 specific provision against receivables B, i.e. a provision against a specific receivable.
  - £8,000 general provision against the other receivables (£400,000 × 2%), i.e. a provision against receivables in general.

Hence, we would evaluate the figure for the balance sheet as follows.

Receivables		**Owed**
	£'000	**£'000**
Receivables listing		
B		70
Others		400
		470
Provisions		
Specific	15	
General	8	
		(23)
		447

Again, it should be noted that all we will see in the accounts is the total figure of £447,000. This breakdown into individual receivables and the deduction of the provision are not separately disclosed.

6.5 Post-balance sheet events

Learning objective

27.2.13 **Explain** what is meant by a post-balance sheet event.

IAS 10 and FRS 21 cover post-balance sheet events. These are events which have occurred subsequent to the balance sheet date, but before the accounts are signed by the directors. These events are categorised as either adjusting or non-adjusting events. For adjusting events, the accounts are adjusted, whereas for non-adjusting events, the accounting standard only requires note disclosure.

An adjusting event is where additional information comes to light about a condition that existed at the balance sheet date. An example of an adjusting event would be the insolvency of a debtor.

Non-adjusting events relate to conditions that did not exist at balance sheet date. An example of a non-adjusting event would be a significant acquisition or disposal.

6.6 Accounting for financial instruments

earning objective

27.3.1 **Identify** the various classifications of financial instrument and outline the accounting treatment of each.

6.6.1 Introduction

There are two core Standards concerning financial instruments:

- IAS 32 Financial Instruments: Presentation – Implemented in the UK as FRS 25
- IFRS 9 Financial Instruments: Recognition and Measurement – Implemented in the UK as FRS 29

Between them these two standards prescribe how financial instruments should appear in the accounts so that the user may fully understand their potential future impact on business assets/liabilities, profits and cash flows.

The primary area that standard setters were originally looking to tackle was derivatives, though in dealing with this issue a far more broadly encompassing standard was developed. The original issue that was identified was that many derivatives, such as future or swaps, have no initial cost but may result in the business having a substantial exposure to some economic factor such as interest rates or exchange rates. Applying purely historical cost accounting would result in nothing appearing in the accounts since they have no initial cost, with the consequence that the user of the accounts may be unaware of the risks faced or the risks that have been hedged.

The standards that have been developed deal with financial instruments. A financial instrument is a contract that gives rise to a financial asset in one entity and a financial liability in another.

Financial assets

A **financial asset** is one of the following

- Cash
- The holding of an equity instrument issued by an entity
- A contractual right to
  - Receive cash or another financial asset from another entity
  - To exchange financial assets or financial liabilities with another entity on terms that may be favourable to that entity
- A contract that will or may be settled by the entities own equity and is a
  - Non-derivative instrument for which the entity is or may be obliged to receive its own equity
  - Derivative instrument that will or may result in the issue of an uncertain amount of new equity by the entity or the receipt of an uncertain amount of cash for an equity issue

Financial liability

A **financial liability** is a contractual obligation to

- Deliver cash or a financial asset to another entity
- To exchange financial assets or financial liabilities with another entity on terms that may be unfavourable to that entity

6.6.2 Liabilities and equity

Financial instruments must be classified according to their substance, not merely their legal form. In particular entities that issue financial instruments should classify them as either financial liabilities or equity. An equity instrument is one that includes no contractual obligation to deliver either cash or any other financial asset.

The critical feature of a financial liability is the contractual obligation to deliver cash or another financial asset. For example, many entities issue preference shares which must be redeemed by the issuer for a fixed amount at a fixed future date. In such instances the issuer has an obligation and the instrument should be classified as a financial liability.

The classification is made when it is first recognised and this classification will continue until the financial instrument is removed from the entity's balance sheet.

6.6.3 Disclosure requirements

IAS 32 (FRS 25) requires a company to describe financial risk management policy and hedging activities and should disclose separately for each hedge

- The nature of the risk being hedged
- A description of the hedge
- A description of the hedging instrument along with its balance sheet date fair value
- For cash flow hedges (eg forward foreign exchange contracts) details of the scales and timings of all cash flows involved

Furthermore, the standard requires any associated financial asset/liability to be reflected in the accounts at their **initial carrying value** from the date that the entity enters the arrangement. Any financial assets that have been recognised (put in the accounts) can only be derecognised (taken out of the accounts) if either

- The rights conferred by the financial asset has expired
- The financial asset has been transferred (sold) such that there can be no recourse to the entity

6.6.4 Disclosure of financial assets

Under IFRS 9 (FRS 29) a company must classify its financial assets under four categories.

A financial asset at fair value through the income statement

Financial assets fall into this category if they are either

- Assets designated as '**held for trading**'. This would be the case if the asset was acquired principally with the purpose of selling in the near term, or if the asset was a derivative.
- Assets designated as a financial asset under this category, ie where the entity want, the asset to be categorised in this way.

In this instance the initial carrying value is the purchase price **excluding** transaction costs (the fair value at acquisition) and the asset is restated each year to its fair value, with the profit or loss going through the income statement. There are two instances where this may arise.

Held-to-maturity investments

These are non-derivative financial assets with fixed or determinable payments and fixed maturity that an entity has the positive intent and ability to hold to maturity.

Loans and receivables

These are non-derivative financial assets with fixed or determinable payments that are not quoted in an active market.

Both **loans and receivables** and **held-to-maturity investments** are measured at amortised cost **including** transaction costs. This involves spreading the benefit through the income statement on a systematic and controlled basis. The security is not therefore revalued to its true market value at the end of the year. Instead its amortised value is shown, and the gain relating to the increase in value is recognised in the income statement.

Available-for-sale financial assets

This is a default category for any financial assets which are not covered by the above three categories.

Available for sale have an initial carrying value of the purchase price **including** transaction costs (in the same way as inventories) and the securities are revalued to their market value at the end of the year. Any changes in value do not go through the income statement, but instead are shown in the Statement of Changes in Equity (SOCIE) so impacting directly on reserves.

6.6.5 Disclosure of financial liabilities

After initial recognition, all financial liabilities should be measured at amortised cost, with the exception of financial liabilities at **fair value through the income statement** (including most derivatives).

6.6.6 Measurement of financial assets and liabilities

When a financial asset or liability is initially recognised it should be at fair value. Where the instrument is subsequently to be disclosed at fair value then transaction costs should not be included in this initial valuation. Where, however, the instrument is to be subsequently disclosed at amortised cost then transaction costs should be included in this initial valuation.

7 Income Statement

7.1 Introduction

The income statement provides a detailed analysis of how the company has generated its profit or loss for the accounting period. As already noted, it reconciles the change in the balance sheet retained earnings figure from one year to the next.

7.2 Format

The Companies Act describes the format of the income statement. As for the balance sheet, the notes normally refer to further detailed analysis, but here refer to additional explanations of the terminology.

All companies in the UK must comply with the requirements of FRS 3 when preparing their income statement. In broad terms, the key difference is that the income statement must give a breakdown on a line-by-line basis of income and expenses:

- Generated from continuing activities.
- Generated from activities acquired during the year.
- Generated from activities that have been disposed of during the year.

XYZ plc
Group Income statement for the Year Ended 31 December 2012

Items	Notes	2012 £'000	2011 £'000
Revenue	1	135,761	141,013
Cost of sales	2	(85,604)	(91,011)
Gross profit	3	50,157	50,002
Distribution costs	4	(22,961)	(21,636)
Administrative expenses	4	(19,620)	(16,752)
Other operating income		100	200
Trading/Operating profit	5	7,676	11,814
Income from fixed asset investments		100	100
Interest receivable and similar income		30	161
Interest payable and similar charges	6	(3,446)	(4,817)
Profit on ordinary activities before taxation		4,360	7,258
Tax on profit on ordinary activities	7	(1,104)	(2,000)
Profit on ordinary activities after taxation		**3,256**	**5,258**
Attributable to			
Equity holders at the parent		3,096	5,058
Minority interest		200	200
		3,256	**5,258**
Earnings per ordinary share		5.08p	9.06p

7.3 Terminology

Learning objectives

27.4.1 Identify and **explain** the classification of expenses based on nature or function.

27.4.2 Explain the principle of revenue recognition.

In accordance with the accruals or matching concept, income and expenses are recognised in the profit and loss account when earned, regardless of when paid. Any difference between the recognition of these items and the corresponding cash flow will be reflected in a balance sheet receivable or payable.

7.3.1 Revenue (Turnover)

The revenue or sales figure represents the total value of goods or services provided to customers during the accounting period whether they have been paid for or not, in accordance with the accruals concept.

Revenue is generally recognised at the point of sale, because at that point the following four criteria will generally have been met.

- The product or service has been provided to the buyer.
- The buyer has recognised his liability to pay for the goods or services provided.
- The buyer has indicated his willingness to hand over cash or other assets in settlement of his liability.
- The monetary value of the goods or services has been established.

7.3.2 Cost of sales

The cost of sales represents the total cost to the business of buying or making the actual items sold.

7.3.3 Gross profit

Learning objective

27.4.3 Identify the following different levels of profit and understand which classes of expenses are considered in arriving at each level: gross profit; trading (or operating) profit and net profit.

Gross profit is the difference between the value of the sales and the value of the cost of goods sold. One measure frequently used in determining the performance of the business is to consider its gross profit margin, which can be calculated as

Formula to learn

$$\text{Gross profit margin} = \frac{\text{Gross profit}}{\text{Turnover}} \times 100\%$$

Clearly, the higher the margin for a particular level of operations, the higher the profit. However, this does not mean that low margins result in low profits. A number of businesses generate very healthy profits through selling very large numbers of items (achieving correspondingly large turnover) at low margins.

7.3.4 Operating costs, exceptional and extraordinary items

Introduction

These costs include all other expenses incurred in generating the turnover for the period, by way of administrative involvement and delivery/distribution.

Direct and indirect costs

Though not evident in a set of accounts, operating costs may be categorised between

Direct costs – costs directly related to the manufacture of the product, i.e. the materials used, labour cost of manufacturing staff, factory running costs etc.

Indirect costs – other costs incurred by the business that are not directly attributable to manufacturing the product. Indirect costs may alternatively be referred to as overheads and include such items as office stationery, telephone costs, sales staff salaries etc.

Extraordinary and exceptional items

Where an expense is abnormally high, say repair costs due to damage arising from a natural disaster, this cost should be separately highlighted on the face of the income statement so that the reader of the accounts can fully appreciate the one-off nature of the cost. This is an example of an exceptional item under IAS 1. Historically, there was a category called extraordinary items but these but these are no longer recognised under any accounting rules.

7.3.5 Interest payable

In common with most other business expenses, any interest payable goes to reduce the company's profit before tax and hence, taxable profit by the gross amount payable. For example, if a company has in issue £100,000 of 10% loan stock, then the interest charge in its accounts each year will be £10,000.

7.3.6 Tax on profit on ordinary activities

UK companies pay corporation tax at the ruling rate on **all** their taxable profits. The element of the total tax charge shown here is the tax on the ordinary activities of the business, excluding any extraordinary items.

7.3.7 Minority interests

Learning objective

27.6.3 **Define** a minority interest and **explain** how it is represented in the financial statements.

Minority interests arise in a similar way as in the balance sheet. Where XYZ plc owns 80% of ABC Limited, it will include all ABC Limited's profit after tax in its own consolidated accounts on the basis that it controls all ABC Limited's operations. However, it does not own all of that profit, with 20% belonging to the minority interests. The 20% of ABC Limited's profit after tax that belongs to the minority interests is deducted from the profit after tax, leaving the amount of profit attributable to the shareholders in XYZ plc.

7.4 Statement of changes in equity

Learning objectives

27.4.4 **Explain** the objective of a statement of changes in equity.

27.4.5 **Identify** the information to be reported in a statement of changes in equity.

International accounting standards require a statement at changes in equity that reconciles the movement in shareholder's equity on the balance sheet from one year to the next as follows

XYZ plc **Statement of changes in equity**	**2012** **£'000**	**2011** **£'000**
Income for the period attributable to equity shareholders	3,056	5,058
Dividends on ordinary shares	(1,374)	(1,988)
New shares issued	73	96
Revaluation of property	881	85
	2,636	3,251
Shareholder's equity at the start of the period	15,792	12,541
Shareholder's equity at the end of the period	18,428	15,792

7.4.1 Dividends

These represent the cash dividends paid out, or proposed to be paid out, to shareholders net of lower rate income tax.

Typically, companies pay out dividends which are less than their profits after tax, i.e. the dividend is being paid from this year's profits and is said to be covered. It is **not essential for a dividend to be covered**, however. It may be financed from previously retained profits which, as we have seen, are accumulated in the balance sheet retained earnings.

In most cases, UK companies pay dividends in two stages.

- **Interim dividend paid** – this is paid out during the year, based on the half-year's performance.
- **Final dividend proposed** – this is paid to shareholders following the approval of the year-end accounts at the Annual General Meeting.

7.5 Capital and revenue expenditure

Learning objective

27.2.3 **Distinguish** between capital and revenue expenditure.

7.5.1 Capital expenditure

Capital expenditure is expenditure on acquiring or enhancing non-current assets or their operating capacity. As such, the benefits will be derived from this expenditure over the remaining life of the asset.

Hence, this expenditure is added to the value of non-current assets (is capitalised) on the balance sheet and will subsequently be **depreciated** through the income statement.

7.5.2 Revenue expenditure

Revenue expenditure is expenditure incurred in

- Acquiring assets to be sold for conversion into cash, e.g. inventories.
- Manufacturing, selling, distributing goods, e.g. wages.
- Day-to-day administrative expenses, e.g. electricity, telephone.
- Maintenance of non-current assets, e.g. repairs.

Revenue expenditure is charged directly against profits for the period to which it relates.

8 Cash Flow Statement

arning objectives	
	27.5.1 Explain the purpose of a cash flow statement.
	27.5.2 Identify the classification of cash flow activities.

8.1 Introduction

The Balance Sheet and Income Statement are prepared on an accruals basis. They give no indication of the effects of the operations of the business on its cash flows. It should always be noted that profits do not correspond exactly to cash. A company may be very profitable, but almost bankrupt (unable to pay its liabilities as they fall due).

Since cash is such an important figure in determining the continuing existence of a company, we need a statement showing how the company's financial resources have been acquired, and have been used, in order to highlight the liquidity position and trends of the company.

IAS 7, *Cash Flow Statements* lays down the rules to be followed in the preparation of such statements, defining

- **Cash**, i.e. what is and what is not cash.
- The **format** to be adopted in cash flow statements.

Note that only larger reporting entities are required to prepare a cash flow statement.

8.2 Cash and Cash Equivalents definitions

IAS 1 defines **cash** as **cash in hand plus deposits repayable on demand less overdrafts repayable on demand**. Deposits repayable on demand are those which can be withdrawn at any time without notice and without penalty, or where a maturity/period of notice of not more than 24 hours has been agreed.

Cash equivalents are **shot-term highly liquid investments** that are **readily convertible into a known amount of cash** and which are subject to a insignificant risk of charges in value.

8.3 Formats

XYZ plc Cash Flow Statement	2012 £'000	2011 £'000
Operating activities		
Cash generated by operations	19,541	10,211
Tax paid	(1,643)	(2,162)
Net cash from operating activities	17,898	8,049
Investing activities		
Purchase of property	(26)	(427)
Sale of property	1,037	261
Purchase of investment	(215)	(183)
Net cash from investing activities	796	(349)
Financing activities		
Issue of ordinary shares	73	42
Decrease in debt	(14,858)	(237)
Interest received	30	30
Interest paid	(3,446)	(4,836)
Equity dividend paid	(1,374)	(1,832)
Net cash from financing activities	(19,575)	(6,833)
Net decrease in cash and cash equivalents	(881)	867
Cash and cash equivalents at start of period	4,804	3,937
Cash and cash equivalents at end of period	3,923	4,804

The aim of IAS 7 is to provide information to the users of financial statements about an entity's ability to generate cash and cash equivalents. IAS 7 has three cash flow headings:

- **Operating activities** are the principal revenue producing activities of the enterprise and other activities which are not investing or financing activities
- **Investing activities** are the acquisition and disposal of non-current assets and other investments not included in cash equivalents.
- **Financing activities** are those that result in changes in the size and composition of the equity capital and borrowings of the entity.

8.3.1 Indirect method

Learning objective — **27.5.3 Calculate** net cash flow from operations given operating profit (or vice versa) and the relevant balance sheet movements.

The indirect method is an approach for identifying **cash flow from operations**. It involves working backwards from the trading profit figure in the profit and loss account to remove non-cash items.

For example:

Co A plc

Trading profit (from the income statement) £500,000

To obtain the cash flow from operations we must adjust this figure for non-cash items. This will include items such as depreciation, changes in inventory levels, changes in payables and changes in receivables.

We can determine whether each number is added or subtracted by considering whether it is good or bad for cash.

BPP LEARNING MEDIA

	£	Good/Bad for cash
Operating profit	500,000	
Depreciation	56,000	Good/Add
Increase in payables	12,000	Good/Add
Increase in receivables	(17,000)	Bad/Subtract
Decrease in inventories	3,000	Good/Add
	554,000	

Depreciation is always added back when undertaking the indirect method, since it represents a cost in the income statement but is not an actual cash movement.

An increase in payables will be good for the company's overall cash position because it indicates the company has been extended credit by its suppliers.

An increase in receivables is bad for cash because it means the company has itself extended more credit to its customers.

A decrease in inventories is good news for cash since stock has been sold resulting in an increase in cash.

8.3.2 Reconciliation to net debt

A reconciliation is required to link cash movements to changes in net debt (borrowings less cash and liquid resources) accompanied by a note analysing the components of the changes in net debt. Where the company has surplus cash rather than net debt, this will be referred to as net funds.

Reconciliation of Net Cash Flow to Movement in Net Debt	
Increase in cash in the period	**2,631**
Cash to repurchase debenture	149
Cash used to increase liquid resources	450
Change in net debt	**3,230**
Net debt at 1 January	**(2,903)**
Net funds at 31 December	**327**

9 Restricted Disclosure Requirements

Learning objective

27.1.3 **Define** 'small companies' for the purpose of financial statement preparation and **explain** the relevance of this definition.

The Companies Act defines two different sizes of company eligible to file abbreviated accounts, each of which have different reporting requirements.

- Small.
- Medium-sized.

9.1 Conditions

9.1.1 Size limits

In order to qualify as either small or medium-sized, a company must satisfy (not exceed) **two of the following three conditions**.

Conditions	Must Not Exceed	
	Small	Medium-Sized
Turnover	< £6,500,000	< £25,900,000
Non-current + Current assets	< £3,260,000	< £12,900,000
Average number of employees	< 50	< 250

9.1.2 Other conditions

In order to qualify as small or medium-sized in any accounting period other than its first, an entity must satisfy the criteria both in the current period and in the previous period. If the appropriate criteria have been satisfied in the preceding two years, there is a year of grace whereby the company is deemed to satisfy the criteria even if it, in fact, does not.

9.1.3 Audit requirements

Though the Companies Act requires all companies to appoint an auditor, there is an exemption available for companies that satisfy both the turnover and total assets criteria for smaller companies.

10 Investments and Group Accounts

10.1 Introduction

When a company buys shares in another company, it is making an investment, the basic accounting treatment for which is outlined diagrammatically below.

Investments

When we invest, the impact on the accounting equation is

- Cash down (assets down)
- Investment up (assets up)

The investment is an asset, but what type?

Current Asset

Definition

Not a non-current asset investment, i.e.

- Speculative.
- For the purpose of resale.

Accounting treatment

- Balance sheet at lower of cost and NRV.
- Income statement: dividends received = income.

Non-current Asset

Definition

- Long term.
- For continuing use, not intended for resale.

Accounting treatment

- Balance sheet at cost, less provision for any permanent diminution in value.
- Income statement: dividends received = income.

The above treatment of current asset investments is appropriate as the interest is very similar to that of holding a unit of inventory for resale. The question is: is this treatment of non-current asset investments appropriate for all the levels of investment? It certainly seems appropriate for very low levels of investment of, say, one or two per cent of share capital of the company in which the investment is held. However, is it appropriate for higher levels of investment? Will this treatment give a true and fair view of the performance of a company and its position at the year-end for significant levels of investment? We will answer this with an example.

Example

A company was formed ten years ago by the investment of £1,200 cash by the shareholders. Its balance sheet today is as follows.

Balance Sheet	**H plc** **£**
Investment in S plc	1,000
Other non-current assets	800
Current assets	800
	2,600
Share capital	1,200
Retained earnings	1,400
	2,600

The £1,000 investment on the balance sheet of H represents the cost of acquiring 100% of the shares in S, formed on the same day as H itself was set up. Neither H nor S have ever paid any dividends, hence, based on these accounts, the only return that the investors are aware of being generated from their initial £1,200 investment is the £1,400 profit in the books of H – not a very exciting return over ten years!

However, if we are now told that the balance sheet of S is as follows, we see a different picture of how well the original £1,200 investment has been utilised.

Balance Sheet	**S plc** **£**
Non-current assets	50,000
Current assets	100,000
	150,000
Share capital	1,000
Retained earnings	149,000
	150,000

As we can see, of the original £1,200 invested in H, £1,000 was immediately invested in S and that £1,000 has managed to generate £149,000 profit over the intervening years. The £1,400 profit we see in H's books is the profit that has been generated on the remaining £200 of the initial capital invested.

Since S has never paid any dividends to H (its shareholder), the shareholders of H have had no indication as to how their cash has been used. Since the directors of H control S through their 100% ownership of its shares and the shareholders of H have effectively financed S, does simply showing S being worth £1,000 in the books of H give a true and fair view of the state of affairs of H plc at that date?

The answer to this question is clearly no. The initial £1,200 invested has been converted into profits of £150,400, of which £1,400 is in H's books and £149,000 is in S's. To give a true and fair reflection to the shareholders of H as to how their cash has been used and what has been generated from it, we need to somehow combine these two businesses together to show the commercial totality of what has been produced; which could be achieved as follows.

Balance Sheet	H plc	S plc	Adjustment	Group
	£	£	£	£
Investment in S	1,000		(1,000)	
Other non-current assets	800	50,000		50,800
Current assets	800	100,000		100,800
	2,600	150,000	(1,000)	151,600
Share capital	1,200	1,000	(1,000)	1,200
Retained earnings	1,400	149,000		150,400
	2,600	150,000	(1,000)	151,600

The adjustments column cancels the cost of the investment in the shares in the books of H against the share capital purchased in S. These are two equal and opposite sides of the coin. What we then get is a combined or group balance sheet that shows that £1,200 has originally been invested by external shareholders, and that £1,200 has been used to generate £150,400 profit in total.

This is the idea behind group accounts. It is an application of the concept of commercial substance over legal form since, legally speaking, H and S are two separate entities. The group is not a legal entity in itself, but a commercial reality nevertheless.

What we actually need in this situation are two sets of accounts, specifically

- H's own individual accounts, which show the distributable profits of H, i.e. what could be paid by H to its shareholders as a dividend.
- Group accounts to reflect the assets and profits controlled by the holding company, reflecting the overall position as if the group were a single entity.

10.2 Conclusion

Learning objectives

27.6.1 Define and **distinguish** between corporate investments, associated companies and subsidiaries.
27.6.2 Explain the purpose of group accounts.

In order to give a true and fair view in the accounts, the treatment of non-current asset investments should depend on the level of influence or control that the investing company has over the company in which it holds its shares.

In basic terms, considering the level of voting influence, the accounting profession has determined three different possible levels.

10.2.1 Trade investment (0% – 20%)

Where our holding is so small as to confer no influence in the other company, then that investment should be treated as a trade investment.

Accounting treatment

The accounting treatment noted above would be suitable, i.e.

- Balance sheet at cost, less provision for any diminutions in value.
- Income statement should record dividends received as income.

10.2.2 Significant influence (21% – 50%)

If the level of voting influence fell in the above range, then the investing company would be deemed to have significant influence in the other company and hence, that other company would be treated as an **associated undertaking** of the investing company.

Accounting treatment

The accounting treatment for associated undertakings is to apply equity accounting, i.e.

- Record as an asset on the group balance sheet at the **group share of the net assets** of the associated undertaking.
- In the income statement record the **group share of the profits** of the associated undertaking.

Rather than bringing in cost in the balance sheet and dividends in the profit and loss account, we are bringing in the group share of assets and profits into those two statements. Hence, if we owned 40% of an associated undertaking, our share of their assets and profits would be calculated as their total assets or profits × 40%.

10.2.3 Control (51% – 100%)

Where one company controls another, that second company is a subsidiary undertaking of the first. This, in fact, is the position we used in our original example to illustrate the problem of accounting for all levels of non-current assets at cost on the balance sheet.

Accounting treatment

The accounting aim for dealing with subsidiaries is identical to that for dealing with associated undertakings. However, the mechanics involved and what will ultimately be seen on the balance sheet are very different. With regards to the accounting aim

- The balance sheet should record the group's share of the assets and liabilities of the subsidiary, though somewhat indirectly as we discuss below.
- The income statement should record the group share of the profit of the subsidiary (again somewhat indirectly).

As we can see, the aim for both equity accounting and consolidations is to show the position of the group as a single entity by including the group share of the assets and profits of the investment in the group balance sheet and income statement. The difference with consolidations is how the group share is calculated.

If we own 70% of another company then, by the method of consolidation, this would be recorded as

$$\text{Group share} = \text{Total} - \text{Other shareholders' share}$$

i.e.

$$100\% - 30\% = 70\%$$

What this means is that we record 100% of the subsidiary's assets on our balance sheet and profit in our profit and loss account, but then make a deduction at the end to reflect the fact that they are not all ours. The end result is that we have 70% of the assets and profits in the group assets and profits, though it has been calculated by an indirect route.

In accordance with accounting standards, all companies who have subsidiaries must produce consolidated accounts incorporating the results and assets of themselves and all their subsidiaries (with some minor exceptions).

10.2.4 Definition

A company S is a subsidiary of another company H, if H has the power to direct the financial and operating activities over the company, i.e. one of the following is true.

- H holds more than 50% of the votes in S as a shareholder.
- H can appoint or remove directors with more than 50% of the votes in directors' meetings.

- H is a member of S, i.e. a shareholder, and controls S through either
  - An agreement with the other members.
  - A provision in the Memorandum and Articles of Association of S.
  - S is a sub-subsidiary of H, i.e. S is a subsidiary of another company and that other company is a subsidiary of H.

Always remember that the aim of group accounts is to show the assets and profits of the group as if it were a single entity, i.e. an application of the concept of commercial substance over legal form.

Chapter Roundup

Financial statements

- A company is a separate legal entity, ie an individual in law.
- A company is owned by its shareholders or members but managed on a day to day basis by its directors
- In small companies the shareholders may be the directors, but in larger businesses the directors are appointed by the shareholders to manage the business on their behalf
- The core financial statements are the balance sheet, the Income statement and the cash flow statement.
- The fundamental accounting concepts underlying the accounts are
  - Going concern
  - Accruals/matching
  - Consistency
  - Prudence
  - Historical cost
  - Entity
- The International Accounting Standards Board sets international accounting standards. They work closely with the Accounting Standards Board in the UK, who set standards for firms following UK standards.
- The directors of UK companies are legally required to prepare accounts that give a true and fair view in accordance with the following rules.

Listed companies	Unlisted companies
■ Must apply IASs and IFRSs ■ These are prepared by the IASB	■ Must apply FRSs and SSAPs ■ These are prepared by the ASB

- UK and International terminology differ but the fundamental approach, and many of the standards followed, are consistent.
- An audit is an independent review of the accounts that confirms to the shareholders that the accounts prepared by the directors do give a true and fair view.
- If an auditor doesn't agree or is unsure whether the accounts give a true and fair view they must give a qualified audit report on one of the following bases:

	Limitation of Scope	Disagreement
Fundamental	**(Disclaimer of opinion)** Unable to express an opinion	**(Adverse opinion)** Do not give a true and fair view
Less significant	Generally give a true and fair view except for a few specific details	Generally give a true and fair view except for a few specific details

- Small and medium sized companies have some reporting exemptions. To be a small/medium sized company two of the following must be satisfied:

Conditions	Must Not Exceed	
	Small	Medium-Sized
Turnover	< £6,500,000	< £25,900,000
Non-current + Current assets	< £3,260,000	< £12,900,000
Average number of employees	< 50	< 250

Balance sheet

- The balance sheet is a statement of the financial position of the business at a specific point in time.
- It is a product of the accounting equation that may be stated as either:
  - Assets = Liabilities + shareholders' funds
  - Net assets (Assets – Liabilities) = shareholders' funds
- Assets are distilled into non-current (fixed) and current. Liabilities are also broken down into long term non-current (long-term) and current. The distinction is to aid the users of accounts and make the accounts useful.
- Any business expenditure will be either
  - Capital expenditure = buying assets
  - Revenue expenditure = paying business expenses

Non-current assets

- All non-current (fixed) assets with a finite useful life must be depreciated in order to match the cost of the asset to the benefit from its use.
- Depreciation may be either:
  - Straight line: $= \frac{\text{Cost} - \text{Residual value}}{\text{Expected useful life}}$
  - Reducing balance: $= 1 - \sqrt[n]{\frac{\text{Residual value}}{\text{Cost}}}$
- Balance sheet value = Net book value (NBV) = Cost – Accumulated depreciation
- If a non-current asset is sold at a price that differs from NBV a profit or loss arises

Current assets

- All current assets are valued at the lower of:
  - Cost = Historical purchase price
  - NRV = Anticipated sales price – selling costs
- Inventory cost allocation methods include:
  - FIFO
  - LIFO – (use not permitted in the UK)
  - Weighted average
  - Any other similar method

Liabilities

- Amounts payable by the company that are split on the balance sheet between:
  - payable within one year.
  - payable after more than one year.
- Provision = amount set aside to meet the probable future costs of a past event (usually a known but unquantified liability).
- Contingency = uncertain liability/possible obligation arising from past events.
- Any pension scheme net assets or liability appears on the balance sheet.

Other balance sheet items

- Post balance sheet event may be:
  - adjusting = new information about balance sheet date values.
  - non-adjusting = relating to conditions not existing at the balance sheet date.

Share capital

- Bonus/scrip issue and split = increase number of shares but do not raise finance, hence NAs and SFs values unaltered.
- Rights issue raises new finance, increasing NAs and SFs.
- Share repurchases consume finance, reducing NAs and SFs.

Reserves

- Retained earnings = accumulated retained profits since the business started.
- Share provision account = non-distributable reserve representing the excess received on issuing shares above their nominal value. May be used to:
  - issue fully paid bonus shares.
  - write off preliminary expenses.
  - write off expenses of issuing shares/debentures.
  - write off the premium on redemption or discount on issue of debentures.
- Revaluation reserve = non-distributable reserve reflecting any change in the value of non-current assets when they are revalued.

Income statement

- The income statement provides detail on revenue and expenses to show how the company has generated its profit or loss.
- Revenue should be recognised if:
  - product/service has been provided to the buyer.
  - the value of the goods/services has been established.
  - the buyer has recognised his liability to pay.
  - the buyer is willing to pay.

- Profit may be measured at a number of levels as follows:

Revenue	X
Cost of sales	(X)
Gross profit	X
Other trading/operating expenses	(X)
Operating profit	X
Non-trading expenses (eg interest)	(X)
PBT	X
Tax	(X)
PAT	X

- The statement of changes in equity shows how the equity shareholders' funds have changed from one year to the next due to:
  - Generation of profits.
  - Payment of dividends.
  - Issue/repurchase of shares.
  - Revaluation of property.

Cash flow statement

- The cash flow statement reconciles the movement in cash on the balance sheet. The statement breaks down into three headings.
  - Operating activities.
  - Investing activities.
  - Financing activities.
- Cash flow from operations may be calculated using either the direct or indirect method.

Indirect method

Operating profit	X
Add: Depreciation	X
Working capital adjustments	
– (Increase)/Decrease in inventory	X
– (Increase)/Decrease in receivables	X
– Increase/(Decrease) in payables	X
Increase in cash from operations	X

Groups

- Investment levels in other companies determine their status:
  - 0%-20% = Trade investment
  - 21%-50% = Associate
  - > 50% = Control, ie subsidiary
- Group accounts = Accounts of holding company + All subsidiaries as if they were a single entity.

TEST YOUR KNOWLEDGE

Check your knowledge of the chapter here, without referring back to the text.

1. What rules may regulate UK company accounts?

2. When does a UK company need to apply international accounting standards?

3. What is the role of the auditor?

4. What are the fundamental accounting concepts?

5. What is the UK accounting terminology for the terms
   - Receivables
   - Inventory
   - Non-current liabilities

6. The balance sheet shows the company's position at a specific point in time. *True/False*?

7. What is the accounting equation?

8. Name three types of non-current asset.

9. Name three types of current asset.

10. What impact will a bonus issue have on the share premium and share capital account?

11. An asset cost £10,000, has a life of five years and a residual value of £2,000. What is the depreciation rate on a
    - straight line basis
    - reducing balance basis

12. You are provided the following information regarding inventories.

Item	*Cost*	*Selling price*	*Selling cost*
A	12	15	2
B	21	24	4
C	18	17	3

Determine the balance sheet value for inventories.

13. The following inventory transactions have occurred.

1 Jan	Buy 100 items at £20 each
3 Jan	Sell 60 items
8 Jan	Buy 40 items at £22 each
10 Jan	Sell 50 items
15 Jan	Buy 40 items at £24 each

Calculate the cost of the closing inventory on
- FIFO basis
- LIFO basis

14. Receivables are shown on the balance sheet net of bad and doubtful debts. *True/False*?

15. Which international accounting standards deal with Financial Instruments?

16. The indirect method of calculating cash flow from operations requires depreciation to be deducted from operating profit. *True/False*?

17. Calculate the cash from operating activities for this year from the following information.

	Last year	*This year*
Operating profit	100,000	120,000
Depreciation	15,000	16,000
Inventories	25,000	28,000
Receivables	39,000	37,000
Payables	31,000	36,000

Test Your Knowledge: Answers

1. Legal rules – the Companies Act

   UKLA rules

   Professional accounting rules

   – IASs for listed companies
   – FRSs for unlisted companies.

   (See Section 2)

2. Since 2005, all UK listed companies have been required to apply international standards to their group accounts. All non -listed companies may apply either IFRSs or UK FRSs.

   (See Sections 2.3)

3. To give an independent opinion as to whether the accounts prepared by the directors give a true and fair view.

   (See Section 3.2)

4. Going concern
   Accruals or matching
   Consistency
   Prudence
   Historical costs
   Entity

   (See Section 4.1)

5. Debtor = Receivable
   Stock = Inventory
   Long term liabilities = Non-current liabilities

   (See Section 4.1.8)

6. True

   (See Section 5.1)

7. Assets = Liabilities + Shareholders' funds
   Net assets = Shareholders' funds

   (See Section 5.2)

8. Property, plant and equipment
   Intangibles
   Investments

   (See Section 5.4)

9. Inventory, receivables and cash

   (See Section 5.4.5)

10. Reduce share premium and increase share capital

    (See Section 5.4.11)

11. **Straight line**

$$\text{Depreciation} = \frac{\text{Cost} - \text{Residual value}}{\text{Expected useful life}} = \frac{10{,}000 - 2{,}000}{5} = \text{£1,600 pa or 16\% on cost}$$

Reducing balance

$$\text{Depreciation rate} = 1 - \sqrt[n]{\frac{\text{Residual value}}{\text{Cost}}} = 1 - \sqrt[5]{\frac{2{,}000}{10{,}000}} = \text{0.2752 or 27.56\% on NBV}$$

(See Section 6.2)

12.

Item	*Cost*	*NRV*	*BS value*
A	12	13 (15 – 2)	12
B	21	20 (24 – 4)	20
C	18	14 (17 – 3)	14
			46

(See Section 6.3)

13.

Total purchases	180 units
Total sales	110 units
Inventory	70 units

FIFO

Cost = Cost of most recently purchased items, ie

40 @ 24 =	960
30 @ 22 =	660
	1,620

LIFO

At each sale, units sold = most recently purchased

	Purchase	*5 Jan sale*	*10 Jan sale*	*Inventory*	*Price*	*Cost*
1 Jan purchase	100	(60)	(10)	30	20	600
8 Jan purchase	40		(40)	0	22	0
15 Jan purchase	40			40	24	960
						1,560

(See Section 6.3)

14. True

(See Section 6.4)

15. IAS 32 Presentation and IFRS 9 Recognition and Measurement

(See Section 6.6)

16. False

(See Section 8.3.1)

17.

Operating profit	120,000
Add: Depreciation	16,000
Increase in inventories	(3,000)
Decrease in receivables	2,000
Increase in payables	5,000
Cash from operating activities	140,000

(See Section 8.3)

16 Analysis of Financial Statements

INTRODUCTION

Ratios may be used by analysts when looking to compare a company's performance against its past period performance, and when comparing a company against similar companies within the same industry. Ratios help condense down information into an easily understandable figure.

Ratios may be broadly defined under profitability, liquidity, financial gearing and investor ratios. Information may be obtained from the balance sheet, the profit and loss account, or the cash flow statement.

CHAPTER CONTENTS

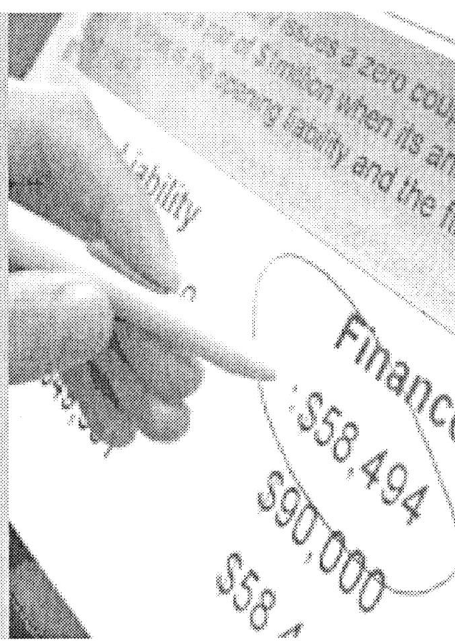

Chapter Learning Objectives

18 Asset classes

Demonstrate an ability to evaluate the characteristics, inherent risks, behaviour and correlation of asset classes

18.3 Equity valuation

18.3.9 **Distinguish** between and evaluate the merits of relative valuation models and absolute valuation models and between historic and prospective measures of value.

18.3.10 **Calculate** a basic earnings per share.

18.3.11 **Explain** what is meant by diluted earnings per share.

18.3.12 **Explain** the rationale for the use of the following ratios in equity valuation.

- Price-earnings.
- Price to book.
- Price to sales.
- Price to cash flow.
- Enterprise value (EV) to earnings before interest tax, depreciation and amortisation (EBITDA).

18.3.13 **Calculate** price-earnings (both historic and prospective), price to book, price to sales, price to cash flow ratios for a company.

18.3.14 **Apply** the company ratios above to the valuation of another given company.

18.3.15 **Explain** the possible shortfalls of using each of these price multiples in corporate valuation.

18.3.16 **Explain** the basics of free cash-flow based valuation methods (FCFF, FCFE) and Residual Income Valuation methods.

18.3.17 **Define** (financial) gearing and understand the effect on required equity returns and thus dividend valuations.

18.3.18 **Explain** the measures of economic value added (EVA) and market value added (MVA).

27 Accounting

Demonstrate an understanding of accounting principles

27.7 Major accounting ratios

27.7.1 **Distinguish** between profitability, liquidity, and gearing ratios.

27.7.2 **Define** and calculate return on capital employed.

27.7.3 **Define** and calculate return on equity.

27.7.4 **Explain** how return on capital employed can be broken down into profit margin and asset turnover.

27.7.5 **Define**, calculate and interpret.

- Operational gearing.
- Financial gearing.
- The current ratio.
- The quick ratio (acid test).

1 INTRODUCTION

Learning objective | 27.7.1 **Distinguish** between profitability, liquidity, and gearing ratios.

The financial statements, the income statement, the balance sheet, the cash flow and all the associated notes contain a vast amount of information. The role of ratios is to distil this information down into a more usable form.

The financial statements are primarily prepared for the shareholders, however, they may have several other users such as lenders, creditors, the government, tax authorities, etc. Each of these will be looking to use the accounts to get some indication of the

- Returns they are receiving.
- Risks they are facing.

A number of fairly standard ratios have been developed to assist with this process.

These ratios can be grouped under four headings.

1.1 Profitability

Ratios which assess the **trading or operating performance** of the company, i.e. levels of trading profits generated and the effectiveness of the use of trading assets.

1.2 Liquidity

Ratios which assess the **trading risk of the company**. In particular, the risk that, as a result of trading activities, the company may be unable to pay its liabilities as they fall due.

1.3 Investors' ratios

Ratios which assess the **returns to the providers of finance**, who may be either shareholders or lenders.

1.4 Gearing

Ratios which assess the **risks to the providers of finance**, by analysing the company's exposure to debt.

Throughout this review of ratios, we will draw our examples from the balance sheet and income statement for Illustration plc at the back of this chapter.

2 PROFITABILITY RATIOS

2.1 Return on capital employed

Learning objectives

27.7.2 **Define** and **calculate** return on capital employed.

27.7.4 **Explain** how return on capital employed can be broken down into profit margin and asset turnover.

This is a measure of the level of profitability generated by the management of a company.

2.1.1 Basic calculation

The return on capital employed is calculated as

Formula to learn

$$\text{ROCE} = \frac{\text{Profit before interest payable and tax}}{\text{Capital employed}} \times 100\%$$

2.1.2 Profit

This profit figure can be viewed as operating profit plus interest receivable and income from other investments, i.e. the profits that management have generated from the resources they have available. It is specifically **before** interest payable, since this will clearly be dependent on the financing of the business – the larger the loans, the larger the interest payable.

	£'000
Profit before tax	3,673
Add back interest payable	3,176
Profit before interest payable and tax	6,849

2.1.3 Capital employed

Ideally, considering capital employed, we would like to consider the average capital employed throughout the year. Our aim is to match the profits generated throughout the year to the capital or assets that have been used to generate them, or the total financing of the business. It is unlikely, however, that this information will be available, and normally the calculation would be based on year-end figures.

Since we are measuring profit as profit before all interest payable, we should consider everything upon which interest is payable as part of the financing in order to be consistent in this ratio, i.e. in this case, we would treat bank overdrafts as part of the financing of the business.

Capital employed could be viewed from either the financing side as

Capital employed = Share capital and reserves + Loans + Bank overdrafts

£54,565,000 = £33,041,000 + £4,445,000 + £17,079,000

or from the trading side as

Capital employed = Total assets – Current liabilities (excluding overdrafts)

£54,565,000 = (£23,499,000 + £57,653,000) – £26,587,000

This is the most consistent treatment of overdrafts for this ratio.

Example

$$ROCE = \frac{£6,849,000}{£54,565,000} \times 100\%$$

ROCE = 12.6%

2.1.4 Potential problems

Ideally, it would be best to use the average capital employed as our aim is to match the profits generated throughout the year to the capital or assets that have been used to generate them, or the total financing of the business.

It is unlikely that this information will be available, and normally the calculation would be based on year-end figures. This can lead to some **major distortions in our ratios**, especially if there have been large changes in capital employed during the year, i.e. from the acquisition of a subsidiary or the raising of funds near the year end.

2.1.5 Analysis points

Having established our return on capital employed, we now need to consider what may have caused any change from one year to the next. This is caused by one of two factors.

- Changes in profit margin.
- Changes in revenue volumes.

We define each of these more fully below, but in outline

$$\text{Profit margin} = \frac{\text{Profit}}{\text{Turnover}}$$

$$\text{Asset turnover} = \frac{\text{Turnover}}{\text{Capital employed}}$$

Hence

$$\text{Profit margin} \times \text{Asset turnover} = \frac{\text{Profit}}{\text{Turnover}} \times \frac{\text{Turnover}}{\text{Capital employed}} = \frac{\text{Profit}}{\text{Capital employed}} = \text{ROCE}$$

2.2 Profit margins

A profit margin is a measure of the profit achieved per £1 of sales generated.

Formula to learn

$$\text{Profit margin} = \frac{\text{Profits}}{\text{Revenue}} \times 100\%$$

Considerations

We may be tempted to use the profit figure from our earlier ROCE calculation, however, this may bring with it the problem that not all elements of this profit have any relationship to the levels of revenue. For example, this profit is stated after

- Interest receivable.
- Income from non-current asset investments.
- Share of profits of associated undertakings.

None of the above three are related to revenue. In practice it might be better, therefore, to use the trading profit figure only particularly if examining the profit margin in isolation. However, we will continue using our 'full' PBIT figure for now.

Example

Again, using information contained in our illustration financial statements at the end of this chapter.

$$\text{Profit margin} = \frac{\text{£6,849 (see ROCE above)}}{\text{£135,761}} \times 100\%$$

Profit margin = 5.0%

2.2.1 Analysis points

Once we have calculated this ratio, we need to make something meaningful out of it. When doing this, it is important to consider the causes and possible consequences, not just the numbers.

If profit margins are up it may appear to be good news – higher levels of profits. However, these higher profits may mean that the company loses customer loyalty if they perceive that they are being exploited. Alternatively, high prices may attract competitors into the field, in which case the company may lose a substantial amount of market share.

Conversely, margins going down may normally be perceived as bad news. However, it may be as a consequence of a policy of penetration pricing; or it may be that the company is incurring high development costs and future years' profitability will be that much higher as a result.

2.3 Asset turnover

The asset turnover ratio assesses the effectiveness of the use of the trading assets available.

Formula to learn

$$\text{Asset turnover} = \frac{\text{Revenue}}{\text{Assets (capital) employed}}$$

2.3.1 Considerations

Once again, we could take all the capital employed used in our ROCE calculation as the denominator in this calculation. However, again, it may be that some assets bear no relationship to revenue whatsoever, e.g.

- Investment in associated undertakings.
- Short-term investments.

In practice, it may therefore be more appropriate to take just those trading assets that have contributed to revenue.

Example

Using information from our illustration financial statements (Section 10.9).

$$\text{Asset turnover} = \frac{\text{£135,761}}{\text{£54,565 (see ROCE above)}}$$

Asset turnover = 2.49×

2.3.2 Potential problems

Again a problem with this ratio, in common with the problem of return on capital employed, is that we are comparing a full year's transactions (revenue) to a year-end balance sheet figure (assets employed). Unless this year-end figure is representative of the assets employed throughout the year, we will not exactly be comparing like with like and there may be some distortions.

For example, if the company buys a subsidiary or raises new finance close to the year end, then the year-end assets employed would be substantially higher than the general level throughout the year.

Another problem is the impact of accounting policies. If, for example, non-current assets are revalued this year then this will have two effects.

- Profits will be down due to increased depreciation charges.
- Capital assets employed will be up due to the increase in non-current asset NBVs.

The result will be that our return on capital employed and asset turnover figures will be reduced, although the effectiveness of our trade, in truth, may be unaltered. It is very difficult to remove these distorting effects. It is probably more convenient to calculate the ratios but to note any distortions.

2.3.3 Analysis points

Again, when considering this ratio, it may be tempting just to state the obvious – but take care. We should **consider the causes**, not just the numbers.

Considering just the numbers, it would be tempting to believe that increased asset turnover is a positive thing. However, it may arise from

- Overtrading, which would result in liquidity problems.
- A deterioration of the capital base, i.e. sales are not rising, rather the asset base is falling.

As the diagram above illustrates, this ratio may be further sub-analysed into, for example, working capital turnover and non-current asset turnover; each of which may be an appropriate ratio for a particular sort of industry. Non-current asset turnover may be an appropriate ratio in a capital-intensive industry where a large amount of the capital of the business is tied up in non-current assets. The analyst needs to decide which ratios to use and how to use them.

2.4 Return on equity (ROE)

Learning objective	27.7.3 **Define** and **calculate** return on equity.

Basic calculation

This looks at the rate of return generated for equity investors, being the ordinary shareholders.

$$\text{Return on equity} = \frac{\text{Profit after tax} - \text{Preference dividends}}{\text{Ordinary shareholder's funds}}$$

Considerations

This ratio looks at the **overall impact of the management's decisions on returns to shareholders**. It reflects the ability of the company to generate returns on its asset base but then reflects how this has been translated into returns to equity by stripping out the debt elements.

Example

$$\text{Return on equity} = \frac{£2,301,000 - £84,000}{£33,041,000 - £837,000} = 6.9\%$$

Analysis points

Shareholders are looking for a rising trend of returns on equity in order to provide them with increasing levels of dividend income and/or growth in the share price.

Returns across different companies in the same sector can be compared but it should be noted that this ratio does **not** produce a yield or return on investment measure. To obtain such a number it would be necessary to use the market value of equity as opposed to the book value (as used to calculate earnings yield).

2.5 Operational gearing

Learning objective

27.7.5 Define, calculate and **interpret**: operational gearing; financial gearing; the current ratio and the quick ratio (acid test).

2.5.1 Purpose and meaning

Operational gearing is a measure of a company's fixed costs compared to its trading profit. Fixed costs are those which relate to a period rather than to revenue or output and as such, they will be incurred by the business regardless of the scale of operations and thus revenue. Other costs are known as variable cost and vary directly in proportion to output and revenue.

Thus, operational gearing is an indicator of the **sensitivity of profits** to changes in sales revenue. For investors, a highly operationally geared company represents a higher risk investment. Companies which would generally exhibit a high degree of operational gearing would be those such as hotel chains or airlines, which both have a large proportion of costs which will be incurred as long as the business is in operation, regardless of the scale of operations.

2.5.2 The ratio

Formula to learn

$$\text{Operational gearing} = \frac{\text{Trading profit} + \text{Fixed costs}}{\text{Trading profit}}$$

NB: Trading profit + Fixed costs = Sales revenue – Variable costs

It should also be noted that operational gearing cannot be calculated directly from the financial statements, as there is no split of costs between those which are fixed or variable. In financial statements, costs are classified according to function rather than nature.

2.5.3 Considerations

This ratio is a measure of operational risk, i.e. risk to the operating profit figure, and is assessing the levels of variable and fixed operating costs in the business. Variable costs are costs whose level varies directly with the level of output, hence if sales increase/(decrease) then variable costs increase/(decrease), e.g.

raw material costs. Fixed costs are costs whose level remains constant regardless of output levels, e.g. rent, rates, depreciation.

3 Liquidity Ratios

These ratios attempt to review the ability of a company to repay its debts through a consideration of its **working capital**. The working capital of a business is the net of its current assets and current liabilities (also sometimes referred to as **net current assets**), i.e.

Working capital = Current assets – Current liabilities

A positive working capital figure indicates that if all of the current assets are realised they will be sufficient to cover the current liabilities and the following ratios examine that comparison in more detail.

3.1 Current ratio

Learning objective

27.7.5 Define, calculate and **interpret**: operational gearing; financial gearing; the current ratio and the quick ratio (acid test).

3.1.1 Basic calculation

The purpose of this ratio is to see whether the assets existing at the year-end, which are recoverable within one year, are sufficient to cover the liabilities at that date which fall due within that year.

Formula to learn

$$\text{Current ratio} = \frac{\text{Current assets due within one year}}{\text{Current liabilities falling due within one year}}$$

3.1.2 Considerations

The term current assets normally refers to assets that are recoverable within one year, hence this would normally be a match. However, care should be taken. It may well be the case, for example, that some receivables are recoverable after more than one year. This particular fact will be noted in the accounts if this is the case.

Example

$$\text{Current ratio} = \frac{£57{,}653{,}000}{£43{,}666{,}000}$$

Current ratio = 1.32×

Analysis points

Analysis points when calculating or using this ratio are as follows.

- **Overdrafts** will be included within creditors falling due within one year but are frequently payable after more than one year in practice. Banks frequently allow companies to continue with overdrafts for several years.
- **Realisation of inventory** – inventory is contained within current assets and therefore is almost automatically assumed to be realisable within one year, but this may not necessarily be the case.

Unlike receivables there will be no note anywhere indicating the recoverability or likely timescale for the realisation of inventory.

- This ratio completely ignores the **timing of cash flows** within the period. In theory it could be possible that all the liabilities are payable now and all the assets are recoverable in 12 months' time. Although in total terms they match, in actual cash flow terms they do not.

3.2 Quick (acid test) ratio

Learning objective — **27.7.5 Define, calculate** and **interpret**: operational gearing; financial gearing; the current ratio and the quick ratio (acid test).

3.2.1 Basic calculation

The quick ratio is an adaptation of the current ratio to remove the problem of inventory. Inventory is a problem, in that it is not easily convertible into cash and therefore may distort the ratio.

Formula to learn

$$\text{Quick ratio} = \frac{\text{Current assets excluding inventory}}{\text{Current liabilities falling due within one year}}$$

3.2.2 Considerations

The quick ratio considers just the readily realisable assets (cash, investments and receivables) and whether they are sufficient to cover the short-term liabilities of the business. Being a modification of the current ratio, it suffers from the same problems, excluding realisability of inventory, of course.

Example

$$\text{Quick ratio} = \frac{£57,653,000 - £19,420,000}{£43,666,000}$$

$$\text{Quick ratio} = \frac{£38,233,000}{£43,666,000}$$

$$\text{Quick ratio} = 0.875\times$$

Our company has a quick ratio of less than one. This does not mean that it is insolvent and unable to pay off its liabilities. However, depending on the type of business, it may be a sign of liquidity problems.

4 Financial Gearing

Learning objectives

18.3.17 Define (financial) gearing and understand the effect on required equity returns and thus dividend valuations.

27.7.5 Define, calculate and **interpret**: operational gearing; financial gearing; the current ratio and the quick ratio (acid test).

These ratios consider the financing side of the balance sheet and consider the relationships between

- Interest-bearing borrowed capital on which the return must be paid.
- Shareholders' capital on which the return is optional.

It is generally accepted that **high levels of gearing** imply **high financial risks** for the company.

4.1 Debt-to-equity ratio

4.1.1 Basic calculation

This is a relationship that our shareholders would consider as a measure of the risk to their dividends.

Formula to learn

$$\text{Debt to equity} = \frac{\text{Interest-bearing loans}}{\text{Equity shareholders' funds}} \times 100\%$$

4.1.2 Considerations

We consider only interest-bearing debt, since this is what is causing the risk to profit before tax hence, ultimately, the profits after tax and amounts available for payment as dividends to our shareholders.

Example

$$\text{Debt to equity} = \frac{£2,372,000 + £17,079,000 + £2,073,000}{£32,204,000}$$

$$\text{Debt to equity} = \frac{£21,524,000}{£32,204,000} \times 100\%$$

Debt to equity = 66.8%

The equity shareholders' funds is given by the equity share capital and all the reserves.

4.2 Net debt-to-equity ratio

4.2.1 Basic calculation

This is an alternative to the above and takes account of the cash that a business may also hold that could be used to repay debt, i.e. the interest-bearing loans.

Formula to learn

$$\text{Net debt to equity} = \frac{\text{Debt (as above)} - \text{Cash and current asset investments}}{\text{Equity shareholders' funds}} \times 100\%$$

4.2.2 Considerations

We should consider the ability of the company to use the cash it has available to repay debt.

Example

$$\text{Net debt to equity} = \frac{£21,524,000 \text{ (as above)} - £6,425,000 - £3,926,000}{£32,204,000} \times 100\%$$

$$\text{Net debt to equity} = \frac{£11,173,000}{£32,204,000} \times 100\%$$

Net debt to equity = 34.7%

4.3 Interest cover

4.3.1 Basic calculation

This ratio considers gearing from the viewpoint of the profit and loss account. It measures the capacity of the firm to meet its interest obligations.

Formula to learn

$$\text{Interest cover} = \frac{\text{Profit before interest payable and tax}}{\text{Interest payable}}$$

4.3.2 Considerations

The interest cover gives a measure of the **ability of the company to pay the fixed interest** on borrowings out of its profits for the year. Clearly, the higher the level of interest cover, the less risk there is to either shareholders or lenders. However, again, there is no optimal level.

Example

$$\text{Interest cover} = \frac{\text{£6,849,000 (see ROCE above)}}{\text{£3,176,000}}$$

Interest cover = 2.16×

4.4 Asset cover (or capital cover)

4.4.1 Basic calculation

In the same way that lenders are concerned about the interest cover, they may also be concerned about the safety of the loan itself, as demonstrated by the assets available to repay it. The asset cover is calculated as

Formula to learn

$$\text{Asset cover} = \frac{\text{Total assets} - \text{Current liabilities}}{\text{Loan payable}}$$

4.4.2 Considerations

If there are a number of loans with different priorities of repayment in a winding up, the asset cover is calculated for each of them in priority order on a cumulative basis.

Example

In order of priority, our debt can be analysed as

Debt	Value £'000	Cumulative £'000
Secured loans	2,073	2,073
Unsecured loans	2,372	4,445
Preference shares	837	5,282

Total assets less current liabilities is £37,486,000.

Hence, asset covers are as follows.

Secured loans	= £37,486,000 ÷ £2,073,000 = 18.1×
Secured and unsecured loans	= £37,486,000 ÷ £4,445,000 = 8.4×
Total debt (including preference shares)	= £37,486,000 ÷ £5,282,000 = 7.1×

5 Investors' Ratios

5.1 Earnings per share

Learning objective

18.3.10 Calculate a basic earnings per share.

5.1.1 Basic calculation

Earnings per share (EPS) is the one ratio for which there are some rules regarding the calculation. These are laid out in the accounting standards, which basically defines the EPS as

Formula to learn

$$\text{EPS} = \frac{\text{Earnings attributable to ordinary shareholders}}{\text{Number of ordinary shares}}$$

5.1.2 Considerations

Earnings is defined as consolidated profit **after**

- Interest
- Tax
- Minority interest
- Preference dividends

Earnings therefore represent the profit available to pay out to the ordinary shareholders.

Example

$$\text{EPS} = \frac{£2{,}301{,}000 - £84{,}000}{17{,}925{,}000 \text{ shares}}$$

$$\text{EPS} = \frac{£2{,}217{,}000}{17{,}925{,}000 \text{ shares}}$$

EPS = 12.37p

The net basic EPS must always be disclosed in a listed company's accounts.

5.1.3 Analysis points

We have already noted that current earnings are calculated as profits after interest, tax and preference dividends. However, it is also worth noting that earnings can also be calculated as retained earnings plus ordinary dividends.

While current earnings of different companies can be compared relative to each other, the EPS for one company should not be compared relative to another, as this is affected not only by actual earnings but also by the number of shares in issuance. Therefore, the EPS is not a good measure for comparing two companies against each other.

5.2 Fully diluted earnings per share

Learning objective

18.3.11 Explain what is meant by diluted earnings per share.

5.2.1 Introduction

The purpose of the fully diluted earnings per share figure is to warn shareholders of **potential future changes in the earnings per share figure** as a result of potential shares that already exist. There are three possible factors that could cause a fully diluted earnings per share to arise.

- Convertible loan stock or preference shares in issue.
- Options in issue.
- Shares in issue not ranking for a dividend this year.

Each of these circumstances may potentially result in more shares being issued and ranking for a dividend in future years, hence leading to a dilution of the current earnings per share.

5.3 Price/earnings ratio (P/E)

Learning objectives

18.3.9 Distinguish between and evaluate the merits of relative valuation models and absolute valuation models and between historic and prospective measures of value.

18.3.13 Calculate price-earnings (both historic and prospective), price to book, price to sales, price to cash flow ratios for a company.

5.3.1 Basic calculation

The Price/Earnings ratio is calculated as follows.

Formula to learn

$$\text{Price/Earnings} = \frac{\text{Current market price per share}}{\text{Earnings per share}}$$

5.3.2 Considerations

The P/E ratio expresses the number of years' earnings represented by the current market price. This represents future earnings growth or, at least, the growth potential of the company anticipated by the market.

Example

If we take our current share price as £2.20 and our EPS figure as 12.37p, then the P/E ratio is

$$\text{Price/Earnings} = \frac{220\text{p}}{12.37\text{p}}$$

Price/Earnings = 17.78

5.3.3 Analysis points

The significance of this relative P/E ratio can only be judged in relation to the ratios of other companies in the same type of business. If the median P/E ratio for an industry sector was 8, then a ratio of 12 for a particular company would suggest that the shares of that company were in great demand, possibly because a rapid growth of earnings was expected, or the company is overvalued, hence the share price is high. A **low ratio**, say 4 for example, would indicate a company not greatly favoured by investors, probably because it has **poor growth prospects**.

5.3.4 Prospective and historic P/E ratios: two approaches

There are two basic approaches for calculating a P/E ratio. A historic (or current) P/E ratio is the most straightforward and simply uses the most recently available EPS from the accounts. Alternatively, we could calculate a prospective P/E ratio. This divides the current share price by a forecasted EPS. This will of course require a forecast being made of expected future earnings.

If next year's profits are on course to be significantly higher than this year's, the prospective P/E ratio will be lower than the current P/E ratio. For companies and sectors in take-off or rapid growth industries this often turns out to be the case. The abnormally high current P/E ratio simply reflects future profit levels – they have already been written into the share price.

The P/E ratio is an example of a relative valuation model in that it is used for comparing companies against one another, and so assessing whether the price is over- or undervalued. This differs from absolute valuation models which look to compute a fundamental valuation by estimating future earnings and computing a present value (using DCF).

5.4 Earnings yield

5.4.1 Basic calculation

The earnings yield expresses the most recent earnings per share as a percentage of the current market price as follows.

Formula to learn

$$\text{Earnings yield} = \frac{\text{Earnings per share}}{\text{Current market price per share}} \times 100\%$$

Example

$$\text{Earnings yield} = \frac{12.37\text{p}}{220\text{p}} \times 100\%$$

Earnings yield = 5.62%

5.4.2 Analysis points

The earnings yield is almost the inverse of the P/E ratio, hence similar comments apply. If the median earnings yield for an industry sector was 10%, then a yield of only 6% for a particular company would suggest that the shares of that company were in great demand, possibly because a rapid growth of earnings was expected.

A higher yield, say 18% for example, would indicate a company not greatly favoured by investors, probably because it has poor growth prospects.

In practice, the earnings yield is used less frequently than the P/E ratio.

5.5 Dividend yield

5.5.1 Basic calculation

The dividend yield of an ordinary share is calculated as follows.

Formula to learn

$$\text{Dividend yield} = \frac{\text{Dividend per share}}{\text{Current market price per share}} \times 100\%$$

Example

$$\text{Dividend yield} = \frac{6.25\text{p}}{220\text{p}} \times 100\%$$

$$\text{Dividend yield} = 2.84\%$$

5.5.2 Analysis points

A high dividend yield implies that the company is paying reasonable levels of income, but is not particularly highly regarded for its growth prospects and vice versa. If the figures show a high yield, then the share price is relatively low, implying that the main factor attracting shareholders to the company is the reasonably high current level of income. Investors who believe that the company has good growth prospects would buy the share, driving the price up and reducing the yield.

It is therefore also true that companies with high P/E ratios tend to have low dividend yields and vice versa.

5.6 Dividend cover

5.6.1 Basic calculation

Dividend cover is used as an attempt to assess the likelihood of the existing dividend being maintained. The dividend cover is calculated as follows.

Formula to learn

$$\text{Dividend cover} = \frac{\text{Earnings per share}}{\text{Dividend per share}}$$

5.6.2 Considerations

As noted under earnings per share above, it may be preferable to use the EPS calculated on a maximum distribution basis for this ratio.

Example

$$\text{Dividend cover} = \frac{12.37\text{p}}{6.25\text{p}}$$

$$\text{Dividend cover} = 1.98\times$$

5.6.3 Analysis points

An unusually high dividend cover implies that the company is retaining the majority of its earnings, presumably with the intention of reinvesting to generate growth.

A company **may**, alternatively, pay a **larger dividend than the year's earnings**, in which case it is drawing on past reserves and is said to be paying an **uncovered dividend**.

The dividend payout ratio is the inverse of the dividend cover. It represents the proportion of earnings belonging to the shareholders that have actually been distributed by way of a dividend.

5.7 Net asset value/net assets per share

5.7.1 Basic calculation

The net asset value or net assets per share is calculated as

Formula to learn

$$\text{Net asset value} = \frac{\text{Net assets attributable to ordinary shareholders}}{\text{Number of ordinary shares in issue}}$$

Where net assets is non-current assets plus current assets less non-current liabilities less current liabilities which may alternatively (and more simply) be calculated as equity shareholder funds.

5.7.2 Considerations

The net asset value represents the 'intrinsic' worth of the shares in terms of the net assets that support that value. This could show an unrealistically low figure in terms of current worth if a strict policy of historical cost accounting has been applied. The shareholder may be more interested in the asset values if the company adopts a policy of revaluation.

Example

	£'000
Total shareholder funds	33,041
Less: preference shares	837
Equity shareholder funds (= Net assets)	32,204

$$\text{Net asset value} = \frac{£32,204,000}{17,925,000 \text{ shares}}$$

Net asset value = £1.80 per share

Note that the net assets figure is after deducting those due to the preference shareholders.

5.7.3 Analysis points

While the company continues to trade, the net assets per share might be considerably higher or lower than the market value of those shares. This is because investors do not think that all of the assets will be sold and they are basing the value of the company on its ability to generate returns using those assets. The 'asset backing' tends to become more significant in the event of a potential takeover. It is also of regular concern to property companies and investment trusts.

5.8 Price-to-book ratio

5.8.1 Basic calculation

The price-to-book ratio examines the relationship between the market value of a share and the underlying assets within the company that a shareholder effectively owns.

Formula to learn

$$\text{Price to book} = \frac{\text{Share price}}{\text{Net assets per share}}$$

5.8.2 Considerations

The price-to-book ratio can be used to evaluate if a company appears to be cheap or expensive compared to its peer group. It can be used to generate valuations (where a comparable company's price-to-book ratio can be applied to the book value of the net assets of the company under consideration to generate a valuation).

5.8.3 Analysis

A low price to book, where perhaps the share price is less than the net assets, may indicate that the company is earning inadequate returns on net assets to satisfy shareholders. The share price will reflect the anticipated value of future earnings for shareholders. If these are poor, the price may well be less than the value of the net assets used to generate that return. A high price to book, where the share price is higher than the net assets, may indicate that the market believes that the company will use its assets more effectively to the satisfaction of shareholders. However, the low net assets figure may be due to older assets that are fully depreciated. Therefore, careful consideration must be given when comparing this measure of a company relative to another.

5.9 Price-to-cash flow ratio

5.9.1 Basic calculation

The price-to-cash flow ratio examines the relationship between the market value of a share and the cash that is being generated by the company from its operating activities, again on a per share basis.

Formula to learn

$$\text{Price to cash flow} = \frac{\text{Share price}}{\text{Cash flow from operating activities per share}}$$

5.10 Price-to-sales ratio

5.10.1 Basic calculation

The price-to-sales ratio examines the relationship between the market value of a share and sales being generated by the company from its operating activities.

Formula to learn

$$\text{Price to sales} = \frac{\text{Share price}}{\text{Sales}}$$

5.10.2 Considerations

While this measure considers sales, that does not necessarily mean profits for the shareholders. Secondly, these sales are generated by both equity and debt finance, which is ignored here. Therefore, the Enterprise Value to sales may be more appropriate.

5.11 Enterprise value

5.11.1 Basic calculations

The following earnings multiples measuring corporate performance are used frequently by analysts as an alternative to the P/E ratio.

Formula to learn

$$\text{Enterprise value to EBITDA} = \frac{\text{Enterprise value}}{\text{Earnings before interest, tax, depreciation and amortisation}}$$

Formula to learn

$$\text{Enterprise values to sales} = \frac{\text{Enterprise value}}{\text{Sales}}$$

5.11.2 Considerations

These earnings multiples work in the same way as the P/E ratio, in that they compare an historic earnings or revenue figure to the market value of the business. Thus, the higher the multiple the more growth expectation is factored into market values and the more positively the company is viewed in relation to its peers.

However, the market value used in these ratios is not the market value of equity, which is used for the P/E ratio. Instead, the enterprise value (EV) is used, which is the market **value of equity** plus the **market value of net debt** (in other words, the value of the business to all providers of finance).

The rationale for using the EV is that this is a figure that is not distorted by the gearing of the business, and therefore can be used to more directly compare companies with different financing strategies. Therefore, whilst the P/E ratio focuses only on earnings available to equity shareholders, EV multiples look at earnings available to all finance providers, being earnings before all dividends and before interest payments.

Earnings before interest, tax, depreciation and amortisation (EBITDA) is used for the following reasons.

- To eliminate distortions caused by different financing structures, tax regimes, depreciation mechanisms and amortisation periods.
- To facilitate cross-border comparisons.
- To calculate meaningful multiples for companies in high growth sectors, such as telecommunications and technology, where traditional P/E measures are not able to be calculated due to the businesses being currently loss making.

There is a further measure, EV to sales, that is used mainly for companies in the technology sector (especially internet businesses), where they are at the early stages of growth and thus any form of profit figure tends to be relatively meaningless. By using sales, or turnover, as the historic measure of performance, all distortions to profit are stripped out.

5.11.3 Analysis points

EV multiples should be analysed in the same way as P/E multiples, to compare different companies within the same sector. Therefore, the same comments can be made, and conclusions drawn, as were discussed for the P/E ratio.

5.12 Economic value added

Learning objective | **18.3.18 Explain** the measures of economic value added (EVA) and market value added (MVA).

5.12.1 The purpose of economic value added

Economic Value Added (EVA, **note that the abbreviation is a registered trademark of Stern Stewart & Co.**) is a measure of performance that is designed to identify the economic profit a company is earning.

It was primarily designed to be a measure of management performance, genuinely assessing the value which management has brought to a company's shareholders by their actions. The benefit of using economic profit for this purpose is that, if carefully calculated, it cannot be affected by accounting choices in the way that accounting profits are.

However, in recent times, it has become fashionable to use EVA as part of an assessment of a company's expected future returns.

The methodology of EVA focuses on the following basic ideas.

- Capital invested.
- Cost of capital.
- Profitability after allowing for the cost of capital.

The idea is that management have to generate a sufficient return to fully satisfy the requirements of the various investors, debt and equity. This should encourage management to use capital efficiently, raising capital where they believe they can earn high returns compared to its cost, and repaying capital if the rate of return on investment is too low.

Definition

EVA is defined as

Formula to learn

EVA = Net operating profit after tax – Cost of capital

Net operating profit after tax

Net operating profit after tax = operating profit before interest, i.e. normal operational profits irrespective of the financing of the company.

Cost of capital

Formula to learn

Cost of capital = Value of the capital invested × Weighted average cost of capital

That is, the after-tax cost to the company of servicing its finance based on the required returns of equity and debt investors and the market values of these sources of finance.

If the EVA is a positive value, then value is being added by the management of the company. If negative, then the opposite is true.

5.13 Market value added

5.13.1 Definition of market value added

Market Value Added (MVA) is defined as the difference between the market capitalisation of the firm's equity plus debt less the capital invested, i.e.

Formula to learn

MVA = Current market value – Capital invested

Current market value

The current market value is the market value of the company's shares and debt, a measure of the total value of the business.

Capital invested

Capital invested is the total value of all finance historically raised by the company, again both debt and equity.

5.13.2 Use of MVA

MVA measures the amount by which the management has increased the value of the capital invested in the firm. It is done by investing in projects with positive net present values, i.e. where the required return exceeds the WACC.

The market value added (MVA) is the present value of all the expected future EVA from the firm's operations.

MVA is linked to the price-to-book ratio in the way it compares the market value of the firm with the value of its assets. As with these ratios, the reason why the MVA is positive is because the management has invested capital received from investors in projects which have positive net present values, where the expected rate of return exceeds the required rate of return.

One feature of MVA is that it can only be calculated on a firm-wide basis, since it is based on the market value of the firm. It cannot be performed on a divisional basis, unlike the other measures highlighted.

6 Illustration PLC

6.1 Balance sheet as at 31 December

	£'000	£'000
Non-current assets		
Intangible		3,926
Tangible		18,731
Investments		842
		23,499
Current assets		
Inventory	19,420	
Receivables	27,882	
Investments	3,926	
Cash	6,425	
		57,653
Total assets		**81,152**

	£'000	£'000
Share capital		
£1.00 NV Ordinary shares		17,925
Preference shares		837
Reserves		
Share premium account reserve		2,455
Revaluation reserve		2,681
Retained earnings reserve		9,143
Shareholders' funds		33,041
Creditors due after one year		
Secured loans	2,073	
Unsecured loans	2,372	
		4,445
Creditors due within one year		
Bank overdraft	17,079	
Trade payables	18,702	
Tax	1,625	
Others	6,260	
		43,666
Total liabilities		**81,152**

6.2 Income statement account

	£'000
Revenue	135,761
Cost of sales	(83,604)
Gross profit	52,157
Distribution costs	(22,961)
Administration costs	(22,712)
Operating profit	6,484
Interest received	365
Interest paid	(3,176)
Profit before tax	3,673
Tax	
Corporation tax	(1,372)
Profit after tax	**2,301**
Dividends	
Ordinary	1,120
Preference	84
	1,204
Earnings per share	12.37p
Dividend per share	6.25p

Chapter Roundup

Ratio analysis

- Ratios are useful for condensing down information which may be used to identify changes in a company's performance from year to year, or to compare the company's performance against other companies in the same industry.
- Ratios broadly go under the heading of profitability, liquidity, investor and gearing.

Profitability

- Profitability ratios assess the trading or operating performance of the company.

$$\text{ROCE} = \frac{\text{Profit before interest payable and tax}}{\text{Capital employed}} \times 100\%$$

$$\text{Profit margin} = \frac{\text{Profits}}{\text{Revenue}} \times 100\%$$

$$\text{Asset turnover} = \frac{\text{Revenue}}{\text{Assets (capital) employed}}$$

$$\text{Return on equity} = \frac{\text{Profit after tax} - \text{Preference dividends}}{\text{Ordinary shareholder's funds}}$$

$$\text{Operational gearing} = \frac{\text{Trading profit} + \text{Fixed costs}}{\text{Trading profit}}$$

Liquidity

- Liquidity ratios measure the risk of a company being able or unable to pay its creditors.

$$\text{Current ratio} = \frac{\text{Current assets due within one year}}{\text{Current liabilities falling due within one year}}$$

$$\text{Quick ratio} = \frac{\text{Current assets excluding inventory}}{\text{Current liabilities falling due within one year}}$$

Gearing

- Gearing ratios measure the risks to the providers of debt and equity finance.

$$\text{Debt to equity} = \frac{\text{Interest-bearing loans}}{\text{Equity shareholders' funds}} \times 100\%$$

$$\text{Net debt to equity} = \frac{\text{Debt (as above)} - \text{Cash and current asset investments}}{\text{Equity shareholders' funds}} \times 100\%$$

$$\text{Interest cover} = \frac{\text{Profit before interest payable and tax}}{\text{Interest payable}}$$

$$\text{Asset cover} = \frac{\text{Total assets} - \text{Current liabilities}}{\text{Loan payable}}$$

Investors

- Investors ratios measure and assess the returns to the providers of finance.

$$\text{EPS} = \frac{\text{Earnings attributable to ordinary shareholders}}{\text{Number of ordinary shares}}$$

$$\text{Price/Earnings} = \frac{\text{Current market price per share}}{\text{Earnings per share}}$$

$$\text{Earnings yield} = \frac{\text{Earnings per share}}{\text{Current market price per share}} \times 100\%$$

$$\text{Dividend yield} = \frac{\text{Dividend per share}}{\text{Current market price per share}} \times 100\%$$

$$\text{Dividend cover} = \frac{\text{Earnings per share}}{\text{Dividend per share}}$$

$$\text{Net asset value} = \frac{\text{Net assets attributable to ordinary shareholders}}{\text{Number of ordinary shares in issue}}$$

$$\text{Price to book} = \frac{\text{Share price}}{\text{Net assets per share}}$$

EVA = Net operating profit after tax – Cost of capital

Cost of capital = Value of the capital invested × Weighted average cost of capital

MVA = Current market value – Capital invested

Test Your Knowledge

Check your knowledge of the chapter here, without referring back to the text.

1. How is return on capital employed calculated?

2. How is the debt-to-equity ratio calculated?

3. A low price to earning ratio indicates that a company is highly rated in the eyes of shareholders. *True/False*?

4. What is EBITDA?

5. How is the dividend yield calculated and what does it tell us about the growth prospects of the company?

6. You are given the following information.

Balance sheet

	Last year	*This year*
Non-current assets	200	220
Current assets	100	120
Creditors	(80)	(90)
Loans	(120)	(130)
	100	120
Share capital	50	50
Retained profits	50	70
	100	120

Income statement

Revenue	100	140
Cost of sales	(60)	(80)
Gross profit	40	60
Operating cost	(25)	(30)
Operating profit	15	30
Tax	(5)	(10)
Profit after tax	10	20

Calculate the following ratios:

- ROCE
- Gross profit margin
- Current ratio
- Debt to equity

TEST YOUR KNOWLEDGE: ANSWERS

1. Profit before interest payable and tax/capital employed.

   (See Section 2.1.1)

2. Interest-bearing loans/equity shareholders' funds.

   (See Section 4.2.1)

3. False. A low P/E ratio indicates investors are prepared to pay only a relatively low amount relative to the current year's earnings of the business.

   (See Section 5.3.1)

4. Earnings before interest, tax, depreciation and amortisation.

   (See Section 5.11.2)

5. Dividend/share price.

   A high dividend yield often indicates a company with low growth prospects, since the company is likely to be paying out a large proportion of its profits as dividends, and so only retaining a small proportion.

   (See Section 5.5)

6. ROCE = $\frac{15}{220}$ = 0.068 or 6.8%

   (See Section 2.1)

   Gross profit margin = $\frac{60}{140}$ = 0.429 or 42.9%

   (See Section 2.2)

   Current ratio = $\frac{120}{90}$ = 1.33×

   (See Section 3.1)

   Debt to equity = $\frac{130}{120}$ = 1.08 or 108%

   (See Section 4.1)

17 Investment Management

INTRODUCTION

Investment management is the process of managing assets on behalf of institutional and private investors. Before investing it is important for the portfolio manager to identify the objectives and constraints of the client.

Asset allocation, market timing and stock selection all contribute to the overall performance of the portfolio. Stock selection approaches consist of both active and passive approaches.

CHAPTER CONTENTS

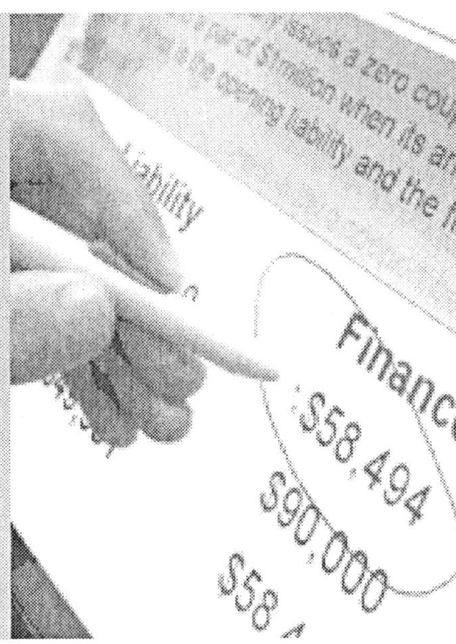

Chapter Learning Objectives

18 Asset classes

Demonstrate an ability to evaluate the characteristics, inherent risks, behaviour and correlation of asset classes

18.12 Correlation between asset classes

18.12.1 **Identify** the correlation between the various asset classes (equity, fixed interest, property, cash, alternative investments) and explain its relevance to asset allocation.

18.12.2 **Explain** the limitations of correlation analysis in extreme market conditions.

18.13 Pricing liquidity and fair value

18.13.1 **Explain** the relationship between pricing, liquidity and fair value for the asset classes of equity, fixed interest, property, cash and alternative investments.

22 Investment management principles

Demonstrate an understanding of the principles of investment management

22.1 Investment management principles – fixed income

22.1.1 **Explain** the following bond portfolio management techniques.

- Cash matching /dedication.
- Immunisation.
- Contingent immunisation.
- Anomaly switches.
- Policy switches.
- Credit risk management.
- Riding the yield curve.

22.1.2 **Calculate** the theoretical gain from riding the yield curve.

22.1.3 **Calculate** duration for a bond portfolio.

22.1.4 **Explain** the benefits and risks of using, barbell and bond portfolio strategies.

22.2 Fund management styles

22.2.1 **Distinguish** between a 'top-down' and 'bottom-up' approach to fund management.

22.2.2 **Distinguish** between active and passive fund management and explain the costs/benefits to the investor.

22.2.3 **Distinguish** between strategic and tactical asset allocation.

22.2.4 **Explain** the major investment styles prevalent in the fund management industry (including socially responsible investing – SRI / environmental social governance investing ESGI).

22.3 Liability driven investment (LDI)

22.3.1 **Explain** the benefits and risks of an LDI strategy.

22.3.2 **Explain** the process of a liability driven investment strategy.

22.3.3 **Explain** some of the techniques used in LDI.

22.3.4 **Explain** the use of basic measures of risk used in LDI.

1 Objectives of Investment Management

1.1 Introduction

1.1.1 Purpose and consideration

Investment management involves the investment of a client's assets in order to meet a number of key objectives. The objectives will vary from investor to investor and, consequently, the process of investment management must start with a detailed consideration of the client's objectives.

To satisfy the client's objectives, the fund manager also needs to appreciate the constraints that he must operate within, i.e. he must know such factors about the client as

- Time horizons.
- Liquidity needs.
- Risk aversion/tolerances.
- Tax status.
- Other preferences and legal constraints, e.g. ethical considerations.

This is needed for at least three reasons.

- It is a prerequisite to the initial portfolio structure.
- It influences the kinds of portfolio adjustment that can be made.
- It consequently influences portfolio performance.

1.1.2 The regulatory framework for the investment manager

The regulation of the UK financial services industry continues to evolve. Prior to the advent of the 1986 Financial Services Act, the industry was completely self-regulating.

The Financial Services Act was not a detailed legal code as one might anticipate, but rather a statutory framework which made provision for the recognition of detailed rules produced by the investment industry itself – the self-regulatory aspect of the regulatory structure.

A key element of the system was the Financial Services Act 1986, which contained the basic premise that those conducting investment business in the UK obtain authorisation. On 30 November 2001, the **Financial Services and Markets Act 2000 (FSMA)** came into force. Whilst practitioner and consumers are actively consulted it is the FSA, a public authority, that co-ordinates the regulation of the industry.

The provision of investment management services constitutes a **regulated activity** as defined by FSMA. Thus, any firm providing these services requires **authorisation**.

On 1 November 2007 further changes to the regulatory environment occurred with the introduction of MiFID, a European directive aimed at opening up the European market.

1.1.3 The role of the investment manager

While an individual investor may choose to manage his own money, the majority of investors in the UK are turning towards institutional investment management to safeguard their assets. One of the reasons for this is that commissions have come down for institutional investors, while commissions for private customers remain high. Unless customers are undertaking large transactions, they may be limiting their access to the marketplace.

Equally, it is important for an investor to buy a range of assets. This restricts the level of risk he may face but, with only a limited amount of capital, it may be impossible at today's commission rates for an investor to spread his money over a portfolio wide enough to minimise risk. Consequently, it makes sense for small investors to pool their money into large funds that can be invested on their behalf by professional fund managers.

To safeguard the assets of the individual investors, funds are frequently managed under trust. This means that **all of the fund's assets** are registered in the name of the trustees, rather than the managers, with the managers only having authority to undertake particular transactions, e.g. buying or selling securities, on behalf of the trustees.

1.1.4 The role of the trustee

Introduction

Sometimes a fund is managed under trust and the role of the trustee is to protect and control the trust property. It is the responsibility of the trustee to invest the trust property, though this role is frequently delegated to a fund manager.

If the fund is managed under trust and there are no specific instructions for its investment in the trust deed, the trustee must invest the funds in accordance with the Trustee Act 2000. Where there are specific investment criteria laid out in the trust deed, the trustee must ensure that these are not breached by the fund manager.

In performing this role, a trustee must, under the terms of the Trustee Act 2000, act with a duty of care, ensuring the suitability of an investment to the trust.

When investing trust money, a trustee has four duties.

- To invest in **authorised** investments, i.e. authorised by either
  - The Trustee Act 2000; or
  - The trust instrument.
- To show the same degree of skill in investment selection as **a man of ordinary prudence would exercise in the management of his own affairs** and to avoid any investments of a speculative character.
- To have regard to S4 of the Trustee Act 2000 with respect to
  - The need for diversification.
  - The suitability of the type of investments to the trust.
  - The suitability of the particular investment of that type.
- To act impartially between beneficiaries.

The provisions of the Trustee Act 2000 do not apply to **occupational pension schemes** or **authorised unit trusts.**

1.2 Client objectives

1.2.1 Introduction

Broadly speaking, the requirements of clients fall into one of two categories, those who seek

- To maximise their returns, i.e. positive net worth individuals looking for a portfolio to match their risk/return preferences.
- To match liabilities, e.g. pension funds, where the aim is to match assets and liabilities or minimise any mismatch.

Return maximisation

Given the choice, most investors would elect to have a high performance fund with minimal risk. However, this is not achievable and some trade-off between the two will have to take place. Understanding this **risk/reward trade-off** is crucial to understanding the overall objectives of a return maximising fund and then to establishing the policy of a fund.

Lower risk aversion or greater risk tolerance results in

- Greater allowable portfolio risk.
- Greater potential gains (and losses).

The primary concern in this type of fund is, therefore, to fully understand the client's risk tolerance, be they private or institutional clients.

Liability matching

The only way to guarantee the matching of any liability is through investment in government bonds where the income and capital inflows exactly match those liabilities.

If the return from bonds is insufficient to achieve this required return then we must use other assets. The result of the use of other assets is that we may achieve the higher return required. However, the risk associated with the use of these other assets means that the liabilities may not be exactly met – there may be a mismatch.

Once again, a key requirement here will be to establish the clients attitude to risk, though here we have more specific financial objectives to meet, ie a future liability to satisfy.

1.3 Constraints on the fund

1.3.1 Introduction

Given the client's objectives, the key to understanding the investment strategy is to appreciate the various constraints that operate on the fund itself.

1.3.2 Time horizons

The time horizons for the attainment of the return, or the matching of the liabilities, will clearly influence the types of investments that will be worthwhile for the fund.

A fund whose purpose is to meet some liabilities in, say, two years' time, may find that the investment vehicle is low coupon gilts. This will especially be the case if the client is a high rate taxpayer as he will be able to benefit from a tax-free capital gain on these gilts at redemption.

For a fund that has liabilities to meet in 20 years' time, such investments would be inappropriate.

The time horizon will also influence the level of risk that can be taken in order to achieve the objectives. A fund with a long-term time horizon can probably stand a higher risk, as any poor returns in one year will be cancelled by high returns in subsequent years before the fund expires. Clearly, this sort of risk cannot be taken in a very short-term fund which may only span a couple of years and, therefore, may not have counterbalancing good and bad years.

1.3.3 Liabilities

As mentioned above, certain funds have liabilities that they are obliged to meet and the investment manager's objective must take these into consideration. For example, pension funds and life assurance companies will have statistical projections of their liabilities into the future and the fund must attempt to achieve these.

A further consideration is the exposure to currency risk. A pension fund may have all its liabilities denominated in sterling. If the fund were to invest heavily in overseas assets this would expose it to an additional risk, other than the risk inherent in the assets themselves. However, if the pension fund has liabilities in, say, dollars, then buying US investments matches their currency exposure and, therefore, minimises risk as well as taking on board an acceptable investment.

1.3.4 Liquidity needs

Within any fund there must be the ability to respond to changing circumstances and, consequently, there needs to be a degree of liquidity. Government fixed interest instruments can guarantee a tranche of the investment portfolio which will give easy access to cash should the fund need it. In general, exchange traded investments (equities and bonds) tend to be highly liquid whilst investments that are not exchange traded, such as property, have low liquidity.

1.3.5 Risk aversion and risk tolerances

We commented above on the risk/reward trade-off and how it impacts on the ways in which the fund's requirements can be achieved.

1.3.6 Tax status

Taxation is a consideration for all investment managers. The investment portfolio and the strategy adopted must be consistent with the fund's tax position. In some cases, such as pension funds, the fund does not suffer taxation. For these **gross funds** the manager should, normally, avoid those stocks which involve the deduction of tax at source. For, even though it may be possible to reclaim any tax suffered, the fund will have incurred the opportunity cost of the lost interest on the tax deducted.

1.3.7 Other preferences and legal constraints

Obviously, when constructing a portfolio for any investor, the manager should consider the legal constraints that may exist. The regulatory framework adopted in the market needs to be adhered to. For collective investment schemes in the UK, there are certain investments into which the fund may not invest, such as derivatives.

Equally, a **trust deed** may exist which binds the investment manager to invest in certain securities and, consequently, the manager must abide by this trust document. Where there is no trust deed, the **Trustee Act 2000** provides guidance on the appropriate mix of investments. This places a duty of care on the trustees to exercise reasonable care in investments.

1.4 Return maximising funds

Return maximising funds include normal retail collective investment schemes discussed earlier in this Study Text, ie

- Unit trusts
- OEICs
- Investment trusts
- ETFs
- Hedge funds
- Structured products

These firms seek to maximise returns whilst remaining within prescribed risk tolerances. They are typically ongoing funds that therefore adopt a long-term investment view, though some have specified terms. They have no specific liabilities to meet, are subject to the tax regulations of the country in which they are constituted and are constrained by their trust deed or published investment policy.

1.5 Liability matching funds

1.5.1 Liability driven investment

arning objectives	
	22.3.1 Explain the benefits and risks of an LDI strategy.
	22.3.2 Explain the process of a liability driven investment strategy.
	22.3.3 Explain some of the techniques used in LDI.
	22.3.4 Explain the use of basic measures of risk used in LDI.

There has been increasing focus in recent years on liability management due to lower overall funding levels on pensions, maturing defined benefit pension schemes, and the change in the accounting environment for pension schemes.

Liability driven investment involves building a portfolio that meets the future liabilities of a scheme. The starting point is therefore to identify the future liabilities, and then to build a portfolio to meet those requirements.

Traditional ways of matching liabilities include immunisation and cash flow matching (covered later) and the use of conventional gilts, index-linked gilts, and corporate bonds. However in the physical market place there are often liquidity and duration constraints, particularly at longer maturities, which may frustrate investors from obtaining the ideal type of securities and the use of corporate bonds introduces credit risk to the arrangement.

As a result other asset types have gained prominence in recent years. **Interest rate swaps** may allow **nominal liabilities** to be closely matched. Inflation swaps, which allow investors to generate a return tied into an inflation index, may help match **real** liabilities.

The primary LDI risks faced are immunisation risk and credit risk (covered later in this section). The investment manager will use a risk framework to decide what risk the portfolio is able to take beyond meeting the required liabilities, e.g. interest rate risk, inflation risk and credit risk. The greater the divergence from the required liability matching portfolio, the greater the risk of both under and over performance.

1.5.2 Pension funds

A pension fund may be a liability matching fund or a return maximising fund depending on circumstances. It represents a pool of money to be invested now, to achieve either

- A specific return based on the employee's salary and number of years' service with the company – a **defined benefit/final salary scheme** (liability matching to the specific return); or

- A general increase in value of the contributions paid on behalf of the employee – a **defined contribution/money purchase scheme** (liability matching and return maximisation).

Occupational pension schemes are schemes set up by the employer for the benefit of the employees, that tend to be defined benefit schemes, though defined contribution schemes are becoming increasingly popular.

Personal pension schemes are set up by an individual who is, perhaps, self-employed or is not a member of an occupational scheme, are defined contribution pensions.

Generally speaking, pension funds have fairly **long-term horizons** and, therefore, are prepared to take on board a higher degree of risk, since any shortfall in the fund can be made up in future investment performance. This **investment policy** depends on the **maturity** of the fund. If the fund beneficiaries are close to retirement, then it would be more appropriate to select relatively short-term safe investments. However, in general the above comment is applicable.

Defined benefit pension schemes are not allowed to make profits or losses so must aim to ensure that their assets cover their liabilities both now and on a projected basis (in the future). Assuming for a fund that assets cover liabilities at present, the primary driver of their required return, the required **Actuarial Rate of Return**, is how rapidly the fund liabilities are growing. This will be driven by such factors as

- Current employee length of service and ages – influencing likely ultimate length of service
- Potential wage inflation rates
- Current pensioner ages and pension rights
- Mortality rates

Pension funds also have to keep control over the real rate of return that they earn since their liabilities, the potential pension payments calculated by the fund actuaries, will be expanding in line with inflation. As a consequence, pension funds tend to invest in slightly more speculative assets often referred to as **real assets**, such as **equities** and **property**, since these offer a degree of protection against the impact of inflation with only a small proportion of the fund in fixed interest instruments. They will tend to be substantial holders of index-linked stocks, partly because these guarantee real returns over a period of time, but also because the bonds themselves tend to have fairly high durations and are, therefore, sensitive to movement in real interest rates.

Equally, the pension fund will need to keep some assets in a liquid form and government bond markets represent a highly liquid market place in which to invest money gaining a moderate but **risk-free** return.

Note that as the age profile of contributions changes, the asset mix is likely to change. With **young** contributors the fund is likely to focus heavily on **equities**. This results in a greater **mismatching** between the assets and the liabilities. However, as the contributors get **older** the focus is likely to switch to **bonds** since they will provide greater price stability in the short term. This also provides more direct matching of the assets against the liabilities.

UK pension funds tend to have a much greater proportion of equities in their portfolios than Continental European pension funds.

Pension funds approved by the Inland Revenue are **gross funds**, i.e. they pay no UK tax on either fund income or capital gains.

1.5.3 Life assurance companies

Life assurance is a form of insurance against an eventuality that is **assured** (hence the name) to arise, i.e. that people will die. As such, it is another form of liability matching fund. Life assurance policies offering some significant levels of protection take a number of forms.

- **Term assurance policies** – where an individual's life is insured for a specific period or term (usually ten years or more) in a similar way to normal car or household insurance.

- **Whole of life policies** – where a capital sum will be paid upon the death of the policyholder, whenever that may be.
- **Endowment policies** – which combine life insurance and savings. These policies are generally associated with mortgages where the savings element is designed to pay off the capital borrowed at the end of the term of the policy, and the life insurance will repay the mortgage should the policyholder die before the end of that term.

In common with pension funds, life assurance companies tend to have reasonably **long-term** liabilities and, as such, are able to take on board a higher degree of risk. Once again, this tends to involve a high proportion of their assets being invested into equities and property with only a smaller proportion being invested into the fixed interest markets.

As a long-term fund, life assurance companies are able to take reasonably higher degrees of risk and again may be tempted towards the higher duration stocks in the bond markets.

Within the industry there are a variety of policies available ranging from with profits policies, which share in the profits of the fund but attract higher premiums, to without profits policies, where the premiums are lower but the profits go to the insurance company.

1.5.4 General insurance companies

General insurance companies clearly aim to be able to match their liabilities. They have a much shorter liability profile than life funds. In essence, insurance is like taking a bet. The insured person pays the company the premium.

The insurance company makes money if they are able to take in this premium and earn investment income on it that exceeds the amounts of any claims arising on the policy.

Since claims are likely to arise in the immediate future, for example in the next year, then they are unable to take substantial risks, forcing them to invest a greater proportion of their fund into **short-term** 'risk-free' government securities. Whilst the returns may not be as high, the fund simply cannot take any risk.

Both life assurance funds and general insurance funds are closely monitored by the FSA to ensure that the solvency of the company is in no way called into question. Overall, this tends to make both of them more risk adverse than pension funds but there is a marked difference between life assurance companies and general insurance companies in the risk/reward profile they adopt.

1.5.5 Charities

Charities may be set up as corporations or as trusts. Charities are regulated by the Charity Commission in England and Wales. The Charity Commissioner's function is to promote the efficient use of charitable resources. In addition, this body encourages better administration and provides charities with advice.

The powers of the Charity Commission permit the removal of trustees and transfer of assets to other bodies. They also maintain a register of charities and have the right to receive the annual report and accounts from each charity, which are then made available for public inspection.

1.5.6 Banks

London has a highly developed banking market ranging from the high-street banks to the large international banks that have a presence in the London Market. The range of services is considerable, from the straightforward deposit-taking and lending to the more sophisticated corporate finance and money market activities run the merchant banks and capital markets divisions. In general, however, bank liabilities are **short term**, since the build of their assets are derived from deposit taking, most of which is repayable on demand.

In recent years, the commercial pressure on the conventional banking activities through the process of diversification has forced the banks to expand their activities into the areas of financial services and, in particular, the provision of investment advice to the individual customer.

1.5.7 Building societies

In the past, building societies have provided an extremely limited range of services mainly linked to long-term lending on property. The Building Societies Act 1986 considerably expanded the range of services that societies are able to provide.

Under the legislation governing building societies, they are able to

- Transact business in the **forex** market.
- Operate estate agencies.
- Establish and manage **ISAs**.
- Provide **investment services**, however, this will bring the society under the auspices of the FSA. In practical terms, many societies avoid their obligation to this end by becoming appointed representatives of a specific firm.
- Make **unsecured loans**. As with many of the other changes introduced in the Building Societies Act 1986, this makes the societies much more like retail banks.
- In a further relation of the controls, societies are now able to obtain up to 20% of their finance from beyond the depositor base by accessing the capital markets. Indeed, with the permission of the regulator, this limit can be extended to a level of 40%

2 Assets Available

2.1 Introduction

Fundamental to an understanding of investment management is an appreciation of the relationship between risk and reward, that is

High risk = High expected return

Investments offer a range of risk and return that can be summarised as follows.

Risk	Investments
Low Risk ↑	National Savings Certificates
	Bank and Building Society Accounts (Including money market deposits)
	Gilts Held to Redemption
	Gilts Sold Before Redemption (Here, there is the risk of a fall in the value of the stock)
	Local Authority Issues
	Corporate Bonds (Dependent on the credit rating)
Medium Risk	Life Assurance Policies
	Unit and Investment Trusts (Obviously, certain schemes, such as GFOFs, carry greater risk than others)
	Shares and Property (Ranging from 'blue chips' to penny shares in small dynamic companies)
↓ **High Risk**	Warrants, Futures and Options (However, there is only a limited risk in purchasing an option or a warrant since, here, only the premium can be lost)

Before offering any investment advice, it is vital to ensure that the risk and returns match the customer's criteria. These assets can be sub-categorised between

- **Nominal** – those whose returns are fixed in value irrespective of future inflation, e.g. bonds.
- **Real** – those whose returns vary as we experience inflation, e.g. shares, property.

2.2 Analysis of those assets

2.2.1 Introduction

In theory, all investment managers should have undertaken a complete analysis of all available investment assets to be in a position to assess them in relation to a client's portfolio.

There are, broadly, four approaches that are adopted.

- Fundamental analysis.
- Technical analysis.
- Quantitative analysis.
- A combination.

2.2.2 Fundamental analysis

Fundamental analysis concentrates on the economic strengths or weaknesses of the market in question and the individual features of the stock within that market. The basic idea behind this approach is that every security has an **intrinsic value** that can be determined from a consideration of these factors.

With government bonds, this form of analysis entails reviewing the economic outlook for the economy and the funding requirement.

With corporate securities, in addition to assessing the economic environment and interest rate profile, it involves assessing the individual credit and operational risk, along with details of its dividend yield and P/E ratio.

2.2.3 Technical analysis

Technical analysts, rather than looking at the fundamentals of the economy, look to the pattern and trading history to determine the appropriate strategy to adopt.

Frequently, through the use of charts, technical analysts develop patterns of market behaviour that they expect to be repeated time and time again. By charting the daily price movement in a stock, they believe they can predict the eventual out-turn of the market. To an extent these predictions will be self-fulfilling because, for example, if the charts predict the price will fall and investment managers react to this sell signal, then undoubtedly the supply and demand factors will force the price down.

The intellectual justification for the use of technical analysis is based on behavioural finance and the theories of crowd behaviour. Basically, the same group of people exposed to the same circumstances will react in the same way: 'history repeats itself.'

2.2.4 Quantitative analysis

Quantitative analysis involves analysing investment instruments according to expected levels of return and risk. It is generally accepted that higher returns can only be obtained at the expense of higher risk. However, investment managers can use computers to generate strategies that allow them to invest making the most cost-effective and efficient trade-off between risk and return.

2.2.5 The combination approach

Many houses tend to use a combination of all three approaches, with fundamental and quantitative analysis dictating the markets and stocks which they need to buy and technical analysis being used to determine the timing of entry into the market place.

Regardless of whether the investment manager believes in technical analysis or not, he will have to keep an eye on the charts, since if sufficient numbers do believe the technical analysts, the market will move in line with their predictions.

3 Approaches to Investment Management

3.1 Introduction

The process of investment management involves the investment of a third party's assets in order to meet a number of key objectives. The objectives will vary from investor to investor and consequently, as noted above, the process of fund management must start with a detailed consideration of the fund's objectives and associated constraints.

3.2 Investment policy or investment strategy statement

The objectives and constraints of the fund lead the fund manager to consider a variety of strategies or possible asset allocations, and within these to select specific stocks that meet the fund objectives. The fund manager will be judged by his performance with regard to the objectives of the fund and, in the highly competitive world of fund management, an under-performing manager will not be given many second chances.

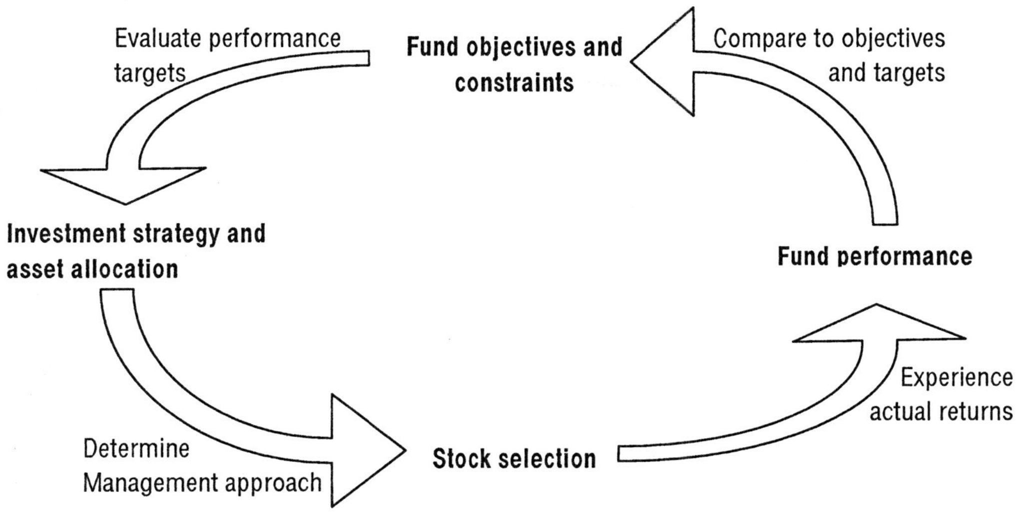

Once the objectives and constraints of the particular fund have been established, the next stage is to develop the investment policy/strategies that will be used in order to achieve these objectives. All these considerations will be detailed as recommended investment policy/strategy options.

These recommendations must then be submitted to the client for approval. In simple situations there may be one obvious approach for the manager to adopt, in more complex situations, several alternatives may be presented to the client forming the basis of a discussion leading to the finally agreed investment policy/strategy statement.

The resultant investment policy/strategy statement forms the basis of the management approach. This strategy will detail the long term strategic asset allocation options selected to achieve the client's objectives. Asset allocations should not, however, be set in stone. Different asset categories perform better in different economic situations and the fund manager must be ready to respond to such circumstances.

Along with the long term strategic asset allocation, the strategy may also detail market timing/tactical asset allocation options that may be adopted by the fund in those differing circumstances. The strategy details asset allocations and limits but will not detail stock or product recommendations.

Finally, the investment strategy will probably detail any performance benchmarks against which the fund performance is to be assessed.

When the overall strategy and policy of the fund have been determined, the final stage is to select the stock that will make up the portfolio and approaches to this are discussed later.

The final stage of the investment process is to evaluate whether the fund is achieving its objectives through a consideration of its performance. Fund performance should be reviewed no less than once a year, certainly more regularly for short term funds, and will look to achieve a number of objectives.

- **Client circumstances** – we should firstly look to determine whether any client circumstances have altered as this may result in an alteration of the client's objectives. Any significant changes may require a modification to the investment strategy.
- **Performance review** – we need to monitor the performance of the fund against the selected benchmark to ensure that it is achieving its objectives.
- **Portfolio rebalancing** – following on from the performance review we should consider whether there is any need to update the agreed asset allocations. Care needs to be taken here in respect of the tax liabilities that may arise from the effects of any rebalancing.

The fund management process cannot, however, be thought of as a step by step process that finishes at this stage, rather it is an ongoing process. This review will establish the strategy for the next period and the process will continue.

Throughout this process there are, however, a number of considerations that must be kept in mind in carrying out this fund management process. These include

- Should the fund management be conducted on an active or a passive basis?
- Should fund management be conducted top-down or bottom-up?
- Should the fund manager be conducting a value or growth style of management?

3.3 Active versus passive

Learning objective

22.2.2 Distinguish between active and passive fund management and explain the costs/benefits to the investor.

3.3.1 Introduction

There are two alternative investment management styles that may be adopted.

- Active investment management.
- Passive investment management.

3.3.2 Active

An active investment manager is one who intervenes in the portfolio on a regular basis, attempting to use individual expertise in order to enhance the overall return of the fund. This means the fund manager constantly takes decisions and appraises the value of investments within the portfolio.

Whilst, to many, this may seem the only thing a fund manager could do, it has to be appreciated that in practice there are costs involved with all transactions and hence, a limit on the number of active interventions taking place that is likely to be to the advantage of the fund holder.

Moreover, from a more theoretical point of view, there are a number of theories that indicate that the market itself is efficient and therefore, the prices currently quoted in the market contain within them all available information. If this is so, then the only reason that a price will move is because of information that is not already known to the market and, as such, fund managers buying and selling (switching between stocks) will only make money if they are 'lucky' and switch to the right stock at the right time.

Active fund managers do not believe that the securities markets are continuously efficient. Instead, they believe that markets and securities can be misvalued and that at times, **winners** can be found. They also attempt to correctly **time** their purchase or sale on the basis of specific stock information, market information, economic factors, etc.

Active fund managers may obtain research from external sources such as investment banks. In this instance analysts are referred to as 'sell-side' analysts. Alternatively they may establish an in-house research department, made up of 'buy-side' analysts. The benefit of generating unbiased internal research needs to be weighed against the costs of setting up the department.

3.3.3 Passive

Passive management involves establishing a strategy with the intention of achieving the overall objectives of the fund. Once established, this strategy should require little active intervention, being largely self-maintaining.

There are, however, few perfectly passive strategies. Most such strategies require some intervention in response to the occurrence of events, the publication of information, or market/stock movements that have occurred. Passive management does not attempt to beat the market, it follows the market.

Passive portfolio management is consistent with two conditions being satisfied in the securities market: efficiency and homogeneity of expectations. If securities markets are efficient, then securities will be fairly priced at all times. There will be no mispriced securities and hence, no incentive to actively trade. Similarly, if securities markets are characterised by investors who have homogeneous expectations of risks and returns then, again, there is no incentive to trade actively.

3.3.4 Hybrids

Increasingly, fund managers are being requested to outperform indexes, rather than merely track them, and this inevitably requires a less passive, more interventionist approach, potentially with an **indexed core fund** and a **peripheral** or **satellite fund** (which is more actively managed and potentially involves the use of derivatives in order to establish larger trading positions than the fund itself can obtain). The regulator of collective investment schemes such as unit trusts, the FSA, has established a number of important rules limiting the extent to which a fund can invest in futures and options.

Alternatively, the fund manager may combine both active and passive fund management methods by **tilting** the fund. That is holding all/a representative sample of the constituents of an index (like a passive tracker fund), but with larger proportions in some areas that he favours and smaller proportions in others, this asset allocation decision constituting the active management component.

3.4 Top-down versus bottom-up

Learning objective

22.2.1 **Distinguish** between a 'top-down' and 'bottom-up' approach to fund management.

Portfolio managers tend to use either a top-down or a bottom-up approach to the investment process.

3.4.1 Top-down approach

The investment manager using a top-down approach first allocates his assets based on the objectives and constraints of the fund and then selects individual securities to satisfy that allocation. The most important decision in this approach is the choice of markets and currencies. Once these choices have been made, the manager then selects the best securities available.

3.4.2 Bottom-up approach

The manager using a bottom-up approach studies the fundamentals of many individual stocks and constructs a portfolio from the ones he considers best satisfy the fund's objectives and constraints. The product of this approach is a portfolio with a market and currency allocation that is more or less the random result of the securities selected. This approach is appropriate when the manager is more concerned with risk exposure in various sectors than with either market or currency risk exposure.

3.4.3 Consequences of the choice of approach

The approach adopted will have an impact upon the organisation of the department. A research department using a top-down approach focuses on country and currency analysis primarily. Such a department will therefore be specialised by country. Financial analysts using the bottom-up approach are specialised by worldwide industry sector.

Empirical evidence has shown that all securities within a single market tend to move together, but national markets and currencies do not. This appears to demonstrate that the major factor contributing to portfolio performance is the choice of markets and currencies (asset allocation), not the individual securities (stock selection). This, in turn, suggests that an investment organisation should be organised along primarily top-down lines with its analysts specialised by country, with possibly a few international sectors such as oil stocks.

Where a top-down approach is adopted, investment management involves three activities.

- Asset allocation.
- Market timing.
- Stock selection.

This top-down approach is the one we concentrate on below since it is drawn directly from a consideration of the clients' objectives and circumstances

3.5 Management style

Learning objective

22.2.4 Explain the major investment styles prevalent in the fund management industry (including socially responsible investing – SRI / environmental social governance investing ESGI).

Management style relates to the idea that investors have different views about key determinants of stock price movements, resulting in different fund managers holding different portfolios in terms of investment characteristics. The various views can be categorised into distinct classes and portfolios can be grouped in the same way.

There are two major classes of style that illustrate the above idea.

- Growth investors.
- Value investors.

There are also two other management styles, market orientation and small capitalisation, that are discussed below.

3.5.1 Growth investors

When looking at a price to earnings ratio, the growth investor is primarily concerned with the earnings. If he believes that the earnings will grow substantially, then he will buy the stock.

Assuming that the P/E ratio stays constant, this will give rise to growth in the stock price.

Growth styles

As noted above, growth investors focus on companies with higher growth prospects for earnings. As a result, they often will have to buy a stock on a relatively high P/E multiple, reflecting the company's strong fundamentals. However, they are trying to identify companies where the growth prospects are not fully reflected in the price so far.

Other characteristics of growth investors are as follows.

- Invest in high quality companies.
- Focus on consumer, service, healthcare and technology.
- Little interest in cyclical and defensive stocks.

The growth style can be sub-analysed into two sub-styles, as follows.

- **Consistent growth** – Where the investor concentrates on high quality companies with a consistent record of growth.
- **Earnings momentum** – Where the investor concentrates on companies with more volatile but above average growth rates.

3.5.2 Value investors

In contrast, value investors are less concerned with future growth in earnings. Instead, they focus on whether the existing price of the company looks cheap on the basis of some comparison, such as price to book or price to earnings.

The value investor will buy the cheap stock, in the expectation that the price will move to a more normal level in the future.

In other words, the value investor expects the P/E ratio to increase even if the earnings stay the same, resulting in growth in the stock price.

Value investing is related to contrarian investing in that both are looking for mispriced investments and buying those that appear to be undervalued by the market.

A **contrarian investor** is one who invests in a manner that differs from the consensus view when they believe that consensus view to be incorrect. A contrarian believes that irrationality exists among investors that can lead to mispricings of securities offering the opportunity for gains.

3.5.3 Value styles

Value styles are based around analysing the price of a company. When looking at price, different investors may focus on different comparisons, as follows.

- Low P/E ratios.
- High dividend yield.
- Low price to book ratio.
- Low price to sales ratio.

Three sub-styles of the value style can be identified.

- **Low P/E** – Where investors concentrate on companies with low prices compared to earnings. Such companies are often cyclical or defensive and may be in an unfashionable industry.
- **Contrarian** – Where investors concentrate on companies with low price to book values. They will often select cyclical companies with low profits or dividends relative to their asset base. The hope is that the assets will provide a base from which price can rebound. This rebound may be due to cyclical factors or be company specific.
- **High yield** – Where investors focus on companies with high yields, since they believe that the companies can maintain or increase their dividend payments. This sub-style is the most conservative, since it is focusing on the ability to maintain dividends.

3.5.4 Market oriented

Market oriented investors are those whose portfolios are closer to the market average than an emphasis on growth or value would suggest.

There are also sub-styles within this category.

- **Value bias** – Where the investor has a tendency towards value stocks but not sufficient to classify him as a value investor, due to his predominant emphasis on the whole market.

- **Growth bias** – Where the investor has a tendency towards growth stocks.
- **Market normal** – Where the investor has a portfolio that is close to the market average in terms of value and growth stocks. Such an investor may shift towards value or growth stocks at any one time, but has no distinct bias one way or the other.

3.5.5 Small capitalisation

This is when the investor concentrates on small companies. The motivation for this is often a belief that such companies are under researched and the investor can therefore find more opportunities for profitable investment through his own research.

Such portfolios have the following typical features.

- Low dividend yields.
- High betas.
- High residual risk.
- Little research done by analysts.

The small capitalisation approach can be analysed into three sub-styles, as follows.

- **Value** – Where the investor concentrates on small companies where the price appears cheap relative to earnings, dividends, assets or sales.
- **Growth** – Where the investor concentrates on small companies with good growth prospects, primarily in consumer, technology and health care.
- **Market oriented** – Where the investor concentrates on small companies that are similar to the overall small capitalisation market.

3.6 Socially responsible investing

Learning objective	22.2.4 **Explain** the major investment styles prevalent in the fund management industry (including socially responsible investing – SRI / environmental social governance investing ESGI).

Socially Responsible Investing (SRI), also known as environmental social governance investing (ESGI), is a term used to describe an investment approach that integrates personal values and social concerns into the investment decision-making process.

Socially responsible investment allows the investor to bring together his values and beliefs with his financial requirements. This allows an investment to be made, for profit, but with principles.

Environmental social governance describes an investment approach that considers environmental issues of sustainability, climate change, carbon footprint, energy efficiency, waste disposal etc.

There are four basic strategies that can be applied by ethical or socially responsible funds when selecting investments for their portfolios:

- **Screening** – The inclusion (**positive screening**) or exclusion (**negative screening**) of investment based on ethical or social reasons. Negative screening looks **to** filter out investments with an unacceptable ethical or social performance, positive screening aims to identify investments with a superior ethical/social stance.
- **Positive or active engagement** – Identifying investments that could improve their ethical, social or environmental behaviour and encouraging them to do so through exercising their shareholder power. The idea is that this form of **shareholder advocacy** will then assist the company in improving their social and environmental performance.

The idea of **engagement** goes beyond mere selection criteria and involves an active process of shareholder activism and lobbying, by investors or institutional fund managers. A fund manager with a substantial stake in a company may be in a position to enter into dialogue with the company in an attempt to encourage the company to pay attention to ethical and SRI objectives where there is a good business case for them, and improved corporate reporting.

- **Best of class** – Rating investments in the same sector based on ethical, social or environmental issues with the fund manager biasing his selection based on this '**best in class**'.
- **Thematic investment** – Where key themes (eg pollution, education) are used to identify investment opportunities that are seeking to improve the ethical and social wellbeing of the world.

4 Strategic Asset Allocation

Learning objective

22.2.3 **Distinguish** between strategic and tactical asset allocation.

4.1 Introduction

Assuming that a top-down approach has been applied, the first stage in the investment management process will be the strategic asset allocation decision.

Strategic asset allocation is the allocation of the funds available between these various instruments or financial markets. At the asset allocation stage, the fund manager decides what proportion of the total portfolio to invest in broad asset categories such as shares, bonds, property, etc. Where a technical or quantitative analysis system has been used, this system may suggest the appropriate asset allocation.

Despite the existence of these techniques, all fund managers require knowledge of asset allocation according to more fundamental principles. This is perhaps the most subjective area of fund management, and one where there will never be a single correct answer. Given the same fund and client, it is unlikely that any two fund managers would produce exactly the same asset allocation and make exactly the same investment decisions. However, it would be reasonable to assume that any allocations would have a broadly similar effect. The justification for this last statement is that the fund manager has a legal and professional duty to base the asset allocation on the client's wishes with particular regard to the criteria discussed above, when identifying the client's objectives, specifically

- Matching liabilities.
- Meeting any ethical considerations.
- Remaining within risk tolerances.
- Maximising fund performance.

There are three basic rules the fund manager should bear in mind when trying to satisfy the client's investment objectives.

- The fund manager should take every step to **diversify risk**, a process requiring an understanding of the different risk factors affecting all the investments in which he may be investing as well as the impact of foreign exchange.
- The fund manager should be aware that the best way to match the client's liabilities if they are fixed in money terms is by investing in bonds (or similar nominal returning assets), since this will generate cash flows from interest and redemption proceeds, which will allow the liabilities to be met as they arise.
- Asset allocation is effectively a compromise between matching investments to client liabilities and investing assets in more attractive markets in order to maximise fund performance.

4.2 Approach

The optimal asset allocation should be based on the objectives and constraints of the fund and the fund manager's estimate of the risks and returns offered by the various securities.

The idea is that the objectives and constraints of a fund direct the investment manager towards certain asset classes and away from others, leading towards the asset allocation decision. For example, if real liabilities are to be met, these must be matched by real assets (equities/property/index-linked bonds), or if high liquidity is needed, then property is inappropriate.

As an illustration of this, we consider in the table below the various constraints for common liability matching funds and a potential resultant asset allocation.

Tutor tip

This is a regularly examined area, especially the aspect of risk.

Constraint	Young Pension Fund	Mature Pension Fund	Life Assurance Fund	General Insurance Fund
Time	Long-term	Short-term	Long-term	Short-term
Liability	Real	Real	Nominal	Nominal
Liquidity	Very low	High	Low	Very high
Risk tolerance	High	Low	Medium/High	Very low
Tax status	Gross fund, no tax on income or gains*	Gross fund, no tax on income or gains*	Tax on income and gains	Tax on income and gains
Asset Allocation				
Equities	60% - 80%	20% - 30%	55% - 65%	0%
Property	5% - 10%	0% (illiquid)	0% - 5%	0%
Bonds	15% - 25%	55% - 65%	15% - 30%	} 100%
Cash	0% - 5%	15% - 25%	5% - 15%	

* Pension funds are no longer able to recover the 10% tax credit on dividend distributions.

The asset allocation decision is extremely important, since it dominates the performance of most portfolios. As we have already noted, this is because returns on securities within each asset category are usually highly correlated, i.e. they generally rise or fall together. This implies that selecting the best performing asset category is more important for performance than selecting the best performing securities within each asset category.

A fund manager should also be aware of the restrictions placed on them by the trustees, as these may mean that they are not completely free in making their asset allocation decisions.

4.3 Diversification

Learning objectives

18.12.1 Identify the correlation between the various asset classes (equity, fixed interest, property, cash, alternative investments) and explain its relevance to asset allocation.

18.12.2 Explain the limitations of correlation analysis in extreme market conditions.

18.13.1 Explain the relationship between pricing, liquidity and fair value for the asset classes of equity, fixed interest, property, cash and alternative investments.

Due to the large number of investments that are liable to be held within any portfolio and the complex interrelationships between them, the economy, etc. computerised portfolio optimisation techniques are frequently used to establish measures such as portfolio yield, total risk (both systematic and unsystematic components), maximum and minimum stock numbers, maximum levels in any one stock, etc. These techniques all tend to be based on diversification ideas, requiring the calculation and input of appropriate measures such as standard deviations and correlation.

4.3.1 Types of diversification

Two types of diversification can be distinguished:

- **Diversification by asset class.** This is achieved by holding a combination of different kinds of asset within a portfolio, possibly spread across: cash, fixed interest securities, equity investments, property-based investments, and other assets.
- **Diversification within asset classes.** An investor can diversify a portfolio by holding a variety of investments within the particular asset types that he holds. This may be achieved by holding various fixed interest securities, by spreading investments across different industry sectors and geographical markets, by holding equities in a number of different companies, and by holding a number of different properties or property-based investments.

4.3.2 Diversification by asset class

As we saw earlier in this Study Text, the greatest diversification benefits arise when we combine securities with low or negative correlations. As a result, diversification between asset classes is the primary route to portfolio risk reduction.

The average correlation coefficients experienced between the major classes of assets over the last ten years are given below.

		Equities			Bonds			Property	Commodity
		Large cap	Mid cap	Small cap	Corp	Gilt	ILG		
Equities	Large cap	1.00	0.78	0.62	0.32	0.21	–0.30	0.84	–0.58
	Mid cap	0.78	1.00	0.90	0.33	0.25	0.11	0.68	–0.40
	Small cap	0.62	0.90	1.00	0.27	0.17	–0.06	0.58	–0.47
Bonds	Corporate bonds	0.32	0.33	0.27	1.00	0.95	–0.41	0.11	–0.26
	Gilts	0.21	0.25	0.17	0.95	1.00	–0.29	0.10	–0.15
	ILGs	–0.30	–0.11	–0.06	–0.41	–0.29	1.00	–0.24	0.67
Property		0.84	0.68	0.58	0.22	0.10	–0.24	1.00	–0.29
Commodities		–0.58	–0.40	–0.47	–0.26	–0.15	0.67	–0.29	1.00

A broadly spread portfolio of equities and bonds should, therefore, be reasonably well diversified and achieve strong risk reduction under normal circumstances.

One limitation of this correlation analysis in determining portfolio risk is that these correlation figures are not static, rather they vary over time. In the extreme market circumstances experienced in the 2008 credit crunch, all of these correlations became more extreme, moving strongly towards either +1 or –1. As a consequence, much of the hoped for risk reduction in many portfolios was not realised and even quite broadly diversified portfolios suffered significant losses.

Another limitation of this analysis is that it takes no account of the **liquidity** of stocks held. Analysis of portfolio risk and return based on individual security returns, risks and correlations assumes that investments can be bought at their **fair value**, ignoring completely any dealing costs and spreads. For large cap stocks or gilts this is probably a reasonable assumption under normal circumstances as they are usually highly liquid.

The liquidity of smaller cap stocks may be much lower and the liquidity of property is very low even in normal circumstances. In more extreme circumstances, however, liquidity in all markets may dry up altogether, making it difficult, if not impossible, to deal at a fair value. In conclusion, more liquid investments are more likely to trade close to fair value, less liquid investments and more difficult market circumstances are likely to result in assets trading some way from their fair values.

4.3.3 Diversification within asset classes

A portfolio that includes a collection of securities will be less exposed to any loss arising from one of the securities.

Using a **spread of shares** across different **sectors** of the market can also reduce risk. In this way there is a reduced concentration of capital in any one sector.

Diversification across different **markets** can also be achieved within an asset class. For example, a portfolio of shares or equity-based collective investments may be spread across different national markets and regions, perhaps with holdings in Asia as well as North America, Europe and the UK. Gaining exposure to particular markets can be relatively difficult – for example, there are currently relatively few investment vehicles providing exposure to China, although new collective investments (such as **exchange-traded funds** or **ETFs**, based on the shares in an index) covering China are now becoming available.

Sometimes a client will have a large holding in one share, perhaps because of an inheritance or as the result of a share option scheme. Such a client should be made aware of the potential risk of such a large holding.

Although different economies and stock markets influence each other, there are differences in how well different regions and national markets perform. Different economies will be at different stages of the **business cycle** than others at any particular time. On the same principle as that of different companies' shares, a **portfolio spread across different markets or regions of the world** will be less exposed to poor performance of a particular economy such as the UK.

5 Market Timing – Tactical Asset Allocation

5.1 Introduction

Strategic asset allocation discussed above is the asset allocation that the fund should operate with in the long term (on average) in order to satisfy its objectives and constraints. The strategic asset allocation is based on long-run estimates of capital market conditions; it ignores short-term fluctuations on the premise that markets are efficient in the long term. As such, the strategic asset allocation is inherently based on the Efficient Market Hypothesis.

Market timing (or tactical asset allocation) involves the short-term variation of the asset allocation of the fund in order to take advantage of market changes or fluctuations. Market timing implies that asset classes are mispriced and looks to take advantage of this mispricing in order to enhance returns. As such, market timing assumes that markets are not efficient in the short term and may overreact to information.

Market timing is the variation of the asset allocation of the fund in anticipation of market movements. It involves adjusting the sensitivity of the portfolio to anticipated market changes. A fund manager engages in market timing when he does not agree with the consensus about the market, i.e. he is more bullish or more bearish than the market, and rebalances his portfolio to take advantage of this view.

In determining the strategic asset allocation it is normal to specify a range of values the fund can move from the strategic allocation, eg the tactical asset allocation limits may be that we can vary up or down by 4% from the strategic limits. The scale of any permitted variation is usually linked to the liquidity and transaction costs of the asset class, more liquid and lower transaction cost assets being allowed a greater degree of flexibility.

The approach to market timing is to adjust the β/duration of the portfolio over time. If the fund manager is relatively bullish, he wants to increase the β/duration of the portfolio, i.e. make it more aggressive. If, on the other hand, the fund manager is more bearish, he will want to reduce the β/duration of the portfolio, making it more defensive.

One way of achieving this result would be to buy high β shares or high duration bonds in a bull market and sell them in a bear market. However, the transaction costs involved would make this an expensive strategy. An alternative is to keep the portfolio of risky assets constant and raise or lower the beta or duration through the use of derivative instruments, such as futures and options.

In summary, the action is

- **Falling market** – reduce the sensitivity to the market fall, through
  - Switching from sensitive (high β/duration) stocks to less sensitive (low β/duration) stocks.
  - A derivatives overlay, such as selling futures or buying put options.
- **Rising market** – increase the sensitivity to the market rise, through
  - Switching from insensitive (low β/duration) stocks to more sensitive (high β/duration) stocks.
  - A derivatives overlay, such as buying futures or buying call options (if these are permitted for the fund).

Many fund managers become involved in market timing. For example, pension funds have regular inflows from their clients that the investment manager may decide to

- Invest immediately, in which case the fund will benefit from pound cost averaging, i.e. the purchases are made at both the peaks and troughs throughout the year, hence the fund acquires the investments at the average cost for the year – a passive strategy; or
- Delay his investment (i.e. hold cash as an asset) and time his acquisitions in the hope that it will be the most favourable price – an active strategy.

5.2 Importance of market timing

As noted earlier, studies have shown that the asset allocation decision has a greater effect on performance than stock selection for most funds, especially international funds where the correlations between markets are low.

It follows that achieving the correct strategic allocation, and responding correctly to market movements with an appropriate tactical move should be the primary objective of most fund managers in order to maximise their funds' returns.

6 Stock Selection

6.1 Introduction

Having decided on the overall asset allocation, the fund manager must now select specific securities within each asset category. This is the stock selection decision. The various approaches to stock selection, either active or passive, depend on the specific asset category being considered.

6.2 Active equity selection strategies

6.2.1 Introduction

Stock selection, or **stock picking**, is important whenever the fund managers are prepared to accept the overall consensus for the market as a whole, but believe that certain individual securities are **misvalued**. A good stock picker believes he knows which securities are misvalued. An overpriced security is one that has an expected return that is less than should be expected on a risk-adjusted basis. An underpriced security has an expected return that is more on a risk-adjusted basis than would be expected.

The approaches involved in active stock selection utilise the application of various fundamental, technical or quantitative techniques.

6.2.2 Comparison to the securities market line

In terms of the Capital Asset Pricing Model and the securities market line (SML), a security is said to be mispriced when it does not lie on the SML. A security that lies above the SML is giving a return above what might otherwise be expected and is therefore undervalued. A security that lies below the SML is giving a return that is too low, and the security is overvalued.

The objective of a stock picker is **to pick portfolios of securities that lie above the SML**. The stock picker will attempt to construct portfolios of securities that, in comparison with the market portfolio, have a more than proportionate weighting of the underpriced securities, and correspondingly less than proportionate weighting of overpriced securities.

6.2.3 Use of investment funds

As an alternative to selecting individual stocks for a client, the fund manager may choose to achieve exposure through the use of funds such as OEICs. This would be particularly appropriate if the client's fund was so small that individual stock management would be impractical or uneconomical.

The factors that need to be considered here include

- **Past performance** – though past performance can never guarantee future performance, it may be regarded as an indication of the fund manager's skill when the manager, his approach and his performance have shown some consistency.
- **Fund charges** – within any fund there are typically two types of charge, initial charges and annual management charges. Initial charges are levied on purchase, though these are sometimes replaced by exit charges that are levied if the fund is sold within five years of purchase. Annual management charges are levied each year on the value of the fund. Management charges for actively managed funds may be 1.5% which can have a significant impact on fund performance. Passively managed funds tend to have substantially lower management fees. As a result, actively managed funds need to significantly outperform passive funds in order to offset these higher fees.
- **Financial stability of provider** – a final issue to consider is the financial stability of the provider. It is most likely that the investment is to be held for a number of years and, as noted under past performance above, we will be looking for management consistency which, in turn, is related to the stability of the provider.

6.3 Passive equity selection strategies

6.3.1 Buy and hold

A buy and hold strategy involves buying a portfolio of securities and holding them for a long period of time, with only minor and infrequent adjustments to the portfolio over time. Under this strategy, investments bought now are held indefinitely, or if they have fixed maturities, held until maturity and then replaced with similar ones. The returns from a buy and hold strategy will be dominated by income flows, i.e. dividends and coupons and, for shares, long-term capital growth. Short-term capital movements are irrelevant for this strategy.

Since there is a consensus view when adopting a passive strategy that all securities are fairly priced at all times, it does not really matter which securities are bought and held. However, by buying and holding only a few securities, a substantial amount of diversifiable risk may remain in the portfolio. Hence, a reasonable number of securities must be held within the portfolio.

6.3.2 Indexation

Introduction

A version of buy and hold that eliminates diversifiable risk is **index matching** or **indexation**. Indexation involves the construction of an index fund that is designed to replicate the performance of a market index.

With indexation, the fund manager selects an appropriate index quoted in the market place. Having established the index, the fund manager builds a portfolio that mimics the index, the belief being that this portfolio will then perform in line with the index numbers.

Approaches to indexation

Indexation can be achieved in a number of ways, including

- **Full index replication** – where all of the securities in an index are held in proportion to their index weighting. This should perfectly match index performance (ignoring management fees) but will need rebalancing every time the index changes which may be costly (adversely affecting performance). This approach may be suitable for an index with few shares but would be problematic for larger indices such as the FTSE All-share index.
- **Stratified sampling/optimisation** – as an alternative, a stratified sampling approach may be adopted where a range of shares are selected that closely mirror the performance of the index. This approach will reduce the need for rebalancing when the index changes, but is unlikely to exactly mirror the index performance. Optimisation is a sampling approach designed to minimise intervention (buying and selling) and management fees.
- **Factor matching** – selecting a portfolio of shares that have the same exposure to various economic factors as that of the index, perhaps based on Arbitrage Pricing Theory ideas.

Results of indexation

Unless our portfolio exactly matches the index in all circumstances we will experience a tracking error. The tracking error is the standard deviation of the difference between the returns on the tracking portfolio and the returns on the index being tracked and will be a function of

- Any differences between the constituents of the portfolio and the index
- Any costs experienced by the portfolio that are not a feature of the index

With respect to the first of these points, a portfolio's tracking error will be a function of

- Any differences in the securities held in the portfolio and the index
- Any difference between the security weightings of the portfolio and the index
- Any differences in pricing methodology of the constituents of the portfolio and the index
- The volatility and beta of the portfolio and the index

In an actively managed portfolio where we are comparing returns to a benchmark portfolio rather than an index, further factors influencing the tracking error would be

- Fund size differences between the portfolio and the benchmark
- Investment style differences (eg market timing activity) between the portfolio and the benchmark

On top of this there are also the transaction costs of setting up and periodically rebalancing the portfolio as a result of either the injection of new funds or changes in the constituents of the index or benchmark. Such costs are never a feature of an index, hence underperformance is an almost automatic consequence.

Apart from the transaction costs involved in setting up and rebalancing, there are other problems associated with running an index fund. The most important of these concerns management fees and the treatment of income payments on the securities.

Indexation is, however, a popular form of fund management. It attempts to avoid, as far as possible, decisions about selection and timing of investment. However, it is not purely passive. At the very least, the choice of index and the reinvestment of income involve active intervention.

Indexation is normally used in conjunction with other active methods whereby there is an indexed core fund with actively managed peripheral funds, again with the objective of enhancing the overall return of the fund.

6.4 Active bond selection strategies

Learning objective

22.1.1 Explain the following bond portfolio management techniques: cash matching /dedication; immunisation; contingent immunisation; anomaly switches; policy switches; credit risk management and riding the yield curve.

6.4.1 Introduction

As with shares, a bond portfolio will be actively managed whenever there are misvalued bonds around. Similarly, with asset allocation decisions having been made, active bond portfolio management operates around the activities of security selection and market timing. However, there is a difference between share and bond portfolio managers. Most share managers engage in security selection, whereas most bond managers engage in market timing.

A bond picker will construct a portfolio of bonds that, in comparison with the market portfolio, has less than proportionate weightings in the overpriced bonds and more than proportionate weightings in the underpriced bonds.

A market timer engages in active management when he does not accept the consensus market portfolio and is either more bullish or more bearish than the market. Expectations of interest rate changes are therefore a crucial input into successful market timing. A bond market timer is interested in **adjusting the relative duration** of his portfolio over time. Market timing with bonds is sometimes called duration switching.

If the fund manager is expecting a bull market because he anticipates a fall in the general level of interest rates, he will want to increase the duration of his portfolio by replacing low-duration bonds with high-duration bonds. If the fund manager is expecting a bear market because he is anticipates a rise in the level of interest rates, he will want to reduce the duration of his portfolio.

Active bond portfolio management is generally not as profitable as active share portfolio management. There are several reasons for this.

- There are more shares traded than bonds in the UK.
- The most liquid bonds are UK government bonds that have only certain maturities.
- The volatility of bond prices is generally much lower than that of shares, hence fewer opportunities for substantial mispricing of bonds exist.

- With only a few bonds suitable for active trading, the portfolio consisting of these bonds will be relatively undiversified.

The cost of active bond portfolio management can be reduced using futures and options.

6.4.2 Riding the yield curve

Learning objective	**22.1.2 Calculate** the theoretical gain from riding the yield curve.

Riding the yield curve is a valid strategy when the yield curve is upward sloping. If this is the case, then an investment manager can buy bonds with maturities in excess of his investment horizon. He proceeds to hold the bonds until the end of his investment period and then sells them. **If the yield curve has not shifted during that period**, the investment manager will have generated higher returns than if he had bought bonds with the same maturity as his investment horizon.

This follows because as the time to maturity declines, the yield to maturity falls and the price of the bond rises, thereby generating a capital gain (hence, the term yield curve ride). These gains will be higher than those available if bonds with the same maturity as the investment horizon are used because the maturity value of the latter bonds is fixed.

Example

An investor has a liability due in one year. Two available bonds (both zero coupon) are

Bond	Maturity	Yield %	Price £	
A	1 year	6%	£94.34	$\frac{£100}{1.06}$
B	2 years	7%	£87.34	$\frac{£100}{1.07^2}$

Determine

- The return from a yield curve ride.
- The extra return from a yield curve ride.
- Comment on the risk of the position.

Solution

There are two alternative courses of action.

Alternative 1 – Invest in the One-Year Bond and Hold to Maturity

This is perhaps the most obvious course of action and would give the following.

Return

The return can be determined from the holding period return calculation, i.e.

$$r = \frac{£100.00 - £94.34}{£94.34} = 6\%$$

Alternatively, it can be taken as the yield on the bond of 6%, since the bond is a zero coupon held to maturity.

Risk

Since this is a zero coupon held to maturity, the risk is zero.

Alternative 2 – Invest in the Two-Year Bond and Hold for One Year, Selling as a One-Year Bond (The Yield Curve Ride)

Return

The return can again be determined from the holding period return calculation, though an assumption is required regarding the selling price in one year. If we assume that the yield curve remains static, i.e. that in one year's time, bonds with one year to maturity are yielding 6% and those with two years to maturity are yielding 7%, then we will have

$$r = \frac{£94.34 - £87.34}{£87.34} = 8.01\%$$

Risk

The risk this time is not zero. Here, the investor is exposed to movements in the yield curve.

Conclusion

The yield curve ride is a strategy by which investors take on some risk in order to enhance returns.

6.4.3 Bond switching

Bond portfolio adjustments involve the purchase and sale of bonds, i.e. switching or swapping of bonds. There are two main classes of bond switches.

- Anomaly switches.
- Policy switches.

Anomaly switching

An anomaly switch is a switch between two bonds with very similar characteristics, but whose prices or yields are out of line with each other.

Substitution switching

The simplest example of an anomaly switch is a substitution switch. This involves the temporary exchange of two bonds that are similar in terms of maturity, coupon, quality rating and every other characteristic, but which differ in terms of price and yield. Since two similar bonds should trade at the same price and yield, this circumstance results in an arbitrage profit opportunity with the expensive bond being sold and the cheap bond purchased initially.

If the coupon and maturity of the two bonds are similar, then a substitution swap involves a one-for-one exchange of bonds. However, if there are substantial differences in coupon or maturity, then the duration of the two bonds will differ. This will lead to different responses if the general level of interest rates changes during the life of the switch. It will, therefore, be necessary to weight the switch in such a way that it is hedged from changes in the level of interest rates but is still exposed to changes in the anomalous yield differential between the bonds.

Pure yield pickup switch

Another type of anomaly switch is a pure yield pickup switch. This involves the sale of a bond that has a given yield to maturity and the purchase of a similar bond with a high yield to maturity. With this switch, there is no expectation of any yield or price correction, so no reverse transaction will need to take place at a later date, which may be the case with a substitution switch.

Policy switching

A policy switch is a switch between two dissimilar bonds, which is designed to take advantage of an anticipated change in

- Interest rates.
- Structure of the yield curve.
- Bond quality rating.
- Sector relationships.

Such changes can be expected to lead to a change in the relative prices and yields of the two bonds. Policy switches involve greater expected returns, but also greater potential risks than anomaly switches.

Changes in interest rates

A market timer will always be on the lookout for changes in interest rates. Switching from low-duration to high-duration bonds if interest rates are expected to fall is an example of a policy switch.

Changes in bond quality ratings

A bond whose quality rating is expected to fall will fall in price. To prevent a capital loss, it can be switched for a bond whose quality rating is expected to rise or remain unchanged.

Changes in sector relationships

An example of a change in sector relationships is a change in taxes between two sectors. For example, one sector may have withholding taxes on coupon payments, e.g. domestic bonds, whereas another, e.g. Eurobonds, may not. If it is anticipated that withholding tax will either be applied to all sectors or will be withdrawn from all sectors, then another switch is possible.

6.4.4 Credit risk analysis and management

Credit risk management is not a management approach per-se, rather it is an overlay that may be applied in order to control the risk exposure within a portfolio. We saw earlier in this Study Text that most corporate bonds have credit ratings that may be used to indicate their credit risk and we considered various measures that could be used for credit analysis purposes in respect of individual bonds. The same approach allied with the principles of diversification may be used for a portfolio in order to establish their credit exposure, and in particular

- How probable is it that a default will take place
- How severe will the loss be if there is a default
- When will any default take place (near term/far term)

If the credit exposure is higher than acceptable levels then the fund must either alter its investments or use, say, credit default swaps to bring the portfolio risk down to an acceptable level (at a cost of some of the portfolio return).

6.5 Passive bond selection strategies

arning objective	**22.1.1 Explain** the following bond portfolio management techniques: cash matching /dedication; immunisation; contingent immunisation; anomaly switches; policy switches; credit risk management and riding the yield curve.

6.5.1 Introduction

There are three types of passive strategy suitable for the management of the bond element of the portfolios.

- Immunisation.
- Cash flow matching (also known as dedication).
- Combination matching.

6.5.2 Immunisation

Using immunisation (bond duration matching), it is possible to create a portfolio to have an assured return over a specific time horizon, irrespective of any changes in the interest rate. Hence, if we need to match a liability, we should select a bond portfolio with the same duration as the liability it is intended to meet.

The concept of immunisation

A bond is purchased with a yield of 10%. Interest rates fall to 8%. Consequently, the price of the bond will rise. However, the reinvestment return on the bond will fall, as it is now only possible to reinvest the coupons received at the rate of 8%. As the bond approaches maturity, this fall in the return will become greater as the reinvestment loss outweighs the gain (which will fall as the bond moves to redemption and the price pulls to redemption at par). Overall, the investor will not receive a return of 10% (the yield).

The same is true of the opposite situation where interest rates rise and bond prices fall. Again, the fall in the bond's price will gradually be repaired as the bond approaches maturity and the bond pulls to redemption. The coupons, however, will have been reinvested at a higher rate, therefore generating greater returns. Under this scenario, the overall return from the investment will have outperformed the quoted yield of 10%.

As we saw earlier, the yield is not an effective measure of the anticipated return on a bond if it is held to maturity precisely because it assumes reinvestment at the same rate as the yield.

The concept of **immunisation** relies on the fact that these two effects (price and reinvestment) are balanced at the point of duration, the **weighted average life** of the bond. Therefore, by holding a bond to its duration and not its maturity, the return can be guaranteed.

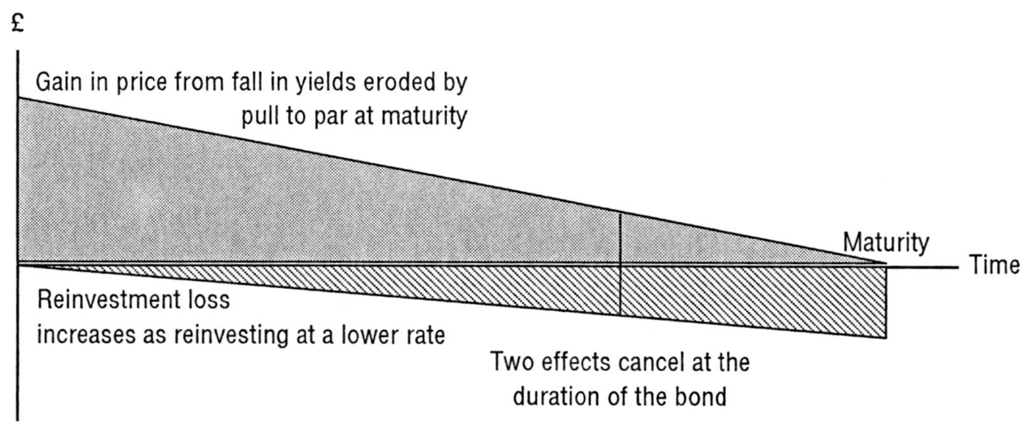

Immunisation is a process whereby the fund manager purchases a bond or portfolio of bonds with a duration equal to the liability. If the manager is able to do this, then it is likely the fund's asset will be close to the liability at the date the liability falls due.

Example

A 13.77% gilt with five years to maturity is currently yielding 10%. Its market value and duration can therefore be shown to be as follows.

Time	Cash Flow £	DF (10%)	PV £	tPV £
1	13.77	0.9091	12.52	12.52
2	13.77	0.8264	11.38	22.76
3	13.77	0.7513	10.35	31.04
4	13.77	0.6830	9.40	37.62
5	113.77	0.6209	70.64	353.22
			£114.29	£457.16

Market value = £114.29

$$\text{Duration} = \frac{£457.16}{£114.29} = 4 \text{ years}$$

If this bond is held for four years (its duration) with income reinvested, the value of the fund at the end of that time (its terminal value) for three possible interest rates (9%, 10% and 11%) will be

Time	Cash Flow	Comp. Fact. (9%)	Terminal Value (9%)	Comp. Fact. (10%)	Terminal Value (10%)	Comp. Fact. (11%)	Terminal Value (11%)
1	13.77	1.09^3	17.83	1.10^3	18.33	1.11^3	18.83
2	13.77	1.09^2	16.36	1.10^2	16.66	1.11^2	16.97
3	13.77	1.09^1	15.01	1.10^1	15.15	1.11^1	15.28
4	13.77	1.00	13.77	1.00	13.77	1.00	13.77
5	113.77	$\frac{1}{1.09}$	104.38	$\frac{1}{1.10}$	103.44	$\frac{1}{1.11}$	102.50
			£167.35		£167.35		£167.35

Hence, whatever happens to reinvestment rates, the fund value at four years will always be £167.35, and the yield will have been

$$\text{Yield} = \sqrt[4]{\frac{167.35}{114.29}} - 1 = 10\%$$

equal to the original yield on the bond. By holding a bond for its duration, it is possible to lock in the initial yield to maturity.

Immunisation of bond portfolio

rning objectives	**22.1.3 Calculate** duration for a bond portfolio. **22.1.4 Explain** the benefits and risks of using barbell and bond portfolio strategies.

The same principles apply to portfolios of bonds. The duration of a portfolio of bonds is simply the weighted average of the durations of individual bonds (weighting by values).

It is possible to construct a portfolio with the specified duration from a whole range of bonds with different durations. For example, a portfolio could be constructed from bonds with durations close to that of the liabilities, this would be a **focused or bullet portfolio**. Alternatively, it could be constructed from bonds with durations distant from that of the liability, a **barbell** portfolio.

Portfolio Duration

Barbell

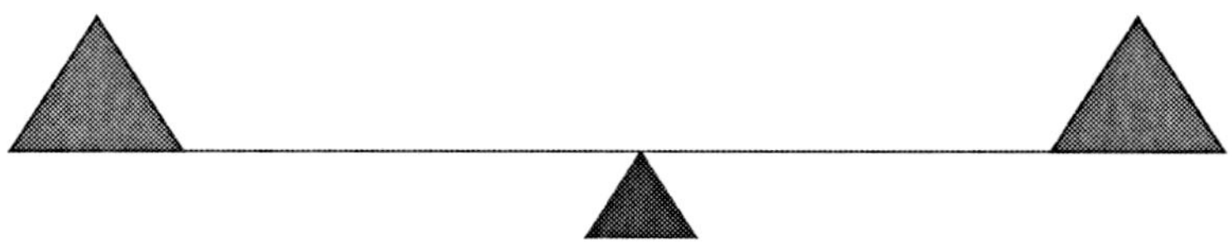

Bullet

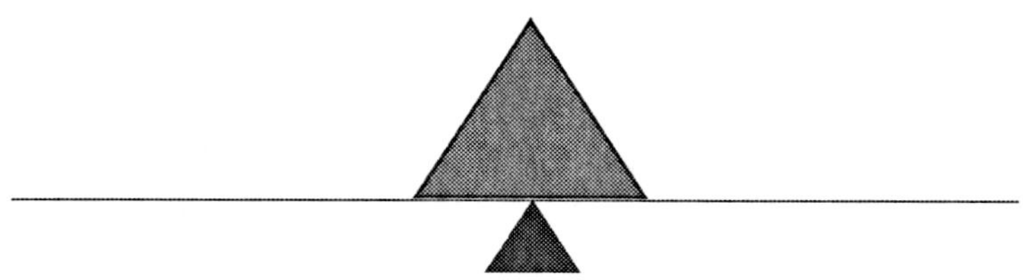

Example

A fund has a liability due in ten years and a set of bonds with durations of 4, 9, 11 and 15 years.

A focused or bullet portfolio would contain the nine and eleven-year duration bonds in equal proportions giving a portfolio of duration

$$(0.50 \times 9) + (0.50 \times 11) = 10 \text{ years}$$

A barbell portfolio would consist of the four and fifteen-year duration bonds with 45.5% of the fund invested in the shorter dated bond and 54.5% in the longer duration bond, giving a portfolio duration of

$$(0.455 \times 4) + (0.545 \times 15) = 10 \text{ years}$$

The advantage of the barbell strategy is that a much wider range of portfolios with different durations can be constructed compared with the focused strategy. However, the disadvantage of the barbell strategy is that it has greater immunisation risk than the focused strategy.

Immunisation risk

Immunisation risk arises whenever there is a **non-parallel shift in the yield curve**. The above example of immunisation showed that it works for parallel shifts in the yield curve, i.e. the reinvestment rate fell from 10% to 9% for each coupon. If this does not happen, then matching the duration of the investment to the liability horizon no longer guarantees immunisation. Non-parallel shifts in the yield curve will lead to the income component and the capital component changing in value by differing amounts.

Immunisation will also only avoid risk completely if there is a flat yield curve, as the example above illustrates.

This risk is reduced if the durations of the individual bonds in the immunising portfolio are close to that of the liability, i.e. a bullet portfolio. In this case, the non-parallel yield curve shift will affect the individual bonds and the liability in similar ways. This is unlikely to be the case if a barbell portfolio had been constructed, since the individual bonds within the portfolio would be affected in different ways.

Rebalancing

Immunisation is not a completely passive approach to investment management because the portfolio will require a continual **rebalancing**. The initial bonds are selected on the grounds of their portfolios' duration, but because duration erodes over time and due to the effects of immunisation risk, new bonds will have to be purchased in order to match the liability.

One possible way around this is to immunise the portfolio using **zero-coupon bonds, as they have a duration equal to their time to maturity**. The advantage of zero-coupon bonds would be that their duration will change in line with time and, therefore, the portfolio will not require a constant rebalancing. However, without the existence of a strips market, there are unlikely to be the stocks that are required as straight zeros.

Contingent immunisation

With **contingent immunisation**, the fund manager actively manages the portfolio attempting to enhance returns subject to an absolute **floor rate of return** which the fund must generate. If active management fails to generate the floor level of return, at that stage, the portfolio is immunised, locking in the minimum rate of return. In this way, the liabilities of the fund are insured against risk, guaranteeing that the rate of return will be sufficient to meet the liabilities as and when they mature.

6.5.3 Other problems

Any uncertainty surrounding a bond's cash flows will present a **problem** to the manager wishing to employ immunisation. For instance, **the existence of callable bonds** in the portfolio will render the duration calculation partly dependent on an estimate of when the issuer might call for redemption.

6.5.4 Cash flow matching or dedication

Introduction

Cash flow matching (also referred to as dedication) is a more straightforward approach to investment management. The approach is simply to purchase bonds whose redemption proceeds will meet a liability of the fund as they fall due.

Under the concept of matching, bonds are purchased to exactly match the liabilities of the fund. Starting with the final liability, a bond (Bond 1) is purchased whose final coupon redemption proceeds will extinguish the liability.

Turning next to the penultimate liability, this may be satisfied in part by the coupon flows arising from Bond 1. Any remaining liability can be matched against the redemption value of a second bond (Bond 2).

This process is continued for each liability, ensuring that bonds are purchased whose final coupon redemption values extinguish the net liabilities of the fund as and when they occur.

If we assume that the bonds are held to maturity, then there is no reinvestment risk and also no interest rate risk, and any changes in the yield curve will not have any effect on the cash flow matching process.

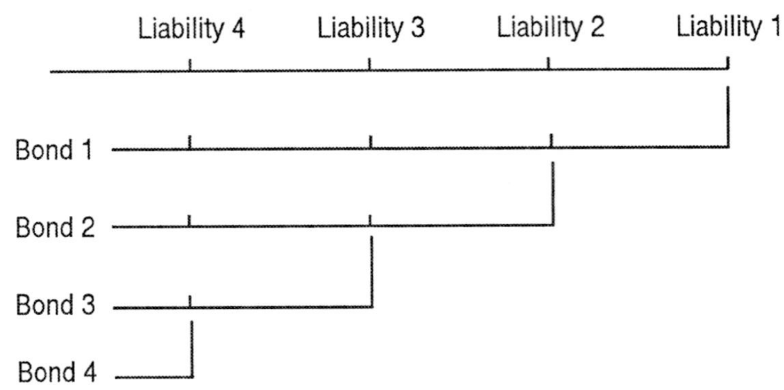

Example

A fund has to meet liabilities of £1,000 arising at the end of each of the next three years. There are three bonds available.

Maturity Years	Coupon %	Redemption Payment, Capital and Coupon £
1	14.29	114.29
2	12.50	112.50
3	11.11	111.11

Construct a portfolio to achieve cash matching.

Solution

Number of Bonds	Coupon £	Maturity (Years)	Cash Flows Year 1 £	Cash Flows Year 2 £	Cash Flows Year 3 £
9	11.11	3	100	100	1,000
8	12.50	2	100	900	–
7	14.29	1	800	–	–
			£1,000	£1,000	£1,000

In effect, this policy is a simple buy and hold strategy and as such does not require a regular rebalancing. Technically, it is inferior to immunisation since, in practice, it is unlikely that bonds exist with appropriate maturity dates and coupons. It involves a greater initial capital outlay but, intuitively, it is easier to understand.

6.5.5 Combination matching or horizon matching

Combination matching is a mixture of the above two approaches to investment management. For example, we could construct a portfolio that cash flow matches the liabilities for the next four quarters but is immunised for the remaining investment horizon. At the end of the four quarters, the portfolio is rebalanced to match cash flow over the subsequent four quarters and is again immunised for the remaining period.

6.6 Mixed management

6.6.1 Introduction

We have considered active and passive strategies separately, but it is possible for fund mangers to use a mixture of the two. For example, the asset allocation decision can be passive, with active security selection. This is known as a security selection style of management. Alternatively, the fund manager may construct a passive portfolio of individual securities but make active allocation decisions. This is known as asset allocation style of management.

6.6.2 Core-satellite portfolio

Another mixed strategy is core-satellite portfolio management. Increasingly, fund managers are being requested to outperform indices rather than merely to track them. This inevitably requires a less passive/more interventionist approach, which could be achieved with an **indexed core fund** and a **peripheral fund**, which is more actively managed and potentially involves the use of derivatives in order to establish larger trading positions than the fund itself can obtain.

This is a management strategy often pursued by very large funds. The fund manager has a large core portfolio that is never traded because doing so would result in adverse market movement. The surrounding satellite portfolios are actively managed in order to generate superior returns.

6.6.3 Portfolio tilting

A fund manager may combine both active and passive fund management methods by **tilting** the fund, that is, holding all/a representative sample of the constituents of an index (like a passive tracker fund) but going slightly overweight in sectors he is bullish about and underweight in others, this asset allocation decision constituting the active management component.

6.6.4 Derivatives

A third type of mixed active-passive strategy involves options and futures. Fund managers may have a passive portfolio of cash market securities that are not traded because of the high transaction costs involved. Instead, the fund managers trade individual stock options. Similarly, they can engage in market timing and shift the beta of their portfolio or the duration of their bond portfolios by buying or selling stock or guilt index options and futures. This is because transaction costs are low and liquidity is generally high in the derivatives markets.

An alternative version of this strategy is using equitised cash portfolios. The entire value of the portfolio is passively held in money market instruments and the active part of the strategy is performed entirely with derivatives.

Chapter Roundup

Objective and funds

- Investment objectives broadly break down into return maximisation and liability matching.
- Investment constraints include time horizons, liabilities, liquidity needs, risk aversion and tolerances, tax status and other preferences and legal constraints.
- Return maximising funds
  - Investment trusts (closed ended).
  - Unit trusts, OEICs, ETFs (open ended).
  - Offshore funds (hedge funds, structured products).

Fund management

- Fundamental analysis focuses on identifying the intrinsic value of a stock using techniques such as discounting future cash flows.
- Technical analysis, also known as chartism, looks at past price movements in trying to establish future performance.
- Strategic asset allocation is the first step in the asset allocation process and is the allocation of funds between various financial markets based on their returns, risks and correlations.
- Market timing involves the short-term variation of the asset allocation in order to take advantage of market changes or fluctuations.
- Stock selection strategies may take a passive approach or an active approach. Passive approaches include buy and take hold strategies and indexation.
- Top down = Strategic asset allocation then stock selection.
- Bottom up = Select stocks first, asset allocation results.
- Active management = Regularly trading within the fund in order to enhance returns.
- Passive = Establish and maintain a policy (assumes market are efficient and hence active trading incurs dealing costs at no benefit).
- Mixed (active + passive) = Core and satellite or portfolio tilting.
- SRI/ESG
  - Negative screening = avoiding certain activities.
  - Positive screening = supporting certain activities.
  - Engagement – enter into dialogue with companies in order to encourage certain behaviour.

Fixed income techniques

- Riding the yield curve = invest in a bond whose term exceeds the term of the liability when there is an upward sloping yield curve in order to enhance returns.
- Anomaly switch = Switching between bonds with similar characteristics in order to take advantage of price anomalies.
- Policy switch = Switching between dissimilar bonds to take advantage of anticipated changes.

- Credit risk management = Analysing a portfolio's credit exposure and altering holdings/using CDSs to achieve on acceptable level of risk.
- Immunisation = Invest in a bond whose duration matches the term of the liability to guarantee the portfolio terminal value irrespective of interest rate movements.
- Contingent Immunisation = actively manage a fund to enhance returns but immune to guarantee the financial value if the return falls below a floor level.
- Cash flow matching = Invest in a bond/bond portfolio whose cash flows exactly match the scale and timing of fund liabilities.
- Immunisation and cash flow matching are both ways of matching future liabilities.

Test Your Knowledge

Check your knowledge of the chapter here, without referring back to the text.

1. What is LDI?

2. Rank the following in order of ascending potential return and risk when used in isolation: ordinary shares, bank deposits, corporate bonds, derivatives

3. A value investor will tend to focus on companies with a low p/e ratio. *True or false?*

4. SRI is:

   A Strategically responsible investing
   B Socially responsible investing
   C Simply reasonable investing
   D Strategically representative investing

5. A young defined benefit pension fund will tend to hold more in the way of equities than a general insurance fund. *True or false?*

6. What is the aim in riding the yield curve?

7. A liability is due in five years. Using immunisation, what duration bond, or weighted duration for a bond portfolio, is required to try and meet this liability?

8. What is a risk when immunising?

9. Name two approaches that combine active and passive management

10. *Without referring back through the chapter make brief notes on the following,*

    (a) Fund objectives and constraints.

    (b) Contrast the approaches of top-down management to bottom-up management

Test Your Knowledge: Answers

1. Liability driven investment involves building a portfolio that meets the future liabilities of a scheme. The starting point is therefore to identify the future liabilities, and then to build a portfolio to meet those requirements.

   (See Section 1.5.1)

2. Bank deposits, corporate bonds, ordinary shares, derivatives

   (See Section 2.2.2)

3. True

   (See Section 3.5.2)

4. B

   (See Section 3.6)

5. True

   (See Sections 4.2)

6. To obtain a higher return by buying longer dated bonds. This strategy only works with an upward sloping yield curve.

   (See Section 6.4.2)

7. Five-year duration.

   (See Section 6.5)

8. Non-parallel shifts in the yield curve.

   (See Section 6.5)

9. Core and Satellite funds and fund tilting.

   (See Section 6.6)

10. (a) Objectives
    - return maximisation
    - match liabilities

    Constraints
    - time
    - liabilities
    - liquidity
    - risk tolerance
    - other, eg SRI

    (See Section 1.2, 1.3)

    (b) Top-down – allocates his assets based on the objectives and constraints of the fund and then selects individual securities to satisfy that allocation

    Bottom-up – select stocks with asset allocation resulting from that selection

    (See Section 3.4)

18 Indices

INTRODUCTION

Indices offer a benchmark of performance for fund managers to measure themselves against. There are a great variety of indices computed and various different ways of constructing them.

We will look at these methods and then focus on the main global and national share indices used when evaluating fund manager performance.

CHAPTER CONTENTS

Chapter Learning Objectives

18 Asset classes

Demonstrate an ability to evaluate the characteristics, inherent risks, behaviour and correlation of asset classes

18.11 Alternative investments

18.11.2 **Identify** the main commodity derivative indices including GSCL, DJAIG and RICI.

18.11.4 **Understand** the role at the Investment Property Databank indices in the market.

26 Statistics and financial mathematics

Demonstrate an ability to apply statistical and financial mathematics techniques

26.4 Index numbers

26.4.1 **Explain** the purpose of an index value.

26.4.2 **Calculate** an index level for the current year, given the base year data and the current year data.

26.4.3 **Explain** the role of financial market indices in fund management.

26.4.4 **Explain** and calculate a price relative for a share.

26.4.5 **Calculate** and interpret a simple arithmetic index.

26.4.6 **Calculate** an index level having re-based the index series.

26.4.7 **Calculate** and interpret a geometric index.

26.4.8 **Calculate** and interpret a market value weighted index.

26.4.9 **Understand** the composition and construction of key global bond and equity market indices.

26.4.10 **Explain** the relevance of free-floating indices.

1 Introduction

Learning objectives

26.4.1 **Explain** the purpose of an index value.

26.4.2 **Calculate** an index level for the current year, given the base year data and the current year data.

1.1 What is an index?

An index is a number that gives the value of something relative to some base value. We have probably all heard of the Retail Price Index (the RPI), which is used as a measure of inflation. It measures prices now relative to those in a base year.

However, indices are also frequently used in relation to stock markets to describe how prices of securities in general have moved over time.

In general terms for any index, a base date is established and ascribed an index value of, say, 100. Subsequent valuations of the items will be carried out and compared to the original base value to establish the revised index value.

There are no rules in relation to the selection of a base date, though it would be more useful if it did not have an extreme or unusual value.

1.1.1 Illustration

If we chose Year 1 below as the base year and set the base index value to 100, we could calculate **price relative** index values using the relationship

Formula to learn

$$\text{Index} = \frac{P_n}{P_0} \times \text{Base index value}$$

Giving the following.

Year	Price £	Index
1	10.00	100
2	10.40	104
3	11.10	111
4	11.50	115
5	12.60	126

1.2 Use of indices

This is the simplest form of index, but it does illustrate the idea. It shows the value for any year relative to the **base year**, enabling us to calculate the **percentage change** relative to the base year or, indeed, between any two years, using

Formula to learn

$$\text{Percentage change} = \frac{\text{Index for later year} - \text{Index for earlier year}}{\text{Index for earlier year}} \times 100\%$$

We could also calculate the **percentage points** movement between any two years which is simply.

Formula to learn

$$\text{Percentage points movement} = \text{Index for later year} - \text{Index for earlier year}$$

NB: These two measures should not be confused, they are different.

Example

What has been the percentage points movement and the percentage change in prices between Years 3 and 5?

Solution

Percentage points movement = 126 – 111 = 15

$$\text{Percentage change} = \frac{126-111}{111} \times 100 = \frac{15}{111} \times 100 = 13.51\%$$

Thus, we would say that prices have increased by 15 **percentage points** over the period, which corresponds to a **percentage change** in prices of 13.51%.

Movements of an index over a period of time can be used by analysts to give an indication of general trends, and also indicate whether the market appears overpriced or underpriced relative to previous years. Clearly, our aim as an investor is to buy cheaply and sell at a higher price. Indices may give us some input into the decision as to when we should buy and sell.

To be useful in this context, however, the index must be comparable over the period being considered, and great efforts must be made to ensure that any index is both **relevant** and **comparable**. If an index is to be used as a performance yardstick against which the performance of a fund is to be assessed, then it must provide a reasonable comparison.

This is particularly important when a client will want to compare the performance of the fund that they are investing in. There are several private client performance indices available, the best known being the WM Performance indices, as well as the FTSE indices.

The WM Performance indices include a series of benchmarks based upon **income** and **growth,** as well as a **balanced fund** index.

In relation to this, in particular, we would need to know how the index deals with the payment of income by a security (dividends for shares and interest for bonds). The normally quoted **FTSE indices** do **not** include dividend income in their evaluation. In contrast, bond indices, e.g. **Salomon Brothers World Government Bond Indices**, most frequently **do** include the value of coupon payments and hence represent **total return indices**.

1.3 Rebasing indices

Learning objective

26.4.6 Calculate an index level having re-based the index series.

Occasionally, indices are rebased, i.e. reset to a new base value. For earlier years' figures to continue to be useful, we will either need to re-evaluate them based on the new base year, or re-evaluate the new index values based on the old base year.

The only time when we can see the connection is in the year when the index is rebased. Looking at that year, we can establish the relationship between the new and old index values. We can then apply the following formula to re-evaluate either index based on the other.

Formula to learn

$$\text{New index value} = \text{Old index value} \times \frac{\text{New index when rebased}}{\text{Old index when rebased}}$$

Example

Based on the following table, calculate

- The old index value for Year 5.
- The new index value for Year 1.

Year	Old Index	New Index
1	100	
2	108	
3	117	100
4		106
5		114

Solution

Old index value for Year 5

Using

$$\text{New index value} = \text{Old index value} \times \frac{\text{New index when rebased}}{\text{Old index when rebased}}$$

gives

$$114 = \text{Old index value} \times \frac{100}{117}$$

hence

$$\text{Old index value} = 114 \times \frac{117}{100} = 133.4$$

New index value for Year 1

Using

$$\text{New index value} = \text{Old index value} \times \frac{\text{New index when rebased}}{\text{Old index when rebased}}$$

gives

$$\text{New index value} = 100 \times \frac{100}{117} = 85.5$$

2 Single Item Index

2.1 Price-relative or unweighted single item index

arning objective	26.4.4 **Explain** and **calculate** a price relative for a share.

If we wished to construct an **index of price changes** for a single item, then we would probably start with a **price-relative** index. A price relative index would simply take the price at the base date (P_0) as the reference price, and measure the current price (P_n) against this. Hence, the index value would be

$$\text{Index} = \frac{P_n}{P_0} \times \text{Base index value}$$

Example

The price of an item at the base date was £36 and its current price is £90. What is the price relative index for this item if the base value was 100?

Solution

$$\text{Index} = \frac{£90}{£36} \times 100 = 250$$

2.2 Weighted single item index

The price relative idea works well when we are considering the change in the price of a particular standard item and while we may be tempted to believe that it can easily be applied in relation to shares, there are a few problems with this.

Example

A share was priced at £1.60 three years ago, when its index was based at 100. Its current price is £2.00. However, there has been a one for four bonus issue in the meantime. What is the index value in relation to this share?

Solution

Price-relative index

If we calculated the price relative index using the above formula, we would get

$$\text{Index} = \frac{200}{160} \times 100 = 125$$

That is a gain of 25%. But does this fairly reflect the return over the period? Consider an individual who held four shares at the start of the period. What return would he have received?

At the start of the period, he held four shares each valued at £1.60 each, a total value of £6.40. At the end of the period, he has five shares valued at £2.00 each, at a total value of £10.00. His investment has increased in value by £3.60 (£10.00 – £6.40), a gain of 56.25% $\left(\frac{3.60}{6.40}\right)$. Clearly, the price relative or unweighted index does not reflect this.

Weighted index

What is missing from the price relative index is the fact that the number of shares held by the investor over the period has increased. In order to deal with this, we need to consider both the price of the share and the number of shares held, i.e. the total value of the shares held. A weighted index will therefore weight the prices by (multiply them by) the number of shares, i.e. the weighted index will be calculated as

Formula to learn

$$\text{Index} = \frac{P_nQ_n}{P_0Q_0} \times \text{Base index value}$$

This gives

$$\text{Index} = \frac{5 \times £2.00}{4 \times £1.60} \times 100 = \frac{£10.00}{£6.40} \times 100 = 156.25$$

The result that we expected.

Hence, weighting an index may provide a more realistic measure or, putting it another way, a price relative measure may be an unrealistic measure.

3 Composite (Multi-Item) Index

3.1 Introduction

The above examples illustrate the ideas, although it is unlikely that we will wish to construct an index to track the changes in the price of a single item. Indices are most frequently used in relation to tracking changes in the prices of a number of items. We therefore need to extend the above ideas to cater for dealing with several items, i.e. producing a composite index.

3.2 Methods of combining indices

3.2.1 Introduction

Whether we are weighting our index or not, we need a way to combine the relative price changes on the individual items to provide the composite index. Broadly, there are two alternative approaches to this, to combine

- Arithmetically
- Geometrically

3.2.2 Arithmetic indices

Learning objective 26.4.5 **Calculate** and **interpret** a simple arithmetic index.

An arithmetic index is calculated using the principle of the arithmetic mean of the selection of prices to be indexed. The arithmetic mean is calculated as

$$\text{Arithmetic mean} = \frac{\text{Sum of prices}}{\text{Number of items}} \text{ or } \frac{\sum P_i}{n}$$

And the arithmetic index can be calculated as

Formula to learn

$$\text{Arithmetic index} = \frac{\text{Arithmetic mean of the current prices}}{\text{Arithmetic mean of the base prices}} \times \text{Base index value}$$

Which, assuming we are considering the same items through time, can be simplified to

$$\text{Arithmetic index} = \frac{\text{Sum of current prices}}{\text{Sum of base prices}} \times \text{Base index value}$$

This may be expressed mathematically as

Formula to learn

$$\text{Arithmetic index} = \frac{\sum Pi_n}{\sum Pi_0} \times \text{Base index value}$$

3.2.3 Geometric indices

Learning objective

26.4.7 **Calculate** and **interpret** a geometric index.

A geometric index is constructed in a similar fashion, using the calculation of the geometric mean of the selection of prices to be indexed. The geometric mean is calculated as

$$\text{Geometric mean} = \sqrt[n]{\text{Product of prices}} \text{ or } \sqrt[n]{x_1 \times x_2 \times x_3 \times \cdots \times x_n}$$

And the geometric index can be calculated as

Formula to learn

$$\text{Geometric index} = \frac{\text{Geometric mean of the current prices}}{\text{Geometric mean of the base prices}} \times \text{Base index value}$$

Which, assuming we are considering the same items through time, can be simplified to

$$\text{Geometric index} = \sqrt[n]{\frac{\text{Product of current values}}{\text{Product of base values}}} \times \text{Base index value}$$

This may be expressed mathematically as

Formula to learn

$$\text{Geometric index} = \sqrt[n]{\frac{P1_n \times P2_n \times P3_n \times \cdots \times Pn_n}{P1_0 \times P2_0 \times P3_0 \times \cdots \times Pn_0}} \times \text{Base index value}$$

3.2.4 Comments

The disadvantage of these methods is that they take no account of the actual quantities of each item held; each item is equally weighted in these calculations.

For example, if a fund invests in the shares of ten companies, holding many shares in each company, the above methods would simply average the ten share prices, taking no account of the numbers of each shares held. It would not, therefore, indicate the value or change in value of the portfolio (Value = Price × Quantity). The method to overcome this would obviously be to weight the prices by relevant quantities, which we consider below.

Considering this share example a little further, of the two alternatives above, the **arithmetic index is the most appropriate alternative for portfolio performance measurement**, since the returns on a portfolio will be the sum of the returns of the individual stocks within the portfolio, not the product.

Indeed, in comparing these two methods, the following comments can be made.

- A geometric index is **unlikely to be representative** of anything that can be achieved (the return on a portfolio is the sum of the constituents, not the product), hence a geometric index is unsuitable as a benchmark.
- A geometric index tends to **understate the performance** relative to an equivalently arithmetic index, since it is less sensitive to large increases in prices and more sensitive to large price falls.

This can be easily seen by considering what would happen to the index if the value of one of the constituents fell to zero. In this case, the arithmetic index would still have a value as long as other constituents had positive values, whereas the geometric index becomes zero regardless of the values of the other terms.

Example

We will illustrate the computation of the relevant indices (assuming a base index value of 100) with the following data, which relates to the calculation of food price inflation rates, although exactly the same approach would be used in relation to share portfolios.

Item	Base		Current	
	P_0 £	Q_0	P_n £	Q_n
A	1.00	22	5.00	8
B	1.20	19	2.40	17
C	1.50	15	2.20	20
D	2.00	10	2.10	21

This example is realistic in relation to inflation because, as we can see that as the price of Commodities A and B have risen dramatically, we have altered our eating habits by substituting more of the other items, C and D. That is, we switch **from** the faster rising products.

Clearly, in relation to a share portfolio, we would be expecting a switch **into** the faster rising shares.

3.3 Price-relative or unweighted composite indices

3.3.1 Arithmetic

The unweighted or price-relative arithmetic index would be calculated as follows.

Formula to learn

$$\text{Unweighted arithmetic index} = \frac{\sum Pi_n}{\sum Pi_0} \times \text{Base index value}$$

Solution

$$\text{Unweighted arithmetic index} = \frac{5.00 + 2.40 + 2.20 + 2.10}{1.00 + 1.20 + 1.50 + 2.00} \times 100$$

$$= \frac{£11.70}{£5.70} \times 100 = 205.3$$

3.3.2 Geometric

An unweighted or price-relative geometric index is calculated as

Formula to learn

$$\text{Unweighted geometric index} = \sqrt[n]{\frac{P1_n \times P2_n \times P3_n \times \cdots \times Pn_n}{P1_0 \times P2_0 \times P3_0 \times \cdots \times Pn_0}} \times \text{Base index value}$$

Solution

$$\text{Unweighted geometric index} = \sqrt[4]{\frac{5.00 \times 2.40 \times 2.20 \times 2.10}{1.00 \times 1.20 \times 1.50 \times 2.00}} \times 100$$

$$= \sqrt[4]{\frac{55.44}{3.60}} \times 100 = 198.1$$

As we can see, the price-relative or unweighted geometric index understates the increase relative to the price-relative arithmetic index.

3.4 Weighted composite indices

3.4.1 Introduction

With regard to weighted indices, there is a question regarding the weighting quantity to use. Should we weight

- By the original quantity for both original and current prices?
- By the current quantity for both original and current prices?
- By the original quantity for original prices and current quantity for current prices?

In relation to arithmetic means, different versions are used for different purposes though the third version is used for investment indices. In relation to geometric means, the third is the only method we need consider.

3.4.2 Weighted arithmetic index

Learning objective

26.4.8 Calculate and **interpret** a market value weighted index.

The date-weighted index weights by the appropriate quantities for the given dates. As such, it calculates the total value of what was actually being considered at that date. The calculation of this index is

Formula to learn

$$\text{Date weighted index} = \frac{\sum P_n Q_n}{\sum P_0 Q_0} \times \text{Base index value}$$

Solution

Item	P_0Q_0 £	P_nQ_n £
A	22.00	40.00
B	22.80	40.80
C	22.50	44.00
D	20.00	44.10
	£87.30	£168.90

$$\text{Weighted index} = \frac{£168.90}{£87.30} \times 100 = 193.5$$

3.4.3 Weighted geometric index

The geometric index works by multiplying together all the constituent items. As a result, if an item appears a number of times, i.e. we are weighting by quantities, it will need to be multiplied in a number of times. Due to the complexity of the calculation it is not in the syllabus for this exam.

4 Benchmark Indices

Learning objective

26.4.3 Explain the role of financial market indices in fund management.

4.1 Introduction

Indices may be used for a variety of reasons. Historically, their purpose was to give an indication of the mood of the market. More frequently now, they are used as a benchmark for performance assessment.

To be appropriate for benchmarking purposes, an index must be indicative of the performance that could realistically have been achieved.

The characteristics that are required to render an index suitable as a benchmark are, therefore, that it is

- Specified and unambiguous.
- Appropriate to the preferences of the fund (e.g. a UK large market capitalisation fund may utilise the FTSE 100 index).
- Appropriate to the currency of the fund.
- Investable, i.e. composed of investments that could conceivably be held in the fund.
- Measurable, i.e. the return can be calculated on a frequent basis as required.
- Representative of achievable performance, i.e. it has an arithmetic weighted composition (remember that the return of a portfolio is an arithmetic weighted average of the individual stock returns).
- Measures the relevant component of performance, i.e. total return indices for total return performance and capital value indices for capital growth.

4.2 Free-float indices

Learning objective

26.4.10 Explain the relevance of free-floating indices.

The idea underlying 'free-float' indices is to ensure that the index satisfies the benchmark requirement of being investable. For example, if only 10% of the shares of a company are available to investors at large, then its index weighting should only reflect this investable proportion rather than the full market capitalisation of the company concerned.

If this were not the case, and a full 100% weighting were given to this security within the index, then there would be significant demand for the few available shares (if only from trackers trying to replicate this weighting from the limited supply available) distorting the price upwards, hence distorting the index.

Most major indices are now prepared on a free-float basis.

4.3 Share and bond indices

Learning objective 26.4.9 **Understand** the composition and construction of key global bond and equity market indices.

4.3.1 Share portfolios

In the UK and worldwide, equity indices developed in the 1960s and there are now a number of universally accepted indices that may be used for share performance evaluation in various countries.

Share indices generally measure the appreciation (or otherwise) of the **capital value** of the relevant shares, taking no account of the income generated. As a result, they will provide a useful benchmark for comparing portfolio capital gains, but not dividend income. To reflect the different sizes of companies in the index the most common construction is arithmetic weighted.

4.3.2 Bond portfolios

Bond indices did not develop in the UK until the 1980s and, unlike share indices, there are no universally accepted indices for evaluation purposes.

Bond indices are generally total return indices that **include both capital gain** and **income reinvested** for bonds with particular characteristics. They are also generally unweighted or price-relative as the level of investment in a bond issue is unlikely to be linked to the size of the issue but is more likely to depend on cash flows, yields and duration.

For UK bond indices, the consideration of the duration primarily dictates which of the available indices is chosen as a benchmark.

4.4 Changes in the constituents of indices

From time to time, it is necessary to replace a share in a share index, perhaps as a result of a closure, merger or takeover, or a bond in a bond index as a result of one reaching maturity or a new bond being issued.

The important point when this occurs is that the index value should **not be altered** by the change. We do not want any discontinuities in the index that will prevent it from being useful.

To avoid this, we need to establish a new divisor (denominator) for the index that will maintain the index value without the old component and with any new component.

Example

Suppose that the earlier price-relative arithmetic index related to four shares and that Share D is to be removed from the index and replaced by Share E, which has a current price of £1.00. The current index must still be 205.3 following the change since the market as a whole has not moved; we have simply changed the constituents of the index.

As a result, we must have

$$205.3 = \frac{5.00 + 2.40 + 2.20 + 1.00}{\text{New divisor}} \times 100$$

Hence

$$\text{New divisor} = \frac{5.00 + 2.40 + 2.20 + 1.00}{205.3} \times 100 = £5.163$$

Originally, we were dividing by the price-relative base date value of £5.70 in calculating the index. Now, we are calculating the index by dividing by £5.163, which is not the base date value of the new constituents.

This type of adjustment is required for all types of index (arithmetic and geometric), the result being that the divisor for any stock index calculation is unlikely to be simply the base value of shares or bonds in the index.

4.5 Changes in the share capital of constituents

If the issued share capital of any of the constituents of an index changes, then this must be dealt with in exactly the same way. When the issued share capital of constituents of an index changes, a new denominator must be calculated based on the new weightings, in order to ensure that the level of the index itself is unaltered by that change.

5 Market Indices

Learning objective

26.4.9 **Understand** the composition and construction of key global bond and equity market indices.

5.1 Stock indices

	Market (Stock Exchange)	Number of Shares	Arithmetic (A) Geometric (G) Weighted (W) Unweighted (U)	Currency	Notes
FT Ordinary Share Index	UK (London)	30	GU	£	
FTSE 100	UK (London)	100	AW	£	Based at 1,000 at 30 December 1983. The FTSE 100 Index represents approximately 70% of the market value of UK listed shares.
FTSE 250	UK (London)	250	AW	£	
FTSE 350	UK (London)	350	AW	£	Combines the FTSE 100 and FTSE 250 shares.
FTSE Small Cap	UK (London)	c. 550	AW	£	All shares in the FTSE all shares index not in the FTSE 350.
FTSE Actuaries All Share	UK (London)	c. 900	AW	£	
FTSE Eurotop 100	UK & Continental Europe	100	AW	€	

	Market (Stock Exchange)	Number of Shares	Arithmetic (A) Geometric (G) Weighted (W) Unweighted (U)	Currency	Notes
FTSE Eurotop 300	UK & Continental Europe	300	AW	€	Calculated by both region and sector.
FTSE APCIMS Private Investor Indices	UK		AW	£	Based on typical private client asset split.
WM Private Client Performance Indicators	UK		AW	£	Various private client indices.
Dow Jones Industrial Average	US (New York)	30	AU	$	Possibly the most widely quoted US index.
Standard and Poor's 500	US (New York)	500	AW	$	
CAC 40	France (Paris)	40	AW	€	
Nikkei 225	Japan (Tokyo)	225	AU	¥	
Nikkei 300	Japan (Tokyo)	300	AW	¥	
Hang Seng	Hong Kong	33	AW	HK$	
DAX	Germany (Frankfurt)	30	AW	€	

Tutor tip

The most commonly examined aspects are the composition (most are AW though there are three exemptions) and the country/currency.

5.2 Bond indices

As for equity markets, there are many bond indices and the table below mentions just a small sample of those published. All are unweighted or price-relative indices.

Index	Market	Currency
FTSE global government bond index	UK, US, Japan, EU countries, Switzerland, Australia, Canada, New Zealand	Currency of country
FTSE corporate bond indices	UK, EU corporates	Currency of country
FTSE Euro emerging markets	Emerging EU markets	€
S&P/BG Cantor US Treasury Bond Index	US T-Bonds	$

Index	Market	Currency
S&P Municipal Bond Index	US Municipals	$
Dow Jones CBOT Treasury Bond index	US T-Bonds	$
Dow Jones Corporate Bond index	US corporates	$
Barclays Capital Aggregate indices	An aggregate index of government and investment grade corporate bonds. Separate indices available for the US, European, Asian and global markets	$
Barclays Capital US Universal index	Global index of $ denominated government, municipal and corporate bonds. The entire universe of all bonds available internationally	$
Barclays Capital US Treasury index	US T-Bonds	$

5.3 Property indices

Learning objective

18.11.4 Understand the role at the investment Property Databank indices in the market.

Many of the major firms of chartered surveyors now produce rental or capital value property indices, in some cases based upon a sample of actual institutional investment performance. In many instances, comparisons are also drawn between performance of property investments against other forms of investment on the basis of these indices. While providing a broad, general, historic trend, these indices may or may not provide a good basis for forecasting future performance. The compilation of indices is beset with many difficulties.

The stock market is an efficient market producing reliable and regular data upon which to base an index of investment performance such as the FTA All Share Index. With its inefficiencies and heterogeneity, the property market is completely different. If a hypothetical portfolio of properties is to be formed and used as the basis for an index, the problem is: Which types of property should be included and what weighting should be used between them?

The FTA Index includes all shares weighted by their market values. When there are problems in establishing a true market value, as with certain properties, such an index will be difficult to establish.

In addition to the issues of establishing the properties in a property index we also have the issue of costs that may distort the index returns. Transaction costs in equity markets are relatively small, however in property markets the transaction costs are significantly larger in relative terms. We would, therefore, expect a portfolio with regular transactions to underperform a more stable one (all other factors being equal). In addition, any management costs that are deducted from the income by a property fund manager will distort returns, especially where the manager earns performance based fees.

Thus, the imperfections in the market cause a real problem in establishing a valid property index. In addition, an investor cannot hold the basic property portfolio being used for the index, unlike most other indices. Some indices that are available are outlined below.

Investment Property Databank (IPD) UK Monthly/Annual Index

The IPD UK Monthly, Quarterly and Annual Indices are based on roughly 3,300 properties worth £27bn at the end of 2008. The indices analyse total return, income return, capital growth and rental value growth by region and according to type of property (retail, offices, industrial and total) based on portfolio returns and valuations. The indices are value weighted in order to provide a realistic benchmark and are compounded monthly.

FTSE Commercial Property Indices

The FTSE Commercial Property Index Series was launched in 2006 based on the the performance of the FTSEpx Fund, a dedicated Guernsey-listed property unit trust. The fund is invested in a diverse portfolio of UK commercial property investment vehicles with a value of over £16bn in 2007 and the index provides details of capital and total returns for each of three sectors (retail, office and industrial) and in total.

Nationwide and Halifax Building Society Indices

The Nationwide Building Society and the Halifax Building Society produce indices of house prices based on mortgage lending at the approval stage of the mortgage process. Between them, these building societies account for almost 30% of UK mortgage lending.

Royal Institution of Chartered Surveyors

The Royal Institution of Chartered Surveyors (RICS) produces a monthly housing market survey, indicating house price changes both nationally and by region. It also produces a number of quarterly surveys such as the residential lettings survey, indicating trends in residential rents both nationally and by region.

These surveys are constructed from information provided by a national panel of over 300 chartered surveyors. The purpose of these indices is to give a good indication of the general trend of prices and rental values.

5.4 Commodity indices

Learning objective	**18.11.2 Identify** the main commodity derivative indices including GSCL, DJAIG and RICI.

There are a number of commodity index providers covering the three commodity categories that may be used for performance assessment of commodities. These include

- **S&P GSCI (formerly Goldman Sachs Commodities Index (GSCI))** – an arithmetic weighted index of commodity sector returns representing for long-only investment in commodity futures that is broadly diversified across the spectrum of commodities. The weightings are reassessed annually based on the five year moving average of world production values.
- **S&P GSCL (formerly Goldman Sachs Crude Oil Index Spot (GSCL))** – an index of spot crude oil prices.
- **Dow Jones-AIG Commodities Index (DJAIG)** – a weighted index that allows investors to track a diversified range of commodity prices. The weightings are rebalanced annually.
- **Dow Jones-UBS Commodity Index (DJUBSCI)** – a broadly diversified index that allows investors to track commodity futures contracts on physical commodities. The weightings are reassessed based on dollar adjusted production values averaged over a five year period with a minimum weighting of 2% and a maximum of 33%.

- **Rogers International Commodity Index (RICI)** – an index of 35 commodities from 11 exchanges, playing a significant role in worldwide (developed and developing countries) consumption. This index is broken down into three sub-indices

  – Agriculture
  – Energy
  – Metals

  and includes any commodity that has a 'significant' role in global consumption as assessed through imports/exports.

- **Thomson Reuters/Jefferies CRB index** – This was originally correlated in 1957 as the **Commodity Research Bureau (CRB)** index. It is an unweighted (or equally weighted) geometric index of 19 categories of commodities from 19 different futures markets.

Chapter Roundup

Indices

- An index is a number that gives the value of something relative to some base value.
- Indices may be used for a variety of reasons including as a benchmark for performance assessment. They may also be used for measuring inflation, the RPI and CPI being two such indices.
- Indices may be weighted or unweighted/price-relative, and calculated on an arithmetic or a geometric basis.

Arithmetic indices

- General calculation

  $$\text{Arithmetic index} = \frac{\text{Sum of current values}}{\text{Sum of base values}} \times \text{Base index value}$$

- Price-relative/unweighted – distorted by movements in highest priced item
  - Single item

    $$\text{Index} = \frac{P_n}{P_0} \times \text{Base index value}$$

  - Composite index

    $$\text{Price-relative arithmetic index} = \frac{\sum Pi_n}{\sum Pi_0} \times \text{Base value}$$

- Weighted – distorted by movements in highest value item
  - Single item

    $$\text{Index} = \frac{P_n Q_n}{P_0 Q_0} \times \text{Base index value}$$

  - Composite index
  - $$\text{Weighted index} = \frac{\sum P_n Q_n}{\sum P_0 Q_0} \times \text{Base value}$$

Geometric indices

- General Calculation

  $$\text{Geometric index} = \sqrt[n]{\frac{\text{Product of current values}}{\text{Product of base values}}} \times \text{Base index value}$$

- Unweighted/price-weighted

  $$\text{Geometric index} = \sqrt[n]{\frac{P1_n \times P2_n \times P3_n \times \cdots \times Pn_n}{P1_0 \times P2_0 \times P3_0 \times \cdots \times Pn_0}} \times \text{Base index value}$$

- Geometric index understates arithmetic index

Market indices

- The majority of indices are arithmetically calculated and weighted, the exceptions are
  - FT ordinary share index = Geometric unweighted, 30 stocks.
  - Dow Jones.
  - Nikkei 225 = Arithmetic unweighted.
- Benchmark index for performance appraisal must be
  - Specified and unambiguous.
  - Appropriate for fund preferences, assets and currencies.
  - Investible, hence the need for free-float indices.
  - Measurable.
  - Representative of achievable performance, ie have an arithmetic weighted composition.
- The FTSE 100, FTSE 250 and FTSE All Share are all indices used by fund managers managing UK equity portfolios.
- Bond indices are usually total return indices, share indices are usually capital value indices.

TEST YOUR KNOWLEDGE

Check your knowledge of the chapter here, without referring back to the text.

1. What is the formula for rebasing an index?

2. Based on the following information

1980	100	
1981	110	
2004	580	100
2005		106
2006		115

(a) What is the old index value for 2006 (to the nearest whole number)?
(b) What is the new index value for 1981?

3. Based on the following information

	Base		Current	
	Po £	Qo	Pn £	Qn
I	2.00	16	5.00	12
II	2.40	14	4.00	14
III	2.80	12	4.60	12
IV	3.20	10	5.40	14

An index value of 1000 was set in the base year for this selection.

(a) What is the current unweighted arithmetic index?
(b) What is the current unweighted geometric index?
(c) What is the weighted arithmetic index?

4. A firm reviews its input costs over a ten-year period and decides to construct price indices to reflect the price changes. The information concerning prices and quantities used of the three main inputs are given below.

	Original		Current	
Input	**Quantity**	**Price per Unit (£)**	**Quantity**	**Price per Unit (£)**
I	500	10	700	5
II	750	15	600	20
III	1,000	10	900	15

What is the unweighted and weighted change in the price of inputs over the period?

5. An analyst wishes to construct a price index of four key inputs used by a large manufacturing company over a period. The table shows the average prices and the quantities of the inputs used.

Input	Price	Quantity	Price	Quantity
A	£7	80	£11	120
B	£3	70	£4	60
C	£9	90	£11	10
D	£3	70	£7	100

What is the unweighted and weighted change in price of inputs?

6. An investor has a small portfolio of four stocks which he has held (in different quantities). Calculate the unweighted and date weighted price changes for this portfolio given the following information.

Share	Acquisition Price (pence)	Number of Shares	Current Price (pence)	Number of Shares
A	28	250	51	300
B	71	100	60	0
C	54	200	120	400
D	92	300	150	400

7. From the following share price information calculate

(a) A value weighted arithmetic index.
(b) An unweighted arithmetic index.
(c) An unweighted geometric index.

Share	Prices (pence)		No of Shares
	Original	Current	in Issue
A	100	150	3,000
B	200	250	4,000
C	300	240	5,000

8. Name an index that may be used for measuring the performance of a portfolio of US government bonds.

9. What are the characteristics required for an index to be a suitable benchmark?

10. How many stocks are there in the Dow Jones index?

TEST YOUR KNOWLEDGE: ANSWERS

1. New index value = Old index value $\times \left(\frac{\text{New index when rebased}}{\text{Old index when rebased}}\right)$

(See Section 1.3)

2. (a) Old index value = $115 \times \frac{580}{100}$ = 667

(b) New index value = $110 \times \frac{100}{580}$ = 18.9655

(See Section 1.3)

3. (a) Unweighted arithmetic index = $\left(\frac{5.00+4.00+4.60+5.40}{2.00+2.40+2.80+3.20}\right) \times 1000$ =1827

(b) Unweighted geometric index = $\sqrt[4]{\frac{500}{2.00}\times\frac{4.00}{2.40}\times\frac{4.60}{2.80}\times\frac{5.40}{3.20}} \times 1000$ = 1844

	Q_0	P_0	Q_n	P_n	P_0Q_0	P_nQ_n
I	16	2.00	12	5.00	32.00	60.00
II	14	2.40	14	4.00	33.60	56.00
III	12	2.80	12	4.60	33.60	55.20
IV	10	3.20	14	5.40	32.00	75.60
					131.20	246.80

$$\text{Weighted index} = \frac{\sum P_nQ_n}{\sum P_0Q_0} \times \text{Base value} = \frac{246.80}{131.20} \times 1{,}000 = 1.8811 \times 1{,}000 = 1881.1$$

(See Section 2)

4.

Input	Q_0	P_0 (£)	Q_n	P_n (£)	P_0Q_0 (£)	P_nQ_n (£)
I	500	10	700	5	5,000	3,500
II	750	15	600	20	11,250	12,000
III	1,000	10	900	15	10,000	13,500
		35		40	26,250	29,000

$$\text{Unweighted index} = \frac{\sum p_n}{\sum p_0} = \frac{40}{35} = 1.143$$

an increase of 0.143 or 14.3%

$$\text{Weighted index} = \frac{\sum P_nQ_n}{\sum P_0Q_0} = \frac{29{,}000}{26{,}250} = 1.10476$$

an increase of 0.10476 or 10.476%

(See Sections 3.3 and 3.4)

5.

Item	P_0	Q_0	P_n	Q_n	P_0Q_0	P_nQ_n
A	7	80	11	120	560	1,320
B	3	70	4	60	210	240
C	9	90	11	10	810	110
D	3	70	7	100	210	700
	22		33		1,790	2,370

Unweighted index = $\frac{\sum p_n}{\sum p_0} = \frac{33}{22} = 1.500$, ie a change of 0.500 or 50.0%

Weighted index $\frac{\sum P_nQ_n}{\sum P_0Q_0} = \frac{2{,}370}{1{,}790}$ = 1.324, ie a change at 0.324 or 32.4%

(See Sections 3.3 and 3.4)

6.

Q_0	P_0	P_n	Q_n	P_0Q_0	P_nQ_n
250	28	51	300	7,000	15,300
100	71	60	–	7,100	0
200	54	120	400	10,800	48,000
300	92	150	400	27,600	60,000
	245	381		52,500	123,300

Unweighted index = $\frac{\sum p_n}{\sum p_0} = \frac{381}{245} = 1.555$, ie a change of 0.555 or 55.5%

Weighted index = $\frac{\sum P_nQ_n}{\sum P_0Q_0} = \frac{123{,}300}{52{,}500}$ = 2.349, ie change of 1.349 or 134.9%

(See Sections 3.3 and 3.4)

7.

Share	No. of Shares (Q)	P_0 (£)	P_n (£)	P_0Q (£)	P_nQ (£)
a	3,000	1	1.5	3,000	4,500
b	4,000	2	2.5	8,000	10,000
c	5,000	3	2.4	15,000	12,000
	12,000	6	6.4	26,000	26,500

(a) Weighted arithmetic index = $\frac{26{,}500}{26{,}000} \times 100 = 101.9$

(b) Unweighted arithmetic index = $\frac{6.4}{6.0} \times 100 = 106.7$

(c) Unweighted geometric index = $\sqrt[3]{\frac{1.5 \times 2.5 \times 2.4}{1.0 \times 2.0 \times 3.0}} \times 100 = 114.5$

(See Section 3)

8. US Treasury Index

(See Section 5.2)

9. Specified, unambiguous, investable, measurable and representative

   (See Section 4.1)

10. 30

    (See Section 5)

19 Performance Measurement and Appraisal

INTRODUCTION

It is important to be able to measure a manager's investment performance periodically. Time weighted return calculations are the most commonly undertaken when measuring a fund managers performance.

Various risk adjusted performance measures exist such as the Sharpe measure and the Jensen Measure. These are used to evaluate whether a fund manager has achieved a suitable risk adjusted return.

CHAPTER CONTENTS

Chapter Learning Objectives

23 Investment performance measurement

Demonstrate an understanding of the principles of investment performance measurement

23.1 Total return and its components

23.1.1 **Explain** the importance of returns analysis in the portfolio management process.

23.1.2 **Identify** the components of total return for a bond or equity portfolio.

23.1.3 **Calculate** the income, capital and total return over a single period for an equity or bond portfolio.

23.1.4 **Calculate** the reinvestment return on income over a specified investment horizon.

23.1.5 **Explain** how returns are decomposed for different asset classes such as equities (sector/stock interaction effect) and fixed income (shift/twist/spread return).

23.2 Money weighted and time weighted returns

23.2.1 **Identify** the data requirements to calculate a

- Money weighted return.
- Time weighted return.

23.2.2 **Calculate** respectively, from such data, the

- Money weighted return.
- Time weighted return.

23.2.3 **Interpret** time-weighted and money-weighted returns.

23.3 Choosing a benchmark, comparisons with investment objectives, base portfolio, indices

23.3.1 **Explain** the purpose of benchmarking.

23.3.2 **Identify** the characteristics of an appropriate benchmark.

23.3.3 **Identify** the key types of benchmark used in the investment management industry.

23.3.4 **Explain** how to construct a benchmark portfolio comprising global equities.

23.4 Performance measurement including risk adjusted returns

23.4.1 **Explain** the importance of risk analysis in performance evaluation.

23.4.2 **Explain** and interpret the following risk adjusted measures of return.

- The Sharpe measure.
- The Treynor measure.
- The information ratio.
- Jensen's alpha.

23.4.3 **Calculate** the Sharpe, Treynor, information ratio and Jensen measure.

23.4.4 **Explain** how total return can be decomposed into the following.

- Risk-free return.
- Return due to choice of benchmark.
- Return due to market timing.
- Return to diversifiable risk.
- Pure selectivity.

1 Introduction

Learning objective

23.1.1 Explain the importance of returns analysis in the portfolio management process.

An investor who has been paying someone to actively manage their portfolio will clearly wish to monitor how well the fund manager is doing his job. Such information can then be used to

- Alter or update the portfolio investment constraints in order to achieve a particular objective.
- Communicate investment objectives to the fund manager, which should affect how the fund is managed.
- Identify strengths and weaknesses of particular fund managers.

When measuring a fund's performance we have three objectives to establish.

- What was the performance achieved? We need to be able to **measure performance**.
- Was the fund performance relatively good or bad? We need to be able to **appraise performance**.
- Did this situation arise due to skill (or lack thereof) or just fortune? We need to be able to **attribute performance**.

2 Measurement of Returns

2.1 Introduction

In order to reflect all the actions of our fund managers, any performance measures must include both income (dividends or coupons) and capital growth. As such, we must always be looking at the market values of any securities held in the fund, as opposed to their historical costs.

2.2 Holding period return

Learning objectives

23.1.2 Identify the components of total return for a bond or equity portfolio.

23.1.3 Calculate the income, capital and total return over a single period for an equity or bond portfolio.

23.1.4 Calculate the reinvestment return on income over a specified investment horizon.

2.2.1 Introduction

Each investment is characterised by a cost and a pattern of cash flows. We could describe a fund's total performance by stating the dividends or coupons plus capital growth (final market value less initial value) as a percentage of the initial amount invested. Alternatively, we could assess the income (dividends/coupon) above as a percentage and the gain as a percentage, decomposing the total return into income and gain.

Example 1

Suppose Investment A costs £100 and at the end of six months, returns £10, before being sold for £110. How can it be compared with Investment B, bought at £50, held for one year and then sold for £70 with no income paid out? Obviously, the different costs must be taken into account, as well as the different returns and time periods involved.

2.2.2 Basic calculation

Calculating the percentage holding period return for each investment avoids the problem of comparing different size investments. This return is simply the total return during the period held (money received less cost) divided by the initial cost, i.e.

Formula to learn

$$r_p = \frac{D_1 + V_1 - V_0}{V_0}$$

where

r_p = holding period return

D_1 = any returns paid out from the investment/fund at the end of the period

V_0 = is the initial cost at the start of the holding period

V_1 = the value of the investment at the end of the holding period

Solution

Using this equation, the holding period returns for Investments A and B along with the income and gain sub-components of that holding period return can be calculated as

Investment A

Total return	Income	Gain
$r_a = \frac{D_1 + V_1 - V_0}{V_0}$	$r_a = \frac{D_1}{V_0}$	$r_a = \frac{V_1 - V_0}{V_0}$
$r_a = \frac{£10 + £110 - £100}{£100} = 0.20$ ie 20% in six months	$r_a = \frac{£10}{£100} = 0.10$ ie 10% income in six months	$r_a = \frac{£110 - 100}{£100} = 0.10$ ie 10% gain in six months

Investment B

Total return	Income	Gain
$r_b = \frac{D_1 + V_1 - V_0}{V_0}$	$r_b = \frac{D_1}{V_0}$	$r_b = \frac{V_1 - V_0}{V_0}$
$r_b = \frac{0 + £70 - £50}{£50} = 0.40$ ie 40% in a year	$r_b = \frac{£0}{£50} = 0.00$ ie 0% income	$r_b = \frac{£70 - £50}{£50} = 0.40$ ie 40% gain

2.2.3 Using the results – annualising

The holding period returns of A and B are not directly comparable, since B was invested for twice as long as A. When A was sold, the proceeds could have been reinvested for another six months, but we do not know what return would have been available to the investor at that time. To compare the returns, they must be for a standard period. This is achieved by using the equivalent period interest rate formula to annualise the returns as follows.

Solution

Investment A

r_a = 20% in six months

Hence, annualising this return, we get

$$1 + r = (1+R)^n$$

$$1 + r = 1.2^2 = 1.44$$

$$r = 0.44 \text{ or } 44\% \text{ p.a.}$$

Investment B

r_b = 40% p.a.

We have now got a standardised measure of return, the annualised holding period return.

However, the problem that arises with this measure is what happens if there have been significant cash inflows to/outflows from the fund during the period, other than the period end dividend? These could significantly distort the results.

Example 2

A fund has a start value of £10m. Halfway through the period, it has the same value and a further £10m is deposited. At the end of the period, it is worth £20m, no dividends having been paid.

What is the fund's performance?

Solution

Using our equation above, we have

$$r_p = \frac{D_1 + V_1 - V_0}{V_s} \times 100$$

$$r_p = \frac{£0 + £20m - £10m}{£10m} \times 100 = +100\%$$

But has the fund really generated a 100% return? In truth, it has generated no return whatsoever. Its terminal value is simply the sum of what was initially held plus the funds added. No return or growth has been generated.

This simple approach is therefore inadequate. We must in some way account for the deposits and withdrawals that occur during the period over which we are determining the performance.

2.3 Money-weighted returns

Learning objectives

23.2.1 Identify the data requirements to calculate a: money weighted return and time weighted return.

23.2.2 Calculate respectively, from such data, the: money weighted return and time weighted return.

23.2.3 Interpret time-weighted and money-weighted returns.

A money-weighted return (MWR) is the internal rate of return (IRR) of the fund opening and closing values along with any deposits into/withdrawals from the fund.

If r is the money-weighted return then, using present value ideas, the current fund market value must be equal to the future fund cash payouts discounted at this rate, i.e.

Formula to learn

$$V_s = \frac{CF_1}{(1+r)^{t1}} + \frac{CF_2}{(1+r)^{t2}} + \cdots + \frac{CF_n}{(1+r)^{tn}} + \frac{V_n}{(1+r)^{tn}}$$

where

V_s = current fund value

CF_n = cash inflow to/outflow from the fund at time t_n during the period, including dividends paid out by the fund

V_n = fund value at the end of the period

r = **money-weighted return**

This has the advantage over our simple holding period return calculation above of considering all the relevant cash flows **and** their timings.

Note that this formula cannot be solved; the money-weighted return (or IRR) must be found through trial and error/interpolation in a normal DCF tabular calculation. Furthermore, in applying this approach, we must assume we buy the fund at the start and sell it at the end.

Solution

Applying this to Example 2 above, we get

Time	Comment	Cash Flow £m	Discount Factor	Present Value £m
0	'Buy' the fund	(10)	1	(10)
½	Further investment	(10)	$\frac{1}{1.00^{½}}$	(10)
1	'Sell' the fund	20	$\frac{1}{1.00^{1}}$	20
				0

Giving a money-weighted return of 0%, the solution we wanted.

Unfortunately, this method does not always give the expected results.

Example 3

Our fund starts the year with a value of £20m. It falls to £10m by the middle of the year when a further £10m is invested bringing the fund back up to £20m in total. It then rises to £40m at the year-end. Calculate the money-weighted return.

Solution

Before we calculate the money-weighted return, let us consider what we expect. Each £1 we held at the start of the period fell in value to 50p by the middle of the period but rose back to £1 by the end. Once more our overall performance has been zero.

Time	Comment	Cash Flow £m	Discount Factor	Present Value £m
0	'Buy' the fund	(20)	1	(20.00)
½	Further investment	(10)	$\frac{1}{1.40693^{½}}$	(8.43)
1	'Sell' the fund	40	$\frac{1}{1.40693^{1}}$	28.43
				0.00

The money-weighted return is 40.693%, clearly not what we expected.

2.3.1 Results

The performance appears good because there was more money invested in the second half of the period when the fund was performing well. The performance has been **money-weighted**, biasing this measure towards the performance during the period when money invested was at its peak.

What is needed is a measure that is unaffected by cash inflows to and outflows from the fund (deposits and withdrawals) over which the fund manager has no control.

2.4 Time-weighted returns

Learning objectives

23.2.1 Identify the data requirements to calculate a: money weighted return and time weighted return.

23.2.2 Calculate respectively, from such data, the: money weighted return and time weighted return.

23.2.3 Interpret time-weighted and money-weighted returns.

The time-weighted return achieves this objective. The method is to calculate the returns between any cash flow dates, using our original holding period formula, and then combine them in a similar fashion to compound interest to establish the return for the full period.

When calculating the returns between each cash flow (deposits, withdrawals, dividends), we will take

V_s = fund value immediately **after** the cash flow that marked the **start** of the sub-period (or start of the period if it is the first sub-period).

V_e = fund value immediately **before** the cash flow that marked the **end** of the sub-period (or end of the period if it is the last sub-period).

For the purposes of clarity of calculations, it is always useful to draw a graphical representation of how the value of the fund has changed over time. This helps to clarify the numbers of use.

Solution

In relation to Example 2 above, we had a mid-period deposit and hence we need to evaluate two sub-periods, the sub-period before that date and the subsequent one.

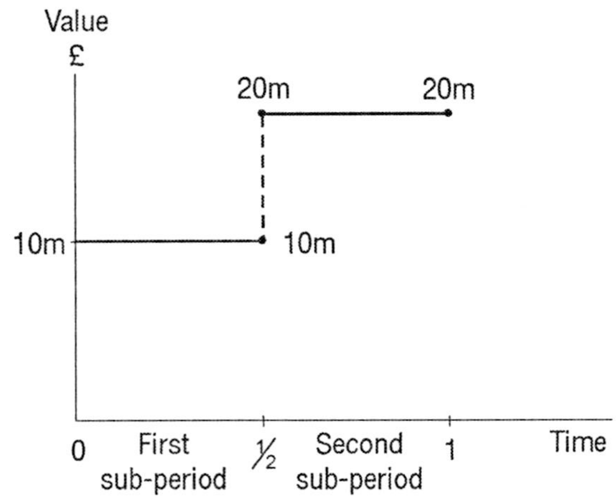

The idea here is that the fund manager controls the change in the fund value over time (i.e. the solid horizontal lines above). He does not control the timing and scale of any cash inflows or outflows (the vertical dotted line). The fund manager should only be assessed on the factors he controls, which is the aim of the time-weighted return.

First sub-period

Using

$$r_1 = \frac{D + V_e - V_s}{V_s} \times 100$$

We get

$$r_1 = \frac{0 + £10m - £10m}{£10m} \times 100 = 0\%$$

Second sub-period

V_s is now £20m following the £10m deposit marking the start of this sub-period, hence

$$r_2 = \frac{D + V_e - V_s}{V_s} \times 100$$

Gives

$$r_2 = \frac{0 + £20m - £20m}{£20m} \times 100 = 0\%$$

Combining

Clearly, if there is no return during either sub-period the combined periods return is zero. Demonstrating this formally to give the full period return r_p

$$1 + r_p = (1 + r_1) \times (1 + r_2)$$

$$1 + r_p = (1 + 0) \times (1 + 0) = 1$$

$$r_p = 0$$

Solution

In relation to Example 3 above, again we have two sub-periods to evaluate.

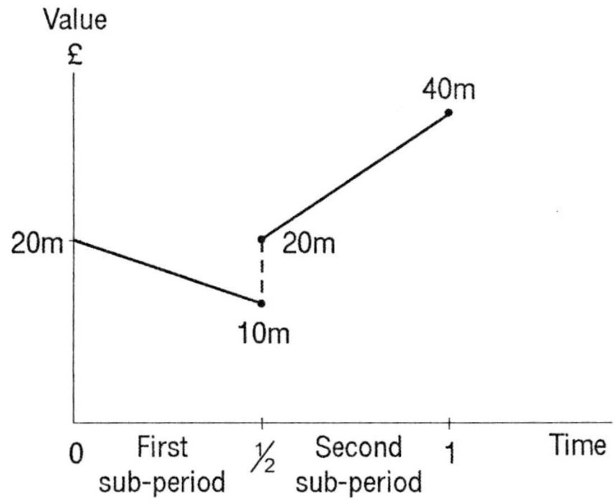

Once again, the fund manager controls the change in value over time (i.e. the solid diagonals), and it is this change in value over this time that he should be appraised on.

First sub-period

The fund starts with a value of £20m which falls to £10m, hence

$$r_1 = \frac{D + V_e - V_s}{V_s} \times 100$$

Gives

$$r_1 = \frac{0 + £10m - £20m}{£20m} \times 100 = -50\%$$

Second sub-period

Following the deposit of a further £10m the fund value starts this sub-period with a value of £20m which rises to £40m, hence

$$r_2 = \frac{D + V_e - V_s}{V_s} \times 100$$

Gives

$$r_2 = \frac{0 + £40m - £20m}{£20m} \times 100 = +100\%$$

Combining

Combining these two sub-periods to give a full period return r_p using

$$1 + r_p = (1 + r_1) \times (1 + r_2)$$

Gives

$$1 + r_p = (1 - 0.5) \times (1 + 1) = 1$$

$$1 + r_p = 0.5 \times 2 = 1$$

$$r_p = 0$$

Hence, the overall periodic return is reported as zero as we felt it should be.

By combining the returns as effectively compound interest in each sub-period we are **time-weighting** the returns.

Results

The time-weighted return is unaffected by either the timing of cash inflows/outflows or the value of funds invested in the period. It therefore represents a good measure of the manager's performance.

Example 4

A fund starts the year with a value of £100m. The value of the fund at the end of each quarter and the cash inflows/(outflows) following those valuations are

	Q1	Q2	Q3	Q4
Value	£105m	£107m	£116m	£117m
In/(out)	(£2m)	£3m	(£4m)	(£2m)

Calculate the time-weighted return for the year.

Solution

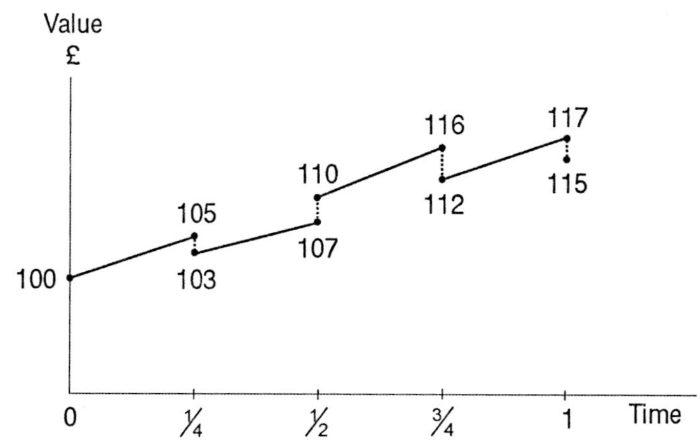

$$r_1 = \frac{105-100}{100} = 0.05 \text{ or } 5\%$$

$$r_2 = \frac{107-103}{103} = 0.0388 \text{ or } 3.88\%$$

$$r_3 = \frac{116-110}{110} = 0.0545 \text{ or } 5.45\%$$

$$r_4 = \frac{117-112}{112} = 0.0446 \text{ or } 4.46\%$$

$$1 + r_{yr} = (1 + r_1)(1 + r_2)(1 + r_3)(1 + r_4)$$

$$= 1.05 \times 1.0388 \times 1.0545 \times 1.0446 = 1.2015$$

$$r_{yr} = 0.2015 \text{ or } 20.15\%$$

2.5 Conclusion

In general, the **money-weighted method** of measuring returns for the purposes of evaluation is considered **inappropriate**, since this measure is strongly influenced by the size and timing of cash flows outside the control of the fund manager.

The **time-weighted** return does not suffer this problem and must be considered **more appropriate**.

3 Appraisal of Performance

3.1 Introduction

We have now established a way of assessing the return achieved, but how can we tell whether this is good or bad, e.g. is a return of 5% good? Clearly, we cannot answer this question unless we have a yardstick to measure against, e.g. interest rates and general market performance.

Given that the basis of most finance theory is that investors are rational and risk averse, it is appropriate to determine whether they are being adequately compensated by way of absolute return for that absolute risk. Methods that we can utilise for this purpose include

- Comparison of total returns to a benchmark index.
- Comparison of total returns to the capital market line or the securities market line.
- Excess return per unit risk measures, determining how well the excess absolute return over the risk-free rate compensates for the total risk.

3.2 Comparison to a benchmark index

arning objectives

23.3.1 Explain the purpose of benchmarking.

23.3.2 Identify the characteristics of an appropriate benchmark.

23.3.3 Identify the key types of benchmark used in the investment management industry.

23.3.4 Explain how to construct a benchmark portfolio comprising global equities.

3.2.1 Introduction

In order to assess how well a fund manager is performing, we need a yardstick for comparison. One such suitable yardstick may be a benchmark index. Once we have determined an appropriate benchmark, we can then compare whether the fund manager outperformed, matched, or underperformed.

The appropriate benchmark is one that is consistent with the preferences of the fund's trustees and the fund's tax status. For example, a different benchmark is appropriate if the fund is a gross fund and does not pay taxes (e.g. a pension fund), than if it is a net fund and does pay taxes (e.g. a general insurance fund).

Similarly, a general market index will not be appropriate as a benchmark if the trustee has a preference for high-income securities or an aversion to certain securities, e.g. rival companies. The FTSE All Share Index would not be an appropriate benchmark if half the securities were held overseas.

There will therefore be different benchmarks for different funds and different fund managers. The benchmark is likely to be an index of one kind or another, hence it is important to understand the structure of the relevant index. The structure of indices has been discussed in an earlier chapter.

As discussed previously, the characteristics that are required to render an index suitable as a benchmark are that it is

- Specified and unambiguous.
- Appropriate to the preferences of the fund (e.g. a UK blue chip fund may utilise the FTSE 100 Index).
- Appropriate to the currency of the fund.
- Investable, i.e. composed of investments that could conceivably be held in the fund.

- Measurable, i.e. the return can be calculated on a frequent basis as required.
- Representative of achievable performance, i.e. it has an arithmetic weighted composition (remember that the return of a portfolio is an arithmetic weighted average of the individual stock returns).
- Measures the relevant component of performance, i.e. total return indices for total return performance and capital value indices for capital growth.

Whilst it is completely appropriate to use an index as a benchmark for a passively managed fund, it is less appropriate for actively managed funds. Alternatives that may be applied are

- **Peer group comparison** – Where the fund performance is compared to the performance of other similar funds, ie funds of a similar size with similar objectives and a similar management style. The aim is usually to achieve top or top quartile performance.
- **Median manager** – Where the fund performance is compared to the median performance of other similar funds.
- **Two-horse race** – Where the fund performance is compared to the closest direct competitor.

It is, however, unlikely that any of these will satisfy the requirements noted earlier for the characteristics that are necessary to render a portfolio as suitable as a benchmark.

3.2.2 Performance appraisal

Once we have established a suitable benchmark we can appraise the fund manager's performance by reference to it. The benchmark performance can be quite simply calculated as the weighted average of the holding period returns on the relevant benchmark indices.

Example 5

A pension fund manager has a portfolio with an initial value of £100m. The company for whom the fund is run is internationally based with 80% of its employees in the UK and 20% in the US. As such, it requires a corresponding international investment strategy concentrating on a diversified spread of shares.

The company feels that the fund manager should be able to at least match the following two indices on the relevant portions of the fund.

- FTSE 100 Index on the UK portion.
- S&P 500 Index on the US portion.

The values on these indices at the start and end of the year were

	FTSE 100	S&P 500
End of Year	4520	1000
Start of Year	4000	920

The fund had a capital value of £113m at the end of the year, there having been no cash inflows and outflows during the year. What return has the fund manager achieved, what return has the benchmark portfolio achieved and has the fund manager achieved his target of at least matching the benchmark?

Solution

Fund performance

Since there have been no cash inflows/outflows during the year, we can use the simple holding period return formula to assess the fund performance, giving

$$r = \frac{D + V_e - V_s}{V_s} \times 100$$

Gives

$$r = \frac{0 + £113m - £100m}{£100m} \times 100 = +13\%$$

Benchmark performance

FTSE 100 Index

$$r = \frac{4520 - 4000}{4000} = 0.13 \text{ or } 13\%$$

S&P 500 Index

$$r = \frac{1000 - 920}{920} = 0.087 \text{ or } 8.7\%$$

Weighted average

$$r = (80\% \times 13\%) + (20\% \times 8.7\%)$$

$$r = (0.8 \times 13\%) + (0.2 \times 8.7\%) = 12.14\%$$

Appraisal

Actual Portfolio Performance	+13.00%	+0.86%	**Total outperformance**
Original Benchmark Performance	+12.14%		

The fund manager has achieved a return of 13% against the benchmark portfolio return of 12.14%. Hence, the fund manager has achieved his target of outperforming the benchmark, his outperformance being 0.86%.

Note, however, that this conclusion is only truly valid so long as the total return achieved was at no higher a level of risk than that of the underlying index. If this actual return has been achieved at a significantly elevated level of risk, this conclusion would be invalid.

In addition, no account has been taken of currency effects in this example.

3.2.3 Equity Performance attribution/decomposition

Learning objective

23.1.5 Explain how returns are decomposed for different asset classes such as equities (sector/stock/interaction effect) and fixed income (shift/twist/spread return).

The above performance appraisal assumed that the fund manager made no decisions regarding asset allocation, rather he simply took the 80:20 split proposed by the company and concentrated on selecting stocks within those sectors. Thus, we have established in the above example that the fund manager is good at stock selection.

The fund manager may however be free to determine his own asset allocation. If this is the case, then we may wish to appraise his performance in the two-key investment management areas of

- Asset allocation/market thing.
- Stock selection.

To achieve this, we need to consider the actual performance and the performance of the following two benchmark portfolios.

- A portfolio with the asset allocation determined by the fund manager – a **timing portfolio**.
- A portfolio with the asset allocation as proposed by the client – the **original benchmark**.

Example 6

Based on the Example 5 data above, but now assuming that the fund manager has decided on a different asset allocation, investing 85% in UK equities and 15% in the US, establish how the fund manager has performed.

Solution

Fund performance

As before, the fund performance is +13%.

Timing portfolio

The performance of the timing portfolio can be calculated in exactly the same way as for the original benchmark but using the actual asset allocation. This portfolio is referred to as the timing portfolio as it only takes account of the market timing (changes in asset allocation) activity that has been undertaken.

FTSE 100 Index

$$r = \frac{4520 - 4000}{4000} = 0.13 \text{ or } 13\%$$

S&P 500 Index

$$r = \frac{1000 - 920}{920} = 0.087 \text{ or } 8.7\%$$

Weighted average

$$r = (85\% \times 13\%) + (15\% \times 8.7\%)$$

$$r = (0.85 \times 13\%) + (0.15 \times 8.7\%) = 12.35\%$$

Original benchmark

The original benchmark performance is unaltered at +12.14%.

Appraisal

The actual performance has exceeded both benchmarks but what does this tell us?

The actual portfolio and timing portfolio have the same asset allocation (85% UK, 15% US), hence any difference in performance must be attributable to stock selection. As a result, we can say that the fund manager has boosted fund performance by 0.65% (13.00% – 12.35%) as a result of superior stock selection, or £650,000 based on our original fund size of £100m (£100m × 0.65%).

The timing portfolio and original benchmark are based on the same indices (same stocks), hence any difference between them must be due to asset allocation. As a result, we can say that the fund manager has boosted fund performance by 0.21% (12.35% – 12.14%) as a result of superior asset allocation, or £210,000 based on our original fund size of £100m (£100m × 0.21%).

We can lay out the calculation quite conveniently as follows.

Actual Portfolio Performance	+13.00%	+0.65%	**Stock Selection Gain**
Timing Portfolio Performance	+12.35%		
Original Benchmark Performance	+12.14%	+0.21	**Asset Allocation/Market Timing Gain**

Through this decomposition we have broken down the total outperformance of 0.86% identified earlier into

	%
Stock selection gain	0.65
Asset allocation/market timing gain	0.21
Total outperformance	0.86%

This analysis or decomposition can be further extended by utilising the Brinson Fachler framework. Under this framework the stock selection gain above is sub-analysed into a selection component and an interaction component reflecting the interaction between the asset allocation/market timing decision and the stock selection decision.

Under the Brinson Fachler method the attribution could be undertaken as above but one extra portfolio would be considered, a portfolio with the asset allocation proposed by the client but the actual selected stock returns – the **stock-selected portfolio**.

Example 7

Based on Example 6 above, decompose the total return into selection, timing and interaction components given that the UK return was 13.6% and an actual US return was 9.6% giving the actual total return of

r = (85% × 13.6%) + (15% × 9.6%)

r = (0.85 × 13.6%) + (0.15 × 9.6%) = 13%

as before

Solution

One way to start would be to complete the decomposition undertaken above giving

Actual Portfolio Performance	+13.00%	+0.65%	**Stock Selection Gain**
Timing Portfolio Performance	+12.35%		
Original Benchmark Performance	+12.14%	+0.21%	**Asset Allocation/Market Timing Gain**

We would then decompose the +0.65% stock selection gain into a selection and an interaction component by comparing the original benchmark performance to the selected benchmark performance.

Stock-selected portfolio

The performance of the stock-selected portfolio is the performance that would have been achieved with the selected stocks had we not undertaken any market timing activity, i.e.

r = (80% × 13.6%) + (20% × 9.6%)

r = (0.80 × 13.6%) + (0.20 × 9.6%) = 12.8%

So we can now see that the gain due to stock selection alone (since we are using the original asset allocation) is

Stock-selected Benchmark	+12.80%	+0.66%	**Selection Gain**
Original Benchmark	+12.14%		

And hence we can decompose the earlier +0.65% stock selection gain as follows

	%
Selection Gain	0.66
Interaction Loss	(0.01)
Stock Selection Gain	0.65%

And our total outperformance of +0.86% has now been decomposed into

	%
Selection gain	0.66
Interaction loss	(0.01)
Asset allocation/market timing gain	0.21
Total outperformance	0.86%

The above discussion is quite long and seeks to explain the idea. The approach to apply in the exam, however, would be

- Determine the total out/underperformance of 0.86% as we originally did in Example 5 above.
- Calculate the asset allocation/market timing contribution to this using the benchmark returns applied to each of the original and actual asset allocations giving the asset allocation component only in the absence of any stock selection effect, ie.

Timing Portfolio Performance	12.35%	0.21%
Original Benchmark Performance	12.14%	

- Calculate the selection gain contribution to this using each of the actual and benchmark returns applied to the original benchmark asset allocation giving the selection component only in the absence of any asset allocation effect, ie.

Stock-selected Portfolio Performance	12.80%	0.66%
Original Benchmark Performance	12.14%	

- Put together the full analysis with the interaction effect as the balancing figure.

	%
Selection gain (calculated)	0.66
Interaction effect (balancing figure)	(0.01)
Asset allocation/market timing gain (calculated)	0.21
Total outperformance (calculated)	0.86%

As we can now see

- The selection gain here is the effect of the stock selection decision without any impact on a change in asset allocation – the impact of pure stock selection alone.
- The asset allocation/market timing gain is the effect of the asset allocation choice alone without any impact of a change in selected stocks.
- The interaction effect that can only ever be calculated as a balancing figure is the impact of changing both asset allocation and stock selection.

Conclusion

We now have three levels of our appraisal requiring us to consider the returns of 2, 3 or 4 different portfolios.

- We firstly calculated the total out/underperformance based on the actual portfolio performance and original benchmark performance.
- We then decomposed this into stock selection and asset allocation components by also considering the timing portfolio performance.
- We then further decomposed the total out/underperformance into a (pure) selection, intervention and asset allocation components by also considering the stock-selected portfolio performance.

We need to take care with the terminology to be sure about what is being asked.

3.2.4 Fixed income performance attribution/decomposition

Index returns are less relevant for bonds and attribution needs to be undertaken by reference to interest rates and the yield curve as follows.

Example 8

A 10 year bond is yielding 6.3% when interest rates are 5%. The term spread on 10 year gilts is 0.8%, decompose the bond's return.

Solution

Actual return on the 10 year bond	6.3%	
		0.5% credit/default spread return
Benchmark return for a 10 year bond (5% + 0.8%)	5.8%	
		0.8% term spread return (shift)
Interest rate	5.0%	

If we were then asked to analyse the change in the yield on this bond from one year to the next then we would need to decompose this into

- The change in interest rates over the period
- The change in the spread return which, from one year to the next, will be due to
  - The reduction in the bonds term
  - Shifts in the yield curve
  - Twists in the yield curve
- The change in the credit/default return

Numerically, the approach to any questions would be exactly as for equities and has three possible appraisal levels.

- Calculate the total out/underperformance based on the actual portfolio performance and the original benchmark performance.
- Decompose this into a credit/default return component and a shift or term spread return component by also considering the timing portfolio (the benchmark return for a portfolio of the actual maturity/duration).
- Further decompose this into a pure credit/default spread, a twist (interaction) and a shift or term spread component.

3.3 Jensen measure/comparison to SML

Learning objective 23.4.1 **Explain** the importance of risk analysis in performance evaluation.

3.3.1 Introduction

We have now established a way of measuring and appraising the return, though measuring return in isolation with no consideration of the risk involved is inappropriate for investment decisions. We must somehow take account of the risk inherent in the portfolio that has generated this return.

The appropriate measure of risk to use depends on whether the beneficiary of the fund's investments has other well-diversified investments or whether this is his only set of investments. In the first case, the market risk or β of the fund is the best measure of risk, in the second case, the total risk or standard deviation of the fund σ_i would be the best measure.

If, on the other hand, the portfolio is a bond fund, then the appropriate measure of market risk is of relative duration.

Hence, as an alternative to simple comparison to a benchmark index with no consideration of risk, we could use the expected returns of the securities based on the capital market line (for total risk) or the securities market line (for systematic risk).

We will illustrate this with the following example.

Example 9

Two fund managers are employed to manage portions of a large pension fund. They both have the same objectives, etc. Details about their portfolios are given below.

Fund	Return %	Beta Factor β_p
A	19%	1.05
B	22%	1.20

Over the same period the risk-free rate was 8% and the stock market generated a return of 18%.

3.3.2 The Jensen measure

If the risk measure is systematic risk, the relevant alpha value is defined with respect to the security market line

Formula to learn

$$\bar{r}_p = r_f + \beta(\bar{r}_m - r_f)$$

The corresponding alpha value is again

Formula to learn

$$\alpha_p = r_p - \bar{r}_p$$

This is known as the Jensen differential performance index.

$$\bar{r}_p = r_f + \beta(\bar{r}_m - r_f)$$

Gives

$$\bar{r}_a = 8\% + 1.05(18\% - 8\%) = 18.5\%$$

$$\bar{r}_b = 8\% + 1.20(18\% - 8\%) = 20.0\%$$

The Jensen measure

$$\alpha_p = r_p - \bar{r}_p$$

Gives

$$\alpha_a = r_a - \bar{r}_a = 19.0\% - 18.5\% = 0.5\%$$

$$\alpha_b = r_b - \bar{r}_b = 22.0\% - 20.0\% = 2.0\%$$

Hence, we can say that on this risk-adjusted basis (systematic risk) fund manager B has outperformed fund manager A.

3.4 Excess return per unit risk

Learning objectives	
	23.4.2 Explain and interpret the following risk adjusted measures of return: the Sharpe measure; the Treynor measure; the information ratio and Jensen's alpha.
	23.4.3 Calculate the Sharpe, Treynor, information ratio and Jensen measure.

3.4.1 Introduction

There are four performance measures that we need to be aware of, each distinguished by the risk measure used. Three of these are relevant to general share portfolios, one is specific to bond portfolios. These are

Share Portfolio Measures

- The Sharpe measure.
- The Treynor measure.
- The Information ratio.

Bond Portfolio Measure

- The excess return to relative duration measure.

We will illustrate these with the following example.

Example 10

Two fund managers are employed to manage portions of a large pension fund. They both have the same objectives, etc. Details about their portfolios are given below.

Fund	Return %	Beta Factor β_p	Total Risk σ_p
A	19%	1.05	20
B	22%	1.20	30

Over the same period the risk-free rate was 8% and the stock market generated a return of 18% at a risk of 19%.

3.4.2 Sharpe measure

The Sharpe measure uses as its measure of risk, the total portfolio risk or standard deviation.

The Sharpe measure is calculated as

Formula to learn

$$\text{Sharpe measure} = \frac{r_p - r_f}{\sigma_p}$$

where

r_p = portfolio return

r_f = risk-free return over the same interval

σ_p = portfolio risk (standard deviation of the portfolio returns)

As noted above, this measure is appropriate where this portfolio represents the full set of investments of the client (**an undiversified investor**). The higher the measure, the better the performance, which can be achieved by either **better stock selection** or **greater diversification**.

Solution

$$\text{Sharpe measure} = \frac{r_p - r_f}{\sigma_p}$$

Gives

$$\text{Fund A} = \frac{19\% - 8\%}{20} = 0.55$$

$$\text{Fund B} = \frac{22\% - 8\%}{30} = 0.47$$

Hence, we can say that on a risk-adjusted basis (total risk) fund manager A has outperformed fund manager B.

3.4.3 Treynor measure

The Treynor measure uses as its measure of risk, the systematic risk or β of the portfolio. The Treynor measure can be calculated as

Formula to learn

$$\text{Treynor measure} = \frac{r_p - r_f}{\beta_p}$$

where

r_p = portfolio return

r_f = risk-free return over the same period

β_p = portfolio beta

The Treynor measure is appropriate where this fund represents just one of many investments held by the client who is well diversified. The higher the measure, the better the performance of the fund when we take account of risk. This measure cannot be improved through diversification, since only systematic risk remains in the portfolio, and can only be improved through **better stock selection**.

Solution

$$\text{Treynor measure} = \frac{r_p - r_f}{\beta_p}$$

Gives

$$\text{Fund A} = \frac{19\% - 8\%}{1.05} = 10.48$$

$$\text{Fund B} = \frac{22\% - 8\%}{1.20} = 11.66$$

Hence, we can say that on a risk-adjusted basis (systematic risk) fund manager B has outperformed fund manager A, the same conclusion as we drew above with the alpha value measure (the Jensen measure) based on systematic risk and the securities market line.

3.4.4 Information ratio

The information ratio considers, in comparison to the benchmark, the excess return of the portfolio against the excess risk. Again, this can be compared to the Sharpe measure for the benchmark in order to determine the impact of active performance.

The information ratio is calculated as

Formula to learn

$$\text{Information ratio} = \frac{r_p - r_b}{\sigma_{b-p}}$$

where

r_p = portfolio return

r_b = benchmark return

σ_{b-p} = known as the standard deviation surplus or tracking error, ie the standard deviation of the difference between the returns on the portfolio and the benchmark returns, $(r_p - r_b)$

If the information ratio exceeds the benchmark Sharpe ratio, then the active performance has been good, as the extra return has more than compensated for the additional risk.

Where this is applied to a tracking fund the surplus return on the top line is the funds **alpha** and the standard deviation surplus is the fund's **tracking error**.

3.4.5 Excess return to relative duration

The excess return duration measure is suitable for **bond portfolios** where the measure of risk is the duration. The measure can be calculated as

Formula to learn

$$\text{Excess return to relative duration} = \frac{r_p - r_f}{d_p / d_m}$$

where

r_p = portfolio return

r_f = risk-free over the same period

d_p/d_m = duration of portfolio (d_p) relative to that of the market (d_m)

Again, the higher the measure, the better the performance and the calculation of this measure is very similar to the above.

Chapter Roundup

Return measures

- The holding period return, money weighted return and time weighted return are methods of measuring a manager's performance.
- Holding period return

  $$r_p = \frac{D + V_e - V_s}{V_s} \times 100\%$$

  and this total return can be decomposed into an income and a gain component.
- Money weighted return is IRR calculation.
- Time weighted return – Plot a chart of the changes in fund values and use the holding period return for each sub-period to assess the return.
- Returns for short periods can be annualised by compounding, ie apply DCF ideas.
- The time weighted return is typically the preferred method of calculation by fund managers since it is not biased by the size and timing of inflows and outflows.

Appraisal

- Performance attribution may be undertaken to establish a manager's skill in asset allocation and stock selection.
- Performance may be assessed by reference to a benchmark, benchmark index, though such an index must be
  - Specified and unambiguous.
  - Appropriate for fund preferences, assets and currencies.
  - Investible, hence the need for free-float indices.
  - Measurable.
  - Representative of achievable performance, ie have an arithmetic weighted composition.
- Decomposition outlines
  - **Total return**

    Actual Portfolio Performance } Total outperformance
    Original Benchmark Performance }

  - **Asset allocation/Stock selection**

    Actual Portfolio Performance } Stock Selection Gain
    Timing Portfolio Performance }
    Timing Portfolio Performance } Asset Allocation/Market Timing Gain
    Original Benchmark Performance }

– **Asset allocation/Selection/Interaction**

Assess total performance

Actual Portfolio Performance
Original Benchmark Performance } Total outperformance

Assess asset allocation gain

Actual asset allocation with benchmark stock returns
Original Benchmark Performance } Asset allocation gain

Assess selection gain

Benchmark asset allocation with actual stock returns
Original Benchmark Performance } Selection gain

Pull together	%
Selection gain (calculated)	x
Interaction effect (balancing figure)	X
Asset allocation/market timing gain (calculated)	X
Total outperformance (calculated)	X

- The Sharpe measure, the Treynor measure and the Information ratio are all performance measures for identifying risk-adjusted return.
- Jensen measure

  $\alpha_p = r_p - \overline{r}_p$

  where

  $\overline{r}_p = r_f + \beta(\overline{r}_m - r_f)$
- Sharpe measure

  $$\text{Sharpe measure} = \frac{r_p - r_f}{\sigma_p}$$
- Treynor measure

  $$\text{Treynor measure} = \frac{r_p - r_f}{\beta_p}$$
- Excess return to relative duration

  $$\text{Excess return to relative duration} = \frac{r_p - r_f}{d_p/d_m}$$
- Information ratio

  $$\text{Information ratio} = \frac{r_p - r_b}{\sigma_{b-p}}$$

TEST YOUR KNOWLEDGE

Check your knowledge of the chapter here, without referring back to the text.

1. What is a weakness of the holding period return?

2. An analyst believes that a firm's dividends will grow at 8% p.a. indefinitely. If the current share price is £4.60, and last year's dividend, which has just been paid, was 20 pence per share, what is the expected annual net holding period return?

3. A US investor buys €1 million at an exchange rate of $1.50: €1 to the dollar to hold for six months in an account yielding 3% p.a. If the euro are sold at the end of the period at an exchange rate of $1.40:€1, what is the dollar holding period return?

4. A firm has just paid a dividend (net of tax) of 20 pence per share. An analyst believes that the firm's dividends will grow at 6% per annum forever. If the current share price is 300 pence, what is the expected annual net holding period return?

5. An investor uses £1m to purchase dollars on the spot market at $1.4625 and places them on a six-month eurodollar deposit at an annual rate of 5%. If at the same time he sells the proceeds forward at $1.4587, what is the holding period return?

6. A company has just paid an annual dividend of 8 pence per share and the current share price is £1.60 per share. If analysts foresee continuing dividend growth of 6% p.a., what is the expected net holding period return from holding this share?

7. An investor buys one million US shares for $20 each, holds them for two years and receives dividends of $1.50 and $2.00 per share at the end of each year. The first dividend is invested in a one-year dollar term deposit paying 4%. The investor sells the shares at $18 each at the end of the second year. When the investor bought the shares the £:$ exchange rate was $1.52:£1.00, and when the shares were sold the rate was €$1.48:£1.00. What is the holding period £ return?

8. A US investor buys £100,000 to hold for three months in a eurosterling account yielding 5% p.a. If the sterling is bought at $1.6283 per £ and sold at $1.5941, what is the dollar holding period return?

9. What is a weakness of the money-weighted return?

10. What is the average annual time weighted return of a £140m investment based on the following portfolio year end values?

Year 1	170	following the receipt into the fund of £10m
Year 2	182	following the receipt into the fund of £5m
Year 3	210	no receipt this year

11. £40m is invested in a fund that pays on annual dividend. The year end dividend and fund value prior to the payment are.

Year End Value	45	47	50
Dividend	3	4	6

What is the average annual time weighted return?

12. A fund manager invests 75% of his portfolio in the UK and 25% in the US. The fund has a value of £30m at the start of the year and £33.5m by the year end. Comparison benchmark indices for each part of the portfolio had the following values.

	UK	US
Start of year	5,000	800
End of year	5,500	900

Based on the above portfolio details, but given that the fund managers asset allocation differs from that suggested by the client of 80% UK, 20% US, what gain or loss has the fund manager generated through the activities of stock selection and asset allocation?

13. A portfolio returns 9%, has a beta of 1.2 and a variance of returns of 16. If the risk-free return is 5% and market return is 8%.

(a) What is the Treynor measure of the above portfolio?

(b) What is the Jensen measure of the above portfolio?

14. A fund returns 14% with a portfolio beta of 1.2 and an overall risk of 12%. The risk free rate is 5%. Calculate the Sharpe measure and the Treynor measure.

15. A fund returns 10.5%, has a beta of 0.8 and a risk (expressed as a standard deviation) of 12%. The risk-free return is 6%, the market return is 10% and the market risk is 11%. The client's stated preference is for a portfolio that has a beta of 0.7 on average. What is the

(a) Sharpe measure of fund performance?
(b) Treynor measure of fund performance?
(c) Jensen measure of fund performance?

TEST YOUR KNOWLEDGE: ANSWERS

1. It does not allow for cash flows made between the start and end dates of the calculation.

   (See Section 2.2)

2. Holding period return = $\frac{(460+20)\times 1.08-460}{460}$ = 0.1270 ie 12.70%

   (See Section 2.2)

3. Cost at the start at \$1.50:€1.00 = \$1,500,000

   Value at end

– € Capital	1,000,000
– € 1 interest (1.5%)	15,000
	€1,015,000
– Dollar value at \$1.40:€1.00	\$1,421,000

   Holding period return = $\frac{1,421,000-1,500,000}{1,500,000}$ = –0.0527

   (See Section 2.2)

4. Holding period return = $\frac{Ve-Vs}{Vs}$

   Current cum-div price = 300 + 20 = 320

   Cum-div price in one year = 320 × 1.06 = 339.2 (growth 6% p.a.)

   Holding period return = $\frac{339.2-300}{300}$ = 0.131 or 13.1%

   (See Section 2.2)

5.

Spot dollar value (£1m × 1.4625) =	1,462,500.00
Interest for six months at 5% p.a. = (1,462,500 × 0.05 × 6/12)	36,562.50
	1,499,062.50

   Sterling proceeds $\frac{\$1,499,062.50}{1.4587}$ = £1,027,670.19

   Holding period return = $\frac{1,027,670.11-1,000,000}{1,000,000}$ = 0.0277 or 2.77%

   (See Section 2.2)

6.

Next years dividend (8 × 1.06)	8.48
Next years share price (160 × 1.06)	169.60
	178.08

   Holding period return = $\frac{178.08-160.00}{160.00}$ = 0.113 or 11.3%

   (See Section 2.2)

7. Value at end

	$m
– shares	18.00
– 1st div 1.50 × 1.04	1.56
– 2nd div	2.00
	21.56 ÷ 1.48 = £14,567,568

Cost at start $20m ÷ 1.52 = £13,157,895

$$\text{Sterling holding period return} = \frac{14,567,568 - 13,157,895}{13,157,895} = 0.1071 \text{ or } 10.71\%$$

(See Section 2.2)

8. Cost = 100,000 × 1.6283 = $162,830

$$\text{Final sterling value} = £100,000 \times \left(1+\frac{0.05}{4}\right) = £101,250$$

Final value in dollars = 101,250 × 1.5941 = $161,403

$$\text{Holding period return} = \frac{161,403 - 162,830}{162,830} = -0.0088 \text{ or } -0.88\%$$

(See Section 2.2)

9. It is biased by the timings of the cash flows.

(See Section 2.3)

10.

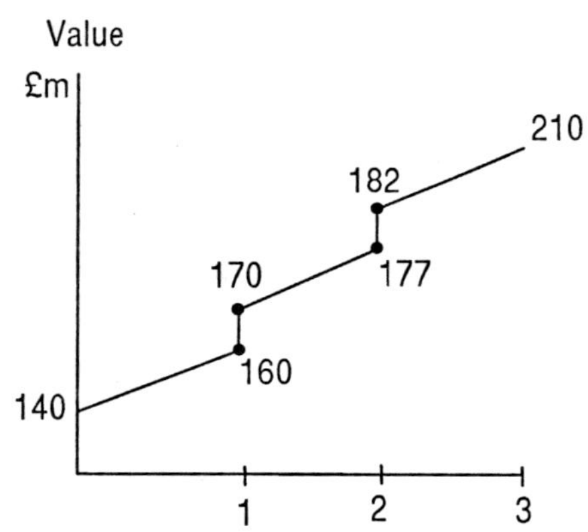

$$r_1 = \frac{160-140}{140} \qquad r_2 = \frac{177-170}{170} \qquad r_3 = \frac{210-182}{182}$$

= 0.1429 or 14.28%   =0.0412 or 4.12%   =0.1538 or 15.38%

$(1+r)^3 = 1.1429 \times 1.0412 \times 1.1538 = 1.3730$

$1+r = 1.1115$

$r = 0.1115$ or 11.15%

(See Section 2.4)

11.

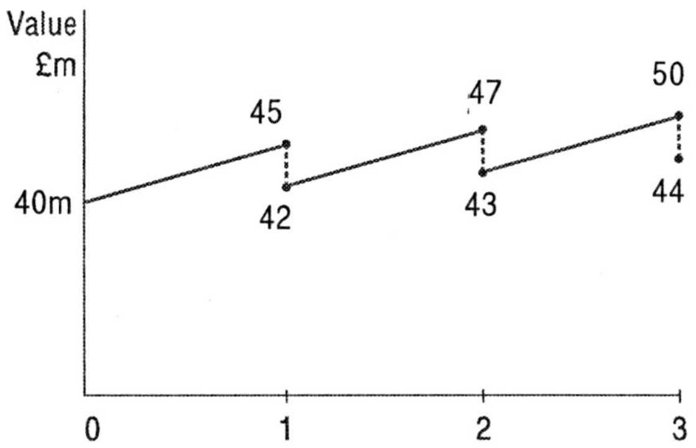

$r_1 = \dfrac{45-40}{40} = 0.125 \text{ or } 12.5\%$ $\quad r_2 = \dfrac{47-42}{42} = 0.1190 \text{ or } 11.90\%$ $\quad r_3 = \dfrac{50-43}{43} = 0.1628 \text{ or } 16.28\%$

$(1 + r)^3 = 1.1250 \times 1.1190 \times 1.1628 = 1.4638$

$1 + r = 1.1354$

$r = 0.1354$ or 13.54%

(See Section 2.4)

12. **Actual performance**

Holding period return = $\dfrac{33.5-30}{30} = 0.1167$ or 11.67%

Revised benchmark performance

$$\left(0.75\times\left(\frac{5{,}500-5{,}000}{5{,}000}\right)+0.25\times\left(\frac{900-800}{800}\right)\right) = 0.10625 \text{ or } 10.625\%$$

Original benchmark performance

$$\left(0.80\times\left(\frac{5{,}500-5{,}000}{5{,}000}\right)+0.20\times\left(\frac{900-800}{800}\right)\right) = 0.105 \text{ or } 10.5\%$$

Giving

Actual Portfolio Performance	+11.670%		
		+1.045%	**Stock Selection Gain**
Timing Portfolio Performance	+10.625%		
		+0.125%	**Asset Allocation Gain**
Original Benchmark Performance	+10.500%		

(See Section 3.2)

13. (a) Treynor measure = $\dfrac{r_p - r_f}{\beta_p} = \dfrac{9-5}{1.2} = 3.33$

(b) $r = r_f + \beta(r_m - r_f) = 5 + 1.2(8 - 5) = 8.6\%$

Jensen measure = $r_p - r = 9.0 - 8.6 = 0.4\%$

(See Section 3.3 and 3.4)

14. Sharpe

$$\frac{14-5}{12} = 0.75$$

Treynor

$$\frac{14-5}{1.2} = 7.5$$

(See Section 3.4.2 and 3.4.3)

15. (a) Sharpe measure = $\frac{r_p - r_f}{\sigma_p} = \frac{10.5-6}{12} = 0.375$

(b) Treynor measure = $\frac{r_p - r_f}{\beta_p} = \frac{10.5-6}{0.8} = 5.625\%$

(c) $r = r_f + \beta(r_m - r_f) = 6 + 0.8(10 - 6) = 9.2\%$

Jensen measure = $r_p - r = 10.5 - 9.2 = 6.3\%$

(See Section 3.3 and 3.4)

INDEX